CW00554785

MACHIAVELLI

ALSO BY ALEXANDER LEE

Humanism and Empire

The Ugly Renaissance

Petrarch and St Augustine

The End of Politics (with T. R. Stanley)

MACHIAVELLI

His Life and Times

Alexander Lee

PICADOR

First published 2020 by Picador
an imprint of Pan Macmillan
The Smithson, 6 Briset Street, London ECIM 5NR
Associated companies throughout the world
www.panmacmillan.com

ISBN 978-1-4472-7499-5

1 3 5 7 9 8 6 4 2

A CIP catalogue record for this book is available from the British Library.

Map artwork by ML Design Ltd

Typeset in Adobe Caslon 11.5/14 pt by Palimpsest Book Production Limited, Falkirk,
Stirlingshire
Printed and bound by CPI Group (UK) Ltd, Croydon, CR0 4YY

Visit **www.picador.com** to read more about all our books
and to buy them. You will also find features, author interviews and
news of any author events, and you can sign up for e-newsletters
so that you're always first to hear about our new releases.

To Marie
with all my love

Contents

List of Illustrations

ITALY IN *c.* 1494

① Republic of Venice
② Duchy of Milan
③ Duchy of Savoy
④ Marquisate of Monferrat
⑤ Republic of Genoa
⑥ Duchy of Modena
⑦ Republic of Lucca
⑧ Republic of Florence
⑨ Republic of Siena
⑩ Papal States
⑪ Marquisate of Mantua
⑫ Duchy of Ferrara
⑬ Kingdom of Naples

A L P S

Bolzano

Trento

② Novara Milan ① Verona Venice ①
③ Pavia Padua
Adda
Turin Cremona ⑪ Adige
Asti Piacenza ④ Mantua Ferrara ①
Genoa ⑤ ② Parma Bologna ⑫
③ ⑥ Modena Imola Ravenna ①
Pistoia Forlì
Lucca ⑦ Prato Rimini
Pisa Arno Florence Urbino Senigallia (Sinigaglia)
Livorno ⑧ Arezzo ⑩
Città di Castello ①
Piombino Siena Perugia

Ligurian Sea

Po
Susa Valley

⑤ Viterbo
CORSICA ⑩ A P E N N I N E S
Ostia Rome ⑬
SARDINIA Gaeta
Capua
Naples

Tiber
Garigliano

Adriatic Sea

N

Tyrrhenian Sea

Palermo

⑬
SICILY

M e d i t e r r a n e a n   S e a

100 miles

200 kilometres

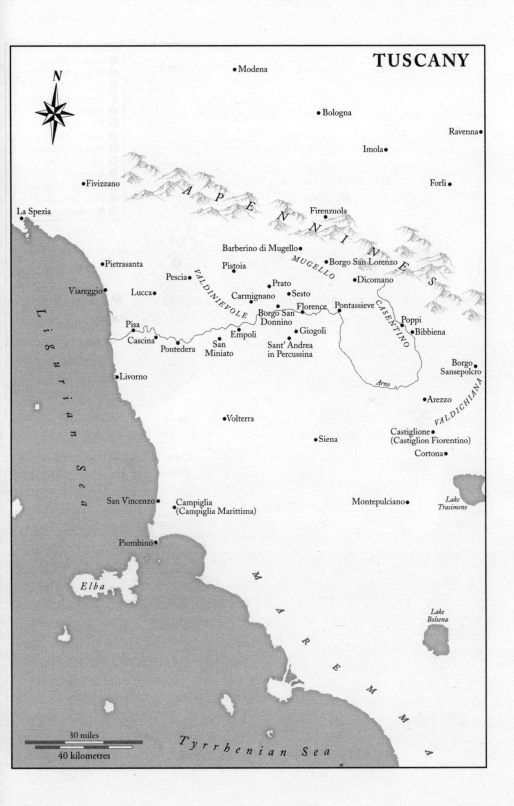

TUSCANY

N

Modena

Bologna

Ravenna

Imola

Forli

Fivizzano

Firenzuola

La Spezia

_A P E N N I N E S_

Barberino di Mugello

Borgo San Lorenzo

Pietrasanta

Pistoia

MUGELLO

Dicomano

Pescia

Prato

VALDINIEVOLE

Viareggio

Lucca

Carmignano

Sesto

Florence

Pontassieve

CASENTINO

Poppi

Bibbiena

Pisa

Borgo San
Donnino

Giogoli

Cascina

Empoli

Pontedera

San
Miniato

Sant' Andrea
in Percussina

Arno

Livorno

Borgo
Sansepolcro

_L i g u r i a n   S e a_

Arezzo

VALDICHIANA

Volterra

Castiglione
(Castiglion Fiorentino)

Siena

Cortona

San Vincenzo

Montepulciano

_Lake
Trasimeno_

Campiglia
(Campiglia Marittima)

Piombino

Elba

_M A R E M M A_

_Lake
Bolsena_

30 miles

40 kilometres

_T y r r h e n i a n   S e a_

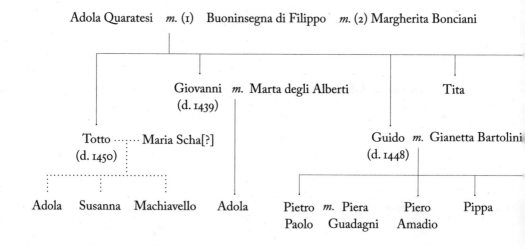

Adola Quaratesi   *m.* (1)   Buoninsegna di Filippo   *m.* (2) Margherita Bonciani

Giovanni   *m.* Marta degli Alberti
(d. 1439)

Tita

Totto ········ Maria Scha[?]
(d. 1450)

Guido   *m.* Gianetta Bartolini
(d. 1448)

Adola   Susanna   Machiavello   Adola

Pietro   *m.*   Piera   Piero   Pippa
Paolo   Guadagni   Amadio

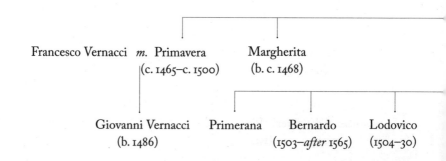

Francesco Vernacci   *m.* Primavera   Margherita
(c. 1465–c. 1500)   (b. c. 1468)

Giovanni Vernacci   Primerana   Bernardo   Lodovico
(b. 1486)   (1503–*after* 1565)   (1504–30)

THE FAMILY OF MARIETTA CORSINI

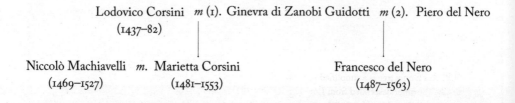

Lodovico Corsini   *m* (1). Ginevra di Zanobi Guidotti   *m* (2). Piero del Nero
(1437–82)

Niccolò Machiavelli   *m.* Marietta Corsini   Francesco del Nero
(1469–1527)   (1481–1553)   (1487–1563)

THE MACHIAVELLI

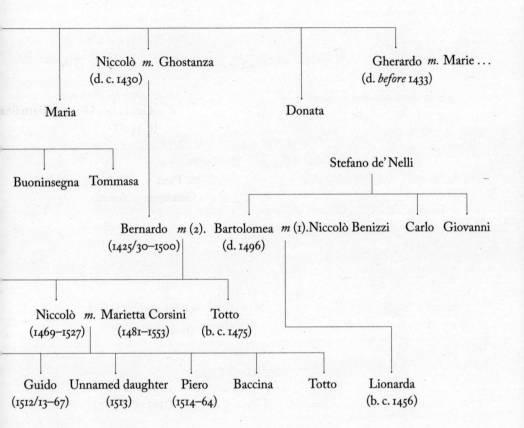

Niccolò *m.* Ghostanza
(d. c. 1430)

Gherardo *m.* Marie ...
(d. *before* 1433)

Maria

Donata

Buoninsegna   Tommasa

Stefano de' Nelli

Bernardo   *m* (2).   Bartolomea   *m* (1).Niccolò Benizzi   Carlo   Giovanni
(1425/30–1500)   (d. 1496)

Niccolò   *m.* Marietta Corsini   Totto
(1469–1527)   (1481–1553)   (b. c. 1475)

Guido   Unnamed daughter   Piero   Baccina   Totto   Lionarda
(1512/13–67)   (1513)   (1514–64)   (b. c. 1456)

N.B. This family tree is a simplified version of one of the two major branches of the Machiavelli family. The other descended from Lorenzo, one of the three brothers of Buoninsegna di Filippo. Its members included Francesco di Lorenzo (d. 1428), Francesco d'Agnolo (d. 1459), Girolamo d'Agnolo (d. 1460), Alessandro di Filippo (d. after 1466), and the 'other' Niccolò – Niccolò di Alessandro.

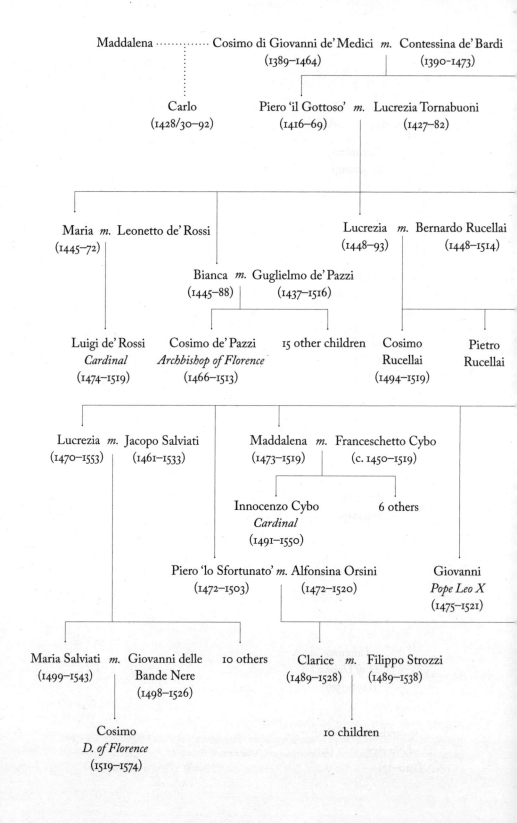

THE
MEDICI

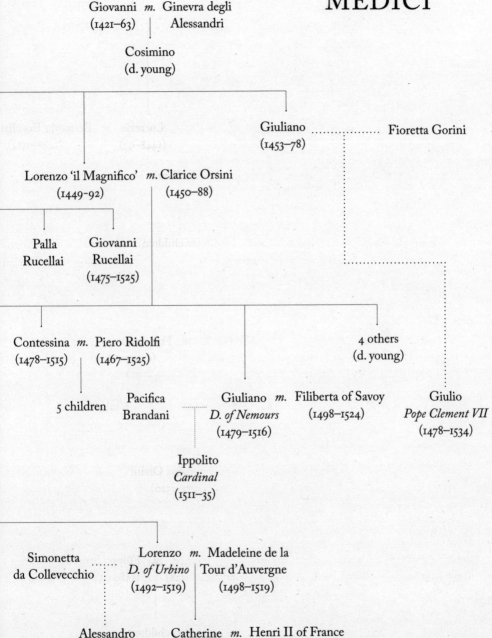

Giovanni *m.* Ginevra degli
(1421–63)   Alessandri

Cosimino
(d. young)

Giuliano .... Fioretta Gorini
(1453–78)

Lorenzo 'il Magnifico' *m.* Clarice Orsini
(1449-92)   (1450–88)

Palla   Giovanni
Rucellai   Rucellai
(1475–1525)

Contessina *m.* Piero Ridolfi
(1478–1515)   (1467–1525)

5 children

4 others
(d. young)

Pacifica   Giuliano *m.* Filiberta of Savoy   Giulio
Brandani   *D. of Nemours*   (1498–1524)   *Pope Clement VII*
  (1479–1516)   (1478–1534)

Ippolito
Cardinal
(1511–35)

Simonetta   Lorenzo *m.* Madeleine de la
da Collevecchio   *D. of Urbino* | Tour d'Auvergne
  (1492–1519)   (1498–1519)

Alessandro   Catherine *m.* Henri II of France
D. of Florence   (1519–89)   (1519–59)
(1510–37)

Preface

It would be hard to overstate the extent to which our understanding of Niccolò Machiavelli's life and times has been transformed since the publication of Roberto Ridolfi's classic study in 1954. Over the past few decades, a veritable torrent of new biographies has appeared, of which those by Francesco Bausi, Robert Black, Sebastian de Grazia, Maurizio Viroli and Corrado Vivanti deserve particular mention. Thanks to the tireless efforts of scholars such as Sergio Bertelli, Denis Fachard, Jean-Jacques Marchand and Mario Martelli, critical editions of an ever-growing number of Machiavelli's works have been made available. And, in almost every field with a bearing on his writings and career, huge strides have been taken. To take just one example, it is fair to say that our approach to his political thought has been revolutionized by those like Erica Benner, Gisela Bock, John Pocock, Quentin Skinner and Gabriele Pedullà. In much the same way, Alison Brown, Anna Maria Cabrini, Marcia Colish, Virginia Cox, Carlo Dionisotti, Victoria Kahn, Brian Richardson and Gennaro Sasso – to name but a few – have not only cast fresh light on his literary, dramatic and historical works, but have also enriched our knowledge of his use of rhetoric, his engagement with the Latin classics and even his attitude towards gender. So, too, our understanding of the turbulent world of Florentine politics has been recast by the pioneering work of Nicolai Rubinstein, Humphrey Butters, John Najemy and John Stephens, while our perceptions of the Italian Wars – and Machiavelli's role in them – have been turned on their head by Mikael Hörnqvist, Michael Mallett and Catherine Shaw. And, every day, new and important discoveries continue to be made.

This biography cannot hope to equal, let alone surpass the remarkable contributions which have been made to Machiavellian scholarship over the past seventy years. Nor, as a consequence, does it attempt to advance an especially radical vision of its subject. Instead, its aim is to bring together the insights of recent years to provide as detailed, accessible and comprehensive a portrait of Machiavelli's life and times as possible. As the endnotes testify, my debt to those who have gone before me is immense, especially insofar as *Il principe* and the *Discorsi* are concerned, but I have not hesitated to suggest new interpretations where I have thought it appropriate, to shine a light into those corners of Machiavelli's life which have hitherto remained in shadow, and to make his day-to-day existence as vivid and immediate as the evidence allows. Throughout, my approach has been guided by three over-arching considerations.

The first is *context*. In the recognition that Machiavelli's intellectual and personal development can only be seen clearly in the mirror of his own times, I have been at pains to situate him firmly in the culture, society and politics of late fifteenth- and early sixteenth-century Italy – more firmly, I believe, than has sometimes been the case in the past. Naturally, I have paid particularly close attention to the ebb and flow of the Italian Wars, the constitutional wrangling by which Florence was beset and the bitter divisions by which the city was wracked, but I have also endeavoured to give as full an impression as possible of the texture of everyday life – from Renaissance attitudes towards the family to the nature of friendships, and from the education of children to the sights, sounds and smells of the urban landscape. Given that Machiavelli spent a great part of his life travelling, I have placed a strong accent on Renaissance journeys, as well: that is to say, on different modes of transport, on the routes available, on the dangers involved and – where it has been possible to determine – on the weather. In doing so, I hope not only to have provided a more 'three-dimensional' portrait of Machiavelli the man, but also to have illuminated more brightly the roots of his thoughts, the reasons for his actions and the extent to which, for much of his life, his fate was affected by vast, sweeping events quite beyond his control – and often beyond his comprehension.

The second consideration concerns *completeness*. Although Machiavelli is best known for *Il principe* and the *Discorsi*, I have endeavoured not to privilege any particular texts, and – as far as possible – to take the full range of his writings into account. This is intended to have two effects. On the one hand, by giving ample consideration to his plays and poems, his letters and carnival songs, I hope to make apparent the full richness of his personality, the vivacity of his imagination and the bawdiness of his humour. And, on the other hand, by removing the privileged status accorded to texts like *Il principe*, I believe it will be possible to examine the meaning and importance which Machiavelli himself attached to them at the moment of their composition, without the baggage of presupposition. For similar reasons, I have also tried to give as exhaustive an account of Machiavelli's actions as I can – reconstructing his movements day by day, even hour by hour, as the evidence permits. This has, I feel, allowed for a more detailed understanding of his motivations, his doubts and his fears, especially at moments of high tension. On a few occasions, it has also made it possible to recognize how frequently he could change his mind, and how great were the uncertainties under which he sometimes had to labour.

The third, and perhaps most important, consideration is *contingency*. In writing this book, I have been acutely conscious that direction is something a person's life acquires only in hindsight, and that events frequently unfold in an unexpected and unpredictable manner. Rather than succumb to the temptation to read Machiavelli's past through his future, as it were, or to ascribe to him a foresight which he may not have possessed, I have therefore treated each moment in his life as it was lived – and *only* as such. This will, I hope, allow for a searching and 'realistic' assessment, and a fuller appreciation not only of his successes, but also of his many failures, disappointments and shortcomings – the latter of which have sometimes been overlooked or minimized.

No biography, however, is ever perfect. There are, inevitably, some gaps in our knowledge, some lacunae in the evidential record, and, while I have attempted to fill them as best I am able, I must acknowledge that, like other works of its kind, my reconstruction of Machiavelli's life, thoughts and motivations is, at times, a matter of informed speculation. I am conscious that not all will agree – and that, as the frontiers of our knowledge are pushed back, the views I have expressed will most likely be challenged. Yet, if this book can impart a small fraction of the pleasure I have derived from writing it, and perhaps even inspire others to delve more deeply into the life of this most remarkable of men, it will have more than fulfilled its purpose.

Lyon
June 2019

PART I

The Pygmy

(1469–98)

1

Inauspicious Beginnings

(1469–76)

On 3 May 1469, the Via Pisana would have been thronged with travellers making their way from Pisa to Florence. It was always a busy road, but now that summer was approaching and the River Arno was becoming too shallow to navigate by boat, it would have been more crowded than usual. Apart from a few ragged journeymen and the occasional pilgrim, the majority of those plying its route would have been farmers from the surrounding countryside or merchants on their way from the wharfs. Some would have been herding animals. Others would have been carrying foodstuffs – from the beans and tripe that are still the mainstays of Florentine cuisine, to aromatic spices imported from the Near East, and richly woven carpets from Persia. Others still would have been driving carts or leading mules laden with the wool and silk on which Florence's economy depended. For all of them, it would have been a difficult journey. Although the Via Pisana followed the course of the Arno for much of the way, the terrain was often rugged, and – except in the few wooded stretches – the heat could be oppressive.

Rounding the hill of Bellosguardo, Florence would at last have come into view. Unlike many of its neighbours, such as Volterra or Siena, which had been founded on easily defensible hilltops, Florence lay in a plain, and could not be seen from further away – at least not along this route. But from the flower-strewn slopes of the *collina*, the whole city would have been visible. Ringed by the blue-tinted mountains and undulating fields dotted with hamlets and villas, it presented a formidable sight, an impression of which can be gained from *The Map of the Chain*, produced by an anonymous artist only a few years later. Writing at the beginning of the century, the chancellor Leonardo Bruni doubted whether there was any city on earth that was more splendid or distinguished. Indeed, so magnificent did it appear that no one – Bruni predicted – would ever possess the eloquence needed to describe the richness and diversity of its citizens' lives.[1]

On both sides of the Arno, Florence was girded by stout walls. Some 8.5 kilometres in length, and boasting no fewer than seventy-three towers, these enclosed an area of more than 600 hectares. They were not, to be sure, so massive as to inspire fear.[2] As the banker Benedetto Dei was to observe a few years later, they did not have a 'moat or a fortified citadel', nor were they attached to 'drawbridges, checkpoints, a fortress . . . or a stronghold'. They were not even guarded by 'sentinels [or] a standing army'.[3] But they could hardly be called imprudent. For more than one hundred years, they had kept Florence safe from attack, and were a symbol of the republican liberty of which its citizens were so proud.

Within the walls, Bruni noted, the city abounded with buildings more magnificent than anything found elsewhere.[4] Dominating the skyline was the great octagonal dome of Santa Maria del Fiore. Designed by Filippo Brunelleschi, it was said to be 'large enough to cover all the Tuscan people with its shadow', and would soon be crowned by Andrea del Verrocchio's golden cross.[5] Aside from the cathedral, however, there were more than a hundred other churches, many of which could clearly be made out, even at a distance.[6]

Not far from Santa Maria del Fiore was the imposing structure of the Palazzo della Signoria. Surmounted by a soaring bell-tower, this fortress-like edifice was the seat of Florentine government. In its great chambers, the councils and committees that administered the Republic's affairs gathered for their deliberation: the Signoria, the most senior executive body, consisting of a *gonfaloniere di giustizia* (standard-bearer of justice) and eight priors, each elected for a two-month term; the *Dodici Buon' Uomini* (Twelve Good Men), an advisory 'college' elected for three months at a time; the *Otto di Guardia* (Eight of the Watch), which oversaw security and policing; the *Dieci di Balìa* – sometimes called the *Dieci di Libertà e Pace* (Ten of Liberty and Peace) – which was called into being to deal with military affairs in times of war; the *Consiglio del Popolo* (Council of the People), a legislative body with 250 members; and a multiplicity of other, more specialized, committees. On the second floor, there were the offices of the chancellery. This consisted of a varying, but not inconsiderable, number of secretaries and notaries, who were each notionally assigned to the different organs of government, but who, in practice, all shared the enormous task of keeping up with the never-ending stream of letters, minutes and reports.

No less striking than these fine public buildings were the many *palazzi* that were dotted about the city. Owned by some of the city's richest families, these were nothing if not ostentatious. According to Bruni, these had been 'designed, built, and decorated for luxury, size, decency, and most especially for magnificence.'[7] They were, however, more than just a statement of wealth. They were also a visible affirmation of the political power that their owners wielded. For, while Florence may have been a republic, its institutions had long been dominated by those merchant bankers to whom the guilds deferred, and upon whose contributions the city's finances depended.

By far the most important of these palaces was the recently completed Palazzo Medici. It had been constructed by Cosimo 'il Vecchio' de' Medici, who, according to Giovanni Rucellai, was 'not only the richest Florentine, but the richest Italian of all time.'[8] From 1434 until his death, thirty years later, he had used his immense wealth 'to control the city government as if it had been his private property.' Having succeeded him as the city's de facto ruler, his son, Piero, was dying of gout in one of the *palazzo*'s many sumptuous chambers at that very moment.

Most of those travelling along the Via Pisana that afternoon would have been heading to the market. After climbing down from Bellosguardo, they would have entered the city through the Porta San Frediano – then, as now, an unpretentious brown-stone structure – and plunged headlong into Oltrarno, one of Florence's humbler quarters. Unlike most of the major thoroughfares on the north side of the Arno, the streets here were largely unpaved, and were filled with mud and filth. The many animals that passed along them naturally left their mark, and, despite the priors' repeated attempts to improve public hygiene, residents routinely failed to construct adequate cesspits, with the result that human excrement often spilled over into the road as well.

Although there were some fairly grand *palazzi* in this area, the majority of the dwellings that lined the streets were more modest. Inhabited mostly by cloth workers – particularly wool carders, combers, and beaters – these had usually been built in a disorganized manner according to the limited resources available. They tended to be narrow, rarely having a frontage more than five metres wide, but they were deep and often very tall, sometimes having as many as four storeys. In several cases, the ground floor would be taken up by a workshop, while the upper floors were given over to living quarters. But, more often than not, there was nothing to distinguish the workshop from the home at all, and it was not uncommon for several families of artisans to live and work under the same roof.

As the travellers approached the Ponte Vecchio, the streets would have become ever more cramped and noisy. But, had they glanced to their right before crossing the bridge and plunging into the bustling confusion of the market, they might have caught a glimpse of one particular house on the Via Romana (now the Via Guicciardini). Sandwiched between all manner of *botteghe* and taverns opposite the church of Santa Felicità, it was unlikely to impress. True, it was a little larger than most, and was sometimes even referred to as a *palazzo*,[9] but, like many other such buildings in the area, it was nothing more than a ramshackle collection of half-connected structures clustered around a small central courtyard.

Inside, it was scarcely any more imposing. Housing four branches of the same family, it was divided into four roughly equal parts. Since it was destroyed in the Second World War, there is no means of knowing precisely how the rooms were arranged in each household. But it was unlikely to have been very different from the home described by Michele di Nofri di Michele di Mato (1387–1463) some thirty years before.[10] On the ground floor, there was a large hall used for storing wine and other produce, such as flax, grain, flour and oil.[11] On the floor above, there would probably have been a single large room that functioned as living and sleeping space. Above that, the second floor would have been dominated by a sizeable kitchen, complete with an open fireplace. And, if there was a third floor (as seems likely), it would have contained two or three rooms, including the servants' sleeping quarters and perhaps a pantry as well.[12]

With almost thirty men, women and children all living around the same courtyard, it would have been a cramped and noisy place. Especially on a warm afternoon like 3 May 1469, the air would have been filled with the sound of wives scolding their husbands, children playing, servants chattering and crockery clattering. Yet, on one of the upper storeys, just as the office of None was beginning, all was happiness and joy. Watched over by her delighted second husband, Bernardo, the exhausted Bartolomea di Stefano was cradling their newborn son in her arms. And, as the bells of Santa Maria del Fiore echoed faintly in the distance, the infant who would shortly be given the name Niccolò Machiavelli opened his eyes onto the world for the very first time.

*

In some senses, Niccolò was born under a fortunate star. As Bernardo was anxious to point out in his *libro di ricordi* (a sort of personal diary), the Machiavelli were an old and well-esteemed family. Originally hailing from near the village of Giogoli, a few kilometres south of Florence, they were descended from the same stock as the lords of Montespertoli, and, though they belonged to the *popolani grassi* (literally 'fat' or 'rich people') rather than the disenfranchised urban nobility, they would always retain an air of distinction.[13] When they took up residence in Oltrarno, at some point in the thirteenth century, they were regarded as being among the foremost families in the vicinity of Santa Felicità.[14] So prominent were they, indeed, that, after Florence's defeat at the Battle of Montaperti on 4 September 1260, they – like others associated with the Guelph cause – were forced into exile.[15] But though at least one branch of the family would establish themselves permanently in Bologna, the Machiavelli proper were soon able to return, and had been fully rehabilitated by the dawn of the fourteenth century.[16] Steadily increasing their wealth, they threw themselves into public service, acting as priors on twelve occasions and as *gonfalonieri di giustizia* no fewer than fifty times.[17] There were, of course, some black sheep. Giovanni di Angiolino (*c.* 1250–1330), for example, was excommunicated for killing a priest while he was studying law in Bologna, and was later accused of rape and pederasty by members of the cathedral chapter.[18] But these were the exceptions rather than the rule. Before long, the more ambitious Machiavelli would find themselves in the first rank of Florentine society. The most remarkable was Buoninsegna di Angiolino (*c.* 1250–1330), the brother of the reprehensible Giovanni.[19] Born in turbulent times, he made a fortune out of his association with the Bardi banking house.[20] Having successfully represented the Bardi at the court of Charles II of Naples, he was chosen to negotiate with the legates of Pope Clement V on Florence's behalf in 1305.[21] He would also serve as prior ten times, as master of the mint twice, and as *gonfaloniere di giustizia* once, in 1326.[22]

After their *palazzo* narrowly escaped being burned down by disenfranchised cloth workers during the Ciompi Revolt (1378),[23] the Machiavelli began to concentrate on consolidation rather than growth. Generally contenting themselves with unremarkable careers in law, banking and commerce, they husbanded their resources carefully and jealously defended their rights, even when it meant engaging in costly legal suits.[24] Yet, the Machiavelli nevertheless remained a 'high status' family.[25] If nothing else, they were still wealthy enough to display their standing through cultural patronage. In 1438, for example, Alessandro di Filippo (d. *post* 1466) received the right to establish a family chapel in the convent church of Santa Felicità – opposite the Palazzo Machiavelli – and commissioned Ridolfo del Ghirlandaio to paint a (now lost) series of frescoes on its walls.[26]

Niccolò's father, Bernardo, had benefitted from the family's prosperity. His childhood had, admittedly, been marred by sadness. Born in early 1430, or a little before, he had lost his father while he was still in swaddling clothes.[27] Since it was customary for a widow to return to her own family after her husband's death, he had been placed in the care of his childless uncle, Giovanni di Buoninsegna. When Giovanni died in 1439, he was once again robbed of a father figure. But Bernardo did at least inherit a good deal of property. From his father – whose taxable assets in 1427 amounted to the not inconsiderable sum of 1,500 *fl.* (florins) – he inherited one of the *case* of which the Palazzo Machiavelli was composed, together with some land in Sant'Andrea in Percussina. He had also been named as Giovanni's principal heir, and received a further share in the family town-house, as well as an *albergaccio* in Sant'Andrea in Percussina, complete with a garden and loggia.[28] What was more, in 1445, another uncle, Totto di Buoninsegna, named him as substitute heir should his own children die or fail to produce offspring, and, five years later, Bernardo duly accepted half of the estate, alongside his illegitimate cousin, Machiavello.[29]

As befitted someone of his background, Bernardo began studying law at the Studio Fiorentino in around 1447. It was not a course for the faint-hearted. Quite apart from the difficulty of the subject itself, the Studio was then entering a period of decline.[30] As his fellow student, the future chancellor Bartolomeo Scala, later recalled, 'there was a tremendous shortage of books and teachers.'[31] But Bernardo was helped by his family's strong connections with the institution. His first cousin once removed, Francesco di Lorenzo di Filippo (d. 1428), had taught there earlier in the century, while his second cousin, Girolamo di Agnolo (1415–60), was among the teachers of law in his own day.[32] Such ties were not to be sniffed at. Like many others, Girolamo combined his legal scholarship with political service. He was in a position to help Bernardo not only with his studies, but also with his career beyond the university. By 1447, Girolamo had already served as a *gonfaloniere di compagnia* ('standard-bearer of the companies', responsible for one of Florence's sixteen districts); as one of the *ufficiali dell'onestà* (officials of decency), who supervised the city's communal brothels; as a member of the *Ufficio della Grascia* (Office of Grace), which controlled the price of goods and services; and on a commission appointed to revise the Republic's laws, statutes and provisions.

Bernardo had an aptitude for learning. Whether or not he ever took his doctorate in law, his legal knowledge – and his abiding faith in legal justice – earned him the respect of his contemporaries. Indeed, so highly was he thought of that he later appeared as one of the two interlocutors in Bartolomeo Scala's dialogue *De legibus et iudiciis* ('On Laws and Legal Judgements').[33] Apparently set during Carnival, this took the form of a debate about whether it was better to be ruled by good laws or a good prince.[34] Pouring scorn on the ineffectiveness of human legislation and the corruption of judges, Bartolomeo's character maintains that only under a wise guardian like Cosimo de' Medici could mankind's natural inclination towards disorder be restrained. Bernardo's character, by contrast, upholds the idea of law as the embodiment of justice and reason. Although he is careful to avoid casting any aspersions on Cosimo de' Medici, he argues that those who hold the reins of power are often tempted to succumb to evil desires. As such, it was far better to place one's trust in a structure of laws, rather than in the goodwill of a fallible prince.

Bernardo's interests were, however, not limited to jurisprudence. He had a voracious appetite for the ancient classics, and he was acquainted with some of the city's leading humanists. Dropping in to see Scala at his magnificent palace in the Borgo Pinti, he came into regular contact with figures such as Angelo Poliziano, Marsilio Ficino and Leon Battista Alberti.[35] He also had a small, but respectable, private library, which he often supplemented with books borrowed from friends or the convent of Santa Croce. By the time little Niccolò had turned seven, Bernardo had purchased or borrowed Cicero's *De officiis*, a compendium of works on logic – including Boethius's *De divisione* and *De topicis differentiis* (a translation of Aristotle's *Topics*) – and Ptolemy's *Cosmographia*.[36] His passion for classical texts was so strong, in fact, that when 'Maestro Nicolò Tedesco' approached him in the Via Calimala in September 1475 and suggested that he compile a topographical index to Livy's *Ab urbe condita* in return for a copy of the text, he jumped at the chance.[37] Evidently relishing the task, he worked quickly, and was able to present Nicolò Tedesco with the index ten months later, in July 1476. No sooner had he done so than he was seeking out other works on historical and geographical subjects, as well as additional volumes on philosophy and rhetoric. Over the years that followed, he would get his hands on Cicero's *Philippics* and *De oratore*, Pliny the Elder's *Naturalis historia*, Macrobius's *Commentary on the Dream of Scipio* and *Saturnalia*, Aristotle's *Nicomachean Ethics* – together with the commentary of Donato Acciauoli – pseudo-Cicero's *Rhetorica ad Herennium*, Justinus's *Epitome* and Flavio Biondo's *Italia illustrata*.[38]

Niccolò's mother, Bartolomea, was no intellectual sluggard either. Hailing from the Mugello, her family had accumulated a modest fortune from trade, and had enjoyed close ties with Petrarch in the previous century.[39] Although her date of birth cannot be known with any certainty, she is known to have been raised in an affluent household which was sympathetic to humanistic studies, and which allowed her to share in the fruits of the new learning. At a relatively young age, she married the apothecary Niccolò di Girolamo di Niccolò Benizi, and soon bore him a daughter, Lionarda.[40] After being widowed in 1457, she married Bernardo, whose family *palazzo* was diagonally opposite the Benizi's home in Oltrarno. By the time Niccolò was born, she had already borne him two further daughters: Primavera (b. *c.* 1465) and Margherita (b. *c.* 1468). But her work was not limited to the home. Despite legal restrictions on the economic role of women, she appears to have conducted business on her own initiative. In his *libro di ricordi*, Bernardo mentions her dealing with fullers and weavers on several occasions.[41] She also played music, read books and wrote whenever she had time. According to family tradition, she composed a number of religious verses (*laudi*), which she dedicated to Niccolò.[42]

Yet, while Niccolò took his first steps in a busy, happy household filled with books, stories and songs, his beginnings were not quite as auspicious as they might seem. Later in life, he claimed that he was 'born into poverty and ... at an early age learned to scrimp rather than to thrive', and, though his judgement was doubtless coloured by a desire to elicit his readers' sympathy, he was not so very far from the truth.[43]

Gifted as Bernardo may have been, he never amounted to much. He never practised law, he never engaged in banking or trade to any appreciable degree and he never took part in the political life of the Florentine Republic. Indeed, compared to many of his contemporaries, one might even say that he was something of a failure – at least in professional terms. This is not, however, to say that he was indolent. He was, instead, a victim of circumstance.

Bernardo had always lived under something of a cloud. From his earliest childhood, he had been dogged by doubts about the legitimacy of his birth. Although the legacies he received from family members suggest that this was never seriously challenged – least of all in a court of law – the possibility that he may have been born after his father's death left room for uncertainty. That he was often vague about his date of birth in later years probably did not help him either.[44] This was no trifling matter. While Florence treated bastards more sympathetically than many other cities, it still subjected them to a range of legal restrictions.[45] They were prevented from joining certain guilds and were prohibited from practising law.[46] They were also precluded from holding public office. In 1404, bastards were forbidden to sit on any of the major executive or legislative councils; and, in 1428, a law was passed imposing a fine of 500 *fl.* on anyone who attempted to do so.[47] Even if Bernardo was not a bastard – as the evidence seems to suggest – gossip could still be damaging. It was a bad start.

As time wore on, however, things only got worse. Just as he was reaching the end of his legal studies, his life was disrupted by political unrest. For some years, opposition to the Medici had been growing.[48] Many of the *ottimati* (literally 'the best', but used to mean 'magnates' or 'elite') – as leading members of the *popolo grasso* now liked to style themselves – had begun to resent attempts to reduce them to the status of mere clients, and the Republic to that of a private enterprise. In 1454, an attempt was therefore made to dismantle the dominant oligarchy and to restore the 'popular' form of government that Florence had traditionally enjoyed. Although this was largely successful, the reforms that were enacted proved fragile.[49] Not only were the *ottimati* unable to prevent the Medici's supporters from holding office, but, as the city's financial situation worsened, they also began to divide against themselves. By 1458, Cosimo de' Medici felt ready to retake control of the government, and set about arranging for the necessary constitutional changes to be made.[50] Some *ottimati* were determined to put up a fight, though. When Cosimo's proposals were put before the *pratica* – an ad hoc committee set up to advise the priors – they were met with unexpected opposition. Among the most vocal was Bernardo Machiavelli's second cousin, Girolamo. Owing in large part to his efforts, the proposals were rejected. Thwarted, Cosimo was forced to appeal to a public *parlamento*, but, before doing so, he took the precaution of having Girolamo arrested on a charge of having induced one of the other members of the *pratica* to vote against his plans. Girolamo was tortured and then exiled to Avignon for twenty-five years.[51] Two years later, however, he was caught conspiring against the newly restored Medici regime in the Lunigiana, and was imprisoned in Florence, where he died a short time later, either from ill-treatment or from torture.[52] Before he succumbed, he confessed all he knew, and, as a result of his testimony, some twenty-five other citizens were banished.[53]

Strictly speaking, Bernardo's kinship to Girolamo need not have been too great a problem. Although a rebel's immediate family were usually made to suffer, more distant relations were seldom treated as guilty by association. Provided that they were eligible to do so, they could even go on to hold public office. One of Girolamo's cousins, Alessandro di Filippo, was chosen as one of the officials of the *catasto* for the Florentine *contado* only weeks after his relation's arrest in 1458, and later served as a member of the *balìa* in 1466.[54] Another, Paolo di Giovanni, even went on to serve as *gonfaloniere di giustizia* in 1478, and as captain of Pisa and Livorno in 1483 and 1488.[55] Like them, Bernardo could probably have shrugged off

Girolamo's fate without suffering any ill effects. But the involvement of his wife's former in-laws made this more difficult. In 1458, four members of the Benizi clan had been sent into exile, and, after Girolamo confessed in 1460, two were declared rebels.[56] With rebels on both sides of his family, Bernardo was bound to be regarded with mistrust, and even if there were never any grounds to launch formal proceedings against him, he would still have been subject to unspoken social constraints. But there was nothing Bernardo could do about it. More so even than the question of his legitimacy, this would have been a serious impediment to any kind of public life.

Bernardo's greatest professional handicap was, however, his indebtedness. Although he had inherited a considerable amount of property from his father and his uncles, he had also inherited their debts. These were not to be sniffed at. The 1433 *catasto* returns indicate that his father had died owing money to twenty-four different people; and, in the same year, his uncle Giovanni identified a further seventeen creditors.[57] Some of these were owed large sums. Giovanni di Barducci – from whom Bernardo's father had apparently purchased land in Sant'Andrea in Percussina – had the figure of 400 *fl.* written against his name; and there were several others demanding the repayment of similar sums.

For a young man with a wife and three children (four, after Totto's arrival, in 1475), this was a heavy burden to bear.[58] Even before Girolamo's conspiracy had been discovered, Bernardo had begun to fall behind with his taxes. Soon enough, he was placed on the *specchio* (the list of tax defaulters). Some of his arrears were waived shortly after Niccolò was born. As he noted in his *libro di ricordi*, those that had accrued since 1458 were set aside in 1475, along with another tax bill dating back a few years earlier. But he was still liable for 245 *fl.* that had been owed since before 1458. And since he agreed to repay this in instalments of 2½ *fl.* every six months – in addition to keeping up with the tax bills that continued to pour in regularly – he would have remained on the *specchio* for the remainder of his life.[59] This destroyed any hopes of pursuing a legal career that he might still have had. In the late fifteenth century, tax debtors were not only subject to a certain social stigma, but were also forbidden from holding public office or practising as notaries.[60] He had to accept that the law was closed to him.

Unable to ply his trade, Bernardo had to rely on his country farms for sustenance. These provided him with a regular supply of basic foodstuffs. There were barrels of oil, red wine and vinegar, tubs of broad beans, and bushels of wheat, oats and barley, albeit of a rather low quality.[61] Sometimes, there were apples and cheeses as well.[62] On certain feast days, Bernardo also took delivery of capons, eggs, geese and fish, and, once a year, he received a number of fattened pigs.[63] This all helped keep his family fed, but Bernardo's properties did not provide him with much in the way of an income. Given that his tenants paid him mostly in kind, rents were low. Even then, they were often difficult to collect. The Tuscan sharecropping system was inefficient at best, and farmers were forever falling into debt.[64] To his credit, Bernardo occasionally provided his tenants with incentives to cultivate difficult plots of land, and worked with them to help ensure a good yield.[65] But they still had a nasty habit of short-changing him. Indeed, he was even obliged to lend *them* money on occasions.[66] Of the little he made, most came from the sale of produce, such as wool, flax and wood. He could also claim a half-share from the sale of certain livestock. This was, however, a time-consuming and thankless practice. Even in the best of years, it brought in a mere pittance.

With few resources at his disposal, Bernardo had to struggle for every last *denaro*. He was not a natural businessman. He found it difficult to make sales, and never got to grips with haggling. But, as his *libro di ricordi* testifies, he was not afraid to kick up a fuss if he believed that someone owed him money. It didn't matter how small the debt was. Indeed, the more trifling the amount, the more tenaciously he would fight. In July 1475, for example, he took two muleteers to court for having failed to pay for some brushwood that they had purchased from him.[67] His most bitter dispute was with a butcher named Rolomo d'Agnolo di Cristofano Cecchi.[68] In early April 1476, Bernardo's tenant, Jacopo di Luca, agreed to sell Romolo nine lambs at twenty *soldi* each. As part of this deal, Bernardo was to receive half of the sale price. When Jacopo delivered the lambs a few days later, however, Romolo claimed that some of the ewes were undernourished and he refused to pay the agreed price, demanding a discount of twenty-one *soldi*. When Bernardo learned of this, he was furious. Storming down to the butcher's shop, he started shouting at Rolomo at the top of his voice. When Romolo cannily drew him into a pointless debate about the sort of cheese that could be made from ewe's milk, he became even angrier. In the end, he had to ask a friend to mediate, and, even then, did not manage to recover the full amount until several weeks later.

But, no matter how hard Bernardo tried, it was never enough. At times, he was so hard up that he had to sell his clothes just to make ends meet.[69] Nevertheless, Bernardo and Bartolomea did their best to keep up appearances. Fiercely proud of their status as members of the social elite, they were determined not to let standards slip at home. Somehow, they always managed to scrape together the money to pay the servants, and they never flinched from taking care of their old retainers when they were too elderly or infirm to work any longer.[70] They continued to visit their wealthy friends, and received visitors in return.[71] But there was nevertheless something shabby about their domestic arrangements. The *palazzo* on the Via Romana had always been a rather tumbledown place, but, during Niccolò's youth, it began to reek of decay. Although the maid, Monna Brigida, was supposed to sweep the house every Saturday, it always seemed to be dusty.[72] Repairs were continually being put off. And there were times when even Bernardo couldn't help feeling ashamed of how he was dressed.[73]

Even when it was at its most bookish, their daily life was fraught with tawdry distractions. While Bernardo was busy composing his topographical index to Livy's *Ab urbe condita*, for example, his wife informed him that her unmarried maid, Nencia, appeared to be pregnant. Since his own honour would be impugned if there had been any immoral behaviour in his household, Bernardo was naturally deeply alarmed. When Nencia was questioned, however, she revealed not only that she was pregnant, but also that she was bearing the child of Bernardo's distant cousin, Niccolò di Alessandro Machiavelli, who lived in another part of the *palazzo*. She claimed that they had been having an affair since the previous November. At first, it was she who had visited Niccolò while his wife was pregnant, sneaking out of the house at night, when the rest of the family was asleep. But, later, when Niccolò's wife was sick, he had come to visit her instead. Tiptoeing across the courtyard, he had slipped in through the kitchen window and had his way with her in front of the hearth. It had been fun while it lasted, of course; but now, Nencia's prospects were ruined. Niccolò was doing his best to escape responsibility, claiming that his friend, Francesco Renzi, was to blame, rather than him. Naturally, Bernardo did not believe a word of this. He was furious with Niccolò. When the two met in the street in front of Santa Felicità, he gave Niccolò a piece of his mind. But he still helped to smooth things over, arranging for Nencia to be looked after discreetly until she gave birth, and compelling his errant cousin to pay for her dowry when she eventually got married.

Little Niccolò was, of course, too young to understand all these comings and goings. But even if he could not comprehend the causes of his hardship, it would shape the course of his life ever after. Family was, after all, still the primary determinant of a person's standing and prospects in the late fifteenth century. If Bernardo did not manage to pay off his tax arrears before his death, Niccolò would be set at a severe disadvantage. Not only would he be tainted with the same social stigma as his father, but he would also be prohibited from pursuing certain careers. Florence's laws forbade the sons of public debtors from practising as notaries, and from standing for public office. From 1476 onwards, restrictions were placed on their ability to inherit, as well. Unless they wanted to repudiate their claims to a legacy, they would be obliged to assume responsibility for any unpaid taxes on the property they had been left.[74] All this was, of course, still in the future. But it was hardly the most dazzling start in life for a young lad.

2

The Golden Age

(1476–85)

Poor though he may have been, Bernardo was ambitious for his firstborn son, and could see which way the winds of progress were blowing. For some time now, Florentines had believed they were living in a new 'Golden Age'. Writing only a few years earlier, Ugolino Verino (1438–1516) had expressed his delight at having been born at a time when the liberal arts had been restored to glory and erudite men were showered with honours.[1] And, since Lorenzo de' Medici had 'succeeded' his father as Florence's *de facto* ruler, the city had risen to even greater heights. Still in the first flower of youth, Lorenzo was a fine figure of a man. Possessing a joyful spirit, he played *calcio* and *palloni*, he went hunting and hawking, and was forever bursting into song.[2] As long as the city was at peace, he kept it 'always celebrating festivities, in which jousts and presentations of ancient deeds and triumphs were to be seen.'[3] Most of all, he exalted the arts. A talented poet in his own right, he took the greatest pleasure in architecture, music, philosophy and literature. More so even than his father Piero – whom Verino had hailed as 'a new Maecenas born on Tuscan soil'[4] – he showered patronage upon those with talent. Playing on the associations of his name, Angelo Poliziano hailed him as 'the laurel honoured by the Muses . . . under whose spreading leaves Phoebus plays his lyre and sings sweetly.'[5] Every summer, he and his handsome brother, Giuliano, would invite a circle of humanistic friends for days of classical discussion and philosophical musings at their country villas at Careggi and Cafaggiolo.[6]

Bernardo had little taste for the Medici. Although he was far too careful to express his opposition openly, he belonged to a lay confraternity (the Compagnia di San Girolamo, or, more commonly, the

'Pietà') known for its anti-Medicean sympathies.[7] But he appreciated that the favours Lorenzo bestowed on leading humanists were a reflection of the practical utility of the liberal arts in Florentine society. Since the late thirteenth century, communal government had grown steadily more complex and sophisticated as its institutional structure had been fixed, and its hold over the surrounding *contado* had tightened. This had necessitated a body of people with a command of Latin, capable of drafting laws, keeping records and dealing with official correspondence with subject towns and neighbouring states. At the same time, there emerged a distinctively 'civic' culture, which 'confronted issues that neither the chivalric culture of feudalism nor the scholastic culture of northern universities could address.'[8] Struggling to preserve its republican liberty against the acquisitive designs of its neighbours, members of the commune had looked to the ancient past for the political vocabulary with which to justify and defend their constitutional structure. As such, the study and emulation of classical literature had soon become an essential prerequisite, not only for a growing class of professional bureaucrats, but also for members of the *popolani grassi* who wished to participate in civic government or pursue a career in law, medicine or the Church. Indeed, so entrenched had this become by the mid-fifteenth century that an understanding of Latin (and, increasingly, Greek) had come to denote membership of Florence's social elite.

While those of humbler stock were content for their sons to learn only enough to be able to read a notary's letter or to manage simple accounts, Bernardo wanted to give Niccolò a thoroughly humanistic education. He was determined that – despite the family's deprivations – there would be no doubt about his son's gentle birth. Much like Leon Battista Alberti (1404–72), he knew that 'no matter how much of a gentleman someone might be, he [would] be regarded as nothing but a country bumpkin' without a solid grounding in Latin.[9] But Bernardo also hoped that it would allow Niccolò to escape the poverty in which he was raised.

With a good classical education under his belt, Niccolò would be able to pursue any of the professions. Even if he did not enter the law, he would be admirably placed to assume a position of prominence in civic government, or even to follow a career in medicine or the Church, should the whim take him. Indeed, if he showed genuine talent, he might even catch the eye of a wealthy patron with an amusing epigram in Latin, or a well-turned translation from the Greek.

When Niccolò began his schooling is not known, but he is likely to have learned to read between the relatively young ages of four and six.[10] Placed in the care of an elementary teacher, Niccolò would have been taught using the *tavola* (hornbook).[11] This was a sheet of paper or parchment on which the letters of the alphabet were written, together with one or two prayers, if space allowed. A piece of transparent horn or mica was usually placed over the paper to prevent damage. Often, the hornbook was also equipped with a rudimentary handle, so that it could be held in one hand while the letters were traced with the other.[12] Once Niccolò had mastered the alphabet with this, he would have progressed to the *salterio* (literally 'psalter'). This was a primer containing pages of syllables, some prayers and perhaps a few psalms. Niccolò would have first learnt all of the two-letter syllables (*da, de, di, do, du*), then all of the three-letter syllables (*ban, ben, bin, bon, bun*), and finally the four-letter syllables (*scia, scie, scii, scio, sciu*). Then, he would have tackled words formed from a pair of two-letter syllables (*Ie-su, Ro-ma*), before moving on to three- and eventually four-syllable nouns.[13] Next, he would have been introduced to phrases consisting of a pair of short phrases; and eventually, he would have read entire sentences.

But, given that the *salterio* was written in Latin – or, more rarely, in Latin and Italian – Niccolò would not have been expected to understand what he was learning to read at this stage. This was, however, less problematic than it might seem. It was, after all, difficult to teach a child to read and write a vernacular language like Italian, which was still subject to tremendous regional variation and which lacked a stable orthography. Latin, by contrast, was regarded as an eternal and unchanging language, with the fixed spellings and well-defined phonetic rules that made it particularly suitable for teaching basic literacy skills.[14] In any case, Latin and Italian were similar enough that a child who had learned to read and write in the former would easily be able to apply his skills to the latter at a later date.

On 6 May 1476, only three days after his seventh birthday, Niccolò began his study of the Latin language in earnest. As his father proudly noted in his *libro di ricordi*, he was sent to learn grammar with Matteo della Rocca (d. 1480), a forty-two-year-old communal master listed on the university roll, whose school was at the foot of the Santa Trinità bridge, on the opposite side of the Arno.[15] But, for whatever reason, he stayed with 'Master Matteo' for less than a year. On 5 March 1477, he instead went to study with Battista di Filippo da Poppi, an independent master, whose school was on the corner of the Via dello Studio and the Via delle Oche, barely fifty metres from the Duomo.[16] This proved more satisfactory. Indeed, as Niccolò's education progressed, Bernardo and the new schoolmaster seem to have become quite friendly, even going so far as to lend one another books over the coming years.[17]

Early each morning, Niccolò would have taken his place on one of the simple wooden benches arranged around the schoolmaster's desk, and opened the copy of the '*donadello*' that his father had bought for him.[18] Also known as the *Ianua* (gateway) because of the opening words of its prologue, this textbook had long been attributed to the fourth-century grammarian, Aelius Donatus – albeit mistakenly – and had dominated the grammar curriculum for at least two hundred years.[19] In some quarters, to be sure, it was already being surpassed by more modern works, such as Guarino da Verona's *Regulae grammaticales* (*c.* 1450), but it was still preferred by many parents like Bernardo, who had studied it themselves and who regarded it as the voice of authority.[20] It was not easy, though. Composed in a catechetical style, it introduced the parts of speech (nouns, verbs, participles, conjunctions etc.) using a series of questions and answers. These were insufferably turgid. '*Poet* is what part?' it began. 'It is a noun. What is a noun? That which signifies proper or common substance and quality by means of case. How many attributes does a noun have? Five. What are they?'[21] And so on. When these definitions had at last been exhausted, it then detailed the conjugation of verbs and the declension of nouns, pronouns and adjectives in the same laborious manner. No illustrative examples were provided. Nor were any other mnemonic devices, for that matter. Niccolò and his classmates were expected simply to read, recite and eventually memorize the whole thing. They would repeat it continually until they were word-perfect.[22]

If Niccolò made a mistake, he could expect to be chastised severely, or even threatened with the rod. But Florentine schoolmasters were a far cry from Dickens' Wackford Squeers. Although beatings were sometimes meted out, teachers generally confined themselves to the most moderate forms of corporal punishment.[23] A slap across the wrists was about as severe as it got; anything more was thought to be counterproductive. As Aeneas Silvius Piccolomini (1405–64) advised in his *De liberorum educatione* (1450), boys of gentle birth were better served by 'praise and blame' than by blows.[24] For, while the latter would lead them to hate their master, the former – if used in moderation – would incite them to virtuous study.

After mastering the *donadello*, Niccolò would most likely have started reading 'proper' Latin using the *Disticha Catonis*. A collection of verse couplets often appended to early printed editions of the *Ianua*, this was widely believed to have been written by Marcus Portius Cato (234–149 BC), and was highly esteemed for its supposedly 'classical' style.[25] Consisting of between twelve and fifteen words, each couplet taught a moral lesson. Many of these emphasized the virtues of patience, humility and temperance. But others conveyed more practical messages that would doubtless have struck a chord with the young Niccolò. 'Since Nature created you as a naked child,' read one, 'Remember to bear the burden of poverty patiently.'[26] 'Scorn riches if you wish to be happy in mind,' read another, 'For those who seek them, always beg as misers.'[27]

*

Just as Niccolò was getting to grips with the *Disticha Catonis*, however, his education was interrupted by civil unrest. Glorious though Lorenzo de' Medici's reputation may have been among the humanists he entertained at his country villas, his *reggimento* was anything but secure. In private, many Florentines had already begun complaining about his haughty manner.[28] Some *popolani* felt that the extravagance with which he greeted foreign dignitaries would have been fitting for a noble lord, but was inappropriate for a private citizen. Wealthier families attacked him for confiscating inheritances or forcing their children to marry against their wishes. The *ottimati* resented his habit of having ambassadors report to him before presenting themselves to the Signoria. And those who had been deprived of their offices for punishing his friends' misdemeanours openly denounced him as a tyrant.

At first, Lorenzo paid little heed to such grumblings, confident that he could weather any domestic storms. But, when his father's old ally, Tommaso di Lorenzo Soderini – who had been one of the *accoppiatori* (the officials entrusted with deciding which citizens were eligible to stand for election) since the 1440s[29] – urged the Signoria to end its relationship with Milan and instead ally with Naples or even Venice, the vulnerability of his position began to dawn upon him.[30] He now saw that, if the carpet was not to be pulled out from under his feet, he would have to tighten his grip on the organs of power.

He first turned his attention to the Signoria. Since 1466, the priors had been elected by the *accoppiatori*, who had themselves been chosen by the Cento (Hundred), a new council set up to scrutinize legislation after Girolamo Machiavelli's coup.[31] But since neither of these could be relied upon to return a Signoria loyal to the Medici if left to their own devices, Lorenzo forced through a measure decreeing that, in future, new *accoppiatori* would be chosen by their predecessors and the Signoria then in office.[32] Given that he could count on most of the priors and *accoppiatori* at that precise moment, he felt confident of being able to control all appointments to the Signoria in future.

Lorenzo then turned to the Cento. Although he could usually muster a good number of votes, he could not always be sure of gaining the two-thirds majority needed to pass legislation. Such a risk was no longer acceptable. In July 1471, a newly elected Signoria obedient to his wishes proposed that a special committee (*balìa*) should be created to reform the Cento's composition.[33] Officially, its first forty members would be chosen by the Signoria and the *accoppiatori*, while the remaining two hundred would be chosen by the forty, the Signoria and the *accoppiatori* together. But, in reality, it was Lorenzo who picked the forty. Once they had then packed the rest of the *balìa* with Medici supporters, they appointed themselves as permanent members of the Cento, appropriating sweeping powers over fiscal and military affairs as they did so.

As Benedetto Dei remarked, Lorenzo seemed to have become the 'master of the shop'.[34] But his reforms actually did him more harm than good.[35] In concentrating all political patronage in his own hands, Lorenzo had denied the *ottimati* any meaningful share in government and had thereby alienated them even further. At the same time, he also found it difficult to maintain the loyalty of the vast network of clients through which he sought to dominate the city's councils and committees. Not only did many prominent families feel rather humiliated by their dependence on the Medici, but the uneven distribution of favours also caused resentment. Whenever Lorenzo bestowed an office or sinecure on one supporter, he earned the enmity of two others who had coveted the same position. Rather than strengthening his *reggimento*, therefore, he had succeeded only in creating a growing body of disgruntled outsiders, who, finding themselves without anywhere else to turn, were soon looking to foreign powers for support against Lorenzo.

The severity of the danger became apparent as the fortunes of the Medici bank took a turn for the worst.[36] For more than a decade, its assets had been shrinking. As Niccolò later recorded, it had even had to call in a number of loans from Florentines, causing many businesses to fail and earning the family much enmity.[37] But a radical restructuring had done nothing to stop the decline. By the time Lorenzo had pushed through his reforms, lending was already being reined in and branches had begun closing. Before long, the Medici's primacy among Florentine banks was in serious jeopardy. The great banking dynasties, the Strozzi and the Pazzi – both strong rivals – even dared hope they might soon oust the Medici as papal bankers.

By selling off lands in the Mugello, Lorenzo was able to secure just enough liquidity to fend off the challenge. But when the recently elected Pope Sixtus IV decided to strengthen his hold over the Papal States, Lorenzo's task became more difficult. Having tried and failed to impose his will on Città di Castello – which had repelled the papal forces with Florentine help – Sixtus had set his heart on wresting Imola from Milan's grasp. Much to the pope's dismay, however, the duke of Milan, Galeazzo Maria Sforza, initially offered to sell it to Florence. But, after being threatened with dire punishments, the duke was eventually persuaded to let the pope have it for 40,000 ducats. Naturally, Sixtus asked Lorenzo, as the papal banker, to lend him the money. At that precise moment, Lorenzo could not afford to finance such an enormous loan. But even if he had somehow been able to scrape together enough money, he could not have acceded to the pope's request without exposing himself to tremendous criticism for acting against Florence's territorial interests. Lorenzo therefore declined the pope's request, and, guessing what his next move would be, urged the Pazzi not to lend him the money either. But the Pazzi could not pass up the opportunity that fate had handed them. They gave Sixtus all that he needed, and even told him about what Lorenzo had said. It was the last straw. Without waiting to hear any more, Sixtus dismissed the Medici as his bankers.

The burgeoning relationship between Lorenzo's rivals and the papacy was strengthened by a dispute over ecclesiastical appointments. For obvious reasons, the Signoria had always been anxious that the seven dioceses in its territory – Florence, Pisa, Cortona, Volterra, Arezzo, Pistoia and Fiesole – should be given to men upon whom it could rely; and, as long as the Medici remained in the ascendant, they had also worked hard to ensure the selection of candidates loyal to the family. When the archbishop of Florence died in 1473, Lorenzo thus petitioned to have his brother appointed to fill the vacancy. But Sixtus IV refused and instead nominated his own nephew, Pietro Riario. When Pietro died the following year, the pope then added insult to injury by choosing Francesco Salviati. He was hardly well suited to a clerical career. According to Poliziano, he was 'devoted to gambling' and was 'guilty of every sort of shameful act'.[38] What was more, he was also 'a great flatterer, very frivolous, [and] very vain'. He was, however, one of Sixtus' closest allies, and a kinsman of the Pazzi. This was too much for Lorenzo to bear. Unwilling to be denied a second time, he induced the Signoria to reject Salviati's candidature, and kicked up such a fuss that Sixtus was forced to appoint Lorenzo's brother-in-law, Rinaldo Orsini, in his place. But the pope was not to be outdone. When the archbishopric of Pisa fell vacant in October 1474, he immediately appointed Salviati. Furious, Lorenzo refused to allow Salviati to take possession of his see. Yet his stubbornness was not as well received as he might have hoped. Lorenzo's enemies criticized him in the councils, and even his supporters urged him to think again.[39] Such opposition only strengthened his resolve. Determined to enforce his will, he held on for a further three years. But the face-off could not last forever. The longer it went on, the more cracks appeared in the Medici *reggimento*. Eventually, he had to give in. Salviati would be allowed to take up his seat. In return, the pope promised that no new prelates would be appointed within Florentine territory without the express consent of the Signoria, and to create a Florentine cardinal to bolster the Medici's standing at the Curia.

But the damage was done. Out of the confrontation emerged a coalition committed to removing the Medici. As early as 1475,

Galeazzo Maria Sforza warned Lorenzo that Sixtus and Salviati were planning to kill him and his brother, Giuliano, with the conniv-ance of the archbishop's brother, Jacopo ('an altogether obscure and sordid person'[40]), and the pope's nephew, Girolamo Riario, the recently created count of Imola. When Lorenzo foolishly passed a law preventing one of the Pazzi's wives from inheriting her father's estate in 1476, Jacopo and Francesco de' Pazzi were also persuaded to join the conspiracy.[41] And when Galeazzo Maria Sforza was unexpectedly assassinated later that year, Bernardo Bandini dei Baroncelli and the humanist Jacopo Bracciolini, too, were drawn into the plot, together with Duke Federico da Montefeltro of Urbino and the mercenary captain, Giovanbattista da Montesecco.[42]

After much discussion, they decided to strike on Saturday, 25 April 1478. Concealed in the retinue of Cardinal Raffaele Riario, they originally intended to present themselves at the Medici's villa in Fiesole and kill the brothers when they were off their guard. But when they learned Giuliano would not be present, they were forced to change their plans. On the pretence that the cardinal wanted to see the splendid ornaments in the Palazzo Medici for himself, they asked Lorenzo to receive him at a banquet the next day, Sunday, 26 April. Suspecting nothing, Lorenzo agreed. At the last moment, however, the conspirators discovered that, once again, Giuliano would not be attending. On learning that both brothers were then at Mass in the *Duomo*, they decided to delay no longer. Though the designated assassin, Giovanbattista da Montesecco, refused to shed blood in a church, two priests agreed to take his place, and together, they hurried off. As the consecrated host was raised aloft, they struck. Bernardo Bandini and Francesco de' Pazzi ran Giuliano through with their swords, killing him on the spot. Lorenzo, assailed by the priests, was badly wounded, but managed to escape to the safety of the sacristy with Poliziano's help.[43]

Meanwhile, Francesco Salviati burst into the Palazzo della Signoria with his brother and Jacopo Bracciolini, demanding that the Signoria hand over control of the city. But the Signoria was not so easily overawed. Raising the alarm, the priors grabbed whatever weapons they could find and fought the archbishop's men back. Seeing that things were not going to plan, Jacopo de' Pazzi then rode to the Piazza della Signoria in the hope of kick-starting a popular uprising. But his cries of *'Popolo e libertà!'* ('The people and freedom!') fell on deaf ears.[44] No effort having been made to court public opinion in advance, the people were wary, and when they learned that Lorenzo was still alive, their scepticism turned to outright hostility. Jacopo knew that the conspiracy had failed. Turning on his heels, he fled; and moments later, Lorenzo de' Medici arrived in the square with bands of armed men. They slaughtered everyone they found. Francesco Salviati, Jacopo Bracciolini and Francesco de' Pazzi had nooses tied around their necks and were thrown out of the windows of the Palazzo della Signoria, soon to be joined by the archbishop's brother and cousin. There, they were left to twist in the wind as the butchery continued below. Casting his mind back to the gruesome scene some time later, Poliziano reported that, as Francesco Salviati entered his last death throes, his eyes were wide open in rage, and 'either by chance or anger' he dug his teeth into Francesco de' Pazzi's chest.[45]

From Battista di Filippo da Poppi's school, Niccolò – who was just a few days short of his ninth birthday – would doubtless have heard the commotion. He would already have been poring over the *Disticha Catonis* for several hours when the first shouts were raised in the Duomo, and from his seat, he would easily have been able to make out the sound of horses' hooves clattering over the cobbles as the conspirators hurried to the Piazza della Signoria. His teacher would probably have been too cautious to allow the boys to see what was happening for themselves, but it is just possible that Niccolò might also have heard the distant cheers of the Medici's supporters as Salviati and his fellow plotters were hurled to their deaths later that afternoon.

He was, of course, far too young to understand exactly what was going on. But, in the weeks that followed, he would have felt the effects the conspiracy had on his family. As Lorenzo started hunting down the remaining plotters, Niccolò's father grew nervous. Although Bernardo had been careful to keep his head down, he was still tainted by the memory of his cousin's conspiracy, twenty years earlier, and could hardly deny his membership of the 'Pietà'. Slight though the danger may have been, there was always a risk that he might be suspected of complicity. What was more, his property was in jeopardy, too. As soon as news of Francesco Salviati's death reached Rome, Sixtus – supported by King Ferrante of Naples – immediately declared war on Florence, and, before he had even had a chance to mourn his brother, Lorenzo prepared for invasion. Accompanied by heavy rainfall, mercenaries were soon marching through the countryside near Bernardo's properties south of the city. Even though they were in Florence's pay, they were a fearsome presence. As Niccolò later argued, professional soldiers tended to be of a criminal disposition, and were known for robbing, raping, and murdering their friends as much as their enemies.[46] Unnerved, Bernardo's tenants asked him to take their attractive sister, Sandra, into the security of his house in Florence,[47] and it was not long before they thought it wise to bring their sheep to safer ground, as well.[48] Given that any unharvested crops would probably have been lost at the same time, Bernardo would have seen his meagre income fall even further; and it is an indication of his straitened circumstances that, at the beginning of the next year, he was embroiled in a bitter dispute over a handful of firewood.[49]

All this had a knock-on effect on Niccolò's education. It was probably at around this time that Bernardo removed Niccolò from Battista di Filippo da Poppi's school and instead placed him in the care of Benedetto Riccardini, who had already been engaged to teach the boy's distant cousin, Alessandro di Niccolò.[50] Feeling the pinch, he was probably trying to cut costs. Although the two families lived in different parts of the same *palazzo*, Alessandro's father was far more successful than Bernardo. Not only had he made a fortune trading in silk, but he had also established himself as a political figure of some note. On 15 March 1479, he took up office as one of the *Dodici Buon' Uomini*; and in January 1481, he was elected to the priorate for the first time.[51] Later, he served in a variety of other roles, as well.[52]

Though Niccolò was always the poor relation, Benedetto had a warm relationship with his two charges. Entrusted with continuing their education in Latin, he composed an intermediate grammar – the *Erudimenta grammatices latinae linguae* – for their benefit.[53] In itself, this was not that uncommon. A number of fifteenth-century teachers are known to have composed textbooks for use by their own pupils.[54] But, even accounting for the usual humanistic hyperbole, his dedicatory letter brimmed over with affection. Seeing the virtues of their fathers and grandfathers reflected in their faces, Benedetto wrote, he had decided to dispense with the brief and conventional methods he usually employed, and instead write a work that would allow them to enjoy the rudiments of grammar through reading, and that would be a constant reminder of the 'eternal good-will' he bore them. He hoped only that they would accept his 'little gift' and that, by embracing the Latin language – 'the true mark of honour amongst citizens' – they would acquire the same merit as their forefathers.[55]

*

After the storms of the Pazzi Conspiracy, this was a welcome period of calm. But it was not to last. Over the past two years, the bubonic plague had returned to haunt Northern Italy. In the summer of 1478, Mantua's population had been decimated; and when Florence was struck in early 1479, the people feared that they would suffer a similar fate.[56] As soon as the pestilence was detected, Niccolò, Totto and Margherita were sent to stay on their uncle's property in the Mugello, while Bernardo tried to ride it out with his wife and eldest daughter in Florence. But by the end of May, Bernardo decided to move the children to somewhere more remote. Hurriedly, Niccolò was sent to stay with his step-uncle, Giovanni de' Nelli, in Montebuiano, a little further to the west.[57] A few days later, a muleteer followed with Totto and Margherita. Still too little to walk such a long distance, Totto rode in one of the baskets that were tied to the mule, cocooned in the innumerable sheets and feather duvets that his parents had insisted they take with them.

As long as the plague lasted, Niccolò's lessons would have to wait. Rather than learning about the uses of the subjunctive or the comparison of adjectives, he was free to play with his cousins, or explore the hills and woodlands that surrounded his uncle's farm. Then as now, it was an idyllic part of Tuscany, and it is not hard to imagine the shouts of laughter that would have been heard as the summer drew close.

In Florence, however, the situation had become grave. Back in April, the Signoria had been sufficiently concerned that it agreed to provide extra funds to accelerate the completion of a new hospital on the Prato della Giustizia.[58] But by early June, it was clear that this would not be finished in time. The city's available facilities had already been overwhelmed. So many people were sick with the plague that the Signoria had to grant the *spedalingo* of Santa Maria Novella permission to house them in the nearby church of Santa Maria della Scala.[59] Within weeks, even this had to be expanded, and, in terror, the Signoria fled to Fiesole.[60]

On 30 June, Bernardo returned from a trip to Sant'Andrea in Percussina with a fever, afraid that he had caught the plague.[61] He had every reason to be worried. Mortality rates were high; and over the next few weeks, no fewer than three members of the Machiavelli clan would die.[62] Shutting himself up at home in the Via Romana, he sent for his cousin, Buoninsegna di Guido. When he arrived, Bernardo passed him a sample of urine through an open window, together with a florin to pay for it to be examined by a doctor. This was held to be an important first step towards a conclusive diagnosis.[63] Plague victims' urine was reputed to be cloudy, pale or 'stinky', and Marsilio Ficino was so convinced of its efficacy as an indicator of infection that he barely even mentioned any other signs in his treatise on the pestilence.[64] What was concluded from Bernardo's sample is not known, but, over the next few weeks, a succession of doctors visited him, each offering a different remedy. He was given bitter rue, sweet electuaries and sickly syrups; he had his abscesses lanced; he was bled; and he was rubbed with all manner of poultices. A barber even applied Spanish flies to his legs. All this cost him a fortune. Every time he saw a physician, it cost him a florin. The medicines he was prescribed were not cheap, either. On average, a 'composite' electuary cost somewhere in the region of 11 s., but in times of crisis, prices could rise as high as 68 s.[65] Somehow, though, Bernardo pulled through. By mid-July, he was well on the way to recovery, and, by the beginning of August, he was once again in fine form.

Now acutely aware of his own mortality, he was galvanized into taking charge of his children's future once again. As soon as the plague had subsided, he first turned to his fourteen-year-old daughter, Primavera, who had recently fallen in love with Francesco di Giovanni Vernacci, eight years her senior. As Bernardo later admitted to the young man's father, their romance was hardly to his taste. Strictly speaking, it was for the parents to arrange a suitable marriage, not for young lovers to choose who they liked. But, since Primavera and Francesco were determined, he didn't have much say in the matter. Shrugging their shoulders, Bernardo and Giovanni summoned a notary to draw up a marriage contract, and the proud Francesco was permitted to present his new fiancée with a ring.[66] The wedding itself would take place after Primavera came of age, four years later, in 1483.

As was customary, Bernardo promised to provide his daughter with a dowry. Fortunately, when he had been more prosperous, he had had the foresight to purchase shares in the *Monte delle doti* for her that would be worth 503 *fl.* 2 *s.* 6 *d.* when they matured. It was, admittedly, not particularly large, but it was better than nothing.

Under pressure from Giovanni, however, Bernardo had also agreed to pay for an impressive trousseau befitting the status of her future husband's family. As he noted in his *libro di ricordi*, this included blue cloth made from goat or camel hair for her undergarments (34 *l.* 4 *s.*), patterned white damask for the sleeves (8 *l.*), a length of blue taffeta for a jacket, together with endless quantities of ribbon, sewing silk, and hooks.[67] All this stretched Bernardo to the limit. Unlike the Vernacci, who could afford to buy Primavera a beautiful wedding dress worth 15 *fl.* without a second thought, he had to buy everything in stages, despatching little Niccolò to give the cloth merchant a few lire here and there whenever he could afford it. Sometimes, he even had to pay for items in kind. The tailor who made Primavera's *giacchetta*, for example, found himself being offered a couple of barrels of wine, in place of the three lira coins he was expecting.

Once Primavera's marriage contract had been signed, however, Bernardo was at last able to take Niccolò's education in hand. The time had come for the boy to learn about the methods of contemporary commerce. There was nothing unusual about this. During the commercial revolution of the twelfth and thirteenth centuries, merchants had developed new arithmetical techniques – known as *abbaco* – to cope with the demands of long-distance trade, monetary exchange and international banking. A specialized curriculum had hence been developed to train young boys in the mathematical skills they would need when they entered the world of business and finance.[68] In Florence – where commercial skills were particularly highly prized, even by esteemed humanists like Leon Battista Alberti[69] – boys generally attended 'abacus schools', which taught nothing but *abbaco*, for around two years after they had learned how to read and write, and either before or after they had mastered the rudiments of Latin grammar.[70] As the *catasto* of 1480 reveals, most

of those studying *abbaco* were between the ages of eleven and fourteen, but some were as young as eight or as old as seventeen.[71]

On 3 January 1480 – the same day as Totto started learning to
read – Niccolò began studying with Piero Maria Calandri (1457–
1533/6),[72] one of the city's foremost *abbaco* teachers.[73] Having previously
only been exposed to the Roman numeric system, Niccolò began by
learning about Arabic numerals and the principle of positional value.[74]
He would also have been introduced to finger reckoning, 'a system
of keeping track of the intermediate steps in long division and
multiplication'.[75]

Skipping over addition and subtraction fairly quickly, Niccolò
then tackled multiplication and division. Although he would probably have been required to memorize multiplication tables in much
the same way as modern children are, the emphasis would have
fallen on their application to units of weight, measurement, and
currency.[76]

Once the basics had been grasped, he went on to the problems
that filled the majority of every *abbaco* textbook. As was only to be
expected, these were oriented towards the issues encountered in
business – prices and produce, partnerships, interest payments and
discounts, even the measurement of the constituent metals in alloys.
In contrast to modern maths problems, however, they were posed in
a conversational manner, and the solutions – which were stated at
the same time – explained all of the steps needed to arrive at the
correct answer in a narrative, rather than symbolic, fashion. No attempt
was made either to explore abstract principles of algebra or geometry,
or to expound general rules that the student could apply to similar
questions. Instead, Niccolò would have been encouraged to rely on
a few straightforward techniques. Perhaps the most important was
'the rule of three'. This was really just simple cross-multiplication. If
you knew three out of the four terms in the proportions:

$$\frac{A}{B} = \frac{C}{D}$$

then it was a simple enough task to deduce the unknown value.
There was also the 'rule of the false'. This was basically guesswork.
If Niccolò's guess was right, so much the better. But if it was wrong,

then he was taught to use the incorrect answer to make a *better* guess, often using the 'rule of three' to home in on the solution. It was all very crude. But it worked, after a fashion. And in the world of commerce and government, there was no need for anything more complicated.

After twenty-two months, Niccolò had completed the *abbaco* course. For many boys, this would have marked the end of their formal education. Only a few years later, for example, Guerri dei Rossi (b. 1485) was sent to work for a merchant immediately after finishing abacus school at the age of thirteen years and seven months.[77] But a different fate awaited Niccolò. On 5 November 1481, Bernardo sent him and his brother to study with Paolo Sassi da Ronciglione,[78] a priest and public grammar teacher, who would also go on to teach a clutch of future humanists, including Pietro Crinito and Niccolò's great friend, Francesco Vettori.[79] While Totto would be taught the rudiments of grammar, Niccolò would study works of classical literature and learn the outlines of Latin composition.

Like most teachers, Paolo Sassi probably confined himself to covering a limited range of classical works very thoroughly, including at least one grammarian, one rhetorician, one poet and one historian.[80] No record of which authors Niccolò studied has survived, but a reasonable guess can be made. Given that Bernardo is known to have purchased a copy of Priscian on 5 February 1481, it is safe to assume that the *Institutiones grammaticae* formed at least part of his son's curriculum.[81] And, if contemporary teachers' contracts are anything to go by, Niccolò would most likely have studied Cicero, Virgil, Terence and Livy as well.[82]

Pride of place was given to Cicero, for, as Aeneas Silvius Piccolomini had noted, there was no better way of learning how to write elegant Latin than by studying and imitating his letters.[83] But, for a student like Niccolò, who had previously only studied the simplest sentences, they would have seemed bewildering at first. Though regarded as paragons of Latinity, they were distinguished by their 'periodicity' or 'periodic style'. Rather than use a straightforward word-order, Cicero had frequently attempted to build a sense of anticipation by postponing some element that the reader needed to understand the sentence. This was most often accomplished by placing the verb at the very end. But it could also be achieved by separating nouns and the adjectives that agreed with them, or by using techniques such as antithesis and parallelism. Clever though this might have been, it meant that, if Niccolò was to understand the meaning of any given sentence, he would have had to get used to relying more on the grammatical inflexion of each word than on the order in which they appeared. To help him see how this worked, Sassi would probably have told him to start by rearranging the words in various sentences to express their meaning more directly; and after a few repetitions, he would soon have got to grips with it.[84]

Niccolò would then have been ready to tackle the letters themselves. As Sassi doubtless explained, Cicero had written twenty-four different types of letter in the course of his long and varied career (congratulatory, advisory, explanatory, apologetic, justificatory, excusatory, etc.). Each of these consisted of five distinct parts: *salutatio* (greeting), *benevolentiae captatio* (making the reader well disposed towards the writer), *narratio* (laying out the facts), *petitio* (the request, or the nub of the issue) and *conclusio* (conclusion). When they examined each letter, therefore, Paolo and Niccolò would have begun by identifying what sort of letter it was, discussing its historical context and summarizing its contents. This done, they would have turned to its rhetorical style. They would first have determined whether the letter was written in a high, middle or low style – depending on its subject matter and vocabulary – and noted the words appropriate to each. Finally, they would have dissected the various techniques Cicero had used, such as anaphora (the repetition of a sequence of words at the beginning of clauses for effect), asyndeton (the omission of conjunctions from a series of connected clauses) and chiasmus (reversing the structure of two related clauses for emphasis). Poetry was taught in a similar manner. In the past, Niccolò had studied simple distichs merely as a means of familiarizing himself with the basics of the Latin language. But now he was introduced to Virgil's *Aeneid* – and perhaps the *Eclogues* and *Georgics*, as well – to learn the subtleties of Latin prosody.

Once Niccolò had been given a thorough grounding in the laws of metre and the rules of quantity, he would have read the *Aeneid* right through, listening attentively as his teacher declaimed, paraphrased and explained each verse, word by word.[85] First, he would express the sense of the line in different words, to make sure that Niccolò understood what was being said. Then, he would discuss its grammatical and rhetorical characteristics, taking care to explain any unfamiliar names or places. And finally, he would offer his own allegorical interpretation of the passage in question. As surviving paraphrase commentaries attest, this could often be excruciatingly laborious.

At the same time, Niccolò received lessons in composition. To get him started, he was given short passages to translate into Latin. Then, he graduated to translating whole letters, always taking care to imitate Cicero's style as closely as he could. Like most other teachers, Paolo Sassi placed great store in this. An exercise book written by Niccolò's schoolfriend Pietro Crinito a few years later contains a record of Sassi explaining its importance:

> Tell me, do you believe that we have become learned only by scorning reading and never composing anything else? I do not believe so, and the reason is this: anyone who has been thought learned or who has composed anything affirms that the art of speaking is of little use without practice, because, unless one practices and strives to imitate someone's speech, the art of speaking is of little value. For how can anyone know what he means if they do not see anything he has written? And so that we may write well, we must learn the art [of composition] and practice it and follow [the example of] Cicero or Terence or someone similar to them . . .[86]

This was more than just a matter of learning for learning's sake. As fifteenth-century pedagogues were keen to stress, the whole point was to prepare students for an active life of civic participation. Every letter that Niccolò was made to translate in the schoolroom was practice for the correspondence someone of his class might be expected to undertake later in life, either in pursuit of his own affairs, or as part of a career in law, government or the Church. While he was always encouraged to ensure that his vocabulary and style were as 'classical' as possible, the letters he was set were designed to simulate real-life situations in the here and now.[87] He might, for example, have been presented with a note of consolation to a bereaved friend, a petition on behalf of a family member seeking a position, or a report on what he might have seen during a journey to a neighbouring city. As he grew more proficient, he might even have been given legal letters or diplomatic missives to translate as well.

Niccolò was being prepared for life in other ways, too. Far from being presented as purely literary works, the Latin classics he encountered in the classroom were also held up as repositories of practical wisdom that could help him through life's ups and downs. Much like his philosophical treatises, Cicero's letters were filled with Stoical reflections on everything from fate and fortune to friendship, ambition, love and loss. Virgil's *Aeneid*, too, could be read as a morality tale, in which virtue was praised and vice vilified.[88] The same was also true of the other authors Niccolò studied. While Terence was renowned for his elegant style, his plays were prized most for the ethical maxims they contained. As Niccolò was reading them, he would have copied down the most striking in his notebook and committed them to memory: 'I am a man, and consider nothing human foreign to me' (*Heaut.*, 1.1.77), 'Time heals all wounds' (*Heaut.*, 3.1.421), 'Fortune favours the brave' (*Phormio*, 1.4.203). Similarly, Livy's *Ab urbe condita* was regarded not only as a polished account of Rome's ancient past, but also as a paradigmatic work of philosophy by example, and Niccolò was instructed to pay close attention to the political and moral lessons contained in its description of events such as the rape of Lucretia and the death of Verginia.

But all this talk of morality must have rung hollow. As Niccolò was being taught about virtue and good conduct, he was being sexually abused by his teacher.[89] He was not the only one. Writing many years later, his schoolfriend Francesco Vettori reminded him that Paolo Sassi had done as he had wished with both of them.[90]

At the time, it was not unusual for teachers to take advantage of their pupils. Works of contemporary literature abound with allusions to sexual abuse in the schoolroom. Some decades earlier, Antonio Beccadelli (1394–1471) had written a number of light-hearted poems about the peccadillos of his former schoolmaster, Mattia Lupi da San Gimignano (1380–1468).[91] According to Beccadelli, Lupi only had three students,[92] but one of them – Hisbo (likely a literary pseudonym) – was his 'houseboy'.[93] Lupi never passed up a chance to sodomize his pupil. Although he was careful to do it in private (usually at night), his 'dirty dick' was always eager for 'boys' thighs'.[94]

Such conduct was, of course, illegal. But, as Beccadelli's jocular tone suggests, it was often tolerated – even accepted. As the historian Michael Rocke has noted, pederasty – involving an 'active' adult male and a 'passive' adolescent, between the ages of twelve and eighteen – was 'the predominant, virtually normative, social form of homosexual behaviour in Florence'.[95] Indeed, it was sometimes viewed as an important part of a young man's education, especially if he was from a wealthy, well-connected family. For its many proponents, it not only taught a young man about love and desire, but it also helped him to learn about social virtues such as courage and respect.

But there were limits. Even Beccadelli recognized that the adolescent had to be willing.[96] Others went further, specifying that the 'passive' partner had to derive physical pleasure from the relationship.[97] Where the older man's attentions were neither pleasing nor welcome, they were clearly unacceptable. The authorities – which would otherwise have turned a blind eye – would step in, ready to mete out the harshest punishments.

How far Paolo Sassi went with Niccolò cannot be known with any certainty. It does, however, seem likely that the experience would have scarred him deeply. Recently uncovered documents have revealed that Sassi was a predatory paedophile who preyed on his charges without compunction or remorse. Although he avoided prosecution, his appalling abuse was uncovered by the ecclesiastical authorities around a decade after Niccolò and Vettori had left his care. On 25 January 1495, he was dismissed from his position at Florence's cathedral school for raping one or more of his pupils in the choir of Santa Maria del Fiore, and was forbidden from entering the *Duomo* ever again.[98]

It was perhaps on account of such mistreatment that Niccolò later tried to distance himself from the education he received from Sassi. At the beginning of *Il principe*, for example, he disparaged the fine rhetoric he had been taught, refusing to adorn his treatise with 'rounded periods or big, showy words',[99] and, in the *Discorsi*, he even poured scorn on the feebleness of modern schooling.[100] But however bitter he may have been, he had drunk deep from the well of classical literature and was steeped in the rhetorical culture of the day. In the years to come, he would be sustained and nourished by Cicero and Virgil, Terence and Livy. And, though the experience of civil unrest, plague and abuse had taught him that the world was a harsh and unpredictable place, he had learned to survive whatever life might throw at him.

3

From a Pygmy to a Giant

(1485–98)

Little direct evidence of Niccolò's life after leaving Paolo Sassi's school has survived. Perhaps preoccupied with more pressing matters, Bernardo made fewer entries in his *libro di ricordi* after 1485, and did not mention any preparations he may have made for his son's further education. But an incidental remark in Paolo Giovio's *De viris et feminis aetate nostra florentibus* suggests that Niccolò was enrolled at the university, and, since this would only have been natural for someone of his background, there is no reason to believe otherwise.[1]

Barring any unexpected interruptions, Niccolò would most probably have matriculated at some point between 18 October 1485 and 18 October 1487.[2] Although there were always some exceptions, young men usually began their studies between the ages of sixteen and eighteen. Francesco Guicciardini – who lived not far from the Palazzo Machiavelli in Oltrarno, and who was later to become one of Niccolò's closest friends – was sixteen and a half when he attended his first lecture in November 1498; Niccolò is unlikely to have been much older.[3]

It was an exciting time to be studying at the Studio Fiorentino. Though there had been a university of sorts in the city since 1348, it had been refounded on a much grander scale by Lorenzo de' Medici in 1473.[4] For various political reasons, the faculties of theology, medicine and jurisprudence were transferred to Pisa, but the faculty of arts was allowed to remain in Florence, where it flourished under the nurturing gaze of its patron. Before long, it had become home to some of the most important humanists of the day – including Cristoforo Landino, Demetrius Chalcondyles and Angelo Poliziano.[5]

Like all young men, Niccolò enjoyed the freedom of student life.

Many years later, Francesco Vettori recalled how their mothers had allowed each of them 'a room on the ground floor with a private entrance and all the other conveniences' so they could 'wallow about' as they wished and invite anyone they liked to visit them.[6] If the lives of other students of the day are anything to go by, this would have involved the occasional night out in the city's hostelries or brothels, and perhaps even the odd drunken fight.[7] But the tone of Vettori's letter suggests that it could also have entailed further homosexual experiences. It would not have been altogether unusual if it had. Though only eight students were recorded as being implicated in homosexual acts by the Office of the Night in the period 1478–1502, there were plenty of students who made themselves available to older men, and even more who experimented within their own age group.[8]

Still, Niccolò would have had to work hard. Even though there were plenty of students who attended only one lecture a day, there was a demanding programme of classes for those who wanted to get on in life.[9] In 1485–6, for example, he would have been able to hear Bartolomeo della Fonte on Horace's *Odes*, and Poliziano on Juvenal's *Satires*.[10] The following year, there was Poliziano on Virgil's *Aeneid* and poetry in general, and Chalcondyles on Homer.[11] And, the year after that, there was della Fonte on Juvenal.[12]

Niccolò does not seem to have been a particularly brilliant student. Compared to someone like Giovanni Pico della Mirandola (1463–94) – who arrived in Florence in 1484, and who composed his 'Oration on the Dignity of Man' two years later, at the age of only twenty-three – he was decidedly ordinary. But he did possess at least *some* literary ability, and had begun to develop tastes that were to stay with him for the rest of his life. It was probably during his first years at the Studio that he produced the annotated transcription of Terence's *Eunuchus*, today preserved in a codex in Rome (MS Vaticanus Rossianus 884). While this was a common school text, and could easily have been produced while Niccolò was studying with Paolo Sassi, his inclusion of a number of unusual readings tends to suggest that it was written at this later stage, as his approach to classical literature was maturing.[13]

Modest though it may have been, however, this burgeoning talent served the young Niccolò well. By the time of Lorenzo de' Medici's death on 9 April 1492, he found himself on the fringes of the wider circle of young intellectuals surrounding Lorenzo's

son, Piero (1471–1503), and his two brothers. In the hope of currying
favour with them, he even started writing poetry. In technical terms,
his verses were nothing special.[14] For the most part, they were
nothing more than a collection of images lifted haphazardly from
the works of other poets and strung together in imitation of contemporary poets, such as Poliziano and Bernardo Pulci. But they
nevertheless reflected a sincere attempt to emulate the style of love
poetry popularized by Poliziano, and betrayed a sincere – even
homoerotic – affection for the youngest Medici.

Two of Niccolò's verses are addressed directly to Giuliano (1478–
1516), the youngest of the three brothers. In the first – 'Poscia che a
l'ombra' – he used themes borrowed from Virgil's pastoral poetry to
request admission into the young man's circle of friends.[15] In the guise
of a lovelorn shepherd, resting beneath a laurel while his flock grazes
nearby, he sings of his beloved 'Iacinto'. At first, he is uncertain
whether he will be able to do justice to this 'heavenly young man'.
But he is soon swept along by his emotions. Wishing to make Iacinto's
name live for ever, he swears to carve it in every stone and tree trunk,
and to do all he can to honour the young man's 'outstanding and
divine beauty'. Of course, Niccolò was not the only one singing
Iacinto's praises. There were plenty of other 'shepherds' vying for the
young man's attention. But Iacinto was so liberal with his affection
that they all went back to their flocks happy. As such, Niccolò asked
him to take pity on one more 'miserable soul'. A few sweet words
would be enough to satisfy his love. Besides, Iacinto had received so
many blessings, that it would surely be no hardship for him to receive
Niccolò into his circle of 'loyal subjects' as well.

In the second – 'Se avessi l'arco e le ale' – Niccolò was somewhat
bolder, appealing to Giuliano less as a humble supplicant than as
the victim of unrequited love.[16] Once again, he employed an array
of suitably evocative mythological allusions, but, in keeping with his
amorous and reproachful tone, drew inspiration more from Petrarch
than from Virgil. He began by drawing a provocative comparison.
If 'young Giulio' had a bow and wings, Niccolò claimed, he could
easily be taken for Cupid.[17] But, in place of a bow and arrows, he
has a mouth and words. With these, he wounds whomever he chooses.
His look could be just as cruel. He only had to flutter his eyelashes
for any man to be enraptured by him. But he had the eyes of Medusa:
in the end, he turned anyone who beheld him to stone. Niccolò's

one consolation was that he was not alone in feeling such bitter love. Just as the sun overwhelms the shade and attracts all animal life, so his beauty exceeded all others and drew all men to him. But, like the sun, he remained forever out of reach – even for the gods themselves.

The remaining verses – comprising one sonnet and two *strambotti* – do not name Giuliano either directly or indirectly.[18] But, since they continue the same themes, they seem likely to have been intended for the same recipient. Their tone is even more anguished. In the first *strambotto* – 'Io spero, e lo sperar cresce 'l tormento' – Niccolò again used a Petrarchan model to explore the pain of hope. Though Giuliano had apparently given him reason to believe that his affections *might* be reciprocated, the fact that it remained just a possibility caused him even more torment. He wept bitter tears; and the more he wept, the more sorrow he felt. So searing was the pain that he eventually came to dread the sight of Giuliano. In the second *strambotto* – 'Nasconde quel con che nuoce ogni fera' – he complained that the young Medici was like a panther that hides its 'horrible face' while showing only a 'delightful and furry back': beautiful, yet cruel and insincere. Poor Niccolò could find no respite. If only he could stop thinking of Giuliano for a moment, he sighed in 'Se sanza a voi pensar', he might find some happiness. Or, if he could explain his sorrow and believe what Giuliano told him, it would be easier to bear the pain. But, since he could do neither, he wept.

Yet, that he could feel such sweet sorrow was nevertheless something to be proud of. After all, he could never have nurtured such affection had he not gained some acquaintance with Giuliano, and been assured that his poems would not cause offence. Even if he had as yet received little in return, he was slowly being accepted into the Medici's society, and was beginning to claim a modest place for himself in Florence's literary circles. Were he to cultivate these connections, there was no telling where it might lead. Despite being five years his junior, Pietro Crinito had already been invited to gatherings at the Medici's villa at Fiesole, and was assisting Poliziano with his teaching at the Studio.[19] With a bit of luck, Niccolò's verses might eventually earn him a similar show of favour.

*

But Niccolò's timing could hardly have been worse. Though Piero de' Medici's succession had been accomplished without any difficulty, he possessed none of his father's political skill and proved unable – or unwilling – to build much-needed support for his fledgling *reggimento* among 'men of quality'.[20] As Francesco Guicciardini later put it, he was a 'proud and bestial' young man who preferred 'to be hated rather than loved'.[21] He had little taste for the broad-based, communal style of government, relying instead on a small group of young men who were loyal to him alone. To make matters worse, he also took to walking around Florence accompanied by a number of foreign bodyguards, as if he expected to be assassinated at any moment.

As Piero Parenti observed, Piero de' Medici 'made the whole city want to throw up'.[22] Though still divided among themselves, the *ottimati* were appalled by the contemptuous manner in which they were being treated, and began openly to denounce him as a tyrant.[23] The *popolani*, too, were growing restive. Fearful that Piero intended to reduce them to servitude, or worse, they lent a ready ear to the apocalyptic sermons then being preached throughout the city, and came to believe that God would wreak vengeance upon those who had oppressed them for so long. After fifty-eight years, Fra Domenico da Ponzo told them, the day when the Medici would be punished for their crimes would soon come.[24]

Matters were brought to a head by news that King Charles VIII of France was planning to press his claims to the kingdom of Naples by marching his army into the Italian peninsula. Since Charles's route would pass through Tuscany, he naturally asked the Florentines to provide him with whatever assistance might be required. But this put Piero in an almost impossible situation. He could not, of course, refuse Charles's request without putting himself in danger. Yet nor could he agree. Ever since the Pazzi War, the Medici's foreign policy had hinged on the cultivation of good relations with both the papacy and the Aragonese kings of Naples. He could hardly give Charles free passage now without throwing them over. Even if he could be sure of receiving French support in return – as some in his own family evidently believed he would – it seemed too great a risk. Uncertain what to do, he decided to play for time.

But Charles was not to be denied. Aware that Florence was already teetering on the brink of revolt, he steadily increased the pressure on the city, hoping either to force Piero's hand or to provoke sympathetic *ottimati* into taking action themselves. In June 1494, he began by expelling all Florentine merchants from France – a well-calculated move that had predictably devastating effects on Florence's economy. As exports tumbled, investments were lost and workshops closed, leading even the most uncommitted merchants to ask whether they might be wiser to throw their lot in with the French.[25] If Piero kept putting Charles off, worse would surely follow.

When news arrived that the king had set out from Grenoble on 29 August, their fears only increased. By September, he had arrived in Asti; on 18 October, he was in Piacenza; and, after recognizing Ludovico Sforza as the new duke of Milan a few days later, he was on his way towards Tuscany. Having not yet received Piero's capitulation, he would treat Florence as his enemy. Fivizzano, the first Florentine fortress he came to, was taken by stealth and the population massacred.[26] Sarzana, guarding the strategically crucial coastal road some fifteen kilometres further west, was next; and despite its formidable defences, there was no doubt that it would suffer a similar fate. Were it to fall, there would be nothing to stop Charles from pushing on to Pisa, and then Florence itself.

For many, the city now had no choice but to accept a French alliance. Some even began to suggest that Charles should be welcomed as a liberator. According to Parenti, the city was already awash with leaflets asking the king to free them from Piero's 'tyranny'.[27] In church, Charles was hailed as the fulfilment of prophecy, the instrument of divine judgement. From the cathedral pulpit, the Dominican friar Girolamo Savonarola – who had once ministered to Lorenzo de' Medici on his deathbed – now predicted that God had sent the king as a 'New Cyrus' to punish the city for its sins and lead His people back to righteousness.[28]

Piero resorted to desperate measures. He first appealed to Venice for help, but, resolved to maintain a strict neutrality, they gave him the brush-off. He then offered Charles the astronomical sum of 300,000 francs to leave the Medici in peace. When this was rejected, he began to panic and went to appeal to Charles in person, overlooking the fact that, technically speaking, foreign policy was the preserve of the Signoria alone.[29] Without even attempting to negotiate, he immediately gave the king everything he wanted. Florence's coastal fortresses would be surrendered, the ports of Pisa and

Livorno would be placed at his disposal and – so it was rumoured – some 200,000 ducats would be handed over to help pay for the expedition.

When the Florentines heard what Piero had done, they were furious. Not only had he overstepped his authority, but he had also given away their most important possessions. It was the last straw. Even some of the Medici's oldest supporters now began to turn against him,[30] some openly declaring that he was ruining the city. According to Guicciardini, they argued that it was high time to strike down the tyrant and restore a 'free and popular' form of government.[31] Somehow, the bell of the Palazzo della Signoria was rung and the people came rushing into the piazza, ready to take arms.[32] But, before Piero could be dealt with, the French question needed to be settled – and quickly. To try to claw back their losses and save the city from Charles's wrath, the *pratica* decided to dispatch an embassy 'in the name of the public and not of the tyrant'. At its head was Fra Girolamo Savonarola, who, having 'publicly predicted this calamity', was widely believed to be 'a prophet'.[33]

Piero was in Lucca when he learned of the Signoria's decision. Realizing the danger, he hurried back to Florence. As he entered the city, his few remaining supporters tried to drum up public enthusiasm by letting off fireworks and handing out wine and sweets. But it was all in vain. The mood had turned against him, so much so that he was blocked from entering the Palazzo della Signoria. If he was to stand a chance of surviving, matters would have to be settled by force. The next day, he returned to the *palazzo* accompanied by a contingent of loyal soldiers. This time, not only were the doors again barred, but the Signoria had also taken the precaution of summoning its own guards. What was worse, Piero's old ally, Francesco Valori, had seized weapons from the Bargello and had led a contingent of angry *popolani* into the piazza, where they were already shouting '*Popolo e libertà!*'[34] Hopelessly outnumbered, Piero retreated, vowing to come back with more troops. But though he ordered the mercenary commander, Paolo Orsini, to march on the city with all haste, it quickly became apparent that reinforcements would not arrive in time. There was no other choice but to flee. Later that evening, he and his brother, Giovanni (who was disguised as a Franciscan friar), slipped out of the San Gallo gate under cover of darkness, and made for Bologna.

The Medici had fallen. Even before they had escaped, Piero and his brothers were condemned as public enemies, their property confiscated and their most loyal advisers executed. Within a matter of days, the institutional foundations of their rule had been dismantled. On the advice of an unusually large *pratica*, the Signoria abolished the Seventy, the *Otto di Pratica*, and the Cento, and called for new *accoppiatori*.[35] A long list of exiles – including the Pazzi – were also recalled. But, though the stage had been set for wide-ranging constitutional reforms, no one could agree what to do next. Some of the priors were in favour of re-establishing a truly popular form of government, while others still wanted power to be concentrated in the hands of a narrow oligarchy.

The worsening of the French crisis only exacerbated the political divisions that were opening up. When the Florentine ambassadors found Charles, he had moved down the coast to Pisa, within easy striking distance of Florence. Seeing no reason to negotiate further, the king refused to discuss any changes to his agreement with Piero and made clear that he would enter Florence with or without the Signoria's permission. Indeed, members of his vanguard were already wandering the city, marking potential billets with chalk – a sight that affected Niccolò so deeply that he was later to note that it was 'with chalk' that Charles had conquered Italy.[36]

But what horrified the ambassadors even more was the discovery that the king's presence had also persuaded the Pisans to rise in rebellion and throw off Florentine rule. The loss of the city was a devastating blow. Pisa had allowed Florence to become a major maritime power, and had given its merchants access to lucrative markets stretching from the Low Countries to the Levant.[37] Now that these vital trade routes had been cut, the economy slumped. That Charles had allowed this to happen only seemed to prove that he was bent on Florence's destruction.[38]

The Florentines panicked. Amid fears of an imminent attack – either by Charles, or by Piero, who was rumoured to be mustering troops in the *contado* – angry crowds took to the streets in an orgy of violence and destruction. Unable to restore order, the Signoria turned in desperation to Savonarola, who had resumed preaching from the cathedral pulpit in the days since his return. At their request, he went to treat with Charles once again. This time, he asked the king not for a new settlement, but merely for an assurance that he would help them recover Pisa. This was, of course, more than Charles was willing to grant at that precise moment. But he was nevertheless gratified to see the Signoria tacitly acceding to his original demands. Professing his concern for the Florentines' welfare, he promised to attend to everything when he entered the city a few days later.[39]

After Savonarola's return, preparations were hastily made to ensure that the king was greeted in a suitably magnificent style. The streets were decked out with olive branches; the Palazzo Medici was adorned with a great triumphal archway; the facade of Santissima Annunziata was decorated with bunting; and the royal arms of France were hung from every building.[40] But, though the people cheered wildly as Charles rode through the Porta San Frediano on the afternoon of 17 November, there was still a sense of foreboding in the air. This was perhaps only natural. Although he had left the greater part of his army behind, he had brought somewhere between ten and twenty thousand troops with him, all of whom were billeted in houses around the city, including, it seems, in the Palazzo Machiavelli. Some of the officers were, of course, quite cordial. In Niccolò's *Clizia*, the character of Cleander recalls that the gentleman quartered with his father was a model of courtesy and deference. But, as his friend Palamed counters, this was the exception rather than the rule. Most of the soldiers were crude and boorish fellows, who were bitter at being denied the chance to loot such a wealthy city and who did all sorts of damage while they were there.[41] As Landucci noted, the majority of Florentines could not stand having the French in their homes.[42] Tensions rose.

On 20 November, rumours began circulating that, despite his promises, Charles intended to allow Piero de' Medici to return. This was the only thing that no one in the city could tolerate. As the Signoria met to discuss how best to proceed, the people were seized with fear. Expecting violence to erupt at any moment, they rushed to lock up their shops, hid their merchandise wherever they thought would be safest and barricaded the doors of their homes. The French, too, were afraid. Taking up their arms, they seized the bridges and took control of the Porta San Frediano, in case they needed to retreat. By the afternoon, scuffles were already beginning to break out. Even Charles could see that, unless something was done, the city would be consumed by conflict. After receiving representations from Savonarola, he swore never again to speak of Piero's return and to act only in Florence's best interests.[43] After a few days of fevered negotiations, he also agreed to hand back all of its possessions, including Pisa and Sarzana. In return, the Signoria promised to lend him 120,000 *fl.*, the first 50,000 *fl.* being payable immediately and the remainder in seven months' time.[44] On 26 November, the two sides solemnly swore to abide by these terms at a ceremony in the *Duomo*, and, two days later, Savonarola persuaded the king that 'remaining in the city any longer was against God's will, and that he should depart'.[45]

By 29 November, the last of Charles's troops had left Tuscany for Naples. But no sooner had they gone than the discussions about Florence's political future began again. On 2 December, a public *parlamento* was called in the Piazza della Signoria. At the urging of the *ottimati* – who temporarily held the upper hand – the people confirmed the annulment of all laws passed since the Medici had come to power in 1434, and ratified the abolition of the Cento, the Seventy, and the *Otto di Pratica*. They convened the newly chosen *Dieci di Libertà e Pace* to oversee matters of war and superintend the recapture of Pisa. They also agreed to replace election with sortition and to appoint twenty new *accoppiatori*, in the belief that this would help keep the Medici's old allies out. But in this last decision lay the seeds of discord. When the *accoppiatori* were chosen the following day, their number included at least three of Piero's former stalwarts.[46] This could, of course, easily be justified in theory. After all, Florence had only narrowly escaped destruction and needed to unite all the competing factions if it was to recoup its losses. But, in practice, the appointments were wholly unacceptable. The Medici had aroused far too much popular hatred for their associates to be trusted with choosing the next Signoria. Denouncing the appointments as shameful, Paolantonio Soderini openly called for a more popular form of government.

As civil unrest loomed, Savonarola moved to the fore. Preaching in the cathedral almost daily, he congratulated the Florentines for having thrown off the tyrant's yoke, but reminded them that there was still much work to be done.[47] Having turned their backs on the excesses of the Medici, they should now 'adopt a simpler life, renounce usury, and reduce the duties and taxes that oppressed the poor, for then the people would be content and peaceful, requiring no public festivals to keep them happy, contrary to what many fools have said.'[48] For this to occur, they would not only have to make peace with one another, but they would also have to reform their entire constitution. Rather than being content with government by the few, they should, he argued, establish a government of the many, in which modest and virtuous men, driven only by a love of God and their city, would be proud to serve. Its structure should be inspired by the Venetian model.[49] What this entailed was slightly unclear. It seemed to point towards some sort of general council. But all that Savonarola specified was the enfranchisement of guildsmen and the use of sortition or election for different magistracies. Perhaps naively, he seemed to believe that the details could be hammered out at public meetings convened by the *gonfalonieri* in each quarter of the city.

It was, however, enough to catalyse political change. Although the *ottimati* had little taste for the populist reforms Savonarola was advocating, and bitterly resented his growing influence over the people, they could see that the public mood was turning against them. Many realized that, if the constitution were not remodelled along Venetian lines, revolution could well break out.[50] Bowing to Savonarola's wishes, the Signoria therefore commissioned five proposals for reform, which would serve as the basis for deliberation. Four of these have survived. Though they differed in some important respects – such as over the question of whether there should be an 'upper house' composed of magnates – all advocated a Venetian-style general council.[51] After several days of heated discussion, the Signoria bowed to the inevitable. At a special *pratica*, they recommended the establishment of a Great Council (*Consiglio maggiore*) with wide-ranging legislative powers and the right to choose candidates for major offices by election and, for minor magistracies, by sortition. Membership was open to any legitimately born citizen whose father, grandfather or great-grandfather had ever been chosen for public office; and it was expected that well over a thousand men would be seated on its benches at any one time. Complementing this would be a Council of Eighty, chosen largely from among the Great Council. This smaller council would be charged with selecting ambassadors and military commanders, and would offer any advice the Signoria might require on a weekly basis. Since these recommendations reflected the essence of Savonarola's programme, they passed almost without opposition when they were put before the Council of the

People and the Council of the Commune on 22–23 December; and, like that, the political character of the Florentine Republic was completely transformed.

Savonarola was now in the ascendant. Although there were some who remained bitterly opposed to his constitutional reforms, and who soon became known as the *arrabbiati* (the angry) for the vehemence of the hatred they bore him personally, he could count on a large – and growing – body of devoted supporters. Known as the *frateschi* (the friar's men), or, more derisively, as the *piagnoni* (the wailers), they came from every walk of life.[52] The majority, of course, were *popolani* who viewed Savonarola as their standard-bearer, and who were exultant at being given a greater role in public life. But there were also middling merchants and even members of the *ottimati*, such as Paolantonio Soderini, Francesco Valori and Jacopo Salviati.[53] Cultural figures, too, were soon under his sway.[54] As Vasari reported, Sandro Botticelli was so ardent a follower that he was persuaded to give up painting, despite having no other source of income and nearly starving as a result.[55]

Confident of his strength, Savonarola embarked on an ambitious programme of moral reform. From his pulpit, he exhorted the Florentines to create a truly godly republic – a New Jerusalem – free from every trace of vice. On 31 December 1494, 'the harshest law against sodomy in Florentines' living memory' was passed.[56] The fines that had previously been imposed were abolished. Henceforth, convicted sodomites over the age of eighteen were to be pilloried. If they were found guilty a second time, they would be marched through the city and branded on the forehead. A third offence was punishable by death. Gambling was prohibited; women were forbidden to wear 'shameless' gowns, showy jewellery or extravagant coiffures; dancing was frowned upon; and even fireworks were banned. Later, the campaign assumed even more dramatic proportions. On 7 February 1497, the first of two bonfires of the vanities were lit in the Piazza della Signoria. Some thirty *braccia* (about 17½ metres) in height, it was piled high with all manner of ostentatious and immodest fripperies, often forcibly snatched from their owners' grasp by the crowds of unruly young boys whom Savonarola had recruited for the purpose. As the chronicle of pseudo-Burlamacchi noted, the flames consumed 'all the . . . lascivious objects of women, disgraceful pictures and sculptures, gambling implements, books of poetry in

Latin as well as the vernacular ... musical instruments ... and all the accursed [trappings] of Carnival'.[57]

*

Like many of his contemporaries – including Michelangelo, who claimed still to be able to hear Savonarola's voice thundering in his ears even as an old man[58] – Niccolò was aware of the power of the friar's preaching.[59] Although he could not say whether Savonarola actually spoke with God or not, he still regarded him as a 'great' man, who had clearly been 'inspired with heavenly vigour', and whose writings revealed 'his learning, his prudence and his mental power'.[60] Looking back many years later, Niccolò even believed that the friar had been right about many things. He had, after all, been quite correct to say that Charles VIII's descent into Italy was punishment for their sins – even if these were to be attributed more to the Medici than to the people as a whole;[61] and he had certainly been justified in arranging for a law permitting those whom the Signoria convicted of political crimes to appeal either to the Eighty or to a committee of the Great Council to be passed in early 1495.[62]

But Niccolò was nevertheless painfully conscious that Savonarola's rise to prominence had dangerous implications for him personally. Although the Machiavelli had a long history of opposition to the Medici, his attempt to ingratiate himself with Giuliano had placed him in a difficult position. That he had met with so little success was, admittedly, in his favour. He could never be accused of having been an intimate member of the Medici's inner circle. But he was still tainted by his association with them. At best, he could expect to be regarded with mistrust; at worst, with contempt. That his affections for Giuliano had been homoerotic only made things worse. Were the finger of suspicion to be pointed at him, the results could be devastating. Whipped along by Savonarola's sermons, the *frateschi*'s appetite for persecuting sodomites knew no bounds, especially where the accused had ties with the Medici. Between November 1495 and November 1497, no fewer than 731 accusations of homosexuality were made; and on 19 December 1497, a law mandating even harsher punishments for offenders was introduced.[63]

Niccolò could well have been forgiven for wanting to keep his head down. But family affairs – which had also been hard hit by Savonarola's rise – demanded his attention. After the death of his mother, Bartolomea, in 1496, his long-suffering father had passed on more responsibility for day-to-day matters, and appears to have asked him to defend the family's interests in a dispute over a Church benefice that had arisen out of the recent political upheavals. For many years, the Machiavelli had enjoyed the patronage of the parish of Santa Maria in Fagna, in the Mugello. When the benefice had fallen vacant, a short time earlier, they had naturally given it to one of their own – a distant cousin of Niccolò named Francesco. Being a rich living, however, it had caught the greedy eyes of the Pazzi, who had lately been allowed to return from exile. Hoping to claim the parish for one of their own, the Pazzi challenged the appointment; and, given the influence they then wielded, they had no difficulty in persuading the bishop of Perugia, Cardinal Juan López, to do as they wished. It fell to Niccolò to seek help. On 2 December 1497, he tried writing directly to the cardinal.[64] Protesting that the Machiavelli were superior to the Pazzi in generosity and *virtù*, if not in wealth, Niccolò begged him not to mark them with ignominy by depriving them of what they had striven so hard to preserve. It was unjust, not to mention disgraceful, for men less worthy than themselves to be decked out in their spoils and boasting of such a victory. In the name of all that was right and good, he asked for clemency – even threatening to take further action if it was not forthcoming. But Niccolò seems to have realized that his chances were slight at best. The previous day, he had drafted a letter to an unknown friend, who was apparently helping them, indicating just how hard he was finding it to swim against the tide that Savonarola had unleashed. Complaining of ill health, he apologized for not having had the strength to reply to the messages he had recently received, but wished now 'to encourage, beg, and pray' his correspondent to redouble his efforts on their behalf.[65] As he was well aware, the Machiavelli were mere 'pygmies' locked in a near-hopeless battle with 'giants'.

*

Times were hard for Niccolò. He had no prospects to speak of, and was already weighed down by family worries. As well as cousin Francesco's troubles with his parish, there was the problem of money. This was even more pressing than usual. Bernardo's income from his country properties had not recovered and, given that neither Niccolò nor his brother Totto could contribute anything more, the family's cupboards were often bare, even when they went to stay in the countryside. As was his way, Niccolò tried to make light of this as best he could. In an entertaining little poem addressed to Bernardo at around this time, he jokingly complained of how hungry he and his companions were during a recent stay in the Mugello.[66] For more than a month, he claimed, they had been living on nothing more than nuts, figs, beans and dried meat. It certainly wasn't a joking matter. Like the ox from Fiesole that looked thirstily down at the River Arno while it licked the snot from its nose, they had been gazing greedily at the market traders' eggs and the butchers' meat. They had even tried to find some consolation in the example of the prophet Daniel. After being carried off into exile in Babylon, Daniel and his three friends had refused the food and wine provided by King Nebuchadnezzar out of religious scruples, but had nevertheless avoided causing offence by accepting vegetables and water (*Dan.* 1:3–16). The only problem was that, whereas Daniel and his friends had grown fatter after ten days on such a diet, Niccolò and his chums had grown as thin as a woodcock's beak after eating bread without any dripping,[67] and were so hungry that they could hardly keep their eyes open. It was hence an immense relief when Bernardo sent them a gift of a goose, and Niccolò asked his father to send Totto over so that he could rejoice over their good fortune. It was just a pity that Bernardo, who had actually bought the goose, couldn't enjoy it too.

But, however much he wanted to make light of the situation, Niccolò knew that the odd bird every now and again did little to alleviate the family's sense of hardship. Feeling dejected and downcast, he tried to distract himself by translating Terence's *Andria* into the Tuscan vernacular.[68] It was perhaps a natural choice. Since his childhood, he had found Terence's comedies to be a source of great comfort. As he had come to appreciate when he had annotated the *Eunuchus* a few years earlier, they weren't just funny. They were full of worldly wisdom, and addressed some genuinely interesting questions, too. But now he saw that they also offered him a quietly satisfying means of venting his frustrations, as well.

His decision to tackle the *Andria* was, in itself, a minor act of rebellion. A bawdy comedy of errors, it was the antithesis of the suffocating austerity preached by Savonarola. The 'hero', Pamfilo (to use Niccolò's spelling), is in love with Glicerio, a low-born woman from Andros, and has even got her pregnant. But his father, Simo, has arranged for him to marry Cremete's daughter, Filomena, with whom his friend, Carino, also happens to be in love. Using bluff and trickery, Pamfilo then tries to get out of the match, while Simo attempts to force him to go through with it, despite the fact that he also has to persuade Cremete – who has since withdrawn his permission in disgust – to agree to the whole affair once again. As always in these cases, everything works out for the best in the end. Thanks to the surprise revelation that Glicerio is, in fact, also Cremete's daughter, Pamfilo can marry his beloved, Carino can wed Filomena, and everyone else saves face – although not before a good deal of comedic confusion has ensued.

This was risqué enough as it was. But Niccolò took Terence's scatological ribaldry even further.[69] Rather than simply translating the original, word for word, he seized on the opportunity to bring the text up to date, and in doing so to sharpen his dig at contemporary mores. Not only did he give modern equivalents for antiquated terms,[70] but he also embroidered the dialogue with the pungent slang of the streets, and even inserted some rather vulgar jokes of his own invention. He evidently had no time for Savonarola's invectives against swearing. When Pamfilo's slave, Davo, is accosted by Simo early in the drama, for example, Niccolò spices up Terence's rather mild original by having him sigh, 'What does this dick (*cazo*) want?'[71] Similarly, when Simo is berating Cremete for suggesting that Pamfilo should, in fact, marry Glicerio – whom he is just about to reveal as his daughter – Pamfilo mutters, 'I think this out-of-towner is going to crap himself.'[72]

To top it all, Niccolò also included a sly dig at Savonarola himself. In Act 1, Scene 2, Simo rebukes Davo for failing to keep Pamfilo on the straight and narrow. As a sort of surrogate father, he should have stepped in to correct the boy whenever he got carried away with one of his girlfriends. In Terence's version of the play, the slave pretends not to understand what the older man is saying, cockily replying, 'My name's Davos, not Oedipus'.[73] But, in Niccolò's version, the slave points out that he could hardly be expected to know how Pamfilo's affairs would turn out. 'I'm Davo,' he says, 'not a prophet – nor even the friar (*frate*).'[74] It was gentle enough, but Niccolò's bitterness can nevertheless be heard seething beneath the surface; for a young man facing what must have seemed like insuperable odds, such an ironic little jibe at Savonarola's prophecies was cathartic, if nothing else.

*

Dark as Niccolò's situation may have seemed, however, a chink of light was beginning to appear in the clouds. At about the same time as he was working on *Andria*, he made the acquaintance of Marcello di Virgilio di Andrea di Berto Adriani (1464–1521), and, though he perhaps did not realize it at the time, this chance meeting would change his life forever.

Marcello and Niccolò came from similar backgrounds.[75] Only five years Niccolò's senior, Marcello had been born into a modest family that lived not far from the Porta Romana in Oltrarno. Although the Adriani could not boast the same history of public service as the Machiavelli, having provided only two priors since the beginning of the fourteenth century,[76] they too had been shunned by the Medici and had been compelled to eke out a threadbare existence on the fringes of Florentine society. Like Bernardo, Marcello's father – messer Virgilio – had trained as a lawyer. To be sure, he was not quite as learned and could hardly boast the same literary tastes as his fellow in the Via Romana, but they did share a common friend in Bartolomeo Scala,[77] and they both had a habit of complaining about their financial difficulties. As Virgilio's *libro di ricordi* testifies, he was always borrowing money to pay for his hare-brained business ventures, and, like Bernardo, had soon fallen behind with his taxes.

Marcello had, however, been blessed with a singularly brilliant mind and a voracious appetite for learning. What was more, he was ambitious and – unlike Niccolò – knew how to navigate the stormy waters of Florentine political life. Enrolling at the Studio in 1480, he attended lectures on medicine and the natural sciences, as well as the usual courses on Latin and Greek literature,[78] and his penetrating intellect and relentless dedication to scholarship soon won him such respect that, when Poliziano died in September 1494, he was appointed as the new professor of poetry and rhetoric.[79]

Only a little more than thirty years old at the time of his appointment, Marcello was an imposing character. As a portrait bust on the facade of the Palazzo dei Visacci reveals, he had a severe, if scholarly, appearance: large, piercing eyes, a pointed nose, a high brow with a receding hairline, and a closely trimmed, Roman beard. It suited his temperament. Though not lacking in sympathy or affection, he was determined and resolute, with a reputation for gravitas. Despite the troubles by which Florence was then afflicted, he never succumbed to fear or anxiety, but greeted fortune's blows with calm equanimity and an unflinching singularity of purpose.

When Marcello and Niccolò first met has not been recorded. Most likely it was at one of the older man's lectures, perhaps soon after he took up his position at the Studio. But, however their paths crossed, Marcello proved to be just the sort of mentor Niccolò needed. In the lectures he delivered at the beginning of each university year, he set out a bold new vision of the role humanistic learning should play in Florentine society, and – in doing so – demonstrated how men like Niccolò could harness the wisdom of the ancients to rise above factional conflicts.

Marcello built his case slowly, adapting himself to changing political circumstances as he went.[80] In his first *prolusio* (1494), on poetry, he discreetly attempted to distance himself from the sort of literature that had been in vogue under the Medici, and that Niccolò still admired.[81] In Marcello's eyes, words and metre were merely a tool, and, like any tool, they could be put to a variety of different purposes, some more appropriate than others. It was all a matter of finding the right one. While there were plenty of so-called poets churning out all manner of tawdry little verses just then, Marcello argued, *true* poetry was a craft that should be used to convey philosophical and theological truths for the benefit of society as a whole. Whatever artistry the poet wished to use should, he believed, serve only to adorn divine truth with beauty and to kindle the fire of goodness in men's souls. This was, after all, exactly what many of the ancient poets had done.

But, if poetry should make men good, oratory should make them free. In his second *prolusio* (1495), which, for reasons of safety, was delivered in Prato, twenty-four kilometres north-west of Florence,[82] Marcello drew a close connection between the rhetorical arts and the health of a republic. Repudiating any obligation he might previously have felt towards the Medici, he pointed out that, while they had held sway, rhetoric had been allowed to decay, with the result that justice had been ignored and liberty overthrown. Though now mercifully far from the city, Piero had left a sorrowful legacy. As Lucretius had said of mankind's early history:

Men could not recognise the common good.
They knew no binding customs, used no laws.
Every man, wise in staying strong, surviving,
Kept for himself the spoils that fortune offered.[83]

In such dangerous times, Marcello thundered, oratory should be cultivated anew, and with added vigour, so that it could teach men to value the common weal over private interest, to uphold an equitable justice against sectional rancour and to defend liberty against tyranny with all their might. For only when their hearts were so stirred would they come together in harmony, allowing the Republic truly to flourish. And, for this, the study of the ancient classics was essential.

Marcello did not expect his students to be easily persuaded. With Florence in the grip of political upheaval, he knew that many of them would see little point in studying the classics as seriously as he wanted. They were too frightened of the unknown and too uncertain of their own abilities to look for solutions in the dusty remains of the ancient past, much less put rhetoric at the service of the Republic. After all, it wasn't as if texts written more than a thousand years before could teach them anything they could use to deal with Florence's current crises. Indeed, Savonarola had even argued that it was positively sinful to look to pagan classics for an understanding of either the present or the future. So, what could Marcello possibly say that would shake them out of their torpor?

In his fourth *prolusio* (1497), he admitted that they would probably have heard all the usual arguments in defence of the *studia humanitatis* already. He had no desire to wheel out tired old clichés, only for them to 'wonder at nothing', as Horace had put it. But in a sense, 'wondering at nothing' was precisely what the classics had to offer. When we embark on life without a knowledge of the *studia humanitatis*, Marcello argued, we are like invaders descending from the mountains into a magnificent city. We are astonished by all that we see, struck dumb with fear and wonder, either because we are ignorant of all that has gone before – as Plato suggested – or because everything really is new and unfamiliar – as Lucretius had argued.[84] By studying the classics, however, we can overcome this sense of amazement, fear and doubt. As philosopher-poets like Lucretius had taught, Fortune, Nature and God were the authors of all that happened in the world. One only needed to read the ancient historians to find proof of this, and to see that – despite what Savonarola had argued – the classical past could be used not only 'to fathom the crisis of contemporary society', but also to predict where things might lead.[85] Once this had been grasped, Marcello argued, all fear and doubt would disappear. Equipped with an understanding of the underlying causes of things, and some sense of where events might lead, one could be sure of having the mental flexibility to tackle anything with perfect equanimity. And, from there, it was but a short step to harnessing rhetoric to the service of republican liberty.

Marcello's words may well have struck a chord with Niccolò. For the first time, he could look past the frustrations of recent years and discover the sense of purpose he had been lacking for so long. At around the time of Marcello's fourth *prolusio*, he began writing an annotated transcription of Lucretius' *De rerum natura*, perhaps under his friend's supervision.[86] As was perhaps only to be expected, Niccolò's primary concern was to establish a reliable text. Sifting through the various manuscript traditions, he weighed the merits of different readings with more care than he had shown in any of his previous endeavours, sometimes following Marcello's own corrections, sometimes proposing his own inventive emendations. But this was more than mere philological zeal. Having possibly taken Marcello's defence of the *studia humanitatis* to heart, he was desperate to stabilize the text so that he could drink more deeply from the spring of Lucretius' wisdom. As his marginal notes testify, he was intrigued by those portions of the *De rerum natura* that suggested that, once man understood the cause of things, he would no longer be bound by his fate.[87] Niccolò was, of course, in no doubt that, as Marcello had explained, Fortune, Nature and God governed all human affairs. But he was nevertheless fascinated by Lucretius' contention that their influence was impersonal, even disinterested. When he read that the gods were moved by neither pity nor anger, he scribbled excitedly in the margins: 'the gods don't care about mortal things'.[88] That their benign, but unalterable, influence in no way constrained the human mind excited him even more. When he read Lucretius' claim that the tendency of atoms to 'swerve' spontaneously and unpredictably (*clinamen*) allows for the existence of free will in an otherwise deterministic universe, he quickly scrawled little summaries, to be sure that he would remember so crucial a lesson. First, he noted that 'in the seeds' – that is to say, in atoms – 'there is weight, blows, and the swerve';[89] then, with barely concealed exuberance: 'from motion there is variety, and from it we have a free mind'.[90] For a young man who had been badly beaten by fortune's blows, this crucial insight bore repeating. Despite the setbacks of recent years, he was free. And, now that he could see this, he was ready to throw his hat into the ring once again.

*

By the time Niccolò started work on Lucretius, Savonarola's grip on Florence had begun to weaken. Only a few weeks after the first bonfire of the vanities, Charles VIII signed a truce with the League of Venice, bringing an end to his involvement in Italian affairs. At a stroke, Florence's diplomatic position was transformed. Having staked everything on the French alliance, the city was now left dangerously exposed. Without Charles to back it up, there was nothing to stop the papacy – or any other members of the league – from taking action against it. And, given that its chances of recovering Pisa by force were now much smaller, it would doubtless face further financial difficulties. This dealt a heavy blow to Savonarola's public standing. For years, he had hailed Charles as the instrument of God's will, the saviour of Florence, the harbinger of a new age. Now, all those stirring prophecies suddenly began to ring hollow.

It did not take long for the league to twist the knife. In Rome, the Florentine ambassador, Ricciardo Becchi, received hints that, if the Signoria would rid themselves of Savonarola and pursue a more sensible foreign policy, good relations with the papacy and Venice might be restored.[91] There was even a chance that a solution to the Pisan question could be found, too. If they continued to heed the friar's counsel, however, they would have to face the consequences. It was their choice.

Savonarola needed to take decisive action if disaster was to be averted. But, strangely, he faltered. In his Lenten sermons, he failed to defend his prophecies, offered no meaningful solutions to Florence's woes and seemed curiously indifferent to the people's concerns. In the councils, a groundswell of opposition began to make itself felt. In March, Bernardo Del Nero – who had previously been one of Piero de' Medici's most trusted advisers – was chosen to succeed the arch-Savonarolan Francesco Valori as *gonfaloniere di giustizia*. And, two weeks later, Del Nero's associates put forward proposals to select minor magistracies by sortition, which was thought to favour a transition to a more oligarchic form of government, rather than by election, as Savonarola had urged in the past.[92] Even though these came to nothing, the ground was clearly shifting beneath Savonarola's feet.

Watching this from afar, Piero de' Medici decided that the time was ripe to make his return. After securing financial support from the Venetians, he mustered a small army and marched into Tuscany, confident of victory. In the event, he was disappointed. Heavy rains delayed his advance, giving the Florentines time to summon their mercenary commander, Paolo Vitelli, and strengthen their defences. When Piero arrived outside the gates, he found them firmly shut against him, and, unable to take the city by force, had no option but to withdraw.[93]

But Florentines were nevertheless badly shaken. Even if Piero had been scared off, the friar seemed to be leading them down the road to ruin. There were many – including members of the Signoria – who now felt that, at the very least, he should refrain from preaching, as the Borgia Pope Alexander VI had commanded him to do.[94] This was, however, exactly what he was determined not to do. The mood turned ugly. On 3 May, the night before Savonarola was due to deliver the Ascension Day sermon, his enemies forced their way into the cathedral through a side door and defaced everything they could. When workers arrived to prepare for the feast day, they found the rotting skin of an ass draped over the pulpit, nails driven into the lectern, and excrement smeared over the walls.[95] Thankfully, they had time to clean everything up before the Mass began, but the trouble was just beginning.[96] As Savonarola was launching into a spirited defence of his right to preach, a great shout went up. A couple of young men – probably those who had committed the outrage of the previous night – dashed for the doors; others, weapons in hand, ran towards the pulpit, evidently planning to stop Savonarola preaching by force. Quick as a flash, a gang of *frateschi* jumped up to block their way. Confusion broke out. Alarmed, Savonarola then held his crucifix aloft, whereupon at least some of the congregation cried out 'Jesu!' and fell to their knees. But even Savonarola realized that he could not go on. Leaving his sermon unfinished, he descended from the pulpit and forced his way through the crowds, back to San Marco.

Despite being divided among themselves, the Signoria attempted to restore calm. Twelve 'peacemakers', representing all shades of opinion, were appointed.[97] It was, however, too little, too late. In June, Alexander VI finally excommunicated Savonarola for his obduracy.[98] The following month, the chancellor, Bartolomeo Scala – who for so long had been a restraining influence on the various factions within the Signoria – died, leaving a void at the heart of the Florentine government.[99] Then, in August, Lamberto dell'Antella – a slimy little schemer with close ties to Piero – made things worse by revealing the existence of *another* conspiracy to restore the Medici, involving a number of the 'peacemakers' appointed in July.[100] Five men, including Bernardo del Nero, were arrested and sentenced to death by a hastily convened *pratica*.[101] Horrified, they immediately claimed the right to appeal. But though most members of the Signoria were minded to approve their request, the *frateschi* among them were outraged. In an impassioned speech, Francesco Valori openly accused the other priors of jeopardizing the Republic's safety.[102] If the *pratica*'s judgement were not upheld, he argued, there would be a public outcry. Denying the conspirators an appeal was the only way of preventing civil unrest. There was no time for further discussion. After a violent scuffle in which Piero Guicciardini – the strongest defender of granting the appeal – was almost thrown out of a window, the priors changed their minds and voted to confirm the sentence. Later that evening, the five accused were taken from the Bargello and executed. Savonarola did nothing to save them. He seemed almost satisfied that they were gone.[103] Indeed, it was even rumoured that he had lobbied for their deaths himself.[104]

Even Niccolò could see that Savonarola's moral authority had been irreparably damaged by the affair. In later life, he would pour scorn on the friar for having divided the city with his 'ambitious and partisan spirit'. For all the fervour with which Savonarola preached forgiveness and reconciliation, Niccolò recalled, he had done nothing to castigate Valori and the other *frateschi* for denying the condemned men the right of appeal that his own law had guaranteed.[105] Such hypocrisy had exacerbated the hatred of those who already regarded him with jealousy.[106] The gulf between the factions was becoming unbridgeable.[107] Little by little, the Republic was being destroyed by the very man whom the people had once acclaimed as their saviour.[108]

These were dangerous times. Yet Niccolò could not have escaped noticing that the divisions within Florentine society also created opportunities for young men like him, who had been forced to sit on the sidelines. After Bartolomeo Scala's death, a debate had opened up about how the new chancellor and his staff should be appointed.[109] Aware of how important these positions were to the conduct of government, the *frateschi* pushed for candidates to be chosen by the Council of Eighty, where the friar's supporters had a solid majority. Their opponents were, however, determined to prevent the chancellery from being so overtly politicized, and to restore the neutrality it had previously enjoyed. To achieve this, they advocated giving the Great Council – rather than the Eighty – the final say. Several weeks of bitter debate ensued. But eventually, the friar's enemies prevailed. Those who had been on the fringes of the Medici *reggimento* or who had been mildly critical of Savonarola were now able to aspire to a career in the chancellery once again, and those who had remained outside the political fray stood the best chance of all.

When the elections were held in late February 1498, Niccolò allowed himself to be put forward for the second chancellorship[110] – a role with responsibility for overseeing Florence's relations with subject towns and dealing with domestic correspondence.[111] Although he had no administrative experience and few intellectual accomplishments to his name, he had every reason to be optimistic. His obscurity was now his greatest asset. In the elections for the first chancellorship, those with clear factional ties were passed over, regardless of experience. Alessandro Braccesi – the secretary of the *Dieci*, and a noted *fratesco* – was not chosen, nor was Francesco Gaddi – a prominent *arrabbiato* who was the incumbent second chancellor.

Niccolò was, however, disappointed. Whether to appease the remaining *frateschi*, or as compensation for the loss of the first chancellorship, Alessandro Braccesi was given the job instead. But even though he had come away empty-handed, Niccolò had evidently been proposed by some influential figures and was at least being spoken of as a suitable candidate for chancellery positions in the Great Council.

What was more, his mentor, Marcello di Virgilio Adriani, had been elected to the first chancellorship. Having publicly distanced himself from the excesses of the Medici *reggimento*, while also offering some discreet criticisms of Savonarola, Marcello had proved an ideal compromise candidate. And since he was already renowned for his erudition, all factions had recognized him as a worthy successor to the humanist chancellors of whom Florence was so proud, as well.

His appointment was less decisive for Niccolò than has sometimes been claimed. Although some scholars have suggested that Marcello was now in a position to bestow patronage on Niccolò,[112] he was, in fact, precluded from appointing or even proposing new chancellery officials.[113] But he could still exert some influence over future elections. As long as he remained above faction, his recommendation would carry considerable weight, and a few well-judged words in the right ears would go a long way.

*

It was not long before another opportunity presented itself. Despite his excommunication, Savonarola had celebrated Mass in the church of San Marco at Christmas, and, after presiding over a second bonfire of the vanities on Shrove Tuesday, had further defied the pope's wishes by taking to the cathedral pulpit to preach the Lenten sermons. He was under no illusions about how provocative he was being, nor about how damaging the consequences could be. As Niccolò reported in a letter to Ricciardo Becchi, the Florentine representative in Rome, the friar's first sermon was nothing if not combative. Meeting the challenge head on, Savonarola prayed that, if he was indeed a false prophet, as his enemies alleged, God would give the city a sign. It was an obvious rallying cry. With this bold gesture, he hoped to 'unite his partisans' – and perhaps frighten the incoming priors enough to bring them back into line. When the new Signoria was revealed the following morning, however, he realized that they would not be so easily intimidated. Fearing for his life, he declared that he would stop preaching in the cathedral and return to San Marco. Once in the safety of his home church, he took to the pulpit once again, railing even more violently against his enemies.

Savonarola had, however, misjudged the political situation. Though most of the priors were, indeed, *arrabbiati*, they were fiercely protective of Florence's autonomy and resented the pope meddling in their affairs. Whatever their personal feelings might have been, they were disinclined to muzzle the friar, especially when doing so might spark civil unrest. They therefore instructed their envoys in Rome to assuage the pope's anger by reassuring him of Savonarola's goodwill.[114] Surprised, the friar abruptly changed his tune. As Niccolò noted, he no longer said anything about the danger of tyranny or the 'wickedness of the people', but instead focused his attacks on the pope, saying of him 'what could be said of the wickedest person you could imagine'.

If he had hoped somehow to strengthen the Signoria's resolve, however, he was mistaken. It was another blunder. In this case, silence – or at least contrition – would have been the better part of valour. After hearing the Florentine ambassadors plead their case, the pope had flown into a rage. He knew full well how violently Savonarola was slandering him, and was furious that the Signoria had done nothing to stop him preaching. If the priors would not respect his wishes, he would have no option but to place the city under interdict.

This put an entirely different complexion on the situation. On 14 March, an unusually large *pratica* met to consider Florence's options.[115] Naturally, all still accepted that Florence's independence was inviolable. But that was as far as the consensus reached. Everyone seemed to have a different opinion about what should be done. Some – like Lorenzo Lenzi – maintained that Florence should stand by Savonarola, come what may. He had, after all, freed the city from the Medici's tyranny. Surely it could not now be expected to surrender both its liberty and its liberator? Others maintained precisely the opposite point of view. While it was undoubtedly beneath Florence's dignity to submit to the pope's will, they argued, the Signoria could not afford to antagonize the papacy any further. Merchants had already been hard hit by the worsening of relations; were an interdict to be imposed, their losses would be even greater. Besides, there was the matter of Pisa to consider, too. It was already costing a fortune to keep Paolo Vitelli's mercenary army in the field; angering Alexander and the League would only drag things out for longer and possibly even jeopardize the whole campaign. Distasteful though it might be, surrendering Savonarola was hence the only sensible course of action. Others still advocated a middle way. The friar's old ally, Paolantonio Soderini, agreed that the pope's demands were unreasonable, but suggested that, since open defiance would do

Florence no end of harm, it was better to make a pretence of obedience, while stopping short of handing Savonarola over.

After two days of arguing, the Signoria could not afford to wait any longer. Word had reached them that Alexander was planning to imprison any Florentine merchants that happened to be in Rome, should they continue to drag their heels. Realizing that he meant business, the priors at last gave in. They would silence Savonarola.[116]

But this only unleashed the whirlwind. Smelling blood, the friar's enemies now moved in for the kill. On 25 March, the Franciscan Francesco da Puglia publicly challenged him to prove whether he was a prophet by undergoing a trial by fire. It was pure provocation and Savonarola knew it. Yet, for whatever reason, the friar's faithful acolyte, Fra Domenico da Pescia, agreed to go through it on his behalf. Alarmed, the Signoria questioned whether they should intervene. But on further reflection, they saw that this was an opportunity to end the uncertainty once and for all, and decided to allow it to proceed. The date was duly fixed for 7 April, and, under the priors' supervision, a list of the propositions to be 'proved' or 'disproved' by the trial was drawn up, together with a set of rules. Both sides agreed, and the necessary preparations were made. But, moments before the *experimento* was due to begin in the Piazza della Signoria, an argument broke out over whether Fra Domenico should be allowed to carry the consecrated host into the flames. When the Franciscans refused to allow such 'sacrilege', Savonarola's champions pulled out of the trial. The *arrabbiati* were outraged. The following day, as the friar was saying vespers, an armed mob attacked San Marco, bent on slaughter. The doors were hastily barricaded, but it was clear that they would not hold for long. Outside, some *frateschi* had already been hacked to pieces. In desperation, Francesco Valori snuck out through a side entrance in the hope of rallying some supporters. As he picked his way through the streets, however, he was spotted, chased back to his palace and killed, along with his wife. Before the same fate could be visited on Paolantonio Soderini, the Signoria decided that the time had come to step in. Savonarola would have seven hours to leave the city. After that, he would be declared a rebel, and anyone who killed him would be handsomely rewarded. It was, however, just a legal nicety. Knowing that the friar was going nowhere, they sent a detachment of soldiers, fully equipped with cannon and artillery, to take charge of besieging San Marco. The ensuing battle raged through the night. As the doors of the church went up in flames, the friars fought valiantly, firing crossbows from the windows and hurling tiles from the roof. But eventually, the troops broke through. Savonarola was found praying in the library. He, Fra Domenico and Fra Silvestro Maruffi were arrested and carted away in chains to the Palazzo della Signoria. Over the next few days, they were tortured and interrogated. When, at last, they confessed to their crimes, they were condemned as heretics and schismatics. On 23 May, all three were hanged in the Piazza della Signoria. Their bodies were burned and, in a final indignity, their ashes were thrown into the Arno.

After Savonarola's death, steps were quickly taken to eradicate the movement he had led. His leading supporters were fined, imprisoned or banished; his writings were proscribed; and discussion of his teachings was prohibited. Even the bell of San Marco was punished: removed from its tower, it was whipped as it was dragged through the streets, and exiled for fifty years. But retribution could only go so far. If Florence was to recover Pisa and prevent the Medici from returning, the bitter divisions of recent years would have to be healed. The *arrabbiati* needed to make their peace with the remaining *frateschi*, and the republican experiment that they had entered upon needed to be brought to fruition. And as part of that, the depoliticization of the chancellery would have to be completed, too.

This was the chance that Niccolò had been waiting for. Among those caught up in the ensuing purge was Alessandro Braccesi, the second chancellor and secretary of the *Dieci* – the committee responsible for military and foreign affairs in times of war. Not only was he too closely associated with the friar for the Signoria's liking, but he had also failed to represent Florence's interests effectively during a recent mission to Rome. Although he was neither fined nor imprisoned, he was summarily deprived of his offices, and the search began for a more politically acceptable replacement.[117] Who proposed Niccolò is not known. But he was the ideal candidate: well connected, yet still relatively obscure; able, but not outstandingly brilliant; and, crucially, untainted by success in any quarter. On 19 June 1498, he was confirmed as the new second chancellor. Quite suddenly, the pygmy had become a giant.

PART II

The Apprentice

(1498–1500)

4

The New Republic

(June 1498–February 1499)

When he stepped into the Palazzo della Signoria for the first time, in June 1498, the twenty-nine-year-old Niccolò Machiavelli presented a striking figure. Although only of average height, he had a penetrating gaze, tightly pursed lips, a long nose and a receding chin. His forehead was broad and open, but his closely cropped hair had already formed a pronounced widow's peak, and, above the neckline of his shirt, a prominent Adam's apple bobbed up and down when he spoke. It was perhaps not the appearance of a 'very acute observer and thinker', as one nineteenth-century historian claimed;[1] but it was nevertheless the look of an energetic man, determined to make the most of the opportunities he had been given.

Gazing around as he mounted the stairs, he could hardly have failed to appreciate his good fortune. Despite his relatively modest background, he had, overnight, become one of the most important bureaucrats in Florence, and, with an annual salary of 200 *fl.*, he now enjoyed an income far greater than his father had ever received. Long accustomed simply to making do, the Machiavelli were on the way up.

In his office, Niccolò found himself surrounded by a large staff. Some were, of course, old hands who may have resented having to serve under a young upstart like him a little at first. Antonio della Valle, for example, was twenty years his senior. Nicknamed 'ser Tightass',[2] he had already been entrusted with a number of important offices,[3] and before becoming Niccolò's subordinate, had even served as secretary of the *Dieci*.[4] Andrea di Romolo had also been around since the days of Lorenzo de' Medici, and had similarly long experience as a coadjutor.[5] Having been nominated for the second chancellorship himself in June 1498, he may still have been smarting from his defeat and the subsequent reduction in his salary.

Others were, however, newcomers. About the same age as Niccolò, many of them would soon be counted among his closest friends. Biagio Buonaccorsi, who was appointed to be his assistant in July 1498, was perhaps the most engaging.[6] Endowed with a lively intellect, he would go on to earn a reputation as a poet and historian. But he was also an inveterate gossip with a taste for off-colour jokes.[7] No less chatty, if rather more sober, was Agostino Vespucci, Niccolò's principal coadjutor in the second chancellery.[8] The cousin of Amerigo, he possessed not only a sharp eye for detail, but also a dry sense of humour that chimed with Niccolò's own.

As Niccolò's correspondence reveals, it was a lively place to work. Even if there was some awkwardness on account of the generational divide, it was soon forgotten, and before long, everyone was rubbing along well. There was always someone ready to share an amusing anecdote or deal a game of cards – so much so, in fact, that Andrea di Romolo would later complain of having sore knees from gambling too much.[9] A frisson of sexual tension may have been in the air, too. If hints dropped by Agostino are to be believed, Antonio della Valle had something of a crush on Biagio, calling him all manner of pet names and keeping him up until the early hours of the morning, playing dice.[10]

But, for all the raillery, Niccolò must have been aware that his position in the chancellery was still far from secure. After all, his predecessor had been removed from office after fewer than five months, and he can have been in no doubt that his career depended on his ability to negotiate the challenges with which Florence was then faced.

By anyone's standards, these were formidable. After Savonarola's fall, the city had been plunged into a constitutional crisis and while there was agreement that there should be a new form of government, there was no consensus about what form it should take.[11] Meeting in what is now known as the *Salone dei Cinquecento*, abutting the chancellery, the Great Council was bitterly divided. New factions, cutting across religious lines, had already begun to emerge out of the old parties.[12] Among the *popolani*, there were many who were determined to preserve some of the more populist features of the Savonarolan constitution. But the *ottimati* had begun to demand that a narrow oligarchy should once again control Florentine government. Regardless of whether they had opposed Savonarola or not in the past, they now called for election, rather than sortition, to be reintroduced for the greater magistracies, so that they could use their wealth and influence to ensure their preferred candidates would always be chosen.[13] Hoping to avert civil unrest, representatives of the two factions met on 26 July 1498. After much debate, a compromise proposal was agreed. A council of '150 or 200 leading citizens, drawn from each of the two parties, would be established, with responsibility for 'the care of the government'.[14] Its members would be chosen by sortition, but on the condition that older and wealthier candidates would have a stronger chance of having their names drawn.[15] Ultimately, these proposals came to nothing, but the discussions seem to have eased the tension for a time, nonetheless.

Florence's ongoing financial troubles provided the catalyst for further confrontation. Over the past four years, the exchequer had struggled to meet the financial demands made of it.[16] The subsidy to Charles VIII needed paying, mercenary commanders had to be supplied with funds, and the Pisan campaign needed to be sustained. Seeing that tax revenues were never sufficient to meet all of their obligations, successive Signorie had been forced to borrow money from wealthy citizens, on the understanding that the loans would be repaid with interest by a certain date. They had hoped that Pisa would soon be recaptured, and that, as their expenses decreased, they could use income from taxes to pay everything off in good time. But as the war ground on, it became clear that they had been wildly over-optimistic. They could never hope to raise enough money from existing taxes to repay the loans; and, to make matters worse, their expenses were rising further. By July 1498, the exchequer was already stretched to breaking point. It needed to raise funds from somewhere. One option was to tax the clergy, who had traditionally been exempt. Through its agents in Rome, the Signoria asked Alexander VI for the necessary licence.[17] But when the pope refused, their only remaining choice was to take out *more* loans.[18] To cover the repayments, however, taxes would have to be raised and, while the *ottimati* were willing enough to acquiesce – not least because of the political influence they would gain by lending the city money – representatives of the *popolo* reacted angrily to the proposal. Already suffering from the decline in trade and the rising cost of foodstuffs, they refused to grant taxes that would effectively take money from the poor and give it to the rich.

When the Pisan War took a turn for the worse, later that summer, this dispute was to have damaging repercussions. After Charles VIII's unexpected death on 7 April 1498, the Florentines redoubled their efforts to reconquer Pisa. Despite their financial difficulties, they began enlarging their forces as quickly as they were able, appointing Paolo Vitelli – one of the most accomplished mercenary commanders of the day – as their new *capitano della guerra*, responsible for directing all the city's armed forces.[19] Over the next few weeks, they went on to retain the services of a host of additional *condottieri*, including Rinuccio da Marciano, Ottaviano Riario – the son of Girolamo Riario and Caterina Sforza – and Jacopo IV d'Appiano, the *signore* of the strategically important coastal town of Piombino.[20] But their hopes of a swift victory were soon extinguished. Scenting an opportunity to weaken a commercial rival and extend its influence in the Tyrrhenian Sea, Venice declared that it would continue supporting the Pisan rebels.[21] In September, Venetian troops – accompanied by a detachment led by Piero de' Medici and his brothers – crossed into north-eastern Tuscany for the express purpose of drawing Florentine troops away from Pisa. Their timing could hardly have been better. Despite some recent successes in Buti and Vico,[22] Florence had been distracted by the outbreak of civil unrest in Siena. Desperate not to lose a vital ally, they had been forced to despatch soldiers to prop up Pandolfo Petrucci's regime in early September.[23] This gave the Venetians an opening. On 23 September, they captured Marradi, on the road between Florence and Faenza.[24] Fearing that this was the prelude to an attack on the Mugello, the Florentines hastily sent Rinuccio da Marciano and Jacopo d'Appiano to meet the challenge.[25] But though the town of Cassaglia was occupied, and preparations for the recapture of Marradi were soon underway, the two commanders found that it had been a feint. The Venetians had already diverted their main force southwards and were pushing on towards the Casentino. On 24 October, they took Bibbiena, on the road to Arezzo. Suddenly realizing that they were in danger of losing a key town, the Florentines ordered Paolo Vitelli to abandon the assault on Pisa and hasten to the Casentino.[26] Amid heavy rains, he fought a bitter campaign. But his progress was hampered by the shortage of money. Despite the gravity of the situation, the *popolani* still refused to approve any new taxes. As Landucci remarked, 'great uneasiness ensued'. Seeing no reason to risk their lives if they were not going to be paid, 'some soldiers deserted, and others threatened to do so'.[27]

This was a grave enough setback in itself, but that it coincided with a series of diplomatic reversals only made it more troubling. At first, the Florentines had regarded the accession of the new king of France, Louis XII, with optimism. No sooner had he ascended the throne than he had made known his determination to conquer the duchy of Milan and, ultimately, recapture the kingdom of Naples. Were he to uphold the agreements made by Charles VIII, Florence could reasonably expect him to support their campaign against Pisa. But Louis was cut from a different cloth. Resolved not to repeat Charles's mistakes, he set about building a series of alliances that shattered any hopes the Florentines might have had. The first was with the papacy. In exchange for a papal dispensation allowing him to divorce his wife, Jeanne, and marry Charles VIII's widow, Anne of Brittany, he agreed to facilitate the marriage of Alexander VI's son, Cesare Borgia, to Carlotta of Naples.[28] In January 1499, Louis' marriage was duly annulled, and, though Carlotta refused to marry Cesare – recently created duke of Valentinois – a suitable alternative was found in Charlotte d'Albret, the king of Navarre's sister. This paved the way for a wider understanding. When the marriage contract was signed in the spring, the Borgias also agreed to support any campaign that Louis might mount against Milan or Naples.[29] Given Florence's fraught relationship with Alexander in the past, and the pope's known affection for the Medici, this boded ill. But Louis' second alliance, with Venice, was still more threatening. According to the terms of the Treaty of Blois, which were kept secret for several weeks, the Venetians agreed to join France against the duchy of Milan. They promised that, whenever Louis invaded from the north-west, they would launch a simultaneous attack from the east, and would provide him with a 100,000-ducat subsidy into the bargain. They would then divide the duchy between them. In return, Louis not only promised to provide them with help in the event of war with the Ottoman Empire, but also agreed to moderate his support for the Florentines and allow Pisa's fate to be settled by the arbitration of Ercole d'Este, duke of Ferrara.

Although the Florentines were aware that Louis had been negotiating with Venice and the papacy, they had no means of knowing
what – if any – agreements had been reached. They had not the
slightest inkling of how severely their chances of recapturing Pisa
had been damaged, or of how seriously their position in the Casentino
was threatened. Nervously debating what to do when the king
descended into the Italian peninsula, they naively believed themselves
to be facing a similar choice to that which they had confronted in
1494. On the one hand, they could stand by France. This way, they
would avoid provoking the king's ire. In their innocence, they also
hoped that, in time, he might even be persuaded to help them to
recover Pisa. But this would also mean that they would have to
sacrifice Milan's support, which could have a devastating effect on
their campaign in the Casentino in the short term. On the other
hand, they could abandon the French. Little suspecting how dramatically the diplomatic landscape had changed, they believed that the
threat of a French invasion might persuade Venice, Milan, and the
papacy to set aside their differences, and join with them in fighting
a common enemy. This was, of course, a high-risk strategy; but if
they succeeded in reforming the League of Venice, it would have
the merit of detaching the Venetians from the Pisans, and securing
both the Casentino and the Mugello.

Unaware of how badly they had misjudged the diplomatic situation, the Florentines decided to delay taking a definite decision,
while they explored their options. On 15 February 1499, ambassadors
were sent to Venice and Rome, in the hope of concluding a peace.[30]
Two days later, they also sent for the image of Our Lady of Impruneta
in the belief that it would somehow help them 'to decide whether
they would be well advised to join the League and abandon the king
of France'.[31] Misguided as they may have been about the choice they
faced, however, they were under no illusions about the gravity of the
struggle before them. Whatever course of action they eventually
chose, it seemed clear that they would not only have to tread a very
fine diplomatic line, but would also have to provide their forces in
Pisa and the Casentino with the support they so desperately lacked.
This was a matter not just of careful negotiation, but also of cold,
hard cash – which could only be delivered if seemingly unbridgeable
political divisions at home were overcome.

These were challenges which Niccolò would have to address. As second chancellor, his duties were, in theory, restricted to managing Florence's relationship with its subject towns, issuing permits granting safe passage and handling any other domestic correspondence. But, in practice, his role was far more expansive. Ever since the second chancellery had been created, incumbents had frequently been asked to help shoulder some of the burden on the first chancellor. While this could entail routine administrative tasks, such as recording the meetings of *pratiche* or disbursing salaries owed to various officials, it could also involve a more active engagement with the conduct of foreign policy. In the past, second chancellors had routinely been asked to correspond with Florentine diplomats, or negotiate with foreign legations on the Signoria's behalf.[32] On occasions, they had even acted as ambassadors, as well. That the Signoria had seen fit to elect Niccolò as secretary of the *Dieci di Balìa* on 14 July, as well – although without any increase in salary – served to formalize his involvement in external affairs further.[33]

*

But, while the retrospective wisdom of some of his later writings (especially *Il principe*) might sometimes give the impression that he was a naturally talented diplomat, Niccolò was almost completely unprepared for what lay ahead. Beyond writing a report on Savonarola's fall, he does not appear to have had any experience with matters of state, and, other than being personable and inoffensive, was but poorly qualified to undertake diplomatic missions. Yet, if he was to survive as second chancellor, he had to learn fast.

5

The First Tests

(March–July 1499)

Niccolò's first test was not long in coming. Although the Signoria had resolved to keep their options open, at least until their ambassadors returned from Venice and Rome, the king of France and the duke of Milan were pressing them for a decision. The more insistent they became, however, the more urgent the re-conquest of Pisa seemed. Whichever alliance the Florentines eventually chose, it was clearly in their best interests to take possession of the rebel city before they declared themselves. If they threw their weight behind Ludovico Sforza of Milan, they would have to end the Pisan campaign before the French crossed the Alps, in order to avoid fighting on two, or even three fronts. If they decided to support Louis XII, by contrast, they would be well advised to recapture Pisa before the city had a chance to appeal to the king or otherwise secure a settlement in its favour. Given that Florence's *capitano della guerra*, Paolo Vitelli, had prevented Venetian reinforcements from reaching Bibbiena, and appeared to be on the brink of retaking the town at the end of February, the time for an assault on Pisa seemed now to be at hand.[1] But this was easier said than done. Despite the military advances, Florence was still in the grip of a financial crisis. As they had done for months past, the *popolani* were resolutely refusing to grant further taxes; and until they changed their minds, the exchequer would struggle to pay troops in the field, let alone bear the cost of a siege. But money wasn't the only problem. Florence's war effort was also undermined by the mercenary commanders that the Signoria had employed.

There was, of course, nothing unusual about retaining such men. Commanding large, professional armies of career soldiers, *condottieri*

had emerged as a distinct military class over the past two centuries
in response to the rapid pace of technological change and the
mounting scale of armed conflict, and, by the close of the fifteenth
century, had come to dominate the practice of war in Italy.[2] But
condottieri were an unreliable breed. Aware that states like Florence
were wholly reliant on their services, they often exploited their
employers' weakness for their own gain. Contemporary chronicles
are filled with accounts of *condottieri* refusing to fight unless their
pay was increased, ransacking their employers' territories and even
switching sides when it suited them.

On this occasion, it was the *condottiere* Jacopo IV d'Appiano who
was causing the difficulty. He had, admittedly, given the Florentines
little trouble in the past. Dispatched to recapture Marradi alongside
Rinuccio da Marciano the previous autumn, he had avoided putting
his troops in the way of danger; but, as Niccolò later recorded in
the *Discorsi*, he had nevertheless succeeded in presenting the
Venetians' eventual retreat in such a way that it reflected favourably
on him.[3] On returning from this expedition, however, he suddenly
became bolshie. Ignoring an order to proceed to Pisa, he pitched
camp at Pontadera, just over twenty kilometres from the city. He
refused to budge unless the Signoria agreed to pay him 5,000 *fl.* – on
top of what they were already going to give him – and authorized
him to raise an additional forty men-at-arms.[4]

On 24 March 1499, the *Dieci di Balìa* sent Niccolò to negotiate.
Even for an experienced diplomat, this would have been a daunting
task. But for a young and inexperienced man like him, it would
surely have been even more taxing. The journey to Appiano's camp
was bad enough. Although Pontadera was only sixty kilometres from
Florence, it would have taken Niccolò about a day to get there.
Travelling on horseback at a grindingly slow pace, he would have
struggled with saddle sores and mud, not to mention the risk of
being surprised by Pisan troops.[5] But when he arrived at his destination, dirty and tired, he discovered that Jacopo, though eloquent,
had no sense of judgement. According to Antonio da Venafro, the
quick-witted chancellor of Pandolfo Petrucci, he was a man of little
sense and bad reputation.[6] What was more, he was also as stubborn
as a mule. Unwilling to take orders at the best of times, he could
be pig-headed when the mood took him – especially where money
was involved.

Over the next two days, Niccolò argued the *Dieci*'s case.[7] Although Florence was grateful for Jacopo's service and bore him nothing but goodwill, the city would not accede to his demands. His original contract clearly stipulated that he was to be paid 2,400 *fl.*, and that no further payments would be made except as the *Dieci* saw fit. Given that he had evidently been content with this arrangement in the past, Niccolò argued, there was no reason why he should be unhappy with it now. Besides, the city simply didn't have the money to pay him what he was asking. Of course, if he really needed an additional forty men-at-arms, the *Dieci* would be happy to discuss the matter with the duke of Milan, who had agreed to shoulder the cost of his expenses when the contract had first been signed. But Jacopo would have to wait for a reply and, given the wider political situation, he would probably be turned down, anyway.

It wasn't what the forty-year-old *condottiere* wanted to hear. Yet it was a testimony to Niccolò's ability – or perhaps ingenuousness – that he made Jacopo understand that Florence wouldn't be browbeaten.

*

Niccolò had acquitted himself well. But, by the time he arrived back in Florence, the political situation had already changed. On 5 April, letters arrived from the ambassadors in Venice which put paid to any hopes of a satisfactory negotiated settlement. The Serene Republic had at last revealed that it had chosen Ercole d'Este to decide Pisa's fate. Nobody was in any doubt he would be pressured into ruling against Florence's interests. When a horseman arrived to acquaint the priors with his decision three days later, however, the terms were even worse than they had feared.[8] Florence was to pay the Venetians a total of 180,000 *fl.* over the next twelve years, while the Pisans were to retain control of their castles and fortresses. All that the Florentines would get in return would be an assurance that one of their own would be elected as Pisa's *podestà*. This was greeted with outrage. Many people even said that since the Venetians' campaign in the Casentino had ground to a halt and their troops were even then being besieged in Bibbiena, they should actually be giving Florence money.[9] When the Eighty met – two days after Bibbena was eventually recaptured – they refused to accept Ercole d'Este's terms under any circumstances.[10]

But there was a silver lining. Although Ercole d'Este's decision displeased the Florentines, it was every bit as repugnant to the Pisans, as well. Indeed, they rejected the duke's terms even before the Eighty did so. While they would be given control of their own fortifications, they felt that they were being asked to hand over the reins of government to the Florentines – which was precisely what they were fighting against. According to Landucci, they declared that 'in no way would they consent to such an agreement, or ever submit to the Florentines'.[11] They had already decided to melt down the silver in their churches to pay their soldiers, and 'would lay down their lives before they gave themselves up'.

That Ercole's judgement had so enraged the Pisans could only mean one thing: Venice was no longer as committed to their cause as it had once been. In fact, the Serene Republic was clearly doing its best to get out of the conflict altogether. The reason for this sudden volte-face was that the Ottomans had begun mobilizing their fleet sooner than expected. As Niccolò reported in a letter to Pierfrancesco Tosinghi – the Florentine military commissioner at Pisa – the Venetians had realized they would shortly have to defend their possessions in the Eastern Mediterranean and were hastily making preparations for the coming conflict.[12] In order to avoid having to fight on two or more fronts, they were now trying to settle the Pisan question as quickly as they could, even if that meant selling out their former allies.

What was more, the Venetians were also trying to get out of their obligations to France, too – or, at least, to persuade Louis to delay his expedition. Passing on information received from the Milanese ambassador in Venice, Niccolò informed Tosinghi that they had already dispatched fresh emissaries 'to justify, under the pretext of the sultan, their not paying the money [they had promised him], and to convince His Majesty that at this point he must attend to matters other than Italian ones.'[13]

This provided the Florentines with the opportunity they had been waiting for. Even though they were still uncertain whether to support France or Milan, Venice's abandonment of Pisa appeared to increase their chances of recapturing the rebel city before they had to make up their minds. The only question was how best to do it. Before settling on a course of action, the *Dieci* asked Niccolò to prepare a report based on the recommendations of Florence's generals. Now known as the *Discorso sopra le cose di Pisa*, this was, by necessity, a rather dry work, cataloguing the various opinions he had been given with wearying thoroughness.[14] But it was nevertheless coloured by the unfavourable view of Jacopo d'Appiano that he had formed during his mission to Pontadera, and conveyed a burgeoning scepticism about the effectiveness of mercenaries, especially against a citizen army.

According to Niccolò, Pisa could be retaken in two ways: 'by love or by force'. Love was, of course, the most appealing. By this, Niccolò meant that the Pisans could submit to Florentine rule without a struggle. This was less implausible than it might have seemed. After so many years of war, they might regard surrender as the better part of valour. They were, after all, weak and alone. They had been 'shunned by Milan, turned away by Genoa, frowned upon by the pope, and given short shrift by Siena'.[15] With no credible means of defending themselves, they were reduced to hoping vainly for 'disunion and weakness' among the Florentines and their allies.[16] But, on balance, it was still unlikely that the Pisans would give themselves up voluntarily. Nor did it seem any more probable that someone who had – hypothetically – taken control of Pisa would hand the city over. If it was taken by force, in some sort of coup, the victor would hardly be willing to capitulate when he would clearly be powerful enough to defend it. If the Pisans had willingly granted their city to some kind of protector, by contrast, he would be unlikely to betray their trust by transferring it to the Florentines. Indeed, the only way that he would allow Florence to acquire Pisa would be by abandoning it and leaving it to her enemies as prey, 'the way the Venetians did'.[17] Thus, Niccolò argued, there did not seem to be any chance of recovering Pisa except by force. Perhaps the most obvious method was to besiege it. If the Florentines could not persuade the Lucchesi to assist them, the *condottieri* recommended constructing three camps – at San Piero a Grado, San Iacopo and Beccheria – each fortified with ditches. If the *Dieci* did not want to go to such expense – as Niccolò seems to have feared – they could always build a bastion and have only two camps. But, in the *condottieri*'s opinion, Pisa could not be taken by siege alone. To their minds, it would be almost impossible to starve the city into submission. Even if they could somehow prevent grain from getting in, the Pisans were so determined that they would find a way of making bread out of other things. As such, the commanders urged the *Dieci* to mount a direct assault on the walls, as well. With enough men and artillery, Pisa would be captured in no time. Indeed, the wisest of the *condottieri* predicted that only a miracle would save the Pisans now. As Niccolò pointed out, however, they were still divided when it came to the details, each no doubt thinking of how best to enrich himself. As ever, money and loyalty would be the sticking points.

*

Despite the disagreements, the *Dieci* decided to take their commanders' advice. Preparations were soon being made for a siege and an assault. At the beginning of June, Paolo Vitelli and Rinuccio da Marciano were recalled from the Casentino, raiding parties were despatched to lay waste to the Pisan *contado* and mortars were sent to hasten the capture of Cascina.[18]

For a time, everything seemed to go smoothly. Confident that victory would be swift, the *popolani* were at last persuaded to grant a new tax, dubbed *la Graziosa* ('the gracious') by Landucci, but more commonly known as *el Piacente* ('the pleasing').[19] A few days later, Cascina fell, leaving the road to Pisa open.[20] Best of all, the Venetians were now at war with the Ottomans. Already, Turkish privateers were raiding the Dalmatian coast, and it was rumoured that more terrible attacks would soon follow. On 5 June, Niccolò informed Pierfrancesco Tosinghi that some believed the sultan to be heading for Sicily.[21] Less than a month later, Landucci even claimed that Bayezid had landed at Zara (Zadar) and was then heading for Raugia (Rovinj) – across the gulf from Venice itself.[22]

But the Signoria's policy of diplomatic equivocation was becoming increasingly hard to sustain. As Niccolò reported in a letter to Tosinghi on 6 July, Louis XII was urgently demanding an answer. He was asking the Florentines to supply him with 500 lancers for his campaign against Milan. In return, he would provide them with 1,000 lancers for their war against Pisa. What was more, he also promised to persuade Alexander VI and the Venetians to commit to Florence's defence.[23] It was a tempting offer. But Ludovico Sforza was – if anything – even more insistent. More than once, he offered to provide Florence with whatever forces it needed to reconquer

Pisa, if only it would agree to supply him with 300 men-at-arms and 2,000 foot soldiers whenever he might require them.[24]

The Signoria had, of course, tried to temporize as best it could, telling the king of France that Florence could not conclude any alliance without exposing itself to 'manifest danger'.[25] The duke of Milan was given a similar answer. As Niccolò explained to Tosinghi, the Signoria deemed it 'both dangerous to clarify their position with respect to French matters, and useless for His Lordship', at least for the moment.[26] But, in contrast to Louis XII, Sforza would not be put off. Even if Venice was too preoccupied with the Ottomans to fight alongside the French, he could not afford to do without Florence's support, and greeted the Signoria's vacillating reply with open contempt. In the hope of assuaging his anger, the priors decided to send Niccolò's chancellery colleague, Antonio Guidotti da Colle, to Milan.[27] The more they tried to justify their position, however, the more furious the duke became. Relations quickly soured.

This all had serious implications for the Romagnol city of Forlì. Were Louis XII to cross the Alps in the coming months – as seemed likely – Forlì would be threatened. Although it was far from Milan, Cesare Borgia had been making plans to carve out a principality for himself by sweeping into the Romagna in the king's wake. As long as Florence and Milan had been of one mind, Forlì had felt reasonably confident of being defended by its allies. But now that they were drifting apart, it was suddenly exposed, and Caterina Sforza – who ruled the city on behalf of her son, the *condotterie*, Ottaviano Riario – had to decide which of the two would offer the best protection. Given that Caterina was Lodovico Sforza's niece, Milan was perhaps the more obvious choice – though, as the duke would be too busy defending his own borders, he was unlikely to send much support. It was, however, doubtful that Florence would be much better. Although Caterina was technically a Florentine citizen by virtue of her marriage to Giovanni 'il Popolano' de' Medici, and had been assured of the Signoria's continuing fidelity towards her, she could not depend on the city to come to Forlì's aid should the worst happen. Unless Florence recaptured Pisa soon, it would clearly be reluctant to commit itself – especially if it decided not to ally with Louis XII.

Knowing that Milan and Florence were both desperate for troops, Caterina hoped that one or the other might be persuaded to guarantee Forlì's safety in return for her son's services. And she was not averse to playing them off against one another in the process. On 12 July, she asked the Florentine Signoria to grant Ottaviano a new contract. 'Anticipating the arrival of the French,' she wrote,

> the illustrious lord, the duke of Milan, my uncle and most attentive father, has conveyed to me his desire . . . for five hundred men-at-arms and a great many mounted crossbowmen as well. Given that our company is now under obligation to your excellent republic, we have not been able to give a definitive response; our goodwill is not lacking, but on the other hand, there is our debt to you.[28]

Cunningly, she went on to remind the priors of the services that Ottaviano had rendered during the Venetian campaign in the Casentino, and gave the impression that she would prefer him to remain in their employ. She also highlighted the advantages this would bring them. By taking Ottaviano on, she argued, they would gain additional forces for use against Pisa, and, in earning Forlì's gratitude, they would secure their eastern frontier at the same time.

The Signoria could see the benefits, and were, in any case, anxious not to lose Caterina to Milan. Hoping to strike some sort of a deal, the priors decided to charge Niccolò with negotiating on their behalf. As Marcello di Virgilio Adriani informed him, his task was simple.[29] He was to inform Caterina that, after consulting a copy of Ottaviano's previous contract, the Signoria had found that – contrary to what Caterina had claimed in her letter – she was no longer under any obligation to Florence, and that Florence was under no obligation to her. Mindful of the splendid services Ottaviano had rendered in the past, however, the priors were willing to grant him a new contract. But it would have to be on new terms. Because of the large number of men-at-arms already in the Florentines' pay, they could not afford to pay him as much as before. They could offer no more than 10,000 ducats, and could only employ him on a peace footing. As they well knew, this fell far short of what Caterina was asking for. It would not be easy to persuade her to agree. But, having been impressed by Niccolò's mission to Jacopo d'Appiano, they were confident – perhaps rather too confident – that he had the experience to carry it off.

*

Setting out from Florence on 12 or 13 July, Niccolò trekked more than a hundred kilometres across the Apennines in the scorching summer heat. Before reaching his destination, however, he first stopped in Castrocaro, a little way outside Forlì. There, he met with the captain, Giovanni di Pietro di Giovanni Capponi, to see if any gunpowder, saltpetre or cannonballs could be spared for the attack on Pisa. As it turned out, Capponi couldn't help,[30] but he nevertheless gave Niccolò some valuable advice for his mission in Forlì. In his experience, Caterina could not be trusted.[31] Although she professed to be a friend of the Florentines, her actions suggested otherwise. Only the day before, some fifteen or twenty of her crossbowmen had attacked the Florentine village of Salutare, about two kilometres away. Three men had been wounded and another had been carried off after his house had been robbed. Similar outrages were committed every day, and a number of country people had already complained to Capponi that not enough was being done to protect them.

Arriving in Forlì on the afternoon of 16 July, Niccolò soon had cause to be grateful for the captain's warning. When he was granted an audience with the countess later that evening, he was captivated by her, as so many others had been before him. At the age of thirty-six, Caterina was still a famous beauty. As a presumed portrait of her by Lorenzo di Credi testifies, she had fine, porcelain skin, well-shaped lips, flowing, strawberry-blonde hair and a long, elegant neck. So renowned were her good looks that Biagio Buonaccorsi even begged Niccolò to send him a drawing of her.[32] She was charming and sophisticated, too. Brought up at the Sforza court in Milan, she had received a thorough humanistic education and had been surrounded by scholars and artists from her earliest days. Most of all, she was a woman of strength and courage. Since her first marriage – to Girolamo Riario, the nephew of Pope Sixtus IV – she had grown used to the cut and thrust of Italian politics, and had been compelled to defend her family's interests with force on more than one occasion.[33] At the age of only twenty-one, she had occupied the Castel Sant'Angelo and repelled attacks by rebellious mobs, despite being pregnant at the time. By the time of Niccolò's arrival, she had been acting as regent of Imola and Forlì for more than a decade, and had been nicknamed 'the tigress'.

But, even at that first meeting, Niccolò could see that Caterina was playing a double game. Rather than receiving him alone, as would have been expected, she was attended by the *condottiere* Giovanni da Casale, who, though now in Caterina's service, still retained close ties with the Milanese and, despite having been in Forlì for only a little over two months, already seemed to 'rule everything'.[34] Knowing that he would relay everything she said to the duke of Milan, Caterina was deliberately cold.[35] After listening to Niccolò outline the Signoria's proposal, she replied by accusing the Florentines of mistreating her. Although her son had served Florence faithfully, she had never received the compensation she deserved. Even if the priors were under no obligation towards her, she had hoped they would at least have expressed their gratitude for the readiness with which she had exposed her territories to the rapacity of the Venetians. They were offering far less than she had expected. She would have to think things over before giving Niccolò a definite answer. When he then passed on the Signoria's request for cannonballs and gunpowder, she replied that she could not help them, and brusquely dismissed him.

This was, however, just a ruse. After returning to his chamber, Niccolò received a visit from Caterina's secretary, Antonio Baldraccani.[36] He had come to reassure Niccolò that her relationship with Milan was not as close as it may have appeared and that she was still well disposed to the Florentines. Indeed, she actively wanted to strike a deal with them. She would, however, need the Signoria to give her more money – not so much because she needed the cash, but rather to provide her with an excuse for choosing Florence over Milan. That very day, she had received a letter from the duke begging her to enter into an agreement with him, and promising the same terms as the Florentines had given her the year before. Unless the Florentines upped their offer, she would find it difficult to turn him down without giving offence. It would, after all, seem dishonourable to accept the Signoria's terms when other *condottieri* had been employed on better terms than before. Besides, she did not know what reasons she could give the duke for accepting an inferior offer when she was bound to him by ties of blood and gratitude.

Baldraccani knew that this was a lot to ask. After all, Niccolò had already explained that Florence was in financial difficulties. But, if the Signoria agreed, Caterina was prepared to offer them something in return. Baldraccani outlined her proposal with characteristic subtlety. Pretending to take Niccolò into his confidence, he claimed that certain members of the Council of Eighty had privately made it known that Ottaviano would be re-employed on two conditions. One, Niccolò already knew. But the other was that Caterina should pledge Forlì to Florence – which she would never agree to do, at least not in public. This was, of course, a patent falsehood. The Council of Eighty had never said any such thing. But that was not the point. In stressing that Caterina would never officially pledge her state to Florence, he was hinting that she might be willing to do so unofficially, if the Signoria agreed to increase its offer. An experienced diplomat would have picked this up immediately. But Niccolò was still too naive to see what was going on. Somewhat flustered, he declined to comment. He could not understand why, if the Eighty had decided on such a condition, he had not been informed of it before his departure. But he promised to ask for clarification nonetheless. This was, of course, not what Baldraccani wanted to hear. Masking his irritation, he reiterated that Caterina would not pledge her state *in writing*, and insisted that Niccolò ask the Signoria for further instructions as soon as possible. Even if the young envoy was unable to grasp his meaning, Baldraccani evidently hoped that someone in Florence would.

While Niccolò was waiting for a reply, Tommaso Totti brought him another letter from Adriani, dated two days earlier.[37] Given his failure to secure any supplies in Castrocaro, he was instructed to ask Caterina to loan or sell the Florentines 10,000–12,000 lbs. of gunpowder. He was also to convey the Signoria's desire that she provide them with '500 good infantrymen under good captains' for immediate use against Pisa. Given the brush-off he had received at his last audience, Niccolò's hopes were probably not high. All the same, he dutifully went to raise the matter with Caterina once again.[38] To his surprise, her tone had now changed completely. As she had explained earlier, she had no saltpetre and very little powder in Forlì, but, as a gesture of goodwill, she would give the Signoria half of the 20,000 lbs of saltpetre that Leonardo Strozzi had recently purchased on her behalf at Pesaro. As far as the troops were concerned, she would happily comply, but pointed out that the Signoria would have to pay for them. If the priors needed them urgently, they should send 500 ducats at once and the infantrymen would be on Pisan soil within two weeks.

This was, however, merely a prelude. What Caterina really wanted to discuss was Ottaviano's contract. Having conferred with Baldraccani, she was aware that Niccolò was out of his depth, and she had no desire to waste time indulging in fruitless discussion. Cutting him off before he could say anything, she spelt out her position as clearly as she dared. It was a pity, she observed, that Forlì was so far from Florence. If it were closer, she could inspire her subjects to embrace the Florentine cause simply by making her own enthusiasm for the Republic known. As things were, she would find it difficult. But it would be much easier if the Signoria would acknowledge her affection openly. This could best be done by showing their gratitude for the services she had previously rendered. In other words, if the Signoria gave her what she asked, she would deliver the Forlivesi's loyalty, pledging the city in all but name.

What was more, Caterina would also provide Florence with any additional troops it might need. As one of her secretaries told Niccolò later that day, the Signoria could choose between two kinds of soldiers.[39] On the one hand, there was a corps of 1,500 men armed for Caterina's own service. Provided that the Florentines paid a month's wages in advance, these could be despatched whenever necessary. On the other hand, there was a body of mercenaries. Although Caterina did not employ them herself, she still decided what contracts they accepted. She would let the Florentines have them, but the priors would have to negotiate the scale of payments for themselves.

Having still not received any further instructions, Niccolò did not know how to reply. But, swayed by the force of Caterina's personality, he had come to feel that it was in the Signoria's best interests to give her what she wanted. 'I truly believe that if Your Lordships were to grant [the countess] some recognition for [her] past service, or enlarge the new agreement,' he wrote that afternoon, 'you will certainly keep [her as a] friend.'[40]

Even at the best of times, diplomatic couriers could be slow. But, after four more days of waiting, Niccolò was getting restless. He did not know how to move negotiations along, but even he could see that something had to be done to secure a deal. Caterina was pressing him for an answer. In desperation, he wrote to the Signoria once again on 22 July.[41] He stressed that the best way of satisfying Caterina would be to assure her that she would be compensated for her previous service, and to offer Ottaviano a new contract at the same rate of pay as before. She would never accept less than the duke of Milan was promising, and her patience was beginning to wear thin. She was so annoyed by the Signoria's hesitancy that Niccolò was finding it difficult 'to judge whether she is more inclined towards Milan or to [Florence].'[42] Even the troops she had offered were beginning to slip out of their hands. On 21 July, she had publicly reviewed 500 infantrymen that she was sending to Ludovico Sforza, and had already mustered a further fifty mounted crossbowmen a few days earlier. If the priors wanted to employ the countess's infantrymen, it could probably still be arranged, but they would have to make up their minds and send the money fast.

On 23 July, the courier Ardingo at last arrived with word from Florence. He was carrying at least four letters. Two – possibly three – were from Biagio Buonaccorsi.[43] Though as chatty as ever, these brought worrying news. Back in the chancellery, people were beginning to complain about Niccolò's lack of progress. Most notable among these was Antonio della Valle, who seems to have believed that he should have been sent to Forlì instead. Of course, Biagio had done his best to defend Niccolò. 'In my judgment,' he told his friend, 'you have executed the commission entrusted to you with great honour to yourself up to now.'[44] According to Biagio, Niccolò was every bit as effective as Antonio, even if he might not have been as experienced. This was, of course, all very touching, but Niccolò must have realized that Biagio was really warning him to bring negotiations to a successful conclusion – and quickly.

The pressure to produce results was all the greater given how rapidly events were moving. As Biagio reported, the French were expected to invade Italy any day.[45] On 10 July, Louis XII had arrived in Lyon, where he would soon be joined by Cesare Borgia. That the king was planning to attack Milan and had concluded a deal with the Venetians was at last becoming obvious to all. Evidently fearing that the kingdom of Naples would be attacked, Federico I of Naples had been urging the pope to abandon Louis and unite Italy against the French. But Alexander VI had reassured him that, if Louis did cross the Alps, it would be merely 'to oppose the Turks . . . and to capture Milan.'[46] If Ludovico Sforza had any doubts about this before, he no longer did. His brother, Cardinal Ascanio, had secretly passed through Florentine territory to be with him on 13 July.[47] Even as

Biagio was writing, the two were discussing how best to repel a French assault, and Forlì was naturally an important part of their plans. Given that the chances of Florence allying with Milan were diminishing fast, it was hence vital to secure an agreement as soon as possible. And since Milan was beginning to look vulnerable, the Signoria had reason to believe that Caterina would be willing to compromise.

The priors' instructions were contained in the remaining two letters.[48] On the most important question, they were clear. Having considered Niccolò's reports carefully, they had decided to accommodate Caterina's demands in the hope of reaching a deal.[49] Niccolò was to inform her that, in recognition of her past services, they were willing to offer her a total of 12,000 *ducati di soldo*. This was the same amount that Ottaviano had been paid under his previous contract, and was as much as the duke of Milan was offering. But this did not mean that they were making negotiations easy for him. On other issues, the priors were equivocal, if not downright evasive. They were, for example, undecided what to do about the infantrymen that Caterina had promised them. As yet, they were unable to establish exactly how many soldiers they would need for the next phase of the Pisan campaign. Hoping to keep their options open, they hence instructed Niccolò to thank Caterina as best he was able, but not to commit himself to anything just yet.[50] And there were other respects in which the priors seemed determined to cause him problems. Alarmed at the offences that had been committed against Florentine citizens at Salutare, they wanted Niccolò to express their outrage and to demand that Caterina rectify the situation immediately.[51]

After scribbling a note acknowledging receipt of Adriani's letters,[52] Niccolò rushed off to see the countess. Evidently delighted, he informed her of the priors' offer, and stressed their desire to satisfy her honour.[53] But Caterina again prevaricated, claiming that she was still afraid of offending her uncle, Ludovico Sforza. She did, however, promise to give him her decision as soon as she could. No doubt irritated, Niccolò urged her to hurry.

*

He did not have to wait long. Later that afternoon, Baldraccani called to pass on the countess's decision.[54] She would accept the engagement on a peace footing for one year, on the understanding that she would indeed receive the 12,000 ducats the Signoria had offered. But, in order to justify her taking this step – or, rather, to guard herself against the wrath of Cesare Borgia – she asked the Signoria to promise to defend, protect and maintain the integrity of her dominions. She also wanted to be paid the money still owed to her under the terms of Ottaviano's last contract – if not in full, then at least in part. Surely, Baldraccani added, the Signoria's financial troubles were not so extreme that they could not pay her what they had agreed.

Sensing that an agreement was now within his grasp, Niccolò replied as amicably as he could.[55] The Signoria would, of course, be delighted to hear that Caterina was ready to accept their terms. But there was surely no need for the priors to commit themselves to defending her dominions. As she herself had observed, they would do this anyway. Florence had a long tradition of looking out for its friends and neighbours, after all. And, besides, he had been given no instructions about such matters. He therefore suggested that she accept Ottaviano's engagement immediately and write to her own representative in Florence to sort out such details later.

Baldraccani, however, could not be brushed off so easily.[56] These discussions had already dragged on for long enough, he replied; Caterina wanted to sort everything out once and for all. Niccolò should therefore write to the Signoria asking for the authority to settle the outstanding issues. Knowing that the priors were unlikely to agree to this, Niccolò protested. He could see the deal slipping through his fingers, and used every argument he could think of to persuade the secretary to set the question of defence aside. But nothing he said would dissuade Baldraccani. He had no choice but to write to the Signoria again.

No sooner had Baldraccani gone, however, than things took another unexpected turn. As Niccolò was about to give his letter to the courier, a message came from Caterina.[57] Despite what Baldraccani had said earlier, she was now satisfied that there was no need to ask the Signoria for any further commitments. She trusted that they would treat her in the same way as she would treat them. As such, she asked Niccolò to come to her on the following morning to sign the engagement. His relief can well be imagined, but he was still too naive to see that Caterina had said this less for his benefit than for that of the Milanese.

When he presented himself in the audience chamber the following day, he discovered that Caterina's real intentions were quite different.[58] Adopting the same line as Baldraccani had taken the previous afternoon, she informed him that she *did* want the Signoria to give her an explicit undertaking that Florence would defend her dominions, after all. She asked him to write again to the Signoria. Poor Niccolò could hardly conceal his frustration. He seems to have known that the agreement was foundering, yet was too inexperienced to save it himself. All that he could do was to pass on Caterina's demands and return to Castrocaro to see if he could put an end to the assaults on Florentines while he waited.

But it was too late. On 27 July, Biagio Buonaccorsi wrote to him with news that Louis XII had at last begun his attack.[59] A few days earlier, the French king's commander, Giangiacomo Trivulzio, had crossed into Piedmont, and he had already captured a number of castles along the border with Milan. The Venetians looked set to launch their own offensive, too. Florence was, admittedly, not ready to break off relations with Ludovico Sforza just yet. Preparations for the offensive against Pisa were almost complete and the Signoria was unwilling to jeopardize anything at such a late stage. But, with each passing day, it seemed less likely that Florence would throw in its lot with Sforza – much less risk incurring the king's ire by agreeing to defend Caterina against Cesare Borgia when the main invasion began.

On the same day, Adriani wrote on the Signoria's behalf.[60] After weighing the situation, the priors did not think it necessary to undertake the obligation Caterina had requested. They would, of course, keep an eye out for her, but a formal commitment was out of the question. Once Niccolò had communicated this to the countess, he was to return to Florence – empty handed.

Evidently aware of the Signoria's instructions, Biagio urged him to hasten back 'as swiftly as possible'.[61] Although the style of Niccolò's reports was much admired, his mishandling of the negotiations in Forlì was openly criticized by his chancellery colleagues. It would do him no good to stay in the Romagna any longer than was absolutely necessary. Indeed, he would be risking his career if he tarried.

Niccolò had failed, and failed badly. As he wended his way back over the Apennines to Florence, he would have had to face the fact that he had not only left Forlì to face Cesare Borgia alone, but had also lost his city an important ally and a force of mercenaries. For all the confidence with which he had offered the Signoria advice in the *Discorso sopra le cose di Pisa*, he had arguably done significant damage to Florence's long-term future and could certainly not claim to have passed his first tests with flying colours.

6

The Fog of War

(August 1499–July 1500)

Although Niccolò's mission to Forlì had been a dismal failure, he returned to Florence to find the city's spirits riding high. After weeks of careful planning, its forces were at last ready to begin the assault on Pisa.[1] A swift victory was expected. Even before the last preparations were in place, Biagio Buonaccorsi had told Niccolò that the Signoria was already certain that Pisa was within their grasp.[2]

On 1 August, Paolo Vitelli gave the order to storm the walls. Within a matter of hours, his troops had captured one of the towers and had cut off the hands of those defenders who refused to surrender. Two days later, the Florentine artillery smashed through the city walls.[3] Soldiers poured in through the breach and, though they were repulsed, they could see that the Pisans were becoming desperate. On 6 August, after a spirited fight, Vitelli captured the Porta a Mare – commanding both the road to the sea, and an important river crossing – as well as the formidable bastion of Stampace.[4] One of the Pisan commanders, Piero Gambacorta, was so alarmed that he snuck out of the city under cover of darkness, and the procurator of the charterhouse even visited the Florentine commissioners to discuss the possibility of peace.[5]

It seemed to be only a matter of time before Pisa fell. Such was the Signoria's confidence that, when they learned Vitelli had captured the splendid Romanesque church of San Paolo a Ripa d'Arno, they gathered to discuss whether the city should be sacked or not.[6] In the event, the Council of Eighty chose mercy over vengeance, but the priors nevertheless sent for the tabernacle of Our Lady of Impruneta, so that the sacred image could be present for what was expected to be a decisive attack on 24 August 1499.[7] And when the branch of an olive tree caught on the Virgin's mantle as it was carried into Florence, it was widely interpreted as a sign of the city's imminent victory.

But for reasons best known to himself, Vitelli hesitated. Despite howls of protest from the Signoria's representatives, he declined to press home his advantage and decided instead to camp beneath the shattered fortifications of his goal. It was a fateful move. Sporadic cases of malaria had been reported over the previous weeks, and the disease now ripped through his tired and ill-supplied army.[8] As the losses mounted, disorder quickly took hold. On 29 August, Pierantonio Bandini, one of the commissioners in the field, came riding into Florence with the news that the army was in disarray.[9] Almost all of the key positions had been abandoned. Unless money and men-at-arms were sent immediately, the Pisans would surely capture their artillery; were that to happen, Bandini warned, the Signoria would have no choice but to abandon the siege altogether.[10]

Like many of his colleagues in the chancellery, Niccolò was appalled that Vitelli had denied the Florentines the victory he had promised them only weeks before. He seemed not only dishonest, but also incompetent. 'We have granted the captain all . . . he desired,' Niccolò complained, 'yet we behold . . . all our troubles brought to naught through his various shufflings and deceit.'[11] Suspicions of treachery were also being voiced.[12] Some reasoned that the captain must either have been corrupted or have succumbed to pressure from those who did not want Pisa to be retaken while Florence was under a popular regime. Others even suspected that he had conspired with the pope and the Venetians to restore Piero de' Medici, and was somehow acting with that end in mind.[13]

For the moment, the priors were prepared to give Vitelli the benefit of the doubt. There was, after all, no proof that he had been disloyal. Given that he was reportedly suffering from malaria at the time,[14] it seemed more likely that he had simply made an error of judgement. Since there was nothing to be gained from recriminations, they decided to provide him with the resources to rectify his mistakes while there was still time. On the advice of a specially convened *pratica*, they agreed to send him the sum of 10,000 *fl.* and to call up an additional 3,000–4,000 infantrymen from the countryside. Under the watchful gaze of two new commissioners, he was to use these to safeguard the artillery and to resume the offensive as quickly as possible.[15]

But it was too late. Without waiting for the reinforcements to arrive, Vitelli took matters into his own hands and ordered the siege to be lifted on 5 September.[16] His weary and demoralized army retreated to Cascina in humiliation, leaving the Pisans to repair the walls at their leisure. To make matters even worse, several boats carrying Florentine artillery to Livorno capsized a little over a week later.[17] Two large bombards and a *dragonetto* – a small, quick-firing cannon – sank beneath the waves. Writing on the Signoria's behalf, Niccolò urged Vitelli to mount a salvage operation.[18] But, despite the gravity of the situation, he did nothing. To the Florentines' dismay, the Pisans recovered the guns instead.[19]

The Signoria's confidence in Vitelli was shattered. To have botched an attack might have been regarded as a misfortune, but to have abandoned the siege and lost much-needed artillery looked decidedly like treachery. And when King Louis XII passed on some letters that appeared to prove Vitelli had conspired with Ludovico Sforza to prolong the Pisan War, the priors realized the time for action had come.[20] Without further ado, Braccio Martinelli and Antonio Canigiani were despatched to the camp at Cascina, ostensibly to finalize arrangements for the retreat, but really to place Paolo Vitelli and his brother, Vitellozzo, under arrest.

Perhaps annoyed that he had not recognized Vitelli's treachery sooner, Niccolò now did everything he could to help bring the captain to justice. On 27 September, he urged Martinelli and Canigiani to be zealous in pursuit of their duty.[21] They must not waste a single moment in apprehending these 'rebels and enemies', he warned; Florence's safety, not to mention its reputation, depended on it. But they must not be too hasty, either. It was better to exercise prudence and circumspection than to give the game away by acting too precipitately. There was, he reminded them, no room for error.

Martinelli and Canigiani did not fail him. The following day, they invited Vitelli to discuss the conduct of the campaign over dinner.[22] When he arrived, they clapped him in irons and locked him up while they went in search of Vitellozzo, who was claiming to be ill. Vitellozzo had, however, realized what was afoot and escaped before he could be captured. It was a little disappointing, but it seemed to confirm the brothers' guilt. The next morning, Paolo Vitelli was conducted to Florence and tortured mercilessly.

While Vitelli was lying on the rack, the Signoria convened a *pratica* to decide his fate. Opinions were divided.[23] Some believed that, since he had disobeyed the Signoria's orders in lifting the siege and had probably conspired with Piero de' Medici, he deserved to die. Florence's honour would only be recovered if he was executed; besides, his death would serve as an example to the other *condottieri*. But others thought he might be innocent, as he claimed. His actions, though reprehensible, were not proof of any criminal intent, and, however damning the letters acquired by Louis XII might have seemed, their authenticity was not beyond question. As such, it was only reasonable to ask whether those baying for his blood had some ulterior political motive. And, as long as there was room for doubt, it would be wrong – perhaps even dangerous – to condemn him to death.

The people who had gathered in the square outside had little taste for such legal niceties, however. Regardless of whether Vitelli's guilt could be proved or not, they wanted vengeance. 'Hang him, hang him!' they shouted.[24] It was enough to settle the matter. Even though Vitelli stubbornly refused to confess, the priors met with their colleagues and decided that he should die.

On 1 October, he was escorted to a scaffold that had been constructed on the parapet of the Palazzo della Signoria. The piazza below was full of people, many of whom testified to his courage. Though his end had come, he showed no fear of death. Even to the last, he maintained that he had never betrayed the Florentine people.[25] At 7:45 p.m., he was beheaded. As Landucci reported, it 'was expected that his head would be thrown down into the Piazza below.' But, instead, it was 'stuck on a spear and shown at the windows of the parapet, with a lighted torch [beside it] so that it could be seen by everyone.'[26] Before the captain's blood was dry, Niccolò had written to inform the commissioners in the Florentine camp at Cascina of his execution.[27]

The Florentine people were satisfied that justice had been done. But uncertainties still remained. Rumours began to spread that the Signoria had acted improperly, even cravenly. In Lucca, a chancellery secretary speculated that Vitelli had lent Florence money, and that the Signoria had executed him to avoid having to repay the debt, rather than because of any treachery on his part. But Niccolò had no such doubts and, having seen a copy of the secretary's letter, felt bound to respond.[28] It was, of course, untrue that Vitelli had loaned Florence any money, but, even if he had, he would still stand condemned. After all, if he had laid so much cash aside that he could make such subventions, he must either have been accepting bribes from foreign powers or keeping the money he was supposed to be paying his troops for himself. If the former was true, then he was a traitor; if the latter, he was a thief who had weakened his own army. In either case, Niccolò argued, he would have deserved 'endless punishment'.

*

Cathartic though Vitelli's death may have been, however, it did nothing to advance the faltering campaign against Pisa. Now under the command of Jacopo d'Appiano and Rinuccio da Marciano, the army was still reeling from the siege. Many troops were still sick with malaria, morale was low and money was short. In his capacity as the secretary of the *Dieci*, Niccolò spent the first week of October trying desperately to find some way to restore order while reducing costs to an absolute minimum.[29] But it was an uphill struggle. Even if the promised reinforcements arrived from the countryside, it was doubtful whether the army would be in a condition to mount another attack, much less recover the ground that had been lost over the past month. If Florence was to make any headway at all, it would need help.

Lacking options, the Signoria turned to Louis XII of France. A few weeks earlier, he had crossed the Alps, and, after a lightning campaign, had succeeded in driving Ludovico Sforza from Milan. He was, moreover, well disposed towards Florence, even going so far as to describe the Pisans who had made their way into his camp as 'traitors'. Indeed, as Niccolò told the Florentine ambassador in Lucca, the reports from the royal court could hardly have been better.[30] But the king still drove a hard bargain. In return for 15,000 gold *écus*, payable in regular instalments over the next three months, and an undertaking to support any future campaign against Naples, Florence would be permitted to hire 5,000 Swiss mercenaries for use against Pisa, at an exorbitant cost.[31]

But if Niccolò was hoping that this would lead to a change for the better, he was bitterly disappointed. When riots broke out in Milan at the end of October, Louis XII decided to leave the city in the hands of his lieutenant, Giangiacomo Trivulzio, and return to France. In his absence, the situation quickly deteriorated. Without the king to restrain him, Cesare Borgia embarked on a campaign of conquest in the Romagna, with the full support of his father, Alexander VI. By mid-December, he had taken Imola, and, in early January, he captured Forlì from Caterina Sforza, threatening Florence's interests directly. Even more worrying, however, was Ludovico Sforza's determination to recapture his duchy. With the gold that he had smuggled out of Milan, he and his brother, Ascanio, had been raising soldiers in the Holy Roman Empire throughout the winter. By mid-January, they were ready. Marching southwards through the Alpine passes in two columns, they quickly seized Ciavenna, Bellinzona and Domodossola. On 2 February, Como was occupied as well.

This put Florence in a difficult situation. Back in December, it had begun making payments to Louis XII, as agreed. But Ludovico Sforza's return made it impossible for Trivulzio to release the mercenaries Louis had promised; and what was worse, the king's representative, Pierre de Sacierges, was also pressing the Signoria to make further payments, ahead of schedule. Naturally, the priors did not want to anger the king, but nor did they want to waste money on what might prove to be a lost cause, especially if they were not going to receive the troops they needed. As they had done so many times before, they decided to temporize. On 27 January, they wrote to Trivulzio to protest about Sacierges' manner.[32] His repeated demands for money were, they claimed, an insult to the warm affection they bore the king. But, being true friends of the French crown, they wished to resolve the matter amicably. As such, they were going to send Niccolò to negotiate with Trivulzio on their behalf, and promised that he would set off in a few days. If nothing else, they hoped to buy themselves a little time to see how the political situation developed.

As Niccolò's credentials were being prepared, however, news arrived that Milan had fallen.[33] There was now no point in sending Niccolò to Trivulzio's camp. Fearing that they had backed the wrong side, the Signoria hurried to congratulate Sforza instead. Fortunately, the duke's success was short lived.[34] Not a month had gone by before he was struggling to pay his troops. By the end of March, no fewer than 2,000 Swiss soldiers had left his army, and his bold attempt to besiege Trivulzio's stronghold at Novara had begun to falter. This gave Louis XII the opportunity he needed. While Sforza was floundering, he despatched the experienced Louis de La Trémoille to come to Trivulzio's aid with a force of 500 lances. On 8 April, La Trémoille arrived at Novara and immediately gave battle. Ludovico fought bravely, but he was no match for the Frenchman. He was defeated and captured. When Ascanio heard of this, he retreated southwards. Before he had gone far, however, he was surprised by a Venetian patrol and taken captive. He and his brother were sent to France as prisoners and, on 14 April, Milan was retaken. The new governor, Cardinal Georges d'Amboise, punished the citizens' contumacy by imposing fines, rather than by shedding blood, and the situation was soon stable enough for the king to return to the city.

Now that Ludovico was out of the way, the Signoria could patch up its relationship with Louis. Shortly after news of the French victory at Novara arrived in Florence, the priors received word that the king was at last willing to place his soldiers and artillery at their disposal for use against Pisa. As a mark of goodwill, he had also sent messengers to demand the Pisans' immediate capitulation, and to instruct Lucca to hand back the possessions it had recently taken from Florence. In return, the priors set aside their former objections to his requests for payment. They agreed to send the necessary sums in a few weeks, well before the troops were due to arrive, and, ignoring howls of protest from the *popolo*, even voted a special tax to raise the money.[35]

But the limitations of French support soon became apparent. In Lucca, the *popolo* rose up in opposition to Louis' demands. They refused to surrender their newly won territories and were confident that the king was still far too busy with Lombard affairs to force them.[36] Only two weeks later, the Pisans attempted to secure their independence by playing on this weakness.[37] They offered to surrender to Louis, on the condition that he would not hand their city over to the Florentines. This was, of course, impossible. Louis replied that they must surrender unconditionally or not at all. But, though they promised to do so, they did nothing further. It was enough that they had indicated their willingness to submit to French rule, were Louis ever to abandon his obligations to Florence.

When the Swiss mercenaries eventually arrived, things did not improve. Although Louis had offered to appoint Yves d'Alègre as his commander in the field, the Florentines had asked him to choose Charles de Beaumont instead.[38] Having restored Livorno to them in 1496 – as Niccolò fondly recalled some years later[39] – he was held in high regard. But he proved to be even more incompetent than Vitelli. No sooner had the attack on Pisa begun than he had lost control of his troops. Even though Niccolò would later describe the Swiss as the 'masters of modern war', they seemed wholly unwilling to fight.[40] It was said that they went in and out of the city as they chose and were already betraying the Florentine cause. To make matters worse, the Signoria antagonized them further by sending them poor quality supplies and delaying their pay. The Gascons who had accompanied the Swiss soon fell to pillaging the surrounding villages, and the attack ground to a halt.[41]

Having been appointed secretary to the commissioners in the field, Niccolò was entrusted with cajoling the recalcitrant mercenaries into action. At the best of times, it would have been an unenviable task, but, for Niccolò, it would have been almost too much. Already worn down by work and travel, he had recently been struck by tragedy. For some time, the aged Bernardo had been ailing, and, on 10 May, his heart finally gave out. Niccolò, who had always been very close to his father, was undoubtedly deeply upset. As the head of the family, he would most likely have made the arrangements for Bernardo's burial, and would have attended the funeral mass in Santa Croce with a heavy heart. Even though he relied on relatives to tidy up Bernardo's other affairs, it is difficult to believe that his conduct in Pisa was not adversely affected by his grief.

At the very least, Niccolò was unable to prevent the discussions with the Swiss mercenaries from breaking down. On the morning of 8 July, a group of them burst into the quarters of Luca di Antonio degli Albizzi, one of the Florentine commissioners, and demanded to be paid for what they said were their past services. Albizzi, of course, knew nothing about any of this, but offered to provide them with the letters they needed to negotiate directly with the Signoria. But they refused and took him prisoner instead. Unless the Signoria paid them what they were asking within forty-eight hours, they would kill him. As Albizzi reported in a hastily scribbled note, Beaumont was deeply shocked, but could see no way of resolving the matter.[42]

The next day, the situation deteriorated further. That afternoon, one hundred Swiss soldiers from another company came to Albizzi's quarters demanding to be paid as well. But, according to Niccolò, who was present at the time, Albizzi was 'unable to pacify them with words or promises'.[43] Enraged, they then led him out of the camp and walked for about half a mile in the direction of Pisa.[44] There, he was brought before their captain. After a long and angry altercation, during which Albizzi was threatened with halberds, he was given a new and even more extortionate ultimatum. In addition to the demands they had already made, the Swiss now wanted the Signoria to pay the 400 or 500 other mercenaries who were then on their way from Rome. If this were not done, the Swiss would not only kill Albizzi, but they would also take all of the Florentine artillery in lieu of payment.

Left behind at San Michele, just outside the walls of Pisa, Niccolò scarcely knew what to do. He wandered around in the hope of gathering more information, but, flustered by all that had happened, was unable to provide the Florentine government with much detail. His reports were sketchy at best, and added little, if anything, to what Albizzi had told them himself. The *Dieci* were not impressed. Writing to another of their commissioners, Giovanbattista Bartolini, they complained about Niccolò's failure to provide them with a clear picture.[45] They urgently needed answers. Where, for example, was Albizzi? What had happened to the artillery? What had become of the mercenaries who had marched towards Pisa and Livorno? Did any other soldiers go with them?

Of one thing, however, the *Dieci* were sure: they would not be blackmailed by the Swiss. It was better to stand and fight. While they were raising the troops to do so, however, Bartolini was to do his utmost to defend the camp at Cascina, where the bulk of the artillery was stored. But the outlook was grave. Writing on the evening of 9 July, Bartolini reported that he was ill prepared for such a task. Everything was in short supply. 'We have neither armour, nor lances, nor bucklers, nor any ammunition, except for quite a few barrels of gunpowder,' he lamented.[46] If he was to stand a chance against the Swiss, the *Dieci* would have to send him the provisions he required as quickly as possible. A bitter struggle seemed inevitable. And Niccolò, bewildered and frightened, seemed likely to be caught in the middle.

But, quite suddenly, the Swiss backed down. Perhaps realizing that Florence would not easily be intimidated, they released Albizzi and left. Last seen marching in the direction of Lucca, they vanished 'almost defeated and tainted with great shame', as Niccolò put it, never to reappear.[47] Unable to continue fighting, Beaumont had no option but to raise camp and abandon the siege.

7

La Chasse

(July–December 1500)

Niccolò's first years at the chancellery had not been a great success. He had achieved little that was positive beyond pacifying Jacopo d'Appiano and composing the *Discorso sopra le cose di Pisa*. Indeed, he had left a trail of diplomatic failures and political missteps behind him. He had failed to reach an agreement with Caterina Sforza; he had misjudged and then persecuted Paolo Vitelli; and he had frozen with fear during Albizzi's captivity. It is perhaps doubtful whether anyone else would have fared much better, but he had certainly not helped Florence's situation. The Pisan campaign was in ruins, the treasury was empty and a talented commander had been put to death, perhaps without just cause. What was more, Forlì had fallen to Cesare Borgia, leaving Florence even more exposed than before.

But though Niccolò had failed to cover himself in glory, he had a remarkable knack for ingratiating himself with the right people. He was competent at handling routine bureaucratic work, and his diligence was always going to be valued. While far from outstanding, his eloquence was appreciated, as well. Whenever he was away from Florence, Biagio Buonaccorsi would read his letters out loud to prominent figures in the Palazzo della Signoria, and reported the warmth with which they were commended.[1] But the esteem in which Niccolò was held was also a function of his charm. Witty, self-deprecating and engaging, he made and kept friends easily. As Biagio observed, he 'so abounded in charm and drolleries' that his colleagues in the chancellery could not help laughing and smiling whenever he was around;[2] and as his brother, Totto, noted, he was no less popular among members of the various magistracies.[3] He was brilliant at casting himself in a positive light, even managing somehow to win the admiration of Albizzi and to convince the priors to reward him for his 'courage' with a sizeable bonus, rather than censuring him, as he probably deserved.[4]

It was no doubt for this reason that Niccolò was entrusted with a delicate diplomatic mission only days after his return to Florence. As he knew from first-hand experience, the Swiss revolt had precipitated a breakdown of relations with France. Furious that Beaumont had been forced to abandon the siege, the Signoria was refusing either to honour the contract it had made with the rebellious mercenaries or to accept any more help from the French unless it could appoint its own commanders. Louis XII was, of course, every bit as angry that the siege had failed. But, to his mind, Florence had been to blame for what had happened. Since the Swiss had been denied the money and food they had been promised, it was hardly surprising they had mutinied. As such, Louis insisted the Signoria not only keep on paying their wages, but also pay for their return journey. To add insult to injury, he wanted Florence to take on more of his soldiers – again under French command – to continue the war against Pisa, as well.

Together with Francesco della Casa, Niccolò was to argue the Signoria's case at the French court. As their instructions made clear, they were to absolve Florence of any responsibility for the failure of the siege, and explain the 'true' reasons for the mercenaries' rebellious behaviour.[5] Although they were to avoid criticizing Beaumont too stridently, they were to point out that he had been unable to exercise any meaningful authority over the troops under his command from the very beginning. Wilfully disregarding his orders, the Swiss captains had openly conspired with the Pisans. What was more, Niccolò and Francesco were to argue, Lucca, Genoa and Siena had secretly been helping Pisa as well, and had even persuaded the Gascons to defect. It was for this reason – and this reason alone – that the Swiss had become mutinous. This should, the priors believed, be enough to vindicate the Florentines. But, just to make sure Louis recognized they were the victims, rather than the perpetrators, of this dreadful misfortune, Niccolò and Francesco were also to speak of Albizzi's capture and of the other outrages the Signoria had been forced to bear. Indeed, the priors wished them to make it clear that, since the French alliance had been concluded, the Florentines had been treated 'more like enemies than friends'.

*

The journey was difficult. Not only were Niccolò and Francesco obliged to divert to Bologna for discussions with the tyrant, Giovanni II Bentivoglio,[6] but their onward path was also beset with dangers. On the way from Parma to Piacenza, they had to go out of their way to avoid several thousand disgruntled Swiss mercenaries on their way home from the Pisan campaign; and, as the summer heat rose in the marshlands of the Po Valley, the spread of malaria and plague posed a constant risk.[7]

When they arrived in Lyon on the evening of 26 July, things did not get much better.[8] Although they had confidently expected to find Louis in residence, they discovered that he had left for the Pays de France five days earlier.[9] They could not go after him. As Niccolò reported a few days later, the court had stripped the city of every means of transport when it left.[10] There was scarcely a horse to be found, and the few battered nags that had been left were being sold for ludicrously inflated prices. Having been granted only a small allowance for the mission, Niccolò and Francesco couldn't afford such heavy expenses. They had no option but to wait either until prices dropped, or until they received more money from Florence.

While they were stuck in Lyon, they at least had the chance to consult with Lorenzo Lenzi, one of the Signoria's permanent ambassadors at the French court, who had remained behind in the hope that he would soon be allowed to return home. After carefully listening to them explain the object of their mission,[11] Lenzi gave them some good advice about how to conduct themselves when they eventually tracked Louis down.[12] Whatever they did, he urged, they were to avoid laying *any* blame on Beaumont. At most, they could say that the trouble at Pisa had arisen out of the natural gentleness of his character, which prevented him from inspiring the fear that he should. They were, however, to stress that he had always manifested the greatest concern for Florence's good and the king's honour. If pushed, they were even to accept that Beaumont had been appointed at the Signoria's request. According to Lenzi, it would be much better to argue that the 'malignity' of Florence's neighbours was 'the cause of all [the] disorders'.[13] There was, admittedly, a chance that the French would accept Lucca's excuses, and for that reason, they would be wise to emphasize just how badly the Lucchesi had behaved.[14] Given that none of them would be present, Niccolò and Francesco could attack them as viciously as they liked.

Most importantly of all, Lenzi advised them to keep in mind those who exercised the greatest influence over the king, particularly Cardinal Georges d'Amboise, whom Louis had recently appointed as his lieutenant general in Milan. It was through him that Niccolò and Francesco would have to approach the king. A brilliant diplomat of undoubted intellect, he was neither to be underestimated nor challenged directly. They should on no account argue with him about any point on which he had formed a definite opinion; instead, they should simply agree, and trust that the king's goodwill would prevail should an agreement be reached.[15] It was good advice – and Niccolò would have done well to have heeded it.

*

On 30 July, Niccolò and Francesco were at last able to set off. Riding as quickly as their wretched horses would travel, they took what they thought was the most direct route. Although details are scant, it seems probable that they passed through Roanne and Lapalisse, before cutting across the marshy woodlands of the Bourbonnais Sologne to Moulins. As Niccolò reported, they felt sure that they would overtake Louis before long.[16] But, unbeknown to them, the king had chosen a different road. At Roanne, he had turned northwards to follow the Loire through Marcigny, Pierrefitte and Decize.[17] The journey was no shorter, but it was easier. Passing through comfortable villages, rolling pastures and well-tended fields, Louis made rapid progress, and, despite the encumbrance of his train, easily outpaced the Florentine envoys.

By the time Niccolò and Francesco finally ran the king to ground at Nevers, on 6 August, they were physically and financially exhausted. Having been forced to provide themselves not only with horses, but also with accommodation, servants and clothing along the way, they were already running up debts. One third of the expenses they had incurred had not been paid, and they seriously doubted that they would be able to afford to despatch couriers over the coming days.[18] Niccolò was even worse off than Francesco. Although he had to spend the same amount and did every bit as much work, he had been granted a smaller allowance, and had even had to ask his brother to lend him seventy ducats to see him through.[19] When he wrote to the Signoria to ask for further funds, he had no choice but to enclose an additional note requesting that he receive as much as his colleague or else be relieved of his duties.[20]

It was an embarrassing situation to be in. But, when Niccolò and Francesco presented themselves to Cardinal d'Amboise ahead of their first audience with the king, they felt even more humiliated. Rather than being greeted with the courtesy and respect that Niccolò had encountered on his previous missions, they were received with barely concealed contempt. Upon hearing the purpose of their mission, the cardinal curtly remarked that the Signoria's explanations for the failure of the siege were largely unnecessary.[21] To his mind, it was far more important to discuss how to recuperate the losses that Florence and the king had sustained as a result. As he led them through the corridors of the royal residence, he began questioning them about the possibility of resuming the campaign. Niccolò and Francesco were, of course, taken aback. But, before they could make any reply, they found they had arrived at the king's quarters.

Having just finished his meal, Louis was resting; but after a few minutes, he was ready to receive them.[22] They were not, however, granted the lengthy private audience they might have been hoping for. No sooner had they had presented their credentials than they were ushered into an adjoining room, where Louis was joined by the cardinal and the treasurer, Florimond I Robertet d'Alluye, as well as Giangiacomo Trivulzio and three members of the powerful Pallavicino family.[23] Overcoming their nerves, they began presenting the case they had tried to outline to Cardinal d'Amboise a little while earlier. But, though they were allowed rather more time to develop their argument and were careful to follow Lenzi's advice, they had no more success. While the king was prepared to admit that the Swiss had behaved badly, and even promised to have the Gascons arrested as soon as they arrived back in France, he maintained that the Signoria had only itself to blame for the revolt.[24] Regarding the matter as settled, he had no intention of being drawn into a debate. When the envoys then tried to bring up the 'brutal' and 'shameless' treatment of Luca degli Albizzi, as they had been ordered, he cut them short, insisting they discuss the resumption of the war instead.[25] Having already been subjected to a barrage of questions from the cardinal, Niccolò and Francesco should have been ready for this. But they floundered. Protesting that they had not received any instructions on this point, they could only observe that, after the lifting of the siege, the Florentines had lost all their confidence and could not summon the strength to attempt anything similar again.[26] They certainly didn't want to risk wasting even more money on another fruitless venture. If Louis were to mount a campaign against Pisa himself, however, the envoys were sure that the Signoria would 'justly and amply' compensate him once the city had been recovered. A more ludicrous suggestion could hardly have been imagined. Even before they had finished speaking, the king and his ministers were crying out in protest. Under no circumstances would Louis consent to wage war on Florence's behalf and at his expense. As far as he was concerned, the treaty they had signed the previous year was binding.[27] He would uphold his end of the bargain by providing troops for the reconquest of Pisa, come what may, but, if the Signoria failed to fulfil its obligations, he would be within his rights to keep Pisa for himself. If Florence wanted its possessions back, it would have to pay. To this, Giangiacomo Trivulzio added that, if the Signoria let this chance slip through its fingers, it would probably never be able to recover Pisa. Shamefaced, Niccolò and Francesco promised to ask the Signoria for an answer, and – seeing that nothing more could be achieved – took their leave.

There was no denying that their first audience had been a serious disappointment. Unaccustomed to being treated like representatives of a second-rate power, they had allowed themselves to be bullied. Still, at least they now knew what to expect. Once they had received further instructions from the Signoria, Niccolò reasoned, they could meet with the king again and make their case more effectively. Perhaps they would even find an opportunity to bring up the points they had been prevented from making. With this in mind, they had some intercepted letters that apparently 'proved' Lucca had plotted against Florence translated into French.[28]

But before Niccolò and Francesco had finished writing to the Signoria, Louis had decided to leave Nevers and continue his journey northwards.[29] Hurriedly packing their things, they saddled their weary nags and set out with the court along the banks of the Loire. As the summer sun glistened on the gently flowing waters, they passed through richly coloured heaths and low-lying woodlands, occasionally catching the gentle aroma of saffron on the breeze. Yet it was still frustrating to have to traipse along in the rear of Louis' train while he continued his stately *pérégrination* through France.

They could neither communicate effectively with Florence, nor transact any business. And as the summer wore on, their morale must surely have flagged.

*

On the morning of 10 August, Louis and his court arrived at Montargis.[30] A delightful medieval town, graced with a magnificent royal château and criss-crossed by canals and bridges, it was an ideal place to stop for a few days. While the king went hunting in the forests nearby, his ministers were at last able to catch up with the affairs of state. For Niccolò and Francesco, it was a chance to resume discussions. On the morning after their arrival, they were granted a private audience with Cardinal d'Amboise.[31] Finding him in a more relaxed mood than before, they naively supposed that it was an opportune moment to raise the subject of Lucca's alleged conspiracy with the Swiss. Confident of success, they handed him one of the letters they had had translated. But the cardinal had no interest in reading it. Cutting them off before they could protest, he affirmed that the Lucchesi had never acted improperly. If anything, he claimed, they had served Louis better than the Florentines had ever done. That very day, in fact, he had received word from the French ambassador, Jean du Plessis, that the Signoria was not only unwilling to pay the Swiss, but was also refusing to allow French troops to remain in Florentine territory. Niccolò and Francesco vainly tried to object. But the cardinal continued to rail against Florence's temerity, blaming it for the failure of the siege and dismissing any suggestion that Louis should undertake the reconquest of Pisa at his own expense.

A little taken aback, the emissaries then tried a different tack. Even if Amboise could not be persuaded of Lucca's complicity in the mutiny, would he at least persuade the king to force the Lucchesi to return some of the territories they had taken? But this, too, met with a stern refusal. The king had promised the Lucchesi that they would only have to do so *after* Pisa had been recaptured, and he intended to keep his word. Although Niccolò and Francesco pointed out that this may have been why the Lucchesi had been trying to sabotage the siege in the first place, the cardinal was unmoved. If the Florentines wanted Lucca to give their lands back, he declared, they would have to honour their agreement with Louis first. Unless they paid the Swiss, agreed to a new offensive against Pisa, and allowed French troops to be quartered on their territory, they could not expect to receive anything – not even what was rightfully theirs.

The next day, Niccolò and Francesco tried again.[32] That morning, they had received news that arrangements were being made to find billets for Louis' soldiers, and were confident of being able to mollify the cardinal's anger a little. But the audience went even worse than before. When they gave Amboise the letters they had received from the priors, they made the mistake of suggesting that du Plessis may have misrepresented – or at least misinterpreted – the Signoria's goodwill. Nothing could have enraged the cardinal more. Barely troubling to conceal his fury, he reminded them that du Plessis was a wise and honourable man, who was greatly beloved by the king. His judgement was beyond reproach – and to suggest otherwise was a gross insult. Only with great difficulty did Niccolò and Francesco manage to make their apologies heard. But the damage was done. Amboise stubbornly refused to discuss Florence's allegations against Lucca again, and was so ill-tempered that they did not even dare mention the Swiss. As soon as they could, they made their excuses and left.

Niccolò and Francesco had reached a dead end. The cardinal had evidently made up his mind. Until they received further instructions from the Signoria, there was nothing they could do to move the negotiations forward. Disconsolately, they wandered around the town, picking up whatever information they could from other diplomats. The news was not positive. The situation in the Romagna was grave.[33] Having already seized Imola and Forlì, Cesare Borgia was preparing to move against Faenza, and his father, the Pope, was asking for Louis' help. If Cesare succeeded, it seemed likely that he would then turn against Bologna, robbing Florence not only of an important ally, but also of the last remaining route across the Apennines. If this weren't bad enough, it was also rumoured that Paolo Vitelli's brother, Vitellozzo, had entered Cesare's service, and was planning to exact a terrible vengeance 'whenever the Pontiff or any other [power] declare[d] war' against Florence.[34]

Already dented, Niccolò's spirits sank even further. Although Biagio Buonaccorsi assured him that his reports were received with great satisfaction in Florence, he knew perfectly well that, so far, the mission had been a resounding failure.[35] He was not even able to console himself with a hearty meal and a flagon of good local wine, as he was almost out of money, and since there were no Florentine merchants to be found in Montargis, he could not draw any more on account.[36] Totto and Luca degli Albizzi were doing their best to get his allowance increased;[37] but there was no guarantee they would succeed. Biagio would have to wait for the gloves and purses he was asking for.[38] And as for the rapier he wanted as a gift – well, that was almost laughable.

*

The next few weeks were a litany of disappointments. During a stag hunt in the countryside around Montargis, the king had been thrown from his horse and had injured his shoulder badly.[39] In need of medical attention, he decided to transfer the court to Melun, in the Île-de-France.[40] Once again, Niccolò and Francesco packed their bags and followed behind. It was not a long journey. Only a little over sixty kilometres away, it would have taken them no more than a day or two. But it was nevertheless dispiriting to have to traipse across country when fortune seemed to be conspiring against them. The landscape reflected their mood. Though the forest of Fontaine-bleau could be beautiful in the summer, it was full of mystery and danger. Sunlit glades quickly gave way to barren gorges, strewn with strange, unsettling rock formations; the songs of woodpeckers and larks were interrupted by the unexpected hissing of snakes and lizards; and the rich soil tempted the unwary traveller with enticing, but poisonous mushrooms.

When they reached Melun, fate dealt them another blow. Although they had assured Cardinal Amboise that the Signoria was arranging for the French detachment to be quartered on Florentine territory, the treasurer, Florimond Robertet, informed them that the troops were not even in Tuscany, and were refusing to return to Pisa on account of how badly they had been treated.[41] The king was, of course, furious. According to Robertet, he viewed this as yet another example of Florentine perfidy. He was starting to question whether there was any point in continuing negotiations if they could not be trusted. That there were rumours of dissension within the Signoria only weakened his faith further. As Robertet intimated, it was widely believed that there were two factions jostling for power, one of which was more anxious to see the return of Piero de' Medici than the recapture of Pisa. Realizing how damaging these charges could be, Niccolò and Francesco tried to rebut them as best they were able. But, having no reliable information of their own, there was little they could do to convince Robertet that the Signoria was still committed to the French alliance.

In desperation, Niccolò and Francesco rushed off to see the cardinal.[42] They found him outside, and for a moment, they allowed themselves to believe that the informal setting might serve them well. But, having already heard the news, he was even more intransigent than before. 'Until now, I have always done you as much good as I could,' he told them, rather disingenuously, 'but now, since you comport yourselves so badly, I really do not know what more I can do to benefit you.'[43] He had no interest in listening to any more excuses. Before Niccolò and Francesco had the chance to say another word, he jumped on his horse and rode off.

Wandering dolefully back to court, they decided to see how the news had been received by their fellow diplomats. But they were horrified to discover that they had become pariahs. No one wanted to be seen talking to them publicly, for fear of seeming too friendly towards Florence.[44] Even their allies kept their distance. Only after much effort did they succeed in persuading one or two of them to talk privately. What they heard alarmed them even more. The Signoria's apparent failure to find billets for Louis' troops was, it seemed, just the tip of the iceberg. The king had also been informed that the priors 'had sent ambassadors to the Emperor [Maximilian] and to the king of Naples, with offers of money, to stir them up against His Majesty'.[45] The Franco-Florentine alliance seemed on the brink of collapse.

Not knowing what to do next, they turned to Jean du Plessis for advice.[46] Having recently returned from Florence, he was the only person who knew both sides of the story, and they seem to have hoped that he might be able to tell them how to rescue the negotiations. He greeted them as friends, but his counsel was not encouraging. In his opinion, Franco-Florentine relations had now degenerated to the point that compromise would no longer be possible. Either the Signoria must pay Louis the 38,000 francs they owed him for the Swiss mercenaries, or have him as an enemy forever.

Du Plessis was not wrong. When Niccolò and Francesco eventually succeeded in securing an audience with the king, on 8 September, he presented them with the same stark choice.[47] Although he claimed to have an affectionate regard for Florence, he was no longer willing to tolerate the Signoria's duplicitous equivocation. If the priors refused to pay the money, he told them, 'I should not consider them to be my friends, and should avail myself of all the means [at my disposal].'[48] If they discharged the debt honourably, by contrast, they could be assured that all other outstanding questions would be settled in their favour.

It was clear that the Signoria would have to pay up, but Niccolò and Francesco did not have the authority to negotiate an agreement on that basis. They had been empowered to avert precisely such an eventuality and, being mere emissaries, could not deviate from their terms of reference.[49] There was, however, no one at the court who *did* have the right authority. At that moment, Florence lacked a resident ambassador in France. Lorenzo Lenzi, with whom Niccolò and Francesco had conferred in Lyon, had returned home and his former colleague, Francesco Gualterotti, had also been recalled.[50] All that Niccolò and Francesco could do, therefore, was to advise the Signoria of the situation and to ask for new ambassadors to be appointed as soon as possible.

Confident that this would not take long, they settled down to wait, sending regular reports back to Florence. For Niccolò, there was even some good news. On 27 August, Totto had written to tell him that his financial difficulties were over.[51] After fifteen days of pleading, Totto had at last succeeded in persuading the priors to increase Niccolò's allowance. Although some had wanted simply to augment his salary, colleagues had convinced the others that he should not have to spend his own money in the service of the state.

But, after a week, Niccolò and Francesco had still heard nothing about the ambassadors. Unbeknown to them, Florence had been convulsed by political turmoil.[52] Since the execution of Paolo Vitelli, many among the *popolo* had suspected that certain *ottimati* had conspired with the disgraced commander to drag the war out in the hope of provoking a financial crisis that would allow them to assert control over the government and restore the Medici.[53] So potent had these suspicions proved that, for more than a year, the *popolo* had refused to confirm the election of any *ottimati* candidates for the *Dieci*.[54] When factional unrest broke out in the subject city of Pistoia in early August, these lingering tensions threatened to erupt into open conflict.[55] Everyone took sides. While the *popolani* favoured the Cancellieri party, many *ottimati* threw their weight behind the Panciatichi faction. By mid-August, the fighting in Pistoia had become severe.[56] Desperate for military support, the pro-Medicean Panciatichi appealed to Vitellozzo Vitelli and his Orsini allies. Horrified, the *popolani* feared that the *ottimati* might be using the unrest in Pistoia as an excuse to bring in foreign mercenaries and restore the Medici by force. By early September, these fears had reached fever pitch; and as *ottimati* and *popolani* eyed each other warily in the councils of state, all foreign policy decisions were put on hold. For the time being, Louis XII's ultimatum would have to go unanswered. Until the crisis passed, no new ambassadors would be appointed.

*

On 15 September, the king left Melun for Blois.[57] Francesco was, however, unable to go any further. He had fallen ill and was suffering from a bad fever, perhaps indicative of malaria. Rather than continue chasing the court around France, he decided to leave for Paris, hoping to find a doctor who could cure him 'before the malady becomes worse.'[58] Niccolò had no choice but to go on alone.

For six long days, he rode across country. Skirting the edge of the forest of Fontainebleau, he traversed the low-lying fields of the Loiret before at last arriving in Blois. It was a magnificent town. A favourite residence of the royal family, it was dominated by an immense château that was still being enlarged. But Niccolò found little to raise his spirits. There was still no news from Florence; he continued to be shunned by the diplomatic community; and he didn't even have a companion to talk to anymore.

By 25 September, he was beginning to get anxious. The king's ministers were constantly asking him when the new ambassadors were expected to arrive, and he was afraid that, unless he could give them an answer soon, Louis would conclude a treaty prejudicial to Florence's interests. He decided to take matters into his own hands. Upon learning that Cardinal d'Amboise was due to arrive the next day, he rode out to meet him at a village about thirty-eight kilometres from Blois, where he was planning to stay overnight.[59] In doing so, he hoped not only to pay the cardinal a courtesy, but also to find an opportunity to talk to him at length. If he could do so, he might be able to change his mind. It was worth trying, if nothing else.

Niccolò arrived too late in the evening to do anything. But, early the next morning, he accosted the cardinal on the road. With all the eloquence he could muster, he described the sad condition in which Florence found itself and begged Amboise not to withdraw his protection. Thankfully, the cardinal was in a good mood. He listened carefully without interrupting, but was too much of a politician to be swayed by fine words. He did not doubt that Florence had suffered greatly, but, as he had said many times before, it had only itself to blame. The king had upheld his side of the bargain; if the Signoria wanted his help, it would have to do the same. That was all there was to it. Over the next few weeks, Niccolò would hear the same refrain over and over again. The king hoped that the city would remain his friend; but if the Signoria wanted to make an enemy of him, then so be it. Either way, Florence would have to pay what it owed.[60] There was no scope for further discussion.

On 2 October, there was at last a glimmer of hope. Niccolò received word that tensions in Florence were beginning to dissipate. When the *popolani* had learned that the Panciatichi were getting the upper hand, they had agreed to a compromise with the *ottimati* and had allowed a new *Dieci* to be elected on 19 September.[61] This had paved the way for further important decisions. The following week, Niccolò was informed that Luca degli Albizzi had been chosen as the new ambassador to France.[62]

But Niccolò's hopes were quickly dashed. Claiming that he already had too many other responsibilities, Luca degli Albizzi turned his appointment down.[63] Several other candidates also declined the job, perhaps realizing how difficult it would be to negotiate a satisfactory agreement. They could hardly be blamed. Even the Signoria was unsure how to proceed.

Their indecisiveness was perhaps only to be expected. Even though everyone knew they would have to back down in the end, no one wanted to jeopardize the fragile peace by suggesting Florence should accept responsibility for the debt when its finances were already strained to breaking point. Such hesitancy was, however, dangerous. As Niccolò warned, Louis would not wait much longer. Besides, Florence might soon need his help with more than just the recovery of lost territories. At court, Cesare Borgia's army was much talked about.[64] Though no one knew whether he would attack Faenza, Rimini, and Pesaro, or link up with the Colonna on the road to Rome, it was clear that he would soon pose an even greater threat to Florence than before. It was even rumoured that he would try to restore the Medici by force.[65] Only the king would be able to restrain him.

*

Wishing to put Brittany in order before returning to Lyon, Louis set out for Nantes on 14 October.[66] Niccolò followed close behind in a state of high anxiety. He knew that, unless the Signoria made up its mind soon, it would be too late. As he travelled along the Loire's winding course, he must have been hoping that a message would be waiting for him when he reached his destination.

When Niccolò arrived in Nantes, however, he received a letter bearing terrible news. His sister, Primavera, had died, perhaps of the plague. Her son, Giovanni, had also contracted the same illness and was fighting for his life. On 25 October, Niccolò wrote to the Signoria to ask for leave to return.[67] He reminded them that, in the last five months, he had lost both his father and his sister. In his absence, the family's affairs were going to rack and ruin. He would need a month in Florence at least. Afterwards, he would gladly go back to France, or anywhere else the priors cared to send him. Totto did his best to help, even persuading Leonardo Guidotti – a member of the *Dieci* – to argue Niccolò's case for him.[68] But it was to no avail. Sympathetic as they may have been, the priors could not grant his request. Although they had still not decided how to respond to Louis' ultimatum, they could not afford to lose their only diplomatic representative at such a critical moment.

Alone and far from home, Niccolò must have found his loss hard to bear. But, through his grief, he continued to work. Grave rumours were circulating about Cesare Borgia.[69] It was said that, since Louis depended more on the pope than on any other Italian potentate, he was ready to acquiesce in Cesare's conquest of the Romagna. Though this would threaten the Venetians' interests, they would not stand in his way. From their perspective, the Ottomans were still the greater threat; and they were prepared to surrender their influence over the

Romagna in return for French support in the Adriatic. If this were true, Florence's fate would be sealed.

The priors were deeply alarmed. On their instructions, Niccolò hurried to see the king. He explained that the rumours about Cesare's 'evil intentions' had caused them much apprehension, particularly as they had no soldiers with which to defend themselves.[70] He begged Louis to send them whatever help he could spare. But the king merely told Niccolò to take the matter up with Amboise. When he did, however, the cardinal immediately turned the situation to his advantage. Provided Louis could be sure of the Signoria's friendship, Amboise affirmed, he would never allow Cesare to attack the Florentines and would gladly furnish them with the means to protect themselves. It was, however, difficult for the king to trust the priors when they were refusing to pay him what they owed. If only they would settle their debts, their safety would be assured.

This was blackmail, pure and simple. But Niccolò was not easily deterred. After receiving another despatch from the Signoria, he tried again – accosting the cardinal in one of the halls of the royal château.[71] He may have been hoping that Amboise would be less belligerent in a public setting. If anything, however, the cardinal was even more uncompromising. When Niccolò pointed out how easy it would be for Cesare to attack Florence if he was allowed to seize Faenza, Amboise took him by the hand and led him towards the Grand Chancellor, who was standing nearby. In a loud voice, he then went over all the old complaints against Florence and expressed his amazement at the temerity of the Signoria's request for help. Unless the priors agreed to the king's terms, he warned, they would be left to face Cesare's onslaught alone.

The cardinal was, however, careful not to push the Signoria too far. For all his invectives against the Florentines, he knew that Louis had treated them badly of late. They had every reason not to trust him. If they suspected he would betray them, they might be inclined to seek allies elsewhere, and, despite Amboise's bluster, the king did not want to have to fight for his money. The cardinal had to give them a sign of Louis' sincerity. On 3 November, therefore, he sent Robertet to speak with Niccolò in private.[72] As Robertet explained, the cardinal had informed Cesare Borgia and his father that the king had been greatly displeased by the rumours that had recently been circulating, and would not permit any attack on Florentine territory. These were, of course, just words. They did not place Louis under any obligations. But, as Niccolò recognized, they showed that he was in earnest.

*

It was enough to tip the balance. After reading Niccolò's reports, the Signoria decided to swallow its pride. If Florence was to hold off Cesare Borgia – let alone stand any chance of recovering Pisa – it would have to come to terms with Louis. In early November, therefore, the priors appointed Niccolò's old friend Pierfrancesco Tosinghi as their new ambassador, and despatched him to conclude the agreement. But they still wanted to avoid further financial difficulties, if they could. Rather than accepting responsibility for the whole debt, they would offer Louis only 10,000 ducats. In the circumstances, they hoped that he would compromise. It was up to Niccolò to inform him of Tosinghi's appointment and prepare the ground for the negotiations.

Louis had already left Nantes by the time the Signoria reached its decision. Niccolò followed behind. Perhaps wanting to seek out cheaper accommodation, he took a different route. By 18 November, however, he had caught up with the court at Champigny-sur-Marne, and was at last able to pass on the news. He went to see the cardinal first.[73] But, when he relayed the Signoria's offer, he received a stern rebuke. If the priors believed that the debt was negotiable, Amboise told him, they were mistaken. Either they paid the full amount, or they would be severely disappointed when their ambassador arrived. Niccolò was crestfallen. As he admitted in his report, this was not the answer he had expected. Knowing that it would only 'humiliate and discourage' the priors, he did not want to communicate it to them. He was afraid that, 'deprived of all hope of achieving any good', they would give themselves up to despair.[74] He decided to try again, with the king this time. Louis was, after all, more generous of heart than Amboise: perhaps he would show Florence a little mercy. But, to Niccolò's dismay, his reply was the same. No sooner had an agreement been within reach than it seemed to be slipping through the Florentines' fingers.

A day or so later, the court pressed on to Tours. There, the outlook threatened to become even bleaker. Niccolò learned that the pope's ambassador was doing all he could to prevent the king from being reconciled with Florence.[75] He was trying to convince Louis that Florence was on the verge of forming a league against France with the Bolognese, the duke of Ferrara and the marquis of Mantua. What was more, he claimed the Florentines were coordinating their efforts with the emperor, whom they had asked to attack Lombardy. With consummate cunning, the ambassador advised the king to avert this danger by severing relations with the Signoria and restoring Piero de' Medici.

Alarmed, Niccolò went to speak with Amboise. He complained of the malignity of Florence's enemies and assured the cardinal that the Signoria had no intention either of forming a league with the Bolognese or of seeking help from Germany. He does not seem to have been expecting Amboise to believe him. Even in his report, he sounds rather desperate.[76] But he was pleasantly surprised. After listening patiently to all that Niccolò had to say, the cardinal reassured him 'that the king was extremely prudent.'[77] Louis knew perfectly well that the papal ambassador was making things up; not for one second did he believe that the Florentines were conspiring with the emperor. He was, in fact, concerned for their safety. As Robertet had intimated a few days before, the Borgias had been warned that Louis would not tolerate any attack on Florentine territory.[78] This was excellent news. Despite the upsets of recent days, everything was as it had been before. Although there could be no discussion about the money the king was owed, he was evidently keen to secure an agreement, and there was no doubt that he would keep his word.

On 24 November, Niccolò had another audience with the king.[79] He was happy to inform Louis that, in light of his recent reports, the Signoria had thought better of its parsimony. It was now offering to pay him 10,000 ducats immediately, if he agreed to return Pietrasanta, and it would be willing to discuss the repayment of the remainder of the debt at a later date. It did, however, require urgent help against Cesare Borgia. He had already taken the Val di Lamona and was about to seize Faenza, too. To this, Louis replied that the priors need have no fear of Cesare. He had already told his lieutenants in Italy that, 'if Valentino should attempt anything against the Florentines or the Bolognese, they should immediately march against [him].'[80] But the money was still a sore point. Once again, he went

over all his old complaints against the Florentines and demanded
that they reimburse him for his losses. Having recently heard from
Tosinghi,[81] Niccolò assured the king that the ambassador was
expected to arrive at court in a few days' time and would be glad to
discuss such matters then. Rather ominously, the king then muttered,
'perhaps he will be too late.'[82] But any fears that Niccolò may have
had were soon dispelled. After leaving the king's chamber, he went
to see Robertet, who advised him not to read too much into the
king's remark. Cesare Borgia's campaign in the Romagna had recently
become 'offensive to this King', the treasurer observed.[83] There was
no chance of him changing his mind and turning against Florence.
The Signoria could rest easy on that account. Louis was just impatient to have the money, that was all. Niccolò was so relieved that
he asked the priors to give Robertet a suitable gift as a token of
their gratitude.[84]

One week later, Tosinghi arrived in Tours. It was now up to him
to guide the negotiations to a successful conclusion. After almost
five months of chasing around France, Niccolò could at last hand
over responsibility. Although he could take comfort from the fact
that an agreement now seemed likely, it had nonetheless been a
draining and disappointing mission, replete with failure and humiliation. As soon as he received the *Dieci*'s permission to leave, on 12
December, he made for Florence as fast as he could travel.[85]

PART III

The Man

(1501–3)

8

The Gathering Storm

(January–October 1501)

On 14 January 1501, Niccolò arrived in Florence. After months of traipsing along dusty roads, he was undoubtedly glad to be home, to put the French court behind him and to pick up the threads of the life he had left behind. His family's affairs were, however, in disarray. Although he had asked one of his relatives to help put Bernardo's estate in order, there were still some matters that demanded his attention. Rents had to be collected, farms had to be inspected, and the *albergaccio* at Sant'Andrea in Percussina probably needed checking, too. There was the aftermath of Primavera's death to deal with, as well. While her concerns had been handled by her husband and Totto, Niccolò had not yet had the chance to mourn properly.

But Niccolò also needed to let his hair down a little. Having been deprived of company for most of his time in France, he would have been looking forward to having some fun with his friends. While he had been away, they had regaled him with tales of their high-spirited romps around Florence. As Andrea di Romolo had told him on 23 August, there had often been parties at Biagio Buonaccorsi's house.[1] At these gatherings, the wine had flowed freely and, more than once, they had ended up in one of the city's many brothels. According to Andrea, there was one particular lady, down by the oratory of Santa Maria delle Grazie, who still had a soft spot for Niccolò and was awaiting his return 'with open figs'.[2] Niccolò – who had jokingly been nicknamed '*il macchia*' ('the spot') – is unlikely to have needed any further encouragement. Together with his chancellery colleagues, he would have cruised the city's taverns, drinking, gambling and fighting until late, before rounding off the evening in his admirer's welcoming bed.

Yet, for all his carousing around Florence, Niccolò must have known that he had reached a turning point in his career. The past three years had been filled with frenetic activity – and he had often found himself struggling. Though he had enjoyed some modest successes, they were far outweighed by his many failures. But it was only now that he had the experience of meeting and being bested by some of the toughest players on the international stage that he could understand what was required of a public servant in such troubled times. Older, wiser, and perhaps a little calmer, 'the spot' was at last ready to become a man of substance.

It was about time. Professionally, he had a lot to make up for. The Palazzo della Signoria was rife with backbiting and chicanery, and, though Niccolò had friends in high places, he was concerned that his uninspiring performance in France might have weakened his position as second chancellor. While he had been away, he had learned that some had begun to question his suitability for such a responsible role. According to Agostino Vespucci, 'a certain very noble citizen' who held him in high esteem had warned that, unless he returned to Florence immediately, he would be in danger of losing his job.[3] At the time, he had, of course, been unable to do anything; but now that he was back, he needed to prove his worth.

*

Within days of his return, he had his chance. After several months of peace, factional violence erupted in Pistoia once again. At first, the Cancellieri had the upper hand and succeeded in expelling a number of Panciatichi from the city. But the exiles soon found new ways of causing trouble. Roaming the hills and valleys to the south-east, one band turned to brigandage, and, by the end of January, were only twenty kilometres from Florence.[4] Another group threw in their lot with Vitellozzo Vitelli and went to help the Pisans fight the Florentines.[5]

The Signoria was alarmed. Such disturbances not only endangered the towns and villages of the Florentine *contado*, but also threatened Florence's control over Pistoia. After all, the exiled Panciatichi had realized that, as long as the Cancellieri remained in control of the city, they would never be able to return home. Unless they wanted to remain brigands forever, therefore, they would have to take Pistoia for themselves – ejecting both the Cancellieri and the Florentines at the same time. That they had already begun forging alliances with Florence's enemies suggested that it would not be long before they struck.

It was imperative to reconcile the rival factions before it was too late. As Niccolò later argued, there were three ways of doing this:[6] the Signoria could kill the leading members of each party; it could remove them from the city; or it could compel them to make peace, imposing penalties on any that took up arms in future. Previously, the Signoria had favoured the latter. With the benefit of hindsight, Niccolò believed this had been a mistake. It was, he argued, the 'most harmful, [the] least certain, and' – as the current disturbances demonstrated – the 'most ineffective', as well. But, now, the Signoria was unwilling to try even this. It had neither the soldiers to constrain the Pistoiesi by force, nor the political will to raise the necessary troops. As Guicciardini later observed, the *gonfaloniere di giustizia*, Piero di Simone Carnesecchi, was a 'good-natured man, but with little experience and poor judgement in the affairs of state.'[7] Carnesecchi could see that the people were 'in a strange mood', and was reluctant to provoke their ire by asking for new taxes to pay for a campaign against a subject town. Since the priors shared his timidity, they were forced to accept that, for the moment, there was nothing they could do to remedy the factional unrest. Until circumstances changed, they would just have to try their best to prevent the Panciatichi bands from doing too much damage in the *contado*, and pray that Pistoia would not slip from their grasp in the meantime.

On 2 February, Niccolò was sent to oversee matters in Carmignano.[8] As the Signoria's commissioner, he had been given the authority to do whatever he thought necessary to avert the danger. But when he arrived, he found that there was precious little he could do. Lacking both money and men-at-arms, he could neither mount punitive attacks, nor improve the defences in any meaningful way. Perhaps all that he *could* do was to inspect the fortress and liaise with its commander. After only a few days, he left. If his later reflections are any guide, he was disappointed at his lack of progress and frustrated with the Signoria's inactivity. Although it has been suggested that he may have travelled on to Pistoia, the evidence is slight: it seems more probable that he returned to Florence, dejected and dispirited.[9]

Unchecked, the violence in Pistoia grew worse. On 5 March, it was reported that a group of Cancellieri had secretly followed, attacked and killed three Panciatichi as they left the city for Florence.[10] On 10 March, news reached Florence that the Cancellieri and the Panciatichi were burning each other's houses down in the countryside around Pistoia. Two days later, it was said there had been a pitched battle in which many Cancellieri had been slain.[11] On 2 April, there was yet another skirmish, in which sixty-four men were killed.[12]

By Easter, it was getting too much even for the Pistoiesi.[13] Overcoming factional loyalties, a delegation of ten leading citizens travelled to Florence to explain the situation to the Signoria on 15 April. At last, the priors were stirred out of their torpor. Since there now seemed to be a reasonable chance of reconciling the warring parties, they were prepared to commit the necessary resources. The new *gonfaloniere di giustizia*, Piero Soderini, was a stronger character than his predecessor, and began marshalling support for military action from both sides of Florence's political divide.[14] Over the next few days, the Signoria despatched a group of commissioners, including Niccolò's kinsman, Niccolò di Alessandro Machiavelli, to restore order in Pistoia by force, and provided them with a contingent of men-at-arms and six pieces of artillery with which to do so.[15]

The commissioners tried their best. They took control of each party's strongholds, manned the fortress and placed guards on all the gates.[16] They also demanded the surrender of all artillery pieces, both large and small.[17] It was, however, to no avail. As Niccolò had warned, factional rivalries ran too deep simply to be forgotten. Violent confrontations continued to occur on a daily basis, and the exiled Panciatichi were still roaming the countryside nearby. On 27 April, Landucci dolefully reported that matters in Pistoia were just as they had been before.[18]

*

The Signoria soon regretted not having taken more decisive action. While it had been fumbling away, Cesare Borgia had captured Faenza. After this success, it was expected he would turn his attention to Bologna. But Giovanni Bentivoglio, the city's *signore*, managed to avert the danger by agreeing to cede Castel Bolognese and provide Cesare with troops.[19] Free to pursue his wider ambitions, Cesare then turned his attention to Florence. Back in March, he had despatched one of his commanders to Pisa; and at the beginning of April, he had concluded a pact with Pandolfo Petrucci, the *signore* of Siena. Now, he could finally strike. Without giving any warning, he began making his way across the Apennines. On 2 May, he was already encamped at Firenzuola. Terrified of what Cesare might have in store for them, the inhabitants panicked and fled to nearby Florence. The priors immediately saw how foolish they had been not to have settled Pistoia's affairs sooner. As Niccolò told the commissioners on 4 May, there was a risk that the exiled Panciatichi would join forces with Cesare and launch an immediate attack on the city.[20] If Pistoia was taken, Cesare would have Florence surrounded. A siege seemed imminent.

The Signoria hurried to stave off the danger as best they were able. Although rumours that Louis XII had dismissed their ambassador had been circulating, the priors remembered how displeased he had been by the growth of Cesare's power the previous year, and still regarded him as their best hope.[21] Despite their financial difficulties, they sent the king 20,000 *fl.* in part-payment of their debt, and as a sign of their continuing loyalty.[22] Such a dramatic gesture was, they felt, sure to persuade him to heed their plight. Now that Cesare was already within striking distance of Florence, there was, admittedly, relatively little Louis could do, but the priors were still praying that, even at this late stage, he might somehow be able to hold the duke back.

Despite the Signoria's worst fears, Cesare had no intention of capturing Florence just yet. He was, he claimed, merely on his way to Piombino. As they must surely have known, his father was then besieging the town to punish Jacopo d'Appiano for his 'disobedience', and had asked him for help – hence his haste. He had not meant to startle the priors, but he hoped that, in the circumstances, they would understand. If they would be so kind as to grant him safe conduct through Florentine territory, he would be on his way.[23] The priors were somewhat reassured by this. His explanation was, after all, plausible enough: if he really was on his way to Piombino, he definitely would not want to become embroiled in a lengthy struggle with Florence. In the hope of hastening his departure, they quickly agreed to his request. But they remained suspicious of him. He was too ambitious – and too cunning – to be trusted entirely. On 7 May, Niccolò told the commissioners in Pistoia that, while Cesare claimed to want Florence's friendship, it was as well to be prepared for anything.[24]

The Signoria was right to be wary. Even if Cesare may not have had the time to besiege Florence, he was more than willing to blackmail it. When its emissaries arrived at his new camp at Barberino di Mugello, he asked to be appointed as the city's captain-general, and to be paid 36,000 *fl.* for his services. What was more, he also demanded a reduction in the Great Council's powers, and either the restoration of the Medici or the establishment of an oligarchic government.[25] The emissaries were aghast. By any standards, this was absurd. But, with 10,000 troops encamped only a stone's throw from the city, Cesare felt that he was in a strong position to dictate terms.[26]

When the duke's demands became known in Florence, there was outcry. According to Guicciardini, the *popolo* came to the conclusion that Cesare must have been invited into Tuscany by leading *ottimati* who hoped to topple the government with his help.[27] Even Piero Soderini was suspected. This was almost certainly unfounded. Although Soderini and a group of close allies had indeed called for the Great Council to be reformed some months before, they had never conspired with the Borgias. But the rumours were potent and it was feared that riots might break out any day.

As disorder took hold, Cesare pressed his advantage. His troops were set loose to wreak havoc. In Barberino di Mugello, they did 'all sorts of damage, burning and robbing, and cutting the [recently planted] grain.'[28] Advancing to Calenzano and then to Campi – the latter barely ten kilometres outside Florence – they did the same.[29] Convinced that they were in great peril, people from the surrounding countryside fled, doing their utmost to get inside the city walls before it was too late. In Florence, shopkeepers closed their businesses, carried their stock back to their homes and barricaded themselves in. On 12 May, the Signoria, fearing a raid on the city, ordered that a light be kept burning in the window of every house all night; and the following day, it was announced that, should the guns fire twice and the bells toll six times, twice over, all able-bodied men should rally to the standards.

On 13 May, three emissaries were sent to Cesare to protest at his conduct, and, if possible, to negotiate better terms.[30] Granted an audience, they managed to persuade him to abandon his demands for constitutional change. But he continued to insist on being appointed Florence's captain-general, with the pay he had stipulated. He also wanted an assurance that the Signoria would do nothing to help Piombino. This was progress. But, when the emissaries returned to Florence, they were greeted with outrage. Together with the peasants who had fled from Cesare's soldiers, the *popolo* wanted to go out and attack him immediately. It was, they argued, 'abominable to let him ruin our countryside so iniquitously'.[31] As Florentines, they should feel ashamed to compromise 'with one who is not worth a threepenny bit.' The Signoria, however, did not feel that it had much choice. As a sign of goodwill, it immediately promised not to hinder his attack on Piombino, and even offered to provide him with 300 men-at-arms.[32] Two days later, it agreed to hire him as its *capitano* at a rate of 36,000 *fl.* per year and to give him 9,000 *fl.* at once.[33]

It was a crushing humiliation. The Signoria was unsure how it would ever pay such an enormous sum. And, though Cesare began heading westwards, he did nothing to restrain his troops. Encamped at Signa, they raided along the banks of the Arno, as far as Montelupo, 'robbing and committing every sort of wickedness.' Some country folk they beat about the head, others they strung up by the testicles, to make them say where their valuables were hidden.[34] The next day, they sacked Carmignano. When they found all the girls from the area hiding in a church, they broke the doors down and carried them off, raping and killing as they went.[35] There was nothing the Signoria could do to stop them. Fearful of provoking Cesare's ire, it maintained a shameful silence.

*

But just when things seemed darkest, a shaft of light broke through the clouds. On 18 May, Niccolò wrote to the commissioners in Pistoia with the happy news that letters had at last been received from Florence's ambassador in France.[36] Alarmed by news of their plight, Louis XII had written to Cesare Borgia warning him not to harm the Florentines or to exact any kind of payment from them. He was, indeed, to leave Florentine territory immediately. If he did not, Louis' forces in Milan would compel him to do so.

Encouraged by Louis' show of support, the priors regretted agreeing to Cesare's terms so readily. While they were not in a position to spurn him openly – he was, after all, still in Florentine territory – they could delay paying him the money they had promised.[37] Sooner or later, he would have to press on to Piombino.

Cesare was not willing to be put off, however. Whatever the Florentines might have thought, he was not unduly troubled by

Louis' letter. He did not believe the king really would take action against him, but, if it turned out that orders had, in fact, been given to the French forces in Milan, he was confident that he could still strong-arm the Florentines into paying him before they reached Tuscany. Seeing that he still had a little time before he had to be in Piombino, he decided to increase the pressure. As he marched his forces to Empoli, he gave his soldiers free rein to pillage at will. According to Landucci, they behaved not like Christians, but 'like the Turks, putting the whole countryside to fire and flame, and carrying off the girls and women.'[38] There were rumours that, at any moment, Cesare might turn back and attack Florence, so that Vitellozzo Vitelli – who had been sent to Pisa[39] – could exact revenge for his brother's death. Within the city walls, the streets grew ever more crowded with 'unfortunate peasants', and householders, fearful of an imminent assault, began stockpiling bread.[40]

Nevertheless, the Signoria held its ground. By 24 May, Cesare had begun to grow agitated. It had dawned on him that he was unlikely to receive the full amount. While keeping up the pressure, he decided to lower his demands. Now encamped at Castelfiorentino, around thirty kilometres south-west of Florence, he announced that he would settle for 8,000 *fl*. If the priors handed the money over promptly, he would leave Florentine territory without causing them any further inconvenience.[41]

But it was too late. To the Florentines' delight, Louis XII proved better than his word. Since returning to France the previous year, he had been making preparations for a campaign against Naples. Realizing that he could not seize the kingdom without arousing the enmity of Spain, which also had a claim, he had agreed to divide it with King Ferdinand the Catholic. According to the terms of the Treaty of Granada (11 November 1500), Louis would take the crown, along with the city of Naples, the Terra di Lavoro and the Abruzzi, while Ferdinand would hold Calabria and Apulia from the papacy as duke.[42]

Having thus secured himself, Louis was now ready to launch his attack. On 26 May, word reached Florence that the king had already despatched some 30,000 troops against Naples.[43] Given that these forces would have to pass through Tuscany, they would be able to put Cesare Borgia in his place on their way.

Advancing rapidly across the Apennines, the French commander, Bernard Stewart d'Aubigny, reached Dicomano, around twenty-five kilometres north-east of Florence, on 6 June.[44] After being joined by a large cavalry contingent, he then marched towards Siena.[45] It was enough to scare Cesare off. Having already thought better of blackmailing Florence, he hastily withdrew.

After a brief pause, he pressed on to Piombino,[46] but, even then, he was not allowed to rest easy. As the French took possession of Siena, he learned that he had been appointed as one of Louis XII's lieutenants and was expected to accompany the French army to Naples. Uncertain of what the king might have in store for him, he tried to delay as long as he could.[47] But he could not put it off forever and had to follow the French forces to Rome, without having received a single penny from Florence.[48] The Signoria at last breathed a sigh of relief.

*

Freed from Cesare's malign influence, Florence could turn its attention to Pistoia once again. Despite the commissioners' best efforts, the city's factional divisions remained as bitter as ever.[49] The Cancellieri were still doggedly clinging on to the organs of communal government, and bands of exiled Panciatichi continued to roam the countryside, spoiling for a fight. On 4 July, hostilities broke out again.[50] A pitched battle took place, in which as many as 200 men, mostly foreign mercenaries, were killed.[51] The following day, there was another skirmish. Although fewer lives were lost, the exchange was no less gruesome. According to Landucci, the heads of a dozen men were stuck on lances and paraded around Pistoia. They were then taken down and used as footballs.

Over the past few weeks, Niccolò had been in constant contact with the commissioners. Keeping himself fully appraised of events, he had written almost every day with fresh instructions from the priors and the *Dieci*. But now it was felt that a more direct approach was needed. On 23 July, the Signoria decided to send him to Pistoia to see things for himself, and to express its displeasure at the Panciatichi's attempts to batter their way into the city.[52] Little is known about this mission. Beyond his letter of credence* and a few instructions from the Signoria about incidental matters, nothing has survived in the way of documentation. It is, however, likely that the

* A formal document appointing Niccolò as the representative of the Florentine Republic.

journey came as something of a shock. Although the country folk from Sesto, Campi and Carmignano had now returned home, their fields had either been stripped of their crops or reduced to ashes. Burned-out houses would have been visible along the roadside and, had Niccolò paused to talk to anyone, he would doubtless have heard tales of property stolen and of honour lost. It is also probable that, once he reached Pistoia, he was surprised by the disorder gripping the city. In the few days he was there, he was certainly unable to do anything to calm tempers or to bring the factions to heel. No sooner had he left than another violent confrontation occurred.[53] Once again, the Panciatichi came off worst. As Landucci reported, seven of their party were hanged from the windows of public buildings. It was even said that the Cancellieri had forced a priest to hang them. Still, Niccolò's mission had been a success in one respect: it was now evident that, if Pistoia was ever to be pacified, the priors would need a clearer strategy. They could not expect to achieve anything by talking anymore – even if they used soldiers to make themselves heard.

*

When Niccolò arrived back in Florence, he found the Palazzo della Signoria abuzz with activity. In the wake of his mission to Pistoia, the priors were feverishly debating what to do. At the same time, sweeping political changes were also under discussion. Now that Cesare was out of the way, certain members of the Signoria believed the time was right to revisit Soderini's proposals for a reformed Great Council. Although this was still a controversial idea, especially among the *popolo*, it was widely felt that the council was too large to be efficient. After much wrangling, a plan for its membership to be reduced to 600 was eventually approved.[54] If this was not already enough, news had also arrived that the French had captured Naples.[55] This was, of course, greeted with tremendous joy. Fireworks were let off and cheering crowds filled the streets.[56] Yet it also provoked a flurry of diplomatic activity. The French were demanding that Florence stump up more money to help pay for the campaign, and new ambassadors had to be appointed to negotiate.[57]

Niccolò's mind was, however, elsewhere. The house on the Via Romana was no longer the happy, bustling place it had once been. Now that Totto – then pursuing a career in business – was the only other inhabitant, it must have seemed very cold and lonely. After the turbulence of recent months, this sense of emptiness began to take its toll. Niccolò decided that a change was needed. As the head of the family, it was his duty to take a wife – and, at thirty-two, he was fast approaching the age at which men were usually expected to marry.[58]

At some point in August, Niccolò married Marietta Corsini.[59] Nothing has survived to shed light on their courtship, but given Marietta's age (she was twenty years old), it is most likely to have been an arranged match.[60] Over the summer, Niccolò would have hammered out the details with her family. There would have been a good deal of haggling – but eventually, they had reached an agreement. In the presence of a notary, they would have signed a marriage contract and exchanged handshakes or kisses.[61] A short while later, there would have been a celebration in her home. Rings would have been exchanged, and Niccolò would have offered a few gifts to his future in-laws, before sitting down to a festive meal. Finally, Marietta – clothed in all her wedding finery – would have been ceremonially escorted to her new home in the Via Romana. There, Niccolò would have thrown another party for the two families and their guests, probably lasting through the night and into the next day.

It was probably not a huge celebration. Niccolò was still short of money and, given the damage recently inflicted on the *contado*, prices were high. But he would still have wanted to push the boat out a little. He was making an advantageous match, after all, and he needed to show that he was worthy of his new bride. Although Marietta's family *palazzo* was not far from his own *casa*, the Corsini were worlds apart from the Machiavelli in social terms. Having made a fortune trading in wool and silk, they had manoeuvred themselves to the heart of Florentine political life during the course of the fourteenth century. They had provided no fewer than forty-seven *gonfalonieri di giustizia* and at least twelve priors. Many of their number had also pursued successful ecclesiastical careers. Pietro Corsini (d. 1403) – whose funerary monument can still be seen in the *Duomo* – had served as bishop of Florence for seven years; and Amerigo (d. 1434) had been its first archbishop. Their star had waned a little under the Medici, but now they had resumed their place at the heart of the Florentine polity. Indeed, it cannot have escaped Niccolò's attention that Marietta's step-father, Piero del Nero, was a prominent member of the *Dieci*, and thus technically his superior.

After the festivities, the young couple settled down to their new life together. Being young and inexperienced, it would probably have taken Marietta a little while to adjust to the exacting social expectations which weighed upon her. As Francesco Barbaro explained in *De re uxoria* (1415), a wife was expected to love her husband, comport herself with modesty and take complete care of domestic matters.[62] Of these duties, perhaps the most demanding was the third. Notwithstanding her age, a well-born woman like Marietta would have been required to manage her servants appropriately, appoint 'sober stewards for the provisions', arrange for food and accommodation for the household staff and order the household accounts.[63] Modesty was a rather more complex obligation. Although Barbaro believed that a wife should wear clothes that would reflect her husband's social standing, he was insistent that she should also be careful to safeguard her honour and reputation.[64] She should not inspire jealousy with the richness of her dress, nor incite lust by revealing too much of her flesh. The same standard of modesty, Barbaro claimed, applied to 'behaviour, speech . . . eating' and even 'lovemaking'.[65] Even in the act of procreation, she was required to protect her virtue. Ideally, she should remain covered – to the point of being fully dressed – while having sex.

Love was a similarly stringent duty. In almost all senses, it was equivalent to subservience. As Barbaro argued, a woman should 'love her husband with such great delight, faithfulness, and affection that he can desire nothing more in diligence, love, and goodwill. Let her be so close to him that nothing seems good or pleasant to her without her husband.'[66] This meant no complaining, under any circumstances. Wives must, Barbaro believed, 'take great care that they do not entertain suspicion, jealousy, or anger on account of what they hear.'[67] If her husband was drunk, or committed adultery, or wasted the household income on gambling, she just had to smile and carry on. Should the man find something to complain about, however, the situation was quite different. Beatings and domestic violence were accepted and even encouraged. As the fourteenth-century poet, Franco Sacchetti, put it, 'good women and bad need to be beaten.'[68]

There is some evidence to suggest that Niccolò sympathized with these views. Certainly, he saw no contradiction between being married and having affairs or visiting prostitutes. Nor did he see anything wrong with getting roaring drunk with his friends, or gambling

wildly when the fancy took him. But, despite this, works like Barbaro's
De re uxoria were more of a construct than a reality. Although we
have few glimpses of their early life together, it is evident that theirs
was a partnership of equals. Niccolò genuinely loved Marietta. As
the many letters they wrote to each other over the years testify, he
always treated her with great tenderness and affection. He adored
her learning, her clever conversation and her wry sense of humour.
He also admired her strength of character. She was certainly able to
hold her own against him. Whenever he stepped out of line, she
was not afraid to let her displeasure be known. She also enjoyed
considerable autonomy. Like many of her contemporaries, she was
able and willing to take control of the family's interests when needed.[69]
Especially when Niccolò was abroad, she looked after the farms in
the countryside, collecting rents, arranging for repairs and managing
debts, always with great aptitude.

*

Niccolò was not able to enjoy married life for long. Only a few days
after his wedding, he was called away to deal with the affairs of
state. His first task concerned Siena. Now that Cesare Borgia had
left Tuscany, the pact he had made with Pandolfo Petrucci earlier
that year no longer seemed as threatening as it once had. But, since
the bulk of Cesare's army was still besieging Piombino, there was a
chance that Pandolfo might be planning some sort of assault. The
Signoria needed to be sure of his intentions. On 18 August, Niccolò
was despatched to Siena, most likely for this purpose.[70] Although
few documents have survived to cast light on this mission, he cannot
have been away for more than four days. During this time, he
accomplished little of note. It does, however, seem that he was able
to reassure the priors that Pandolfo had no designs on Florentine
territory – at least for the moment.

Once the Sienese question had been settled, Niccolò was required
to devote his full attention once again to Pistoia, where the Cancellieri
and the Panciatichi had grown tired of fighting and were holding
secret meetings to discuss peace terms.[71] This was, of course, what
Niccolò and his colleagues had been working towards for so long.[72]
But the fact that the two factions had consulted neither the Signoria
nor the commissioners before opening negotiations worried them.

They were afraid that, if Florence was cut out of the agreement, its hold over Pistoia would be greatly weakened. Instinctively, the priors despatched two new commissioners to take the place of the *capitano del popolo* and the *podestà*.[73] But this was just a temporary measure. They knew they would have to intervene more decisively soon.

Before they did so, action was first taken to streamline Florence's foreign policy. In the past, there had seldom been much scope for tension between the *Dieci* and the priors. Since the *Dieci* were only called into existence to deal with short-term military situations, they generally did not trespass on the priors' responsibilities for long, if at all. But, given that Florence had now been at war for almost seven years, the situation had become rather confused. The *Dieci*, traditionally dominated by *ottimati*, had accustomed themselves to interfering in foreign affairs rather too regularly, leading to a lack of clarity in diplomatic negotiations and considerable resentment among the *popolani*, who tended to be better represented in the Signoria. Perhaps in retaliation for the reform of the Great Council, the *popolani* decided to simplify matters – and, in doing so, to curtail the influence of the *ottimati*. The *Dieci* would be allowed to lapse, and the Signoria would assume responsibility for both foreign and military affairs.[74] Such a drastic move is likely to have alarmed Niccolò at first. Stripped of his role as secretary of the *Dieci*, he might have feared that his position was being undermined. But it soon became clear that, whatever political changes were taking place, he was well enough respected to be secure. Although he had lost his title, his duties remained virtually unchanged. In addition to dealing with subject towns, he would continue to have some responsibility for military matters and foreign affairs – especially where they concerned the Pistoiesi.

With the new constitutional arrangements in place, the Signoria felt ready to take control of the peace talks in Pistoia. These were, admittedly, already further advanced than the priors would have liked. While they had been dealing with the *Dieci*, the fighting had died down. The two factions had then agreed to appoint a new Signoria of their own, with four priors from each.[75] The commissioners had been unable to do anything to stop them: one was reportedly sick, and the other felt he did not have sufficient troops to impose his will, and retreated to the citadel. On hearing this, the Florentine Signoria was initially at a loss to know how best to respond. The priors did not, of course, want to react too harshly. If they tried to impose their will by force, there was a risk that *both* factions would turn against them. But, if they did nothing, it might seem that they were allowing Pistoia to slip from their grasp. For the moment, all they could do was to gather more information; and in early October, Niccolò was despatched for precisely this purpose.[76] What he advised the priors on his return is not known, but whatever insights he may have gleaned evidently did little to alter their views. They would just have to await further developments.

Fortunately, the peace was still fragile.[77] Old rivalries had not yet been forgotten, and, soon enough, violence began to flare up once again. Fearing that public order might collapse, the priors of Pistoia appealed to the Florentines for help.[78] This gave the Signoria the opportunity they had been waiting for. On 18 October, it named Niccolò Valori as its new commissioner general, and appointed Niccolò Machiavelli to assist him.[79] Accompanied by a sizeable body of troops, they were to travel to Pistoia as quickly as possible. There, they were to do everything possible not only to shore up the agreement, but also to ensure that Pistoia's dependence upon Florence would be put beyond doubt.

Over the coming days, they worked feverishly to reconcile the two factions. As Niccolò later recalled, they imposed harsh penalties for public disturbances and obtained guarantees of good behaviour from leading families on both sides.[80] It cannot have been an easy task. But their efforts were not in vain. On 20 October, peace was restored. The exiled Panciatichi were allowed to return to their homes and a guard was established to prevent any further feuding. It seemed that Pistoia's woes were over, at least for the time being.

After checking that the provisions were holding, Niccolò returned home, arriving no later than 26 October.[81] For once, he was able to hold his head high. Although the past few months had been fraught with danger, Florence had come through it unscathed. Against all the odds, it had seen off Cesare Borgia and kept hold of Pistoia – thanks in no small part to his efforts. The failure of his mission to France was now firmly behind him. He had redeemed himself. His position in the chancellery was more secure than ever before and, despite the demise of the *Dieci*, he could look forward to playing a more prominent diplomatic role in future. Best of all, he had a beautiful young wife with whom to share his success. There could be no question that 'the spot' had at last become a man.

9

The Whirlwind

(October 1501–July 1502)

If the Florentines believed that they had seen the last of Cesare Borgia, they were mistaken. After Louis XII's forces had taken Naples, there was no need for Cesare to remain with the French army any longer. Taking his leave of the harem he had assembled for himself at Capua, he wended his way northwards to Rome. There, the fires of his ambition were rekindled. With the connivance of his father, Pope Alexander VI, he once again began formulating plans to enlarge his newly created duchy of Romagna.

Cesare's timing was propitious. For the moment, Louis XII was unlikely to trouble him. Though Naples had fallen, French rule was still far from secure. Already struggling to keep order, the king's viceroy, Louis d'Armagnac, had become embroiled in a territorial dispute with the Spanish which threatened to destroy the alliance.[1] And on top of all this, Louis was also making preparations for a campaign against the Turks.[2] Even if he had wanted to, he would have struggled to hold Cesare back.

With the French out of the way, Alexander VI swung into action. Realizing that Cesare's northern frontier would remain vulnerable unless Ferrara could be counted upon, he quickly arranged a marriage between his daughter, Lucrezia, and Ercole d'Este's eldest son, Alfonso.[3] After lavish – and reputedly debauched[4] – celebrations in Rome, Cesare was ready to launch his campaign. He would first strike at Urbino and Camerino. Once they had been dealt with, he would push on to Bologna. Naturally, Cesare would have preferred to have Florence as an ally from the outset. He knew that it had enjoyed a long and friendly relationship with all of the states at which he was tilting his lance, and wanted to be sure that it would not consider coming to their aid. He had also not forgotten that the Florentines had signed a *condotta* (contract) in May, and was anxious to be paid the money he was owed. This being so, Alexander VI despatched ambassadors to propose a formal alliance in October.[5] The Florentines rebuffed the idea in no uncertain terms, but Cesare was confident he could bring them round. There was no lack of opportunity for bringing pressure to bear on them. Pisa was still in open rebellion, the peace in Pistoia was fraying at the seams, and the towns of the Valdichiana were beginning to strain under the Florentine yoke.[6] Now that Piombino had been captured and fortified, Vitellozzo Vitelli was already raiding the countryside nearby: it would not take Cesare much to persuade him to put his soldiers to good use in any one of these theatres. The Orsini would doubtless be ready to lend a hand, too. As soon as the Florentines felt threatened, Cesare was sure they would come crawling.

Even before he had made his first move, the situation began to swing in his favour. In November, the Pisans reached out to the pope of their own volition. As the Florentines discovered after capturing six of their soldiers outside Cascina, they had been tormented by poverty and had not received any relief from other powers for some time.[7] They had been hoping Vitellozzo Vitelli might come to their aid, but their situation had become so grave that they could wait no longer. In desperation, they wrote to Alexander VI, begging him to send Cesare to restore the Medici to power in Florence and save Pisa from its plight.[8]

At the same time, the Signoria received word that the king of France was thinking about consenting to the Medici's return. Despite his longstanding ties with Florence he had grown tired of the priors' tardiness in providing the money they had promised him for the Neapolitan campaign, and was prepared to entertain other possibilities. Piero de' Medici's brother, Giuliano, was even then locked in discussions with Georges d'Amboise.[9] As Parenti reported, it was rumoured that he was prepared to offer the king 30,000 *fl.* over three years in return for Louis' support.[10] A short time later, he upped the offer, promising Louis an immediate lump sum of 70,000 *fl.* if he agreed.[11]

The Signoria was deeply alarmed. Florence was in no state to deal with this. Plagued by financial troubles, it was 'full of confusion and disorder'.[12] Attempts to restructure the *Monte* (the public debt) only seemed to generate further resentments, opening up the old divisions between *popolo* and *ottimati* again. The priors were not sure how – or if – they would cope if the rumours were true. They braced themselves.

In early December, news arrived that Cesare's commanders were on the march. To the Signoria's surprise, however, they appeared to be making not for Pisa, but for the Valdichiana. Vitellozzo Vitelli had already taken up position in Città di Castello, his family's traditional stronghold, while Paolo Orsini was following behind, arriving at Perugia at about the same time.[13] From these stage-posts, they would be able to mount a pincer movement against Arezzo. Even to the untrained eye, it was obvious that Vitelli would march northwards towards the Florentine town of Borgo Sansepolcro, and then turn to attack from the east, while Orsini would head across country towards Cortona, and then approach from the south.

The Signoria scrambled to block the *condottieri*'s paths as best they could. Judging Vitelli to be the most immediate threat, they despatched a sizable force to Borgo Sansepolcro and sent as many infantrymen as they could afford to strategically important locations elsewhere.[14] Now that the first winter snow was beginning to fall, the priors hoped this might be enough to hold them in check for the time being. But it was, at best, a stopgap measure. Once the spring came, Vitelli and Orsini would surely sweep them aside without difficulty.

In the chancellery, Niccolò and his colleagues desperately searched for a diplomatic means of averting the danger. The wedding of Lucrezia Borgia and Alfonso d'Este seemed to offer an ideal opportunity to reach out to their enemies. They first tried currying favour with the Ferrarese. When the groom's uncle, Cardinal Ippolito d'Este, passed through Florence on his way to fetch Lucrezia from Rome, on 14 December, they hastened to ingratiate themselves with Cesare's future in-laws. After welcoming the cardinal and his retinue 'with great honour', they despatched a special delegation to offer him the Signoria's most obsequious congratulations.[15] When this failed to produce any positive results, they tried their luck with the pope. Although they could scarcely afford it, they sent two ambassadors to present Lucrezia with a wedding gift of gold and silver cloth, reputedly worth 800 ducats.[16] But even such largesse could not sweeten the pontiff's mood. He would not lift a finger to restrain Cesare's commanders.

The Signoria's only remaining option was to appeal to Louis XII. Relations had, admittedly, become rather strained of late, but the priors nevertheless believed that he was someone with whom they might be able to negotiate. He was a pragmatist, after all – a tough negotiator, but open to reason. They had, however, underestimated quite how much they had tried Louis' patience. When their ambassadors appeared before him, asking for Florence to be released from its previous obligations and offering to conclude a new agreement in return, they met with a stern refusal. Not only did Louis intend to hold them to the old terms, but he also demanded that they pay him the outstanding balance in one year, instead of over the next four.[17] It was rumoured that he might expect further concessions, as well. Most likely, he would ask for 'exiles to be recalled, and the magistrates to be nominated according to his wishes.'[18] Louis also made it clear that he did not want to wage war 'against any other Christian potentate, except to recover or defend his own lands.'[19] He would only mobilize his forces against the infidels.

The priors were aghast. As things stood, they could not possibly agree to such terms. But, if they did not, they were afraid that Louis might accept the Medici's offer and allow Cesare's *condottieri* to return Piero to power.[20] A compromise clearly had to be found. To this end, Florence's ambassadors were instructed to propose a more modest arrangement. If Louis agreed to provide the city with military assistance, the Signoria would be prepared to consider paying at least *part* of what it owed, in some manner.

Louis refused to budge, however. Unless Florence was willing to discharge its financial obligations in full, the king would not even discuss military support. Given the parlous state of the city's finances, however, the Signoria was reluctant to give way. The priors still hoped that, in time, they would talk him round. But time was the one thing they did not have.

While the ambassadors were arguing their case, Florence found itself confronting a series of crises. The first concerned Pistoia, where civil unrest had again broken out.[21] On 23 February 1502, the Cancellieri had driven the Panciatichi out of the city and burned many of their houses to the ground. The Florentine commissioners did their best to contain the violence, even going so far as to hang some of the leading rebels, but, when this proved inadequate, the Signoria decided to assume direct control over the city. Orders were given to raise a force of 700 foot soldiers and ninety mounted cross-bowmen, and to despatch it to Pistoia by the middle of March.[22] There, it was to set up guard-posts at strategic locations, dismantle all the fortifications, confiscate weapons from both parties and punish anyone who broke the peace. It was also to compel the leaders of the two factions to come to Florence for talks.

Uncertain of how to proceed, the Signoria turned to Niccolò for advice. Drawing on his experiences the previous year, he composed a report 'On Pistoiese Affairs' (*De rebus pistoriensibus*).[23] Although the attribution has been challenged, it is possible that he also drew up two further documents (the '*Sommario della città*' and the '*Sommario del contado*') containing a series of recommendations.[24] In keeping with his later views on faction-torn cities, these were uncompromising. Within the city, the first text argued, the two parties should immediately be prohibited, the exiles allowed to return and harsh punishments imposed on those who broke the peace.[25] Restitution should also be made to those who had lost their property, and the perpetrators brought to justice. Under the commissioners' supervision, a new government (priors, colleges and council) should be chosen for a term of four months, during which time every effort should be made to reform the city. In the *contado*, meanwhile, all towns and villages should be brought under the authority of the Florentine Signoria, and the remaining bands of rebels should be hunted down without mercy.[26]

After briefly debating whether to lay waste to the Pistoiese *contado*, the Signoria decided to approve the majority of these recommendations.[27] But, before they had had a chance to take effect, Florence was faced with a second crisis – this time from Pisa. Emboldened by the advance of Cesare's *condottieri*, the Pisans had recently taken to raiding the Florentine countryside.[28] On 23 March, they captured the town of Vicopisano, almost without a fight.[29] From its fortress, they would be able to menace not only Cascina, but the whole of the lower Arno. As Biagio Buonaccorsi later recalled, a cavalry detachment was immediately despatched to the area,[30] and a quantity of artillery and bombards would soon follow.[31] But it was clear to everyone in the Palazzo della Signoria that Florence's situation was now critical. Were Vitellozzo Vitelli and Paolo Orsini to cross the frontier, there would be little it could do to stop them. Its only hope was to accept Louis XII's terms, however punishing they might be.

On 16 April, a new agreement was signed. The Florentines would pay Louis 150,000 ducats and, in return, the king would guarantee their safety. As a mark of his commitment, he also promised to provide a force of 400 men-at-arms to defend them against anyone who might threaten their city. It was, admittedly, far from perfect,[32] but, as Biagio noted, the priors were confident that it would be enough to dispel the shadow that had fallen across the city.[33]

Feeling heartened, Florence prepared to renew its campaign against the Pisans. On 23 April, a vote was passed to lay waste to the territory around Pisa. As Landucci reported, 'more soldiers were continually being hired to go there'.[34] A host of new *condottieri* were taken on. Overall command was given to Ercole Bentivoglio, who was also accorded the lofty title of 'governor general'.[35]

As these preparations were being made, the incoming Signoria sent Niccolò to Bologna to meet with its *signore*, Giovanni Bentivoglio. Since only his letter of credence has survived, the exact purpose of this mission is not known.[36] It may simply have been an act of diplomatic courtesy. Given that Bologna was in a similar situation to Florence, it would not have been unreasonable for the priors to have informed its *signore* about the pact with France. It is, however, more likely to have been connected with the forth-coming attack on Pisa. As Bertelli has pointed out, Florence's 'governor general' was a kinsman of Giovanni Bentivoglio, and it would hence have been natural for Niccolò to have been deputed to give him advance notice of the measures that were going to be taken.[37]

Whatever his task may have been, Niccolò did not remain in Bologna long. Within a matter of days, he was back in Florence, in time for the opening assault against the Pisans. The early reports were positive. On 10 May, Florentine troops ravaged the countryside, destroying 'corn, vines, fruit and whatever else there was'.[38] The following week, a steady flow of prisoners began to arrive in the city. On 26 May, it was reported that no fewer than 130 Pisan horsemen had been captured, together with a hundred mules laden with supplies.[39] Three days after that, the Signoria was informed that

Vicopisano and its fortress had been recaptured.[40] The Florentines were overjoyed. That Louis XII had also despatched messengers to the pope and all the other powers to declare that 'no one was to make any move against [them], under pain of his displeasure' only added to their delight.[41] They seemed to have come through the worst.

*

Yet such hubris was to prove the source of Florence's perdition. In their haste to secure an agreement with Louis XII, the priors had not paused to consider how little Cesare's *condottieri* would be deterred by the king's warning. Four hundred men-at-arms were, after all, nothing much to write home about, and, since Louis was then preoccupied with Neapolitan affairs, it seemed unlikely that he would jeopardize his relationship with the Borgias by taking any more decisive action. Cesare's men decided to try their luck. As Niccolò later recalled, while the Florentines were busy with Pisa, Vitellozzo, still 'burning with anger' at his brother's death, set out for Arezzo.[42] His advance galvanized the opponents of Florentine rule into action. On 4 June, the city rebelled.[43] In panic, the Signoria ordered their troops to raise the camp at Vicopisano and head for Arezzo without delay.[44] But it was too little, too late. On 10 June, Vitellozzo entered the city 'with many foot-soldiers and plenty of artillery';[45] and the following week, the citadel was taken, although not without a struggle.[46]

As Landucci reported, the Florentines were greatly dismayed.[47] They knew that their forces had no chance of dislodging Vitellozzo. Situated on a steep hill, Arezzo was virtually impregnable. All their soldiers could do was stand guard over the Val d'Arno and protect their remaining possessions nearby as best they could. But this left them vulnerable elsewhere. Now that the camp at Vicopisano had been raised, there was nothing to stop the Pisans raiding and looting at will, and it was not long before rumours began spreading that Cesare Borgia might be approaching from the direction of Siena, as well.[48] Although the Great Council had approved a slew of new taxes to pay for more troops, the priors knew it would be impossible to fight on two – or even three – fronts at once.[49] In desperation, they re-established the *Dieci* to take charge of the crisis[50] and sent one of their number, Piero Soderini, to Milan to beg the French for more help.[51]

Before Soderini had presented the Signoria's request, however, another hammer blow fell. On 20 June, news reached Florence that Piero de' Medici had entered Arezzo to a hero's welcome. As he rode through the streets, there were cries of '*Marzocco!*' (the traditional symbol of Florence) and '*Palle!*' (referring to the balls on the Medici's coat of arms). The Florentines were horror-stricken. There could no longer be any doubt about the Borgias' intentions. It was only a matter of time before they attacked Florence. But what was the Signoria to do? Aside from ordering all able-bodied men to rally to the city's defence, the priors were at a loss.[52] Although they still hoped Louis XII would come to their aid, they were forced to accept that, unless he came to Italy in person, the Borgias would not pay any heed. But they had no other allies upon whom they could call – or at least none who could stop Cesare's *condottieri*. Frightened and alone, they reluctantly concluded that their only chance of averting disaster might be to despatch an embassy to negotiate with Cesare himself, then rumoured to be moving northwards towards Urbino. For this task, they chose Francesco Soderini – the bishop of Volterra and brother of Piero – and Niccolò Machiavelli.[53]

It was not easy for Niccolò to undertake such a mission. Only a few months earlier, Marietta had discovered that she was pregnant, and by June, they were preparing for the arrival of their first child. Although there were servants to help her, Niccolò was still needed at home, and Marietta cannot have been impressed that her husband was leaving her alone, perhaps for several weeks. What was more, embassies were a costly business and they could ill afford the expense. With a baby on the way, they needed every *soldo* they had. Yet he had to go. It was, after all, his duty. And even if his function was merely to assist Francesco Soderini, rather than conduct negotiations in his own right, he wanted to shine – both for Florence's sake, and his own.

*

On 22 June, Niccolò and Francesco rode out of Florence. Since they could not pass through Arezzo, they were forced to take a rather indirect route. Heading eastwards, they reached the hamlet of

Ponticelli, nestled in the hills above Consuma, by evening. There, they chanced upon one of Cesare's messengers, on his way to Florence.[54] From him, they learned that Cesare had already captured Urbino and was expecting its deposed duke, Guidobaldo da Montefeltro, to take refuge in Florentine territory. Niccolò and Francesco were stunned. They had not expected Cesare to make such rapid progress. Early the next morning, they set off again. They knew that their horses were tired, and were probably in no fit state to travel,[55] but they could not afford to hang around looking for fresh mounts. Spurred on by anxiety, they made rapid progress. By the morning of 24 June, they had arrived at Mercatello and expected to reach Urbino before vespers.

It had previously been agreed that they would be met at one of the main gates by Cesare's secretary, Agapito Gerardini, and his *cameriere*.[56] But, by the time Niccolò and Francesco reached the city, night had already fallen and the gate had been locked. They shouted to the guards to let them in, but strict instructions had been given to keep the doors firmly closed. They had no choice but to search for another entrance. After picking their way around the walls in darkness, they eventually managed to creep in through a small gate, not far from the fortress, and, feeling rather shamefaced, made their way to the Bishop's Palace, where they were to be lodged. To their relief, they found Gerardini and the *cameriere* waiting for them there, having evidently guessed what had happened. The two envoys were perhaps a little embarrassed at first – not to mention nervous. But Gerardini put them at their ease. Welcoming them on Cesare's behalf, he invited them to rest awhile. When Cesare was ready to receive them, he would send word.

Gerardini and the *cameriere* came to collect them early the next morning. Together, they walked a short distance to the *Palazzo Ducale*, where Cesare was staying 'alone, with [only] a few of his men'.[57] Passing through the richly decorated entrance, they were led into the courtyard and up the stairs to the audience chamber. There, they found themselves face to face with Cesare himself. Even in the dazzling surroundings of the *Palazzo Ducale*, he presented a marvellous sight. Not yet twenty-seven years old, he was tall and athletic, with a long mane of thick black hair and piercing blue eyes. He commanded attention and respect. Niccolò could not help being impressed.

As the Signoria had instructed, the envoys began by congratulating

Cesare on the conquest of Urbino. But Cesare was in no mood for pleasantries. Barely pausing to acknowledge their good wishes, he pointed out that his success would have been sweeter had Florence kept its promises to him. Despite signing an agreement the year before, the priors had so far failed to pay the money they owed him. Nor had they sent him any artillery. Such bad faith was unacceptable. The time had come for Florence to make up its mind. He would give the priors one more chance to keep their promises. If they did, then all would be forgiven. If they decided to reject his friendship, however, there would be consequences. Niccolò and Francesco must surely see that he could not feel safe as long as Florence was his enemy. He would have to take steps to ensure the security of his states. With a menacing smile, he reminded them that he could easily have restored the Medici to power the year before; it would be even simpler to do so now.

Alarmed by Cesare's threatening tone, Niccolò and Francesco tried to mollify him with facile excuses and empty assurances.[58] If Florence had been slow in paying, they claimed, it was not because the city wanted to avoid its obligations. It had simply been short of money and the priors had been reluctant to use unlawful methods to acquire the necessary funds. They were, however, keen to satisfy his wishes as quickly as possible. Cesare should trust that the Florentines wanted his friendship as much as he wanted theirs.

But Cesare was too shrewd to be taken in so easily. 'I know only too well that your city is not well disposed towards me,' he growled; 'in fact, it treats me like an assassin.'[59] He was well aware that the priors had already tried to stir up trouble with the pope and the king of France; and though these efforts had been in vain, his confidence in the Florentine Republic had been eroded. 'This government does not please me,' he added. 'I cannot put any faith in it; it needs to change, and it needs to reassure me that it will keep to what it promised. If not, you will very quickly realize that I am not prepared to live like this; and if you do not wish to be my friend, you will prove to be my enemy.'[60]

Niccolò and Francesco gamely replied that Florence had the best government it could wish for.[61] It satisfied the citizenry, even if it did not satisfy Cesare. And, as far as keeping faith was concerned, the Signoria did not believe there was anyone in Italy that had a better track record – even though Florence had suffered more than most. Perhaps if Cesare were to give them some proof that he was the friend he professed to be, the priors might be willing to reciprocate more openly. If he were to order Vitellozzo to withdraw from Arezzo, for example, they would certainly regard him as their truest ally, and would act accordingly.

Such horse-trading was not to Cesare's taste. They could hardly expect him to do them any favours, he argued, especially given how badly they had treated him.[62] But, even if he did want to do something for them, he could not help with Vitellozzo. Though Vitellozzo was his man, he claimed to know nothing about what had happened in Arezzo. As far as he could see, Vitellozzo was merely trying to avenge the death of his brother. Neither he nor any of his other commanders were mixed up in it. Indeed, Cesare claimed to have done his best to stay aloof from it all. Although some of the towns that had rebelled against Florentine rule had offered themselves to him, he had turned them all down.

It was a patent lie, of course. But it was enough to scotch any ideas of a quid pro quo. If the Florentines wanted Cesare to stop Vitellozzo, they would first have to agree to his terms – and fast. After all, Cesare could not keep his army in Urbino for long. It was far too exposed.[63] Besides, he had plans elsewhere. If they left it too late, he would not be able to help them. He knew perfectly well that Florence would stand little chance against Vitellozzo's forces. With wicked glee, he reminded the envoys that the city was far too disunited and badly governed to defend itself.

Niccolò and Francesco knew he was right, but they could hardly admit it. There was only one line of argument left to them. They reminded Cesare that the Florentines had signed an agreement with Louis XII, and could count on French support in the event of an attack.[64] They also pointed out that – according to a report received by the Signoria – the king had been deeply displeased by the fall of Urbino, and would not tolerate Cesare's expansionism for much longer.[65] Cesare reacted angrily. The envoys were right that he had been frustrated by Louis' recent warning, but they were mistaken if they believed Louis would really come to their aid. The king would never sacrifice the Borgias' support for their sake – especially when tensions were rising in the south. Louis had made fools of them.[66] And, that being so, Cesare saw no reason to change his mind.

There was nothing more to discuss. Cesare said that he would give the emissaries a little time to think things over, but he would send for them again before long. And, like that, Niccolò and Francesco were dismissed.[67]

*

Returning to their lodgings in the Bishop's Palace to wait for Cesare's call, they felt sure he would summon them soon. But, as the hours slipped by, their confidence waned. By the time evening fell, they had still not heard anything and they were getting anxious. Even if a deal could not be reached today, the Signoria would still need some idea of Cesare's intentions. With this in mind, they decided to pay a visit to two of Cesare's commanders, Paolo and Giulio Orsini, who had recently arrived from Perugia.

At first, the Orsini were reassuring. They spoke about Florence with affection. As Niccolò explained in his report, it even seemed as if they might be willing to intercede with Cesare on the Signoria's behalf.[68] But no sooner had Niccolò and Francesco begun explaining their position in greater detail than the Orsini turned nasty. Cesare was right, they said: Louis would never come to Florence's aid. Surely the envoys could see that the king had already decided to abandon Florence to its fate? 'Do you really believe that . . . we would have embarked on such a campaign if the king had not consented to it?' they asked.[69] That Cesare had captured Urbino was surely proof enough that Louis was willing to acquiesce in his plans. In any case, Pandolfo Petrucci's ambassador to France, Pepo da Corvaia, had confirmed it only a few days before.

Even if Louis *did* send the Florentines more troops, however, it would be to no avail. They would be no match for Cesare's *condottieri*. 'We are already masters of a good portion of your *contado*,' the Orsini said; 'we have a large army and much artillery.' It would not be hard to sweep the French aside, and then Florence would be at their mercy. Sooner or later, the Orsini predicted, they would be top dogs in Tuscany. It would be better for the Signoria to accede to Cesare's demands now, rather than suffer the wrath of his *condottieri* later.

Niccolò and Francesco were shaken. They had not anticipated such violent resolve. But at least they could now be sure that Cesare was not bluffing. The Orsini had revealed that he was indeed planning a campaign against Florence, and was even struggling to hold his commanders back. The only question was when he would launch his attack. Given everything they had heard so far, Francesco was prepared to bet that it would be soon.[70] Writing up their report in the dead of night, Niccolò intimated that the Signoria might have to bow to the inevitable.

*

When they awoke the next morning, however, the outlook began to brighten. Soon after they had breakfasted, they were informed that Pepo da Corvaia and Cornelio Galanti – one of Vitellozzo's men – had just arrived in Urbino.[71] Puzzled as to what this might portend, Niccolò and Francesco hurried to ask them why they were there. Naturally enough, they refused to say. But, from a few incidental remarks they made, Niccolò and Francesco divined that they had come to discuss Louis XII's letter of warning. Vitelli and Petrucci wanted to be sure the king would not come to Florence's defence before they took any further action. Sensing an opportunity to sow doubt into their minds, Niccolò and Francesco tried to persuade Pepo and Cornelio that Louis was, in fact, firmly behind the Florentines. Whatever else Cesare might tell them, they would soon see that the king was 'not a man to play with loyalty or his friends'.[72] Pepo and Cornelio were sceptical at first. They had no reason to trust the Florentine envoys. After all, diplomats were always trying to pull the wool over their enemies' eyes in one way or another. But, at the same time, they could not ignore the possibility that Niccolò and Francesco might be telling the truth. Fearing they had already given away too much, they went on the offensive. Regardless of whether Louis sent the Signoria help in future, Cornelio said, the Florentines would never be able to stop Vitellozzo now. Their soldiers and commanders were a joke.

Cornelio's jibes must have been painful to hear, but they were nevertheless revealing. Niccolò and Francesco realized he would not have been so malicious had Louis' intentions been a matter of indifference to him. It now appeared that the king's relationship with the Borgias was more equivocal than Cesare had claimed. Vitellozzo seemed genuinely worried. Far from making ready to attack

Pontassieve, he was hesitating. And as long as he remained uncertain, Florence would have time. This would not only allow them to negotiate with Cesare with greater confidence, but it would also give them a chance to secure French support.

As the day wore on, Niccolò and Francesco's sense of hope grew. After making careful enquiries, they discovered that the Orsini had spent all morning trying to persuade Cesare to break off negotiations with Florence.[73] Whether this was because they wanted to launch an attack before Louis XII had a chance to stop them, or because they were simply impatient was unclear. Either way, Cesare had refused. He wanted to continue talking – at least for a while. This seemed to confirm that he was not as confident as he had made out the day before. Even if he *was* planning a campaign against Florence, Niccolò and Francesco reasoned, he might be trying to put it off for as long as he could, evidently hoping that he could still scare the city into giving him what he wanted. And, on top of everything, there appeared to be tensions opening up between him and his *condottieri*.

At terce, Cesare summoned Niccolò and Francesco once again.[74] This time, however, his bearing was different. Though as stern as before, he was not as confrontational. He began by repeating his grievances against Florence. As he had the previous day, he made it clear that he would not allow the Signoria to vacillate any longer. He wanted an answer. He would give the priors four days to make up their minds. There was, of course, an implicit threat lurking behind this, but something about it seemed weak. Four days was an awfully short amount of time for the Signoria to make such a momentous decision. Cesare could hardly be serious. Given all that Niccolò and Francesco had heard that day, they may well have asked themselves if he might just be trying to get Florence to make him an offer. Still, it was better not to take any chances. Not wanting to lose any time, they decided that Niccolò would ride back to Florence as quickly as possible and deliver his report to the Signoria in person.

*

After Niccolò had left, Francesco began making enquiries about the disposition of Cesare's forces, in the hope this might reveal whether he was really serious. At first, no one seemed to know what the duke had in mind. His troops were too widely dispersed and the routes they could take too numerous to judge.[75] But, by 30 June, Francesco had seen his worst fears confirmed. Rather than heading north, towards Bologna, Vitellozzo had encamped outside Anghiari – in Florentine territory – where he would soon be joined by Paolo Orsini.[76] Another, even larger force was approaching from the east.[77] There could no longer be any doubt that Cesare was massing his forces for an attack on Florence. Horrified, Francesco could not help wondering whether he and Niccolò might have misunderstood Louis XII's warning, after all.

In Florence, however, the Signoria and the *Dieci* held their nerve. Unbeknown to Francesco, they had recently heard that Louis XII was growing tired of Cesare and would have no hesitation about sending the Florentines the troops he had promised them. These were expected to arrive very soon.[78] Provisions were already being arranged – perhaps by Niccolò himself. What was more, it was even said that Louis was thinking about coming to Italy to set Cesare straight in person. This buoyed everyone's spirits. There seemed to be a chance that Florence might be able to face Cesare down, after all. The *Dieci* were so confident they decided to reject the duke's demands out of hand.[79] Francesco was ordered to tell him that they would certainly not pay the exorbitant sums he was asking for, and resented the suggestion that their form of government needed changing.

When Francesco received the *Dieci*'s instructions, he rushed off to Fermignano to give Cesare the news straight away. As was to be expected, the duke was not happy.[80] He railed against the Florentines with such vehemence that Francesco found it hard to get a word in edgeways. Calling on God as his witness, he swore that he wanted only Florence's friendship. They should not let themselves become arrogant because of the French soldiers who had arrived, he warned. He knew perfectly well how many and of what sort they were, and he was also better informed about what Louis XII was thinking, too. It was absurd to suppose the king would ever favour Florence over the Borgias. This being so, he was confident the Florentines would want to come to some sort of an agreement. Since he would not negotiate with the *Dieci*, however, he once again demanded that they consider a change of government.

But Cesare had played his hand poorly. Francesco could see he was rattled. Suspecting that he might already have tried to call his *condottieri* back in the hope of avoiding Louis' wrath, Francesco decided to stand his ground. With calm self-assurance, Francesco replied that, since the *Dieci* were all men of good quality, there was no need to replace them.[81] He even gave their names. It was a small point, but it was enough to show that Florence would not be bullied anymore. At this, Cesare buckled. Seeing that Florence's government was so constituted, he said, he would be happy to treat with it.[82] When he had asked them to change their government, he had not meant to suggest that they should change their constitution. Far from it. He had no preferences, as far as that was concerned. He trusted the Signoria to know what was best. He just needed to be confident of any alliance they signed, that was all.

Regarding the details of this agreement, Cesare was prepared to be rather more accommodating than before. Even though he preferred to leave the question of money aside for the moment, he was keen to discuss some form of mutual security.[83] In order to be sure that the Florentines would keep their word, he wanted them to hand over a number of fortified towns for a certain period of time. In return, he would offer the Signoria a pledge of his own goodwill. He would, for example, be willing to return the territories that had been taken from them – presumably including Arezzo. With a smile, Francesco promised to pass his offer on. There was hope, after all.

*

While Cesare was softening his stance in Fermignano, however, his *condottieri* were running rampage around the Val Tiberiana. Heedless of his calls for restraint, Vitellozzo and Paolo Orsini were pursuing their own interest with wanton abandon.[84] On 2 July, the *Dieci* wrote to their envoy with news that Borgo Sansepolcro had rebelled the previous day and Anghiari had been captured.[85] Frightened, the nearby communes of Pieve Santo Stefano, Caprese and Montedoglio had given themselves up, rather than be taken by force.

Although the arrival of the French troops reassured the Florentines a little, the realization that Vitellozzo and Paolo Orsini might now be acting independently was cause for alarm. Divisions started to open up. While most of the *ottimati* still wanted to negotiate with

Cesare, the *popolani* had their doubts. What was the point of dealing with Cesare if he could not control his *condottieri*, after all? Were the *ottimati* really so blind? Or were they secretly in league with Cesare? Matters soon threatened to turn violent.[86] If the *ottimati* wanted to avert civil unrest, they realized they would have to demand more favourable terms from Cesare, or else abandon the negotiations altogether and trust to the French alliance. It would be a big risk, but they had no choice.

On 5 July, the Florentines learned that Vitellozzo and Paolo Orsini were now encamped at Poppi and Chiusi, fifty-eight kilometres and eighty kilometres from Florence, respectively.[87] What was more, there were dark rumours circulating about the Pistoiesi. In Urbino, two Pisan ambassadors gleefully told Francesco that Pistoia would go the way of Arezzo within a week.[88] These were frightening developments, but, under pressure from the *popolani*, the *ottimati*-dominated *Dieci* felt obliged to play it tough with Cesare. As they explained in a letter to Francesco that afternoon, they had decided that they did not want to be held to the agreement they had made the previous year.[89] They now felt that 36,000 ducats was too much to ask when the men Cesare would supply would not be under a commander of their own choosing. They also refused to pardon all those who had committed offences against Florence the previous year, since that would mean absolving the Medici and their partisans. Cesare could put any thought of security from his mind, too. As far as the *Dieci* were concerned, there was no question of handing over any fortified places, least of all those that were still in Florentine hands. To cap it all, Cesare was going to have to respect their agreement with Louis XII as well. What Niccolò made of all this is not known. As secretary to the *Dieci*, he would have been party to their discussions, but it is uncertain whether he approved. Given the tenor of his earlier reports, it seems doubtful.

Barely a day after taking their decision, however, the *Dieci*'s gamble started to pay off. While their letter was on its way to Urbino, events took a turn for the better. On 6 July, they learned that Louis XII had finally lost patience with Cesare and his men. Having 'sworn upon his crown to avenge all the insults to the Florentines', the king had set off for Italy, and had already reached the frontier.[90] Two days later, it was reported that Louis was at Asti and had despatched an extra 150 lances to help Florence with its travails.[91] This was exactly what Cesare and his *condottieri* had feared most. Even before Louis had reached Asti, Vitellozzo had begun retreating in fear. Abandoning the siege of Poppi, he withdrew to Arezzo and immediately set about strengthening its defences, while the combined French and Florentine forces marched south from Pontassieve.[92] Niccolò's relief can only be imagined.

On 9 July, Francesco finally received the *Dieci*'s letter. As soon as he read it, he wanted to talk to Cesare. A few days earlier, however, the duke had fallen from his horse during a hunt and had been badly hurt.[93] Doctors had been summoned, and had warned him against overtaxing himself. Not until evening did he muster the strength to receive Francesco. Having evidently realized the tide was turning against him, he was desperate to secure an agreement while he still could. After listening patiently to the *Dieci*'s terms, he let it be known that he was prepared to give way on almost everything.[94] Not only did he promise to recover all of the territories that Florence had lost that year, but he also offered to lighten the city's financial burden. Rather than paying him all of his *condotta* at once, it could settle the account by instalments – over a long period of time, if need be. What was more, he was content for half of the men provided for in the contract to be stationed in Florentine territory, and for them to be commanded by an officer of the Signoria's choosing. He still wanted Florence to hand over a number of fortified sites as a token of its goodwill, but he was eventually persuaded to let even this pass.[95] Only with regard to pardons did he remain intractable. These had been agreed more than a year ago, he argued; there was no reason to renegotiate them now. He did, however, agree to a three-day ceasefire before the rebels returned home.

This was almost better than Francesco had been expecting. He thanked Cesare for his graciousness and assured him that the Signoria wanted nothing better than to be his ally. But Cesare was too weary and too embittered to return his courtesy. There was no pride or dignity left in him. Without any hint of a smile, he muttered that the Signoria should authorize Francesco to conclude the agreement as quickly as possible.[96]

*

But, just when it seemed as if the end might be in sight, things took a turn for the worst – at least in Urbino. Contrary to what the

Florentines had believed, Francesco had heard rumours that Louis had come to Italy without any soldiers other than his personal guard.[97] It had also been suggested that he was concerned only with the kingdom of Naples and had no intention of helping Florence, after all. If this were true, Francesco reasoned, the king would be unable to rein in Vitellozzo and the Orsini. Once they had got over their initial shock, they would go back on the offensive once again. And, if this proved to be the case, Florence would need Cesare's help more than they had thought. As such, Francesco advised the *Dieci* to sign an agreement while Cesare was still on the back foot. If they waited too long, the envoys warned, Florence would lose its advantage and Cesare would start demanding harsher terms.

But Francesco should have known better than to listen to court gossip. The reality was that Louis XII was still firmly committed to the Florentines and was determined to bring Cesare to heel. So confident were the *Dieci* of the king's support, in fact, that they were even reconsidering the terms they had proposed. On the morning of 12 July, they instructed Francesco to offer Cesare half, or at most two thirds, of the money he had asked for.[98] By the afternoon, however, they began to think that even this might be too generous. Having received an extremely encouraging report from their ambassador in France, Luca degli Albizzi, they now wondered whether they needed an agreement with Cesare at all – as the *popolani* had been arguing for the last two weeks.[99] While they made doubly sure about Louis XII's relationship with the Borgias, especially with Alexander VI, Francesco was therefore ordered to slow the negotiations down as much as possible.

Cesare was unused to being outmanoeuvred like this. Even before the *Dieci*'s letters reached Urbino, his temper had begun to fray. On 13 July, he summoned Francesco to complain about the behaviour of Florence's ambassador to France.[100] Furious that the ambassador had been speaking ill of him to Louis XII, the duke demanded that Francesco write both to the Signoria and to the French court to set the record straight. Reluctantly, Francesco agreed.[101] But Cesare's mood only grew worse. When the *Dieci*'s instructions arrived on 15 July, Francesco again requested an audience. He could not have anticipated how badly Cesare would react. Before Francesco had said a word, the duke started shouting like a petulant child. He had come to the Florentines like a brother, he whined.[102] He had shown nothing but concern for their liberty. Yet they evidently did not want his friendship. They were, in fact, trying to trick him. They knew perfectly well that he could not accept less money without losing face. It was obvious they were playing for time. Were they planning to launch a campaign against him? At this point, he became more menacing. Given how their relationship had soured, he growled, perhaps it would be better to put this matter before Louis XII, after all? They should know that, if the king was forced to choose between them, he would ultimately decide in Cesare's favour. But even he knew that this was a hollow threat. Changing tack, he then suggested that, if the Florentines had so little time for him, he might be tempted to dismiss Vitellozzo from his service.[103] This would, of course, come as a blow to Vitellozzo, but Cesare was sure he would get over it. And then, he would be free to wreak whatever vengeance on the Florentines he wished. They could kiss goodbye to Arezzo forever, and they could expect Vitellozzo to team up with the Medici, as well. Did the Florentines not realize, Cesare asked, that, if they were only to accept his friendship, he would force Vitellozzo to withdraw and would even help them to recover their lost possessions? He would give them one last chance.

The *Dieci* were, however, unmoved. They saw Cesare's bluster for what it was and were no longer willing to pander. While he had been fulminating, they had received letters from Asti which confirmed that Louis XII would take Florence's side against the Borgias, and that troops were already on their way to Tuscany.[104] There was evidently no point in negotiating with Cesare any further.[105] On 16 July, the *Dieci* therefore instructed Francesco to extricate himself from discussions however he thought best.[106] Three days later, he bade the duke farewell and rode off to attend to his affairs in Rome.[107]

Cesare was unnerved by news of Louis XII's approach. Realizing the enormity of his miscalculation, his confidence failed him. In the hope of escaping the king's wrath, he ordered Vitellozzo to abandon Arezzo and withdraw from Florentine territory.[108] This done, Cesare made haste to explain himself to Louis XII as well as he could. Disguised as a knight of St John of Jerusalem, he rode out of Urbino and made his way swiftly to Milan.

*

The Florentines were exuberant. By the end of the month, as Niccolò recalled a few years later, Vitellozzo had marched away and Cesare had humbled himself before the king.[109] The spectre of tyranny had been lifted. But, despite everything, Niccolò found it difficult to share in the excitement. During his brief encounter with Cesare in Urbino, he had been struck by the duke's dashing appearance and martial spirit:

> This lord is very splendid and magnificent. In [the profession of] arms, his courage is such that he can accomplish the greatest undertakings with ease. [When he means to acquire] glory and enlarge his domains, he neither rests, nor knows either fatigue or danger. No sooner is his arrival in a place known than he is gone . . . He has employed the best troops in Italy – and these things, together with perpetual good luck, make him a fearful and victorious [adversary].[110]

In part, such lavish praise was, of course, a reflection of Niccolò's own social aspirations. Still acutely aware of his humble origins, he was anxious to show his superiors in Florence that he was refined enough to appreciate the courtly virtues of a great *signore*. But Niccolò's assessment of Cesare was also born of careful observation. Having realized how badly he had misjudged members of the French court the previous year, he had made a particular effort to redeem himself with the accuracy of his analysis. And amid the jubilation of victory, he could not help sounding a note of caution. While Cesare may have been foiled on this occasion, it would be foolish to underestimate him. Something told Niccolò that he would bounce back, bolder and more brilliant than before. Having just weathered the whirlwind, Florence would soon have to pass through the eye of the storm.

10

The Eye of the Storm

(August 1502–January 1503)

As the autumn drew near, the Florentines could have been forgiven for breathing a sigh of relief. After months of anxiety, they at last seemed to be safe. Although Louis XII had given Cesare Borgia a warm welcome in Milan and had reaffirmed his affection for the pope's family, he had made it clear that he would not allow France's allies to be threatened so brazenly again.[1] At the same time, Cesare's relations with his *condottieri* were also becoming more strained. Those who had harried Florence hardest during the summer were outraged to find themselves now in disgrace with the king of France, and condemned Cesare for having placed the blame on them.[2] Of these, none was more furious than Vitellozzo Vitelli.[3]

Florence was more politically stable, too. For years past, the city's ability to respond to military crises had been hampered by the rapid turnover of magistrates and seemingly endless disputes over taxation. It was often difficult to raise troops at short notice, and virtually impossible to develop consistent policies in the longer term. Several attempts had, of course, been made to address this problem. Each time, however, political rivalries had put paid to any chance of constitutional reform. But the revolt of Arezzo had finally brought matters to a head. In early July, the Signoria had decided that Florence could no longer afford to go on like this.[4] *Pratiche larghe* were convened to discuss 'how to organize the city well and to introduce good government.'[5] A variety of different proposals were put forward, some more radical than others. All, however, agreed there was a need 'for a greater degree of continuity in government' and for a more efficient means of managing the city's finances. In early August, after various disagreements, the possibility of electing a *gonfaloniere* for life – rather than just for two months – was mooted. This was, of course, not an altogether novel suggestion. After all, the Venetians had already been electing their doges for life for centuries. It was a system the Florentines had long admired. Eight years before, Savonarola had argued in favour of remodelling Florence's constitution along Venetian lines and, early that same summer, some members of the *Dieci* had also mentioned it. But now there was genuine support for the idea. The *popolani* were satisfied that a *gonfaloniere a vita* would bring continuity to government, without detracting from the authority of the Great Council or of the priors, and the *ottimati* reassured themselves that further reforms would surely follow. On 22 August, the Eighty ratified the proposal and, four days later, on 26 August, the Great Council gave its approval. The task of choosing someone suitable then began.[6] After a series of votes, Piero Soderini emerged victorious. He was the perfect compromise. Although he came from a prominent political family and had been a vocal proponent of constitutional reform in the past, he was not associated with any particular faction. He was, however, tremendously experienced. For four of the last six years, he had been away on diplomatic missions. This had allowed him to develop particularly close ties with France. He had served as ambassador to Charles VIII in July 1493, to Louis XII in June 1498 and to Cardinal Georges d'Amboise in 1500.[7] Most importantly, he had also negotiated the agreement with Louis XII in April 1501.

This was all good news for Niccolò. Not only did the dissipation of the Borgia threat reflect well on his recent diplomatic efforts, but the election of Piero Soderini also seemed to bode well for his career at the chancellery. During his mission to Urbino, he had struck up a firm friendship with Piero's brother, Francesco.[8] By the beginning of August, the two had already begun an affectionate correspondence, in which Francesco addressed Niccolò as his 'very dear friend'.[9] Over the weeks that followed, Niccolò had no hesitation about capitalizing on this relationship. No sooner had Piero been elected than he dashed off a 'charming' letter to Francesco, congratulating the bishop on his brother's success. Although the text has not survived, it was evidently designed to curry favour – and it worked. On 29 September, Francesco wrote him a reply that must have gladdened his heart. '[S]ince you are second to none in ability [*virtute*] and affection,' the bishop assured him, 'you will not only be with us, but far dearer and more welcome [than before].'[10]

Satisfied that his position was now secure, Niccolò was able to enjoy family life a little. Having been absent for the birth of his daughter, Primerana, he would doubtless have wanted to make up for lost time. Even if child-rearing was regarded as a matter for women, Niccolò was still a doting father.[11] Dandling the infant in his arms, he would have delighted in her every smile. He was solicitous to a fault. Huddled around the crib, he and Marietta would have fretted over their choice of wet nurse and worried about whether the swaddling was too tight.[12] He was keen to have more children, too. Indeed, he and Marietta were already trying for a second child.

*

It was a blissful time for Niccolò and his young family. But, before the grape harvest had been gathered in, their peace was interrupted. On 2 September, Cesare Borgia at last took his leave of Louis XII.[13] Having arrived at court in disgrace, he was now departing in triumph. Over the previous weeks, he had learned of the growing tensions between the French and Spanish forces in southern Italy,[14] and had seized on the opportunity to remind Louis of how useful the Borgias could be if it came to war. It did not take him long to win the king over. By the beginning of September, he had even managed to talk Louis into granting him further concessions in return for his support. His sins were to be forgotten, he would be allowed to proceed against Bologna and he would even be provided with soldiers, should he feel the need to put his former *condottieri* in their place.

Vitellozzo and his like-minded friends were furious. While Cesare had been at court, they had allowed themselves to believe the ludicrous rumour that he was going to be sent back to France in chains.[15] Only now did they realize the extent of their folly. Though they did not yet know of the help Cesare had been promised by Louis XII, they could see he once again enjoyed the king of France's favour. It was obvious that, sooner or later, he would move against them. As Niccolò later wrote, they feared that, after conquering Bologna, 'he would try to destroy them in order to be the only armed man in Italy'.[16]

They had to strike first. At the end of September, all the disgruntled *condottieri* gathered on the shores of Lake Trasimeno, near Magione, and agreed to form an alliance.[17] Their objective was not, as has sometimes been claimed, to get rid of Cesare altogether.[18] Although Vitellozzo and Pandolfo reportedly swore to kill him, they knew it would be impossible. However strong their combined forces might be, they could never hope to do away with a figure who boasted a pope for a father and a king for a friend. Instead, they wanted simply to cut Cesare down to size. By presenting a united front, they felt sure they could put him off taking action against them. They even thought that they might be able to bully him into giving them what they wanted, as well. If all went to plan, Guidobaldo da Montefeltro would regain the duchy of Urbino, Giovanni Bentivoglio would have his safety guaranteed, and the dissatisfied *condottieri* would be re-employed on more favourable terms than before – and with a freer hand to pursue their own interests.

No sooner had the conspirators concluded their pact than they swung into action. As Niccolò later reported, messengers were immediately despatched to stir up rebellion in Cesare's domains.[19] The citizens of Urbino needed little encouragement. Tired of smarting under the Borgia yoke, they rose up and ejected the garrison.[20] The same day, they captured the strategically important fortress of San Leo, which commanded both the crossing over the River Marecchia and the road towards Rimini.

Flushed with their success, the conspirators began readying their troops 'to assail any city in that territory which had been left in the duke's power.'[21] Before doing so, however, they tried to use the rebellion of Urbino to tempt the Florentines into joining them.[22] It was an enticing prospect. More than once, they had been the victims of Cesare's acquisitive designs. But they felt bound to decline. Florence could never join an association of which Vitellozzo Vitelli was a member. Nor could it afford to alienate Louis XII by making war on Cesare.

Yet the Florentines saw that, if they were clever, they could still take advantage of the situation. For the first time, they had an opportunity to negotiate an alliance with Cesare from a position of strength. Clearly, he was no longer in a position to intimidate them. Since Louis XII had guaranteed their safety, he could neither invade their territory, nor threaten them with the restoration of the Medici. As long as he was weakened by this struggle with his *condottieri*, they would have the upper hand. Naturally, they would have to consult with Louis XII before actually signing anything, especially if it involved any sort of military action, but otherwise they would be able to call the shots.

On 5 October, the Signoria despatched Niccolò to conduct talks with Cesare, who was then in Imola.[23] He was, in some ways, a natural choice for such a mission, but it appears he may actually have put himself forward. The following week, Agostino Vespucci wrote him a letter complaining about his eagerness 'for riding, wandering, and roaming about'; and, from the context, it seems it was this wanderlust that had impelled Niccolò to volunteer.[24] However delightful family life may have been, he had evidently developed a taste for the road, and, having already fallen under Cesare's spell, was desperate not to miss out on such an exciting trip. Of course, Marietta was not very happy about it, but he promised her he would be away for no more than eight days.[25]

Once in Imola, Niccolò was quickly granted an audience. As he had been instructed, he began by informing Cesare that, though Florence had been approached by the conspirators, the Signoria had 'resolved to remain good friends with our Lord [Louis XII] and his Excellency'.[26] They felt bound to inform him about what was going on and 'to do [their] duty as good friends.' With warm words, Niccolò reassured the duke that they wished him only the best. But, for the moment, he said nothing about an alliance; the Signoria wanted him to test the waters before they made any definite proposals. Cesare was, however, embarrassingly eager to conclude an agreement.[27] He had, he claimed, always wanted an alliance with Florence. That he had not concluded one was due more to the malice of his *condottieri* than to any fault of his own. Vitellozzo and the Orsini were to blame for threatening Florence in the past. They had been responsible for invading the Valdichiana in the spring. It had been difficult to hold them back. But now that they had rebelled against him, he was at liberty to treat with the Florentines as he wished. As was only to be expected, he was reluctant to disclose what he would be willing to offer Florence in return for their friendship. Such details could be discussed later. Cesare did, however, add that he would greatly appreciate it if Florence would send soldiers to Borgo Sansepolcro, in order to dissuade Vitellozzo from making any further incursions into his lands.

Although Niccolò was encouraged by the warmth of Cesare's response, he could not agree to the duke's request. The Signoria had forbidden him to give any undertakings just yet. After politely reaffirming Florence's friendship, he therefore thanked the duke for his time and excused himself. It was perhaps a pity to have had to stall, but negotiations had still got off to a positive start. Indeed, there seemed to be a good chance that Niccolò's mission might actually be a success.

*

Over the coming days, Niccolò and Cesare resumed the negotiations. If anything, Cesare was even more anxious to secure an alliance than before. Although he was still determined to put off discussing any details, he tried to persuade Niccolò that it would be to Florence's advantage to commit itself, in principle, sooner rather than later. Every day, he boasted, there was more good news. The king of France had already offered his support, and Cesare was confident that troops would soon arrive from Milan.[28] The Venetians, too, had shown their willingness to stand by him. Although they had given refuge to Guidobaldo da Montefeltro, they had promised Cesare that they had nothing to do with Urbino's revolt and would not give any aid to the rebels.[29] What was more, the Orsini had begun to show signs of wavering. When the pope's envoy arrived in Perugia, 'they threw themselves into his arms, saying that they were soldiers of the Church, and did not wish to deviate from the pontiff's will'.[30] Best of all, Vitellozzo Vitelli was said to be ill with fever.

Of course, Cesare was not so foolish as to believe that his victory was assured. As Livy had once observed, nothing was as uncertain as war.[31] But whether Cesare triumphed or not, it was still in the Florentines' interest to take his side now.[32] If Florence agreed to an alliance, he argued, it would be sure to benefit. No matter who won in this struggle, it would have earned his lasting gratitude. It could rest easy in the knowledge that, if he won, he would be able to help it resolve the Pisan question; and if he lost, he would still do his best to protect it from his former *condottieri*. But, if Florence remained neutral, Cesare pointed out, it could only lose. Were he to emerge victorious, he would find it difficult to live with a hostile neighbour on his doorstep and might need to take steps to ensure its safety. Were the conspirators to defeat him, however, he would have no reason to stop them from resuming their campaign against Florence.

Cesare appreciated that terms would still have to be settled before a formal alliance could be signed, but, if the Florentines could give him some indication of their intentions right now, that would suffice. If they were to send a detachment of soldiers to Borgo Sansepolcro, as he had already suggested, he would feel much more confident of their friendship.

Niccolò could see the merit of Cesare's argument. So could everyone back in Florence. No one doubted the advantages of an alliance with the duke. After all, that was why Niccolò had been sent to Imola in the first place. But they did not want to commit themselves just yet. Before they agreed to anything, they would first have to know exactly what Cesare would offer them; and then, they would have to secure Louis XII's consent.[33] They were not in a position to make the sort of goodwill gesture Cesare was asking for, either. Writing on behalf of the *Dieci*, Marcello di Virglio Adriani informed Niccolò that it was 'neither possible nor convenient' to move troops to Borgo Sansepolcro.[34] All of Florence's forces were currently committed to recovering Arezzo and Pisa. Indeed, it was already running short of soldiers. On 10 October, the *Dieci* had even had to employ Francesco II Gonzaga, marquis of Mantua, as the city's new *capitano* – even though they were afraid this might not go down well with Cesare.[35]

Despite this, Niccolò felt sure some sort of agreement could be reached. When he told Cesare about the letter he had received from Adriani, the duke did not seem to be as disappointed as might have been expected. Cesare was not overly troubled that the *Dieci* could not spare any troops, and he even seemed happy that Florence had employed the marquis of Mantua. As Cesare explained, there was no reason for him to feel differently.[36] Francesco Gonzaga was, after all, a talented general, and – unbeknown to the Florentines – had recently offered to come to his aid, should he have need. Of course he was happy! It was just another reason why he and Florence should be allies.

Even if this seemed a little insincere, others at Cesare's court confirmed that an agreement was likely.[37] According to the duke of Ferrara's secretary, Ercole d'Este was pushing Cesare to ally with the Florentines – and with some success.[38] That Cesare was slow to discuss details should not alarm them. He probably just wanted to make sure he was in step with the pope. Alternatively, he might just be waiting until Piero Soderini took office on 1 November before getting down to serious negotiations. All would be well, they would see.

*

As Niccolò's first week in Imola drew to a close, he had good reason to feel pleased with himself. Back in Florence, his progress had not gone unremarked. As Piero Guicciardini observed, he was 'giving satisfaction to everyone'.[39] Piero Soderini was especially impressed. After listening to Agostino Vespucci read one of his most recent letters, Soderini had praised Niccolò's talent, noting that he was evidently 'endowed with much judgement, and also no little wisdom'.[40] Even Biagio Buonaccorsi was forced to admit that Soderini appeared 'to love [Niccolò] particularly'.[41] Like everyone else, Soderini was struck by how quickly he had established a rapport with Cesare and his courtiers. As Vespucci related, it seemed as if he was already held in great honour there.[42] This would have been a rare accomplishment for a diplomat in any circumstances, but that Niccolò had earned the respect of so formidable a prince was quite remarkable.

Niccolò was so puffed up with his own success that he felt able to ask for some leave. Now that he was in Piero Soderini's good books, he did not want to miss the new *gonfaloniere*'s inauguration on 1 November. It was an unusual request, to say the least. Envoys were not usually given permission to return home in the middle of a mission. The affairs of state took precedence – even over the death of a loved one, as Niccolò had found out during his mission to France, two years earlier. But Niccolò evidently felt that an exception should be made in this case. He seems to have believed that negotiations with Cesare were progressing so well that a few days' leave would not do any harm. To boost his chances further, he asked Biagio to put in a good word for him, as well.[43]

But not everything was as rosy as Niccolò liked to believe. Although his reports were well received, his absence was causing serious problems in the chancellery. While he was away, his colleagues had to take on his responsibilities – including taking the minutes of the *Dieci*'s meetings, liaising with Florence's commanders in the field and corresponding with the various subject cities. But no one wanted the extra work – and they were all starting to get pretty annoyed. As Agostino Vespucci reported, Biagio was forever reviling Niccolò with insults and curses.[44]

Niccolò was beginning to put his colleagues' noses out of joint in other ways, too. Although his letters were as charming as ever, he had begun to adopt a rather haughty tone with them. A never-ending stream of instructions issued from his pen. Leonardo Guidotti was charged with arranging for his wife to receive some money;[45] and poor Biagio was told not only to buy him some cloth for a new mantle, but also to track down a copy of Plutarch's *Lives* for him to read while he was away.[46] It was not long before Biagio began to tire of being treated like a skivvy. On 15 October, he was already complaining that Niccolò did not appreciate him enough. All of their other friends received long, affectionate letters, but he had scarcely received anything. He didn't ask for much in return for his efforts: a kind word now and again – that was all.[47] By 21 October, however, he had become bitter. While Niccolò was 'rustling about' in the Romagna, he was 'shit[ting] blood' for him in Florence – and for what? It hardly seemed worth the effort. Biagio hadn't even bothered asking about Niccolò's leave, and, if Niccolò didn't like the cloth he had purchased, Biagio told him that he could 'go scratch [his] arse'.[48] This cut Niccolò to the quick. Realizing that he might have been a bit too high-handed, he hurriedly dashed off a few friendly letters to Biagio. These went some way towards healing the rift. A few days later, Bartolomeo Ruffini told Niccolò that his letters to Biagio had gone down very well, 'and the jokes and witticisms' he had written in them had made 'everyone split their sides laughing'.[49] But some rancour still remained, nonetheless.

Marietta, of course, was desperate to have him back.[50] But even she was getting upset with him. Niccolò had promised her faithfully that he would not be away for more than eight days, and it had already been more than that. She didn't mean to pester him, but he had to recognize how hurt she was. Even Biagio took pity on her. On 15 October, he urged Niccolò to 'come back, in the name of the devil, so the womb doesn't suffer'.[51] When Marietta found out that Niccolò had asked Biagio to buy cloth for a mantle, however, her sorrow gave way to anger. Writing on 21 October, Biagio reported that she was 'making a big fuss' about it.[52] She knew that, if her husband was having a new mantle made, he was obviously expecting to stay at Cesare's court until the winter. And he hadn't even bothered to tell her! What was more, he was supposed to be helping to arrange the marriage of Bartolomeo Ruffini's girl.[53] If it was all to go off without a hitch, Marietta would need to know more about the dowry, the nuptial gifts and all the other things that went with a wedding.[54]

*

Worst of all, negotiations soon began to founder. Although Cesare was still anxious to conclude an agreement, the *Dieci*'s tentativeness was starting to try his patience. On 15 October, Niccolò saw the first signs of his growing exasperation. Early that evening, Niccolò had received word that Vitellozzo had moved some of his infantry and artillery from near Borgo Sansepolcro towards Fratta (probably the town now known as Umbertide, halfway between Città di Castello and Perugia).[55] Realizing the importance of this information, he immediately rushed off to see Cesare. As it happened, the duke was busy inspecting some detachments of infantry, but Niccolò was able to talk to one of Cesare's secretaries, and asked him to pass on the news. Later that night, Cesare called Niccolò back to discuss it further. He began by offering his thanks. Although he suspected that Vitellozzo's movements were likely to be a feint, he was still grateful to the *Dieci* for having kept him informed.[56] Such acts of goodwill were always appreciated. But, he added, they were not enough. They whetted his appetite, rather than sating it. What he wanted was an alliance – and quickly. There was, he argued, no reason for the Florentines to hesitate.[57] They should not worry about France. He was certain that Louis XII would want them to join his cause. Nor should they worry about having too few soldiers. He was only asking for a token force of fifty to sixty cavalrymen and 300 to 400 conscripts, after all. They could raise this many men in the field, if necessary. If they were afraid that even this would weaken them too much, however, he would be willing to make up the shortfall by helping them with their campaign against Pisa. All that he wanted was for his enemies to be able to *see* that Florence was on his side.

Niccolò had no choice but to temporize as best he could. The *Dieci* had given him strict instructions not to commit them to anything just yet, but he knew he would not be able to stall for much longer. Cesare was demanding an answer. Whatever reservations the *Dieci* might have, it seemed that it would be wisest to close the deal sooner rather than later. As far as Niccolò could see, Cesare's position had greatly improved. It was said that the Venetians had resolved not to offend him, and that in Urbino – which had been regarded as lost only a few days before – he had regained the upper hand.[58] What was more, it was rumoured that the Orsini might be about to break with the rebels and submit to Cesare, as well. Unless the *Dieci* acted quickly, Niccolò warned, it would be too late.

The *Dieci* were, however, unconvinced. Having heard Cesare make similar claims before, they had learned not to take him at his word – especially insofar as the king of France was concerned. Even if his position had improved as much as Niccolò seemed to believe, they did not think it wise to risk the French alliance. Until Louis XII had given them his blessing, they would not agree to anything. And they would not – could not – send Cesare the soldiers he had asked for, either. He would just have to wait. A few more days would not make any difference, anyway. Niccolò was probably being hysterical, they told themselves. Cesare's position could not have improved *that* much.

It was a grave miscalculation on both parts. Niccolò had, indeed, overestimated Cesare's strength.[59] But the *Dieci* were wrong to suppose that Cesare would wait. The more precarious his situation grew, the less willing he was to tolerate their excuses. If the Florentines did not make up their minds soon, he would have to consider other options.

Cesare tried to explain this to the Florentines. On 17 October, he informed Niccolò that he had received word from Siena.[60] It appeared that the Orsini had moved their troops towards Cagli, about twenty-one kilometres south of Urbino. This was, he claimed, a sign that the Orsini could indeed be detached from the rebels. He had recently told them that, if they withdrew towards the duchy of Urbino, he would regard them as friends. And, for their part, the Orsini certainly seemed ready to make a deal. They had indicated that they would come to terms with Cesare if he would agree to abandon his attempt on Bologna, and instead attack either Florence or Venice. As yet, however, Cesare had not taken them up on their offer. 'You see with how much [good] faith I act towards you,' he said, 'believing that you will come to be my friends with good will, and that your Signoria will not deceive me.' 'They really should have more confidence in me than in the past,' he added.[61] But behind the duke's honeyed words there lurked an unmistakable threat. If the *Dieci* did not ally with Cesare, he would cut a deal with the Orsini, and turn against Florence.

Later that day, Niccolò met with one of Cesare's staff.[62] He confirmed that Cesare's threat was in earnest. The Florentines really should hurry up and make a deal with the duke, he said. Their interests aligned so neatly, it would be foolish not to do so. Their hesitation only bred suspicion. And, if the duke suspected that they might betray him, they could hardly blame him if he threw in his lot with their enemies.

Ruffled, if not unduly alarmed, the *Dieci* tried to reassure Cesare of their commitment. Still convinced that they were in a strong bargaining position, they tried the duke's own technique. On 20 October, Niccolò informed Cesare, on their behalf, that they had again been approached by the conspirators.[63] Although they had been offered an attractive deal, they had turned it down. As Niccolò explained, this only showed how strongly Florence identified itself with Cesare's cause. The *Dieci* were hoping to receive word from Louis XII very soon; when they did, they would be only too happy to conclude a formal alliance with the duke. Cesare replied as graciously as ever. He asked Niccolò to thank the *Dieci* 'for the marks of friendship which [they gave] him on every occasion', and went on to denounce the actions of his former *condottieri* 'in very scornful terms'.[64]

But Cesare was far from satisfied. Despite the *Dieci*'s little show of loyalty, his faith in the Florentines was beginning to dissipate. Although nothing was said openly, Niccolò soon got the feeling that the duke was becoming more distant. It was as if he was being shut out. There was a 'remarkable secrecy' observed at Cesare's court, he reported; no one ever spoke of things that were not to be discussed.[65] Indeed, it was quite possible that the *Dieci* had a more accurate impression of what was going on than he did. He had, however, begun to suspect that he might have misjudged Cesare's situation, after all. From what he could gather, the conspirators seemed to be gaining the upper hand. He had heard rumours that Cesare's troops had been forced to abandon Fossombrone, about fifteen kilometres east of Urbino, and had retreated to Fano, on the Adriatic coast.[66] What was more, it was said that Guidobaldo da Montefeltro had left Venetian territory and was expected to arrive in Urbino before long.[67] If this were true, Cesare might indeed be thinking about cutting his losses and reaching an arrangement with the conspirators while he still could.

At last, the *Dieci* realized their mistake. Without waiting to hear further from France, they hurried to give Cesare what he had been asking for. Although they could still not spare any troops, they despatched two constables to the area around Borgo Sansepolcro, with orders to call up all able-bodied men in Anghiari and Bagno [di Romagna?].[68] Then, they turned their attention to the terms of an alliance. Fortuitously, Gasparre Pou, one of the papal chamberlains, had arrived in Florence to begin negotiating on the pope's behalf. He indicated that, if the *Dieci* paid Cesare the money that it had promised him the year before, provided a sizeable number of men-at-arms and dismissed the marquis of Mantua from their service, Alexander VI would persuade his son to help the Florentines recover Pisa and defend their borders.[69] Greatly encouraged, the *Dieci* despatched Alessandro di Rinaldo Bracci to continue discussions with the pope in Rome, while Niccolò was ordered to do the same with Cesare in Imola.

When Niccolò raised these proposals with Cesare, however, he received a mixed response. Much to his surprise, the duke was willing to agree to much more generous terms than his father.[70] He did not want any more troops, nor did he expect any money. He was even happy for the marquis of Mantua to continue in the Florentines' service, for the moment. But he was not prepared to wait any longer. Indeed, he was so anxious to conclude an alliance that he even seemed ready to do so without waiting for his father's consent. Rather menacingly, Cesare observed that, since their last meeting, the Orsini had presented him with a plan to change the government of Florence. So far, he had rejected this. Florence was, after all, a friend of Louis XII, and he still had hopes of reaching an agreement.[71] But, if the *Dieci* did not oblige him very soon, he would seriously consider accepting the Orsini's suggestion.

*

Niccolò advised the *Dieci* to accept Cesare's terms without hesitation. To be sure, it was still tempting to believe that the conspirators had gone too far to be reconciled with the duke. After all, their differences were striking:

Anybody who examines the qualities of the one side and the other recognizes this lord [i.e. Cesare] as a man courageous, fortunate, and full of hope: favoured by a pope and by a king, and injured by the other side, not only in a state that he wanted to conquer [Bologna], but [also] in one that he had acquired. Those others have come to be jealous of their states; they were fearful of his greatness before they injured him; and now they have become much more so, having done him this injury. There does not seem to be any way he can forgive the injury, and they can let go of their fear; nor, as a result, does there seem to be any way for one to yield to the other regarding the expedition against Bologna and the duchy of Urbino.[72]

But, if they could find a common enemy, Niccolò argued, they could still be reconciled.[73] There were, however, only two possible states against which they could turn: Florence and Venice. While the conspirators were likely to favour the latter, Niccolò believed that Cesare would prefer the former. It would not be an easy target, but it was richer. Besides, Louis XII would be more willing to consent to the restoration of the Medici than to the loss of Venice's friend-ship.

Although Biagio Buonaccorsi was soon to express his disapproval of judgements like these, the *Dieci* agreed with Niccolò's analysis.[74] Even before reading his report, they had come to the conclusion that they had dragged their heels for long enough. And having finally received confirmation that Louis XII would not object to an alliance between Florence and Cesare Borgia, they could see no reason to tarry.[75] But it was already too late. On 26 October, Paolo Orsini arrived in Imola.[76] He had come in disguise, 'dressed as a courier'. His purpose was, however, unmistakable. As Niccolò reported, Cardinal Ludovico Borgia had given himself to the Orsini as a hostage while negotiations took place, and the other conspirators had already halted their attacks on Cesare's possessions in expecta-tion of an agreement. Deeply alarmed, Niccolò went to speak with the duke as soon as he heard the news. Given that Bolognese troops had been spotted near Florence's northern border, he was afraid the city's fate might already have been sealed.[77]

Over the next few days, there was a flurry of activity. Everywhere Niccolò looked, there were people dashing back and forth, passing messages to and fro, and whispering with one another in corners.

No one was busier than Paolo Orsini. After several rounds of discussions with Cesare, he rode to Bologna to confer with Giovanni Bentivoglio, and then rushed back to Imola.[78] Terms were evidently being hammered out. By 29 October, it was openly said that a treaty had been concluded. Niccolò was not able to learn the particulars, but it was rumoured that 'all the old compacts that this Lord [i.e. Cesare] had previously had with Messer Giovanni, and the Vitelli, and the Orsini [were to be] renewed; and that the duke [would] be reinstated in Urbino, and that the duke of Ferrara [would stand] surety for both parties.'[79] There did not seem to be any room for doubt. Florence's hopes for an alliance appeared to have been shattered. After dinner that night, Cesare's treasurer, Alessandro Spannocchi, even took some pleasure in telling Niccolò that the *Dieci* 'had had the time to ally with the Duke, [but] that it had now passed.'[80]

Cesare had reassured Niccolò that the Florentines were not in any danger. 'I shall never conclude anything against your Signoria,' the duke told him. 'I will not allow a single hair on their heads to be harmed.'[81] In the circumstances, however, it was cold comfort. There was no telling whether he was being truthful or not.

*

By the morning of 1 November, news of Cesare's reconciliation with the *condottieri* had not yet reached Florence. It was therefore in a spirit of cheer that Piero Soderini was installed as *gonfaloniere a vita* on the stepped platform on front of the Palazzo della Signoria. As Landucci reported, the whole city seemed to be in the piazza.[82] Young and old, rich and poor alike were there, all jostling for a better view. There was a sense of excitement and possibility in the air. '[E]veryone seemed to have hopes of living in comfort.'

When Niccolò's despatches arrived that afternoon, the mood in the *palazzo* quickly changed. Fear and confusion took hold. The *Dieci* could hardly believe what had happened.[83] They had heard that Camerino, in Le Marche, had just rebelled against Cesare; it seemed incredible that the duke had reached an agreement with conspirators who were still intent on doing him harm. They did not know what to do. As Marcello di Virgilio Adriani related, they could only await further developments. Until the *Dieci* decided how best to proceed, Niccolò was to keep his eyes and ears open.

It was a nerve-wracking time. Although Niccolò did his best to pick up information, he found himself cold-shouldered by the court. He saw almost nothing of Cesare. Apart from a few key figures, no one was allowed to speak to the duke. Cesare did not even come out of his antechamber 'until eleven or twelve at night'.[84] Everything was shrouded in mystery – and Florence's fate seemed to hang in the balance.

Niccolò began to despair. He was already in trouble back home.[85] Although he had sent the *Dieci* regular reports, his couriers had been slow in delivering them. The *Dieci* had been furious. They had accused him of neglecting his duties, and had rebuked him severely for withholding crucial information.[86] He had, of course, protested,[87] but it had been to no avail. Even Biagio had upbraided him.[88] Now that Cesare was keeping him at a distance, he was worried the *Dieci* would construe the lack of news as wilful idleness on his part, and reprimand him even more harshly.[89] His career was in jeopardy. What was worse, he was also short of money. After much effort, Biagio and Niccolò Valori had managed to rustle up thirty ducats for him, but there was some doubt whether he would get it safely.[90] They were wary of sending coins by courier when the political situation was so dangerous. It was all too much for Niccolò's nerves. On 2 or 3 November, he asked Piero Soderini to be relieved – albeit in vain.[91]

But just when things seemed darkest, a ray of hope broke through the clouds. Although negotiations between Cesare and the *condottieri* were already well advanced, Niccolò learned that the treaty had not yet been definitely settled. Shortly after Paolo Orsini had left Imola to circulate a draft among the conspirators, Cesare had suddenly asked for an additional clause – concerning the *stato* and honour of France – to be included in the text. Whether or not the *condottieri* would agree to this was unclear. But to Niccolò, it looked as if Cesare might simply be stalling. This would hardly have been surprising. As they stood, the terms were, after all, injurious to him. Although he stood to regain the duchy of Urbino, he would effectively be at the *condottieri*'s mercy. But he also knew that he was not yet strong enough to fight them openly. By stringing the negotiations out like this, he would buy himself the time he needed to raise more troops without risking anything. Regardless of whether the conspirators accepted his new clause or not, he would be in a better position to face them on the battlefield when they eventually made up their minds – and, best of all, he would be sure of catching them off their guard. As Niccolò was told by one of Cesare's bodyguards, who had previously served as Florence's master of the horse, the duke had been driven more by a desire for 'revenge against those who had imperilled his state' than by 'a desire for or inclination towards peace' all along.[92]

While the conspirators deliberated, Cesare's preparations continued apace. As Niccolò later recalled, the duke 'kept increasing the number of his cavalry' the whole time, 'and in order that his preparations might not be evident he scattered his soldiers through all the towns of Romagna.'[93] He also raised the possibility that he might still be prepared to enter into an alliance with Florence. On 7 November, he summoned Niccolò to test the waters. 'Secretary,' he began, 'I ask you to tell me whether these *signori* of yours will go further with me in its friendship.'[94] When Niccolò replied that the *Dieci* were certainly interested in forging closer relations, the duke then asked him about Florence's military dispositions.[95] He was particularly anxious to know whether the city would employ him as its *capitano*. Niccolò had to admit that, at present, the *Dieci* were happy with the marquis of Mantua. But this might still change, especially given that they had sent Francesco Soderini to France to seek further instructions from Louis XII.[96]

Niccolò must have realized that, after his recent run-ins with the *Dieci*, there was always a chance that they might not agree with his assessment of Cesare's intentions. After taking his leave of the duke, he therefore took the precaution of talking to a friend at court.[97] This person – who is likely to have been one of Cesare's secretaries – confirmed all of his suspicions. Like Niccolò, he believed that Florence should not let the opportunity to conclude an alliance slip through its fingers again. Even before Urbino had rebelled, he argued, Cesare had been thinking about how best to secure his position in the long term. He knew the pope was nearing the end of his life, and was hence anxious to establish some other foundation on which his power could rest. He could always count on the strength of his own armies and on the support of the king of France, but – as the conspiracy had revealed – these were not enough. He therefore wanted 'to make friends of his neighbours, and of those who would be obliged by necessity to defend him in order to defend themselves' – namely, Florence, Bologna, Mantua and Ferrara.[98] He had already secured an agreement with Ferrara, and was in discussions with Mantua, too.[99] He was also hopeful that he would be able to detach the Bolognese from the rebels and conclude a separate treaty with them. This only left the Florentines. As things stood, Cesare regarded them as friends; and since they were also allies of France, he would never do anything to harm them. But, if they were to become his allies, the Florentines would see 'what a difference there is between his friendship and that of others'. Of course, Niccolò's friend knew that it was tempting to keep relations flexible. But it was worth bearing in mind that, if the Florentines needed help in future, Cesare would not be bound to come to their aid. And since Louis XII was currently their only ally, it was probably unwise to shy away from a formal compact. In any case, the advantages were clear. If the Florentines employed Cesare as their *capitano*, he would help them recover Pisa and would keep them safe from Vitellozzo. They knew this already. Indeed, they had proposed a similar quid pro quo only a few weeks earlier. There was, of course, the matter of the treaty. But this should not cause them any alarm. As Niccolò had already guessed, it was just a ruse. Cesare was only trying to buy some time, and, if possible, to separate some of the plotters from the others. As such, the Florentines would be well advised to press ahead with an agreement of their own.

*

Progress was hampered by another breakdown in communications. Although Niccolò was sending regular reports back to Florence, nothing was getting through.[100] On 11 November, Marcello di Virgilio Adriani wrote to complain that the *Dieci* had not received anything from him for more than a week, and that without further information, they could not do anything.[101] This, in turn, caused difficulties for Niccolò, for, without further instructions from the *Dieci*, he was unable to continue discussions. He was in danger of losing the initiative. The day before Adriani wrote, news had arrived that all the conspirators except Giovanni Bentivoglio had consented to Cesare's new clause. Although some of them were uncomfortable about the implications of the treaty – especially for Guidobaldo da Montefeltro – Niccolò felt sure that, with a little more persuasion, they could be induced to ratify it before long.[102] As Cesare had hoped, Bentivoglio – who had some differences with the Orsini – was even willing to negotiate a separate agreement, and was interested in having Florence stand surety for the two sides. At the same time,

Cesare was busily continuing with his preparations, recruiting ever
more soldiers and soliciting support from the conspirators' enemies
everywhere. He was also pressing Niccolò for an answer – and warned
Florence against delaying too long.

When Niccolò's letters eventually arrived in Florence, however,
the hoped-for decision failed to materialize. Although Piero Soderini
wrote to assure him that the 'entire city' was 'well disposed toward
His Excellency [i.e. Cesare]', and would soon be ready 'to do more
than talk',[103] the *Dieci* were not so enthusiastic. They could, of course,
see the attraction of an alliance with the duke, but they wanted to
know more about what he was offering before they agreed to
anything. While the arrangement Cesare had sketched out did seem
to resemble the terms they had suggested a few weeks earlier, a lot
had changed since then, and they were worried that what he had in
mind would benefit him more than them. In particular, they wanted
Niccolò to find out exactly what he planned to do with Vitellozzo
and what he would do to help them recover Pisa.[104] They also wanted
to know whether he would be willing to enter into an alliance *without*
being employed as their *capitano*, since such an arrangement would
certainly be beyond their means.

Niccolò's heart must have sunk when he read the *Dieci*'s instructions. He could see they were making a mistake, but he knew that
nothing he said would make any difference. As long as he was in
Imola, however, he was duty bound to obey. On 19 November,
therefore, he went to see Cesare.[105] After briefly reiterating the
Florentines' affection for the duke, he explained the *Dieci*'s position
as delicately as he could. Cesare listened patiently, without the least
sign of displeasure. But, when Niccolò had finished speaking, his
manner changed. 'See now,' he growled,

> this doesn't amount to anything ... what we have to decide now is
> whether we shall have a general friendship, or a special [alliance]. If
> we are to have a general friendship, then there is nothing more for us
> to say, since I have always told you ... that I shall not permit a single
> hair on your Signoria['s head] to be touched, that I shall do everything
> I can to please them, and that their citizens shall enjoy every conveni-
> ence in my territories. But if we are to have a special alliance, without
> a contract [of employment], then there is nothing for me to do, because
> they reject the first principles [of such an alliance].[106]

This was, of course, the sort of response that Niccolò expected. But, good public servant that he was, he tried to change Cesare's mind all the same.[107] He pointed out that relationships built on friendship alone could not be relied upon, but strong and lasting alliances were often contracted without one party employing the other. The duke was, however, unmovable. No *condotta*, no treaty. That was all there was to it. He would not even answer any questions about how he proposed to deal with Pisa and Vitellozzo. The only faintly encouraging thing he said was that his contempt for the conspirators was undimmed.

There was nothing more to say. Taking his leave, Niccolò trudged back to his lodgings. There, he sank into a deep depression. He was in an invidious position. Not so very long ago, he had set out from Florence with such high hopes. He had been confident that here, at last, was a chance to cover himself in diplomatic glory. But now, through no fault of his own, the mission was in tatters. It was obvious to him that the *Dieci*'s hesitancy was destroying any hope of an alliance. Unless they changed their minds soon, there was no telling what might happen. Only one thing seemed sure: Niccolò's own career was in danger. Thanks to his couriers' ineptitude, his reputation had already been damaged; if there were any further setbacks, he would really get it in the neck – regardless of whether it was his fault or not. Although Piero Soderini spoke up for him at public meetings, it did little to stem the tide of criticism.[108] Things were so bad that he feared he might not even be reconfirmed as second chancellor when he came up for re-election.[109] He once again asked to be recalled. At least if he were in Florence, he reasoned, he would be able to lobby potential supporters. But, once again, his request was denied. Piero Soderini promised him that, when the time came, he would be relieved. For the moment, however, he was to remain in Imola.[110]

Niccolò had no choice but to stay put. Having nothing further to discuss with Cesare, he saw no point in seeking another audience. He could only watch glumly as events unfolded around him.[111] As far as he could see, Cesare's ploy appeared to be working admirably. Negotiations with Giovanni Bentivoglio were proceeding faster than anyone had expected and, on 2 December, an agreement was signed.[112] This stipulated that Bentivoglio would provide Cesare with a hundred men-at-arms and a hundred mounted crossbowmen for one year, at his own expense.[113] In return, the pope would confirm Bentivoglio as *signore* of Bologna, thus assuring his safety. The agreement forced the other conspirators' hands. Even before Cesare's pact with Bentivoglio had been signed, Paolo Orsini had been striving to persuade them to set their misgivings aside. As was only to be expected, Vitellozzo had tried to dig his heels in, but, in the end, he, too, had agreed. On 27 November, Orsini had returned to Imola with news that *all* of the confederates were now ready to sign a treaty.[114] Two days later, Orsini even ordered his men to march on Urbino and retake the city in Cesare's name. It would not be long before Cesare was master of the Romagna once again. Only three questions remained. What would he do with all the troops he had assembled?[115] How would he take vengeance on the conspirators, now that they had been lulled into a false sense of security? And why on earth did the *Dieci* not do a deal with him while they still could?[116]

*

On 10 December, Niccolò reported that Cesare had finally decided to leave Imola. Setting out early that morning, he had led his army south-eastwards along the ancient Via Aemiliana through heavy snow, bound for Cesena.[117] Niccolò was reluctant to follow. The last thing he wanted to do was traipse across country in the freezing cold. He was not feeling well, and he was desperately short of money.[118] But there was no avoiding it. Pulling on his warmest clothes, he mounted his horse and took to the road on the morning of 11 December.[119] Perhaps to avoid paying inflated prices, he did not take exactly the same route as Cesare, even though it was the most direct. At first, he made good progress. Before nightfall, he had arrived at the Florentine subject-town of Castrocaro, around ten kilometres south-west of Forlì. Since he had got to know the town well during his mission to Caterina Sforza three years earlier, he decided to spend the night. But, when morning came, he decided not to go out into the cold again just yet. He spent the whole day there, warming himself by the fire. After a good rest, however, he was ready to set out again. Covering the remaining twenty-four kilometres in reasonable time, he finally arrived in Cesena on the evening of 13 December.

At any other time, Cesena would have presented a charming aspect. Lying halfway between the Adriatic Sea and the foothills of the Apennines, it enjoyed a more temperate climate than many of the Romagna's other cities. Not far from the gently flowing waters of the River Savio stood a fine fortress that is even now regarded as a masterpiece of military architecture, and a little further to the north-east could be found the magnificent Biblioteca Maletestiana, the first public library in the whole of Europe. When Niccolò first set foot within its walls, however, it was in a pitiable state. Cesare's troops were everywhere. Although the majority were encamped outside, there were still a great many who were billeted in houses inside. Pounded by countless feet, the streets had turned into swamps. Worst of all, there was almost nothing to eat. Although Cesare had purchased 30,000 bushels of wheat from the Venetians to alleviate the pressure on the local area, every last grain had already been consumed.[120] 'Even the stones' had been eaten, Niccolò observed.[121] So grave was the shortage of food, indeed, that, before long, Cesare had commandeered all the private granaries in the city and summoned his governor-general, Ramiro de Lorqua, to explain what had become of the usual stores.[122]

On presenting himself at court, Niccolò found no more comfort than in the city's streets. It appeared that Cesare was planning to remain in Cesena for a few more days to conduct talks with representatives of Vitellozzo and the Orsini, who were still campaigning in the duchy of Urbino.[123] Now that he had re-employed them, they wanted to know where they were to attack next. Oliverotto da Fermo presented Cesare with a choice of two possibilities on the *condottieri*'s behalf. 'If [the duke] wished to carry on a campaign in Tuscany,' Oliverotto said, 'they were ready for it'; if not, they would be willing to lay siege to Sinigaglia (Senigallia) instead.[124] Cesare 'replied that he would not begin war in Tuscany because the Florentines were his friends', but he would certainly be very happy if they went to Sinigaglia. Some ninety kilometres further down the Adriatic coast, it was, in many senses, a natural target. Though too small to rival Ancona, its port was still large enough to be respectable. It also boasted a redoubtable castle, which had recently been improved. But its real importance – at least from Cesare's point of view – lay in the fact that it was then governed by Giovanna da Montefeltro, the widow of Giovanni della Rovere and the sister of Guidobaldo da

Montefeltro, the deposed duke of Urbino. As long as she held the town, it would provide Guidobaldo with both a base from which to mount military operations against Cesare, and a secure line of supplies throughout a campaign. If Cesare's *condottieri* could capture it, he would be much more secure.

Niccolò was, of course, relieved that Cesare had refused to attack Florence. But his decision to attack Sinigaglia instead did not seem particularly encouraging. If Cesare was embarking on such bold ventures with his *condottieri* now, there was no guarantee that he would not turn on them in future. There was always the possibility that he might have decided to forgive the *condittieri's* transgressions, after all – in which case, he might not be so willing to entertain an alliance with the Florentines, even if the *Dieci* changed their minds about engaging him as its *capitano*, which, given that they had recently despatched Giovanni Vittorio Soderini to negotiate with the pope in Rome, seemed unlikely. It looked like there could be a long and unrewarding diplomatic road ahead.[125]

For Niccolò, this was the last straw. The day after his arrival, he wrote to the *Dieci* begging to be relieved for the third – and last – time.[126] His tone was more plaintive, more sorrowful than ever before. He had now lost faith in his ability to carry out his duties. All his confidence had gone. 'There is no advantage to my staying here any longer,' he wrote. He had come to realize that he was not – and never would be – up to the job. If the *Dieci* wanted to conclude an agreement with the duke, he argued, they should send someone else – 'a man with more discretion, more reputation than I have, who understands the world better'. Giovanni Vittorio Soderini would be ideal. He had all the right qualities: he was from a wealthy patrician family, he was well educated and he was the *gonfaloniere's* brother, to boot. He was just the sort of person Cesare would listen to. What was more, he would be of more use in Cesena than in Rome. After all, the *Dieci* would need Cesare's support far more than the pope's, if they were to negotiate a settlement. Of course, Giovanni would have to come with a clear sense of purpose, which would require the *Dieci* to make up their minds, but, if this could be assured, 'without doubt, things would be settled, and soon.'[127]

Poor Niccolò was so desperate that he even sought the aid of some powerful friends. He wrote countless letters to Piero Soderini, most of which have not survived. He also wrote to Alamanno Salviati, the *éminence grise* of Florentine politics, entreating him to intercede with the *gonfaloniere* on his behalf. Neither of them could help him, though. As Alamanno pointed out, there was no chance of him being relieved just yet.[128] But he need not worry too much. Although Biagio Buonaccorsi had told Niccolò that he was being called a 'cold fish' by everyone in the chancellery,[129] Alamanno did not believe his absence would hurt his chances of being reconfirmed.[130] He would still have a job when he eventually returned. Besides, he wouldn't have to wait much longer. Piero Soderini promised him that, as soon as he found out what Cesare's intentions were, he would be allowed to return home.[131] In the meantime, he would just have to make the best of things – even if his wife continued to berate him because she was short of money.[132]

*

But just as Niccolò's spirits were at their lowest ebb, things suddenly changed. Quite unexpectedly, three of the companies of French lances that had been with Cesare left Cesena and returned to Lombardy.[133] The court was stunned. No one could understand why Cesare appeared to be deliberately weakening his own forces. As Niccolò told the *Dieci* a few days later, 'this Lord is very secretive . . . I do not believe that what he is going to do is known to anybody but himself . . . he does not tell [even his chief secretaries] anything except when he orders it, and he orders it [only] when necessity compels and when it is to be done, not otherwise . . .'[134]

The departure of the French lances did not, however, slow down the conquest of Sinigaglia. The *condottieri* were keeping up the pressure regardless, and, the same day, Cesare was joined by 1,000 Swiss and 600 Romagnol infantrymen from the Val di Lamone.[135] So overwhelming were the forces massed against Giovanna da Montefeltro that her brother-in-law, Cardinal Giuliano della Rovere, advised her to surrender before more blood was shed.[136] It was only a matter of time before the town was taken.

Early on the morning of 26 December, before the sun had risen, Cesare set out for Fano, where he intended to await news of Sinigaglia's fall.[137] When dawn broke, however, the citizens of Cesena were horrified to discover the body of their governor-general, Ramiro de Lorqua, lying 'in two pieces in the *piazza*'.[138] His body was dressed in fine clothes and his hands were still wearing gloves, but his head had been set on a pike nearby. It was a grisly sight. As Niccolò reported, however, the reason for his death was unclear. Even before Cesare had summoned him to answer for the misappropriation of grain in Cesena, Ramiro had been repeatedly warned about his corrupt practices and abuse of justice. Perhaps the duke was simply unable to tolerate his behaviour any longer. Or perhaps Cesare had needed to execute him to appease the hunger-stricken people of Cesena. There was, however, another – more sinister – possibility. As well as his other crimes, Ramiro was rumoured to have concluded a secret treaty with Vitellozzo and the Orsini against Cesare.[139] Had the duke learned of this, he could be forgiven for having had his treacherous governor-general beheaded. But, if this was the case, then Cesare must also be preparing to exact a similar revenge on his *condottieri*, as well – the same *condottieri* who were then about to conquer Sinigaglia on his behalf. It was all very puzzling.

On 29 December, Cesare arrived in Fano. The following day, he received word from Vitellozzo that Sinigaglia had capitulated, but the citadel was still holding out, because its commander, Andrea Doria, wished to surrender it to the duke in person.[140] Vitellozzo therefore urged him to come. Clearly delighted, Cesare agreed to meet them outside the city gates on the morrow. Almost as an afterthought, he also asked Vitellozzo to prepare quarters for his soldiers in the town. This would, of course, require the *condottieri*'s own troops to be dispersed, but Cesare was sure this would not be a problem. He looked forward to celebrating their shared triumph together soon.

That night, however, Cesare revealed his true intentions to eight of his most loyal followers.[141] The time for vengeance had finally come, he told them. '[A]s soon as Vitellozzo, Paolo Orsini, the duke of Gravina, and Oliverotto [da Fermo] . . . arrived for the meeting,' the next day, Cesare ordered, they were to be 'brought to his quarters and arrested.'[142] Cesare also gave instructions that his entire army – comprising some 2,000 cavalrymen and 10,000 infantry – were to assemble on the banks of the River Metauro, just outside Fano, at daybreak, and wait for him there.

Neither Vitellozzo nor his confederates suspected anything. The next morning, they were waiting for Cesare outside the gates.[143] As agreed, their soldiers had been withdrawn to towns ten or eleven kilometres away. In Sinigaglia, there remained only a token force. Having been assured everything was in order, Cesare approached, pausing at the bridge over the Savio to allow his infantry to enter the town ahead of him. Vitellozzo, Paolo Orsini and the others stepped forward to greet him, and then accompanied him to his lodgings. The moment they crossed the threshold, Cesare sprang his trap. Before any of them knew what was happening, they were taken captive and dragged off to prison. At the same time, their troops were being disarmed, still in their camps. Cesare's plan had gone off without a hitch.

Niccolò had come to Sinigaglia expecting to see a triumphal entry. The events of the morning had stunned him. As Cesare's troops sacked Sinigaglia later that evening, he scribbled a hasty note to the *Dieci*, but he scarcely knew what to make of all that he had witnessed.[144] His head was spinning. In the early hours of the morning, however, Cesare summoned him to an audience.[145] The duke greeted him with a broad smile, and 'with the best spirit in the world rejoiced . . . in this success.' Somewhat to Niccolò's surprise, he then spoke most affectionately of Florence, repeating all the reasons why he desired its friendship, and asking once again for an alliance. To this end, he asked Niccolò to write to the *Dieci* with three requests. The first was that they rejoice with him at the destruction of his enemies; the second was that they immediately send their cavalry to Borgo Sansepolcro, whence they might march on Città di Castello or Perugia together with Cesare's troops, as necessary; and the third was that they should immediately have Guidobaldo da Montefeltro – who was then at Città di Castello – arrested, in case he should try to take refuge in Florentine territory.

Niccolò knew that these were not so much requests as commands. He could see that Cesare was now in a position to dictate terms to the Florentines, should he so wish. If the *Dieci* did what he said, however, he might still be willing to reach an equitable agreement. Everyone Niccolò spoke to confirmed this. He therefore urged the *Dieci* to set aside their reservations – and quickly. This could be their last chance.

Cesare was in no mood to mess around. A few hours before summoning Niccolò, he had ordered that Vitellozzo and Oliverotto da Fermo be put to death. As one of his officers related on 2 January, it was his intention to do the same with Paolo Orsini and the duke of Gravina.[146] Once the pope had arrested Cardinal Giovanni Battista Orsini, Archbishop Rinaldo di Jacopo Orsini of Florence and some others of their party, he would bring them to Rome, have them condemned as traitors against the Church, and execute them. Thereafter, Cesare planned to reduce the states of the Church to obedience, and firmly establish himself in his duchy of Romagna as the papacy's most loyal defender. First, however, he meant to confiscate the Vitelli's lands and deal with Pandolfo Petrucci.

The *Dieci* did not need telling again. When they learned of all that had happened, they immediately wrote to Niccolò, asking him to pass on their congratulations to the duke, and to assure him of their immediate compliance with his 'requests'.[147] They despatched Jacopo Salviati to act as a special ambassador, with a view to negotiating a formal alliance as Cesare wished. Given that the duke had already set off for Siena, they expected Salviati to be with him in a matter of days.[148]

*

While he waited for Salviati to arrive, Niccolò resigned himself to following in Cesare's train as the duke marched across the Apennines, settling old scores en route. Giampaolo Baglioni – the rebellious *signore* of Perugia – just slipped through his grasp, having fled the city a few days before. But others were not so lucky. On 13 January, Cesare reached Castello della Pieve, where Paolo Orsini and the duke of Gravina were being held prisoner; five days later, he had them strangled.[149] Satisfied that justice had been done, he then took to the road once more, determined to revenge himself on Pandolfo Petrucci without further delay.

Along the way, Niccolò did his best to keep the duke apprised of the situation in Florence. It was not easy, though. Coupled with the bad weather, their rapid progress hampered communications more than usual. Many of Niccolò's despatches went missing, and the *Dieci*'s instructions were often out of date by the time they reached him.[150] He was always having to excuse himself for failing to carry out their orders, or repeat news he had already imparted. He could scarcely conceal his frustration. In the circumstances, he hoped the *Dieci* might show him a little more understanding.[151] But they wouldn't stop complaining. His patience was beginning to snap.

Rather testily, he reminded them that, if it hadn't been for their mistakes over recent months, the situation might have been very different. Had they not shilly-shallied so much, there wouldn't have been any need for him to traipse through the cold while Cesare exacted such brutal revenge on his former *condottieri*.

As Cesare's forces were setting out for Pienza, however, Jacopo Salviati finally caught up with them.[152] Niccolò's relief was palpable. After so many months of heartache and so much bloodshed, he would finally be able to go home. Once he had briefed Salviati on his recent discussions with the duke, he mounted his horse and rode off as quickly as he could, stopping only to scribble the *Dieci* a brief note at Castiglion Aretino.[153] He may not have wreathed himself in glory, but at least he was in one piece.

11

The Wind Changes

(January–December 1503)

On 23 January, Niccolò arrived back in Florence. Striding through the doors of the family *casa*, he would have been greeted by Marietta's smiling face. For all her complaints, she had missed him dearly. Since Biagio Buonaccorsi had come to tell her that Niccolò was on his way back to Tuscany two weeks earlier, she had been counting the days until his homecoming; and now that he was back, she could not contain her joy.[1] She could forgive all the privations his absence had caused. All that mattered was that they were together again at last, and, once he had gone to see their infant daughter, Primerana, they were free to rekindle the fires of their love once more. It was no surprise that, within a few weeks, Marietta was pregnant again.[2]

Later that afternoon, or perhaps the next morning, Niccolò returned to work at the Palazzo della Signoria. He could have been forgiven for being a little apprehensive. After all, he had been reprimanded by the *Dieci* several times over the past few weeks and his relations with his colleagues had been badly strained. But when he arrived in the chancellery, he was pleasantly surprised. His position was more secure than he had supposed. Despite the perceived failure of his mission to Cesare Borgia, he had been reconfirmed as second chancellor without any difficulty and continued to enjoy the esteem of Florence's leading men. Thanks in no small part to Niccolò Valori, who loved him 'like a brother',[3] the *gonfaloniere a vita*, Piero Soderini, had come to value his judgement highly,[4] while Alamanno Salviati, whom Guicciardini later described as the 'true leader' of the Signoria, declared himself to be Niccolò's 'devoted friend'.[5] He could also count on the respect of Luca degli Albizzi, Lorenzo Lenzi and his kinsman,

Niccolò di Alessandro Machiavelli – all of whom continued to play a prominent part in Florentine politics.[6]

Over the following weeks, Niccolò's advice was eagerly sought. However harshly he may have been chastised in the past, even his critics had to admit that Florence needed his expertise. After Niccolò had left Cesare's camp, the duke had advanced to within striking distance of Siena. As he had told Niccolò earlier in the month, he intended to expel Pandolfo Petrucci and assure himself of Siena's loyalty.[7] Ideally, he would have liked to take the city for himself, but, since it was under Louis XII's protection, this was clearly not possible.[8] His only option was to force the Sienese to eject Petrucci themselves. On 27 January, he therefore informed them that, if Petrucci had not been expelled within twenty-four hours, he would order his soldiers to lay waste to the *contado* and to regard every inhabitant as an enemy.[9] As soon as Petrucci was out of the city, Cesare would then send fifty men-at-arms to capture him on the road. But Petrucci was too fleet of foot. Slipping out of Siena under cover of darkness, he managed to escape to Pisa, being 'helped . . . by the providential intervention of the Florentine commissary at Cascina, who barred the way to Borgia's soldiers, having received no orders from Florence to let them pass.'[10] This was, of course, frustrating, but it was not a serious setback. Believing that Siena had been cowed, Cesare felt secure enough to answer his father's call to return to Rome.[11]

The Florentines were, at first, jubilant.[12] Although they would have preferred Petrucci to have been captured and killed, they had still been freed from a perennially hostile neighbour. And, now there was a new *reggimento* in Siena, it might even be possible to negotiate for the return of Montepulciano. Optimistically, the *Dieci* sent Jacopo Salviati to see if the Sienese would be amenable. It was, however, in vain. Even though Petrucci had gone, Siena's government was still dominated by his supporters.[13] Under no circumstances would it discuss Montepulciano, let alone consider handing it back.

The Florentines were not too discouraged, though. The Sienese government might be full of bluster just now, but soon enough, they would change their tune. The current regime could not survive for long. Either the Sienese would have to acclaim Cesare as their *signore*, or they would have to ask the king of France to restore Pandolfo Petrucci. The former was, of course, unpalatable, but the latter entailed considerable risk. Although Louis XII seemed willing to agree, Siena would still need help defending itself against Cesare. With this in mind, the French ambassador, Francesco da Narni, was despatched to invite the Florentines to form an anti-Borgia league with Siena, Bologna and Lucca.[14] This would, of course, have required Florence to accept Petrucci's return, but the suggestion was not as absurd as it might first have seemed. Not only were the Sienese now prepared to sweeten the deal by offering to return Montepulciano, but the king of France's involvement also held out the prospect of a wider shift in Italy's balance of power. If Louis XII was prepared to reinstate Petrucci, then he was evidently prepared to disregard Cesare's wishes, too. This might well be an indication that he was no longer willing to tolerate the duke's dominance of Central Italy and was on the brink of breaking with the Borgias for good. If so, an alliance with Siena, Bologna and Lucca might not be such a bad idea, after all.

The Florentines were certainly tempted. But it seemed almost too good to be true. Even if the Sienese were sincere, it was hard to believe that Louis would risk conflict with the Borgias when the situation in the kingdom of Naples was grave. Since the previous autumn, the French and Aragonese had been at war.[15] At first, Louis' viceroy, Louis d'Armagnac, duc de Nemours, had enjoyed the upper hand, but, by the New Year, his fortunes had taken a turn for the worse. With more reinforcements arriving from Spain every day, it was only a matter of time before the Aragonese commander, Gonzalo Fernández de Córdoba, mounted a major counteroffensive. As far as the Florentines could see, the last thing Louis needed was to push the Borgias into the arms of the Spanish just then. It would be foolish to read too much into his support for Petrucci. After all, he hadn't actually done anything to help Petrucci beyond issuing a few rather bland statements. Even if he were to put Petrucci back in power, what guarantee was there that he'd come to Florence's aid if Cesare turned against it? It seemed better to think things over a little more carefully before taking the Sienese offer any further.

While they were weighing their options, however, the Borgias seemed to be doing their best to alienate the king of France. Determined to stamp out any remaining opposition, Alexander VI ordered Cesare to lay siege to Giovanni Giordano Orsini in the fortified town of Ceri, heedless of the protection Louis XII had accorded him.[16] When the king's ambassador came to protest the very next day, the pope greeted him with 'ill humour', and then refused to grant him any further audiences.[17] As the siege intensified and additional towns belonging to the Orsini fell into the duke's hands, relations deteriorated further. Although Louis was not ready to put his wider interests at risk just yet, he did not intend to let Cesare get away with flouting his authority. He had to remind the Borgias who was in charge, and Siena offered him the perfect means of doing so. On 11 March, the Venetian ambassador to Rome, Antonio Giustinian, reported that the king had informed the Florentines of his intention of returning Pandolfo Petrucci to power in Siena, regardless of what Cesare might think, and had asked the Signoria to give him every aid.[18] The following day, Petrucci was already said to be in Poggibonsi, just twenty-three kilometres away.[19] Within three weeks, he would re-enter the city in triumph.[20]

Whether the Florentines decided to join the Sienese or not, Piero Soderini could see they urgently needed to start raising more money. Louis XII had already asked them for funds to help cover the costs of the war in the kingdom of Naples (usually referred to simply as the *Regno*),[21] and common sense demanded that they began making preparations in the event that hostilities should break out in Tuscany, as well. But Soderini was only too well aware of how difficult it would be to persuade the *popolani*-dominated councils to grant any new taxes. On the very day that Niccolò had returned to Florence, they had rejected one such request.[22] Soderini was worried they might do the same again. To avoid such an eventuality, he asked Niccolò to draft a speech for him to deliver when he presented his new proposals.[23] This was not the sort of task Niccolò was used to handling. But Soderini, who had written to him about the parlous state of Florence's finances the previous year,[24] seems to have believed that his familiarity with both Cesare Borgia and the French court would allow him to write authoritatively about the dangers facing the city.

Soderini's confidence was not misplaced. The result – the *Parole da dirle sopra la provisione del danaio* ('Words to be spoken on the provision of money') – was by far the most insightful and compelling piece that Niccolò had yet written.[25] It began with a simple enough observation:

> All the cities that have at any time been ruled by an absolute prince, by aristocrats, or by the people, as this one is, have had for their protection [armed] forces combined with prudence; because [the

latter] is not enough on its own, and [the former] either do not lead
to anything, or, if they do lead to something, do not maintain it.
These two things, then, are the lifeblood of all the governments
[*signorie*] that ever have been or ever will be in the world. Hence any
man who has considered the change of kingdoms [and] the ruin of
provinces and of cities has not seen them caused by anything other
than the want of arms or good sense.[26]

If the members of Florence's governing councils granted this, Niccolò
reasoned, they must want their city to have both of these things,
and would do their utmost to maintain them, if they were already
there, or to provide them, if not. How, then, was it that Florence
did not have the armed forces it needed? Its custodians were clearly
not lacking in good sense. Only the year before, they had established
the office of *gonfaloniere a vita* to deal with the crisis that followed
Arezzo's rebellion. So why were they refusing to increase military
expenditure? Did they really think the city was safe? If they answered,
'What need do we have for [armed] forces? We are under the king's
protection; our enemies are destroyed; Valentino has no reason to
attack us,' they were deluding themselves.[27] As long as the Florentines
were unarmed, Niccolò argued, Louis XII would not pay any heed
to his treaty obligations unless it suited him to do so; Venice would
seize any opportunity it got to recover the 180,000 ducats it believed
it was owed; and the Borgias would break any agreement they made
as soon as they got the chance. Even Florence's own territories could
not be counted upon.[28] Recent experience had shown that, unless
subject towns were certain of being defended against attack or
punished for their transgressions, they were liable to revolt.[29] Only
if Florence had a strong army of its own could it command the
loyalty of its allies and the obedience of its subjects.

Even if this were true, however, the Florentine assemblies might
argue that the danger was still quite remote. But this would be
equally misguided. As Niccolò pointed out, they had already seen
where such thinking led. Back in September 1500, when Cesare had
first threatened the city, penny-pinching councils had refused to
grant new taxes on the grounds that 'the danger did not seem
immediate'.[30] After the fall of Faenza in April 1501, however, they
had regretted being so blithely parsimonious. As Cesare's forces
advanced, they had rushed to approve new taxes. But they had been

too late. Within days, they had 'learned that Firenzuola had been reached by the enemy army.'[31] The city had been in confusion. Unable to put up any defence, they had seen their houses burned, their goods plundered, their subjects killed or taken prisoner, their women violated, and their property laid waste. '[T]hose who, six months before, had not wanted to pay twenty ducats [in additional taxes], had two hundred taken from them, and they had to pay the twenty just the same.'[32] It was no different now. However distant the threat might seem, the councils should remember that Cesare could be in Tuscany in eight days, and the Venetians in two. They should also recall that Louis XII was preoccupied with the *Regno* and could not be counted upon. But, above all, they should keep in mind that Florence was weak, and Fortune fickle. If they wished to preserve their liberty, therefore, they *must* approve new taxes – and quickly.

The *Parole da dirle sopra la provisione del danaio* is usually said to have been written at some point between 25 and 31 March.[33] A close inspection of the communal records, however, suggests it may have been composed towards the beginning of this period, and delivered by Piero Soderini on 28 March. On this date, the *gonfaloniere* is said to have addressed a meeting of the colleges, the *Dieci*, the Council of Eighty and 200 leading citizens 'with great effect'.[34] Since his exact words were not recorded, it is, of course, impossible to be absolutely certain that he was using Niccolò's text. But the brief summary that the scribe set down does seem to follow the thrust of his argument closely enough for it to be a reasonable supposition. Even if Soderini delivered the *Parole* at a later gathering, however, the effect of Niccolò's words was still the same. On 1 April, the new taxes were granted. Soon afterwards, military preparations began in earnest.

*

Following the success of the *Parole da dirle sopra la provisione del danaio*, Niccolò's relationship with Piero Soderini grew steadily closer. Now confident that the younger man could be depended upon, Soderini began turning to him for advice on a more regular basis. And as international tensions worsened over the coming weeks, he would also rely on Niccolò to help him steer Florence through the diplomatic storms that lay ahead.

In the first week of April, after a ferocious bombardment, the fortress of Ceri surrendered to Cesare.[35] Only the castle of Bracciano now remained in Giovanni Giordano Orsini's hands. But before the Borgias could deliver the coup de grâce, Louis XII decided to bring them to heel. Fortunately, he was now in a position to do so. Not only had he settled a long-running dispute with the Swiss in Lombardy,[36] but he had also opened negotiations for a settlement of the Neapolitan conflict with Archduke Philip of Austria, the son of the Emperor Maximilian I and – as the husband of Joanna of Castile – the son-in-law of Ferdinand of Aragon.[37] So encouraged was he by these developments that he put his preparations for a new expedition on hold, and even called back troops he had previously ordered to embark for Genoa. With peace apparently within his grasp, Louis was able to force the Borgias to adhere to an agreement which placed Giovanni Giordano's lands in his own hands.[38]

The pope was, however, furious. In his eyes, the king had no right to meddle in the affairs of the Papal States, least of all when it placed limits on the Borgias' territorial ambitions.

Although the moment had not yet come, conflict was inevitable. This being so, Alexander immediately began trying to form an anti-French league; and within days, he had already reached out to Ferdinand of Aragon (whose complicity in the peace negotiations he doubted), Pandolfo Petrucci and Giovanni Bentivoglio of Bologna.[39] But he was shrewd enough to realize that, if the League was to succeed, he would need Florence's support, as well. It would not be easy to talk them into joining, though. He knew that, if he was too brazen about his purpose, they would turn him down flat. He therefore tried to tempt them with the offer of an accord which ostensibly had nothing to do with Louis XII. This stipulated that the border between Florence and the new duchy of Romagna would be formally recognized, and a force of 1,100 men-at-arms would be raised to guarantee their mutual safety. Of these, 600 would be provided by the pope. The remaining 500 were to come from Florence.

The Florentines were not so easily fooled. While the *Dieci* brought the pope's offer before a *pratica* on 10 April, his sleight of hand was quickly spotted.[40] Everyone could see that, if they accepted, they would risk angering Louis XII – and might even be drawn into a war against France. Yet they believed they could still turn it to their advantage. Shrewdly, they asked the pope to insert two additional articles into the treaty, stipulating that any existing agreements with

Louis XII would be respected and that the king's consent would have to be obtained before any military action could be undertaken. If the pope did so, they would gladly sign. Of course, they did not seriously expect Alexander to agree. From his perspective, the second clause in particular would have defeated the whole point of the treaty. But by opening negotiations with the pope, Florence could strengthen its hand with Siena. As the *pratica* knew only too well, Pandolfo Petrucci was an unscrupulous rogue. Even though he had been restored to power by Louis XII, he was seriously thinking about joining the Borgias' anti-French league. If he did so, he would almost certainly renege on his promise to return Montepulciano. But, if he believed that Florence might ally with Alexander VI *and* Louis XII, he would have no choice but to hand it over.

Sure enough, the pope rejected the Florentines' request. While he was happy enough to allow existing agreements with Louis XII to stand, he could not allow the king to have a veto over military action. On 23 April, therefore, Piero Soderini summoned another *pratica* to advise him on how best to respond.[41] Opinions were somewhat divided. While some wondered whether the pope's concession might be enough, most still believed the treaty could not be signed unless he accepted *both* clauses. This was, however, even more unlikely than it had been two weeks ago. Only a few days earlier, French forces had been crushed at Seminara, in Calabria and, despite Louis XII's hopes for a negotiated peace, the balance of the war in the *Regno* seemed to be shifting in Aragon's favour.[42] But the *pratica* saw no need to abandon the negotiations just yet. The longer Florence strung them out, the more likely it was that Petrucci would hand Montepulciano over.

On 26 April, the *Dieci* ordered Niccolò to ride to Siena as quickly as possible.[43] The moment he got there, he was to seek an audience with 'the magnificent Pandolfo'. After the usual courtesies had been made, he was to inform Petrucci of the pope's offer and to assure him of Florence's intention of standing by its alliance with the king of France. No mention was to be made of Montepulciano, but the implication would be clear. Once Niccolò had made sure that Petrucci understood the situation, he was then to communicate the same message to the Sienese *balìa* and the French ambassador as well. If all went well, Florence might soon have something to celebrate.

*

The Sienese, however, demurred.[44] They could not believe that the Borgias would allow the Florentines to equivocate for much longer. As such, they did not want to be rushed into making a decision they might regret later. The Florentines were bitterly disappointed. But, within a matter of days, even they had to admit that the Sienese had been right.

On 1 May, Alexander VI revealed in public consistory that Louis XII's peace negotiations were a sham.[45] Letters had arrived from Barcelona indicating that Philip of Austria had been acting without his father-in-law's knowledge all along. It was highly unlikely that Ferdinand the Catholic would ratify any agreement, especially after Gonzalo's victory, a couple of days earlier, at the Battle of Cerignola (at which Louis d'Armagnac himself had perished).[46] Even Louis' own commanders now regarded peace as an impossibility. It seemed obvious that, soon enough, Louis would have to mount the expedition he had put on hold only a few months before. And, when he did, conflict with the Borgias would be inevitable.[47] As such, the Borgias began accelerating their preparations. Although Cesare was formally bound to support the king of France's campaign in the *Regno*, he made one excuse after another to explain why he could not go.[48] Meanwhile, Alexander was doing his best to strong-arm various states into joining his anti-French league, albeit with little success. Venice, admittedly, seemed to be favourably disposed towards him,[49] as did Maximilian I, who was still hoping to receive an imperial coronation in Rome;[50] but Bologna seemed uncertain, and Siena was still leaning towards Louis.[51] This left Florence. As the Sienese had suspected, the pope wanted a decision – and he was prepared to use force to get the answer he wanted.

Alexander's timing could not have been better. On the same day as his revelation in the consistory, the Florentines had decided to renew their assault on Pisa.[52] At the time, it had seemed like a reasonable proposition. The Pisans were, after all, badly provisioned and poorly led, and, if the king of France did venture into Italy, it could only help the Florentine cause. But no sooner had Florence's troops been despatched to lay waste to the Pisan *contado* than they realized they had left themselves exposed to the resurgent Borgia menace. On 10 May, Niccolò warned Antonio Giacomini, the commissary in charge of the Pisan campaign, that an attack might be imminent, perhaps from the direction of Piombino. 'In light of the news we have received from Rome,' he wrote, 'we have thought it necessary to send a commissary to Campiglia, with responsibility for finding out what is happening in Piombino, so that he can advise us what would be needed to block the path of certain cavalry-men, and whether it could be done easily.'[53] The Borgias certainly did not waste any time. Not only did they begin building up their forces in Piombino, as Niccolò had anticipated, but they also started sending support to the Pisans, too.[54] On 14 May, Niccolò informed Bernardo de' Medici, the commissary in Livorno, that 500 Swiss mercenaries were on their way to Pisa, and that Don Michele had brought Cesare's treasure to Piombino, with a view to hiring more soldiers.[55]

The Florentines were deeply alarmed. But they refused to be bullied into joining the Borgias' anti-French league. Instead, they appealed to Louis XII for help. The king agreed to let them retain the services of Jacques de Seuilly, 'a captain renowned in war'.[56] According to the terms of the contract, de Seuilly would command a force of one hundred lances, half of which would be paid for by Louis and half by the Florentines. It was not the largest body of men, but the *condotta* was nevertheless a clear sign that, despite setbacks in the *Regno*, the king was prepared to stand by his allies. This stopped the Borgias in their tracks. Even if war with France was on the horizon, they did not want to risk open confrontation just yet – least of all if it entailed losing Florence for good.

Greatly relieved, the Florentines were able to resume their campaign against Pisa. With de Seuilly's help, they soon succeeded in recapturing not only Vicopisano, but also Librafatta and the castle of Verrucola.[57] The Pisans' increasingly desperate raids were easily defeated, and a good deal of booty was captured into the bargain. As Landucci noted, 'things looked bad for them, poor things!'[58] Every day, the Florentines seemed to get stronger.

But the Borgias had not given up hope. Though they had failed to bully Florence into an alliance, they believed they might still be able to tempt the Republic into joining them. While the Florentines had been busy fighting the Pisans, things had not been going well for Louis XII's forces in the kingdom of Naples. Following his victory at the Battle of Cerignola, Gonzalo had rapidly continued his advance westwards, forcing the French to abandon the strong-holds of Capua and Aversa.[59] On 16 May, he had entered Naples.

A small band of diehards had tried desperately to hold him back from the Castel dell'Ovo and the Castel Nuovo, but supplies were already running short and, with no prospect of reinforcements, it was only a matter of time before they would be overrun. As the Venetian ambassador in Rome observed, their situation was desperate.[60] This was all to the Borgias' good. Although Louis XII was already preparing an army, the kingdom of Naples seemed as good as lost. This being so, the Borgias thought it might be possible to persuade the Florentines to change their minds. While the French alliance had seemed advantageous a few days ago, it could easily turn out to be a liability in a couple of weeks' time. Surely it would be better to join the winning side before their final victory?

It was a persuasive argument. The Borgias were, however, reluctant to trust to reason alone. They wanted to ensure the Florentines got the message – and, as they knew from long experience, bribery was usually the simplest way of making people see what was best for them. With a republic, this could be problematic, but, now that Piero Soderini headed the government, things were a little easier. If the Borgias could persuade him that his family would benefit from an agreement with Rome, he might talk the priors and the *Dieci* round. All that was needed was a suitable incentive. Evidently, Piero could not be bribed openly, but his brother, Francesco, could receive ecclesiastical preferment without difficulty. On 31 May, therefore, Alexander VI created him a cardinal.[61]

The red hat was, of course, not unwelcome, either to the Soderini or to the Florentines. As Landucci reported, news of Francesco's elevation was greeted with enthusiasm. A great *festa* was held, complete with bonfires and fireworks.[62] But it was not enough to sway either the *gonfaloniere* or the rest of his government. At about the same time as the new cardinal arrived in Florence to say his first Mass in Santa Maria del Fiore, news arrived that Louis XII's expedition was already underway.[63] A force under La Trémoille was expected to enter Tuscany within a matter of weeks. This being so, it would be the height of folly for the Florentines even to think about switching sides. Indeed, the news only strengthened their commitment to France. They severed all ties with the Borgias and prepared themselves for war. Not used to being denied, Cesare and his father would almost certainly want to hit Florence as quickly as possible, so as to be ready to meet Louis' army when it arrived and perhaps also to strong-arm others into joining their proposed anti-French alliance, too.

*

Niccolò was wracked with anxiety. Having devoted the greater part of his career to averting just such a conflict, it seemed as if all his worst fears had suddenly been realized. Perhaps better than anyone else, he knew what a formidable adversary Cesare could be – and what cruelty the duke was capable of. But he doubted whether his fellow Florentines really knew what they were up against. The more Niccolò thought about what might lie ahead, the more he found himself going back over the bloody events at Sinigaglia earlier that year, and wondering if history might be about to repeat itself.

As so often in moments of tension, he took up his pen and started writing. Before the first week of August had passed, he had completed the *Descrizione del modo tenuto dal duca Valentino nell'ammazzare Vitellozzo Vitelli, Oliverotto da Fermo, il signor Pagolo e il duca di Gravina Orsini* ('Description of the method used by Duke Valentino in killing Vitellozzo Vitelli, Oliverotto da Fermo, the Lord Paolo and the Duke of Gravina Orsini').[64] What function this text was intended to serve is, admittedly, somewhat obscure. Given its narrative style, it was evidently not meant to be either an official report or a public speech. It was, perhaps, an early experiment in historical writing. As Robert Black has noted, there are certainly 'features characteristic of literary history in the text, including geographical digressions . . . and touches of human interest'.[65] But there is no way of being completely sure. There is, however, no mistaking the warning it was meant to convey. Rather than write an objective, dispassionate account of *il bellissimo inganno*, Niccolò crafted a narrative that showed just how cruel and cunning Cesare could be.

As was only to be expected, Niccolò drew on the despatches he had written at the time. But he did not stick to them rigidly. To his mind, it was more important to get his message across than it was to adhere to the facts. He had no compunction about embroidering his text with dramatic flourishes, glossing over inconvenient details and changing the order of events where it served his purpose. The effect is certainly arresting. Cesare's diabolical brilliance is on full display. Although he is initially taken aback by the *condottieri's* rebellion, he quickly regains his composure and begins drawing the conspirators into a trap.[66] Whereas, in reality, he was plagued with self-doubt and hesitant to the point of inaction, Niccolò instead portrays him as calm, confident and assured. His enemies' advance almost seems to be part of his plan. Indeed, he is credited with *tricking* them into believing they could take what was his. '[B]eing a very skilful dissembler,' he draws them into negotiations, and even agrees to a peace treaty that is more to their benefit than his – by design, rather than by compulsion.[67] Having thus lulled them into a false sense of security, he sends them off to besiege Sinigaglia, having evidently selected it as the site of his vengeance in advance. His confidence is overpowering. Before leaving to take the surrender, he even dismisses his French troops – an obvious distortion that makes him seem far more commanding than he was at the time, not to mention far less reliant on the king of France.[68] By the time he reaches Sinigaglia, it seems that his plan can hardly fail. At this point, however, Niccolò was compelled to indulge in a rather more surprising flight of imaginative fancy. Realizing that Cesare's might would hardly be shown to good effect if the conspirators were portrayed as too trusting and guileless, he decided to make them seem wary, even suspicious. Rather than inviting Cesare to Sinigaglia, as had actually been the case, they have to be persuaded to join him there with 'crafty and prudent words'.[69] As befitted Vitellozzo's status as the de facto leader of the rebellion, he was made to appear even more cautious. Although he had, in reality, enthusiastically reaffirmed his loyalty to the duke, he is said to be 'very reluctant'. But he, too, is brought round. It is not that he believes Cesare's assurances. Quite the reverse. Unlike his co-conspirators, he seems to sense that Cesare is plotting something terrible. He is, however, unable to resist. He knows that Cesare is now too strong – and too brilliant – to be denied. The effect of this is to transform him into an unexpectedly tragic figure.[70] Outmatched and outmanoeuvred, he bows to the inevitable. Taking his 'final leave' of his troops, he goes to meet Cesare outside the gates, 'unarmed, in a cloak lined with green, very disconsolate, as though he was aware of his coming death'.[71] There is no escape. Though Cesare greets the conspirators with 'a pleasant face', he has them arrested the moment they enter his chamber. Later that night, he decides to have Vitellozzo and Oliverotto da Fermo strangled. But their final words are nevertheless 'unworthy of their past lives'. Crushed, Vitellozzo begs for forgiveness, while Oliverotto tries to blame Vitelli 'for any injuries done to the duke'.[72]

The implication was plain. Even when Cesare seemed to be at a disadvantage, Niccolò warned, he was still stronger and more resourceful than anyone expected. It would be difficult for anyone to stand up to him – let alone the Florentines. After all, if Vitellozzo Vitelli had been defeated after nearly bringing Florence to its knees, Florence itself would surely stand little chance a mere eight months later, even with Louis XII's support. As far as Niccolò could see, its only hope was to be realistic. It must keep Cesare's cunning in mind at all times, and it must take care never to underestimate him.

*

This was sage advice. But, if Florence was to resist the Borgias effectively, it would also have to resolve a pressing strategic matter. All agreed that an attack was imminent. Wanting to strike before Louis' army arrived, Cesare had already begun making preparations. He had instructed every household in the Romagna to furnish him with one man-at-arms; he had hired more arquebusiers, purchased more cannon, devised a new uniform for his troops and ordered a steel helmet and breastplate for every man serving under his banner.[73] But from which direction would he come?

Piombino seemed the most obvious choice. After all, there were already troops and stores in place. But, while it was a good position from which to launch occasional raids, it was hardly the ideal place from which to mount a large campaign. Cesare would either have to transport the rest of his forces by ship, or else march along the coastal road, through Sienese territory. Pisa was another possibility. He already had mercenaries fighting there under some of his most trusted commanders. But it suffered from the same drawbacks as Piombino. And, what was worse, the Florentines still had the bulk of their army encamped outside the city. This left the Valdichiana. As Vitellozzo Vitelli and the Orsini had proved the previous year, it was the soft underbelly of the Florentine state. Although Arezzo and its neighbours had been brought back under Florence's control, they were liable to revolt at the earliest opportunity. Were Cesare to approach, they would surely flock to his banner. And, if they did, the road to Florence would be open. The question for the Florentines was: how could the danger be averted?

Industrious as ever, Niccolò tackled this problem in *Del modo di trattare i popoli della Valdichiana ribellati* ('On the manner of dealing with the rebellious people of the Valdichiana').[74] Written at some point in late July or early August, this incomplete discourse may have been conceived as a report for the *Dieci*, or perhaps even as a speech to be read by a prominent figure at a public meeting.[75] Its argument was, admittedly, not entirely novel. There are, for example, several parallels to be drawn with the *Discorso sopra le cose di Pisa*. But it was nevertheless quite different in style from any of Niccolò's previous works. For the first time, he argued that Florence's actions should be guided by the lessons of Roman history.

Drawing on Livy's *Ab urbe condita* (8.13–14), he pointed out that Rome had confronted a similar situation after the First Samnite War (343–341 BC). Although the cities of Latium had either surrendered or been reconquered, they kept rebelling and putting Rome in peril. When the Senate met to decide how best to remedy the situation, Lucius Furius Camillus observed that only two courses of action were possible. Either Rome could punish Latium harshly, making 'a solitude out of a land that [had] often provided [it] with an army of auxiliaries', or it could forgive the Latins their past offences and win their loyalty with a show of generosity.[76] The senators praised Camillus's speech, but nevertheless noted that, since not all the rebellious cities were alike, it would be unwise to pass a general resolution. Instead, each should be dealt with separately. Some were treated mercifully. The Lanuvini were granted Roman citizenship, and the holy objects that had been taken during the war were returned to them. The Aricini, the Nomentani and the Pedani also received citizenship on the same terms, while the people of Tusculum were allowed to keep their privileges. But others were treated more severely. The Veliterni – who had rebelled several times, despite having long held Roman citizenship – had their city destroyed and their citizens sent to live in Rome.[77] A similar fate befell Antium. To be sure that the city would no longer pose a threat, the Romans despatched new settlers to dilute the rebellious element, confiscated all of the Antiates' ships and prohibited the building of any more.[78]

For Niccolò, the key point was that, although the Romans had judged each city on its own terms, they had clung to these two extremes: either winning the rebels' loyalty through benefits (*benefizi*), or treating them so cruelly that Rome need never fear them again. They had regarded any middle way as harmful – and with good cause. The Florentines would be wise to follow this example in dealing with the rebellious peoples of the Valdichiana. To be sure, they had already done so in some regards. Like the Romans, they had decided to judge each town according to its own offences, rather than adopt a more general approach. In many cases, they had also tried to foster fidelity with kindness. Just as the Romans had granted citizenship to the Lanuvini, Arcini, Nomentani and Pedani, so the Florentines had allowed Cortona, Castiglione and Borgo Sansepolcro to keep their communal assemblies. But the Florentines had failed to apply the Romans' policy consistently – particularly insofar as Arezzo was concerned. Until now, they had tried to strike a balance between severity and generosity, and, sure enough, no good had come of it. As Niccolò observed:

> One cannot say that it has benefitted [the Aretines] to have been made to come to Florence every day, to have been stripped of their honours, to have been forced to sell their possessions, to have been disparaged publicly, [or] to have had soldiers quartered in their homes. Yet nor can one claim that we have made ourselves safe by leaving their walls in place, by allowing five-sixths of their citizens to continue living there, by not sending in new settlers to keep them down, and by not ruling them in such a way that, in any future war, we will avoid spending more money in Arezzo than we will in fighting the enemy.[79]

The Florentines had already seen how draining Arezzo's instability could be in times of crisis. In 1498, and again in 1502, they had been obliged to divert much-needed resources to maintaining order – and, even then, had been unable to keep it in check. Neither comforted by kindness nor cowed by cruelty, it had rebelled time and again.[80] Now that Cesare Borgia was on the brink of launching an all-out attack, Florence could not afford to indulge in such folly any longer. If it wanted to hold onto Arezzo, it would have to choose whether to be generous or severe. Niccolò's own preference is clear. Since Arezzo had behaved much like Velletri and Antium, it followed that it should receive the same treatment.[81] Its walls should be destroyed, it citizens resettled and new colonists installed in their place. There was, admittedly, not much time. But this was the only way Florence could be sure that Arezzo would not be a threat to its security.

Sadly, the *Dieci* did not agree. They evidently felt that it would be foolhardy to punish Arezzo at just that moment, particularly given how close Cesare Borgia was rumoured to be. They suspected that, far from frightening the Aretines into submission, any reprisals might actually spark off a revolt. It seemed far wiser simply to take troops away from the Pisan campaign and send them to reinforce the garrison at Arezzo.[82] There, the *Dieci* reasoned, they would be able to quell any dissent and guard against an attack at the same time – at least until the French arrived. When that might be, however, was anyone's guess. Partly because of the Venetians' ambivalence, Louis' army was moving painfully slowly, and there were even rumours that Louis de La Trémoille had been taken ill.[83] If the French got their act together, all would be well. But, if they continued to tarry, Arezzo might be harder to hold. It was worth taking the gamble.

*

For once, the Florentines' luck was in. Five days after the redeployment, La Trémoille's vanguard reached Pescia[84] – much sooner than the Borgias had expected. Cesare had not yet had time to complete his preparations, much less mount an offensive against Florence. Given that his father had failed to assemble a viable anti-French alliance in time, he dared not take the field against Louis XII. His moment had passed. To allay any suspicions, Cesare meekly agreed to leave Rome to join Louis' army on its way south, just as a good vassal should.[85]

Yet, if the Florentines had hoped the king would allow some of his troops to remain in Tuscany, they were disappointed. So severely had the French position in the *Regno* deteriorated that Louis could not spare them even a single detachment. Indeed, he even had to ask *them* for help, requesting supplies for the main body of his army, which was still a little way behind. Unable to refuse, the Signoria grudgingly sent Niccolò to Fivizzano to make the necessary arrangements.[86]

A few days later, the Florentines watched with a heavy heart as the last French troops left Tuscany. Though Cesare had been thwarted on this occasion, it seemed highly likely that, as soon as he could excuse himself from Louis' service, he would pick up where he had left off. Without the French around to deter him, Florence would be a sitting duck.

*

But Fortune smiled on Florence once again. On 10 August, Cesare and his father were invited to dine at Cardinal Adriano Castelli da Corneto's villa in Suburra, on the southern slopes of the Esquiline Hill. It promised to be a sumptuous affair. Having once served as the pope's personal secretary, Cardinal Castelli had become immensely wealthy, and was well known for entertaining on a lavish scale. What transpired at that meal, however, remains unclear. According to an anonymous story later inserted into the famous diaries of Marino Sanudo the Younger, Castelli had discovered that the Borgias were planning to poison him so they could take his fortune for themselves, and cunningly bribed the person they had hired for the task to give the poisoned wine to Cesare and Alexander instead.[87] The historian and diplomat Francesco Guicciardini thought this perfectly plausible.[88] The Borgias were, after all, known to be fond of poisoning. But there is nevertheless room for doubt. As Burchard and Giustinian testify, malaria was rife in Rome just then.[89] Earlier that month, it had carried off the pope's kinsman, Cardinal Juan de Borja Lanzol de Romaní, and it is not impossible that, in the heat of Castelli's vineyard, the mosquitos struck again.[90] Whatever the truth of the matter, the effects of the meal were certainly devastating. On the morning of 12 August, the pope fell ill. The following day, Cesare, too, took to his bed with a fever.[91] At first, the son appeared to be in greater peril than his father.[92] After a violent bout of vomiting, Cesare was said to have run so high a temperature that he had himself plunged into a vat of iced water. The pope, by contrast, appeared to recover slightly. Having been bled, he even felt well enough to play cards with some of his household.[93] But soon their positions were reversed. Still young and vigorous, Cesare was able to muster enough strength to put on a brave face for a few visitors. Alexander, however, had a serious relapse. By 17 August, his condition had become grave. His fever grew worse and he began slipping in and out of consciousness.[94] The following evening, he received the last rites; and as darkness fell, his heart gave out.[95] The pope was dead.

Though still wracked by his sickness, Cesare immediately recognized the danger in which he now stood. With Alexander's death, the foundation of his power had been swept away. He knew it would not be long before his enemies tried to revenge themselves on him. His most pressing need was for money, which would be essential to any stratagem. Without shedding so much as a tear for his father, he therefore ordered his most trusted lieutenant, Michele de Corella, to take possession of the papal treasure. This Michele did in his usual, uncompromising fashion. After forcing Cardinal Jaime de Casanova to hand over the keys at knifepoint, he carried off caskets of gold and jewels worth almost 300,000 ducats, leaving the servants to ransack the rest of the papal apartments.[96] This done, Cesare then applied himself to the upcoming conclave. If he could somehow arrange for the election of a sympathetic candidate, he might still be able to save his territories in the Romagna. That he still commanded a large army was certainly to his advantage. But his mind was not what it once was. Still confined to his bed and afflicted by violent headaches, his thoughts had begun to wander. He could no longer find his way through the tangle of Church politics with the same ease. Despite his earlier hostility, he first approached the French, promising to support Cardinal d'Amboise in return for their protection. But no sooner had he reached an understanding with them than he entered into a similar agreement with the Aragonese.[97] Such clumsy duplicity was quickly discovered, and cardinals from both sides began clamouring for him to leave Rome. This, of course, was the last thing he wanted. Though he might have sacrificed any chance of influencing the election, he still hoped to bully the winner into confirming him as *gonfaloniere* of the Church, and his best chance of doing this was to remain in the city. Ignoring the cardinals' requests, he therefore fortified the Vatican and sent for reinforcements from the Romagna. But, with the French army only a short distance away, he must have realized that he could not hold out for long. Over the next few days, he desperately tried to negotiate some sort of settlement with the cardinals. He even offered to go quietly if his position was guaranteed. It was, however, in vain. Under pressure, he eventually bowed to the inevitable. On 2 September, he left Rome for Nepi.[98]

The Florentines were overjoyed.[99] All their worries seemed to have been dispelled. The danger of an attack had receded, the Valdichiana was now more secure, the Pisans had been dealt a heavy blow, and they were receiving reports that Cesare's forces were already being driven back on all fronts.[100] By the end of August, Jacopo IV d'Appiano had recaptured Piombino.[101] Soon afterwards, Giampaolo Baglioni re-entered Perugia.[102] A little further north, Guidobaldo da Montefeltro was meeting with similar success. Supplied with troops by the Venetians, he first seized the fortress of San Leo, and then massacred the Borgias' garrison in Urbino a few days later.[103]

The future looked bright – especially given how the papal election seemed to be shaping up. Although the conclave had not yet convened, Georges d'Amboise was already the front runner. The Florentines could not suppress a thrill of anticipation. Were d'Amboise to win, as seemed likely, they would be all but invulnerable. With excitement running high, the *Dieci* decided to send Niccolò to Rome to observe the conclave.[104]

*

For reasons that remain unclear, however, Niccolò's departure was postponed.[105] It must have irritated him to have to stay in Florence, but it was probably just as well that he did. Although Georges d'Amboise was hailed as the new pope by crowds of admiring Romans when he entered the city, his plans soon came unstuck. An outsider, Cardinal Francesco Todeschini Piccolomini, was elected with a handsome majority. Somewhat taken aback, he announced that he would take the name Pius III, in honour of his uncle.[106]

Pius had seemed like a reasonable compromise. After all, he had looked harmless enough. More of a scholar than a politician, he had never been particularly ambitious. Though he had been entrusted with a number of important offices over the years, he had not actively sought advancement and had shown no sign of aspiring to the papacy. Just recently, he had been more preoccupied with the library he was building in his native Siena than with garnering votes in the conclave.[107] Indeed, the papal office actually seemed to unnerve him. As one of the six cardinals appointed to draw up a programme for the reform of the Church six years before, he had expressed his opposition to the concentration of power in the pope's hands and had put forward proposals that would have allowed the cardinals to share in the government of the Church to a greater extent.[108]

Best of all, Pius was far from robust. At the age of sixty-four, his health was already failing. Indeed, he was so sick that he had even missed his own election. With any luck, he would last just long enough for the French to work out a deal with the Aragonese, and then make way for d'Amboise to ascend the throne in his place.

When Pius held his first public audience on 25 September, he initially seemed to justify d'Amboise's hopes.[109] True to his reformist tendencies, he announced his intention to overhaul the papal finances and establish a council of cardinals. But he then shocked everyone by suddenly reconfirming Cesare Borgia as *gonfaloniere* of the Church. Why he did so is unclear. As the Venetian ambassador later recalled, he had harboured a strong dislike of Cesare when he was a cardinal.[110] Most likely, Pius felt he had no choice. Although Cesare's power in the Romagna was crumbling, he was still a force to be reckoned with. After all, he had several thousand troops under arms and now that the French army had left for the kingdom of Naples, he could easily use them against the pope if he so wished.[111] For someone as timid as Pius, it might have seemed wise to give him what he wanted, at least for now. If he destroyed himself later – as the pope suspected he might[112] – then so much the better; but, for the moment, it was probably best not to provoke him.

On 2 October, Cesare re-entered Rome.[113] Though he was still gravely ill – so much so that he had to be carried in a litter – he revelled in his triumph. According to the Venetian ambassador, he 'spoke arrogantly, and said that he would soon take possession of all that was his once again.'[114] But, if he was expecting to receive a hero's welcome, he was cruelly deceived. Appalled by his reappointment, his enemies in the city had already begun to mobilize against him.[115] Taking the lead were the Orsini. They had suffered too greatly at his hands to allow him to return unpunished. Heedless of the pope's protection, they were determined to take their revenge. The violence of their assaults took Cesare by surprise. Having brought only a handful of troops with him, he was unable to mount a proper defence.[116] He tried to leave the city and find his way back to Nepi, where he could gather more men, but his way was blocked. Without anywhere else to turn, he took refuge in the Castel Sant'Angelo and was immediately besieged.[117]

Cesare's fate was, for the moment, in the pope's hands. The pontiff could, if he so wished, negotiate for his release with the Orsini (who were showing signs of tiring) and allow him to bring the Romagna to heel. But Pius could equally well leave the duke where he was and try to rid himself of his troublesome *gonfaloniere* by coming to an arrangement with the French or the Aragonese. For a brief moment, it seemed as if the pope might be inclining towards the latter. He was certainly under pressure to do so. On 10 October, the *condottiere* Bartolomeo d'Alviano had arrived in Rome to demand the duke's expulsion, with the blessing of the Aragonese, and, though many cardinals bemoaned the damage he was wreaking in the Papal States, it was hard for the pope to ignore him.[118]

Before Pius could take a decision, however, his physical weakness caught up with him. The excitement of his coronation had taken more of a toll on his health than anyone had realized. On the evening of 13 October, he was suddenly overcome by a cold sweat.[119] Taking to his bed, his chill turned to a high fever and he began vomiting uncontrollably. His condition quickly deteriorated.[120] By 16 October, his doctors were fearing for his life.[121] On 17 October, he confessed his sins and received extreme unction.[122] The following night, he died. He had reigned for less than a month.

For the second time, Cesare had been deprived of his position. His enemies were, of course, jubilant. They knew that, without papal support, he was dangerously vulnerable. Apart from Louis XII, he had no allies to speak of, and even Louis was of doubtful utility. After all, the French army was far too preoccupied with the affairs of the *Regno* to offer any meaningful assistance. Scenting blood, an assortment of dispossessed *signori* pressed their attack on the Romagna. Tormented by his impotence, Cesare's first instinct was to break out of the Castel Sant'Angelo. If he could somehow smash his way through the Orsini's lines, he might still be able to marshal his forces in time to defend his remaining territories.[123] But he nevertheless restrained himself. Sick though he may still have been, he recognized that his best hope of recouping his losses was actually to remain in Rome. As long as he remained in the city, he reasoned, he could influence the forthcoming conclave. If he was able to engineer the election of a sympathetic candidate, he would surely have no difficulty in being reappointed as *gonfaloniere* of the Church. And, from there on, he told himself, the reconquest of the Romagna would be straightforward.

This turned out to be much easier than Cesare had expected. Even before Pius III's body was cold, Giuliano della Rovere – the nephew of Pope Sixtus IV – had emerged as the favourite to succeed him.[124] He had made a strong showing at the previous conclave, and had been working hard to increase his support over the past weeks. Putting his wealth to good use, he purchased the votes of some cardinals with lavish gifts. Others were talked round by powerful allies. So successful was this strategy that he even gained the backing of Georges d'Amboise, who had been forced to acknowledge that his own chances were now slim. Only Ascanio Sforza seemed set to challenge, and his standing was low at best. But della Rovere was determined not to leave anything to chance. Mindful that Cesare still controlled the votes of at least eleven cardinals, none of whom had supported him in August, he therefore set out to woo the captive duke.[125] In return for all eleven votes, he offered to confirm Cesare as 'captain-general and *gonfaloniere* of the Church', and to give him every assistance 'in his own states'.[126] Scarcely able to believe his luck, Cesare agreed. He could hardly wait for the conclave to begin.

*

As soon as the Florentines learned of Pius III's death, Niccolò was instructed to go to Rome 'with all speed'.[127] Equipped with letters of introduction to a number of leading cardinals, he was to assist the four newly elected ambassadors and report on preparations for the conclave as often as he could. He was also ordered to stay in close contact with his old friend, Cardinal Francesco Soderini, whom the *Dieci* regarded as their man in the Sacred College, and who might need his help negotiating with colleagues.

It was an exciting mission. But Niccolò's feelings about it were nevertheless rather mixed. As far as his family was concerned, it could hardly have come at a worse time. Marietta was heavily pregnant and was expected to give birth in the next few weeks. She would not have wanted him gadding off to Rome when she needed him at home. He was probably keen to be there for her, too. After all, he'd missed the birth of their first child, the previous year, and did not want to do the same again. But the opportunity was simply too great to miss. Over the past few weeks, Niccolò had been preoccupied with the affairs of the Romagna, writing letters on the *Dieci*'s behalf to commissaries and *podestà* in an effort to secure 'the return of the old *signori* of Faenza and Forlì, or to keep those lands loyal to Cesare Borgia, or at least under the Church's submission' – anything, in short, to stop a Venetian advance.[128] He knew how much was at stake. In Rome, he would be able to shape Florentine policy actively; what was more, he would also have the chance to make the acquaintance of the leading cardinals – including the man who would be pope. A lot of faith was being placed in him: if he carried out his task successfully, he would strengthen his diplomatic credentials immeasurably.

*

When the conclave convened on 31 October, there was little doubt about what the result would be. A few hours after the doors had been sealed, Niccolò began writing a letter informing the *Dieci* that Giuliano della Rovere was expected to win 90 per cent of the vote.[129] But the result was even more decisive than he anticipated. Before Niccolò had finished writing, one of della Rovere's servants came rushing into his chamber with news that the cardinal had been elected unanimously at the first ballot. It had been the shortest conclave in history. Indeed, to Niccolò, everything about it seemed 'extraordinary'.[130]

Taking the name Julius II, the new pope was greeted with adulation. Though undoubtedly still tired from the previous night, Niccolò was amazed by the outpouring of enthusiasm from all sides.[131] When he reflected on how many promises the pontiff must have made to win so much support, he couldn't help feeling that it was almost 'miraculous'. Everyone seemed to be expecting wonderful things of Julius. Even the bitterest of enemies seemed to join in welcoming his election – each believing they were going to receive his special favour. The kings of France and Spain had already sent words of goodwill, and, before long, 'even the barons of the opposite faction had given [the pope] their support', as well.

The Florentines in Rome were especially excited. Before the conclave had begun, it had been rumoured that, if della Rovere were elected, Florence could hope for 'great advantages'.[132] In fact, he had already made 'greater promises than customary'. Now that he was pope, expectations were raised even higher. On the afternoon of 1

November, Cardinal Soderini told Niccolò that 'there had not been a pope for many years from whom our city had reason to hope for so much as from [Julius II].'[133] Provided the priors 'knew how to adapt themselves to the times,' they would soon be rewarded with his favour. People were already saying the archbishop of Florence was going to be made a cardinal. Perhaps there was even a chance Julius would further their cause in the Romagna, too.

But Niccolò had his doubts. Like the Ferrarese ambassador, Beltrando de' Costabili, he had realized there was no way Julius could keep all of the promises he had made – particularly given that some of them were openly contradictory.[134] Soon enough, the pope would have to decide what course he was going to take, and who he was going to disappoint. For the moment, however, there was no telling what he would do.

Even Cesare began to get nervous. Although Julius had arranged for him to leave the Castel Sant'Angelo and take up residence in the Apostolic Palace, the duke could not be sure that he would keep his word.[135] Pacing up and down the lavishly decorated apartments now known as the 'Raphael Rooms', Cesare debated what he should do.[136] Now that he was free to leave, he was, of course, desperate to mount a campaign in the Romagna as soon as possible. As Niccolò noted in a letter to the *Dieci* on 4 November, the duke could take a boat to Genoa, where he still had many friends, and then go to raise troops in Lombardy. From there, he could descend upon the Romagna from the north. But this was risky. Julius could always renege on his promises after he left. It seemed safer to stay in Rome until Julius's coronation. This way, Cesare could at least be sure of being made *gonfaloniere* of the Church. It would, of course, be frustrating to sit idly by while the Romagna descended further into chaos, but it would be worth the wait. Once he had been reconfirmed, he told himself, he would be in a much stronger position to recover his lost territories.

But some had already begun to suspect that the pontiff might be stringing Cesare along. As Niccolò observed, Julius had little to gain from keeping his promise. Indeed, he could only lose. After all, he could not give Cesare command of the papal armies without making himself dependent on the duke and sacrificing any chance he had of bringing the Patrimony of Saint Peter back under his own control. But, as long as Cesare still had some hope of being made *gonfaloniere* of the Church, the pope would have the upper hand. If Julius wanted, he could keep the duke hanging on in Rome for weeks, if not months. This would give him time not only to deal with the Papal States, but also to find a way of getting rid of Cesare for good.[137]

Niccolò did not think this unlikely. As he reminded the *Dieci*, the pope's 'natural hatred' of Cesare was 'notorious'.[138] Julius had endured 'ten years of exile' in France under Alexander VI. It was only natural for him to want revenge. And, if he was clever enough to get himself elected pope, he was clever enough to lure Cesare to his doom with empty promises.

*

But there was no way of being sure. Whatever Julius had in mind, he was keeping it to himself.[139] The uncertainty made the Florentines uneasy. Until Cesare's fate was settled, they would not be able to make any firm plans – least of all about the Romagna. Indeed, it would be enough just to know what Julius thought about them. Anxious to find out more, Niccolò immediately requested an audience with the pope.[140] He could not, of course, ask Julius outright, but, by extending the hand of friendship, he might elicit some clues. After kneeling at the foot of the throne, he therefore began by telling Julius how delighted the Florentines were with his election. With a winning smile, he assured the pope that they would do all they could to 'enhance the glory and prosperity of his pontificate'. This seemed to delight Julius. He replied that he had always counted upon Florence, 'but now that his power and authority had increased, he wished to show his affection for her in every possible way,' particularly given how much he owed to Cardinal Soderini, who had been by his side throughout the conclave. This was more than Niccolò had dared hope for. Although he was careful not to sound too excited in his report, he evidently believed that Florence would be able to count on Julius's support, regardless of what happened to Cesare Borgia.

It was not long before this was put to the test. After returning to his lodgings, Niccolò received two letters from the *Dieci* informing him of further setbacks in the Romagna.[141] Only a few days earlier, the Venetian cavalry had suddenly descended upon the Val di Lamone, accompanied by the *condottiere*, Dionigi di Naldo da Brisighella.[142] They first attacked Imola. After capturing the citadel and killing its commander, they then pushed on to Faenza, where they had already taken the fortress. Disturbed, the *Dieci* ordered Niccolò to inform the pope of what had happened and to impress upon him the danger of letting 'this province' fall into the Venetians' hands. If Julius agreed to help them, they would gladly follow whatever course of action he thought best.

After conferring with Francesco Soderini and Georges d'Amboise, Niccolò rushed off to speak with Julius once again.[143] Scurrying through the halls and corridors of the Apostolic Palace, he must have been praying that he had not misinterpreted the pope's words earlier that morning. But any fears he may have had were quickly dispelled. After listening carefully to what Niccolò had to say, Julius promised to help. He was sure that he could stop the incursion by bringing Dionigi di Naldo to heel. This would not be difficult. Up to now, the pope claimed, Dionigi had always been more willing to support Cesare Borgia than the Venetians. He was probably only fighting alongside them because he had not heard of Julius's election. As soon as he was told, 'these matters would take a different shape'. But, just to be sure, the pope undertook to have a word with Georges d'Amboise, as well.

Niccolò was, of course, thrilled by the prospect of papal support. But only after taking his leave did he realize quite how dramatically the pendulum had swung in Florence's favour. Going back over the audience in his mind, he noticed that the pope had avoided saying anything about his relationship with Venice. This was unusual, to say the least. Of course, Julius might just have been trying to keep things simple, but his silence seemed too pointed. The only plausible explanation was that he was planning to break with the Venetians and wanted to keep it under wraps until he was ready to strike. If so, his support would effectively guarantee Florence's interests in the Romagna. Even more tantalizing was Julius's vagueness about Cesare. During the audience, he had seemed to suggest that, once Dionigi di Naldo heard of his election, the *condottiere* would go back to following Cesare. But the pope might also have meant that Dionigi would march under the *papal* banner – in which case, Cesare would be cut out of the equation and the Florentines would be rid of one of the most persistent thorns in their side.

Before reporting any of this to the *Dieci*, however, Niccolò wanted to check if his suspicions were right. He first went to see Ascanio Sforza, Raffaele Riario and Federico di Sanseverino – all influential cardinals with ties to France.[144] Repeating the *Dieci*'s news, he stressed the danger posed by Venetian expansionism – not only to Florence, but also to the Church. 'If the Venetians were permitted to increase their power beyond what it was already,' he warned, 'the pope would end up being nothing more than the Venetians' chaplain.' It was imperative to stop them. Much to Niccolò's relief, the cardinals did not contradict him – as they would surely have done if Julius was still hoping to reach some sort of understanding with the Venetians. Instead, they 'showed that they understood the importance of the matter and promised to do everything possible' to ensure the pope held firm.[145]

Niccolò then went to talk with Cesare Borgia.[146] Although the duke could not give him any insights into what Julius was thinking, his reactions might nevertheless reveal whether a breach was opening up between them. How obvious these would be was another matter. As Niccolò knew from first-hand experience, Cesare had always been a master of dissimulation. He rarely gave anything away. But, when Niccolò presented himself at the 'new apartments', he found the duke a changed man. Though as charming and courteous as ever, Cesare was no longer in control of his emotions. As soon as he heard the *Dieci*'s news, he exploded with rage. To his mind, the Florentines, rather than the Venetians, were to blame both for the death of his commander in Imola and for the attack on Faenza. Had they sent one hundred men to the Romagna, both cities might have been saved. The Florentines had always been his enemies, he complained, but he would make them pay. He 'would personally hand over all that he had left to the Venetians', and with their help, he would soon see Florence ruined. Then it would be his turn to laugh. 'As to the French, they would either lose the *Regno*, or they would have such difficulty holding it that they would not be able to help [the Florentines]' at all. And so he went on, ranting and raving 'with words filled with venom and passion.' Poor Niccolò hardly knew what to say. For a while, he tried to soothe the duke's temper. But eventually, he lost the will to continue. As adroitly as he could, he broke off the interview – 'which seemed . . . to have lasted a thousand years' – and beat a hasty retreat. The experience had shaken him deeply. Yet, he could now be sure that Cesare was not a part of Julius's plans for the Romagna – and that Florence would stand to reap the benefits.

*

Cesare's fate now seemed all but sealed. When Niccolò told Soderini and d'Amboise about his interview with the duke, later that evening, they were incensed by his arrogance. Setting aside his usual reserve, d'Amboise growled menacingly, 'Until now, God has not let any sin to go unpunished, and he will surely not let those [of Cesare] pass.'[147]

But Cesare had not yet seen the writing on the wall. Though anxious and unsettled, he still believed he could manoeuvre his way back into power. After recovering his composure, he tried to repair the damage he had done to his relationship with Florence. Summoning Francesco Soderini to his apartments on the morning of 7 November, he put on an air of self-assurance.[148] He claimed that, contrary to the reports the *Dieci* had received, Imola was still loyal to him. There was no reason to believe that it was in any danger. An attack by Ottaviano da Campo Fregoso had been repulsed without difficulty, Dionigi da Naldo was still fighting under his banner, and the Venetians had no forces worth speaking of. Soon enough, he would lead an army into the Romagna and retake the territory he had lost. Any day now, he boasted, Julius would reconfirm him as *gonfaloniere* of the Church. It was therefore in the Florentines' interests to maintain friendly relations with him.

But Cesare wasn't fooling anyone except himself. The very next day, the *Dieci* wrote to Niccolò refuting the duke's claims.[149] The Venetians were pouring across the frontier in ever greater numbers; they had already taken the whole of Faenza and it would not be long before they pushed onwards, perhaps towards Forlì and Cesena. The day after that (9 November), Julius held his first consistory, but, according to what Niccolò had been told, Cesare's reappointment had not even been mentioned.[150] There was talk of him being offered safe passage out of Rome, maybe even to Florence. But wise people were already predicting that he would soon come to a bad end.

*

For the moment, however, Julius was prepared to bide his time. As the situation in the Romagna deteriorated, he began to wonder if Cesare might first be put to some good use. On 13 November, he invited the duke to a meeting with Georges d'Amboise, Francesco Soderini and the Spanish cardinals.[151] After the usual pleasantries, he asked Cesare to help him fight the Venetians. If Cesare agreed, he would depart in two or three days and rendezvous with his men at Imola. From there, Julius promised, he would be able to begin reconquering his states. He could count on every support. Even the Florentines would lend a hand. Of course, none of this last part was true. No one actually wanted Cesare to recover his lands in the Romagna – least of all the pope. But, if Cesare could be persuaded to hold the Venetians back for a while, then so much the better. When he had served his purpose, Julius could always hand him over to his enemies, or have him killed surreptitiously.

It was a clever ruse – and Cesare nearly fell for it. He was certainly tempted by Julius's offer. Ever since his father had died, he had been itching to return to the Romagna. And now that the pope was promising him the resources to do it – or so he believed – he felt he had a real chance of reversing his losses. But he could not find the strength to commit. As Francesco Soderini confided to Niccolò, Cesare appeared 'irresolute, suspicious and unstable'. Whether because of his nature, or because 'these blows of fortune have bewildered him', he was incapable of making a decision.[152] Indeed, he seemed so confused that his kinsman, Cardinal Francisco de Lloris y de Borja, thought he had lost his mind entirely.[153]

Over the next few days, Cesare's mood swung violently. Desperate to assure himself that the pope's proposals really were feasible, he had sent an emissary to ask the Florentines for the safe passage he would need if he were to travel to Ferrara. But, when they failed to give their approval as quickly as he expected, he flew into a temper.[154] If they tarried any more, he warned Niccolò, 'he would come to terms with the Venetians and with the Devil himself; and . . . he would go to Pisa, and would spend all his money, his power, and what friends remained to him to harm [the Republic].' On 19 November, however, he had another change of heart. After ordering his troops northwards, he left the Vatican and went to Ostia.[155] If the weather permitted, he intended to embark for La Spezia.[156] But no sooner had he arrived at the port than his paranoia got the better of him. Fearful of leaving, yet unwilling to stay, he remained beside the shore, angrily denouncing the pope's 'fickleness' and the Florentines' 'duplicity'.

Such mad ravings weakened Julius's faith. Although he did not want to close any doors just yet, he was rapidly coming to the conclusion that Cesare was too unpredictable to be of any use. He would try negotiating with the Venetians instead. After all, he could always deal with the duke later. And, if the Florentines – or anyone else, for that matter – felt like taking a pop at Cesare in the meantime, he wouldn't object.[157]

But Julius' patience soon came to an end. On 20 November, Francesco Soderini came to discuss the affairs of the Romagna with him.[158] Alarmed that the Venetians were still making rapid progress, and fearing that they might even attack Florence,[159] the cardinal tried to persuade the pope to employ stronger measures. To Soderini's mind, Francesco Filipperi, the legate of Le Marche, should immediately move forward with his cavalry; a new legate should be appointed for the Romagna, to bring all those who owed the Church their loyalty back to obedience; and international pressure should be brought to bear on the Venetians, without delay. The pope, however, disagreed. He still wanted to see if the Venetians would come to their senses before declaring war on them. But, after spending a sleepless night worrying about the Romagna, he summoned Soderini back again. Although he had not changed his mind about the cardinal's proposals, he thought it might be a good idea to ask Cesare to hand over the castle of Forlì and any other places he still held in the Romagna. That way, Julius would at least be able to stop them falling into the Venetians' hands. Accordingly, Soderini set out for Ostia with Cesare's former preceptor, Cardinal Francisco de Remolins, early the next morning.[160] They stayed for two days, arguing and cajoling from morning to night, but Cesare stubbornly refused to hand over his last remaining possessions – especially as he had no guarantee that he would ever get them back.[161] As soon as Julius was told, he erupted with fury. This was the last straw. If Cesare wouldn't cooperate, the pope had no use for him, either in Rome or in the Romagna. He would have to be brought to heel. Though it was still the middle of the night, Julius ordered his immediate arrest.

*

By dawn, Cesare had been taken prisoner. Kept under lock and key aboard his galley, he was now 'at the pope's mercy'. As Niccolò noted, Julius wanted 'by all means to obtain possession of those fortresses that [Cesare] still held, and to assure himself of [the duke's] person.' Unless Cesare cooperated, the pope might decide to do away with him altogether. Wild rumours were already flying around. Someone even told Niccolò that Cesare had 'been thrown into the Tiber on the pope's orders'.[162] This struck him as unlikely. But even it if turned out to be untrue, it would surely come to pass before long.

Despite the danger Cesare was in, he did nothing to help himself. It was not that he lacked the opportunity. Shortly after Julius's coronation, the duke's old friend, Francisco de Remolins, had intervened on his behalf. Prostrating himself before the papal throne, he implored Julius to show the duke some mercy.[163] The cardinal was certain that he had learned his lesson by now; with a little more persuasion, he would surely agree to hand over his fortresses. Since this was all Julius really wanted, he could see no harm in trying – after all, Cesare's governors would be much less likely to resist if they knew he had gained possession of their towns by agreement, rather than force.[164] On 28 November, he therefore sent his guard to bring Cesare back to Rome.[165] That same afternoon, he informed a group of fifteen leading cardinals that there would soon be an end to hostilities in the Romagna.[166] They all knew the Venetians were fighting Cesare, not the Church; once Cesare signed over his remaining possessions, the pope claimed, peace would surely follow.[167] Two days later, he told Niccolò much the same.[168] He was optimistic that Cesare would come round, and hinted that, if the duke did so, he might even set him free. But Cesare still refused. To make matters worse, there were anti-papal riots in the towns he controlled, as well.

Julius could not afford to waste any more time talking. The Venetians had already acquired control of Rimini,[169] and were on the brink of capturing Forlì, too.[170] If Cesare would not comply with the pope's demands willingly, he would be forced to do so. And Julius knew exactly how to put pressure on him. On 1 December, word was received that Cesare's most trusted lieutenant, Michele de Corella, had been captured by Giampaolo Baglioni 'on the frontier between [Florence] and Perugia', and his troops disarmed.[171] This, of course, weakened Cesare's forces in the Romagna greatly. But it also gave the pope 'the chance to find out about all the cruel robberies, murders, sacrilege, and endless other crimes that had been committed during the past eleven years in Rome against God and man.' Once Michele had confessed, Julius would have all the justification he needed to condemn Cesare – and then he could do whatever he pleased.

Cesare saw the game was up. Bowing to the inevitable, he glumly surrendered his fortresses the following morning. Triumphant, Julius wasted no time in capitalizing on his success. When Niccolò met Francesco Soderini in the Apostolic Palace a short time later, he discovered that the pope had already ordered Carlo Monchier to leave for the Romagna that very day.[172] Knowing how loath Cesare's commanders would be to surrender, Julius also took the precaution of sending one of the duke's own men, Pietro d'Oviedo, to reason with them, as well. Niccolò felt confident they would meet with success. As such, he advised the *Dieci* – on Cardinal Soderini's behalf – to do everything they could to help, even if it meant spending a good deal of money. For, if the pope did indeed gain control of Forlì and Cesena, 'apart from the good that would result [for Florence] from this impediment to the Venetians, the pontiff would also acknowledge himself to be most obliged' to them.[173]

Having been at the centre of affairs for so long, Cesare now found himself pushed aside with unseemly haste. Before the morning was out, he had been forcibly removed from his lodgings in the treasurer's apartments and transferred to the residence of Cardinal d'Amboise, where he could be kept under close observation.[174] He watched forlornly as the whirl of events swept along without him. D'Amboise – who had been none too keen about acting as his keeper – was busily preparing to leave for France, where he was to negotiate an agreement between Louis XII and Maximilian 1 on the pope's behalf. Every so often, one of the cardinals would appear with an urgent matter to discuss, or a messenger would arrive with further instructions from the pope, but they all did their best to avoid Cesare's eye. He had become an embarrassing irrelevance. What his ultimate fate would be, however, remained unclear. Most believed that his end would be a bad one – and Niccolò was inclined to agree. As he told the *Dieci* on 3 December, 'the duke is little by little slipping into his grave.'[175]

*

When Cesare's fall became known in Florence, there was open rejoicing. Landucci was exultant that he was at last being paid in full for all his cruelties.[176] The *Dieci*, too, were gleeful. Though the Romagna was still a matter of grave concern, they were glad the door was finally closing on their years of suffering. Seeing no need to maintain so large a diplomatic presence in Rome anymore, they instructed Niccolò to accompany d'Amboise on his journey northwards and return to Florence.[177]

Niccolò could hardly find the words to express his relief. However exciting his mission had been, he had found life in Rome disagreeable.[178] It was far too expensive – especially for someone on his salary. His lodgings alone cost him 10 *carlini* (6 *lire* 5 *soldi*) a day.[179] Coupled with the heavy expense of couriers, he was often short of money, and complained of the 'many discomforts' he had to endure as a result.[180] The city was also dangerous. Though Bartolomeo d'Alviano and the Orsini had long since left, groups of armed men still prowled the streets, looking for a fight. People in Niccolò's position were simply not safe.[181] If that were not enough, the plague was still raging, as well. As Niccolò told his brother, Totto, he was terrified of getting sick.[182] Everywhere he looked, there were dead bodies. He was convinced it would only be a matter of time before he too fell victim to the pestilence.

But most of all, Niccolò had missed his family. Despite his fondest hopes, he had still been in Rome when Marietta gave birth to a 'bouncing [baby] boy' in the first week of November.[183] He had not even been able to sneak away for the baptism.[184] To be sure, his friends kept him up to date with news. According to Biagio Buonaccorsi, who looked in on the Machiavelli household whenever he could, little Bernardo was the very picture of health and had quickly settled down with the wet nurse.[185] He was the spitting image of his father, with pale white skin and a shock of black, velvety hair.[186] Indeed, Luca Ugolini believed that not even Leonardo da Vinci could have done a better portrait.[187] But, while all these letters must have warmed Niccolò's heart, they can only have made him regret his absence more keenly.

Marietta was just as keen for him to return. Although Piero di Francesco del Nero assured Niccolò that she was 'feeling fine' and lacked nothing,[188] she had run a fever for several days after the birth and could 'find no rest either day or night' on account of the baby.[189] She needed her husband by her side. She had only had three letters from him all the time he had been away, and was beginning to feel a little neglected – particularly as she was still sewing clothes for him from her sickbed. Though he teased her for her 'neediness', she told him that she 'would be flourishing more' if he were at home in Florence with her. Even Biagio had noticed that she was 'in great distress' about his absence.[190] There was, in fact, 'no way to get her to calm down and take comfort.'[191]

But Niccolò would have to wait a little longer before he could set off. By the time the *Dieci*'s orders arrived, he was suffering from a cough and catarrh. This affected his head and chest so badly that the 'violent agitation' of riding on horseback would probably do him 'serious injury.'[192] Had it been left up to him, he would gladly have taken the risk, but Cardinal Soderini 'would not consent to [his] leaving'. However ill Niccolò might have been, Soderini needed his help. There was no one else he could rely upon, and he feared that 'it would be burdensome' for him, not to mention 'detrimental to the city, if he had to remain [there] without some amanuensis of whom he could avail himself in public matters.'[193]

Six days later, however, Niccolò was at last able to leave. Riding out of the city along the ancient Via Cassia, he felt well pleased with himself. He had acquitted himself with distinction. Before his departure, Soderini had even given him a letter apologizing for the delay and urging the *Dieci* to take good care of him because of his remarkable 'loyalty, diligence and prudence'.[194] Although Biagio had hinted that some people in the chancellery had been complaining about his friendship with the cardinal, a letter like that would ensure he was well received by the *Dieci* – and especially by Piero Soderini.[195]

*

If Niccolò had any regrets, it was doubtless that he did not stay long enough to see the last act in the drama of Cesare Borgia's life. There was, however, a grim inevitability about it. The day after Niccolò's departure, the pope's envoy, Carlo Monchier, came rushing back with news that Pedro Ramires had not only refused to surrender Cesena until Cesare was set free, but had even hanged Pietro d'Oviedo as a traitor.[196] Horrified by such violent contumacy, Julius immediately ordered the confiscation of Cesare's remaining treasure, finally destroying any hope the duke may have had of rebuilding his army. Only the question of how best to dispose of him remained, but even this was soon settled. On 31 December, it was reported that the Aragonese had inflicted a crushing defeat on the French at the

Garigliano.[197] Under pressure from the Spanish cardinals, Julius agreed to let Cesare leave Rome, on the understanding that he would never again bear arms against the Church.[198] Relieved, Cesare sailed straight to Naples, where he hoped to receive a warm welcome. At first, his hosts showered him with kindness. Gonzalo even offered to put him in command of a proposed campaign against Tuscany. But Julius had already taken steps to thwart his plans. He made it clear to Ferdinand of Aragon that, were Cesare to receive any further support, Julius would be forced to regard the king as his enemy. Ferdinand did not need telling twice. On his instructions, Gonzalo placed the unsuspecting Cesare under arrest. A few months later, he was sent back to Aragon in chains – condemned to pass from Italian history forever. But, for Niccolò, safe and sound in Florence, the duke would always remain a figure of terrible fascination.

PART IV

The Hand of Fate

(1504–8)

12

The Militant

(January 1504–February 1506)

On 1 January 1504, Florence's churches were filled to the rafters with people celebrating the Feast of the Circumcision. It was a bitterly cold day – too cold to be outdoors, in fact. The snow was already lying thick on the ground and an icy wind was blowing off the Arno. But nothing could have kept people at home today. It was, after all, an important moment in the religious calendar. As Jacopo da Varagine explained in his *Legenda aurea*, it marked the occasion when Christ's blood was first shed, and hence looked forward to his sacrifice on the cross, when the sins of mankind would be washed away.[1] But this year, the promise of redemption seemed to be overlaid with political meaning. With the fall of Cesare Borgia, the greatest threat to Florence's safety had been swept away, and many Florentines hoped peace might soon return.

Niccolò was not a particularly religious man, but even he could not have helped being caught up in the spirit of optimism.[2] If not God, then at least Fate did indeed seem to be smiling on the city once again. And while he may not have been in the little church of Santa Felicità that day, he was no doubt looking forward to the year ahead.

But Fate was nothing if not fickle. Only three days later, news of Gonzalo Fernández de Córdoba's victory at the Battle of Garigliano reached Florence.[3] This delivered the kingdom of Naples into Aragonese hands. But so 'greatly had [Louis XII's] forces been weakened by the loss of such an army and by the death of so many captains' that even Lombardy was now in peril.[4] Should Gonzalo or the Emperor Maximilian decide to move against the duchy of Milan, Louis was unsure whether he would be able to mount an effective defence.

For the Florentines, this was a worrying development. At a *pratica* convened on the afternoon of 4 January, Piero Soderini spoke at length about the danger in which the city found itself.[5] As always, it was desperately short of money, and was already struggling to contain Pisan attacks in the countryside.[6] Without French support, there would be little it could do to check Venetian ambitions in the Romagna, let alone resist a German or Aragonese invasion. It was imperative to clarify Louis' intentions as soon as possible.[7] On 12 January, Soderini and the *Dieci* therefore decided to send Niccolò Valori to France as their new ambassador, and despatched his old friend, Niccolò Machiavelli, to Firenzuola, where Valori was then living, to give him his instructions in person.[8]

Shortly after Niccolò's return, however, Fate dealt Florence another blow. On 18 January, the *Dieci* received a letter from Alessandro Nasi, one of their ambassadors in Rome, informing them that Giampaolo Baglioni, whom they had employed as their *condottiere* jointly with Louis XII the previous year, was no longer in French service and that they would henceforth be solely responsible for providing him with 10,000 *scudi* 'at the time of every fair'.[9] Since they could not possibly afford to pay such an astronomical sum, Louis had effectively deprived them of their most important captain, and two hundred men-at-arms, to boot. But it was also a clear sign that the French were cutting them loose.[10] At a stroke, Florence had lost the bulk of its army and its only ally. The city, which had thought itself safe only a few days ago, was now dangerously vulnerable.

The *Dieci* had to act quickly. Rather than send Valori new instructions, they decided it would be safer to send Niccolò to France, as well. Although he may not have been as well born as Valori, he was far more up to date with Florence's current political situation and already had a good working relationship with Louis XII's ministers.[11] Using these advantages to the full, his task was to make the king understand how gravely the Florentines would be affected by his decision – and to convince him to change his mind.[12] Ideally, Niccolò should also persuade Louis to re-employ Baglioni on the same terms as before, and perhaps even come to Lombardy himself.

*

The following day, Niccolò set out. Wrapped up in his warmest clothes and, bracing himself against the cold, he headed northwards. It was hard going. Where the snows had been trodden down by travellers, the unpaved roads would have been turned to mud, but a heavy frost could just as easily rob his horse of its footing. To make matters worse, winter shortages coupled with the threat of conflict would have made food expensive, even in the fertile fields of the Po Valley. By the time he reached Piacenza, early on the afternoon of 21 January, he would have been tired, hungry and chilled to the bone.

Arriving in Milan the following morning, Niccolò went straight to see the French governor, Charles II d'Amboise, seigneur de Chaumont, who, as well as being one of Louis XII's most trusted lieutenants, was also the nephew of Cardinal Georges d'Amboise. Without mincing his words, Niccolò explained the reasons for his mission and related the *Dieci*'s hope that Louis XII would continue to stand by his allies. To his relief, Charles was reassuring. He did not believe that Gonzalo would march northwards, but, if the Aragonese did make a move, Louis XII 'would take good care' of Florence.[13] And, besides, he was sure the pope 'would be a good Frenchman', too. The same applied to the affairs of the Romagna. Although he did not want to go into much detail, he assured Niccolò that, if the Venetians attempted anything further, the king would 'make them attend to [their] fishing'.[14] He even seemed confident that Baglioni would continue to take orders from the French, despite having had his contract cancelled.

Niccolò was, of course, encouraged by this. Shortly after taking his leave, however, he was approached by Count Piccino da Novara, who recognized him from their time together at the French court and who had an affectionate regard for Florence.[15] Drawing Niccolò aside, Piccino dolefully suggested that the French were in a far worse condition than the governor had led him to believe. At present, they only had a small number of men-at-arms in Lombardy, who were dispersed throughout the countryside, and no infantry at all. It would take a long time for more troops to be raised; but, since Louis XII had not been able to raise any more money, no preparations had yet been made. The enemy, by contrast, 'were ready in their saddles, fresh, and buoyed by good fortune and victory.'[16] This being so, it was difficult to see what help the French could be. Piccino feared for Florence's future.

As Niccolò admitted in his despatches that evening, he did not know whom to believe.[17] While Charles d'Amboise was in a better position to know Louis XII's intentions, Piccino had less reason to lie about the strength of the French army in Lombardy. After a sleepless night, he decided he would not be able to give the *Dieci* a better idea of how things really stood until he had a chance to discuss the situation with Louis' ministers.

*

At midday on 23 January, Niccolò left Milan, his brow still furrowed in thought. On reaching Turin late in the evening of 24 January, he gathered his strength in readiness for crossing the Alps. Following the old pilgrim route through the Susa Valley, he at first encountered only gentle slopes and light woodlands. But his journey would soon have becme more arduous. In the Maurienne Valley, great snow-capped mountains loomed threateningly above the road, the trees became denser, and the cold was savage. As he pressed on further, the landscape became even more forbidding: a barren, rocky expanse, bereft of vegetation, where the mountains, whipped by a ceaseless, icy wind, must have seemed like needles. Yet, his progress was swift. Even here, he travelled around a hundred kilometres each day. By the evening of 25 January, the worst of it was behind him. By Aiguebelle, vertiginous peaks had given way to gentler slopes, and wide river valleys dotted with fields began to open up before him. From then onwards, it was easier going – and he arrived in Lyon late on the night of 26 January.[18]

However tired he may have been, Niccolò did not have long to rest. Early the next morning, he and Valori quickly brought each other up to speed and then headed off to court. They first tried to secure an audience with Louis XII, but were told it would be impossible to see the king that day 'as his catarrh was giving him some discomfort'.[19] They therefore decided to speak to Cardinal d'Amboise instead. After presenting his credentials, Niccolò explained their purpose in as businesslike a manner as he could, without any of the animation the subject might have been expected to arouse. But the cardinal was not impressed – especially when Niccolò suggested that, unless Louis helped the Florentines, the *Dieci* might be forced to make terms with their enemies. As Valori later reported, d'Amboise 'show[ed] himself to be very irritated'.[20] He rebuked Niccolò for daring to say such things. The Spanish were expected to sign a truce fairly soon and, in any case, Louis would stand by his allies. If the Florentines weren't happy with this assurance, he added, they could do as they pleased, but they should think carefully before doing something they might later regret. But Niccolò would not be brushed off so easily. As delicately as he could, he tried to raise the issue of Baglioni's *condotta*, but d'Amboise cut him short. With or without a *condotta*, the cardinal snapped, Baglioni would do as he was told. And, with that, d'Amboise stormed out.[21] This was, of course, exactly what His Eminence's nephew had told them in Milan, but his bluntness still came as something of a shock. Bemused, Niccolò and Ugolino Martelli – another of Florence's representatives – went to talk to the king's treasurer, Robertet.[22] Given that he and Niccolò had got on so well in the past, the Florentines were evidently hoping he would be able to shed a little more light on the matter. But Robertet could tell them nothing more than they had already heard. It was a very disappointing start – and, given the rather sarcastic tone of Valori's report to the *Dieci*, it appears that he may have held Niccolò responsible for the lack of progress.

On 28 January, however, things seemed to change for the better. Shortly after dinner, d'Amboise summoned Niccolò, Valori and Martelli to his lodgings.[23] There, they found him in the company a dozen other high-ranking courtiers, including Robertet, and evidently in a much more cheerful mood. The cardinal began by apologizing for his former reticence. He had not been able to say everything he wanted before conferring with the council, but, now, he was happy to discharge his duty to them more fully. Within a week, he predicted, there would be a truce with Spain, but, if not, Louis XII stood ready to protect Florence with arms. Indeed, 1,200 lances had already been given orders to assemble in the duchy of Milan, in readiness for just such an eventuality. It was Valori who replied. This was, he said, all very well and good, but the extra lances would only be useful against Gonzalo if they were *already in* Lombardy. In any case, Gonzalo wasn't Florence's only problem. If there was to be a truce, Louis would also have to confirm the city's rights over Pisa and support it against the Venetians in the Romagna. In the excitement, Valori forgot to mention Baglioni, but the cardinal nevertheless went out of his way to assuage his concerns – so much so, in fact, that Valori was completely reassured. Niccolò did not share his friend's confidence, though. Everything was still rather vague. Even if the French *did* conclude a truce with the Spanish, he told the *Dieci* two days later, Cardinal d'Amboise had not yet given the Florentines any firm guarantees – least of all about Baglioni.[24] They might still be left out in the cold.

Over the next few days, the French seemed to go out of their way to allay any such doubts. On the evening of 30 January, Niccolò, Valori and Martelli were at last invited to an audience with the king, who was still recuperating in bed.[25] They found him in an effusive mood. After repeating everything that Cardinal d'Amboise had told them, he added that he was also 'organising a new corps of 1,400 lances and 20,000 infantry,' and had already given orders to strengthen the duchy of Milan's defences. What was more, the pope was also proving to be 'a good Frenchman' and had placed a newly hired body of mercenaries under the command of the duke of Urbino. Of Baglioni, Pisa and the Venetians, the king admittedly said little, but Valori seems to have been greatly encouraged.

There was more good news from other quarters, too. After the Florentine envoys had taken their leave of the king, Valori went to see the Aragonese ambassador and was given an assurance that a truce would certainly be signed.[26] Later that day, there were even rumours that the imperial ambassador had dined with Cardinal d'Amboise and, although no one could be sure of what passed between them, it seemed possible that Louis was trying to conclude an agreement with the Emperor Maximilian, as well.[27] When Valori wrote his report to the *Dieci* that night, he could scarcely contain his excitement.

But Niccolò's concerns were soon proved justified. The following morning, he and Valori bumped into Cardinal d'Amboise in chapel and were horrified to learn that Gonzalo was doing everything he could to derail the peace negotiations.[28] Of course, the cardinal hoped he would be brought to heel before long, but there was still a chance that, if a truce were signed, Gonzalo might ignore its terms and march north. If that happened, Florence would bear the brunt of the attack.

Worse was to come. On 2 February, Valori was visited in his lodgings by Claude de Seyssel, a Savoyard lawyer in the cardinal's service.[29] Somewhat nervously, Claude intimated that Pisa might be in much greater danger than the Florentines realized. Despite the ongoing negotiations between Louis XII and the Aragonese, Gonzalo was making overtures to the Pisans, in conjunction with the Venetians. If his offer was accepted, Claude pointed out, the effects would be 'more ruinous . . . than anything that could be imagined at present.'[30] Of course, the French would try every diplomatic means to prevent this from happening, but they were evidently not in a position to commit either troops or money. Florence would be on its own. Rather weakly, Claude suggested that the *Dieci* could try opening communications with the Pisans to encourage them 'not to . . . throw themselves [into the arms of] the Spaniards or the Venetians',[31] but, other than that, he had no advice to give. More worrying still, Maximilian had resolved to mount an expedition into Italy 'with a large body of his own troops' in the summer – which, though it would probably antagonize the Spanish, would almost certainly result in him taking Pisa under his protection.[32] To cap it all, Baglioni was already demanding his money.[33]

Back in Florence, the situation was no better. Despite the cold weather, the Venetians were making rapid gains in the Romagna. The *Dieci* had received confirmation that they had taken Forlì and were unlikely to hand it back over to the Church.[34] Such boldness took them a little by surprise. Given that Louis XII was said to enjoy a strong relationship with Julius II, they would have expected the threat of French retribution to dissuade the Venetians from treading on the pope's toes so brazenly. It hardly seemed worth the risk. That is, unless Louis had secretly come to an arrangement with the Venetians before opening negotiations with the Aragonese. The prospect was almost too awful to contemplate. Terrified, the *Dieci* immediately ordered their envoys to seek clarification.[35]

On 7 February, Niccolò hurried off to see the king with Valori and Martelli.[36] Louis was still in bed with catarrh, but he looked better than he had the last time. It was again Valori who took the lead. From the 'fragmentary' conversation that ensued, he surmised that the king was indeed in talks with the Venetians. Naturally, he did his best to put Louis off, but found himself clutching at straws. The Venetians were untrustworthy, he spluttered. They didn't really want a deal with France; they were just trying to obtain better terms from the Spanish and the Germans, with whom they were also negotiating. Even from his own account, it seems clear he was starting to flounder. Fortunately, Louis stopped him from going any further. Though Valori's outrage did him credit, he said, there was no need for Florence to worry. He would never make terms with the Venetians; he was just stringing them along. The Milanese had offered him 100,000 ducats to make war on them, and he would, in any event, come to agreement with Maximillian, whereby they would jointly fight Venice and Spain if Gonzalo should succeed in derailing the peace. This was, however, just a precaution. He was sure the Spanish would sign a truce soon enough.

To be sure, this did not help with the situation in Pisa. Nor did it resolve the problem of Baglioni's *condotta*. But it was something, at least. The envoys would just have to keep their ears to the ground and hope for the best. Niccolò was, admittedly, ready to leave. Given that a truce seemed to be imminent, he may have felt that he could be of more use in Florence. He may also have been tired of playing second fiddle to Valori, whose cattiness was putting a strain on their friendship. But Valori, who was beginning to doubt his own abilities, insisted that Niccolò stay on.[37] He knew he had been a bit out of line recently, but in an effort to patch things up between them, he made a great point of praising Niccolò in his letters to the *Dieci*.[38] Luckily, Niccolò was not one to hold a grudge.

*

Over the following week, the court was abuzz with activity. As the negotiations continued behind closed doors, Niccolò, Valori and Martelli rushed around, trying desperately to find out what was going on. At first, almost no one would talk to them, and the few reassurances they received did little to allay Valori's fears.[39] But on the morning of 11 February, Cardinal d'Amboise informed them that the Spanish had agreed to the truce. A little later, the king himself confirmed that a formal ratification had been received.[40] A peace with the emperor was also assured.[41] Best of all, Louis now felt that he was in a position to 'punish those who had offended him' – that was to say, the Venetians. 'Whatever the cost,' he growled, 'they must be destroyed'.[42] Naturally, Valori was delighted.

For several days, Louis' desire to revenge himself on the Venetians was all that people could talk about. According to Louis de Villeneuve, who had recently returned from a stint as France's ambassador to the

Curia, there was a chance the king might even persuade Julius II, Maximilian and Ferdinand to join him in wresting the Romagna from their grasp and securing the duchy of Milan 'against their power and malevolence'.[43] But, even if he did not succeed in putting together such a grand coalition, there was still no doubt that Florence would be among the principal beneficiaries of any campaign. On 13 February, Cardinal d'Amboise assured Valori that, if Venice ever wanted peace with France, it would have to show 'regard for [Louis'] friends in Italy', as well.[44]

Yet Louis had got ahead of himself. When the final text of the truce was published on 17 February, it was discovered that the Spanish had craftily taken the Venetians under their protection.[45] It would now be impossible for Louis to take any action against them. Even more troublingly, the Spanish ambassadors revealed that they had deliberately delayed discussions so that Gonzalo could use the intervening period to consolidate his hold on the kingdom of Naples, meaning that he would now be in a much stronger position to push further north, should he decide to do so.[46] And to cap it all, the compact didn't say a thing about Florence's rights over Pisa.

As soon as this became known, Niccolò and Valori went straight to see the king.[47] Although they did not dare criticize him for being outfoxed by the Spaniards, they urged him not to forget his enmity against the Venetians. But Louis merely told them to be patient. Another opportunity would doubtless present itself before long – and, when it did, he would be ready. The treaty with the emperor was nearly concluded, and he had already retained a further 16,000 Swiss troops. Of course, this was not what the envoys had hoped to hear, but they tried to make the best of a bad situation. Given that the king had employed so many new Swiss mercenaries, they asked, could he not find it in himself to employ some *Italian* captains as well? Baglioni, for example? But Louis refused to bend. He would only hire Italians if Florence and Julius II did so first.

Niccolò had finally had enough. Since Louis clearly wasn't going to change his mind, there was no point in staying any longer. Once the (largely meaningless) treaty with the emperor had been concluded,[48] he cast around for a suitable travelling companion,[49] and set off for home, feeling thoroughly disappointed.

*

By the time Niccolò arrived in Florence on, or shortly after, 5 March,[50] news of the Franco-Spanish truce had already reached the *Dieci*'s ears. Although their hopes had not been high, they had not expected Louis to let them down quite so badly. They could see it was now only a matter of time before Gonzalo attacked – and that, when he did, they would have to fight him alone.

Florence could hardly have been in a worse position. It was surrounded by enemies on three sides: Venice to the north-east, Siena to the south, and Lucca and Pisa to the west. Of its neighbours, only Jacopo IV d'Appiano remained, but even he could not be counted as a friend. Although he had recovered Piombino with the Florentines' help only a few months earlier, his attitude towards the Republic was much less favourable than they would have liked. It was not that he was ungrateful; he was just wary. He had not forgotten that, when Cesare Borgia's forces had been expelled, the Piombinesi had initially declared themselves for Florence and Genoa, rather than for him.[51] Fearing that friendship with the Florentines might cost him the city once again, he had therefore made overtures to Pandolfo Petrucci of Siena, and even to Bartolomeo d'Alviano, who had fought under Gonzalo at the Battle of Garigliano. Given how strategically important Piombino was, the *Dieci* could not afford to sit by and let it drift into the enemy camp without putting up a struggle. Hoping that Jacopo d'Appiano had not yet committed himself, they decided to send Niccolò to talk with him.[52] As his instructions made clear, he was to gather whatever information he could about the wavering *signore*, the disposition of his men and the feelings of the Piombinesi. Above all, he was to plant doubts about Petrucci and Alviano in Jacopo's mind, and to assure him that he would be handsomely rewarded if he either rejoined the Florentines or remained neutral.

Niccolò did his best to talk Jacopo round. Although his despatches have been lost – if any were written at all – Jacopo Nardi later recalled that he had used all his skill to make the *signore* 'suspect that he would lose possession of Piombino to the Spanish' if he continued his dalliance with Bartolomeo d'Alviano.[53] But it was no use. The gruff old *condottiere* would not be persuaded. Although he did not actually spurn the *Dieci*'s offer openly, he left their emissary in no doubt about where his sympathies lay. Only a day or two after arriving, Niccolò returned to Florence with the news that Piombino had gone over to the enemy.

Friendless and exposed, the Florentines tried to ready their forces as best they could. There had already been some discussion about employing a new captain.[54] At a *pratica* on 27 February, Fabrizio Colonna and the marquis of Mantua had both been mooted as possible candidates,[55] but there was no time to negotiate with either of them just now. So urgent was Florence's need that the *Dieci* would have to cobble an army together out of a variety of smaller mercenary bands. But even this would be difficult. As Soderini had warned two months earlier, the Republic was painfully short of money. At present, it could not afford to hire more than a handful of troops – barely enough to continue the war against Pisa, let alone stand up to Gonzalo.[56] To remedy this, Soderini asked for new taxes to be granted, hoping that threat of invasion would overcome any objections. Much to his dismay, however, the Great Council rejected his proposals twice in quick succession. Only after much wrangling did he succeed in getting a modified bill passed on 15 April.[57] It was far from ideal, but at least it enabled the *Dieci* to start hiring more mercenaries while there was still some time.

*

As the Florentines waited for Gonzalo to declare himself, an eerie calm fell over the city. Though May Day was only two weeks away, there was none of the usual excitement in the air. The dances and jousts that had previously been the highlight of the celebrations were now too martial for the tastes of a nervous populace.[58] In the Palazzo della Signoria, the tension brought the chancellery almost to a standstill. To keep his mind off things, Niccolò threw himself into family life. Most of his attention would probably have been taken up with his pregnant wife and two young children, but he still found time to deal with other matters, too. Totto had recently decided to pursue an ecclesiastical career and was in search of a suitable benefice.[59] Wishing to help, Niccolò wrote to their mutual friend, Giorgio dell'Antella, in Rome, in the hope that he would intercede with various cardinals on Totto's behalf.[60] Niccolò even managed to write a few poems, as well. Unfortunately, there is no way of telling which poems these were,[61] but, judging by the appreciative remarks of a

Roman correspondent known only as 'V', to whom Niccolò had sent them, they were evidently meant to be set to music and sung.[62] If his other 'songs' are anything to go by, they were probably quite ribald, to boot. Either way, they provided him with a bit of light relief – a break from the political worries by which he was plagued. But no amount of levity could make him forget Florence's peril altogether.

*

In May, Gonzalo at last made his move. Recognizing that Pisa was Florence's Achilles heel, he ordered Rinieri della Sassetta to march northwards and place his troops at the city's disposal. With characteristic cunning, he then informed the Florentines that King Ferdinand of Aragon had taken Pisa under his protection and would not tolerate any further attacks on the city. Of course, he did not expect this to have any actual effect. He knew that Florence could not afford to release the pressure on Pisa, even for an instant. They were bound to try another attack sooner or later. But when they did, he would have all the justification he needed to attack Florence directly – and then use it as a springboard from which to invade the duchy of Milan.

The *Dieci* immediately sent Pierfilippo Pandolfini to negotiate with Gonzalo in Naples,[63] but the best he could do would be to buy Florence a little more time. Everyone could see that war was now inevitable. Even before Pandolfini had set off, the *Dieci* had begun rallying their forces. New *condottieri* were hired, and those already under contract were soon en route to Pisa.[64]

Despite the danger, the Florentines' morale was high. As Landucci wrote, the sight of so many troops marching through the city streets with drums playing and banners flying filled everyone with confidence. On 14 May, the completion of Michelangelo's *David* helped lift their spirits even further. Brought out of his workshop near the *Duomo*, it was slowly moved to the Piazza della Signoria, where it was to be placed on the *ringhiera*.[65] Some people were a little wary. Feeling that it was a little too reminiscent of the Medici – who had commissioned a bronze *David* from Donatello some sixty years earlier[66] – they pelted it with stones at night. But most regarded it

FIORENZA

1. (*Above*) Florence as it would have appeared a few years after Machiavelli's birth. Francesco Rosselli, *The Map of the Chain* (c. 1480).

2. (*Below left*) View of the Via Romana (today the Via de' Guicciardini), looking towards the Ponte Vecchio. The site of the Palazzo Machiavelli is on the left.

3. (*Below right*) The ideal of a Renaissance classroom, from Niccolò Perotti's *Rudimenta grammatices* (1474). Note the *tavola* (hornbook) on the floor in the foreground.

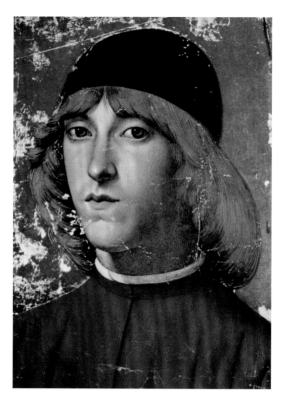

4. Gherardo di Giovanni del Fora, *Portrait of Piero de' Medici* (*c.* 1488). According to Guicciardini, Piero was a 'proud and bestial' young man, who preferred 'to be hated rather than loved'.

5. The hanging and burning of Girolamo Savonarola, as depicted by an anonymous seventeenth-century artist.

6. Santi di Tito, *Portrait of Niccolò Machiavelli* (late sixteenth century).

7. Lorenzo di Credi, *La dama dei gelsomini* (1481–3), thought to depict Caterina Sforza.

8. Portrait of Louis XII of France, as he appeared towards the end of his life, by the workshop of Jean Perréal (*c*. 1514).

9. Pope Alexander VI, as portrayed by Cristofano dell'Altissimo (late sixteenth century).

10. Altobello Melone's *Portrait of a Gentleman* (*c.* 1513),
thought to depict Cesare Borgia.

11. The Palazzo Ducale in Urbino, where Machiavelli first met
Cesare Borgia on the night of 24 June 1502.

12. Machiavelli's despatch from Cesare Borgia's camp in Imola, 4 November 1502.

13. Piero Soderini, elected *gonfaloniere a vita* in 1502,
in an early-sixteenth-century portrait attributed to Ridolfo del Ghirlandaio.

14. Raphael, *Portrait of Pope Julius II* (*c.* 1511–12).

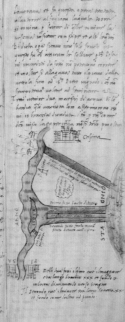

NICOLAI MALCLAVELLI FLO
RENTINI COMPENDIVM RE
RVM DECENNIO IN ITA,
LIA GESTARVM AD
VIROS FLORENTI
NOS INCIPIT
FELICI
TE.
R.

IO cantero litalice fatiche
Seguite gia ne duo passati lustri
Sotto lestelle alsuo ben inimiche.
Quanti alpestri sentier, quãti palustri
Narrero io, di morti & sãgue pieni
Pel uariar deregni & stati illustri.
O musa questa mia cetra sostieni,
Et tu apollo per darmi soccorso
Dalle tue suore accõpagnato uieni.
Haueua ilsol ueloce sopral dorso
Di questo mõdo ben termini mille
Et quattrocen nouãtaquattro corso,
Dal tempo che Iesu lenostre uille
Visito prima, & col sangue che pse
Extinse lediaboliche fauille:
Quando in se discordãte italia aperse
Lauia agalli, & q̃do esser calpesta
Dalle genti barbariche sofferse.

a ii

15. (*Top left*) Biagio Buonaccorsi's sketch of the attempted diversion of the Arno.

16. (*Top right*) The first page of Machiavelli's *Decennale primo*, printed by Bartolomeo de' Libri in 1506.

17. (*Left*) Portrait of Maximilian I, as he would have appeared during Machiavelli's mission to the imperial court in 1508, by Bernhard Strigel (early sixteenth century).

18. Jean Pichore, *The Wheel of Fortune*, from a French translation of Petrarch's *De remediis utriusque fortune* (*c.* 1503).

19. Pope Leo X with Cardinals Giulio de' Medici (*left*) and Luigi de' Rossi (*right*), by Raphael (*c.* 1518–19).

as a fitting symbol of the city's defiant stand against foreign invaders, and took heart from the implication that God was on their side.

Such self-assurance was soon put to the test. Having provided himself with a ready-made casus belli, Gonzalo saw no need to wait for the Florentines actually to threaten Pisa before mobilizing his army. As Niccolò explained in a letter to Giovanni Ridolfi, the *Dieci* had received word that Bartolomeo d'Alviano had left Naples on 25 May with 250 men-at-arms and 3,000 infantrymen.[67] On Gonzalo's orders, he was heading towards Rome, 'in order to move on Tuscany, and to attack Florence'. It had also been reported that Siena and Lucca would give Gonzalo their every support and were already sending Alviano money.

Now that war was upon them, the Florentines needed to decide on a strategy – and quickly. Flushed with success after retaking Ripafratta, Antonio Giacomini, the commissioner-general in the field, suggested an all-out attack on Pisa.[68] If the city could be captured *before* Bartolomeo d'Alviano reached Tuscany, Giacomini argued, Florence would stand a much better chance of beating him back. Soderini agreed. On 31 May, a *pratica larga* was summoned to consider the idea.[69] There was no lack of opposition, especially among the *ottimati*. Some doubted whether Florence had the money to mount such an offensive. Others disliked it simply because of Giacomini's friendship with Soderini. But the *popolani* ardently supported it, and – much to Soderini's relief – their votes were enough to carry the day.

For all its popularity, however, Giacomini's plan was never put into practice. Shortly after the *pratica*'s vote, a group of captured Pisans revealed that the city's defences were far stronger than anyone had expected. Thanks to the arrival of Rinieri della Sassetta, Pisa now boasted a garrison of 2,000 well-armed soldiers, as well as '500 foreign foot and 300 light horse paid for by Siena and Lucca'.[70] Fearing stiff resistance, the Florentines decided not to risk a frontal assault, after all.

Disappointed, but undeterred, Soderini decided to try a different approach. Back in February, an architect named Colombino and an engineer, Giovan Berardi, had put forward a daring plan to divert the Arno, and thereby dry up Pisa's port.[71] This would deprive the Pisans of the help they had been getting by sea; and if the surrounding countryside was ravaged at the same time, they would quickly be starved into submission. It was, of course, an ingenious idea. There had, however, been some doubt about its practicability. At a *pratica* on 23 February, Lorenzo Morelli had queried whether the modest budget that Colombino and Berardi had proposed would be sufficient for such an enormous undertaking.[72] It could end up costing twice as much. Morelli's colleagues were inclined to agree. Though they praised the scheme's boldness, they feared it might prove to be an unsustainable drain on Florence's finances. Even Soderini had seen the merit of this argument. But, now, he saw things differently. As far as he was concerned, any price was worth paying to recapture Pisa before Alviano arrived. Despite howls of protest in *pratiche*, Soderini succeed in talking the *Dieci* round; and Colombino and Berardi's hare-brained plan was set in motion.[73]

*

On 20 August, work began at Riglione, just a few kilometres south-east of Pisa.[74] Since Colombino knew the project better than anyone, the *Dieci* had had no hesitation about placing him in charge, but, just to be sure, they had also taken the precaution of asking Niccolò to keep an eye on things. Seeing that he could not be on site all the time, however, Niccolò delegated many of the everyday responsibilities to Biagio Buonaccorsi, and relied on regular updates from Giuliano Lapi and Tommaso Tosinghi, the commissioners in the field.

From the first, Niccolò had his doubts about Colombino's character. As he told Antonio Giacomini, Colombino was 'so reserved' that he did not 'stand out among such a multitude of men and preparations'.[75] But Niccolò was willing to grant that he might still be 'an excellent expert on . . . hydraulic engineering', nonetheless. Besides, it was only right to give him the support he deserved – especially given that the site was under constant attack from Pisan raiders.

Before long, however, Niccolò had cause to regret his fair-mindedness. Back when the project had been approved, Colombino had promised that, with 2,000 navvies, each paid a *carlino* a day, he would be able to dig two canals from the Arno to a nearby pool in fifteen to twenty days.[76] But, by the beginning of September, it had become clear that he had been wildly over-optimistic. In a letter to the *Dieci*, Niccolò opined that, unless they could find the money to hire more labourers, the canals might not *ever* be finished.[77]

As the work ground on, Niccolò started to worry that Colombino and Berardi's designs for the canals might be at fault, as well. On 20 September, he explained his concerns in a letter to Giuliano Lapi.[78] Having compared Colombino and Berardi's plan with one that had been drawn up by Leonardo da Vinci, he could not help feeling that the latter might have a greater chance of success. The next day, he wrote to Lapi again, evidently in a state of some agitation. Now that he had looked over the site more carefully, it seemed as if the canals were shallower than the Arno. If this were true, he noted, the water would not flow as Berardi and Colombino expected, 'and the entire project could be destroyed'.

Niccolò was not mistaken. When the first of the two canals was completed – several weeks behind schedule – it proved to be an embarrassing failure.[79] Although the river water flowed over the weir rapidly enough at first, it soon stopped. Within minutes, the canal had discharged the little it had received into the pool and was starting to dry out. Meanwhile, the Arno continued along its usual course, completely unaffected.

Colombino assured the *Dieci* that this was just a temporary hiccup. All he needed to do was make a few small changes to the weir, and the river would correct the problem by itself. But, while he was scrambling around at one end of the canal, further difficulties arose at the other. This time, it was the pool that was at fault. It was too small to hold all the water that had been poured into it. As Biagio noted, 'the whole plain of the Vettola [where Pisa Airport is currently located], all the way to S. Pietro a Grado' was flooded.[80] Crops were destroyed and a great many farms were ruined.

Alarmed by the mounting chaos, Soderini asked two experts from Lombardy to assess the situation. After making a careful survey of the site, they concluded that one of the major reasons for the inadequacy of the first canal was Colombino's failure to account for a number of important topographical features. With a few more labourers and a little more time, this oversight could perhaps be corrected. Soderini was willing to give it a try. But political opinion was against him. Having already wasted more than 7,000 ducats on the project, most of Florence's political elite believed the time had come to call it a day. After much heated debate in *pratiche* on 27 and 28 September (both of which were minuted by Niccolò, just days before the birth of his third child, Lodovico[81]), the decision was taken to abandon the canals and find some other way of damaging the Pisans.[82]

*

Although Soderini was not mentioned by name in *pratiche*, the speakers made it quite clear that they held him responsible for the whole debacle. In a thinly veiled attack, Giovanbattista Ridolfi suggested that such a ridiculous scheme could only have been undertaken by someone with more regard for the demands of the mob than for the counsel of wise men.[83] No less vindictive was Piero Parenti, who insinuated that, once work had begun, the *gonfaloniere*'s 'negligence' had scuppered any chance of success.[84]

Before Soderini could defend himself against these charges, he received news from Giovanni Acciaiuoli, the Florentine ambassador in Rome, that his perceived failure had reawakened support for the Medici. As was their custom, the Medici had held a banquet to celebrate the feast day of their family's patron saints, Saints Cosmas and Damian, on 27 September.[85] In the past, this had always been a lavish affair, but, this time, they had taken the unusual step of inviting most of the Florentine community in Rome to join them. Despite the law prohibiting Florentine citizens from having anything to do with the Medici, around forty well-placed merchants came along.[86] Some had tried to convince Acciaiuoli that they had only gone out of concern for their financial interests, but there was no concealing the fact that they had all doffed their hats to the twenty-five-year-old Giuliano de' Medici and hailed him as their 'magnificent' lord.

Soderini knew he had to reassert his authority. On 5 October, he therefore had the Signoria convene a *pratica* to discuss how best to punish those who had attended the Medici's banquet.[87] He was no doubt expecting the *pratica* to be so horrified by the prospect of the Medici's return that it would rally behind his regime and demand harsh penalties for the 'traitors' in Rome, but, to his dismay, there was little appetite for retribution. The *pratica* saw no need for the Signoria to stir up trouble over something as trifling as a party. It would be better to forget the whole thing.

Soderini had no choice but to give way. It was obvious to everyone that he now had so little support that he could no longer enforce the law, let alone defend the Republic against its enemies. Such weakness only encouraged the growth of opposition. Two main groups now began to emerge.[88] The first was led by Bernardo Rucellai.[89] Meeting in the magnificent gardens of his *palazzo*, or the nearby church of San Pancrazio, its members included Niccolò's old schoolfriends Francesco Vettori and Pietro Crinito. Generally conservative in outlook, they had long resented Soderini's failure to give Florence a more Venetian constitution and were furious at what they perceived to be his growing sympathy for the *popolani*. The second group was headed by Jacopo and Alamanno Salviati, both of whom Niccolò knew well.[90] Though they had been instrumental in ensuring Soderini's election as *gonfaloniere a vita*, they had been offended by his refusal to take their advice. Enjoying close ties to the Medici, they resolved to use their dominance of the councils to hamper Soderini in every way they could.

As the chronicler Filippo de' Nerli later observed, government now became a bitter struggle between Soderini and his opponents. Blocked at every turn in the Council of Eighty, the *gonfaloniere* found himself 'unable either to hire soldiers, or elect . . . commissioners or ambassadors', while, in *pratiche*, he was prevented from 'concluding any business, unless the two [other] parties agreed'.[91]

*

Such rivalries put Florence's future at risk. Now that winter was coming, Bartolomeo d'Alviano was unlikely to advance much further. The Florentines should be using the respite to renew their campaign against Pisa, but, as long as the councils were deadlocked, the chances of mounting another attack were slim at best.[92] Someone needed to reach across the factional divide and rally support. Since none of his colleagues seemed willing to do anything, Niccolò took it upon himself to appeal directly to Alamanno Salviati – not by making representations in person, as might have been expected, but, in true humanistic style, by presenting him with a skilfully woven poem, now known as the *Decennale primo* ('First Decennial').[93]

Written in Dantean tercets, the *Decennale* offered a dramatic retelling of Italy's recent past, shot through with flattery and polemic.[94] Beginning with Charles's descent into the peninsula, it first charted the French conquest of Milan and Naples. After a tantalizingly brief account of Savonarola's ascendency in Florence, it then turned to the campaigns of Cesare Borgia. Though unable to suppress a lingering admiration for the speed of the duke's conquests, Niccolò brilliantly captured the sense of fear by which the Florentines had been seized as the duke ranged across the Romagna. As Niccolò recalled, Florence might easily have succumbed to Cesare's rule. Despite the city's friendship with Louis XII, it had already suffered four 'mortal wounds' that left it weak and vulnerable: Pistoia was 'in part rebellious'; Pisa and the Valdichiana had been lost; and the city itself was 'full of confusion'.[95] That it had survived, Niccolò argued, was due solely to Alamanno Salviati. During his 'rule', he had healed three of Florence's wounds: he had 'brought Pistoia back to perfect peace', led 'Arezzo and all Valdichiana back beneath their ancient yoke' and established the office of *gonfaloniere a vita*.[96] Only Pisa had eluded him – albeit through no fault of his own.

Since then, Florence had been rid of the Borgia menace. But Fortune had not yet put an end to her suffering. Even in Cesare's absence, Italy was still divided: the pope was trying to 'cure the Church of its wounds'; the emperor was intent on receiving a coronation in Rome; the French were reeling from the shock of defeat; and Spain 'who holds Apulia's sceptre' was menacing her neighbours.[97] War was looming – and Florence still had not taken Pisa. Niccolò could not help being afraid. He longed to know in which direction Florence's little barque would sail, weighed down as it was with 'such heavy weights', or 'into what harbour, with such winds'. Though he placed his trust in its 'skilful steersman' – that is, Piero Soderini – 'in the oars, in the sails, in the cordage', he felt that the voyage would be much shorter and easier if the city 'reopened the temple of Mars.'[98] The implication was clear. If Florence ever wanted to enjoy peace, it would have to take up arms against Pisa once again. Though Salviati could be forgiven for resenting Soderini's failure to 'turn [the] Arno aside through different courses',[99] he should put his enmity aside, and help the *gonfaloniere* complete the task he had begun only a few years before.[100]

The *Decennale* was a remarkably elegant piece of writing. When Ercole Bentivoglio read it a few months later, he could not help admiring the skill with which Niccolò had described the gravity of the danger facing Florence.[101] But Alamanno Salviati was unmoved. Though he was happy to accept Niccolò's dedication, he saw no reason to change his mind about Soderini's Pisan policy. If anything, he was even more implacably opposed than before.

*

But Soderini had an ace up his sleeve. However bitterly Salviati and Rucellai might hate him, he reasoned, they would not be able to block him forever. Unless they wanted to see Florence fall to Bartolomeo d'Alviano – which, despite their recent flirtation with the Medici, still seemed unlikely – they would eventually have to give way.

Soderini soon had the chance to put this to the test. In February 1505, he asked the Great Council to approve a series of new taxes.[102] At Salviati's instigation, however, the Council refused. Taxes were already too high, his spokesmen argued; it would be folly to raise them further, especially given how wantonly the *gonfaloniere* had wasted Florence's money in the past. Undeterred, Soderini petitioned the Council a second time, only for his proposals to be rejected once again. This time, it was decisive. Rather than risk a third defeat, Soderini withdrew his request. It was a humiliating blow. Never before had he seemed so utterly powerless. Almost as soon as the final vote had been cast, leaflets calling for him to be forced out of office were being circulated in the streets. Salviati was, of course, delighted. But it was not long before the tables began to turn. Without the new taxes, Florence could no longer afford to pay Louis XII the money it owed. Only a few days after the Council voted Soderini's proposals down, in fact, an instalment of 10,000 *scudi* was missed. Since this was a breach of trust, Louis would have been within his rights to abandon the city to its foes. Admittedly, to some of Soderini's opponents, this would not have been too great a loss. After all, Louis had not done Florence many favours recently. They even wondered whether the time had come to stop payments altogether. But, for most Florentines, it was a frightening prospect. On 26 February, a specially convened *pratica* acknowledged that, however painful the payments might be, Florence could not do without France's support. [103] More money would *have* to be found. The Great Council had no choice but to agree. Setting aside their dislike of Soderini, its members duly approved the taxes he had originally requested, with only minor amendments.

Buoyed by this success, Soderini now felt confident enough to tackle the Pisan question again. Two weeks after a Florentine army under Luca Savelli was defeated by the Pisans at Ponte a Cappellese, he called for a direct attack on the rebel city.[104] This would not, of course, be cheap. At a *pratica* on 25 March, he estimated that it would cost 48,000 ducats to keep the necessary forces in the field for two months. What was more, an additional 20,000 ducats would be needed for siege equipment.[105] There was less opposition to the idea than in the past, but opinion was still divided. No consensus having been reached, it was decided that a larger *pratica* should be summoned.

Soderini might still have got his way. Before the *pratica* could be convened, however, the *Dieci* received word that Giampaolo Baglioni had refused to serve in Florence's army any longer.[106] This put paid to any hopes of attacking Pisa. But it also raised a frightening possibility. Up until now, Baglioni had remained loyal to Florence out of self-interest. Though the Republic might not have paid him top dollar – especially in recent months – he had always believed that defending its position in Tuscany was the best way of preserving his own hold over Perugia. That he had now abandoned the Florentines meant that he had either decided to take his chances alone, or had secretly thrown in his lot with their enemies.

On 9 April, the *Dieci* ordered Niccolò to ride to Perugia 'with all speed'. As Marcello di Virgilio Adriani explained in his instructions, he was to make Baglioni understand how furious the Florentines were with his conduct.[107] Most particularly, he was to complain about the *condottiere*'s 'want of gratitude . . . and faith as a soldier'. His real purpose was, however, to provoke Baglioni into 'revealing the true motive for his decision'.

Niccolò was probably quite glad of the chance to get out of Florence. Since finishing the *Decennale primo*, he had been rushed off his feet trying to get Soderini's tax proposals approved and making preparations for the *gonfaloniere*'s abortive attack on Pisa. What was more, Totto had been badgering him about a benefice – even asking him to make enquiries about a provostship at the sanctuary of Santa Maria in Cigoli, twenty kilometres west of Florence.[108] All the while, his three young children must have been screaming the house down from morning to night. It would have been a relief to get away.

Riding out the next morning, he reached Cortona by nightfall.[109]

Seeing that it was too late to make it to Castiglione del Lago, where Baglioni was reportedly staying, he decided to spend the night at the lodgings of Florence's ambassador, Pietro Bartolini. Early the next morning, he was on his way once again, and, by midday, he had arrived at Baglioni's magnificent castle overlooking Lake Trasimeno.

Still in his riding dress, Niccolò was granted an audience. As he had been instructed, he began by telling Baglioni how distressed the *Dieci* had been to hear of his decision – especially so close to the beginning of the campaigning season. At the very least, he might have told them earlier. Baglioni admitted that his timing had been unfortunate, but he could not have told the *Dieci* any sooner. Even a few weeks ago, he had been unaware of 'the machinations of the Colonnas and of his other enemies', and of 'the intrigues which they had been carrying on, even within Perugia itself'. Once he had discovered the danger in which he stood, however, he had realized that 'it would be impossible for him to accept any obligations to others without manifest danger of losing his own state, and that it would be better . . . to [take] care of his own interests than to have accepted [Florence's] money, and then to have had to leave in the middle of his contract.'[110]

It was a plausible enough explanation. Had Baglioni stopped there, Niccolò might perhaps have believed him. But the *condottiere* could not resist complaining about how badly Florence had treated him the previous year.[111] For appearances' sake, Niccolò mouthed a few bland excuses, but he was careful not to interrupt Baglioni's flow. Evidently warming to his theme, Baglioni then poured scorn on Florence's decision to hire Luca Savelli and Marcantonio Colonna as its captains, arguing that it would have been better for the city to have struck a deal with him, Bartolomeo d'Alviano and the remaining Vitelli. That way, Siena could have been brought to heel and Pisa would have surrendered of its own volition. Surprised by the bluntness of Baglioni's remarks, Niccolò defended Florence's captains as skilfully as he could, in the hope that it might goad the *condottiere* into showing his hand more clearly. But Baglioni knew he had already said too much. He refused to answer any more questions, leaving Niccolò uncertain how to take his allusion to Alviano.

Later that afternoon, Niccolò tried again.[112] This time, Baglioni was more guarded. In the course of a 'rather confused and desultory discussion', he repeated his determination to stay at home that year, but would give no clue as to his reasons. He added that he did not believe Florence would be in a condition to attack Pisa any time soon, but that, if Soderini was determined, the *gonfaloniere* should not employ the Colonnas under any circumstances. But that was all he would say. Niccolò could not help feeling frustrated. It was obvious that Baglioni was not telling him the whole story, but he knew he would not be able to trick the *condottiere* into revealing any more.

Fortunately, Niccolò came across two Florentines who happened to be in Baglioni's employ.[113] Whether by appealing to their patriotism, or by offering them some sort of incentive, he persuaded them to spill the beans. The reality was worse than he had feared. They told him that Baglioni had been persuaded to defect by Pandolfo Petrucci as part of a wider plot involving Lucca, the Orsini and Ascanio Sforza. They did not know whether any others were implicated, but they were certain that a good deal was going on behind the scenes. Every night, Baglioni received news from a courier, and Goro Gheri da Pistoia, a partisan of the Medici, was often seen at court. The previous Sunday, Baglioni had also met with Petrucci somewhere near Chiusi, around fifteen kilometres to the south-west, under the pretence of hunting. Although specifics were hard to come by, there was no doubt that they were planning to prevent Florence from recapturing Pisa, and to do the Republic even more harm if they could – most likely in conjunction with Bartolomeo d'Alviano, at whose disposal Baglioni would probably place his troops. Undoubtedly, the restoration of the Medici figured in their plans, as well. Of course, they expected all this to be discovered sooner or later, but Baglioni had waited until the last minute before telling the Florentines that he would not fight for them, so as to give the *Dieci* as little time as possible to make preparations.

Having now discovered the truth, Niccolò did not want to waste another moment in Castiglione del Lago. After scribbling a letter to the *Dieci*, he mounted his horse and rode off as quickly as he could.[114] That evening, he spent the night at Cortona, and, the following morning, took the precaution of stopping at Arezzo to speak with its captain, most likely about the status of the city's defences. He did not tarry, however. By the morning of 13 April, he was back in Florence.

*

Having received Niccolò's letter the previous afternoon, the *Dieci* were already debating who they should hire to replace Baglioni.[115] The most obvious candidate was Fabrizio Colonna.[116] No more than fifty years old, he was known to be a commander of extraordinary ability and a sworn enemy of the Orsini. He was, moreover, keen to join the Florentines' cause. Only a few weeks before, he had actually offered his services. This was enough to convince Soderini, who made no secret of his desire to employ Colonna at once. But Fabrizio was not without his faults. As some of the *gonfaloniere*'s opponents had pointed out when the *condottiere*'s name had first been mooted the year before, Colonna was currently in the service of the Aragonese and had actually fought under Gonzalo at the Battle of Garigliano.[117] It would surely be foolhardy for Florence, which was still allied with France, to engage a Spanish commander to protect it against Alviano and his new confederates.

Seeing that opinion was divided, Soderini agreed to allow a panel of twelve specially elected citizens to decide who to employ as Florence's captain general.[118] Among those chosen to serve on this body were Alamanno Salviati and Lanfredino Lanfredini. At their urging, the panel turned Colonna down and instead settled on the marquis of Mantua, Francesco II Gonzaga. He was not an unreasonable choice. Though only thirty-eight years old, he had already won a reputation for courage in battle. What was more, he had close ties to Florence's allies. After almost a decade in Venetian service, he had recently fought for Louis XII in Naples, and Julius II in the Romagna.

Even Soderini had to admit that the marquis would make a fine captain. With his approval, the *Dieci* began drafting a contract stipulating that the marquis would provide Florence with an additional 300 men-at-arms and would receive 33,000 ducats in return.[119] This was not an ungenerous offer. But the marquis was not an easy man to please. He insisted on having 500 foot soldiers, on top of what the *Dieci* had already asked for, but would not provide any more than 150 men-at-arms.[120] Naturally, the *Dieci* could not accept such terms. But they hoped that, with skilful negotiation, it might still be possible to reach an agreement. To this end, they asked Niccolò to ride by post to Mantua and use his unrivalled knowledge of the situation to bring the marquis round.

*

Leaving Florence, Niccolò headed northwards. Most likely taking the road through the Mugello and Bologna, he would have crossed the River Po within two or three days and, no later than 8 May, he would have beheld the domes and towers of Mantua's skyline reflected in the shimmering waters of the lake. It is still a bewitching sight, but he did not have time to savour its beauty. As was his habit, he would have ridden directly to the Palazzo Ducale and there secured an audience with the famously ugly marquis.

Since Niccolò's despatches have not survived, there is no way of knowing exactly what was said at that first meeting. But the marquis was evidently reluctant to change his mind. Niccolò therefore found himself some lodgings and settled in for what promised to be a wearying round of negotiations.[121]

*

While Niccolò was locked in talks, Florence was facing a serious food shortage. Following their victory over Luca Savelli at Ponte a Cappellese in March, the Pisans had successfully prevented any shipments of corn reaching Florence from Livorno. Prices soon started to rise. Scenting an opportunity for profit, unscrupulous speculators began stockpiling grain in the knowledge that this would drive the cost up even more. By mid-May, the price of corn was higher than it had been since the beginning of the century.[122] Hungry peasants began flocking to the city out of desperation. Soon enough, starvation set in – and, for the first time in living memory, Florence was convulsed by bread riots. According to Jacopo Nardi, private houses were in constant danger of being sacked,[123] Soderini was denounced in the streets and people openly called for the Medici to be restored.

Decisive action by Soderini stemmed the growing tide of unrest. With the support of a large *pratica*, he swiftly banned any more peasants from entering Florence, and ordered consignments of corn to be sent to the surrounding villages. This eased pressure on the city, and – coupled with measures already put in place to tackle hoarding[124] – helped bring prices down a little. Even the *gonfaloniere*'s opponents could not help admiring his resolve. When news arrived that Ascanio Sforza – whose participation in Alviano's alliance was central to the Medici's plans – had died unexpectedly, Soderini's position was further reinforced.

Support for the marquis of Mantua was, however, starting to dwindle. By quibbling over money in the midst of a famine, he had made himself look unscrupulous. Even some of his former supporters were disturbed by such a brazen display of self-interest. Although they were not yet ready to throw him over, they did not know how far they could trust him.

*

When Niccolò returned to Florence, no later than 22 May, the mood became more hostile. Although the marquis had eventually been persuaded to accept the *Dieci*'s terms, he had only done so on the condition that his obligations to Louis XII should take precedence over his service to Florence. This meant that, if Alviano attacked, he would be able to excuse himself from fighting by claiming that it would be a violation of Louis' truce with Ferdinand of Aragon. Understandably, the Florentines were furious. They had not expected him to pull such a cheap trick. Many now questioned whether there was any point in ratifying his contract if he was going to abandon the city when it most needed him.[125]

Soderini's government began looking for some way of backing out. On 23 May, a *pratica* decided to send an emissary to Gonzalo to determine how threatening Alviano's movements really were. If Alviano had no immediate plans to march on Florence, perhaps the city could do without the marquis – at least for the time being. During the debate, Piero del Nero – Marietta's step-father – suggested that Niccolò would be the perfect person for such a mission.[126] But others felt that someone of a higher social status was needed. In the end, Niccolò's old friend, Roberto Acciaiuoli, was chosen.[127] Niccolò wouldn't have been too disappointed, however. As he must have known, it was likely to be a fruitless mission. Even the most optimistic members of the *pratica* must have realized the odds of Alviano holding off were slim at best.

Six days later, another *pratica* debated whether Fabrizio Colonna should be hired instead.[128] If nothing else, some reasoned, he might be able to stir up trouble against the Orsini in the countryside around Rome, and thereby prevent Alviano from marching any further northwards.[129] He was, however, still as flawed a candidate as he had been a few weeks earlier. Given Colonna's close association with

Gonzalo in the past, there was always a chance that he might decide
to abandon the Florentines and join forces with Alviano without
any warning. For Niccolò, who took the minutes at the *pratica*'s
second session, later that afternoon, the risk would probably have
seemed too great, and the majority of speakers thought the same.[130]

The *Dieci* had no choice but to let the deal with the marquis go
ahead as it stood.[131] Time was, in any case, running out. Though they
were frantically trying to stall Alviano by raising the possibility of
peace talks, they knew they would not be able to hold him off for
much longer.[132] The crops would soon be ripe; if Alviano was going
to attack, he would have to do so before the harvest was gathered
in. Trying hard to forget their reservations, the *Dieci* therefore
confirmed the marquis's contract, and braced themselves for the
coming battle.

*

Only a few days later, the *Dieci* received word that Alviano was
already on his way, planning to cross the Maremma and link up with
Jacopo IV d'Appiano in Piombino, where a force of 1,000 Aragonese
infantrymen had already disembarked. Together, they would then be
able to march on Pisa – which, because of Florence's recent weakness,
had been able to recover some of its strength and was sure to welcome
them with open arms.[133]

The *Dieci* were reluctant to send the marquis of Mantua into the
field just yet. As such, they hurriedly began casting about for some
other way of blocking Alviano's approach.[134] At a *pratica* on 29 June,
some favoured cutting a deal with Gonzalo. It was, however, unlikely
to work. Although Gonzalo had recently told Roberto Acciaiuoli that
he might be willing to withdraw his support for Alviano's campaign,
he would only do so on the condition that Florence refrained from
attacking Pisa for a year.[135] Such terms were clearly unacceptable. This
being so, others suggested it might be better to try detaching Alviano
from his Tuscan allies. This was not as impracticable as it might once
have seemed. A few days earlier, Pandolfo Petrucci had intimated
that, if Florence were to give up its rights over Montepulciano and
Pietrasanta, Siena and Lucca would be prepared to change sides.[136]
At a stroke, this would close off Alviano's route through the Maremma
and make any attempt on Pisa considerably more difficult. Even if

the price was a little high, Giovanni Vittorio Soderini argued, it would be foolish to let such an opportunity pass.[137] Someone should be sent to talk to Pandolfo as soon as possible. The *Dieci* agreed.

On 16 July, Niccolò was sent to Siena to begin negotiations.[138] Despite the tumultuous events of recent years, Pandolfo did not seem to have changed much. Though his hair might have been a little greyer, his cold, grey eyes still flashed with their familiar cunning, and the same sardonic smile played about his lips. Niccolò knew he would have to be on his guard. He began cautiously, hoping to gain a sense of Pandolfo's sincerity before showing his hand. Instead of saying anything about an agreement, he claimed to have been sent merely to pass on news of Alviano's approach and to ask how His Lordship intended to proceed. But Pandolfo had been expecting this.[139] Even before Niccolò had finished speaking, he interrupted to say that he had already been giving some thought to the matter, and implied that his sympathies lay with the Florentines. A short time before, he had learned that Alviano was planning to make for Campiglia, some ten kilometres north-east of Piombino. On learning this, he said, he had immediately sent word to Piero Soderini and had urged Alviano not to march any further. Alviano would, he promised, receive no support from Siena.

Pandolfo was clearly angling for some expression of gratitude or friendship, but Niccolò refused to take the bait. It was impossible to say whether any of this was true. Rather than say anything about how their two states might cooperate more closely in future, he politely took his leave. It was a shrewd piece of gamesmanship. Later that evening, Pandolfo sent for Niccolò once again. This time, he was more direct. Without being asked, he revealed that Alviano had broken camp that very morning. He had large reserves of money, infantry and artillery. Of course, Pandolfo claimed to be deeply alarmed by this. If only he could reach some sort of agreement with Florence, he sighed. He then outlined how this might look. In return for Montepulciano, he would offer the Florentines his full support against Alviano in the Maremma, and would provide them with fifty men-at-arms for their own defence. He also seemed to be suggesting that he would bring Baglioni over to their side, as well.

Niccolò was troubled. Although Pandolfo's terms were as expected, his reasons for wanting such an agreement didn't make any sense. If he really was afraid that Alviano might attack him, why wasn't he asking the Florentines for more help? Something wasn't right. Sensibly, Niccolò said he would have to write to the *Dieci* before he could give Pandolfo an answer. But Pandolfo was nothing if not persistent. It was a simple agreement, he repeated. There wasn't anything to think about, especially as they would both benefit. As soon as it was settled, he would send his men to the Maremma, and Florence would be free to concentrate its forces on Campiglia. If this wasn't enough to satisfy them, he would try to talk the Vitelli into joining them, too.

Pandolfo's badgering did nothing to allay Niccolò's concerns. If he was so determined to resist Alviano's advance, the secretary asked, why did he have to wait for the Florentines' decision before sending troops into the Maremma? Surely it would be better to act first? If he did, he would reassure the Florentines considerably. As Niccolò slyly pointed out, they had not forgotten how deceitfully he had treated them in the past and would doubtless view his hesitation with suspicion. This stung Pandolfo. Realizing that he had said too much, he brought the audience to an abrupt end.

Writing to the *Dieci* later that evening, Niccolò confessed that his faith in Pandolfo's offer had been shaken. He was beginning to wonder if Pandolfo might be playing a double game. As things stood, Niccolò reasoned, Pandolfo's fate was bound up with the success or failure of Alviano's campaign. If Alviano succeeded, then so much to the good; but if he did not, Pandolfo could easily find himself exiled from Siena once again. Were the Florentines to accept his terms, however, Pandolfo could be sure of winning either way – and without having to lift a finger. He would just have to wave Alviano through Sienese territory and let the chips fall where they may.

This was, of course, just a suspicion. But, when Niccolò learned that Pandolfo was secretly receiving money from the Venetians and had urged Alviano to advance as quickly as possible, rather than stop, he couldn't help feeling that his misgivings might be justified.[140]

Over the next few days, Niccolò's concerns steadily grew. On 18 July, he was approached by a Paolo di Pietro di Paolo in the *Duomo*.[141] Affecting to have a deep affection for Florence, Paolo reassured Niccolò that Pandolfo had no dealings with Florence's enemies and wanted nothing more than to frustrate Alviano's plans. Time was, however, running out. Paolo urged Niccolò to talk the *Dieci* into signing a deal as soon as possible. But, the very next day, Pandolfo undermined any confidence that Paolo had managed to inspire.[142] Although he seemed desperate to push the Florentines into a deal, he refused to move against Alviano until he could be sure of their friendship. He then started to back-pedal on his earlier claims about Alviano's confederates, too. Despite what he had told Niccolò at their last audience, he could no longer be sure of enticing either Baglioni or the Vitelli to join him. On 21 July, Pandolfo made things even worse for himself. He now claimed to have heard that Gonzalo had ordered Alviano to desist from his attempt on Tuscany. Alviano was, however, still determined to press on, and had asked Baglioni for help. This might, of course, have been true, but it was too much for poor Niccolò. All these intrigues were making his head spin. Nothing Pandolfo said – either about his own intentions, or about Alviano – made any sense.[143] As long as he kept changing his story, it was hard to know what to believe.

Back in Florence, the *Dieci* were beginning to have doubts about Pandolfo, as well.[144] Although they were unwilling to abandon the negotiations just yet, they decided to test him by offering more modest terms. Rather than simply handing over Montepulciano, they now proposed that Louis XII adjudicate between Florence and Siena. If Pandolfo was serious about an agreement, they reasoned, he would at least give it some thought.

When Niccolò broached the idea, however, he met with a gruff refusal.[145] As Antonio da Venafro explained, Pandolfo was afraid the king might decide in Florence's favour. But he still hoped they might be able to reach an agreement. If this was so, Niccolò replied, Pandolfo just had to show a little goodwill to prove to the *Dieci* that he could be trusted. Antonio, however, remained firm. Montepulciano was non-negotiable.

Niccolò had finally reached the end of his tether. It was obvious the discussions were not going anywhere. Florence would either have to accept Pandolfo's original terms, or abandon the agreement altogether.[146] On balance, it might be better to walk away. Reluctantly, the *Dieci* had to agree. Although they had learned that Pandolfo had been telling the truth about Alviano's rift with Gonzalo, they simply couldn't trust him. Niccolò was to bid Siena farewell and return to the chancellery with all haste.

*

With Alviano's army only a few days' march away, the Florentine Republic hurriedly began readying its forces for the defence of Campiglia.[147] Niccolò's old friend, Antonio Giacomini, was appointed commissioner general in the field and, under his watchful eye, the necessary orders were drawn up. Soon, soldiers were marching through Florence's streets on their way southwards, cannons rumbled along country roads and supplies were brought in from near and far. But then disaster struck. At the last possible moment, the marquis of Mantua refused to serve, on the spurious grounds that the king of France had not approved his contract. The French also refused to send help, because Florence had not been keeping up with its payments.

Political unrest erupted. As Guicciardini later reported, Soderini's opponents blamed him for the marquis' defection – albeit unjustly.[148] Although Florence urgently needed to hire a new captain, they stubbornly refused to approve the *gonfaloniere*'s proposals for new taxes.[149] Tempers quickly flared. At a meeting of the Council of Eighty, Soderini even had to apologize for shouting abuse at Lionardo Guidotti, after the latter had put forward a rival plan benefitting the *ottimati* more than the Republic. Such a display of weakness only emboldened his enemies further, and the more obstinately they blocked him, the worse Florence's military prospects became. With only a few ragtag bands of mercenaries to rely upon, the city seemed to be heading for certain defeat.

*

On 17 August, the Florentine army came upon Alviano at San Vincenzo, just north of Piombino. Much to the surprise of Florence's commanders, Ercole Bentivoglio and Antonio Giacomini, Alviano's forces were not as numerous as had been feared.[150] He had no more men-at-arms than they did, and there was nothing to suggest he could expect to receive reinforcements any time soon. Realizing they would never get a better chance, they decided to give battle. A long and bitter struggle ensued. But after several hours of hard fighting, the Florentines routed their enemy. In terror, Alviano fled, leaving behind 'almost all of his baggage train'.[151]

Back in Florence, news of the victory was greeted with wild delight. People rushed out of their houses to see Alviano's captured banners being carried through the streets in triumph, and cheered with joy as they were put on display in the hall of the Great Council. Soderini was especially thrilled. Having been blamed for everything that had gone wrong over the past few months, he felt justified in taking full credit for the army's success.[152] His policies and his leadership seemed to have been vindicated.

Shortly after the battle, Antonio Giacomini called on the *gonfaloniere* to press Florence's advantage and launch an immediate attack on Pisa.[153] Having received detailed intelligence about the city's defences, he was confident it could be taken. Soderini was, of course, easily persuaded, but his opponents were more sceptical.[154] Just because Alviano had been defeated did not mean Pisa would be a pushover, they warned. The Pisans still had plenty of well-trained soldiers, a large number of artillery pieces and plentiful supplies. They could also count on the support of Gonzalo and their other allies. Rather than rushing in, the Florentines would do better to exercise caution. A *pratica* convened to discuss the matter agreed.[155] After rousing speeches, its members unanimously recommended that further thought be given to the proposed assault. Soderini was, however, unwilling to be put off. Disregarding normal procedure, he appealed to the Council of Eighty, where he enjoyed much greater support. Far less cautious than the *pratica*, the Eighty voted overwhelmingly in favour of making an attack as quickly as possible. To facilitate this, they passed a series of new tax measures that same afternoon.[156] The Great Council's approval, two days later, was a mere formality. Soderini had got his way.

As the secretary of the *Dieci*, Niccolò was responsible for making the necessary preparations. He threw himself into the task with gusto. Having long argued for such an assault, he was determined to make sure it succeeded – no matter how great the sacrifice, or how questionable the means. On 19 August, he wrote to Giacomini with orders to proceed towards Pisa. Before taking any action against the city, however, Giacomini was to fall upon Lucca's territory and prevent it from hampering the Florentine attack. As Niccolò put it, he was to 'plunder, ravage, and lay waste to [the land] with fire and sword in the most hostile manner, leaving nothing undone that [could] damage [the Lucchesi]'.[157] Above all, Giacomini was to destroy Viarregio – Lucca's only port. Warehouses were to be razed, houses burned and, if necessary, the inhabitants killed, as well. Whatever Giacomini needed to carry this out, he would get.

Two days later, Niccolò was sent to Giacomini's camp to check on his progress. By this point, the harrying of Lucca's territory had largely been accomplished and Giacomini was beginning to turn his attention towards Pisa. Not wishing to leave anything to chance, Niccolò informed the *Dieci* that more artillery and ammunition would be needed, and asked for additional funds to be sent to Ercole Bentivoglio's constables, so they could raise more troops. He also recommended letting it be known that Florence would employ anyone able to bear arms, so as to encourage Pisan soldiers to desert.

Confidence was running high. Despite their earlier scepticism, even Soderini's opponents believed Pisa might soon be retaken. Jacopo Salviati was so concerned that he tried to patch up his relationship with the *gonfaloniere* by hastening the marriage of his wife's cousin, Pierfrancesco de' Medici, to Soderini's nephew, Tommaso – a match he had violently opposed only a year before.[158] And, in Rome, Genoese merchants were saying that, this time, Pisa was bound to fall to the Florentines.[159] But difficulties soon arose. Even before the Florentine army had reached Pisa, divisions started to open up between its commanders. Out of the blue, Ercole Bentivoglio demanded to be appointed captain general, as a reward for his role in securing the victory at San Vincenzo.[160] This put the *Dieci* in a difficult situation. If they agreed, they risked upsetting their other *condottiere*. As Niccolò confided to Antonio Giacomini, Marcantonio Colonna was already threatening to 'raise the devil'.[161] If he left Florentine service, Jacopo and Luca Savelli would doubtless join him. If the *Dieci* turned Bentivoglio down, however, there was a danger that he might storm off – taking a sizeable number of troops with him. After much deliberation, they decided to compromise.[162] The 'insolent' Bentivoglio would be given his title, albeit grudgingly, and the other *condottiere* would be placated with promises and assurances. But this failed to satisfy anyone. Amid the storm of recriminations that followed, any unity of purpose was quickly forgotten.

No less troubling was the news from Naples. On hearing of Florence's plans, Gonzalo had announced his intention to send troops to Pisa. At first, Soderini had been dismissive. As Guicciardini later reported, he confidently predicted that Pisa would be taken before they arrived.[163] But, a few days later, he had to admit they were advancing far more rapidly than he had expected. It was reported that 1,500 Spanish soldiers had already reached Rome, and would soon board ships bound for Tuscany.[164]

On 6 September, the Florentine army appeared before Pisa.[165] After pitching his camp between the convent of Santa Croce in Fossabanda and the church of San Michele degli Scalzi, Bentivoglio immediately had his cannons brought up and placed opposite the Porta Calcesana (today known as the Porta Garibaldi).[166] The following morning, an hour before sunrise, he unleashed a furious barrage; and by nightfall, a twenty-four-metre-long hole had been blown in the walls. Before the Pisans could repair the damage, Bentivolgio ordered 3,000 of his men to attack. But haste had got the better of his judgement. Unprepared for such a sudden action, the infantry rushed forward without any sense of order. No sooner had they poured through the breach than they were fallen upon by a crack contingent of Spanish soldiers who – unbeknown to Bentivoglio – had arrived from Piombino a few days before. Although the Florentines' numbers were greater, the confined space acted against them. Those not cut to pieces in the melee fled in panic. It was a humiliating rout. The other *condottieri* were furious, but Bentivoglio was determined to try again. Under cover of darkness, the artillery was moved to a position near the Torre del Barbagianni. For three solid days, the guns bombarded the walls once again, until, on the afternoon of 12 September, another large section was brought down. This time, Bentivoglio was more cautious. Rather than making a massed assault, he sent two smaller units into the breach, one after the other. The first achieved little, but sustained no real harm. The second, however, captured nothing and suffered serious losses – much to the Pisans' delight. Bentivoglio now had no choice but to admit defeat. The other *condottieri* had lost all confidence in his leadership; the Lucchesi were said to be sending Pisa reinforcements; and Gonzalo was reported to have despatched a further 2,000 soldiers. There was no point in trying to go on. On 15 September, the shattered remains of the Florentine army struck camp and slunk disconsolately back to Cascina.

Soderini's credibility had been dealt a heavy blow.[167] Having pressed so hard the previous month for the attack on Pisa, he was now held responsible for its failure. For his *ottimati* opponents, whose earlier

scepticism seemed to have been vindicated, it was a damning indict-
ment of his whole approach to government. Had he respected
Florence's constitutional norms and listened to the *pratiche*'s advice,
they cried, the whole debacle might never have happened. For many
popolani, however, it was yet 'another costly government failure.'[168]
They had agreed to higher taxes in the belief that their money would
be used to keep Florence safe, but they had received nothing in
return.

If anything, the city was in a worse position than before. Far from
having been recaptured, Pisa was now more secure in its defiance.
Its walls had been repaired, morale was high and Spanish troops
were pouring in by the thousand.[169] There were even rumours that
Gonzalo might be planning another attack on Florence itself. If this
were true, Florence would find it difficult, if not impossible, to mount
an effective defence, at least as things currently stood. Almost half
of its army had been lost, and, unless the Great Council could
somehow be persuaded to approve a further tax rise, it could not
afford to hire any more mercenaries. An alternative was desperately
needed.

*

According to Guicciardini, it was Niccolò who came up with the
solution.[170] He persuaded Soderini that the only way to meet
Florence's military needs would be to raise a citizen militia. This
was, admittedly, not a new idea. Florence had maintained a militia
until the late fourteenth century, and there had been calls for its
re-establishment ever since. Niccolò himself had suggested it only
a few years before. On 29 May 1504, Cardinal Francesco Soderini
had replied to a (now lost) letter, in which Niccolò had outlined his
plan.[171] The cardinal had agreed that a militia was both 'necessary'
and 'sound'. It had, however, faced stiff opposition. As the cardinal
noted, some of Soderini's enemies had speculated that the *gonfaloniere*
might use it to set himself up as a tyrant rather than to attack Pisa.
But the cardinal had urged Niccolò to persevere, all the same. His
chances had, however, been spoiled by the failure of the Arno project.
Although Niccolò had kept pressing his case, there was no longer
any political appetite for a militia. Even Soderini had lost interest.
Already facing intense criticism, he could not risk being accused of

harbouring tyrannical designs, no matter how unjustly.[172] Besides, Florence had enough mercenaries to be getting on with. But now, things were different. Soderini had no choice but to go along with Niccolò's plan.

It was not going to be easy.[173] There was little support for the project among Florence's political elite.[174] Indeed, the Pisan debacle seemed actually to have strengthened opposition. Even some of the *gonfaloniere*'s former allies were now baulking at the idea. Soderini doubted he would have enough votes to get the militia approved by the Council of Eighty, let alone by the Great Council. He dared not put it before a *pratica*, either. Yet he needed to push it through somehow. Frustrated by the inefficiency of the Florentine constitution and the short-sighted intransigence of his fellow citizens, he decided to sidestep normal procedure altogether. On the Signoria's authority, he simply gave orders for recruitment to begin in the *contado*, and left the troublesome business of formally establishing the militia itself until later.

On 30 December, Niccolò was sent to the Mugello to enlist any men 'who seemed . . . fit to bear arms.'[175] Trekking through heavy snow, he went first to Borgo San Lorenzo, a fortified commune lying some twenty-two kilometres to the north-east.[176] As he related in a letter to the *Dieci*, the response was positive.[177] Most of the inhabitants turned up to the enrolment quite happily, and those who stayed at home did so only because they thought he was a tax assessor. Everyone there welcomed the revival of the militia and counted on it to succeed. Taking into account the neighbouring villages, Niccolò estimated that he could recruit around 180 men. After stopping in the nearby town of Vicchio – where he hoped to recruit as many as a hundred more – he then pressed on to Dicomano, San Godenzo and Pontassieve. There, he met with less success. As he explained to the *Dieci*, the people in this mountainous region had a long tradition of disobedience and the villages were divided by bitter rivalries.[178] After many weeks of pleading and cajoling, he had managed to enrol only 200 men, and, of these, no more than 150 could be counted upon. He was, of course, a little disappointed. But the *Dieci* were still content with his progress. As Marcello di Virgilio Adriani intimated, Soderini was especially delighted.[179] If Niccolò carried on at this rate, it would not be long before Florence's army was returned to full strength. Fate seemed to be smiling on him once again.

On 15 February, Niccolò was able to unveil the first contingents of his new model army in the spectacular processions laid on for the carnival. Decked out in their fine red and white uniforms, 400 of his recruits paraded through the banner-filled Piazza della Signoria. The crowds were bowled over by the sight. As Landucci recorded, it was 'the finest thing ever organised by the city of Florence.'[180]

13

Fortune Favours the Brave

(February–December 1506)

Since the fall of Cesare Borgia, Niccolò had tried hard to shield himself from the cruel blows of Fortune, but he was still worried that he might be powerless to resist her whims. Shortly before composing the *Decennale primo*, he had taken the precaution of seeking advice from Bartolomeo Vespucci, a professor of astrology at the University of Padua and a relation of his chancellery colleague, Agostino.[1] Perhaps fearing he might have been born under an unfavourable star, he wanted to know whether a man could ever escape the influence of the heavens. Vespucci's reply was encouraging.[2] While Fortune was an unyielding mistress, the astrologer argued, Niccolò could shape his own destiny by seizing the opportunities he was offered and adapting to changing circumstances.

Niccolò was tempted to believe him. Just recently, he had felt he had at last begun to take control of his life again. Though the militia was still awaiting legal sanction, he had already trained an impressive number of troops – despite having no military experience of his own to draw on. Since the carnival parade, in fact, he had been inundated with praise. On 21 February, Leonardo Bartolini, a banker in Rome, had applauded his achievement in setting up such a 'wonderful' force,[3] and, on 4 March, a few days after he left Florence to drum up some more recruits in the Casentino,[4] Cardinal Francesco Soderini had congratulated him in even more fulsome terms.[5] He was also enjoying his first taste of literary fame. At some point in February, Agostino Vespucci had arranged for an emended version of the *Decennale primo* to be printed by Bartolomeo de' Libri; and before long, Niccolò's poem was being commended by some of Florence's leading men.[6] Even Ercole Bentivoglio had written that he could not help but 'admire and praise profoundly' what Niccolò had accomplished.[7]

But, just as Niccolò thought he was getting the upper hand, he was buffeted by Fortune once again. While he was traipsing around the Casentino,[8] he received word from Agostino Vespucci that a printer named Andrea Ghirlandi da Pistoia was selling a pirated version of the *Decennale primo*.[9] Agostino had, of course, reported this to the *Otto di Guardia* straight away, and assured Niccolò that all of Ghirlandi's books would be confiscated. But it was upsetting, all the same. Trudging home through heavy snow, Niccolò probably could not help wondering if some people might still have seen Ghirlandi's version and attributed its glaring orthographic mistakes to him, rather than to the printer.

This was not all. Arriving in Florence towards the end of March, Niccolò found the militia mired in controversy. After failing to convince the Great Council to grant new taxes to pay for equipment, Piero Soderini had surprised everyone by appointing Cesare Borgia's former lieutenant, Don Michele de Corella, as the militia's commander.[10] In all probability, this was a purely pragmatic decision. Though Don Michele may have been a 'cruel, terrible, and fearsome man', he was also a talented soldier, capable of clamping down on disturbances in the *contado* and making sure the militia would be ready to defend Florence against any external threats in future.[11] But the *gonfaloniere*'s opponents were horrified. They believed that Soderini would not have chosen Don Michele unless he was *actually* planning to use the militia to stifle dissent in Florence. According to Guicciardini, Bernardo Rucellai was so alarmed that he fled to Avignon.[12] Hoping to assuage these fears, Soderini sent Niccolò to reason with Francesco Gualterotti, Giovanbattista Ridolfi, Piero Guicciardini and a few others, but they proved implacable. Rather than risk putting the matter before a *pratica* of the *Dieci*, Soderini therefore decided to have Don Michele's appointment ratified by the Council of Eighty, where he could count on the support of the *popolani*. In doing so, however, he weakened the credibility of the militia and undermined much of Niccolò's hard work.

Niccolò started to doubt that he would ever be master of his own fate. Feeling thoroughly dejected, he withdrew from the public gaze and buried himself in his work. Even then, he confined himself to routine matters.[13] Though he may have been behind the decision to send Don Michele to quell rebellious grumblings in the Mugello in mid-April, he took little interest in the *condottiere*'s brutal progress over the weeks that followed.[14] He seems to have played no role in reforming the *Monte* in mid-May, either.[15] He even shied away from family business. On 25 May, Totto wrote him a rather stern letter, reminding him that there was a court case that urgently needed settling, and a property deal that required his attention, as well.[16]

Just as Niccolò was surrendering himself to Fortune, however, developments on the international stage convinced him that Fortune *could* be mastered, after all.

*

Although Cesare Borgia's fall had rid Italy of a pernicious menace, Alexander VI's legacy of debt and disorder had thus far prevented Julius II from recuperating the states of the Church from the Venetians. Now that he had pacified the Roman barons and restored some order to the papal finances, however, he felt the time had come to start putting things right by ousting Giampaolo Baglioni from Perugia and Giovanni Bentivoglio from Bologna.[17]

It was not going to be easy. As Niccolò related in a letter to Giovanni Ridolfi, the Emperor Maximilian was once again making preparations for an expedition to Italy.[18] Should he cross the Alps, he would most likely support the Venetians' claims in the Romagna – and perhaps even the tyrants that the pope wanted to unseat, as well. The king of France could be a problem, too. Already uneasy about Bentivoglio's removal, Louis XII was afraid that Maximilian might actually be planning to strike a deal with Julius, instead. Since this would put Milan at risk, he was already trying to dissuade the pope from marching northwards.[19] On top of everything, Ferdinand of Aragon was rumoured to be coming to meet with Gonzalo in Naples, or even Piombino. Julius was, however, undeterred. Confident that he would prevail, he began readying his forces. Supplies were laid in, fresh mercenaries were hired and allies were prevailed upon to honour their agreements.

A few days before setting out from Rome, Julius asked Florence to send him one hundred men-at-arms under the command of Marcantonio Colonna, who had been instrumental in securing the victory at San Vincenzo and who was still in the city's employ.[20] This put the Florentines in a difficult position. They were still not sure whether Julius really would go through with his plans. If his expedition turned out to be nothing more than hot air, it would surely be unwise to part with one of their best commanders, especially given that the Pisan War was still raging and the militia was not yet up to strength. But if Julius *did* march against Bentivoglio, it was unclear whether they should support him or not. Obviously, they did not want to risk antagonizing Louis XII, least of all if there was a chance of war, but nor could they afford to upset the pope, particularly as he was likely to pass through their territory on his way to Bologna. At the *pratiche* convened to consider the pontiff's request, opinion was sharply divided, even among Soderini's enemies.[21] While Francesco Gualterotti, Francesco Pepi and Alamanno Salviati were adamantly opposed to sending any help whatsoever, partly out of a desire to harm the *gonfaloniere*, Landredino Lanfredini, Giovanbattista Ridolfi and Guglielmo de' Pazzi spoke strongly in favour of sending troops.[22] With no agreement in sight, the *Dieci* despatched Niccolò to play for time until the situation became clearer.[23]

*

Niccolò caught up with the pope at Civita Castellana, a fortified garrison town near Viterbo, early on the morning of 28 August.[24] After gulping down a quick breakfast, he rushed off to the papal apartments and was immediately granted an audience. Though Julius was still sitting at table with Cardinal Francesco Soderini and a few others, Niccolò could not have failed to notice how much the pope had changed since their last meeting in Rome, almost three years before. No longer hesitant and uncertain, he was brimming over with self-confidence. He had insisted on riding at the head of his army, often in full armour, and, with his knee-high boots and jaunty manner, he seemed more like a warrior than a cleric.

Choosing his words carefully, Niccolò explained the *Dieci*'s position. He assured Julius that the Florentines would be very glad to see Bologna and Perugia reduced to obedience. Had he told them about his plans earlier, they would have been only too glad to have given him their full support, but they could not spare him any troops at the moment. They needed to deal with Pisa first. In a few weeks' time, however, they might be of more help. Once the campaign against Bologna was underway, they would probably be able to send him what he wanted. That is, Niccolò added, if the pope *really* meant to attack Bologna. Given Louis XII's opposition, Niccolò claimed, the Florentines found it hard to believe that Julius would actually do so. Some wondered if he might simply come to terms with Bentivoglio instead. In this case, there would be no point in the Florentines sending any troops at all.

Julius seemed to have been expecting these sorts of excuses. After listening 'attentively and cheerfully' to what Niccolò had to say, he explained that the Florentines were worrying themselves unnecessarily. France was not as firmly opposed as they thought. Although Louis XII had expressed some reservations about removing Bentivoglio in the past, he was already coming round. With a theatrical flourish, Julius produced a letter in Louis' own hand, in which the king encouraged him to act quickly and offered to provide him with 400–500 lances for the campaign. Nor should the Florentines doubt his own resolve, Julius went on; as Niccolò could see, he was already on the march. After he had dealt with Baglioni, he would eject Bentivoglio from Bologna and make sure he would never return. As such, the Florentines should not have any reservations about sending him the troops he had asked for – when they had put their own affairs in order, of course.

Naturally, Julius added, they would be amply rewarded. After whispering a few words to Cardinal Francesco Soderini, he turned back to Niccolò and assured him that, in return for Florence's support, he would 'bestow a signal gift' on the city – irrespective of how his campaign against Bologna turned out. What this 'gift' would be was not explained, but Niccolò could be forgiven for thinking that it might involve help against Pisa, or even a grant of land.

Rising to his feet, Niccolò then took his leave. He was somewhat reassured. Perhaps Florence would be able to support the pope, after all. Provided France was on side and Julius was serious about his 'gift', there might be a chance that a *pratica* could be persuaded to give its approval when the time came. Just as Niccolò stepped out of Julius's apartments, however, he was unexpectedly approached by Pierre de Filleul, the archbishop of Aix.[25] Having recently served as an intermediary between Louis XII and Julius II, Pierre seems to have felt the need to qualify some of what the pope had said. Julius had, of course, been telling the truth about Louis' change of heart.

As Pierre explained, Louis had held off from supporting the enterprise only because he had not believed it would ever take place; but now that it was underway, 'the king's desire to serve [the pope] had redoubled.' But Julius had been less than honest in leading Niccolò to believe that Louis' support would be unconditional. Although Louis was willing to help Julius recover Perugia, he would not allow his troops to be used for any other purpose – least of all against Bologna. Whether he expected his allies to follow suit was not clear; but if he did, Florence would clearly not be able to send Julius any help – even at a later stage in the campaign – without jeopardizing its alliance with France. But then again, perhaps Pierre de Filleul was not telling Niccolò the truth, either.

Brooding over this unexpected twist, later that evening, Niccolò went back to Julius's apartments to get a better view of the recently constructed Forte Sangallo.[26] While he was there, the pope spotted him and called him aside. After repeating all of the reassurances he had given about France earlier in the day, Julius went on to claim that Florence need not worry about Venice or the Holy Roman Empire, either. According to his sources, the Venetians were no longer sure that Maximilian was going to mount an expedition to Italy. Realizing this would weaken their position in the Romagna, they had therefore started making overtures to the Holy See. They had even offered to help Julius retake Bologna – if he recognized their right to Faenza and Rimini. Julius had, of course, turned them down – not only because he refused to 'concede to them what they had taken from the Church', but also because he knew how much this would harm Florence's interests. The Florentines should therefore rest easy in the knowledge that his path to Bologna was clear, and that, insofar as the Romagna was concerned, his interests coincided exactly with theirs. As such, there was no reason why they should not send him the troops he had asked for.

Niccolò did not know what to believe anymore. There was simply no way of telling what was really happening with France, Venice or the Holy Roman Empire – at least for the moment. The only thing Niccolò could be sure about was Julius's resolve. Rather than waiting for Fortune to smile on him, he was evidently determined to shape his own destiny. As long as the wider international situation remained fluid, he would do and say whatever was necessary to achieve his objectives – even if it meant breaking the commandment against bearing false witness. Whether he would succeed, however, was another matter.

*

Over the next few weeks, Niccolò accompanied Julius on his march northwards.[27] Along the way, Julius received a steady stream of bad news. Despite what he had assured Niccolò in Civita Castellana, Louis XII appeared to be having second thoughts. Charles II d'Amboise, the governor of Milan, had so far failed to send any troops, and the marquis of Mantua had been forbidden to leave French service.[28] The Venetians were also reported to be levying troops in the Romagna.[29] Though they assured Julius that they did this whenever one of their neighbours took up arms, it was difficult to believe they were not trying to frighten him into making concessions. To cap it all, there were rumours Maximilian had already crossed into Friuli.[30] As Niccolò reported, Bentivoglio was thrilled.[31] Perhaps he would hold on to Bologna, after all.

Julius was furious, but he refused to be deflected from his purpose. Indeed, as Niccolò noted, each new setback only seemed to make him bolder.[32] Brushing aside another offer from the Venetians, he pressed on towards Perugia, certain that, if he could recover it quickly, he would be able to force the king of France's hand and ease his own path to Bologna.[33] At first, negotiations seemed to bear some fruit. The townspeople had already placed themselves under his protection, and offered him their services. But Baglioni was not going to give in easily. He was still in control of the fortifications and could count on the loyalty of a large garrison. Confident that he could withstand any assault, he steadfastly refused either 'to leave, or to remain as a private citizen, without any men-at-arms.'[34]

After much discussion, a compromise was eventually reached.[35] Baglioni would surrender 'all the fortresses of the state of Perugia' and, in return, Julius would employ him as a *condottiere* for the duration of the campaign against Bologna. From Baglioni's perspective, it was undoubtedly a good deal. Though he might have lost his city, he had retained his soldiers and been given a position of considerable responsibility into the bargain. There was every chance he could win another state in future, or even regain his old one. But it was still unclear whether he would keep his word. At the last moment,

he might hole himself up in Perugia and dare Julius to do his worst.
Given how precarious the pope's situation was, he might even attempt
something more foolhardy, safe in the knowledge that, if he succeeded,
he would win favour with the Venetians and perhaps even the king
of France.

When the time came for Julius to take possession of Perugia,
however, he took the apparently suicidal decision to leave his army
outside the walls.[36] Baglioni could hardly have wished for a more
perfect opportunity. As Niccolò observed, Julius was at his mercy.[37]
In the blink of an eye, he could have taken the pope prisoner and
had the world at his feet. Curiously, however, Baglioni did nothing.
Seemingly cowed by Julius's daring, he stood meekly by as he was
deprived of his state.[38]

*

Niccolò was deeply impressed. Hurrying back to his lodgings, he
began drafting a letter to Giovanbattista Soderini – the gonfaloniere's
nephew – admitting that Bartolomeo Vespucci had been right about
man's ability to conquer Fortune, after all.[39] Now known as the
Ghiribizzi ('caprices'), this enthusiastic, but badly structured, letter
began with the observation that Fortune could never be second-
guessed. Sometimes, the same action, if repeated, could have very
different outcomes; at other times, different actions could have the
same effect. Of course, most men found this difficult to cope with.
Too indecisive to remain constant, or too stuck in their ways to
change, they invariably ended up doing the wrong thing – with
disastrous results. But a wise man knew how to turn Fortune's fickleness to his advantage. Rather than waste time worrying about what
had happened in the past, or what might happen in the future, he
took care to adapt himself to changing circumstances in the here and
now. Provided he then acted with as much boldness as he could
muster, he was sure to be successful, regardless of what others might
be doing elsewhere. If Giovanbattista needed proof of this, he would
find history full of examples. Take Hannibal and Scipio Africanus.
Each had adopted a different strategy during his campaigns. In Italy,
Hannibal had been cruel, deceitful and impious, while, in Spain,
Scipio had been kind, honest and devout. Because these different
strategies had been suited to local conditions, however, both had

achieved the same end. They had kept their armies united, they had gained the admiration of the people and they had won 'victory upon victory'.[40] There were plenty of more recent examples, too. Guidobaldo da Montefeltro, the commander of the papal armies, had held on to the duchy of Urbino by tearing down castles, while 'Count Francesco in Milan and many others [had] constructed fortresses in their territories in order to secure them'.[41]

Julius II had shown that he understood this perfectly. Since setting out from Rome, he had expended almost no effort on planning how best to retake Perugia. As Niccolò put it, he had 'neither scales nor measuring stick in his house'. But, by adapting himself to circumstances and acting boldly, he had obtained 'by chance – and unarmed – what ought to have been difficult to attain even with organization and with weapons.'[42]

Though Niccolò was too discreet to say so explicitly, he evidently felt that Giovanbattista's uncle, the *gonfaloniere*, would do well to learn from Julius's example.[43] It is not difficult to see why. Over the past few years, Piero Soderini had suffered all manner of failures – not because he had been buffeted by ill fortune, as Niccolò had once believed, but because he had refused to adapt to changing circumstances. The abortive attempt to divert the Arno, the defeat beneath the walls of Pisa and the near-constant political deadlock had all been the result of his stubbornness. By contrast, when Soderini at last consented to try something different – that is to say, the militia – he had met with immediate success. At the time of Niccolò's departure, however, the *gonfaloniere* had been on the brink of undoing any good this might achieve. However talented Don Michele was, his methods were harsh in the extreme – so harsh, in fact, that they might fan the flames of rebellion in the rough hill-country of the Mugello. While 'cruelty, treachery, and impiety are effective in providing a . . . ruler with prestige in [a] region where human kindness, loyalty and piety have long been common practice,' Niccolò argued, Soderini might do well to realize that 'human kindness, loyalty, and piety' could sometimes be more effective 'where cruelty, treachery, and impiety' had previously reigned.[44] The only problem was that, like most men, Soderini might not be able to change his nature, and would hence be condemned to be buffeted by Fortune for evermore.

*

Before Niccolò had finished developing this point, however, he had second thoughts about his letter. It was already quite long, and – as his marginal notes suggest – he was beginning to lose his thread. Perhaps recalling the works of fifteenth-century poets like Luigi Pulci, Antonio Bonciani and Antonio da Meglio, he decided to attempt a more abstract meditation in verse. Setting the unfinished *Ghiribizzi* aside, he therefore started work on a lengthy (and rather misogynistic) poem, now known as the *Capitolo di Fortuna*.

Written in terza rima, this depicted Fortune as a capricious princess. After a brief exordium – again, addressed to Giovanbattista Soderini – Niccolò began by reminding the reader of how fickle she could be.[45] Shifting and inconstant, she keeps the good down and raises up the wicked. If she ever makes a promise, she never keeps it. She turns kingdoms upside down as she pleases, and robs the just only to enrich the iniquitous. She times events as suits her and acknowledges neither right nor law.

No one could escape Fortune's 'hard bite, her rough blows, violent and cruel', any more than he could change his own character, Niccolò warned.[46] Those who try to hide, she seeks out, while those who struggle against her power, she 'resists with the greatest might'.[47] But this need not be cause for resignation or fear. Those who are anxious, regretful, lazy or envious invariably suffer greatly.[48] Like all cruel women, Fortune delights in afflicting them with servitude, infamy, sickness and poverty. But he who 'takes her for his star . . . adjusts himself to her variation' and slaps her about with 'manly' courage will surely win her respect – and her favour. Indeed, he will be rewarded with power, honour and riches, and will 'always be happy and blessed'.

Niccolò again illustrated this with examples taken from history. Long ago, he argued, Fortune had built up kingdoms and empires, only to bring them low when it took her fancy. Egypt, Babylon, Carthage, Jerusalem, Athens, Sparta and Rome had risen and fallen in turn according to her whims.[49] So too, she played with men – even the great. Cyrus and Pompey, Cicero and Marius had all been raised up, only to fall from a greater height because they could not adapt to her ways.[50] But those like Julius Caesar and Alexander the Great, who pushed, shoved and jostled Fortune, had enjoyed triumph without end.[51]

*

Although Niccolò never mentioned Julius II in the *Capitolo di Fortuna*, he evidently believed the pope was destined to follow in the footsteps of these great men. Since Baglioni's capitulation, Fortune had continued to shower him with rewards. Even before Niccolò had finished writing his poem, Julius had received word that Louis XII was at last prepared to support a campaign against Bologna.[52] Although Charles II d'Amboise, seigneur de Chaumont had not yet been authorized to despatch any troops, the marquis of Mantua duly arrived in Perugia to join the pope's army on 17 September.[53] Maximilian's long-awaited expedition to Italy also seemed to be off the cards. On 19 September, Niccolò informed the *Dieci* that no one at court seriously expected him to venture beyond the Alps;[54] and a week later, the sudden death of his son Philip the Fair put paid to any remaining chances of him doing so.[55] This prompted the Venetians to abandon their former hostility, too. Though their demands for Faenza and Rimini precluded any agreement,[56] they nevertheless gave Julius to understand that they would not obstruct Bentivoglio's removal.

Julius was now 'keener [than ever] for [his] enterprise against Bologna'.[57] Leaving Perugia on 21 September, he set out across the Apennines towards Gubbio and Urbino. From there, he would strike out in the direction of Imola, just thirty-four kilometres from Bologna. As yet, he had given no indication of his plans, but Ercole Bentivoglio, who had recently arrived from Florence, told Niccolò that the pope would most likely try to wear Giovanni down by attrition.[58] From Imola, Julius would be able 'to spread some 600 or 700 men-at-arms and 5,000 or 6,000 infantry around [the area between the two cities], and raid it during the winter'. When spring came, he could then raise a larger force and threaten the countryside with devastation. Since Giovanni would find it difficult to bear the cost of such a protracted campaign, he would eventually have no choice but to surrender.

When the Bolognese realized this, they were horrified. They had no desire either to take up arms on Bentivoglio's behalf or to endure the hardships of a lengthy struggle. Shortly before Julius left Urbino, Niccolò reported that they seemed ready to submit.[59] When their ambassadors arrived in Cesena, however, negotiations quickly collapsed.[60] At an audience on 3 October, they offered to surrender their city to the pope, asking only that he would allow them to administer their own affairs, and respect their existing agreements with other powers. It was not an unreasonable request. Had it been made a few weeks earlier, Julius might well have granted it. He had, after all, treated the Perugians with some indulgence. But, now, things were different. Having received word that Chaumont was at last sending him a detachment of French soldiers, Julius no longer needed to bargain. He was going to reduce Bologna to obedience whether they liked it or not. If, once Bentivoglio had been expelled, the city's government pleased him, he would confirm it; if not, he would change it – by force, if necessary. For he had 'provided himself with an army that would make all Italy tremble, let alone Bologna'. And, with that, the stunned ambassadors were dismissed.

Later that afternoon, Julius summoned Niccolò to an audience.[61] Without wasting any time on pleasantries, he demanded that the Florentines send him the troops he had requested, without delay. Niccolò knew the *Dieci* would find it hard to refuse. Julius's determination was beyond any doubt, and – now that Louis XII had committed himself – his success seemed assured. Florence had everything to gain by obliging him, and nothing to lose. But the *Dieci* could be fickle – especially in situations like this. Should they convene a *pratica* to discuss the matter, there was no telling what might happen. Though the Great Council had recently approved Soderini's proposal to raise custom duties, there was still a chance the *gonfaloniere*'s opponents might try to harm him by refusing to sanction Marcantonio Colonna's release.[62] Niccolò could only hope they would see sense.

The *Dieci*'s political fickleness was not Niccolò's only concern. He was desperately short of money. He had not expected this mission to go on for so long and, though Biagio Buonaccorsi had been trying hard to keep him solvent – even asking Michelangelo to take him a few coins on one occasion – he was really beginning to struggle.[63] It was starting to get chilly and costs were devilishly high. Whenever the pope's army arrived in a town, the price of food and accommodation immediately went up. He had already tried to avoid using (expensive) couriers, instead sending his despatches through the sculptor, Andrea del Monte Sansovino.[64] But he couldn't hold out for much longer. He begged the *Dieci* to send him some more money – or else allow him to come home.[65]

The *Dieci* were, however, slow in making up their minds. Never a patient man at the best of times, Julius was quick to show his irritation. On 12 October, shortly after arriving in Forlì, he summoned Niccolò to another audience.[66] Through gritted teeth, he explained that, though he did not *need* Florence's troops, he still expected the *Dieci* to send them – as a sign of obedience. He was a reasonable man, he added. He wanted to show the Florentines his favour – so why wouldn't they let him do so? Were they *trying* to offend him? Trying hard to assuage the pope's anger, Niccolò promised to inform the *Dieci* of his wishes and assured him he would receive an answer in four days or so. But this was far too long for Julius. Making no attempt to conceal his anger, he ordered Niccolò to write *immediately* and, with that, brought the audience to an abrupt close.

While Niccolò was waiting for the *Dieci*'s reply, Julius continued his journey towards Imola. 'After much deliberation about what route he should take . . . without placing himself under an obligation to the Venetians' – who were still firmly in control of Faenza – he decided to follow the mountain road, through Castrocaro, Modigliana and Palazzuolo sul Senio.[67] This took him into Florentine territory – and hence also served as a reminder of just how easily he could punish the *Dieci* if they omitted to show him the respect he was owed.

At last, the *Dieci* took the hint. The day after the marquis of Mantua took Castel San Pietro (just nineteen kilometres from Bologna), they sent word that they had approved the pope's request and that Marcantonio Colonna would arrive in a matter of days.[68] What was more, they were also sending Pierfrancesco Tosinghi, their commissary general in the Romagna, to help arrange provisions for the papal army and to present the pontiff with a suitable gift. In due course, a new ambassador would be chosen to relieve Niccolò, as well.

As soon as Niccolò received the news, he rushed off to see the pope.[69] Julius was delighted – not so much with the troops as with the *Dieci*'s compliance. He called his datary, Giovanni Gozzadini and the *condottiere*, Carlo degli Ingrati, 'most cheerfully' to hear how isolated Bentivoglio now was; then, summoning 'all who were near', he spoke of the *Dieci* in the 'most honourable and affectionate manner'.

Despite the heavy rain and the discomforts of the march, a feeling of exuberance gripped the papal court. Julius was sweeping all before him. There seemed to be nothing he could not do. Arriving at Palazzuolo on 19 October, Niccolò was able to report that everyone was 'of the opinion that, if the pope succeeds against Bologna', as seemed increasingly likely, he would 'lose no time in attempting still greater enterprises'.[70] Indeed, people were openly saying that 'now or never [would] Italy be relieved of those who had planned to devour her' – namely, the Venetians.

Even Giovanni Bentivoglio could see that his position was now grave. Bologna was virtually surrounded. By the time Julius arrived in Imola, on 21 October, the French had reached Modena – less than half a day's ride away.[71] Raiding parties were already scouring the countryside, right up to the city walls.[72] Bentivoglio did not have much time left, but he still thought he might be able to negotiate some sort of settlement. After all, he reasoned, Julius would surely want to avoid the expense of a potentially lengthy siege; and that could give him at least some leverage. Through the marquis of Mantua, Bentivoglio therefore made an offer to recognize papal suzerainty in return for certain assurances for himself.[73] But it was too late. Dismissing his proposals out of hand, Julius – who had already excommunicated Bentivoglio for rebelling against the authority of the Church[74] – made it clear the time for negotiation had passed. As Niccolò reported, the only terms on which the pope was prepared to treat with Bentivoglio were 'either that he should quit Bologna,' never to return, 'or that he should come to place himself unconditionally in [papal] hands'.[75]

In a fit of fury, Julius ordered all the Bolognese at his court to write 'to their relatives and friends . . . exhorting them . . . to bring Bentivoglio to [him] as a captive, or to expel [that tyrant] from Bologna . . .' If they did not do so within four days, he added, he would order the French to fall upon the city, plunder its wealth and burn its houses to the ground.[76] Just to make sure, he also summoned the Bolognese ambassadors and instructed them to pass on the same message. Fearing that such dreadful threats would only encourage the people to rally behind Bentivoglio, however, they said nothing and did their utmost to prevent members of the court from sending any letters, too.[77]

But it was to no avail. On 25 October, Chaumont informed the Bolognese that, unless they obeyed the pope's order within the stipulated period, Louis XII would consider himself absolved of any responsibility towards the city and would treat them as his enemies along with Bentivoglio. The next day, Niccolò watched as the Bolognese ambassadors prostrated themselves before the pope, promising undying obedience.[78] But they were still reluctant to eject Bentivoglio themselves. Even now, it was a dangerous proposition, and the risk of bloodshed probably seemed too great. It fell to Chaumont to break the deadlock. Pointing out that there was nothing to be gained from holding out any longer, he promised to take Bentivoglio under his protection, provided he left quietly. At last, Bentivoglio saw the game was up. On 1 November, under cover of darkness, he and his sons slipped out of Bologna and into exile.[79]

In Imola, news of Bentivoglio's departure was greeted with jubilation. Festive bonfires were lit in the streets and, in the fortress, cannons were fired 'to mark the liberation of [Bologna] from tyrannical captivity'.[80] But Niccolò was not around to share in the excitement. Following the arrival of the new ambassador, Francesco Pepi, a few days earlier, he had taken his leave;[81] and by the time Julius's triumph had become apparent, he was already back in Florence – tired and penniless, but still dazzled by Julius's mastery of his own destiny.[82]

*

Returning to his duties in the chancellery, Niccolò resolved to follow the pope's example. He would be Fortune's master, rather than her slave. He would regard nothing as fixed, but would adapt himself to every change and act upon it with as much daring as he could muster. He would fear no one, use any methods and seize every opportunity – and, with a little luck, he would achieve the success he knew he deserved.

He would start with the militia. In his absence, recruitment had continued apace. By early November, some 5,000 men from thirty *podesterie* had been enrolled,[83] some good captains had been chosen[84] and the new *Dieci* were already beginning to look on the endeavour more favourably.[85] But it still had not been formally established, and the chances of passing the necessary legislation any time soon looked slim at best. While Niccolò had been away, Biagio Buonaccorsi had frequently complained about the 'endless' objections being made.[86] Some of these were, admittedly, born more of personal animus than political principle.[87] But others were more serious. Though the controversy over Don Michele had abated somewhat, there remained grave doubts about the utility of the militia and the wisdom of arming some of Florence's more rebellious subjects.

In the hope of overcoming these concerns, Niccolò was asked to prepare a detailed report on the militia, which could be used as the basis for a future bill.[88] Entitled *La cagione dell'ordinanza* ('The reason for the ordnance'), this was his boldest and most self-assured piece of political writing to date, and was deeply influenced by his new understanding of fortune.[89]

Recalling some of his earlier correspondence with Cardinal Francesco Soderini, Niccolò began by claiming there was no need to waste time asking whether it would be 'good or not to organise the Florentine state for arms'.[90] Everyone knew that, in order to survive, a state – be it empire, kingdom, principality or republic – needed two things: justice and arms. At present, however, Florence had 'little justice, and no arms at all; and the sole means of regaining the one and the other' was 'to organise [the Republic] for arms through public deliberation and with good order, and to maintain [a militia]' for as long as necessary.[91] Of course, some critics might argue that Florence had gone on well enough without a militia for more than a hundred years. But times had changed, and the city could no longer maintain its liberty in the same way. It had already seen how unreliable mercenaries could be, and it couldn't afford to hire many of them, in any case. As Niccolò had argued in the *Ghiribizzi* and the *Capitolo di Fortuna*, Florence's only hope was to adapt to its circumstances and be bold.

The only *real* question was how recruitment should be handled – and, most importantly, *where* it should occur. At that time, the Florentine state was divided into three very different areas: the city, the surrounding countryside (*contado*), and the outlying district (*distretto*), comprising subject towns such as Arezzo and Pistoia. If troops were levied in all three at once, Niccolò argued, it would only cause confusion. Therefore, it would be better to concentrate on just one. But which should it be? The *distretto* was obviously out of the question.[92] As Niccolò knew from bitter experience, its people were constantly agitating for independence and could not be given arms without putting Florence itself in danger. The city would also have to be excluded, at least for the moment.[93] As Niccolò explained, any army worth its salt needed a good mixture of 'men who command and men who obey; and . . . men who fight on foot and men who fight on horseback.' But Florentine citizens were mostly cavalrymen and, having grown used to giving orders, would not relish being told what to do. This left the *contado*.[94] It was not ideal. As Niccolò had found in the Mugello and the Casentino, its people were sometimes uppity and were often divided by village rivalries. But they were not as rebellious as their cousins in the *distretto* and could more easily be checked by discipline. Provided they were given good captains, there should be no problem.[95]

All that remained was to establish who should be in control of such a militia. Mindful of the *ottimati*'s earlier concern that Soderini might use it to set himself up as a tyrant, Niccolò was careful not to suggest placing it under the Signoria's authority. Instead, he proposed to divide responsibility between a number of different bodies. In time of war, overall control would be given to the *Dieci*, while remuneration and provisions would be entrusted to the priors, the *Dieci*, the colleges and a new magistracy.[96]

*

Although there is no means of knowing how widely Niccolò's report was disseminated, it seems to have calmed the *ottimati*'s nerves enough to make legislation a viable possibility. Within a matter of days, he was already helping to draft a bill, in collaboration with Soderini and the *Dieci*. Now known as the *Provisione della ordinanza* ('The provision of the ordnance'), this was an impressively thorough document.[97] It picked up from where *La cagione dell'ordinanza* had left off. After a brief preamble lamenting the unreliability of mercenaries and reiterating the need for a militia, it first explained how the new magistracy – the *Nove ufficiali della ordinanza e milizia fiorentina* ('Nine officials of the Florentine ordnance and militia') – was to be chosen.[98] Then it turned to explain their responsibilities a little more fully. As well as recruiting, training and arming troops, they would be expected to organize battalions under suitable banners, select constables, punish malefactors and disburse salaries as appropriate. No detail was left to chance. The age of recruits, the weapons each soldier was to carry, the amount each man was to be paid, the number of troops that were to be maintained in different areas, the arms that were to be stored in the Palazzo della Signoria, even the design of the *Nove*'s seal were all set out in exhaustive detail. Indeed, so precisely did Niccolò explain the workings of the proposed magistracy that all but the most embittered of Soderini's opponents came to regard it not merely as a useful expedient, but as a valuable necessity.

On 6 December 1506, the Great Council passed Niccolò's bill, almost without alteration.[99] The militia was now set on a sound legal footing and, as he had envisaged, the *Nove ufficiali della ordinanza e milizia fiorentina* was established to oversee its operation. It was only fitting that, once the first members of the new body had been elected, they chose him as their chancellor.[100] This would, of course, mean more work, and there was no prospect of any more pay. But, for Niccolò, the office was a reward in itself. Having worked so hard to make the militia a reality, he asked for nothing better than the chance to ensure its success.

*

As the year drew to a close, Niccolò had every reason to congratulate himself. Following in Julius II's footsteps, he had been bold and he had succeeded where no one else would have dared make the effort. Not only had he provided Florence with a viable militia – which, to Cardinal Francesco Soderini, seemed a 'God-given thing'[101] – but he also held three of Florence's most important administrative offices and enjoyed unparalleled influence over foreign and military affairs.

Yet, at the same time, he does not seem to have appreciated that his success had been purchased at a high political price. As Cardinal Francesco Soderini reminded him, there were still some *ottimati* who feared that the *gonfaloniere* was planning to use the militia to stamp out domestic opposition and set himself up as a tyrant.[102] Perceived as a willing accessory to this wicked plan, Niccolò was no longer the 'neutral' figure he had once been, but had become a major target for the aristocratic opposition and – despite all his efforts to curry favour – had earned the lasting animosity of Alamanno Salviati.[103] Even before the militia had been formally approved, Biagio Buonaccorsi had overheard Salviati denigrating Niccolò as a 'rascal' and vowing to do everything in his power to prevent his reappointment as second chancellor.[104] For all his breezy self-confidence, it remained to be seen whether Fortune actually had favoured the brave Niccolò, after all.

14

The Emperor

(January 1507–June 1508)

Returning to the chancellery after the Christmas holidays, Niccolò enthusiastically set about transforming the rudimentary militia he had assembled over the past few years into a fully-fledged citizen army. His first task was to bring it up to strength. As he was well aware, the *Provisione* had stipulated that 10,000 soldiers were to be recruited within the first six months of the *Nove*'s existence; and though a little over 700 men were already under arms, there was still a long way to go.[1] Despite what he had promised in *La cagione dell'ordinanza*, he therefore extended recruitment to the *distretto* and ordered each village to provide him with a list of all able-bodied men over the age of fifteen who could be pressed into service.[2] He then turned to the question of discipline. Hoping to instil in his new recruits the martial spirit of Swiss mercenaries, he appointed reliable men to serve as constables[3] and laid down harsh punishments for deserters.[4] He also provided Don Michele with a special force of thirty mounted crossbowmen and fifty foot soldiers for the express purpose of stamping out any trouble in the ranks.[5]

Given that Niccolò had no direct experience of military life before establishing the militia, his self-assurance is truly remarkable. It is not easy to explain how he achieved so much in such a short space of time. It may simply be that he was an unusually acute observer of military affairs. During his missions – particularly to Cesare Borgia and Julius II – he had had ample opportunity to see how successful armies were organized and to reflect on how the methods of other commanders might be applied back in Florence. Another possibility is that the administrative challenge of raising a militia was not as great as it might have appeared. Although the practice of war was changing hugely in the early sixteenth century, it was still far less 'professional' than it would later become. As such, the task of raising, training and equipping troops probably did not require any more specialist skills than those with which Niccolò handled his other chancellery work. The most likely explanation, however, is that Niccolò was simply resourceful, dealing with problems whenever they came up as best he could. Indeed, his inexperience may actually have been an asset. Untroubled by habit and unencumbered by preconceptions, he could be more adaptable – and hence more effective – than many battle-hardened captains might have been.

Within a matter of weeks, enough troops had been enlisted and trained for him to begin despatching some of the new *bandiere* to trouble spots in the countryside, allowing the rest of Florence's army to concentrate on raiding the Pisan *contado*.[6] So successful did this prove that, by the beginning of spring, order had been restored to the Republic's domains and a host of Pisan prisoners had already been taken.[7] This caught the attention of Florence's neighbours. According to the chronicler, Bartolomeo Cerretani, the militia had soon gained such an impressive reputation that 'the whole of Italy was keeping an eye on it'.[8] Indeed, the Venetians even sent experienced soldiers to spy on Niccolò's recruits being drilled in the Casentino.[9]

*

It would still be some time before Florence would be able to use the militia for any major offensives, but its growing renown nevertheless emboldened the city to canvas support for a future campaign against Pisa. Two sets of negotiations were opened.[10] The first was with Ferdinand of Aragon.[11] Shortly after his arrival in Naples the previous year, he had dismissed Gonzalo de Córdoba and overturned many of the former viceroy's policies.[12] This had led the Florentines to believe he might be persuaded to withdraw his support from the Pisans, too. He was not unamenable to the idea, but, in return, he demanded that Florence defend Naples against *any* aggressor and allow Aragonese troops to be stationed on its soil. Such conditions were clearly unacceptable, but the *Dieci* were still hopeful and allowed the talks to continue. For a time, it even seemed as if an agreement might be within reach. In May, the *Dieci* announced that, if Ferdinand *forced* the Pisans to surrender, Florence would indeed commit to

Naples' defence. Eventually, however, they realized that Ferdinand was not in a position to compel the Pisans to do anything, after all, especially as he would soon have to return to Spain. Disappointed, the *Dieci* had no choice but to let the matter drop.

The second set of negotiations, with Louis XII of France, seemed more promising, at least at first. Although the king had refused to come to the Florentines' aid the previous year, he was now prepared to be more forthcoming. If they helped him put down a revolt in Genoa, he told their ambassador, Francesco Pandolfini, he would help them against Pisa.[13] The *Dieci* were delighted; and on 30 March, a *pratica* agreed to send Louis the troops he had requested.[14] Within a month, Genoa had capitulated. But Louis failed to keep his side of the bargain.[15] Fearing that Maximilian might cross into Italy at any moment, he decided not to risk provoking him by marching any further south. The Florentines were, of course, furious, but Louis had already made up his mind to return to France. Rather desultorily, he suggested that he and Ferdinand – who were shortly to sign a convention at Savona, settling many of their differences[16] – could arbitrate between Florence and Pisa instead. This, however, only added insult to injury. In May, a disgusted *pratica* rejected the proposal out of hand, and the *Dieci* glumly resigned themselves to yet another diplomatic disappointment.

Having drawn a blank with Spain and France, the *Dieci* began to wonder whether it might be worth approaching Maximilian, instead.[17] He had been talking about mounting an expedition to Italy for years, but this time he seemed serious. His successful resolution of the War of the Landshut Succession had not only strengthened his authority among the princes, but had also allowed him to seize a number of strategically important territories along the Alpine frontier.[18] Once the fallout from Philip the Fair's death had been dealt with, he had begun making preparations in earnest. In April 1507, he convened the Diet of Constance and, though there were still a few hurdles to overcome, it seemed likely he would be granted all the money and soldiers he would need to mount a successful campaign.[19]

Florence would still be taking a risk, however. Though Louis XII had returned to France rather than provoke Maximilian after the fall of Genoa, he had made it clear that, if the emperor crossed the Alps, he would have no choice but to take up arms against him.[20]

Louis had already started fortifying Milan, and was trying to persuade Julius II to join him in forming an anti-imperial league. Were the Florentines to negotiate openly with Maximilian, they would surely arouse Louis' anger and thereby put the whole French alliance in jeopardy. After several ferocious debates in *pratiche*, it was decided that, since Maximilian's expedition was still far from certain, it would be too dangerous to send ambassadors just yet.[21] Instead, the city would despatch an envoy to keep an eye on the situation instead.

On 19 June, Niccolò was chosen as Florence's *mandatario* (emissary). According to Guicciardini, his appointment had been arranged by Soderini, who wanted such an important mission to be handled by someone he could trust.[22] Niccolò's delight can easily be imagined. Although he had already grown used to parlaying with kings, cardinals and pontiffs, this was by far the most prestigious posting he had yet been given. It was an opportunity to shine. His excitement was, however, short-lived. There were many *ottimati* – no doubt including Alamanno Saviati – who believed such a mission called for someone of higher social standing. On 25 June, they annulled Niccolò's election and appointed his old schoolfriend, Francesco Vettori, in his place.[23]

It was not the first time Niccolò had been knocked back like this, but he was still bitterly disappointed, especially as he and Salviati had recently been working together on the militia.[24] His friends did their best to console him.[25] Writing from Fivizzano, Filippo Casavecchia told him that he had nothing to reproach himself for – least of all insofar as Salviati was concerned.[26] Sooner or later, Filippo reminded him, even the closest of political allies became enemies. Adopting a slightly different approach, Alessandro Nasi pointed out that it was probably for the best, anyway. 'I am glad that you have shat out the imperial commission,' Nasi wrote, 'since you are entirely purged.' Indeed, it could be 'a very good thing' for him 'to be in Florence rather than in Germany . . .'[27] This might well have been true, but, for Niccolò, it was cold comfort, all the same.

*

No doubt feeling thoroughly miserable, Niccolò went back to his work in the chancellery. There was plenty to be getting on with, especially insofar as the militia was concerned. Over the coming weeks, he took steps to prevent Venetian constables from poaching Florentine troops in Fivizzano, San Miniato and Val di Cecina;[28] he attended to the disposition of *bandiere* around Arezzo;[29] and, all the while, he continued to oversee recruitment. This flurry of activity should have cheered him up. Others were delighted with his progress. On 3 August, Don Michele confessed that nothing had ever given him so much pleasure as the battalions he had just inspected near Fivizzano. 'I swear . . . that men who have been in the service for twenty years could not have satisfied me more,' he explained.[30] But Niccolò could not be shaken out of his depression, even by the militia. His heart just wasn't in it. And who could blame him? Compared to what he *could* have been doing in the German lands, it must all have seemed rather dull.

Niccolò was, however, far too experienced a diplomat to be left on the sidelines for long. Events were moving rapidly. In mid-July, the Diet of Constance had agreed to provide Maximilian with 12,000 men and 120,000 guilders.[31] This would not be enough for him to challenge Louis XII directly, but it would be more than sufficient to mount an expedition of sorts. The only question was whether Maximilian would attempt to punish the Venetians for failing to help him against France the previous year, or work with them in the hope of easing his journey to Rome. It was difficult to say what he might do, but that his troops had already been heard singing the marching song '*Vom Romzug*' ('On the Road to Rome') suggested the latter might be more likely.[32] Julius II was horrified. He saw that, were Maximilian to ally with the Venetians, all of his gains in the Romagna would be lost. In a desperate bid to deflect the emperor from such a ruinous course, he decided to despatch a legate to the imperial court; and for this most delicate of missions, he chose Cardinal Bernardino López de Carvajal, who was known to enjoy warm relations with the Habsburgs.[33]

The Florentines were even more alarmed. Though they had learned that Julius was sending a legate to the emperor, they did not know why. As Landucci reported, it was feared that Maximilian might have reached an understanding with both the Venetians *and* the pope.[34] If this were true, it would spell disaster for Florence: Pisa's liberty would be assured; access to the Adriatic ports would be cut; and there was even a chance some of the towns in the Mugello might be lost, as well. It was imperative to find out what the pope's intentions really were, and, if necessary, to change his mind. Since Carvajal's journey would take him through Tuscany, the Florentines therefore decided to send Niccolò to meet him in Siena, where he was expected to remain for a few days. Niccolò was to take careful note of the manner in which he was received, so a suitably lavish welcome could be prepared in Florence, and, if possible, to make discreet enquiries about the purpose of his mission at the same time.[35]

Niccolò could hardly have been more delighted. Dashing out of the Palazzo della Signoria, he saddled his horse and set off at once. Riding as quickly as the summer heat allowed, he reached Siena on the evening of 10 August.[36] Carvajal had not yet arrived. At present, the legate was still at Acquapendente, some eighty kilometres to the south, and was not expected for at least another three days. So as not to waste any time, Niccolò decided to try to meet him en route. But this was easier said than done. On learning that Carvajal had stayed in Paglia on the night of 11 August, Niccolò headed to the picturesque village of San Quiricio d'Orcia, which he believed the legate would have to pass through on his way to Buonconvento, the next day. To his frustration, however, Carvajal changed his plans at the last minute and decided to go to nearby Pienza, where he was entertained by the Piccolomini, sending only a portion of his suite on to San Quiricio d'Orcia. This not only robbed Niccolò of the chance to learn more about the legate's object, but it also made it impossible to gauge how many were in his train. He had no choice but to go back to Siena and wait.

On 14 August, Carvajal finally arrived. As Niccolò observed, however, he was treated less bountifully than might have been expected. Although the Sienese provided him with all sorts of marvellous food, they let his retinue 'shift for themselves'.[37] This boded well. After all, if Pandolfo Petrucci had believed that Maximilian really had done a deal with Julius and the Venetians, Niccolò reasoned, he would surely have spared no expense. That he was erring on the side of parsimony could only mean he thought such an agreement unlikely.

Niccolò's suspicions were soon proved correct. On making further enquiries, he learned that, about a month before, Maximilian had sent the Sienese a letter informing them of his intention to cross into Italy and advising them to make no further payments to Louis XII.[38] But Pandolfo had refused to believe Maximilian's expedition would actually go ahead. He was convinced the Swiss and, more importantly, the Venetians would break faith with the emperor and,

together, put paid to it. Even more gratifyingly, Niccolò also discovered that Maximilian had not concluded an alliance with Julius II,
either. From one of Carvajal's attendants, he learned that the true
purpose of the legate's mission was 'to do all in his power to *prevent*
the emperor's coming.'[39] So desperate was the pope to attain this
end, he had even authorized Carvajal to offer to crown Maximilian
in Germany – something that had never happened before. If the
legate really could not change the emperor's mind, however, he was
at least to persuade him to bring as few soldiers as possible, and to
assure himself of France's friendship beforehand.

*

When Niccolò's reports reached Florence, the *Dieci* breathed a small
sigh of relief. That Maximilian would not ally with the pope and
would be opposed by the Venetians was reassuring, to say the least.
If he could be talked into repairing his relations with Louis XII,
too, then so much the better for them.[40] All that remained was for
the emperor to prove Pandolfo wrong and cross the Alps. But the
Dieci were starting to have doubts about whether he actually would.
At the Diet of Constance, it had been agreed that Maximilian would
receive his men and money in October. When the time came,
however, he was disappointed. Instead of the 120,000 guilders he
had been promised, only about 40,000 guilders was handed over,
and, of the 12,000 troops he was expecting, fewer than 1,000 actually
materialized.[41] Given that winter was approaching, he would, of
course, have plenty of time to raise additional funds, recruit soldiers
and hire mercenaries before the campaigning season began again,
but his progress so far did not exactly inspire confidence.

The *Dieci* wanted to wait until Maximilian's situation became
clearer before deciding whether or not to send ambassadors. Keen
though they were to recover Pisa, they had no desire to rush into
something they might later regret. But Maximilian had other ideas.
Already struggling to raise money, he wanted to draw the Florentines
into an agreement sooner rather than later. In early November, he
surprised them by making an offer of his own. In return for a payment
of 50,000 ducats, he would take the city under his protection and
defend it against all comers. Exactly what this might entail, however,
was unclear.

It was a tempting offer, even if it didn't say anything about the recovery of Pisa. But it made many Florentines uneasy. At a *pratica* to discuss the city's response, Francesco Pepi argued that it smacked of desperation.[42] Although the sum of 50,000 ducats was excessive, it was still far less than Maximilian might have been expected to demand had his expedition to Italy been certain. In other words, it was a sign that he probably *wasn't* coming. Nevertheless, Pepi thought it might still be worth sending ambassadors, just in case. Francesco Gualterotti disagreed. He saw no point in opening talks when the costs were so high and the chances of reaping any benefits were so low. If ambassadors *had* to be appointed, he argued, their departure should be delayed until later. The other members of the *pratica* agreed. No action was to be taken – for the moment, at least.

Within a matter of weeks, however, the Florentines had cause to recant their scepticism. On 30 November, Francesco Vettori informed the *Dieci* that Maximilian was certain to come. By threatening legal action, he had compelled many of the recalcitrant German princes to cough up the money they had promised, and was in the process of negotiating a loan with the Fuggers, a prominent German banking family, as well.[43] He was, moreover, in talks with the Swiss, and would soon begin recruiting additional troops in the Tyrol. All being well, he would set off as soon as spring arrived. This changed everything. Already, some Florentines had begun to wonder how long their city could afford to remain neutral. Only a few days earlier, Piero Guicciardini had pointed out that, sooner or later, it would *have* to reply to Maximilian's offer.[44] At *pratiche* on 13 December, Francesco Gualterotti announced that the time had come to send ambassadors.[45] Amid loud cheers, some – including Guicciardini – reinforced his point by adding that an agreement with the emperor had now become imperative. Before a vote could be called, however, Pierantonio Carnesecchi pointed out that, instead of despatching an embassy, the talks could simply be entrusted to Vettori – at least to start with. Once a deal was within sight, the ambassadors could then be sent to thrash out the final details. Most agreed this was by far the most efficient option; and when proceedings resumed the following day, Carnesecchi's proposal was easily passed.[46]

Everything now depended on Vettori, but not everyone was convinced he was up to the task. At thirty-three years old, he was still comparatively young and, though he was well-born, he had little experience of diplomacy, especially at this level. At a *pratica* on 15 December, Piero del Nero suggested Vettori might benefit from having a companion – someone who could not only tell him about his new commission in person, but who could also guide him through the negotiations that lay ahead.[47] Piero was too discreet to propose any names, but those present can have been in no doubt that, as Marietta's stepfather, he was thinking of Niccolò, who, by rights, should have been sent to Germany in the first place. The *pratica* took the hint; and the next day, the delighted Niccolò was duly appointed.[48]

*

On 17 December, Niccolò set out on what was to be the longest and most arduous journey of his career. Expecting to find Vettori at Maximilian's court in Augsburg, but needing to avoid Venetian territory, he decided to travel through Lombardy and the foothills of Savoy. He knew the road well and no doubt thought he would be out of harm's reach. But he was in for a nasty shock. Along the way, he was set upon by French soldiers and searched – apparently with some violence.[49] Of course, legally speaking, his assailants had no right to touch any of the diplomatic correspondence he was carrying,[50] but Niccolò didn't want to take any chances. 'Fearing that he might not be safe ... he ... destroyed all of his letters' as soon as they released him, and thereafter was always looking over his shoulder.[51]

Passing through the Maurienne Valley in heavy snow, he reached Aiguebelle on 22 December and, by Christmas, was in Geneva. He did not, however, waste any time on festivities. Early on Boxing Day morning, he was back in the saddle and heading towards Fribourg. Taking the opportunity to speak with other travellers along the road, he made careful enquiries about Swiss affairs, in the hope of gaining some insight into how Maximilian's negotiations might turn out. From a former mercenary captain, he learned about the peculiarities of the cantonal system and surmised that, while the Swiss did not want to oppose the French, they would probably still be willing to fight for Maximilian in Italy, if the price was right. Even if they did not, however, the emperor could still be reasonably sure of securing the support of the Grisons and the Valais – which could act independently of the rest.

After leaving Fribourg, Niccolò crossed the River Aare outside Bern and rode on through the valleys of Emmenthal, towards the picturesque little town of Schaffenhausen. Pausing to catch his breath, he struck up a conversation with two Genoese merchants who were on their way back to Italy from the imperial court. When he pressed them for news of the emperor, they told him that Maximilian had recently secured a loan of 100,000 *scudi* from the Fuggers. As Niccolò had suspected, he was also on the point of making 'an agreement with the Swiss, according to which they would serve him, but not against France'. This was, of course, tremendously encouraging. But when Niccolò asked them whether Maximilian was still in Augsburg, he got an unpleasant surprise. 'By this time,' they said, 'the Emperor has left Augsburg for Italy and we don't think you'll find him until he reaches Trento'.[52]

Niccolò's heart must have sunk, but there was still a chance the Genoese merchants might be mistaken. After all, he had seen neither hide nor hair of any troop movements since Geneva.[53] Nevertheless, he spurred his horse on, determined not to lose a moment. At Constance, at the year's end, he tried desperately to pick up hints about the emperor's movements, but no one seemed to know anything other than that his preparations were continuing apace, and that the Venetians were readying for war. According to the Savoyard ambassador, Maximilian was so secretive that, when he changed his lodging, he ordered his cook to leave an hour after him to prevent anyone from knowing when or where he was going.[54] Poor Niccolò had no choice but to head for Memmingen, and then turn southwards towards Innsbruck and Trento.

By now, he was starting to grow tired of the journey.[55] Since leaving Florence, he had already travelled more than 1,000 kilometres; and, if the Genoese merchants turned out to be correct, there could be another 400 kilometres to go. The roads were in terrible condition, the weather was dreadful and his horses were fit only for the knacker's yard. To make matters even worse, he was also running short of money. Alone among the icy peaks, he must have wondered why he had been so keen to come on this mission in the first place. How he must have missed his cosy office in the chancellery and the warmth of the family hearth.

It was not until 11 January – almost a month after his departure – that Niccolò caught up with Maximilian's court, at Bolzano.[56]

Located at the confluence of three rivers, this little Tyrolese town presented a glorious sight, even in the depths of winter. Having grown rich off trade, it boasted some splendid churches and a large number of fine castles. The slopes of the surrounding hills, still blanketed with snow, were thick with vineyards; its markets were filled with rich cheeses and fruit conserves; and everywhere there were artisans producing the tapestries and ceramics for which it was justly famed. But, for Niccolò, its greatest attraction was simply that it marked the end of his journey – at least for a while.

Niccolò lost no time in tracking Vettori down. After patching up their friendship – which must have been sorely strained by the younger man's appointment, back in July – they settled down to the tricky business ahead. In his usual purposeful manner, Niccolò informed Vettori of his new commission, and, relying solely on his memory, passed on the *Dieci*'s instructions.[57] Vettori was to begin by offering Maximilian the sum of 30,000 ducats, but, if necessary, he could go as high as 50,000. This would be paid in three instalments: the first when the emperor reached an unambiguously Italian city; the second when he entered Tuscany; and the third when he arrived in Rome, or at some other point, to be decided upon later. In return, Vettori was to ask for the restitution of *all* Florence's possessions, including Pisa, as well as confirmation of its 'present state and dominion'. If restitution proved to be an obstacle to an agreement, however, the *Dieci* were prepared to yield – but, in that case, they would insist on Maximilian recognizing the rightfulness of Florence's claims over Pisa. Lest there be any doubt, the *Dieci* repeated that their offer of 50,000 ducats was final, and that, once an agreement had been reached, they would not countenance any further demands.

*

The next day, Niccolò and Vettori went to request an audience with Maximilian.[58] The imperial court was famously grand, even on campaign; and as the two Florentines were ushered through richly decorated courtyards and magnificent hallways, they would doubtless have marvelled at the aura of majesty. Following Vetorri into the emperor's reception chamber, however, Niccolò would quickly have realized how mistaken his first impressions may have been. As a portrait by Bernhard Strigel reveals, the forty-eight-year-old Maximilian was far from imposing. Like all Habsburgs, he had a long, aquiline nose, a large, fleshy chin, and a protruding lower lip that made it difficult for him to articulate clearly. He was, moreover, already showing signs of age. His flaxen hair was turning grey, his brow was etched with worry and his eyelids drooped heavily. Though the smile that occasionally played about the corners of his mouth hinted at a lively mind, he lacked vitality and purpose.

Kneeling at the steps of the throne, Vettori carefully outlined the *Dieci*'s proposals.[59] No sooner had he finished, however, than the emperor's secretary, Johannes Collauer, jumped in to express his disapproval. The sum they were offering was, he claimed, far smaller than Maximilian had been expecting. Indeed, it was smaller even than Florence had offered back in 1502. The *Dieci*'s demands were, by contrast, much greater – absurdly so. There was no point even discussing restitution. If they wanted a deal, he argued, they would have to be more reasonable. The force of Collauer's attack seems to have taken Vettori by surprise. Rather guilelessly, he immediately upped his offer to 40,000 ducats and dropped the idea of restitution. Instead, Florence would ask the emperor merely to confirm its rights. This pleased Maximilian. As Vettori later recalled, he seemed inclined to accept the proposal right then. But Collauer quickly stepped in. Speaking on the emperor's behalf, he promised to give Vettori a reply the following day.

Rising to their feet, Vettori and Niccolò made to leave. Before they did so, however, Maximilian called Pigello Portinari – a Florentine serving in his chancellery – aside, and asked who Niccolò was, adding that the Florentines seemed to be making a good start.[60] This was no small matter. For Niccolò to have been noticed, despite saying very little, testified to how confidently he bore himself – and perhaps also to how well he compared with his nervous and inexperienced friend. What Pigello told the emperor cannot be known, but it seems likely that he, too, remarked on Niccolò's self-assurance, albeit rather scurrilously. At an audience with the Pisan ambassador, Francesco del Lante, a few days later, Maximilian revealed that Niccolò was rumoured to have been sent 'because Soderini did not trust Vettori' to carry out the mission alone.[61] This was, of course, not so very far from the truth – and was, in some ways, a great compliment to Niccolò. But it cannot have made

Vettori's task any easier, to have been so obviously overshadowed by his assistant.

*

Despite what Collauer had promised, there was no reply the next day, or the day after that. For an old hand like Niccolò, this would probably have been a bad sign, but Vettori was cheerfully optimistic. Someone had told him that Maximilian was pleased with the *Dieci's* offer, and, though two of the emperor's closest advisers – Paul von Lichtenstein and Zyprian von Serntein – were known to be agitating for better terms, he was confident a deal could be reached.[62]

It was not until 17 January that Vettori and Niccolò received a response.[63] Summoned to an audience, they found Maximilian in the company of von Serntein and the formidable Matthäus Lang von Wellenburg – who, as bishop of Gurk, had fought beside the emperor in the War of the Landshut Succession, and who had recently been instrumental in securing the loan from the Fuggers.[64] It was Lang who took the lead. Without wasting any time on pleasantries, he told the two Florentines that, 'in view of the importance of their city', the sum they were offering was far too small. Therefore, Maximilian would have to decline. He was, however, still hopeful that more satisfactory terms could be negotiated. As such, he was prepared to offer the Florentines an interim agreement. If the *Dieci* would consent to *lend* the emperor 25,000 ducats immediately, he would gladly write them a letter in which he would guarantee their 'state and dominion'. This letter would be deposited with the Fuggers for safe keeping. When a treaty was eventually signed, Maximilian would hold the 25,000 ducats on account of whatever sum the Florentines undertook to pay him, and the *Dieci* would be given the emperor's letter. If no treaty was concluded, the letter would be returned to Maximilian and Florence's money would be repaid.

Lang went to great lengths to explain 'the fairness of this proposition', adding that, if the *Dieci* wanted to win Maximilian's favour, they would have to give him some proof of their affection.[65] But Vettori was appalled. This was almost an insult. Had he not been in the emperor's presence, he would doubtless have shown his anger, but he managed to compose himself enough to give a brief answer. Though he assured Maximilian that the *Dieci* were determined not to 'fall short of [their] ancestors in recognising' him as their 'father and protector', he could not see how they could possibly accept such a proposal.[66] Nevertheless, he promised to pass it on to the *Dieci*.

Fortunately, Vettori was able to express himself more frankly over dinner with Lang that evening.[67] He began by pointing out that, under the terms Maximilian was proposing, Florence would be risking a huge sum of money without gaining anything concrete in return; and that, for this reason, the *Dieci* would almost certainly reject his offer. Lang argued for a bit – more for form's sake than anything else – and then asked what terms the Florentines *would* accept. Had Vettori been a more seasoned diplomat, he might well have seen this as an opportunity to negotiate seriously, but he let it pass. He replied that he had already stated the *Dieci*'s terms, and the ball was now in Maximilian's court. Lang saw there was no point in arguing further. Having reached a stalemate, they agreed it would be best to wait until Vettori heard from the *Dieci* before discussing the matter again.

What Niccolò made of this is not known, but he cannot have been pleased. Whatever the reasons for Maximilian's curious fixation with a loan,[68] there would be some difficult negotiations ahead – and it was becoming increasingly clear that Vettori was not up to the job.[69]

*

Had Vettori received a quick reply from the *Dieci*, it might still have been possible to mitigate the effects of his inexperience. But the gravity of the international situation made communications difficult. Letters from Florence were frequently intercepted and destroyed by the Venetians, while those that got through were often too badly damaged to be of any use.[70] Shortly after Vettori's dinner with Lang, for example, a courier arrived with a note from the *Dieci*, but, since he had concealed it in his shoe, it had become completely illegible.[71] To combat this, Vettori urged the *Dieci* to send any future correspondence through the emperor's envoy in Bologna.[72] But even this was risky, and it did nothing to speed things up.

When a letter finally did arrive, it was less than helpful. At the time it had been written, on 29 January, the *Dieci* had only known about Vettori's first meeting with Maximilian.[73] As such, they had no idea about the emperor's rejection of their offer, or about his own proposal. But they were still sharply critical of Vettori's conduct. They rebuked him for having been so quick to raise his original offer, and so slow to make the case for restitution. They had expected him to fight a lot harder. When he next saw Maximilian, they commanded, he was to repeat their offer of 40,000 ducats and to stress that the first instalment of 15,000 ducats would be paid when the emperor's forces reached an Italian city which did not belong to him. If this was not accepted, he was to offer 50,000 ducats and promise that the first 20,000 would be paid when Maximilian reached Trento. One way or another, Vettori was to get a deal done. But this he clearly could not do – at least not on the terms they had outlined.

While Vettori and Niccolò were debating how best to proceed, however, Maximilian surprised them by suddenly declaring war on Venice.[74] At first, all seemed to go well. Within a matter of days, Maximilian had taken possession of the plateau of Asiago, just nineteen kilometres from Vicenza, and Niccolò, who had hastily been sent to observe his progress, expected that the Vicentines would soon rise in rebellion. Similarly, the margrave of Brandenburg quickly surrounded Rovereto; and, despite the presence of a large Venetian garrison, he was confident the threat of a siege would induce the town to surrender.

But the attack soon faltered. Before any signs of revolt had been seen in Vicenza, Maximilian abruptly turned back and set up camp at San Michele all'Adige, on the road between Trento and Bolzano. This caused some puzzlement. As Niccolò related, some people thought the Venetians might have persuaded Maximilian to withdraw with a (false) promise of friendship.[75] Others believed the emperor had allowed himself to be swayed too easily by his advisers at the outset. The most likely explanation, however, was that he had simply been unnerved by the speed of his advance and had fallen back from a surfeit of caution.

*

Poor Vettori was at a loss to know what to do. Though he did not lack the courage or the conviction to carry out his mission, he found it difficult to assess the situation.[76] There was just no way of being sure about what Maximilian would do next, or how he would fare. As Niccolò explained (on Vettori's behalf), the only way of gauging Maximilian's chances of success was to look at 'the multitude and quality of [his] troops . . . how [well] he could keep them together, and how he govern[ed] his men and himself.'[77] But this gave a very mixed impression. Though Maximilian had plenty of good soldiers, it was not clear that he would be able to keep them in the field for long, being so short of money. His character was similarly uncertain. He was, admittedly, 'careful, extremely skilled in the art of war, hardworking, and highly experienced.' But he was 'so good and humane a lord that he [had] come to be too easy-going and credulous.'[78] On this basis, some people had grave doubts about the success of the emperor's enterprise, and, though Vettori had not yet given up hope, he could not help sharing some of their fears.

Despite having been told to stay in Bolzano, Vettori's first thought was to race off towards Vicenza in the hope of learning more, but on learning that Niccolò was already on his way back from Asiago with the emperor, he decided to await further instructions in Trento.[79] Maximilian had, however, heard that Vettori had received a letter from the *Dieci*; and, on reaching San Michele all'Adige, summoned him to an audience – evidently expecting to be made an offer.[80] But, when Lang asked him if he had anything to communicate, Vettori had to reply in the negative. He knew there was no point in offering Maximilian the sum of 50,000 ducats, as the *Dieci* had asked, but he did not want to say anything more about a loan, either. Feeling rather silly, he tried to make up some excuse to explain why he had come to Trento, but it didn't convince anyone and he was immediately sent back to Bolzano. It was all very embarrassing. The *Dieci* would be furious, and Vettori – whose nerves were already frayed – must have known it.

*

On 10 February, Maximilian, too, returned to Bolzano. To make room for his soldiers – who were due to follow shortly – he ordered Niccolò, Vettori and all the other diplomats to transfer their residence to Merano, about thirty kilometres to the north-west. Four days later, he took to the road once again. No one knew for certain where he was going, but he was said to be heading towards Innsbruck, or possibly Brunico (Bruneck), a strategically important town in the Puster Valley.

Vettori was now beside himself with worry. Although Maximilian had given up hope of receiving a coronation in Rome, he was evidently gathering his strength for another attack on the Venetians.[81] There was, of course, no telling when this might happen, but Vettori was scared that, if the emperor moved forward while he was stuck in Merano, he would be severely reprimanded by the *Dieci* for failing to seize the opportunity when he had had the chance.[82] At his wits' end, Vettori fired off another letter to the *Dieci*, assuring them that, though the costs would be higher and the risks greater, a deal could probably still be done. In his opinion, two courses of action were open to them if they wanted Maximilian to recognize their rights over Pisa.[83] Perhaps the safest was to offer the emperor at least 100,000 ducats, the first instalment of which would be paid when he reached an Italian city not subject to him. Alternatively, they could offer a smaller amount – say, up to 50,000 ducats – but make the first payment immediately. Needless to say, these could only be put to Maximilian before he entered Venetian territory successfully; after that, it would be too late. To sweeten the deal, the *Dieci* might also raise the possibility of lending Maximilian an additional 10,000 to 15,000 ducats once a deal had been signed. But these were just suggestions; Vettori meekly promised to do whatever they wanted. He would, however, need an answer soon.

Niccolò saw things differently. Writing to Piero Soderini on 17 February, he admitted that he was no longer sure if an agreement should be made or not.[84] 'I am completely up in the air', he wrote. If pushed, he would probably say that the advantages still outweighed the disadvantages, but there wasn't much in it. Truth be told, he didn't much care either way. By now, he was heartily sick of the whole mission. Though Merano wasn't an unattractive town, the Tyrol was not to his taste. The people were uncouth, the food was awful and the weather was perpetually freezing. He was also painfully short of money.[85] Most of all, he hated having so little to do. Apart from writing a few letters on Vettori's behalf and sending dirty jokes to his friends in diplomatic code,[86] he had nothing to keep him occupied.[87] He dearly wanted to come home, but he had a nasty feeling the *Dieci* might recall the incompetent Vettori and hand responsibility over to him. Claiming that this would only harm

Florence's interests, he begged Soderini not to leave him there alone. He would rather stay there a bit longer and take Vettori in hand – or, as he put it, 'make a mere chancellery secretary out of Francesco'. He still thought his presence would be 'completely superfluous', but, to avoid being stuck there on his own, he would gladly do 'what little good [he could] think of'.[88]

*

Even with Niccolò calling the shots, much would now depend on good information and careful timing. If they coordinated effectively with the *Dieci* and followed Maximilian's movements carefully, they should be able to choose the right moment to get the best deal. It was, however, a big 'if'.

Over the next week, the two Florentines felt as if they were trapped 'on a lost island'.[89] For reasons of security, Maximilian had forbidden anyone to leave Merano for Italy without his express authorization, thus severing their lines of communication with Florence. It was not until 23 February that Vettori was able to secure the permission he needed to despatch a courier.[90] Even then, he doubted whether the courier would make it past Rovereto. Out of desperation, he gave a copy of his letters to two 'vagrants' who were on their way to Italy. But nothing seemed to be getting through.

More worryingly, they were also cut off from Maximilian's headquarters. From their vantage point in Merano, they could see he was preparing to attack the Venetians fairly soon, most probably through Friuli. They had received word that he had moved from Bressanone (Brixen) to Brunico (Bruneck) and they had spotted great columns of infantry and cavalry marching down from the Alps, towards Bolzano and Trento.[91] But it was impossible to estimate the size of his army, or to guess where – and when – he would strike. Unable to communicate with the *Dieci* and without a clear idea of what was going on, Niccolò and Vettori were impotent.

*

While the two Florentines were still scratching their heads, Maximilian had already launched his attack. His plan was simple. A diversionary force under Paul Sixt von Trautson would first occupy the strategically important region of Cadore, 'through which the road leads to Venice by way of Treviso'.[92] While he was holding down the Venetians there, Maximilian would send his main army south from Trento, towards Verona. Provided everything went well, this would cut the Venetians' land empire in two and prevent any further French reinforcements from reaching them.

At first, everything went swimmingly. Within a matter of days, Trautson had occupied Pieve di Cadore and the Val Comelico, and was already pushing on towards Belluno. But difficulties soon arose. Contrary to Maximilian's expectations, the Swiss had agreed to provide France with troops, and the Venetians already had several thousand at their disposal. To make matters worse, Maximilian was also running out of money. Desperate for additional funds, he left his troops to continue their preparations alone and rushed back to Innsbruck 'to raise money and to pawn certain of his jewels'.[93]

Details were slow to reach the two Florentines. They had little sense of what was happening, even a fortnight after the campaign had begun. Like many of their colleagues in Merano, they were reluctant to hazard any guesses as to how Maximilian's enterprise might turn out. On the one hand, wrote Niccolò, 'it seems to everybody that it will be difficult for the Emperor to make any headway against the Venetians and France without the pope's help'; but on the other hand, 'the power of Germany is so great that, if she so chooses, she can resuscitate an enterprise that is dead in a moment – and can strengthen one that is still alive even more easily.'[94] When, on the evening of 7 March, the governor of Tyrol arrived with news that, despite his shortage of money, Maximilian had decided to carry the war into Switzerland, however, the Florentines' calculations were very much altered.[95] In obedience to an imperial summons, they hastened to Innsbruck to learn more – no doubt expecting to receive bad tidings. But the situation was even worse than they imagined.

Barely had Niccolò and Vettori set out than they heard of a disaster in the Cadore.[96] Shortly after Trautson had captured the region, the Venetians had despatched Bartolomeo d'Alviano – who had recently re-entered their service – to counter the imperial advance.[97] Leading a small force of crack troops across the mountains, d'Alviano caught Trautson unaware at Pieve di Cadore. Reluctant to risk an engagement, the Germans started to fall back, but d'Alviano, scenting blood, rushed forward to block their path. While his pikemen held their infantry back from behind a dry stream, his mounted crossbowmen and light cavalry fell upon them from both sides. With no way out, the Germans were cut to pieces. Several thousand, including Trautson, were killed; fewer than 300 escaped. Over the following days, d'Alviano quickly recovered the Cadore; and, by the time Niccolò and Vettori learned what had happened, he had already swept into imperial territory, further to the east.

Maximilian was horrified, but he had now gone too far to pull back. His only chance was to press the attack elsewhere. Before any more Swiss reached Venetian territory, he therefore ordered the main body of his army to march southwards from Trento. Its progress was rapid: pontoon bridges were thrown across the Adige; a bastion was built near Folgaria; and Rovereto was almost overwhelmed.[98] But, as Maximilian's troops neared the shores of Lake Garda, they found their path blocked by a Venetian army and a number of French troops under Alessandro Trivulzio. The two forces eyed each other warily, but, within a matter of days, Maximilian's lack of funds began to tell against him. Tired of not being paid, 2,000 mercenaries from the Grisons deserted.[99]

Maximilian was now in a dreadful fix. He desperately needed more soldiers. His most obvious recourse was, of course, to the German princes, but they had never been willing to provide him with more than a couple of thousand men, and, even then, only on a short-term basis. If Maximilian wanted to swell his ranks beyond their current size, he would have to pay for mercenaries, and, in order to do this, he would need to secure fresh subsidies. With this in mind, he called an imperial diet at Ulm, and hastily set off for Swabia.

Unsure of whether Maximilian would be able to carry on with his campaign, Vettori was keen to follow, but, having recently hurt his arm, he decided to send Niccolò to observe the diet instead.[100] Niccolò probably did not raise too many objections to this. Although the prospect of traipsing across the Alps in pouring rain cannot have appealed to him, he would doubtless have relished the opportunity to learn more about imperial politics, and, having already struck up a friendship with some of the leading humanists at Maximilian's court, would have been looking forward to getting his hands on some of the splendid books then being produced by German printers.[101] But, at the last moment, Vettori changed his mind. Now that he had come to depend on Niccolò's guidance, he felt he could not do without him, especially at such a critical time. It was a bit pathetic, of course, but Niccolò was used to it. Shrugging his shoulders, he dashed off a note to a friend in Cologne, asking for help in procuring the books he had wanted to buy;[102] and in a few days, he and Vettori were preparing to return to Bolzano to await further developments.

By the time they left Innsbruck, the diplomatic situation seemed to be shifting in their favour. Confident that subsidies would be granted, Maximilian was still hopeful of breaking the deadlock – and perhaps even of recouping some of his losses. But, having already suffered so many setbacks, he had now come to recognize that his task would be much easier if he could reach some sort of under-standing with the French.[103] Encouraged by the Aragonese ambassador and the papal legate – who hoped that an accord might pave the way for a wider anti-Venetian alliance – Maximilian had already reached out to Louis. This was tremendously good news on its own, but, when Niccolò and Vettori arrived in Bolzano, they were delighted to learn that Maximilian was also keen to reopen negotiations with Florence, having no doubt realized how much difference its money could make. At his request, Paul von Lichtenstein came to offer them new and more reasonable terms.[104] In return for a subvention of 60,000 ducats, to be paid in three instalments – the first on conclusion of the agreement, the second when the imperial armies reached a certain point in Italy, and the third two months after that – Maximilian would gladly confirm their rights over Pisa. Vettori was certainly tempted. Though the amount was still more than the *Dieci* had been prepared to offer at first, he had just received a letter authorizing him to go higher.[105] Nevertheless, he felt he had to refuse. As Niccolò pointed out in his report, no location had been specified for the second payment, and the third was too soon afterwards. Whether Maximilian could be persuaded to alter these terms was unclear, but, given how great his need for funds appeared to be, Vettori was cautiously optimistic.

Over the next few weeks, Maximilian's position deteriorated rapidly.[106] Fearing the enterprise might now be a lost cause, the diet at Ulm was less supportive than he had expected. Though no deci-sion had yet been taken, the princes were minded to refuse the emperor the subsidies he had requested.[107] To make matters worse, the negotiations with France were also floundering. Rather than simply agreeing to a truce, Louis XII wanted a more comprehensive peace treaty that would settle all of the outstanding areas of dispute between him and Maximilian. In the long term, this would be to the advantage of both sides, but right now the emperor did not have time for such drawn-out negotiations. Realizing he might not be able to continue his campaign for much longer, Maximilian reluctantly decided to open talks with the Venetians.[108]

Back in Trento, where they had since repaired, Niccolò and Vettori felt they would never get a better chance to do a deal. Now that Maximilian's army was 'as good as disbanded',[109] they were sure he could easily be persuaded to make further concessions – not only about the schedule of payments, but also about the amount itself.[110] But would such an agreement be worth it? Vettori thought not. At present, Maximilian didn't seem to be strong enough to carry the war into Italy 'in opposition to the will of France and Venice', and it seemed highly unlikely the German princes would supply him with any more money, now that he was withdrawing the forces they had previously funded.[111] As such, Vettori held off from signing anything.

It was just as well he did. On 8 June, Niccolò and Vettori reported that, two days earlier, a truce had been concluded for three years between Maximilian and the Venetians.[112] As his allies, the emperor named the pope, Hungary and England, while Venice cited Spain and France. Having not been consulted, Louis XII was much aggrieved by this arrangement, especially as it ruined any he had of concluding his own agreement with Maximilian.[113] But, for Florence, it could hardly have been better. With his campaign drawing to a close, Maximilian was willing to accede to the *Dieci*'s requests without demanding any more money in return – and without quibbling too much over the schedule of payments, either. Yet, at the same time, the truce vindicated Vettori's concerns. Now that Maximilian had secured a peace, he would be even *less* likely to come to Florence's defence.

Feeling thoroughly pleased with himself for having held his nerve, Vettori went to join the emperor, and there await his recall.[114] Niccolò, however, left for home straight away. A few days before the truce had been signed, he had fallen seriously ill. As Vettori related, he had great difficulty passing water, and the physicians in Trento did not know whether it was caused by a bladder stone or by something else.[115] Had the roads been open, he would have gone to seek medical attention in Florence before the end of May, but it was only now peace had been concluded that was he able to do so safely.

It was a painful journey. However carefully he picked his way across country, he was constantly being jolted about in his saddle, often causing him to double up in agony. But at least his route was direct. No longer needing to avoid Venetian territory, he headed southwards across the battle-scarred fields by Lake Garda, towards Verona and Modena. By 14 June, he was already in Bologna; and two days later, he was back home in Florence, sick and exhausted.[116]

*

Niccolò had been away for almost six months. By anyone's standards, it was a long time. More than any of his other embassies, the mission had taken a heavy toll. But, as he surrendered himself to Marietta's care, he probably felt that it had been worth it. He had scored a victory over his doubters. Though Florence may not have had its rights confirmed, it had been saved from making a costly mistake, and, given the growing appetite for an anti-Venetian alliance, it was now in a strong position to build support for its campaign among the other Italian powers. If the *Dieci* played their cards right, they might even be able to talk some of Pisa's strongest supporters over to their side. And if they could do that, their chances of recapturing the city would be immeasurably enhanced.

Looking back on the mission as he lay recuperating in bed, Niccolò could not help feeling it was a validation of all that he had written about fate since first penning the *Ghiribizzi*. Though Florence had started at something of a disadvantage, it had successfully adapted itself to changing circumstances and, by waiting for exactly the right moment, it had reaped the rewards. The same could not, however, be said of Maximilian.

As soon as Niccolò was well enough, he hastily took up his pen and began putting his thoughts down on paper. Now known as the *Rapporto di cose della Magna* ('Report on German Affairs'),[117] this took the form of a 'classic diplomatic memoir composed at the end of an embassy',[118] but its true subject was fate – and the emperor's inability to master it. After a lengthy summary of events, from the Diet of Constance to the conclusion of the truce with Venice, Niccolò turned to examine the reasons for the abject failure of Maximilian's campaign. Perhaps the most obvious was political – or, rather, constitutional. Rather than being a strong and cohesive state, the Holy Roman Empire was a patchwork quilt of petty principalities and free cities, each more preoccupied with its own private concerns than with any common purpose. Indeed, for more than a century, the Swiss cantons had even enjoyed de facto independence. Deeply attached to their 'rough and free' way of life, the German peoples had little affection for the emperor's authority, and even less enthusiasm for vainglorious ventures abroad. Unable to draw on the resources of his Empire or to depend on the fidelity of his troops, it was perhaps no surprise that Maximilian had failed. But the most compelling explanation for Maximilian's rout was his own character. He was, admittedly, not without his good points. As Niccolò explained, he had 'infinite virtue'. He was a 'perfect leader', who governed his nation with 'great justice' and who had a boundless capacity for making himself loved. But the two qualities which earned him the greatest praise – his generosity of spirit and easy-going nature – were also his greatest weakness. Rather than asking for advice from particular courtiers, he allowed himself to be advised by them all; and since he was unwilling to show more favour to one than to others, his views changed by the minute. This made him inconstant and irresolute. As such, he was incapable either of adapting himself to changing circumstances or of seizing opportunities. Even had he enjoyed the Empire's unwavering support, Niccolò argued, he had been almost doomed to fail. If fate was to be beaten, a sharp eye and a strong will were needed.

They were wise words. But whether Niccolò would heed his own lesson still remained to be seen.

PART V

The Prisoner of Fortune

(1508–13)

15

Old Scores, New Enemies

(June 1508–June 1509)

To the Renaissance mind, there was no more potent image of the capriciousness of fate than that of the *rota fortunae* (wheel of fortune). A common theme in poetry, art and music, its character was perhaps best captured by a miniature painted by the French illuminator Jean Pichore in *c.* 1503.[1] Gracing a lavish edition of Petrarch's *De remediis utriusque fortune* presented to Louis XII by Cardinal Georges d'Amboise, this shows the wheel being turned by Joy. As she does so, the victims caught in its spokes are carried aloft, helped by a female figure, most likely representing Prosperity. But, no sooner do they reach the summit of glory than they are brought low once again and pulled from the wheel by Greed, Pain and Suffering. Meanwhile, the blindfolded figure of Fortune stands above the scene, distributing crowns and money to those on her right, only to snatch them away from those on her left. For the religious, it was an illustration of the vanity of mortal concerns. For those of a more earthly persuasion, it was a warning against complacency – and despair. But most of all, it was a reminder that nothing in life was certain beyond the turning of the wheel.

It was an image which would have had particular resonance for Niccolò as he picked up the threads of his existence in Florence in the summer of 1508. Change was in the air. At the family home in the Via Romana, everything was topsy-turvy. With three children aged between four and six running around and a worn-out wife complaining about his all-too-frequent absences, the house would have been a riot of noise and activity. Although his friends had done their best to keep an eye on his affairs while he had been away, his finances were a mess, and he soon found himself being dragged into an ugly dispute with a crooked broker named Mariotto d'Amerigo.[2]

His brother, Totto, had also announced that, after much hemming and hawing, he was at last ready to enter the priesthood,[3] and, on 21 June, signed over his share of their father's legacy in preparation for his vows of poverty.[4] On top of everything else, Niccolò was probably wracked with anxiety about his position, as well. Though he had saved Florence from entering into a costly and futile agreement with the emperor, he had done himself few favours on his mission to Germany. Aside from Cardinal Francesco Soderini – who expressed his admiration for the *Rapporto di cose della Magna* before he had even read it[5] – Niccolò does not seem to have pleased many people. Indeed, his modest success may actually have alienated some even further.

By the beginning of July, Niccolò's head must have been spinning. Tired of all this change, he desperately needed to restore some order to his life. If nothing else, he hoped to get his work at the chancellery back on track. Returning to the Palazzo della Signoria, – which was then being repaired after a recent fire – he immediately set about tackling the militia.[6] Shortly before his departure for Germany the previous winter, the Florentine Republic had dismissed Don Michele de Corella, apparently for misappropriating funds.[7] No doubt Niccolò had expected his colleagues to appoint a replacement while he was away. To his dismay, however, no one had yet been found – in part because of lingering doubts about the nature of the role[8] – and, in the absence of a commander, discipline had started to suffer. Clearly, Niccolò could not allow this to continue and, within days of returning to his desk, he was already firing off letters to Rome, asking Florence's resident ambassador to keep his eyes peeled for a suitable candidate.[9] With a bit of luck, he might have the militia back in shape before long, and he could then start repairing some of the damage done by his German holiday.

*

Yet, as the wheel of fortune continued to turn, Niccolò soon found himself caught up in a greater – and potentially more dangerous – process of transformation. Following the collapse of negotiations with the emperor, the *Dieci* convened a series of small *pratiche* to discuss whether Florence should now attempt to bring the rebellious Pisans to heel without him. As ever, Piero Soderini was strongly in favour of attempting another siege. But most of the speakers – all *ottimati*

– were opposed.[10] To their minds, the risks were simply too great. Some argued that, since Pisa could always count on receiving succour from Genoa and Lucca, it 'might not be taken, even if great hardships were inflicted upon it'. Others pointed out that, even if the kings of France and Spain reached an understanding with the emperor – as seemed increasingly likely – the Venetians would never be content for the Florentines to have Pisa, and would do all they could to prevent it from falling into their hands. And others still feared that a campaign against Pisa 'would lead many peasants into great difficulties, such that many families, and especially the women, would suffer.'

Soderini was, however, not to be denied. Seeing that he would never get his way in small *pratiche*, he had the Eighty convene a *pratica larga*, which, by virtue of its size, would be likely to contain more of his supporters.[11] Once again, the *ottimati* expressed their doubts, and, for a time, it seemed they might prevail. But Soderini was ready for them. After vehemently arguing his case, he whipped out a series of letters from Niccolò di Piero Capponi, who had recently been appointed to succeed Alessandro Nasi as commissioner general at Cascina. In these, Capponi predicted that, if a siege were to be attempted, the Pisans would either suffer such great hardships that they would rise up in rebellion against their leaders, or would eventually be starved into submission. His confidence proved decisive. Despite the *ottimati*'s continued objections, the *pratica* gave its approval for the campaign to begin.

Although it was already late in the season, the *Dieci* decided to start preparing for a siege straight away – and, in the hope of depriving the Pisans of as much food as possible, called on the militia to destroy their crops before they could be harvested. Poor Niccolò's heart must have sunk. Though he is likely to have agreed with Soderini's plan in principle, he would have known that the militia was in no state to hold a parade, let alone mount a major offensive. He had not yet found a replacement for Don Michele, much less straightened out the problems that had arisen in his absence. Particularly if the Pisans continued receiving help from abroad, as the *ottimati* suspected, his under-manned and poorly disciplined units would stand little chance. But the *Dieci* had made up their minds, so he would just have to make the best of it.

On 16 August, Niccolò summoned up his courage and set off along the Arno to begin recruiting in Pescia and San Miniato.[12] Setting up his little table wherever there was space, he and his assistants pressed every likely looking local they saw into service with almost reckless speed. He knew full well there would be no time to train these unsuspecting yokels properly, but, right now, numbers were his only concern; and in four days, he had enlisted enough to be going along with. On 21 August, he led his new battalions towards Pontedera, where, as ordered, he began laying waste to the Pisan countryside.[13]

*

Almost immediately, things began to go wrong. The day after Niccolò reached Pontedera, ambassadors from the kings of France and Spain arrived in Florence with a request that the Pisans should not be molested.[14] Though this soon proved to be nothing more than a crude attempt to extort money from the Florentines, it appeared to validate some of the *ottimati*'s concerns. Even Soderini began to suspect that, if the campaign against Pisa was to continue, it might be wiser to come to an agreement with Louis and Ferdinand, after all. On this occasion, at least, he was able to make some common cause with his *ottimati* opponents. All agreed that, 'if no pact were reached with these kings, Pisa would not be had'.[15] But, though ambassadors were soon on their way to France, no one was in any doubt about how long and difficult the negotiations would be.[16] It might take months to agree on suitable terms – and, by then, there was no telling what might have happened.

While the Florentines were talking these matters over, the Pisans took heart. Even if the French and Spanish had not been sincere, their request had at least given the rebels some breathing space – and they lost no time in capitalizing on it. Within days, Niccolò's green-horned militiamen started running up against some stiff resistance, and, though he had previously been well supplied with money, he now found himself struggling to pay for weapons and supplies.[17] As the Pisans may have been expecting, however, the *Dieci* were unwilling to offer him any support. Still unsettled by the Franco-Spanish scare, they refused to acknowledge the difficulty of his situation and fell back on parsimony and recrimination. On 26 August, they reprimanded him for not harrying the Pisans harder, and, after turning down his demand for additional funds, ordered him to redouble his efforts.[18] Even Piero Soderini – who was usually quick to defend his protégé – complained about his lack of progress. 'My dear Niccolò,' wrote the *gonfaloniere*, '[t]o our group here, it seems as if this laying waste is going very slowly ... [I] urge you to press for it to be finished, in such a way that the least possible fodder is left to the enemy and with the greatest possible swiftness.'[19]

Such rebukes must have stung Niccolò badly. But there was little he could do. Outmatched and undersupplied, his militia could only look on helplessly as the Pisans gathered in the last of the harvest and retreated safely behind their walls. It was an ignominious, if not unexpected, end to the operation – and, for Niccolò, it was bitter vindication of his fears. He must have hoped the Signoria would learn from its mistakes and wait a while before attempting anything of the sort again.

But now that the Florentines had recovered from their diplomatic shock, they were more determined than ever to bring the Pisans to their knees. Disappointing though Niccolò's failure may have been, they knew there was more than one way to starve a city – and they lost no time in trying again. Just three days after Soderini's letter to Niccolò, the *Dieci* made an attempt to block Pisa's access to the sea.[20] Under the command of a Genoese captain called Bardellotto, a fleet of ships was sent to Porto Pisano, where it was to stand guard over the mouth of the Arno. But this too went awry. No sooner had Bardellotto taken up his post than Louis XII ordered the captain – who was one of his subjects – to leave Florentine service, apparently in the hope that, by robbing the Signoria of most of its ships, it might be induced to forget about a siege and offer him more favourable terms.

Undeterred, the Florentines tried a different approach. Leaving the remains of their fleet to guard the Arno as best it could, the *Dieci* launched an attack on Lucca, which was still keeping the Pisans well supplied with men and provisions. Meanwhile, the *Nove* ordered Niccolò to begin recruiting again in preparation for a larger and more direct attack on Pisa's supply routes as soon as the winter was over. In October, he was back in Pescia,[21] and, at the end of November, he was on his way to San Miniato, Pomerance and the villages of the Val di Cecina – no doubt filled with foreboding.[22] It cannot have escaped his notice that, if this latest attack failed, as seemed eminently likely, he would get the blame – and perhaps even the sack.

*

Quite suddenly, however, the wheel of fortune turned in Florence's favour. After a lightning attack on Viareggio – in which Florentine troops had captured 10,000 *fl.* in booty and burned wool worth a further 10,000 *fl.* – the Lucchesi had already had enough. On 18 November, they empowered a specially appointed *balìa* to sue for peace, and, on 11 January, they signed a treaty guaranteeing that they would not 'give aid to the Pisans openly or secretly' for three years.[23] The Signoria lost no time in capitalizing on its advantage. Before the month was out, Niccolò had been sent into Lucchese territory at the head of a small army, with orders to close off Pisa's access to the sea by land. Confident of his territory, he moved quickly. By the middle of February, he had already reached the mouth of the Fiume Morto (a strategically vital canal linking Pisa with the coast) and had erected a network of palisades, piles and pontoons to prevent any traffic getting through.[24] His despatches were necessarily brief – so brief, in fact, that Niccolò Capponi even complained about them – but his sense of excitement was palpable.[25] Pisa was now virtually cut off; provided the last remnants of the Florentine navy continued to maintain a blockade of sorts at the mouth of the Arno, the rebels could no longer count on receiving provisions from abroad. And, when the harvest ran out, they would begin to starve. As Biagio Buonaccorsi related, the Florentines were exultant. Eagerly looking forward to 'ending the Pisan business' once and for all, they resolved to spare no expense.[26] Niccolò would have everything he needed to finish the job.[27]

The Pisans could see how perilous their situation had become, but they were not yet ready to give up hope. They reasoned that, if they could just keep the Florentines busy for a while, they might be able to find some more allies – or at least gather the strength to hold on for a bit longer. To buy themselves time, they therefore feigned interest in negotiating a peace through the mediation of Jacopo IV d'Appiano. Convinced the Pisans were already dying of hunger, the Florentines were all too willing to believe their offer, and it was decided that –after checking that Lucca would keep its word not to help the rebels – Niccolò should be sent to Piombino to open talks for Pisa's surrender.[28]

Riding as quickly as he could, Niccolò presented himself before Jacopo d'Appiano on 14 March.[29] The audience began promisingly enough. Expressing an ardent desire to see Tuscany at peace, the old *signore* of Piombino assured Niccolò that he had done everything possible to facilitate an agreement. But, when he then revealed that the Pisan envoys had not, in fact, been granted full authority to treat with the Florentines, it became clear the rebels were not in earnest, after all. Naturally, Jacopo tried to persuade Niccolò that he might as well stay to hear them out, but Niccolò was unconvinced. Since there was no prospect of negotiating seriously, he felt he should leave. Only the desire to pay them back for their deceit made him change his mind. Once the Pisan envoys had been led in, he bluntly informed them that Florence was no longer to be trifled with. Unless they were prepared to hand over their city, with 'all its territory and jurisdiction, exactly as it had been before the rebellion', they could forget any further talks. Just for good measure, he took the opportunity to sow a little discord, as well. Turning to the envoys of the Pisan *contado*, he told them that, however the war ended, they would be sure to lose. If Pisa emerged victorious, he argued, her citizens would 'not want the country people as their companions, but as slaves'; but if Pisa were taken, then the *contadini* would 'lose their properties, their lives, and everything else'. Far better that they come over to the Florentines' side now, he winked. And, with howls of protest ringing in his ears, he took his leave.

*

Returning to Florence two days later, Niccolò seems to have been given permission to resume his duties in the chancellery.[30] After so many months of rushing around, it must have been a pleasant relief to work in a warm office and sleep comfortably in his own bed. But he was not able to enjoy it for long. The diplomatic winds were changing. Back in December, the Emperor Maximilian had formed an anti-Venetian league with Louis XII of France, Ferdinand of Aragon and Pope Julius II at Cambrai;[31] and now, after many months of preparations, they seemed to be on the brink of launching a coordinated attack.[32] The Florentines were, of course, delighted. This ensured that Venice would be too busy readying its own defences to help the Pisans in future. Even more gratifyingly, it smoothed the way for an agreement with France and Aragon. Less than a fortnight after Niccolò's return, news arrived that Florence's ambassadors had at last concluded a treaty.[33] To be sure, it had not been cheap. In return for their support against Pisa, Florence agreed to pay Louis and Ferdinand

50,000 *fl.* each. But it was worth every penny. Pisa was now completely isolated. All that remained was for the *Dieci* to tighten the noose – and, to do that, it needed Niccolò to return to the army.

On 14 April – just as the League of Cambrai was launching its attack against Venice[34] – Niccolò was ordered to set up base in Cascina, where the commissioner Niccolò di Piero Capponi required his help in securing arms and provisions for the coming siege.[35] He was, of course, happy enough to go for a day or two, but, having now smelt victory, he balked at the suggestion that he should remain there indefinitely. Writing to the *Dieci*, he observed that supplies could be arranged by any man:

> whereas if I remained [in Cascina], I could no longer be of any service
> to the army, nor be in any other way of use [elsewhere]. I am aware
> that that posting would expose me to less danger and fatigue, but if I
> wanted to avoid danger and fatigue, I should not have left Florence. I
> therefore beg your Lordships to allow me to remain among the [troops
> in the field] to work with the commissioners on all the things that are
> going on. For here, I can make myself useful, but at Cascina, I should
> not be good for anything, and should die of sheer desperation.[36]

Such forceful words evidently impressed the *Dieci*. Though he would still be responsible for arranging 'provisions for the whole army', he was given permission to go wherever he thought fit, and do whatever he felt necessary.

Over the following weeks, Niccolò shuttled feverishly between the three camps into which the army had been divided – inspecting troops, gauging numbers and supervising the dispersal of funds.[37] His energy was boundless and his attention to detail extraordinary to behold. He seemed to be everywhere and to miss nothing. The men loved him for it and, soon enough, came to regard his authority as superior to that of their own commanders. But not everyone was happy. Having recently been chosen as one of the new commissioners general in the field, Alamanno Salviati was appalled to see this low-born bureaucrat taking on a role that was rightly his.[38] Bristling with wounded aristocratic pride, Salviati unleashed the pent-up frustrations of many months past in a savage reprimand. 'Although [the men] may wish to acknowledge you,' he wrote, 'know that you are not always to command them everywhere you go. That they should love you, and they should think highly of you, I approve, because, being every day under your gaze, they will be so much more obedient and shall know better what they have to do. But do not forget that they must also answer to this Commissioner . . .'[39] Had it been allowed to escalate, this argument might very easily have disrupted the whole campaign – and brought an untimely end to Niccolò's involvement in the coming siege. But Niccolò was too wise to take umbrage at Salviati's tone, or to argue needlessly about their relative status. With a shrug of his shoulders, he meekly accepted the commissioner's rebuke and backed off. There were, after all, much more important things to be getting on with; and as long as he could be in at the kill, he would be happy.

On 16 May, Niccolò had to go to Pistoia for a few days to deal with a shortage of bread.[40] It was a fairly routine matter, and he did not expect to miss much. Though the Florentine army had been advancing rapidly through the Pisan countryside in recent weeks, there was every reason to suppose a long struggle still lay ahead.[41] But no sooner had he returned to the camp at Mezzana than it was all over. Now that a Florentine victory seemed inevitable, the rebels saw no point in fighting on. Rather than suffer the horrors of a siege, they thought it wiser to sue for peace. On 20 May, Niccolò was present when a Pisan delegation arrived in the Val Serchio to offer terms. Once the commissioners had satisfied themselves that, this time, their offer was serious, Niccolò had the honour of giving the *Dieci* the news that the end was at last in sight.[42]

During the heady days that followed, Niccolò found himself at the centre of everything. Dashing off countless letters in the commissioners' names, he took careful notes of the preliminary discussions with the rebels, while simultaneously overseeing the defection of Pisa's leading general, Corrado Tarlatino, and dealing with the sudden influx of Pisans fleeing the beleaguered city.[43] When the time came for the Pisan ambassadors to go to Florence, he was chosen to accompany them; and when, on 4 June, the instrument of surrender was eventually signed, his name appeared on the first page, immediately below that of Marcello di Virgilio Adriani.[44] Four days later, the Florentine commissioners formally took possession of Pisa, bringing an end to fifteen long years of war. Following behind, at the head of the militia he had so painstakingly created, marched Niccolò, revelling in the triumph.

The Florentines went wild with excitement. According to Agostino Vespucci, it was not possible 'to express how much delight, how much jubilation and joy, all the people here have taken in the news of the recovery of that city of Pisa; in some measure *every man* had gone mad with exultation'.[45] Shops were shut, bonfires were lit in the streets and 'great fireworks were placed on all the towers and on the Palazzo [della Signoria].'[46] As the architect of the militia – to which at least part of the victory could be attributed[47] – Niccolò was praised to the skies. One of the commissioners, Filippo Casavecchia, wrote to wish him 'a thousand benefits from the outstanding acquisition of that noble city, for truly . . . to a very great extent, your person was the cause of it . . .'[48] Even Alamanno Salviati was beginning to soften towards him. Though they would never be completely reconciled, Niccolò's role in the recapture of Pisa seems to have earned the aged patrician's respect – and perhaps even a little of his former affection, too.[49]

All the battles that Niccolò had fought over recent years had been worth it. All the struggles in the chancellery, all the missions through rain and snow, all the financial hardships, all the domestic woes, all the frustrations and disappointments were forgotten. Triumphant in war, vindicated in politics and freed from the enmity of his greatest foe, Niccolò was on top of the world.

*

Had Niccolò been as serious a student of Fortune as he often claimed, however, he would have noticed that her wheel had not yet stopped turning. Even as he reached the summit of his ambitions, he was already on his way down.

While the Pisan campaign had been getting underway, another, more subtle, transformation was taking place that was to erode the foundations of Soderini's *reggimento* and have a devastating effect on Niccolò's career. Since Piero de' Medici's death at the Battle of Garigliano in December 1503, his brother, Cardinal Giovanni de' Medici, had been plotting his family's return. While an attempted coup in 1505 had collapsed almost as soon as it had begun, this early failure had taught him a valuable lesson. Although Soderini was bitterly opposed by the *ottimati*, the cardinal realized he would never be able to force the *gonfaloniere* from power unless he could persuade the various opposition factions to throw in their lot with the Medici. Of course, this was not going to be easy. Many of the leading *ottimati* families had been enemies of the Medici for generations and would rather put up with Soderini than allow them to return. But the cardinal was confident that, if he could make them understand how much they stood to gain from the Medici's return, they would soon come round.

The cardinal's campaign had begun shortly before Niccolò had set off for Germany. Having fallen out of favour with Julius II, the archbishop of Florence, Rinaldo Orsini, had decided to resign his see, and had asked his nephew, Cardinal de' Medici, to help him find a suitable successor.[50] The cardinal first proposed Guglielmo Capponi, a long-term Medici ally. But when Soderini, who may have been hoping to secure the vacant see for his brother, blocked this, the cardinal transferred his support to Cosimo de' Pazzi, the popular bishop of Arezzo. It was a shrewd move. Since Pazzi was acceptable both to the Signoria and to the pope, Soderini had no choice but to acquiesce in his appointment. Thus, the cardinal won not only the gratitude of the new archbishop, but also the friendship of a family that had been vehemently opposed to his own for almost fifty years.

Emboldened, Giovanni de' Medici then upped his game. In July 1508, just as Niccolò was returning to work in the chancellery, the cardinal secretly began negotiating to marry his niece, Clarice, to Filippo Strozzi the younger.[51] Though Filippo was only nineteen years old, such a match promised huge political rewards. Even more so than the Pazzi, the Strozzi were old enemies of the Medici. Almost seventy years earlier, Filippo's forebear, Palla Strozzi, had been exiled from Florence, together with the rest of his family, for his opposition to Cosimo 'il Vecchio'; and when Filippo's father, Filippo di Matteo, had eventually been allowed to return, more than three decades later, he had swiftly become one of the leading voices against, first, Piero 'il Gottoso', and then Lorenzo.

There were, of course, risks to the match, as well – especially for Filippo. But, for such a dazzling constellation of support, the cardinal was prepared to pay handsomely. Provided Filippo and Clarice married within eight months, he agreed to provide his niece with a staggering dowry of 6,000 *fl*. This overcame any concerns that Filippo may have had; and, as soon as the contract was signed, he was packed off to Rome to stage a romantic assignation with his fiancée that, it was hoped, would make the whole thing look like a youthful elopement.

It was, however, impossible to keep such an alliance secret for long;

by December, rumours had already begun circulating in Florence. Predictably enough, Soderini's supporters reacted furiously. Rightly denouncing it as a plot to restore the hated Medici, they whipped the *popolo* up into a frenzy of anger. This alarmed the Strozzi. Fearful of being sent into exile yet again, they hurried to the Palazzo della Signoria to protest their innocence.[52] Filippo was just a foolish young man, they claimed. Having filled his head with romantic nonsense, he had contracted the marriage on his own, without consulting the rest of the family. There was, of course, nothing political about the match, and they promised to get him out of it, if they possibly could. But Filippo stubbornly refused to change his mind.

At this, Soderini exploded with rage. Without bothering to convene a *pratica*, he forced the Signoria to summon Filippo before them to answer a charge of consorting with rebels, and accused twelve of his most highly placed opponents – including Cosimo de' Pazzi and Bernardo Rucellai – of conspiring against the *stato*. As loyal as ever, Niccolò went along with it all. According to Filippo's older brother, Lorenzo, he even wrote some of the most vitriolic accusations himself.[53]

But Soderini and Niccolò had gone too far. As Guicciardini later recorded, the *gonfaloniere* was widely criticized for disregarding constitutional norms and for 'treating this case not as a public matter, pertaining to the city [as a whole], but as a private affair'.[54] Unnerved by his apparently authoritarian tendencies, his colleagues in the Signoria were no longer willing to support him. When Filippo Strozzi returned to Florence at the end of December, they refused Soderini's request to prevent him leaving Florentine territory. On 19 January 1509, the *Otto di Guardia* ruled that, rather than suffer the harsh punishments demanded by Soderini, Filippo was merely to be exiled to the kingdom of Naples for three years and pay a fine of 500 *fl.* Following representations by Clarice, even this was later set aside. Filippo was given permission to serve out the remainder of his sentence in Florence, and no restrictions were placed on his movements. The following month, amid lavish celebrations, Filippo and Clarice were married in Rome, cementing an alliance between the two families and consolidating a Medici-led coalition that was rapidly emerging as the dominant force in Florentine politics.

The battle lines had been drawn for a decisive confrontation – and, though he may not have realized it, Niccolò was on the wrong side.

16

Walking the Tightrope

(July 1509–September 1510)

While Florence had been recovering Pisa, the League of Cambrai had been advancing rapidly through Venetian territory.[1] On 14 May, Louis XII had defeated the Venetian army at the Battle of Agnadello, and had quickly taken possession of Bergamo, Brescia and Crema.[2] Meanwhile, Julius II had pushed northwards into the Romagna, seizing Faenza and Rimini with the help of Alfonso d'Este, who had also expelled the Venetians from Ferrara and recaptured the Polesine for himself along the way.[3] By the end of the month, only a handful of towns had remained under Venetian control and, having been left undefended, the three most important – Padua, Verona and Vicenza – had surrendered to Maximilian's ambassadors before imperial troops had even left Germany.[4]

For a time, it had seemed that Venice itself might fall. But no sooner had Maximilian crossed the Alps than the League's fortunes began to turn. As vacillating and inconstant as ever, the emperor proved incapable of putting the enormous army he had brought with him to good use, and soon lost much of what his allies had won for him.[5] On 17 July, Venetian troops retook Padua and, in spite of his overwhelming numerical superiority, Maximilian was unable to dislodge them. Running short of money and supplies, he was forced to lift the siege and withdraw to Verona, whence he appealed to Louis XII for help. When Louis failed to reply as quickly as he had hoped, he tried to buy himself some time by offering the Venetians a truce, but, having now recovered their confidence, they were in no mood to parlay. Humiliated, Maximilian retreated to Trento, leaving what was left of his army to continue the struggle without him.

Before leaving Verona, however, the emperor signed an accord with the Florentines, stipulating that, in return for 40,000 ducats – payable in four instalments – he would confirm them in their possessions and take them under his protection.[6] Perhaps understandably, the Florentines had not been particularly enthusiastic about this. They had, after all, rejected a similar agreement only a year before and, now that they had recaptured Pisa, they had little need for another. But Louis XII had foisted it on them. He had been alarmed by the speed of the Venetians' recovery and was afraid that, if Maximilian was to lose heart, the whole campaign might be jeopardized. Anxious to strengthen the bonds of friendship without spending any more money of his own, Louis had therefore asked the Florentines to come to some sort of understanding with the emperor; since they were still dependent on French support, they felt they could hardly refuse.

The first instalment had been handed over by the Florentine ambassadors straight away. But, when the second fell due, the *Dieci* chose Niccolò to deliver the money.[7] He was a natural choice: reliable, a seasoned diplomat and already familiar with Maximilian's court. Most importantly, however, he was a keen observer – and the *Dieci* knew they could trust him to keep a discreet eye on what the emperor was up to while he was away. Accompanied by 'two or three mounted soldiers' carrying 10,000 ducats in gold, Niccolò was to proceed to Mantua, where he would find one of Maximilian's representatives waiting for him. Once he had made the payment, he was to send his escort back to Florence and then make for Verona, 'or wherever may seem most convenient' to learn more 'about the Emperor's affairs, and especially about his Italian enterprise.' During his stay, he was to change his lodgings regularly – so as to conceal the true purpose of his mission – and report back on 'anything worthy of note'. But on no account was he to leave until he received orders from the *Dieci*.

*

Leaving Florence on 10 November, Niccolò rode northwards through the Mugello and towards Bologna. It was a familiar road and he usually loved nothing better than being in the saddle. But he felt none of the excitement he had in the past. As he confessed in a (now lost) letter to Biagio Buonaccorsi, he was wracked with anxiety.[8]

Although he had been showered with praise for his role in recapturing
Pisa, he was keenly aware that he had antagonized a good many
people with his arrogant behaviour in the field, and with the violent
denunciations he had written during the affair of the Strozzi marriage.
Nothing had been said to his face as yet, but he must have known
his enemies were simply biding their time. More than ever, he needed
to shine on this mission. Even Biagio agreed. 'If ever you were dili-
gent in your reports,' he wrote, 'you need to be so now in order to
shut the mouths of the bench-sitters.'[9]

What Niccolò learned en route only unnerved him further. Shortly
after he set out, Venetian forces under Niccolò di Pitigliano had
renewed their offensive, easily pushing back the remains of
Maximilian's army. Feltre and Belluno had been retaken, and it was
rumoured further attacks might soon be attempted. Worse still, the
League was starting to buckle. Having now achieved his objectives
in the Romagna, Julius II felt there was nothing more to be gained
from the alliance. He was not yet ready to risk antagonizing Louis
and Maximilian by withdrawing openly, but he was no longer willing
to participate actively, either. If the League continued to fragment
like this, there was no telling what might happen. Were Venice to
recover its former strength and Julius to go his own way, the whole
balance of power in Italy would be upset – and the consequence for
Florence could be dire.

Still turning these grim thoughts over in his mind, Niccolò arrived
in Mantua on 15 November. Even cloaked in winter fog, it would
have been a bewitching sight, but he was probably too preoccupied
to notice. Riding straight to his lodgings, he was soon visited by the
emperor's secretary, Pigello Portinari.[10] After a hearty meal the
following day, Niccolò 'counted out . . . 9,000 ducats' to Portinari's
factotum, Antimaco, and was given an imperial letter, together with
an acquittance, in return. Antimaco then presented Niccolò to a
young man from Verona, who was supposed to receive the remaining
1,000 ducats, but, since the fellow had not brought any authorization,
Niccolò sent him away with a flea in his ear. Until he could present
the proper paperwork, Niccolò grumbled, he would not get a penny.
This could, of course, take days, but Niccolò was willing to wait.

Hanging about that evening, Niccolò questioned Antimaco about
the war.[11] Happily, the situation did not seem to be as bad as he had
feared. According to Antimaco, Maximilian had renewed his friendly

relations with Louis and was planning to lead an army against the Venetians any day now. But Niccolò's delight was short-lived. Later that night, Antimaco received a message revealing that, the previous day, Vicenza had revolted and the Venetians had taken possession.

When Niccolò went out into the town, a little after dawn, everyone was already talking about the dreadful news, but their accounts varied wildly. Some said the Vicentines had stripped the imperial garrison and taken its commander prisoner, while others said they had sent the troops away without harming them. Niccolò had no idea which was true, but, either way, it was a terrible development. Many believed that, unless Louis XII intervened, Verona might soon follow Vicenza's example; and if that happened, Maximilian's involvement in the war would effectively be over. Niccolò desperately needed more information, but how was he to get it while he was stuck in Mantua?

*

In an effort to forget his worries, Niccolò went to pay his respects to Isabella d'Este, who was ruling the city on behalf of her husband, Francesco Gonzaga, while he languished in a Venetian prison.[12] By any standards, Isabella was a remarkable woman. Cultured and intelligent, she was a patron of the arts, a leader of fashion and a tireless correspondent. She was also a formidable ruler. In her husband's absence, she had staved off unrest, taken control of the city's forces and readied its defences for an attack. Most visitors were captivated by her. But Niccolò was unmoved. Though she greeted him 'in the kindest manner', he was still too preoccupied with Vicenza to notice her accomplishments, and was disappointed to find that she knew no more about it than he did.[13]

*

To Niccolò's relief, his Veronese contact received his mandate two days later. Hurriedly making the transfer, Niccolò then scribbled a quick note to the *Dieci*, mounted his horse and rode out of Mantua as quickly as he could, towards the Alps. Without an armed escort to slow him down, he made rapid progress; and by the next morning, 20 November, he was already in Verona.[14]

Even in winter, it was a sight to behold. Passing through the imposing arches of the Portoni della Brà, Niccolò would have seen the vast edifice of the Roman amphitheatre towering above him. This would have been impressive enough – especially for an ardent admirer of classical literature – but, as he delved deeper into the city, he would have found yet more monuments to the ancient past and an abundance of fine medieval architecture. Though more restrained than anything in Florence, the Romanesque facades of the cathedral and the Basilica of San Zeno had a beguiling grace; while the gothic baldachins that topped the Scaliger tombs were a potent reminder of Verona's historic dominance of the March. And running through the city were the gentle waters of the Adige, spanned by a bridge that, by common accord, was a marvel of engineering.

Verona was, however, anything but quiet. Just then, its streets were thronged with troops. On 29 November, Niccolò estimated that there were at least 4,500 infantrymen and 2,500 cavalry.[15] Another 4,000 German foot soldiers were expected the next day, and more would soon follow. But what 'such a considerable force' was doing there was a mystery. No one seemed to have any idea what was going on. The emperor was supposed to have met Chaumont just outside Cremona to 'decide how this war [was] to be carried on', but the French commander was still dallying on the banks of Lake Garda and Maximilian had not even left Trento. A rift seemed to have opened. If the rumours were to be believed, Louis XII was refusing to send Maximilian any more troops unless he received some more castles in return. But Niccolò had heard it said that Maximilian would not give Louis 'a single battlement of all that belonged to him; and that the king ought to be satisfied with having the emperor's states as a buffer' between him and Venice.[16]

While the two monarchs squabbled, the imperial troops were growing restless. Having nothing better to do, they occupied themselves 'with plundering and ravaging the surrounding country.'[17] This only served to strengthen the common people's affection for Venice and turn them against the emperor. 'Every day we see and hear of the most wretched [and] unprecedented things,' wrote Niccolò, 'such that the minds of the country people are filled with a desire for death and vengeance; for they have become more determined and angry against the enemies of the Venetians than the Jews were against the Romans.'[18] Indeed, every day 'one of them, taken prisoner, allows himself to be killed rather than renounce the Venetian side.' Less than a week after Niccolò's arrival, one *contadino* was brought before the governor, 'and he said he was a *Marcheso* [that is, a partisan of Venice], and a *Marcheso* he would die, and he did not want to live as anything else, so the [governor] had him burned. And neither a promise to let him live nor any other favour could shake him from this belief.'[19] Naturally, the Venetians were quick to take advantage of this. With the help of local villagers, they ranged through the countryside, seizing one castle after another.

Niccolò could not conceal his alarm. As he admitted to the *Dieci*, he was afraid that, unless Louis or Maximilian backed down, the campaign would collapse and the Venetians would be free to reassert their dominance in the north. Indeed, tensions were soon running so high that he was worried the emperor might actually be ready to 'make terms with the Venetians and drive [the French] out of Italy'.[20] It was agonizing not to have better information. As he told Luigi Guicciardini, he was 'high and dry' there in Verona.[21] It was all very well watching soldiers come and go, but if he was to be of any use to the *Dieci*, he needed to be where the decisions were made. He was so frustrated that he almost set out for Trento there and then, but, since he did not have the proper diplomatic authorization, he was afraid he might be arrested as a spy.[22] He would just have to stay put and see what happened.

*

To while away the time, Niccolò began writing a lengthy poem in terza rima for his friend, Luigi Guicciardini. Now known as the *Capitolo dell'ambizione* ('Tercets on Ambition'), this was, in many senses, a continuation of themes Niccolò had touched on in the *Capitolo di Fortuna* and the *Ghiribizzi*,[23] but its tone was very different. Having been deeply affected by what he had seen in recent weeks, Niccolò was less enamoured with man's capacity to master fortune, and far more scathing about the effects of greed and ambition.[24] Embroidering his poem with references to Maximilian, Louis XII and the Republic of Venice, he bemoaned the suffering inflicted by war and issued a dire warning against taking up arms heedlessly.

Purportedly written in answer to a letter from Luigi, in which he expressed his amazement that a power struggle had recently broken out within the Petrucci family, the poem begins by observing that, if he reflected more carefully on 'human appetites', he would not be surprised at all.[25] Ambition and avarice were everywhere – and had been since the dawn of time. 'When man was born,' wrote Niccolò, 'so they too were born.'[26] Hardly had Adam and Eve been banished from Paradise than they had come to deprive humankind 'of peace and to set us at war'.[27] With 'pestilential poison' they drove Cain to kill his brother, Abel;[28] and from that moment on, they had only spread their wings further – until, by Niccolò's day, they were virtually ubiquitous. No one could escape them:

> Every man hopes
> To climb higher more by pushing down now this one, now
>   that one,
> Than through his own virtue.
> To each person, another's success is always maddening;
> And therefore, always with grief and suffering
> For another's ill he is vigilant and alert.
> To this natural instinct draws us,
> By its own impulse, and its own attraction,
> If law, or a greater force, do not rein us in.[29]

Of course, not everyone could come out on top, but why does one succeed and the other fail? Much as in the *Capitolo di Fortuna* and the *Ghiribizzi*, Niccolò claimed it was a matter of boldness and good judgement. If ambition was joined by a 'strong heart, armed virtue, then for his own ill, a man rarely fears.'[30] But, if not, then sorrow, grief and suffering would surely follow.

What was true of men was also true of states and even provinces. If a region was governed by good laws, then 'Ambition uses against foreign peoples that violence which neither the law nor her king permits her to use against herself'.[31] But, if a country is servile, cowardly and ill governed, 'every sort of distress, every kind of ruin, every other ill comes quickly.'[32]

This, Niccolò explained, was why Siena was then convulsed by civil strife, why Alfonso of Naples had lost his kingdom, and why Venice had been deprived of its territory. But it also explained what was then happening in the Veronese *contado*. Were Luigi to cast his gaze in that direction, Niccolò claimed, he would clearly see that, while ambition drove the imperial forces to rob and pillage, it also inflicted terrible suffering on the country folk who were loyal to Venice. Behold, Niccolò exclaimed, here

> A man weeps for his dead father, a woman for her husband;
> This other man, from his own bed, in sorrow,
> Beaten and naked, is dragged outside.
> O how many times, when a father has held tight
> In his arms his son, a single thrust
> Has pierced the breast of one, and then the other!
> [. . .]
> Foul with blood are the ditches and streams,
> Full of skulls, of legs, and of hands,
> And of other limbs, slashed and severed.
> Birds of prey, wild beasts, dogs,
> Are more their family tombs now.
> O sepulchres cruel, fierce, and strange!
> [. . .]
> Wherever your eyes are fixed and turn,
> The earth is soaked with tears and blood;
> And the air [full] of cries, sobs, and sighs.[33]

But people – and states – could nevertheless change. That ambition should be married to 'judgement and sound intellect, with order and ferocity' could be learned through suffering.[34] Alluding to the Lion of Saint Mark, which was often represented with the Gospel in its paw, Niccolò observed that Venice had realized it needed to hold 'the sword and not the book' in its hand – albeit 'perhaps in vain'.[35] But it could be forgotten just as easily – with potentially calamitous results. No doubt thinking of Maximilian, Niccolò noted that the more a man gained, the sooner he lost it, and 'with greater shame'.[36]

That ambition, which had wreaked such devastation on the Veronese countryside, might soon change the direction of the war troubled Niccolò deeply. Yet he was 'oppressed by an even greater fear'.[37] As he confessed in the closing lines of his poem, he saw 'Ambition, with that swarm, which at the world's beginning Heaven granted her, flying over the Tuscan mountains'.[38] Having already 'sowed so many sparks' among the Sienese, she would 'burn down their farms and their towns', if 'better rule' did not stop her soon.[39]

And, if Siena could be torn apart by the lust for power, what was there to stop Florence from suffering the same fate?

*

For days, Niccolò waited vainly for some news. As a thick fog settled over the city, a steady stream of soldiers arrived – from Germany, from Gascony, even from Spain. The Venetians continued ravaging the countryside[40] and the French noisily demanded the fortress of Valeggio sul Mincio.[41] But, of the emperor, nothing was heard.

Fortunately, Niccolò found other ways to amuse himself. In reply to a gossipy letter from Luigi Guicciardini, filled with titillating stories of his recent sexual exploits, Niccolò offered a darkly comical tale of his own less-than-savoury adventures.[42] Not long after arriving in Verona, tormented by 'conjugal famine' (*carestia di matrimonio*), he had found an old woman to do his laundry. She lived in a house that was 'more than half underground'.[43] Since it had no windows, the only light you saw when you entered came from the door. One day, when Niccolò happened to be passing, the old woman greeted him and offered to show him some shirts she thought he might like to buy. 'Gullible prick' that he was, Niccolò thought she was serious and agreed to take a look. No sooner had he stepped into her house, however, than he 'saw in the gloom a woman with a towel half over her head and face, affecting shyness, and crouching in a corner'.[44] Taking Niccolò by the hand, the old slattern then led him over to her, saying, 'This is the shirt which I wanted to sell you; but I want you to try it on first and pay later.' At first, Niccolò was terrified, but as soon as the old bawd had left the room, shutting the door behind her, he soon fell upon the woman in the corner and 'fucked her one':

> Although I found her thighs flabby and her cunt damp and her breath a bit rancid, I was still so desperately horny that I went at it. And once I had done it, feeling like taking a look at the merchandise, I took a burning piece of wood from the fire that was there, and lit a lamp that was hanging above it; but no sooner was the lamp lit than it almost fell from my hands. Ye gods! I nearly dropped dead on the spot, that woman was so ugly. The first thing I saw was a clump of hair, part white and part black – in other words, sort of whitish, and

although the crown of her head was bald (thanks to this baldness, one could see a few lice parading around), a few isolated wisps of hair still came down to her eyelashes. In the middle of her little, wrinkled head, she had a fiery scar that made her seem as if she had been branded at the column in the Mercato [Vecchio]; at the end of each eyelash, towards her eyes, there was a bouquet of lice; one eye looked up and the other down, and one was bigger than the other, the tear-ducts were full of rheum, and the edges of her eyelids were mangy. She had a turned-up nose, stuck low down on her head, and one of her nostrils was slit open, and full of snot. Her mouth resembled that of Lorenzo de' Medici, but it was twisted to one side, and from that side a bit of drool was oozing, because, since she had no teeth, she couldn't hold back her saliva. On her upper lip she had a longish, but wispy, moustache. She had a long, pointed chin that twisted upwards a bit, from which hung a flap of skin that dangled down to the join of her neck. As I stood there, totally bewildered and astonished to behold this monster, she noticed and tried to say: 'What's the matter, sir?'; but she could not get the words out, because she stuttered; and as soon as she opened her mouth, there issued a breath so smelly that my eyes and nose – the two portals to the two most easily offended senses – were assaulted by this stink, and my stomach was so appalled that it was unable to bear such an outrage; it gurgled, and having gurgled, it started to retch – so much that I threw up all over her.[45]

With that, he departed – swearing that, as long as he was in Lombardy, he'd be damned before he got horny again.

*

By the time Niccolò had recovered from his shock, the political situation had started to change for the better. Although the Venetians were 'acting with renewed vigour', Maximilian had at last given in to the French demands;[46] and, once Valeggio sul Mincio had been handed over, Louis was happy to send help. On 8 December, Maximilian's Spanish soldiers were paid with French gold, more Gascon units arrived, and it was said that Chaumont would soon be on his way with a large army.[47]

Niccolò was delighted. This was great news for Florence – and it wasn't so bad for him, either. He had heard that, if Chaumont came to Verona, Francesco Pandolfini, one of the Florentine ambassadors to Milan, would come too; and, since Pandolfini was bound to keep the *Dieci* well informed about what was going on, there would be no point in Niccolò remaining there any longer.[48] As he made abundantly clear in his reports, he was more than ready to leave. Although he had told Luigi Guicciardini a few days earlier that he might be able to save enough money from this mission to start a little business on the side, he was already running out of cash.[49] Of the fifty ducats he had been given when he left Florence, only eight remained, and most of that would have to be spent on couriers.[50] He had begged the *Dieci* for money, to no avail,[51] and there was no one left in Verona for him to borrow from.[52]

Even before the offensive had begun, however, it seemed to falter. On 16 December, there was still no movement. Chaumont had apparently been ordered back to Milan to repel an unexpected attack by an army of Swiss mercenaries,[53] and, although Maximilian was on his way from Trento,[54] his character was as 'changeable' as ever.[55] He had not yet given any orders, and, until he arrived, Niccolò could not see how the army could take to the field. At the same time, there was a serious danger of famine if such a large number of troops stayed in Verona much longer – and, if that were to happen, it would only take a handful of Venetians to take the city by storm.[56]

Niccolò did not want to hang around a moment longer. Conveniently remembering that the *Dieci* had told him privately that he could return to Florence when the emperor was on the road, he left Verona for Mantua, where he proposed to watch things unfold until he heard from them in writing.[57] But even Mantua wasn't safe. Without waiting to be formally recalled, he jumped on his horse and made for home.

The journey was slow and difficult. It was an unusually cold winter and, in the low-lying plains of the Po Valley, the ground would have been frozen hard. Food was expensive, innkeepers were suspicious of strangers, and the countryside was filled with danger. Bands of brigands roamed freely and, even this far south, Venetian raiding parties were occasionally sighted. Niccolò was dangerously vulnerable. Picking his way along icy roads, his cape pulled tightly about him, he travelled by short stages of no more than a few kilometres each

– with the result that the journey, which would have taken around four days in summer, took him more than a fortnight.

As Niccolò was nearing Bologna, a ray of hope broke through the wintry gloom. On 22 December, a Ferrarese fleet commanded by Alfonso d'Este inflicted a crushing defeat on the Venetian navy at Polesella, on the River Po.[58] At least 2,000 Venetian troops were killed, nine galleys were captured and six were sunk. As the survivors retreated, Alfonso pushed south-eastwards with his army, recapturing the crucial coastal town of Comacchio.

But Niccolò's delight was short-lived. Soon after Christmas – at about the time he would have reached the Mugello – Biagio Buonaccorsi wrote with worrying news from Florence. The week before, 'a masked man had appeared at the house of the notary of the *Conservatori* with two witnesses, and in their presence' handed over a formal denunciation, alleging that, since Niccolò's father had been a public debtor, Niccolò could 'in no way exercise the office' he held.[59] As Biagio noted, the law was technically in Niccolò's favour, but, 'given the nature of the times', that hardly mattered. Everyone had been gossiping about the accusation and some had even demanded that Niccolò be removed from his post. Biagio had, of course, been doing his best to set the record straight, and had already succeeded in 'softening up the minds of some people quite a bit'. But Niccolò's enemies would stop at nothing. As such, Biagio warned Niccolò not to come home until things had quietened down.

Even accounting for Biagio's tendency to exaggerate, Niccolò must have been deeply alarmed. He had never been attacked like this before. Not even Alamanno Salviati, who had died a few months earlier, had been so vicious. Niccolò was in more danger than he had realized. But he still had a few cards up his sleeve. As long as Soderini remained in power and the League of Cambrai held, he might yet weather the storm.

*

By the time Niccolò returned to a snow-covered Florence on 2 January 1510, the trouble seemed to have died down, and, to his undoubted delight, he would have been just in time for Totto's ordination.[60] It would have been a joyous occasion. Whether Niccolò was present is unknown, but if he was there to see the presiding bishop lay hands on his brother's head, his heart must have swelled with pride, love, and perhaps a touch of envy, too. Totto was making a sacrifice, it was true – perhaps the greatest sacrifice a man could make – but he could look forward to a comfortable benefice, a clerkship in the household of Cardinal Louis d'Amboise and, at the end of it all, peace.

There was, however, little time for celebration. While Niccolò had been dallying in Verona, Julius II had finally repudiated his alliance with Louis XII.[61] Though Julius had previously been content simply to withdraw from active participation in the League of Cambrai, he had come to believe that a strong French presence in eastern Lombardy would present as grave a threat to the enlargement of the Papal States as an over-powerful Venice; and given that the pope was already casting avaricious eyes at Ferrara – then still a French ally – he had decided to treat the king as his enemy. As yet, Julius was not strong enough to challenge Louis openly, but he had lost no opportunity to undermine France's position in Italy. He had hired the Swiss mercenaries who had attacked the duchy of Milan in mid-December; he had fomented rebellion in Genoa; and, most provocatively, he had extended the hand of friendship to the Venetians. At first, the Republic of Saint Mark had rejected his overtures out of hand, but the defeat at Polesella had persuaded a frightened Senate to accept his terms. On 15 February, a treaty was signed, and a few days later, the interdict was lifted. Conflict loomed.

From Florence's perspective, nothing could have been worse. If war broke out between France and the papacy, the city would be put in a perilous position. Though it was still bound by its obligations to Louis XII, it could not afford to make an enemy of Julius II by providing the king with military and financial aid. Since the city was surrounded by papal territories, Julius – who had already been won over to the Medici's side – could sweep down and remove Soderini from power whenever he pleased. If Florence was to stand any chance, it would have to find some way of defusing the crisis, or, if all else failed, of walking the tightrope between the two powers.

Since the Florentine ambassador, Alessandro Nasi, had just been recalled from the French court, the *Dieci* sent Niccolò to negotiate with Louis. Such was the gravity of the situation that his instructions were written by the *gonfaloniere* himself.[62] As Soderini explained, Niccolò's most essential task was to reassure Louis of Florence's undying loyalty, while simultaneously making excuses for why it could not send troops. But Niccolò was also to impress upon the king the necessity of preserving his alliance with Maximilian against the Venetians – and, if possible, to prevent an open rupture between France and the papacy. As the *gonfaloniere*'s brother, Cardinal Francesco Soderini, wrote in a separate letter, nothing was more important to the wellbeing of Florence – and of Italy – than that 'they should not be divided from one another.'[63]

Despite the heavy responsibility that had been placed on his shoulders, Niccolò was probably glad to be leaving Florence. Since Totto's ordination, life had, admittedly, resumed its familiar pattern. In mid-March, he had travelled to Monte San Savino on the *Dieci*'s behalf to settle a border dispute between the Florentine village of Gargonza and the Sienese community of Armaiolo.[64] In late May, he had then gone to San Miniato and the Valdinievole to recruit more men for the militia.[65] While he had been away on the latter trip, however, he had received word that another anonymous accusation had been levelled against him. This time, his morality, rather than his father's indebtedness, was in question. It was alleged that he had committed an 'unnatural sexual act' – that is to say, sodomy – 'with a certain Lucretia, known as La Riccia, a courtesan'.[66] The charge was, we assume, false, and it was quickly dismissed. But it was a stark reminder that his enemies had not given up. It can hardly have made things easy at home, either. An embassy, however difficult, would have been a welcome change.

*

Setting out on 20 June,[67] Niccolò followed the now familiar route past Turin, through the Susa Valley and on towards Chambéry. Somewhere along the journey, he ran into his old friend, Alessandro Nasi, who was on his way back to Florence, and Niccolò eagerly questioned him about how things stood at the French court. He may, perhaps, have tarried for a little longer than he intended, but it was worth it.[68] On 7 July, he was in Lyon; and, after pausing for a few days to catch his breath, then made for Blois.[69]

While Niccolò was riding through Auvergne and Berry, troubling developments were taking place in the Veneto. Despite Soderini's most ardent hopes, Louis' relationship with Maximilian was under serious strain.[70] Throughout the winter, the two monarchs had argued bitterly about money, and though a compromise had been reached, mistrust had remained. No sooner had the spring come than disagreements about the conduct of the war had resurfaced. Tired of bankrolling the conflict while Maximilian remained in Germany, Louis had refused to pay a penny more until the emperor came to Italy – which, of course, he was unwilling to do. This was a blessing for Julius. Seizing the opportunity, he tried to tempt the emperor into abandoning the French with the offer of bribes; and so impecunious did Maximilian seem just then that the pope was confident of turning him.[71]

On 17 July, Niccolò finally arrived at court to find it abuzz with talk of Julius's offer.[72] As Robertet explained the following morning, Niccolò had come just in time.[73] Louis XII was apparently furious that the Florentine ambassador had been recalled without being replaced, and that the *condottiere*, Marcantonio Colonna, had been allowed to leave Florence's service to lead a papal army against Genoa. The king was on the point of sending an emissary to demand an explanation from the *Dieci* when Niccolò arrived. Naturally, Niccolò smoothed things over as much as he could. But, when he presented his credentials to the king later that afternoon, he ran up against a more serious challenge.[74] Though Louis claimed always to have been assured of the Florentines' good faith and affection, he now felt obliged to ask for more concrete proof of their loyalty. Given his growing rift with the emperor, he wanted to know exactly 'what and how much they would do in [his] favour if the pope or anyone else were to molest or attempt to molest [his] possessions in Italy'.[75] Somewhat flustered by the king's abruptness, Niccolò promised to write to the Signoria immediately.

Over the next few days, Niccolò spoke to some of the other members of the king's council, in the hope of finding a way round Louis' demand. But they all gave him the same answer. Etienne Ponchier, the bishop of Paris, a wise and even-tempered man, told him Florence should not have any concerns about opposing the pope, and should hastily declare itself for France.[76] The chancellor, Jean de Ganay, 'a more hot and violent tempered man', bluntly told him that Florence should stop temporizing, and give the king what he wanted.[77] Niccolò could not help suspecting that, if Florence wanted to keep Louis' friendship, it might have to do his bidding, after all.[78]

The *Dieci* hurriedly tried to appease the king by promising they would not allow Marcantonio Colonna to pass through Tuscany.[79]

But this only made Louis more insistent. On 25 July, he told Niccolò that Florence should now have no hesitation about committing itself properly.[80] The situation was, in any case, starting to swing in Louis' favour. He was more confident of the emperor; he had put down the revolt in Genoa; he had signed a treaty with the king of England; and he was seriously thinking about attacking the Swiss. Besides, he had already told people that Florence was with him. Realizing Louis was not going to take 'no' for an answer, Niccolò started to worry.

*

Just then, however, Niccolò's luck changed for the better. Now that Genoa had been pacified, 'it seemed to the good and sensible men at court that an agreement between the king and the pope might be hoped for' – that is, if a suitable mediator could be found.[81] One evening, Robertet sent for Cardinal Francesco Soderini's representative, Giovanni Girolami, and suggested that Florence might be ideally suited for this purpose.[82] When Girolami relayed this to Niccolò, the secretary could hardly conceal his excitement. Resolving to do all he could to speed things along, he immediately rushed off to confer with the pope's ambassador, Angelo Leonini, 'a thoroughly respectable man, most prudent and practical in matters of state',[83] who promptly went to the king himself. To Niccolò's delight, Louis welcomed the proposal. He did not want to fight the pope if he could help it, and he would be happy to have Florence intercede between them. He was, however, adamant that Julius would have to make the first move. 'I shall never be the first to bend,' he said; '[b]ut I promise you faithfully that, if the pope makes any demonstration of affection towards me, be it only the thickness of my fingernail, I will go [the length of] my arm [to meet him]; but otherwise, I won't budge.'[84] This was all the encouragement Niccolò and his colleagues needed. That very night, they agreed that Girolami should go to Florence and urge the *Dieci* to send ambassadors to the pope right away.

For a time, it seemed as if there might be a real chance of averting the crisis. On 8 August, Niccolò rode with Robertet to where the king had gone to hunt.[85] During the journey, the two men discussed, if somewhat guardedly, 'all the affairs of Italy'. As Niccolò told the *Dieci*, the French 'do not trust us altogether, and will never trust your Lordships until they see you, weapons in hand, by their side.'[86]

But it nevertheless gave Niccolò heart. The French seemed to have their thoughts fixed on making peace with the pope, or, if that proved impossible, preserving their alliance with Maximilian.[87] Either way, Robertet led Niccolò to believe that the Florentines would stand to benefit. He suggested they might be given Lucca, or even Urbino.[88] Naturally, Niccolò took this with a pinch of salt, but it was encouraging, all the same – and it was a sign that Louis' council thought highly of Florence.

*

Yet, the promise of those balmy midsummer days soon receded. On 13 August, Louis again pressed Niccolò for military aid – this time more forcefully.[89] Despite all the talk of peace, he had heard that the pope was about to renew his attempt against Genoa; if Louis was to defend his possessions, he would need the Florentines to send Chaumont their troops immediately. Somewhat taken aback by the king's impatience, Niccolò pointed out that Florence could not do this without exposing itself to attack from the pope, whose territories surrounded its own. But Louis was not to be put off. France only needed Florence's troops for a few days, he said. Besides, the *Dieci* ought to remember that he 'was as solicitous about its honour and interests as about his own'.[90]

The situation quickly worsened. Although Florence's ambassadors in Rome had been confident of persuading the pope to accept mediation,[91] Julius made it clear that he was not interested in making peace with Louis on any terms. Barely a week after Niccolò's last audience with the king, a papal army under Cardinal Francesco Alidosi captured Modena, and there were rumours – albeit false – that Ferrara and Reggio had also been taken.[92] Louis was incensed. After hastily despatching Chaumont to prop up the ailing Alfsono d'Este, he began canvassing support for a General Council of the Church to judge – and possibly even depose – the pope.[93] Now that a full-scale war seemed likely, he was more determined than ever that Florence should send troops, or, at the very least, lend Alfonso d'Este some money.[94]

Stuck in the middle of the tightrope, Niccolò was beginning to lose his balance. He desperately needed instructions from Florence, but many of the *Dieci*'s letters were getting lost in transit. A few weeks earlier, it had been reported that a courier had been intercepted in Piacenza.[95] The coded messages he had been carrying had been opened and at least one had been sent to Milan. Now, almost nothing seemed to be getting through at all.[96]

*

It was all getting too much for Niccolò. Thanks to the sky-high prices at court, his money worries were worse than ever. He was even afraid he might have to sell his horses and return to Florence on foot.[97] His health was also suffering. Shortly after he had left Florence, the city had been struck by a virulent strain of influenza. Known locally as the *mal di tiro* (shooting sickness), on account of its having appeared after a mock battle during the festival, it caused a painful cough and a fever, lasting four or five days.[98] In the weeks that followed, almost everyone had suffered from it. Since then, it had spread to France – and Niccolò was among its victims. On 24 August, he was still suffering from the effects of the cough, which had left his stomach in 'such a wretched condition' that he had 'no appetite for anything'.[99]

Niccolò was feeling very sorry for himself, but he was even more worried about his family. Although he had been happy enough to sleep with a local prostitute called Jeanne while he had been well, penury and illness had made him apprehensive. Having not heard anything from home for weeks, he could not help fearing the worst. What if Marietta and the children had fallen sick? What if – like Biagio Buonaccorsi's wife – they were even at death's door?[100] More than anything, he longed to go home.

Fortunately, all was well – or at least as well as could be expected, at any rate. On 29 August, a grieving Biagio reassured Niccolò, 'Your wife is here, and she is alive; your children are running around; there is no smoke to be seen in your house; and there will be a meagre harvest at [Sant'Andrea in] Percussina.'[101]

*

From the *Dieci*, however, there was no comfort. Despite Niccolò's urgent entreaties, the *Dieci* were still unwilling to declare for France. 'Your letters have made everyone yawn,' wrote Biagio, 'people think and think again, and then nothing is done.'[102] They did not seem to realize that, unless they acted soon, it would be too late. Caught between the two warring parties, the Florentines would be helpless. Quoting Livy, Biagio mournfully predicted that '[w]ithout favour, without honour, we shall be the prize of the victor.'[103]

Florence's fate now rested in Niccolò's hands. He knew that, without the *Dieci*'s approval, he could not commit Florence to providing either troops or money. But, if he could make Louis believe that Florence's support would actually be a disadvantage, there might still be a chance of getting the city out of trouble. It would not be easy, but he had to try.

On 27 August, Niccolò went to visit Robertet, who, like him, was recovering from the flu.[104] With his customary subtlety, Niccolò began by pointing out that, if the conflict escalated, the king would soon have to decide exactly how he wanted to avail himself of Florence's aid; and, since this was already under consideration, it was just as well that they discuss what the city would *actually* be able to do for him. Naturally, the Florentines had great respect for Louis and would be only too happy to render whatever services they could, but they would not be able to offer him much. Having incurred huge expenses during the Pisan War, they were still very poor and if they were to declare themselves for France, they would have to devote most of their meagre resources to defending themselves against the pope. Indeed, having Florence's help might even harm Louis' campaign. If, after sending soldiers to Lombardy, the Florentines were attacked, Louis would not only be obliged to pay them back for any assistance they had provided, but he might also have to use some of his *own* troops to defend them against their enemies. Since he was already busy defending Ferrara, Genoa, Friuli and Savoy, this could prove dangerous. As such, Niccolò concluded, Louis would have to decide whether it would really be worth having Florence's aid, after all. Amazingly, Robertet agreed.

Over the next few days, Niccolò put his case to the king's council and to Louis himself.[105] There was a great deal of toing and froing, but, on 30 August, the chancellor, Jean de Ganay, informed him that the council, 'having found the reasons [he] had adduced sound', had decided to accept the *Dieci*'s goodwill 'the same as though [they] had actually sent them the . . . troops.'[106] The following day, Louis himself approved the council's decision.[107]

It was a success. Florence would not have to participate actively in the conflict; and, on 2 September, Louis also agreed to send soldiers to assist in its defence, should need arise.[108] Most encouragingly, Robertet assured Niccolò that Louis would soon lead an army into Italy himself. Provided 'the king lives, and England and the Emperor stand firmly by him,' Niccolò wrote on 5 September, the *Dieci* could 'count upon seeing him in Florence next March.'[109]

But would it be enough? Niccolò was under no illusions. He could see that it would not fool the pope for a moment. Since the fall of Modena, Julius's anger against Louis had been growing by the day. Enraged that Louis was pushing ahead with preparations for a General Council of the Church,[110] Julius was determined to 'deliver Italy from servitude and out of the hands of France'.[111] He had already made it clear that this included Florence. No longer in any doubt about its loyalties, he dismissed the Florentine ambassadors who had come to discuss peace, and resolved to punish the city for its impudence. As Niccolò reported, word soon reached the French court that Julius was now set on changing the government of Florence.[112]

*

Before Niccolò could see how things would unfold, his mission came to an end. Having at last woken from their slumber, the *Dieci* had appointed Roberto Acciaiuoli as the new ambassador. When he reached Tours, where the court had recently repaired, Niccolò spent a few days bringing him up to speed, and then set out for home.[113] How Italy would fare in the months to come, he did not know, but, as he made his way slowly across the mountains, tired and penniless, he could take comfort in the knowledge that he and Soderini would be safe – for the time being, at least.

17

Things Fall Apart

(September 1510–September 1512)

By the time Niccolò reached Florence, the conflict between Louis XII and Julius II had already begun to escalate.[1] Emboldened by the fall of Modena, the pope had assumed command of his army and had headed to Bologna to direct operations in person.[2] Although he had fallen ill a few days after his arrival, he had succeeded in giving the campaign a much-needed boost. Within a matter of weeks, a French attack had been repelled, Ferdinand of Aragon had been bribed into changing sides and Venetian troops were pouring into the Polesine. By early November, Julius was raring to strike against Ferrara, but, before doing so, he thought it wisest to deal with Mirandola in order to cut off Alfonso d'Este's supply routes and prevent French reinforcements from getting through.

In Florence, the *Dieci* watched these developments with unease. Although Louis XII had not yet been seriously threatened, there was concern that he might still try to draw Florence in to the conflict. Despite the assurances he had given Niccolò in the summer, the *Dieci* had already been obliged to send him 200 men-at-arms. After much pleading, Louis had promised that Florence's troops would not be used against the pope, but the *Dieci* knew Julius would still be furious that the city was providing the French king with support. Fearing that the pope might turn against Florence at any moment, the *Dieci* hurriedly began readying its forces.

But here lay a problem. For many years, Florentine strategy had been founded on an abiding faith in the power of infantry – so much so that, when Niccolò had drawn up plans for the militia, he had provided only for the recruitment of foot soldiers, at least to begin with. This had been all very well when Florence had been fighting

337

Pisa, but now the city was facing an enemy who could attack at any point along its frontier, it also needed a lightly armed cavalry, capable of patrolling the countryside and responding quickly to incursions.

On 7 November, the *Dieci* asked Niccolò to prepare a report on how this might be raised.[3] Though hastily written, his plans were characteristically expansive.[4] Rather than being recruited only in the city, as he had previously imagined, he now recommended that the cavalry be raised in towns and villages throughout the *dominio*.[5] There were to be at least 500 horsemen, all properly trained and equipped, and organized into appropriately sized squadrons. To ensure a wide defence could be maintained at all times, each squadron was to be assigned to a specific location along the frontier, a good supply of horses was to be laid in and no leave was to be allowed, except with the express permission of the *Nove*.[6]

The *Dieci* were delighted. Giving Niccolò's report their whole-hearted approval, they ordered him to begin recruiting at once; and on 13 November, he set out for the interior of the state.[7] For the next two weeks, he rode around the countryside with feverish haste, pressing every likely looking young man he came across into service. When he returned to Florence on 29 November, the city was already well on its way to having the home-grown cavalry it so desperately needed.

The *Dieci* then turned its attention to diplomatic concerns. For several years, Florence's truce with Siena had held. There had been plenty of ups and downs, largely as the result of Pandolfo Petrucci's constant scheming, but it was now coming up for renewal and Florence could not afford to let it lapse. Unreliable though Petrucci may have been, the *Dieci* urgently needed to secure his neutrality – in principle, at least. Given his experience of dealing with Petrucci in the past, Niccolò was asked to handle the negotiations. Unfortunately, his despatches have not survived. But whatever Niccolò said to Pandolfo during the two weeks of intense negotiations which followed seems to have done the trick. On 19 December, he was back in Florence, agreement in hand.[8]

*

Although the city was now in a stronger position than it had been a few weeks before, anxiety was running high. Reports of Julius II's rapid advance through the Emilian plain were flooding in and, on the very day of Niccolò's arrival, the pope had laid siege to Mirandola itself.[9] This was bad enough on its own, but, before the *Dieci* had had the chance to consider their response, their fears were exacerbated by the discovery of a plot against the *gonfaloniere*.

Recently returned from Bologna, a young Florentine *ottimate* named Prinzivalle della Stufa had tried to persuade Filippo Strozzi to help him kill Soderini. Unwilling to risk his neck so soon after the controversy caused by his marriage, Strozzi refused, and, after allowing Prinzivalle time to escape, informed the authorities. The *Otto di Guardia* moved quickly. On 29 December, Prinzivalle was declared a rebel in absentia and, two days later, his father, Luigi, was confined to Empoli for a period of five years.

It had been a risible plot, poorly planned and badly executed.[10] Although Prinzivalle had told Strozzi that the pope and Cardinal Giovanni de' Medici had offered their support, no evidence was ever found, and it is unlikely that either of them would have had anything to do with such an amateurish affair. On the strength of Strozzi's testimony, however, the *Dieci* convinced themselves that Julius II *must* have been behind it and instructed their ambassador in Rome, Pierfrancesco Tosinghi, to lodge a formal protest. Julius was, of course, furious, and – not without reason – denounced the Florentines as liars.[11] Realizing how foolish they had been, the *Dieci* feared an attack might now be imminent.[12]

Heavy snow impeded preparations. By early January, it was almost a *braccio* (*c*. 58 cm) deep in some places.[13] But the Florentines' hearts still burned with patriotic fervour. Forced to stay at home when they would much rather have been taking up arms, they showed their defiance by building snowmen in the shape of civic symbols. All around the city, leading artists left their workshops to build beautiful snow-lions – evidently representing the *Marzocco* (the traditional symbol of Florence). According to Landucci, there was a particularly 'large and fine one next to the bell-tower of Santa Maria del Fiore, and [another] one in front of Santa Trinità.'[14] Some nude snow-figures – most likely modelled after Michelangelo's *David* – also appeared at the Canto de' Pazzi and, in the Borgo San Lorenzo, someone even created a snow city, complete with miniature castles and galleys.

When the snow eventually cleared, around a week later,[15] the *Dieci* rushed to make up for lost time. Troops were put on the alert, Florentine merchants abroad were warned to be wary of arrest, and emergency measures were put in place to ensure the continuity of government, should Soderini or any of the other leading magistrates be assassinated.[16]

Niccolò was soon dashing around the countryside, trying desperately to bring Florence's defences up to scratch.[17] On 14 January, he was sent to Arezzo to inspect the condition of the fortress and to arrange for any repairs that might be necessary.[18] A month later, he went to Poggio Imperiale 'to see what needed to be done in that place';[19] and, on 14 March, he was sent to the Val d'Arno and the Val di Chiana to get his newly recruited cavalry ready for action.[20] For this last task, he was given just two weeks, but, on his return, he was expected to bring no fewer than a hundred mounted soldiers to Florence, where they were to remain for the whole month of April, when it was thought the pope would be most likely to attack.

*

But no attack came.[21] Though Julius had captured Mirandola on 20 January, his attempt on Ferrara came to nothing. Finding a French army blocking his way, he returned to Bologna and, after placing his troops under the command of his nephew, the duke of Urbino, made for Ravenna.[22] In his absence, the campaign foundered, and, before long, Louis' soldiers were threatening Modena. Fearing that he might not be able to hold it, Julius handed the city over to the emperor, rather than allow it to fall into French hands.

Still bitterly disappointed by the collapse of the League of Cambrai, Maximilian seized the opportunity to propose a peace conference. For a moment, there was a glimmer of hope. Ferdinand and Louis both declared themselves willing to talk. But Julius was bitterly opposed. Despite his recent setback, he had no interest in a negotiated settlement. He declined to send a representative to the conference when it opened, and he refused to listen to the emperor's ambassador, Matthäus Lang von Wellenburg, when he tried to persuade him to reconsider.[23]

With Maximilian's conference in tatters, the conflict resumed in earnest. The French quickly seized the upper hand. Although Chaumont had died at Correggio in February 1511, Louis had found a worthy replacement in Giangiacomo Trivulzio. Driving south-eastwards from Mantua, Trivulzio promptly recaptured Concordia. Stunned by the speed of his advance, the combined papal-Venetian army hastily fell back to protect Bologna.

*

The Florentines were delighted, but they dared not get their hopes up just yet. Keeping the militia in a state of constant readiness, the *Dieci* set about tackling a threat to their sea routes. The previous month, a Florentine galleon on its way to Genoa had been stopped at sea by a Monégasque galley.[24] When its captain had refused to pay for the privilege of sailing in Ligurian waters, his ship had been boarded, his sails taken down and his cargo stolen. This was piracy at its most brazen, and the Florentine government had been swift to protest to the French governor of Genoa. But since the lord of Monaco, Lucien Grimaldi, did not acknowledge his authority, there had been little he could do. An appeal to Louis XII had also met with failure, for the same reason. This left the Florentines with no choice but to negotiate directly. Grimaldi despatched one of his most trusted ambassadors, Antonio di Luca Lantieri, who, with remarkable skill, persuaded the Florentines not only to ransom the galleon that had been taken, for 400 *scudi*, but also to allow Monégasque ships to use their ports – effectively granting them a licence to practise piracy.[25]

On 12 May, Niccolò was sent to Monaco to sign the treaty on the *Dieci*'s behalf.[26] Before he had gone far, however, the *Dieci* realized the enormity of the concessions they were about to make and ordered him to strike out the final clause of the agreement – thus limiting his task to the recovery of the ship and its cargo.[27] Reaching Menton some two weeks later, he renegotiated the terms without difficulty, and signed the accord, for the first time in his career, as a fully fledged ambassador of the Florentine Republic.[28]

*

On returning to Florence, Niccolò found that Julius II's fortunes had deteriorated even further. Following the withdrawal of the papal army, the Bolognese had risen in rebellion and recalled the exiled

Bentivoglio. Taking fright, the papal legate, Cardinal Francesco Alidosi, had fled, and the army had followed suit, pursued by the French. Amid cries of joy, Michelangelo's great bronze statue of the pope, which had stood above the main doorway of San Petronio since 1508, was toppled.[29] A few days later, Trivulzio recaptured Mirandola on his way back to Milan and, soon afterwards, Alfonso d'Este succeeded in clawing back the territories he had lost in the Polesine the year before.

Julius's fury knew no bounds. At an audience in Ravenna on 24 May, he blamed the loss of Bologna not only on Cardinal Alidosi, but also on his nephew, the duke of Urbino. This was certainly unjust. Although Alidosi's cowardice, compounded by his reputation for cruelty, had effectively guaranteed the rebellion's success, there was little the duke could have done to prevent the rout that followed. But Julius was too angry to split hairs. The duke, however, was deeply stung by his injustice. Striding out of the pope's apartments, he dragged Alidosi from his mule and stabbed him to death in the street.[30]

Louis had dealt a severe blow to Julius's ambitions. Now that the route into the Papal States had been opened, the king was poised to sweep all before him. The Florentines could hardly contain their joy. If not peace, then at least security seemed to be at hand. Even were Louis to ask for more troops, the *Dieci* reasoned, the threat of invasion appeared to have dissipated.

*

Before the summer was over, however, Florence again found itself in peril. Since Niccolò's mission to France the previous summer, Louis had been toying with the idea of convening a General Council of the Church; now that he had Julius on the ropes, he felt the time had come to act. Having already secured the support of five cardinals hostile to the pope, he wrote to the *Dieci* on 19 July, asking for permission to hold the council in Pisa the following September.[31] The *Dieci* were horrified. Even before Louis' letter had arrived, Julius had placed Pisa under interdict and anathematized the schismatic cardinals.[32] If Florence allowed the council to be held in its territory, Julius would surely treat the city as its enemy and take the war to its door. Realizing that this could spell disaster for Soderini's government, the *Dieci* hurriedly despatched Niccolò – who had spent much of the summer recruiting in the countryside[33] – to stall the cardinals, who were already on their way to Pisa, and to persuade Louis to cancel the council, transfer it elsewhere or, at the very least, postpone it.[34]

Riding northwards at breakneck speed, Niccolò intercepted four of the cardinals at Borgo San Donnino (today known as Fidenza) on 12 September.[35] He explained the gravity of the danger facing Florence, and, after discreetly querying the legitimacy of their endeavour, pleaded with them not to go any further – at least for the time being. But he met with a sharp rejoinder. Speaking on behalf of the others, Cardinal Federico di Sanseverino pointed out that the Florentines had been given ample time to prepare for the council. He could not see how further delay could be of any use to them. There was nothing to fear from Julius. The king of France had 'never had so many soldiers in Italy as now,' and would not allow the pope to molest them.[36] Nor could the Florentines have any doubt about the council's validity. Sanseverino recalled that, in 1409, they had allowed a small group of cardinals to convene a council in Pisa against 'a holy pope', so why should they worry now, when the pontiff in question was so plainly reprehensible?[37] In any case, the council would not be in Pisa for long. After two or three sessions, it would probably be transferred somewhere else.[38] Niccolò tried to reply, but it was to no avail. The cardinals did, however, agree not to rush and to travel 'to Pisa by way of Pontremoli', rather than through Florence.[39]

Disappointed, Niccolò rode on to Milan. Stopping briefly to explain his mission to the king's representatives, he then made for France,[40] and, on 22 September, arrived in Blois.[41] The following day, he and the ambassador, Roberto Acciaiuoli, went to meet with the king. After all the usual ceremonies, they read a statement prepared from the *Dieci*'s instructions. Louis listened 'cheerfully and attentively', but he stubbornly refused to abandon the council – even in the name of peace.[42] His purpose in calling the council had only ever been 'to bring the pope to some agreement,' he claimed; if he were now to dissolve it, 'the pope would not want to hear anything more of peace'. Naturally, Niccolò and Acciaiuoli objected that the council was more likely to provoke war than lead to peace, but the king was having none of it. Nor would Louis transfer the council elsewhere.[43] He could not do anything without the consent of the cardinals and the emperor, he said. In any case, he had already told the French clergy to gather in Pisa. At least one session would *have* to be held there. Louis was, however, willing to postpone the proceedings for a while. He promised that nothing would happen before All Saints' Day, and ordered that letters immediately be sent to defer the cardinals' departure.[44]

Niccolò breathed a sigh of relief. He had felt sure Louis would not let Florence down; and now that his faith seemed to have been justified, he was anxious to restore his countrymen's confidence in the French alliance. On his way back across the Alps, he penned a brief 'Portrait of French Affairs' (*Ritratto di cose di Francia*).[45] Detailing 'the power of the French monarchy, the military strength of France, its natural resources, its administrative and military organization, and the French court', as well as 'the French character and way of life', this was designed to illustrate France's superiority as an Italian power, and to convince sceptics that Florence's best interests would be served by maintaining good relations with Louis XII.[46]

But Niccolò's confidence was misplaced. While he had been negotiating with Louis, Florence's attempt to appease the pope had already ended in failure. Heedless of whether the council would be postponed or not, the papal nuncio had left the city on 20 September, having given orders for it to be placed under interdict two days later.[47] Worse was to follow. On 5 October, Julius formed a 'Holy League' with Ferdinand of Aragon and the Republic of Venice.[48] Though this was officially a defensive alliance, no one was in any doubt that its real purpose was to drive the French out of Italy. Within a matter of weeks, the confederates were joined by Maximilian and Henry VIII of England, whose support had been crucial to Louis XII's campaign.[49] And when Ramón de Cardona was appointed the League's new commander, Julius named Cardinal Giovanni de' Medici as his legate.[50]

The *Dieci* panicked. Realizing that Julius now had Florence squarely within his sights, they hurried to rid themselves of Louis' council. Just hours after Niccolò returned from France, on 2 November, he was ordered to ride to Pisa and confront the cardinals.[51] Since they were due to open the council in three days' time, it was already too late to stop them, but Niccolò hoped that, by drawing attention to the famine then ravaging Pisa, he might convince them to leave after only a few sessions. When Niccolò put this to Carvajal on the morning of 6 November, however, the cardinal refused to budge.[52] He and his colleagues did not mind a bit of hardship, he claimed. When they had chosen Pisa, they had known perfectly well 'that the palazzi were not as nice as those in Milan, nor life as agreeable as in Paris.'[53] In any case, they could not change the council's venue without consulting the king of France. Niccolò's frustration can well be imagined, but there was nothing he could say to change the cardinal's mind. On 9 November, however, food shortages, made worse by the council's presence, sparked a popular uprising. In the streets between the Ponte di Mezzo and the church of San Michele in Borgo, a pitched battle was fought between gangs of armed citizens and the cardinals' French guards.[54] As the casualties mounted, the cardinals were forced to admit Pisa was no longer safe. The day after Niccolò returned to Florence, on 12 November, the council was adjourned and proceedings transferred to Milan.[55]

But it was too little, too late. Although Julius agreed to a brief suspension of the interdict, he could not – would not – forgive the Florentines their offence.[56] Unless they repudiated their alliance with France and joined the Holy League, he would make them pay. But this Soderini's government could not do. Though the *Dieci* promised not to declare war on Julius and allies, they adamantly refused to abandon Louis XII.[57] Aware of how great a risk they were taking, they had no choice but to send the already exhausted Niccolò into the *dominio* to begin raising more troops.[58]

Some measure of hope was restored by the new French commander, Gaston de Foix. Though only twenty-two years old when Louis XII appointed him governor of Milan, he was already a seasoned campaigner, and quickly proved to be one of the outstanding military leaders of his generation. Tearing through Lombardy and the Romagna in the depths of winter, he repelled a Swiss attack on Milan, prevented Bologna from being besieged by the Spanish, and massacred a Venetian army that had taken control of Brescia.[59] On 11 April 1512, he then inflicted a crushing defeat on Ramón de Cardona at the Battle of Ravenna – albeit at the cost of his own life.[60] Several of the League's best captains, including Fabrizio Colonna, were taken prisoner, along with Cardinal Giovanni de' Medici, and the whole of Emilia-Romagna was captured for France. Believing that Julius's enterprise had been dealt a fatal blow and the chances of a Medici restoration dashed forever, the Florentines sent their heartiest congratulations to Louis XII and eagerly renewed the French alliance.[61] So confident did the *Dieci* feel that they even sent troops to Lombardy to help with mopping-up operations.[62]

But the Florentines' optimism was ill-judged. Though Julius had been badly beaten, he was determined to fight on, and soon persuaded his allies to renew the offensive with a series of coordinated attacks on different fronts. In mid-May, Henry VIII of England invaded Gascony,[63] Maximilian marched south-westwards from Trento[64] and the Swiss provided a further 6,000 mercenaries for an attack on Lombardy.[65] Lacking supplies and still reeling from the loss of Gaston de Foix, the French soon found themselves being pushed back. A few weeks later, a combined Swiss-Venetian army retook Cremona and Bergamo, while Julius's forces captured Rimini, Ravenna and Cesena.[66] By late June, Milan had fallen to the Swiss, Genoa had risen in rebellion and papal troops had taken possession of Bologna, Modena, Reggio, Parma and Piacenza. Horrified, Louis decided to cut his losses. At the end of June, his troops were recalled and, by early July, they were back in France. Barely three months after the Battle of Ravenna, the French presence in Italy was at an end, Giovanni de' Medici was free and Julius was triumphant.

This spelled disaster both for Soderini and for Niccolò. Deprived of its only ally, Florence was now at the pope's mercy. On 30 June, Julius sent the *Dieci* a letter bragging about having 'liberated Italy and the Church from the French', and demanding that they organize 'processions and other manifestations of joy'.[67] A few days later, he summoned representatives of the League to Mantua to discuss the division of France's former territories and to decide Florence's fate. Spitefully, Julius chose the Medici partisan Lorenzo Pucci to deliver their demands, but, even before Pucci arrived, Soderini and Niccolò had guessed that the League would demand the *gonfaloniere*'s removal from office and the complete dismantlement of his *reggimento*.[68]

Julius did not wait for an answer. While Pucci was still in Florence, Ramón de Cardona's army set out for Tuscany, accompanied by Cardinal Giovanni de' Medici. Fear quickly spread through the *contado*. As Landucci reported, hundreds of villagers fled the Mugello and took refuge in the city.[69] Carts, mules and cattle thronged the streets; and food supplies soon began to run low. Opinion was divided over what should be done – and for a time, the city was paralysed by indecision.[70] At a *pratica strette* convened by the *Dieci*, many *ottimati* were in favour of giving in to the pope's demands, saying this 'was the only way to save the city'.[71] The Council of Eighty agreed. According to Cerretani, several *ottimati* even intimated to Pucci that they would be ready to help the Medici return, if it would avert the crisis.[72] But a *pratica larga* – made up largely of *popolani* who supported the *gonfaloniere* – refused even to discuss an accord.

Soderini resolved to stand his ground. With tension rising by the minute, Niccolò hurried to rally the militia and to strengthen fortifications in Firenzuola,[73] while Soderini prepared for the defence of Florence itself. Its forces were not inconsiderable. According to Cerretani, it had 12,000 infantrymen, 500 light cavalry and 350 knights.[74] But this was still too few either to give battle or to mount a defence across a wide front. It was therefore decided to send 2,000 foot soldiers 'as rapidly as possible to Firenzuola . . . so that the Spaniards – in order not to leave such a large detachment behind them – would opt for besieging that town', and so the Florentines would have more time to dig in at Prato, where they had decided to make a stand.[75]

But Cardona had no interest in attacking country towns, however well fortified. Bypassing Firenzuola entirely, he crossed the Apennines and arrived at Barberino di Mugello, a stronghold twenty-seven kilometres north of Florence. On the advice of his commanders, Soderini decided to withdraw most of the troops from Prato and concentrate his forces in Florence itself, where, 'with the aid of the populace', it was thought there would be enough to defend the city. It was to prove a costly mistake.[76]

Cardona was now within easy striking distance. Hoping to avoid unnecessary bloodshed, he sent envoys to assure the Florentines that he had not come as an enemy. He did not wish to deny their city its freedom or change its constitution, but wanted merely to be sure that it would 'withdraw from the French cause and join the League'.[77] Since this would not be possible as long as Soderini was in office, however, he asked that the *gonfaloniere* relinquish his position and the Florentine government name someone else of their choosing. When these demands were discussed before the Great Council and the Eighty, Soderini defiantly refused. As Niccolò related in a letter to Isabella d'Este a few weeks later, he declared that, he had not come into [his] office through either fraud or force but that he had been put there by the people. Therefore, even if all the kings in the world heaped together should order him to relinquish it, he would never do so; but if the people of Florence wanted him to leave it, he would willingly – just as he willingly took it when it was granted him without any ambition on his part.[78]

As soon as the envoys had left, Soderini then turned to the council members and asked them to decide. If they truly believed his departure would bring about peace, he would immediately quit his post and return home. His offer was unanimously rejected. This was, of course, hardly a surprise. As Guicciardini explained, the *popolo* was still overwhelmingly in favour of maintaining popular government.[79] But what *was* surprising was that, at the same meeting, the Great Council and the Eighty also voted in favour of allowing the Medici to return as private citizens. This reflected a significant shift of opinion, and revealed the underlying weakness of the *gonfaloniere*'s position. Among the *ottimati*, too, opposition was hardening. Many were now adamant that the pope's demands should be accepted, and some were openly plotting to restore the Medici to power.

On 27 August, Cardona's troops took the fortified town of Campi Bisenzio – just ten kilometres north-west of Florence – 'without resistance', and, having entered it, 'massacred a band of men and stole everything they could carry, burning flax and many other things, and taking away many prisoners'.[80] They then marched to Prato and 'attacked it vigorously'.[81] Confident this would be enough to scare the Florentines into submission, Cardona again offered to negotiate. Although Soderini's departure was non-negotiable, he suggested the League would be satisfied with a large sum of money, and indicated that the question of the Medici would be handed over to Ferdinand of Aragon, 'so he might request – and not force – the Florentines' to accept them.[82] But Soderini mistook Cardona's offer for weakness. Having been told the Spanish were in such a weakened condition that 'they might die of hunger', and that Prato was sure to hold out, he put off replying, in the belief that the longer he waited, the stronger his position would be. What Niccolò thought of this cannot be known but it is unlikely he would have shared the *gonfaloniere*'s confidence. Fearing the worst, Biagio Buonaccorsi urged him to finish up what he was doing as quickly as possible.[83]

On 29 August, Cardona's troops stormed Prato. Breaking through the walls with little difficulty, they put the city to the sack 'and massacred the . . . population in a pitiable spectacle of calamity.'[84] According to Niccolò, more than 4,000 men were killed and many more taken prisoner. In his letter to Isabella d'Este, he refrained from giving too many details, but he did note that no mercy was shown, even to 'the virgins cloistered in holy sites, which were all filled with acts of rape and pillage.' So horrified was the chronicler Bartolomeo Cerretani that he feared, if he were to tell of all 'the inhumanity and unheard-of cruelty' committed on that terrible day, it would make his reader believe 'the earth would open itself up in pity.'[85]

News of the sack struck terror into the Florentines' hearts. But Soderini, 'relying on some chimeras of his own', remained insensible to the danger.[86] Refusing to step down, he still clung to the hope that, if he offered Cardona enough money, he would be able to keep the Medici out. It was, however, too late. His envoys, Baldassare Carducci and Niccolò del Nero, were left in no doubt that, unless he accepted the Medici, Florence would suffer the same fate as Prato.[87] The last of his support now evaporated. Appalled by the *gonfaloniere*'s failure to defend Prato, the Council of Eighty voted to accept the League's terms.[88] On the evening of 30 August, ambassadors were instructed to conclude an agreement with Cardona, 'come what may'.[89] But Soderini still showed no signs of giving in.

Enraged, the *ottimati* decided to take matters into their own hands. The next morning, four young nobles – Paolo Vettori, Gino Capponi, Bartolomeo Valori and Antonfrancesco degli Albizzi – burst into the Palazzo della Signoria and threatened Soderini with violence unless he resigned.[90] Fearing that he would be murdered the second he did so, however, Soderini again refused. At this, Antonfrancesco – the youngest and most hot-headed of the four – seized him roughly by the tunic, and, for a moment, it looked as if blood would be shed. Luckily, Niccolò was on hand, having most likely come rushing from his office when he heard the plotters' shouts. With a quavering voice, Soderini immediately asked him to fetch Paolo's brother, Francesco Vettori – who had recently been put in charge of the city's defences – to break the deadlock.

When Francesco heard what had happened, he was terrified. Knowing he could not oppose his brother without putting himself

in danger, but unwilling to harm either the *gonfaloniere* or the government of Florence, he considered fleeing the city. But Niccolò
somehow managed to talk him round and, together, they hurried
back to the Palazzo della Signoria. By the time they arrived, however,
Soderini's will had already been broken. Although he still refused
to believe that he had done anything wrong, he now agreed to go.

Alone and terrified, Soderini was spirited out of the *palazzo* to
Vettori's house. As soon as night had fallen, he rode for Siena, where
he would remain until finally finding refuge in the Adriatic city of
Ragusa (Dubrovnik).

Now without patron or ally, Niccolò was left to face the consequences alone.

18

'Ministers of Violence'

(September 1512–March 1513)

On 1 September, Giuliano de' Medici re-entered Florence. Yet, if he felt any sense of triumph, he was careful not to show it. According to Cerretani, he wanted to be seen merely as 'a private citizen'.[1] Having shaved his beard and put on civilian clothes, he strolled about the city with his friends, just like anyone else. For, while Soderini had been driven from office, the Medici's position was still far from secure. Though Cardona had compelled the Signoria to accept the Medici's return and enter into an alliance with Ferdinand of Aragon and the Emperor Maximilian, the Medici had yet to raise the 150,000 *fl.* he had demanded in return.[2] Most of the *popolani* were hostile. Still loyal to Soderini, they refused to appoint Medici partisans to the Signoria or the *Dodici Buon' Uomini*;[3] they voted down Medici proposals in the Great Council; and they murdered Spanish soldiers in broad daylight.[4] Worst of all, Soderini's *ottimati* opponents – to whom the Medici instinctively turned for support – were divided into two rival groups, each with its own vision of how Florence should be governed.[5]

The first was a heterogeneous collection of 'radicals'. Its most prominent members were the young noblemen who had forced Soderini to leave Florence a few days earlier. All tremendously ambitious, they saw in the Medici an opportunity to enrich themselves and to gain the positions of prominence from which they had previously been barred by age or political disposition. There were, however, some older faces, too – men like Giovanni Rucellai and Bartolomeo da Bibbiena, who had faithfully supported the Medici while they had been in exile, and who now expected some recompense for their long years in the political wilderness. Together, they

351

called for the Florentine government to be completely restructured. Every last vestige of the popular republic should be swept away – especially the Great Council; and, in its stead, the Medici should rule with a rod of iron, assisted by a coterie of dedicated adherents. According to Cerretani, some even favoured replacing the republic with a principate. The Medici were, of course, sympathetic to such views. But they were wary of putting too much faith in the radicals, especially at this early stage. Though some, like Rucellai, were independently wealthy, they could not provide the Medici with the sort of money they needed; besides, they were not the sort of people around whom the Medici could build any kind of consensus. Having been political outsiders for almost two decades, they had few friends among Florence's political elite, and did not have the networks of patronage needed to build a stable regime.

The second group was composed of so-called 'moderates'. Unlike the radicals, they were men of some political standing. They were also somewhat older, and many had previously had ties to the *frateschi*. Their leaders were Jacopo Salviati and Giovanbattista Ridolfi, but their ranks also included figures such as Lanfredino Lanfredini, Francesco Guicciardini and Filippo Strozzi. Conservative by nature, they had long advocated a 'Venetian' system of government. Now that Soderini was gone, they were quite content to see the Great Council remain. They simply wanted the constitution to be amended to give the patricians a greater share of power. They were, however, wary of allowing the Medici too much sway. Although some, like Ridolfi, were bound to the Medici by marriage, they had bitter memories of the family's last period of dominance and had no desire to go back – even to the days of Lorenzo the Magnificent. As such, Giuliano de' Medici and his brother, Cardinal Giovanni, found them much less attractive allies, but, since they had a wide networks of clients and a great deal of political influence, they commanded attention.

Uncertain of their footing, the Medici tried to balance the groups – no doubt hoping some sort of compromise might still be reached. When the question of constitutional reform was debated, however, the moderates, being by far the stronger, easily prevailed. On 6 September, the Eighty passed two laws, similar in substance to the proposals outlined in Francesco Guicciardini's *Discorso del modo di ordinare il governo popolare*.[6] The first decreed that, henceforth, the *gonfaloniere di giustizia* would serve a one-year term and that his powers would be greatly restricted. He could no longer negotiate with foreign powers without the colleges' express approval; he could not open any letters – even those addressed to him – without two members of the Signoria being present; he was forbidden to accept any gifts while in office; and he was barred from serving again for five years after the end of his term. The second law created a Senate. Consisting of former members of the *Dieci*, former *gonfalonieri di giustizia* and the Eighty, this would have a greater role in passing legislation, and would elect the *Dieci*, the *Otto* and the Signoria. The following day, both laws were approved by the Great Council, and, on 8 September, the moderate Giovanbattista Ridolfi was elected as the new *gonfaloniere*.[7]

The radicals were horrified. Fearful that, once the Spanish left, they and the Medici would be swept aside, they hurried to persuade Cardinal Giovanni de' Medici – then still in Prato – to abandon the moderates and push for a more restrictive constitution. This would not be easy. According to Cerretani, Jacopo Salviati tried to make the cardinal see that the *popolo* would not allow the Great Council to be taken from them without putting up a fight.[8] Of course, the Medici could always call a *parlamento*, but even if they managed to get their reforms passed, they would still find it difficult to govern with the radicals as their sole supporters. Naturally, the radicals dismissed this as nonsense. They felt sure that, despite their small numbers, they could still mount a successful coup. Once a new government had been installed, they told the cardinal, it would soon be accepted by the citizenry. After all, most people were more interested in having food in their bellies and a safe home for their kids than in constitutional technicalities. It was a persuasive argument, but the cardinal was not quite convinced. Still wary of acting precipitately, he wanted to see the city for himself before throwing in his lot with the radicals.

On Tuesday, 14 September, Cardinal Giovanni de' Medici rode back into Florence accompanied by a large retinue of soldiers and supporters.[9] But if he had been hoping for a rapturous welcome, he was cruelly disappointed. Cries of '*palle*' were few and far between, and the *popolo* glowered at him menacingly. He was doubtless rather crestfallen, but the radicals were delighted. As Cerretani reported, this allowed them to argue that the Medici were in greater jeopardy than they had realized and that only a *parlamento* could save them from ruin. After a day and a night of heated discussion, the cardinal reluctantly agreed.

At about 3 p.m. on Thursday, 16 September, Giuliano de' Medici, accompanied by thirty-three of his most ardent supporters, stormed into the Palazzo della Signoria, carrying weapons and shouting, '*Palle, palle*'.[10] Finding it undefended, they quickly took possession. Meanwhile, the *condottieri* Rinieri della Sassetta and Melchiore Ramazotto filled the piazza outside with troops. Helpless and frightened, the Signoria had no choice but to do as they were told and summon a *parlamento*. According to Bartolomeo Masi, fewer than 4 per cent of the *popolo* turned up – far fewer than the quorum required.[11] But such details hardly mattered. Frightened by the soldiers, yet reassured by the bread that Giuliano's men handed out, those present readily became instruments of the Medici's will. After 'confirming' that they constituted two thirds of the adult male population, they agreed to the establishment of a *balìa*, made up of the Signoria and forty-six other nominees, to reform Florence's constitution. Two days later, the *balìa* elected a new *Otto di Guardia*; and, after the requisite funds had been approved, the Spanish finally agreed to leave Tuscany.

The moderates had been dealt a heavy blow. But it was not as crushing as it might have been. Even now, the Medici hoped it might be possible to rule by consensus. Rather than stack the *balìa* with radicals, the cardinal ensured that it included a number of leading moderates, including Jacopo Salviati and Lanfredino Lanfredini, and even some of those who had played a role in Soderini's regime. It also excluded the former radicals Giovanni Rucellai, Prinzivalle della Stufa and those who had driven the former *gonfaloniere* from power the previous month.[12] Of course, there were still some moderates who refused to come round. Francesco Guicciardini saw in the *balìa* the death of Florentine liberty,[13] while Francesco Vettori described it as a form of 'tyranny'. But most seem to have been convinced that some sort of compromise might still be achieved.[14]

*

While the political maelstrom had been raging outside, Niccolò had been in his office. He had almost no work to do anymore, and seems to have had no enthusiasm for anything, either. Though none of his letters from this period have survived, he was doubtless worried about his future. Not only had he lost his principal patron, but he was also badly tainted by his association with the former *gonfaloniere*. He had, after all, devoted the greater part of his career to keeping the Medici out of Florence and, at times, had gone out of his way to antagonize their friends. Now that they had returned, he must have been afraid they would take their revenge.

Niccolò's fears were somewhat assuaged by the *balìa*. He reasoned that, if the Medici were prepared to work both with moderates and with members of Soderini's government, they might be willing to work with him, too. If he could prove his worth as a counsellor – and his loyalty to the new regime – he might still be able to secure a future for himself. Indeed, given that he and Giuliano de' Medici had known each other as young men, he may even have been quietly optimistic.

Giuliano had evidently not forgotten Niccolò and, perhaps recalling the carefree days of laughter and song they had enjoyed together before Piero de' Medici's fall, he decided to give Niccolò a chance. A few days after the *parlamento* on 16 September, Isabella d'Este, the marchioness of Mantua, asked Giuliano for news of what had been happening in Florence, and it has convincingly been argued that Giuliano asked Niccolò to write a suitable reply.[15] Jumping at the opportunity, Niccolò worked quickly; and by the end of the month, he had produced his famous 'letter to a noblewoman'.[16] It was no doubt painful to look back on Soderini's fall, but his account of those turbulent weeks nevertheless painted the Medici in as favourable a light as possible. Dubious decisions were excised, shameful actions were glossed over, and laudable – even patriotic – motivations were ascribed to them. Indeed, some episodes were so heavily rewritten that they erred closer to fiction than to history. The cardinal's presence in the Spanish camp during the sack of Prato, for example, was conveniently forgotten; Giovanni and Giuliano were shown negotiating with Cardona for Florence's safety, rather than for their own return; and the *parlamento* was portrayed as a popular response to civil unrest, rather than as a Medici-led coup. Towards the end of the letter, Niccolò was even rather fawning. Now that the 'Magnificent Medici' had been reinstated 'in all the honours and dignities of their ancestors', he wrote, the city was 'quite peaceful' and hoped, 'with the help of these Medici, to live no less honourably than it did in times past, when their father Lorenzo the Magnificent, of most happy memory, governed.'[17]

Emboldened by the favour Giuliano appears to have shown him, Niccolò then wrote to Cardinal Giovanni, offering some advice about how to avoid a potential misstep.[18] On 29 September, a committee of five officials had been appointed to identify and recover all the goods that had been confiscated from the Medici, eighteen years before.[19] This was, of course, only to be expected, but Niccolò warned that it might do the Medici more harm than good. He pointed out that everything the Medici had lost had been sold in a lawful fashion. If they now tried to deprive the buyers of their purchases, they would cause lasting offence. For, as Niccolò drily put it, 'men complain more about a farm that has been taken from them than about a brother or a father who has been killed; because death can sometimes be forgotten, but property never.'[20] Indeed, the Medici might even provoke a revolution, for everyone knew that, while a change of regime (*mutazione d'uno stato*) would not bring a dead relative back to life, it could give a man back his farm. If the Medici needed proof, Niccolò claimed, they had only to look to their own past. When Cosimo de' Medici had been on his deathbed, he had told his son Piero to entrust all his affairs to his friend, Dietisalvi Neroni, and 'to look on him as a father'.[21] On learning that various Florentines owed Cosimo's estate some 20,000 ducats, however, the cunning Dietisalvi had advised Piero to demand payment, aware this would provoke the undying hatred of his debtors. Capitalizing on Piero's unpopularity, Dietisalvi had then launched a revolt that had very nearly succeeded in driving the Medici out of Florence. As such, Niccolò counselled the cardinal that magnanimity might serve his family better than greed. By allowing the new owners to keep their possessions, and accepting an annual payment of between 4,000 and 5,000 ducats in return, he argued, the Medici would not only avoid causing any resentment, but would even win new friends.

*

Yet, if the Medici were ready to forgive, the radicals were determined they should not. According to Cerretani, they pointed out that the cardinal had already been far too trusting. In appointing so many moderates, they argued, he had created a *balìa* he could not control.[22]

If Salviati and Ridolfi wished, they could quite easily reimpose a 'Venetian' constitution and consign both the Medici and the radicals to the fringes of political life. Suitably alarmed, the cardinal was persuaded to appoint eleven more men to the *balìa* – including his brother, Giuliano, and a number of prominent radicals.[23] Thus equipped with the numerical advantage they had coveted, the radicals quickly set about dismantling the last vestiges of the old regime. They first abolished Niccolò's militia and the magistracy of the *Nove*, then the Great Council and the Eighty. Soderini and his brother were formally banished, and, to add insult to injury, the *Salone dei Cinquecento* – the very symbol of the popular republic – was turned into a barracks.[24] For good measure, the Senate was disbanded, as well. Too late, the moderates realized how precarious their position had become. Following an ugly disagreement over appointments to a new scrutiny council, Giovanbattista Ridolfi was forced to resign as *gonfaloniere* and Jacopo Salviati found himself packed off to serve as Florence's ambassador in Rome.[25]

Niccolò was deeply shaken. Although he was no friend of the moderates – least of all Salviati – their sudden demise signalled that he, too, was in danger. Having received no reply from the cardinal to his last letter, he hastily scribbled another. Now known as the *Ai Palleschi* ('To the Mediceans'), this was again designed to prove his worth as a counsellor.[26] But, in a desperate bid for political relevance, Niccolò now attempted to be more radical than the radicals themselves. Though the Medici would instinctively want to rebuild relations with the great families once things had settled down, Niccolò warned them against listening to the moderates' advice any further. However laudable it might be to seek consensus, he argued, it would be foolish to trust those who had distanced themselves from the Medici in the past simply because of their virulent attacks on Piero Soderini. Indeed, the Medici should actually regard the moderates as their greatest enemies. For, while the moderates were now calling for Soderini's supposed crimes to be exposed publicly, they were doing so not to help the Medici, but to curry favour with the people and strengthen their own position. They still wanted to preserve elements of Soderini's regime, and were clearly trying to make sure their political influence would not suffer if the Medici faltered. It would be far wiser, Niccolò claimed, to cut them down to size, bury the old republic, and rule Florence with a firm hand.

Though badly written and crudely argued, the *Ai Palleschi* showed just how much Niccolò was prepared to sacrifice to earn the Medici's trust. In a few confused paragraphs, he had repudiated everything he had worked for since becoming second chancellor. He had poured scorn on Soderini, spat on his regime and rejoiced over the destruction of the militia. Even if he had not said so openly, he had silently promised that, in return for his livelihood, he would betray everything and say anything.

But the *Ai Palleschi* was not enough to save him from the radicals' wrath. He possessed neither the money nor political influence for his 'conversion' to be of much significance, and he was not so brilliant an administrator that his services were irreplaceable. On 7 November, just six days after the first radical-dominated Signoria had taken office, Niccolò was dismissed from all his posts.[27] The following week, he was forbidden to leave Florentine territory; and, at the end of the month, he was subjected to a humiliating enquiry into his handling of the militia.[28] His friend, Biagio Buonaccorsi, was sacked at the same time. But Marcello di Virgilio Adriani, who had always taken care to remain above party politics, was allowed to remain as first chancellor.

It was a crushing blow. Damned by association, as much as by his own actions, Niccolò had become a political outcast, a nobody. Worse still, he was staring poverty in the face. Although his salary had never been large, the sudden loss of a regular income would have hit Niccolò's pocket hard. With nothing but the rent from his farm at Sant'Andrea in Percussina to fall back on, and with a wife and children to support, the future must have looked bleak.

Niccolò could not help feeling bitter, and it was not long before his natural caution gave way to vocal resentment. Over the Christmas period, while the cardinal was away in Bologna, he began to criticize the Medici openly, attacking them both for their weakness and for their political naivety.[29] According to his friend, Giovanni Folchi, he went around telling people that the regime 'could rule only with difficulty, because it lacked someone at the rudder, where Lorenzo de' Medici had stood so firmly.'[30] He also suggested that the Holy League – upon which the Medici regime ultimately depended – 'could not remain as it was forever, and . . . would probably fall apart someday.' His rancour made his friends nervous. Though an avowed enemy of the Medici, even Folchi did his best to keep away, while

Paolo Vettori admitted that Niccolò was causing too much bother for his own good.

Niccolò didn't see any harm in sounding off, though. He was, after all, quite right about the Medici's weakness. Although the popular republic had now been dismantled, the Medici had still not 'resolved the question of who should manage the regime, or how.'[31] The cardinal was, perhaps, the natural choice, but Church affairs often drew him away from Florence, especially now the pope's health was declining,[32] and his brother, Giuliano, was too soft-hearted to take his place. Much like Niccolò, the radicals had realized that stronger leadership was needed. The Medici still had many enemies in Florence; and if they were not to become a threat, Paolo Vettori argued, the Medici would have to govern 'more with force than skill'.[33] According to Cerretani, some radicals even believed the Medici would have to become 'ministers of violence' to survive.[34] The Medici were, however, reluctant to accept this. Although they allowed the *Otto* to banish Martino della Scarfa and a mace-bearer called Piero for speaking ill of the government in late January 1513,[35] they were still wary of being too heavy-handed.[36]

But all that was about to change. In mid-February, a certain Bernardino Coccio came bursting into the Palazzo della Signoria and demanded an audience with the *Otto*. When he was shown in, he produced a list of 'eighteen or twenty young men' which had 'accidentally fallen from [the pocket of] Pietro Paolo Boscoli' while the two of them had been at a party hosted by some of Soderini's relatives.[37] Given that Boscoli was known to be hostile to the Medici, the *Otto* realized this could be evidence of a conspiracy and immediately had Boscoli and his friend, Agostino di Luca Capponi, arrested. At first, they denied having done anything wrong, but under torture they confessed to having conspired to assassinate Giuliano de' Medici, along with his cousin, Giulio, and his nephew, Lorenzo di Piero.[38] Some sources suggest they may have wanted to kill the cardinal as well, but this is far from certain.

Their chances of success were never high. As Giuliano himself noted in a letter to Piero da Bibbiena, they knew more about books than about weapons.[39] They had few followers and they had probably not even spoken to half of the people on the list. But the violence of their intentions was nevertheless clear. It seemed no coincidence that among those they had named were several prominent opponents of the Medici, including Niccolò Valori and Giovanni Folchi.[40] Neither the *Otto* nor the Medici wanted to take any chances. That evening, Boscoli and Capponi were condemned to death, and orders were given for all those on the list to be arrested.[41] Niccolò was among them.

Shortly after midnight, several constables forced their way into his house on the Via Romana. But Niccolò was nowhere to be found. As Ridolfi has suggested, he may well have been hiding, having been tipped off by one of his friends in the chancellery.[42] The *Otto* were, however, not to be denied. The following morning, 19 February, a warrant was issued for Niccolò's arrest.[43] Anyone who was giving him shelter or who knew where he was hiding had an hour to give him up, on pain of being declared a rebel. Soon enough, Niccolò handed himself in. Hauled off to the *Stinche*, a forbidding, fortress-like prison, less than 200 metres from his old office in the Palazzo della Signoria, he was thrown into a stinking dungeon to await interrogation.

That Niccolò had played no role in the conspiracy is almost certain. Even had Boscoli and Capponi approached him – which seems unlikely – he would doubtless have refused to have anything to do with them. Bitter though he may have been about his dismissal, he was no revolutionary. But it made no difference. Having been a key player in Soderini's regime, he was already suspect; and when Folchi revealed Niccolò had been criticizing the Medici in public, the *Otto* had no difficulty in believing the worst.[44]

Locked away in the depths of his prison, Niccolò was tortured using a cruel technique known as *strappado*. His hands were first tied together behind his back. Using a rope slung over a beam, or through a ceiling hook, he was then lifted into the air by his wrists. He may also have had weights tied to his feet.[45] Although he was never more than a few centimetres above the ground, the pain would have been excruciating. His shoulders were dislocated, his neck was in agony and his back felt as if it were about to break.

Six times Niccolò was pulled aloft. He tried to bear it as manfully as he could, but it was too much even for him.[46] Had he anything to confess, he would surely have done so, but there was nothing he could say to make his tormentors stop. Lying in his cell at night, with chains around his ankles and handcuffs on his wrists, he cursed his fate.[47] He could see the Medici were bound to be suspicious – he had himself advised them to rule with a firm hand – but he had never dreamt that an innocent man could be treated so cruelly. He knew that his brother, Totto, had sent a messenger to Rome to ask Francesco Vettori to intercede with the cardinal, but he must have held out little hope of ever seeing the light of day again.[48]

Before dawn on 23 February, Niccolò was woken from his sleep by the sound of funeral chants being sung as Boscoli and Capponi were led to the scaffold. Struck with terror, he saw the grave open up before him. Slipping the gaoler a few coins, he hurriedly got hold of some paper and ink, and scribbled a heartfelt appeal to the only man he thought could save him: Giuliano de' Medici. Unlike Boscoli, who had made a long, self-pitying confession to Luca della Robbia the previous night, Niccolò did not try to protest his innocence or excuse his indiscretions. Instead, he turned to poetry. It was, admittedly, a slightly unusual decision. As he was well aware, the best-known examples of prison poetry were found in classical epics, chivalric romances and philosophical treatises, and recommended that unjust incarceration be met with either heroic fortitude or stoic detachment – neither of which lent itself to supplication, or, indeed, to sympathy. But Niccolò realized that by subverting or even parodying these poetic norms, he might be able to persuade Giuliano to show him some mercy.

Harking back to the halcyon days of their youth, Niccolò penned two verses, each depicting his suffering with unsentimental clarity, each coursing with black, self-mocking humour, and each pleading for forgiveness – not from a master, but from an old friend. The first – 'Io ho, Giuliano, in gamba un paio di geti' – was perhaps the most vivid.[49] Neither elegy nor jeremiad, it is rather a *sonetto caudato* (literally 'a sonnet with a tail'), a form usually reserved for pieces of comic realism, and derives its force from the repudiation of 'heroic' virtue. In the opening lines, Niccolò portrayed himself sitting with 'a pair of jesses' on his legs and suffering badly from 'six pulls of the rope'. But he decided not to recount his other miseries – 'because that's how poets always carry on', and because there was also a danger that Giuliano would not believe him if he tried to paint himself as too much of an anguished hero. He therefore turned to describe the cell in which he found himself – and, in doing so, sent up some of the tropes familiar not only to chivalric romance, but also to classical epic. Here, there were neither monsters nor battles, gods nor saints:

About these walls crawl lice
So big and double-bodied that they look like butterflies;
There was never such a stink in Roncesvalles,
Or among those glades in Sardinia,
As there is in my dainty lodging-house;
And there's a sound that's exactly like the thundering
Of Jove and Etna put together.
One is chained up, and another freed
With the clattering of locks, keys, and bolts:
Another shrieks 'You're lifting me too far off the ground!'

For someone like Giuliano, who was familiar with poems like the *Aeneid* and the *Chanson de Roland*, it would have been hard to suppress a chuckle at Niccolò's literary jokes. But the twist was in the tail. Having made it clear he was no hero, Niccolò was free to express his fears openly – and to plead for mercy without shame. With striking economy of language, he described the horror he had felt on hearing the prayers that had been sung as Boscoli and Capponi were led from the prison. But he felt no pity for them – and he certainly had no intention of following them, either! They could rot, for all he cared, just so long as Giuliano would set him free.

The second – 'In questa notte, pregando le Muse' – is equally tongue-in-cheek.[50] This time, however, Niccolò used a parody of Boethius's *Consolation of Philosophy* to distance himself from Soderini, and thereby ask Giuliano's pardon. It begins in mock-serious style. The previous night, while Niccolò had been 'beseeching the Muses that, with their sweet cither and sweet songs,' they would visit Giuliano and make his excuses, one of them suddenly appeared before him. 'Who are you, who dares to call me?' she thundered. But when Niccolò stammered out his name, she refused to believe him. Slapping him about the face and clamping his mouth shut with her fingers, she told him that, since he had his legs and feet bound and was sitting 'chained like a madman', he was clearly not Niccolò Machiavelli, but the poet Andrea Dazzi. As Giuliano would doubt-less have known, Dazzi had been a pupil of Niccolò's former colleague, Marcello di Virgilio Adriani, and had dedicated a number of syco-phantic verses to Soderini while himself serving as a professor of Greek at the Studio.[51] Naturally, Niccolò tried to convince the Muse that he was who he said, but she only mocked him further. In desperation, he then begged Giuliano to prove that he was not Dazzi – by removing his chains.

They were clever, funny and charming verses, but it is impossible to know if they had any effect – or if they were even delivered. Fortunately, Niccolò's friends were still working hard on his behalf. At Totto's insistence, Francesco Vettori had already petitioned Cardinal Giovanni for his release,[52] but it was Francesco's brother, Paolo, who had the most success. Unlike Francesco, whose ties to the old regime made him rather suspect, Paolo was a dedicated supporter of the Medici. He had been instrumental in forcing Soderini from office, and may already have been serving as Giuliano's major-domo.[53] In contrast to many radicals, however, he valued friendship above partisan concerns, and now used his considerable influence to persuade Giuliano that Niccolò was not the traitor he had been made out to be.[54] It cannot have been easy, but – helped by the abatement of the Medici's desire for vengeance – he eventually succeeded.

On 7 March, the interrogations were wound up. Niccolò Valori and Giovanni Folchi were found guilty of conspiracy and sentenced to two years' imprisonment in Volterra.[55] Others were confined to Florentine territory and some were let off with little more than a fine. Niccolò was among the lucky ones. Subject to the payment of a 1,000 fl. bond, he was to be released. All he had to do now was raise the money – and, for that, he could count on the help of Francesco Vettori and his kinsmen, Filippo and Giovanni Machiavelli.

*

But Fate had one more surprise in store. Shortly after Niccolò's arrest, Julius II had died following a long illness; and, a few hours before the execution of Boscoli and Capponi, Cardinal Giovanni de' Medici hastily left for Rome. He had few hopes for himself in the forthcoming conclave. Though he could count on the support of some of his younger colleagues, few thought him papabile. As the imperial ambassador noted, the leading contenders were Raffaele Riario, Luigi d'Aragona and Niccolò Fieschi.[56] Besides, Giovanni was suffering from a painful fistula on his rump and had to miss the opening sessions of the conclave so he could undergo surgery. When he was sufficiently recovered to join the rest of the Sacred

College, however, he found the situation much changed. In the first ballot, on 10 March, Riario received not a single vote, and, of the sixteen candidates who could boast some support, none had emerged as the favourite.[57] Crestfallen, Riario realized his only hope of retaining some influence in the Curia was to throw his weight behind Giovanni. Amid a flurry of bribes, the other cardinals rallied to the Medici banner, and, on the morning of 11 March, Giovanni was unanimously elected Pope Leo X.

Even before the scrutiny had been held, rumours of Giovanni's election had reached Florence. Though dawn had not yet broken, the citizens went wild with elation.[58] Bells were rung and 'bonfires were lit in many places throughout Florence, with such joy and happiness, and with such continual cries of "*Palle!*" that it made everyone . . . get up and go to the windows.'[59] As yet, nothing was known for certain, but, as Landucci admitted, it was 'impossible' not to join in. When confirmation was finally received at around 10 p.m., the celebrations were even more extravagant. All night, fireworks were let off from the Palazzo della Signoria, the cupola of Santa Maria del Fiore, the gates and any number of houses and *palazzi*; cannons blazed in triumph and shouts of '*Palle! Papa! Leo!*' rang throughout the city.[60] The bonfires were stacked high with brushwood and branches, baskets, barrels and anything else that happened to be nearby. To Landucci, it seemed 'as if the city had been turned upside-down'.

With Leo X seated on the papal throne, the Medici's position in Florence was unassailable. Whereas only recently they had been obliged to be ruthless, they could now afford to be merciful. That same afternoon, they issued a general pardon. With the exception of Valori and Folchi, who were to remain incarcerated in Volterra for the duration of their sentence, everyone associated with the conspiracy – including Niccolò – was released from prison.

PART VI

The Outsider

(1513–19)

19

Slumming with the Lice

(March–December 1513)

Late in the evening of 11 March, or perhaps early the following morning, the doors of the *Stinche* swung open and from the dark recesses within stepped the bent and battered figure of Niccolò Machiavelli. Pulling his tattered cloak tightly about his shoulders, he would have squinted up at the sun and filled his lungs with air. It was thick with the stench of celebration – of bonfires still burning in the streets, of stale wine, of sweat and swill. But to Niccolò, it must have smelt only too sweet. After more than three weeks locked in a dank cell, tortured and beaten, he must have felt as if he had awoken from a long nightmare. And having been saved only by 'God and [his] innocence', he was determined not to slumber a moment longer.[1]

He was confident of returning to the Palazzo della Signoria – or, if not, then of finding some post at the papal court. He had, after all, played no part in Boscoli's conspiracy. Now that the times were becoming 'more liberal and not so suspicious',[2] his career in the chancellery would surely be less of a stumbling block. Though he may have worked closely with Piero Soderini for many years, his friends reminded him that he had been appointed as second chancellor long before Soderini became *gonfaloniere*, and had only ever wanted the best for Florence.[3] If he could only convince the Medici of his abilities, he felt sure they could not fail to give him a position.

Soon after his release, Niccolò sent a gift of thrushes to Giuliano de' Medici, together with a witty *sonetto caudato*. Turning the puny birds into a metaphor for himself, he urged the young *signore* to judge him by his merits, rather than by the scurrilous gossip put about by his enemies:

I am sending you, Giuliano, a few thrushes,
not because they are a good and handsome gift,
but to remind Your Magnificence
of poor Machiavelli.

And if you have someone who bites next to you,
you could shove my gift between his teeth,
so that, while he is eating that bird,
he might forget to tear others to pieces.

But you might say: 'Perhaps these will not have
the effect that you say, because they are neither tasty
nor fat: and no-one would eat them.'

To such talk I would reply
that I, too, am rather thin, as they well know,
but they still take a few good bites out of me.

Ignore all the chatter,
Your Magnificence: finger and touch,
and judge with your hands, rather than your eyes.[4]

Whether Giuliano ever replied is not known, but no sooner had Niccolò sent his poem than he realized that, if he wanted to find favour with the Medici, he might be better advised to petition Leo X, rather than the pontiff's wayward younger brother. For this, he sought the help of his old friend, Francesco Vettori – who, despite his republican tendencies, was then serving as one of Florence's ambassadors in Rome. On 13 March, he sent Vettori the first of a long series of letters. After thanking him for having helped secure his release from prison, Niccolò asked him not only to find his brother Totto a position in the papal household, but also to remember him to the pope, 'in order that, if it should be possible, either he or his family might start engaging my services'.[5]

Vettori's reply was encouraging. He had been profoundly disturbed by Niccolò's imprisonment and regretted not having been able to do more. Now that Niccolò had been released, however, he was sure that, together, they would find him something. '[T]ake heart,' he urged, 'and . . . hope that, since things have settled down and the fortunes of [the Medici] are beyond imagining and debate, you will not always have to stay down.'[6] In the meantime, he invited Niccolò to come and stay with him for as long as he wanted.

Niccolò was deeply moved. Having suffered so greatly and so unjustly, the kindness of a true friend was worth more to him than gold. All that he had left in life he owed to the Vettori and 'the Magnificent Giuliano', he wrote. As for setting his face against Fortune – well, Vettori need have no worries on that account. He had borne his sufferings more manfully than he had expected, and he would accept whatever else Fortune had in store for him with the same stoic equanimity. '[I]f these new masters of ours see fit not to leave me lying on the ground,' he declared, 'I shall be happy and believe that I shall act in such a way that they too will have reason to be proud of me. And if they should not, I shall get on as I did when I came [into the world]: I was born in poverty and at an early age learned how to scrimp rather than to thrive.'[7]

Difficulties, however, soon arose. On 30 March, Vettori dolefully informed Niccolò that, although he *had* obtained a post for Totto in the papal household, the appointment had since been overturned by the *camera*, 'because the clerics say that offices are being wasted'.[8] When the uncertainty caused by the new pope's election eventually died down, he would, of course, try again, but he could not promise anything. Of Niccolò himself, Vettori said not a word. Either his request had been met with a stern refusal, or – more likely – he had not yet dared to put Niccolò's case before the pope, who was known to dislike being asked for 'private favours'.[9] That Niccolò would be angry, he did not doubt, but he nevertheless implored his friend to show him a little understanding. His position was already uncertain, and, having failed utterly to foresee the outcome of the conclave, he had no faith in his ability to anticipate the shifting currents of Curial politics. He could not push any harder without putting himself in jeopardy.[10] As it was, he was afraid he might be recalled any day now. Still, he promised always to be at Niccolò's disposal, and once again invited his friend to visit.

Niccolò was, of course, disappointed. But, being generous of heart, he was more concerned for Vettori than for himself. 'Your letter terrified me more than the rope,' he wrote, 'and I am sorry you thought that I could be annoyed – not on my own account ... but for your sake.'[11] He knew only too well how anxiety and self-doubt gnawed at the soul. He advised Vettori not to waste time trying to second-guess everything; more could be gained from instinct and persistence than from intelligence and prudence. As for Totto's position in the papal household, there was no need to worry; he knew that Vettori had done his best. For himself, however, Niccolò had not yet given up hope. He had recently learned that his old friend, Cardinal Francesco Soderini, had forged an unlikely alliance with Leo X at the conclave, and had since become one of the pontiff's closest advisers.[12] Spying an opportunity, Niccolò asked Vettori whether it would be appropriate to ask Soderini to recommend him to the pope, or whether it might be better for Vettori to speak to the cardinal on his behalf.[13]

A week later, Niccolò wrote to Vettori once again, evidently in a state of some excitement. In a few days' time, he explained, Giuliano de' Medici would be coming to Rome, and Vettori would no doubt find him 'naturally disposed to please me'. The same was true, he thought, of Cardinal Soderini. The presence of such powerful allies would doubtless be a great advantage. Indeed, provided his case was 'managed with some skill,' he believed he would 'succeed in being put to some use, if not on Florence's behalf, then at least on behalf of Rome and the papacy'.[14]

Niccolò's optimism was, however, misplaced. He found no support from Giuliano de' Medici and, on 19 April, Vettori advised him not to bother contacting Cardinal Soderini either.[15] Although the cardinal was 'in good credit with the pope', there were still many Florentines who were opposed to him, and Vettori feared that, if he put Niccolò forward, he might easily arouse suspicion. Indeed, Niccolò was still so much of a political liability that Vettori did not even know whether Soderini would want to be associated with him anymore. There was nothing Vettori could do to help. While he had still not been recalled, he too had been badly tainted by his former republicanism and was regarded with deep hostility by the Medici's partisans.[16] Perhaps his brother, Paolo, might be able to get Niccolò permission to leave Florentine territory, but there was no chance of finding him a job – either in Florence or in Rome.

*

Until now, Niccolò had been content to enjoy the festive atmosphere that had taken hold of Florence. Together with a group of similarly down-at-heel former bureaucrats, he had whiled away his time drinking, laughing and whoring. Every day, he and his friends had visited 'the house of some girl to recover our vigour';[17] and every night, they had lounged about on public benches, chatting about everything and nothing.[18] The old gang had, admittedly, changed a bit since their days in the chancellery, but Niccolò still cherished them and must have chuckled as he recounted their foibles in his letters to Vettori. One friend, Tommaso del Bene, had become 'eccentric, churlish, irritating, and shabby' to such an extent that he seemed almost to be another person.[19] Tommaso had also become rather tight-fisted. The previous week, he had bought eight pounds of veal, but, since he had spent far more than he intended, he had tried to get his money back by inviting friends to eat it with him.[20] '[I]nspired by pity,' Niccolò had gone along with two others. When the dinner was over, Tommaso had presented them a bill for fourteen *soldi* each. Niccolò, however, only had ten *soldi* on him. Since then, Tommaso had badgered him incessantly for the four he owed, and, after cornering him on the Ponte Vecchio, forced him to cough up. Another, Girolamo del Guanto, had recently been widowed. For three or four days, he had been inconsolable, but after that he perked up and decided to take another wife – much to the amusement of Niccolò and the rest of the gang. Still another, Donato del Corno, had opened a new shop, which, judging by Niccolò's rather arch description, was actually a male brothel – and it seems that Donato was not above sampling his wares.[21] '[A]t one time, he goes with Vincenzio,' wrote Niccolò, 'at another time, it is with Piero'; despite this, Niccolò had 'never seen him have a falling out with Riccio', who must have been his 'regular', or at least a boon companion.

By the middle of April, however, these frivolous distractions had already begun to lose their appeal. Realizing his chances of rehabilitation were waning, Niccolò slid into a deep depression. Though he still joined in the merrymaking, he had 'resigned himself to desiring nothing passionately any longer'.[22] Quoting one of Petrarch's sonnets, he confessed that,

> . . . if at any time I laugh or sing,
> I do so because I have no other way
> to hide my anguished weeping.[23]

When Vettori told him the worst, however, he could contain his sorrow no more. He had lost everything: his position, his income, his dignity – and now his hope. He was an outsider, a pariah. All he had left was bitterness and regret. Being in Florence only compounded the pain. He no longer wanted to be reminded of his former life or have anything to do with politics anymore, let alone waste any more time carousing with chancellery has-beens. Packing his bags, he left for his farm at Sant'Andrea in Percussina[24] – vowing 'not to think about affairs of state, nor to discuss them' anymore.[25]

*

Some eleven kilometres south of Florence, Sant'Andrea in Percussina was scarcely more than a hamlet. There was a little church, with its ramshackle bell-tower, an inn, a butcher's shop, a mill or two and at least one kiln. The houses were nothing fancy. Most were made of roughly-hewn stone that had been robbed from ruins or picked up haphazardly in the fields. The Machiavelli family's house – known affectionately as the *albergaccio* – was the only substantial dwelling; even then, it was not up to much. A long, low building, set into the slope on the lower side of the road, it had been built in the same crude manner as all the others.[26] Still, the rooms were spacious and, apart from the chatter of women washing their clothes at the nearby well, it was peaceful.

All around, there were fields and vineyards, and, on the horizon, gently rolling hills, crowned by swaying cypress trees. To the south-east, there was a wood, dotted by pools and springs, and bounded by the Greve – notionally a river, but, in reality, little more than a stream. Just then, the air would have been heavy with the smell of wild onions and the ground carpeted in mushrooms, ripe for the picking. Thrushes sang from the branches, while hares scampered through the undergrowth and roe deer grazed timidly behind tree trunks. Now and then, wild boar could even be seen snuffling among the bracken.

Here, Niccolò felt safe. He had spent much of his childhood at the *albergaccio* and, even now, it was warmed by the memory of happier times. It may not have had much in the way of creature comforts, but it offered a simple, wholesome way of life – far from the anxieties of the city. Here, at last, he could relax. He could also live quite cheaply – a consideration which, given his straitened financial situation, was of no less importance. The farm provided him with wood for the fire, oil and vegetables, and he could always catch game for the pot. With Marietta – then around six months pregnant – and the children by his side, he could build a new life.

Despite his best intentions, however, his mind kept drifting back to politics. Even before he had left Florence, he had told Vettori that, since he did 'not know how to talk about the silk or the wool trade, or profits and losses', he *had* to talk about affairs of state.[27] Though he was often frustrated that things turned out differently from how he expected, he felt a great need to discuss the latest news and fill Vettori's head with 'castles in the air'. Now that he was in the country, surrounded by yokels who spoke only of haystacks and harvests, that need had become acute.

*

Happily, Vettori came to his rescue. On 21 April, the ambassador wrote to Niccolò, asking for advice about a matter that had recently been puzzling him. Since the expulsion of the French, the Holy League had started to crumble.[28] Prevented by the Swiss from dominating the new duke of Milan, Massimiliano Sforza, the emperor had endeavoured to seize the cities east of the River Adda, over which the Venetians had a prior claim. He had been supported by Julius II, who – along with Ferdinand of Aragon – had been anxious to see the long-running tensions between the two powers settled once and for all. In return for Maximilian's repudiation of the schismatic Conciliabulum of Pisa and recognition of the Fifth Lateran Council, then in session, Julius had agreed to use whatever military and spiritual means necessary to force the Venetians to give way. This had created an unhoped-for opportunity for Louis XII of France. Soon after the League's forces had captured Brescia, he had persuaded the Venetians to enter into an alliance. In exchange for certain territorial concessions, they had agreed to help him recover the duchy of Milan.[29] Much to Vettori's amazement, however, Louis had also signed a truce with Ferdinand of Aragon, at Orthez, on 1 April.[30] The benefits to Louis were clear enough. Although the truce only covered the Franco-Spanish frontier, leaving Ferdinand free to oppose the French in Italy, it allowed Louis to devote far more resources to a campaign in Lombardy. But Vettori was at a loss to know what Ferdinand hoped to gain from it – or why he had agreed to it in the first place.[31] It was tempting to believe that, with this truce, Ferdinand simply hoped to safeguard Navarre against attack and thereby avoid having to maintain two armies – one along the French border and the other in Italy. But, if this were the case, Ferdinand would have been just as secure had he *not* signed the truce. As Vettori observed, the duke of Milan, the Swiss and the pope were so anxious to keep Louis out of Italy that they would gladly have helped Ferdinand maintain an army in Navarre, just so as to force Louis to fight on two fronts. Vettori therefore surmised that something else must be afoot. What it was, however, he could not say. He had stayed in bed for two hours longer than usual trying to figure it out, but had failed to come to any conclusions. He dearly wished that he could walk with Niccolò 'from the Ponte Vecchio through via de' Bardi as far as Cestello and discuss what the king of Spain's fancy might be',[32] but, since he could not, he asked Niccolò to tell him what he thought. 'I shall agree with your judgement,' he added, touchingly, 'because, to tell the truth without flattery, I have found it more sound in these matters than that of any other man I have spoken with.'[33]

This was just the sort of problem that Niccolò loved. Although he worried that his thoughts might seem 'higgledy-piggledy',[34] his reply – written with evident glee – was a masterpiece of political reasoning, more thorough and balanced than anything he had written for years.[35] Of course, he began, if Ferdinand was as wise as he was reputed to be, it would indeed be strange for him to have concluded a treaty that would bring him nothing but ill. Therefore, something about this syllogism must be at fault.

One possibility was that Ferdinand was not, in fact, all that astute. This was not inconceivable. For his part, Niccolò had always considered Ferdinand to be 'more cunning and fortunate than wise'.[36] He had, after all, taken a great many unnecessary risks in the past. There had, for example, been no reason for Ferdinand to join the Holy League. He could very easily have concluded a peace with Louis XII and secured himself for years to come, but instead he had chosen war, even though, in one decisive engagement, he might have lost all his Italian possessions, as had nearly happened after the Battle of Ravenna. That he had not was due more to good luck than to sound judgement. Having made a mistake once, Niccolò argued, he was more than likely to make a thousand more mistakes in future – and the Treaty of Orthez could well be one of them.

Alternatively, the truce might not be as disadvantageous as it seemed. Here, it was instructive to ask, not 'Why did Ferdinand throw in his lot with Louis?' but 'What else could Ferdinand have done?' Were Ferdinand to have continued his campaign against Louis in Navarre – as he had seriously considered doing – he would have needed the pope to send him money, the emperor to attack Burgundy and the king of England to invade from the north. But he could count on none of these. The pope had only ever sent money in 'dribs and drabs', the emperor had refused to commit himself, and the king of England had offered nothing but 'debilitated troops that could not be united with his own men'.[37] What was more, Louis XII had ample funds of his own, and had not only secured an agreement with the Venetians, but was also in talks with the Swiss. Unable to fight on, Ferdinand had therefore thought it better to 'forestall the king [of France] however he could, rather than continue in such great uncertainty and muddle and lay out an intolerable sum of money.'[38] Either the truce would 'remove the war from his own backyard' and oblige his allies to ratify an agreement with Louis, or it would 'compel the emperor and England to declare war in earnest'.[39] Whichever the case, Ferdinand would find himself in a stronger position.

Niccolò did not know enough about what was going on to say whether the truce or Ferdinand was more likely to have been misjudged, but he no doubt looked forward to discussing the matter further with Vettori. It would, however, be almost two months before either of them would write again – partly because Vettori was inundated with work, and partly because Niccolò thought he would soon be returning to Florence, anyway.[40]

*

During this time, a great deal happened. Just two weeks after Niccolò's letter, Louis XII launched his campaign to reconquer the duchy of Milan.[41] Under the command of Louis de La Trémoille and Giangiacomo Trivulzio, a French army – reinforced by a large number of German landsknechts – crossed the Alps and, after rendezvousing with their Italian allies in Piedmont, quickly captured Asti and Alessandria. Meanwhile, a Venetian army under Bartolomeo d'Alviano took Valeggio, Pescheria and Cremona, and, in Genoa, Antoniotto Adorno was installed as Louis' governor, with the help of a French fleet. Massimiliano Sforza seemed powerless to resist. Though he had been rumoured to have 1,200 Spanish and Neapolitan men-at-arms, 800 Spanish infantry and 3,000 Lombard foot soldiers at his disposal, in addition to 7,000 Swiss mercenaries, Cardona had abruptly withdrawn his troops on Ferdinand's orders and retreated to Piacenza. Facing little opposition, the French army then advanced rapidly; by early June, most of the west of the duchy had been occupied. Besides Milan, only Como and Novara remained – and these looked ripe for the taking. While La Trémoille laid siege to Novara, where Massimiliano had taken refuge, Trivulzio used threats and promises to persuade the terrified Milanese to place themselves under French protection.

But, just as victory seemed to be within grasp, disaster struck.[42] On 5 June, La Trémoille raised the siege of Novara, having learned that up to 8,000 Swiss reinforcements were on their way. Weighed down by artillery and baggage, however, his forces had travelled no more than a few kilometres by the time night fell, and made camp where they stopped, still almost within sight of the city. They were dangerously exposed and, worse still, they had grossly underestimated the speed of the Swiss advance. Shortly before dawn, the Swiss fell upon them. Although few in number and poorly equipped, they had the element of surprise and exploited it to the full. The French were routed. Nearly all of their artillery was captured and hundreds – if not thousands – were killed.

Following this defeat, the French position quickly crumbled. Ferdinand at last gave Cardona permission to join up with the Swiss; Antoniotto Adorno was driven out of Genoa; and soon, the tattered remains of the French army were chased out of Lombardy, pursued by Swiss mercenaries intent on plunder. Louis XII's campaign was at an end, and it was painfully clear that he would not be able to launch another before the following year – if at all. Now, the only question was: what would the peace look like?

*

By 20 June, Niccolò could bear the lapse in discussion no longer. Having heard all about Louis XII's humiliation, he desperately wanted to share his thoughts with Vettori. Now he was sure the ambassador would be staying in Rome for the time being, he penned a long and thoughtful letter. His stance was, however, striking. Rather than offer a general assessment of how the conflict might affect Italy as a whole, as might have been expected, he attempted to place himself in the pope's position and scrutinize 'in detail what I may now have to fear and what remedies I might use.'[43] This may, of course, have been nothing more than an amusing intellectual exercise. But it is perhaps more likely to have been inspired either by his desire to be of some help to Vettori, who was, after all, at the pope's side, or by a lingering belief that, through his friend, he might still prove his value to the Medici as a counsellor.

His advice was, however, unexpected. Whereas, in his earlier works, like the *Ghiribizzi* and the *Capitolo di Fortuna*, he had argued that the only way to receive Fortune's favour was to seize her by the throat, he now suggested that the pope's best course of action would be 'to rely entirely on Fortune until an agreement could be drawn up, providing for a total, or almost complete cease-fire.'[44] It was not that he had changed his mind about *Fortuna*, but rather that there was almost nothing else for the pope to do – or at least not without leaving himself worse off. Unless Louis XII defeated the English (which seemed unlikely), Leo X had no reason to fear him, and, though Ferdinand and the Swiss were both untrustworthy, they were at least predictable. Naturally, Ferdinand dearly wanted to make himself sole master of Italy, but the Swiss were still far too strong for him. Yet he also knew that, if he attempted to come to an understanding with them, Leo might easily deprive him of the kingdom of Naples – which was, after all, a papal fief. Ferdinand's only option was therefore to conclude a treaty with France, Venice and the papacy. Such an agreement would benefit them all. The Venetians would probably be satisfied to possess Verona, Vicenza, Padua and Treviso; the king of France to regain the duchy of Milan; the pope to keep his own territories; and Ferdinand to be confirmed in the kingdom of Naples. What was more, this alliance would 'harm only an ephemeral duke of Milan, the Swiss, and the Emperor, who would all be left to attack France.'[45] For Louis XII to protect himself against them, he would 'always have to wear his cuirass', with the result that his three allies – Venice, Ferdinand and Leo – would be safe from him, and could concentrate on keeping an eye on each other. Thus, provided the pope allowed the situation to unfold as Niccolò expected, he would not be disappointed.

After so long an interval, Vettori was delighted to receive Niccolò's letter – and was intrigued by his friend's predictions.[46] He did not agree with them entirely, though. While an agreement between Ferdinand of Aragon and Louis XII did indeed seem likely, he could not help feeling that a wider treaty, involving Leo X and the Venetians, might prove elusive. The pope and the *Serenissima* were, he believed, too suspicious of one another to be easily reconciled, and, besides, he did not see how a peace could be achieved without removing Massimiliano from Milan – which, of course, the Swiss would never allow. This being so, Vettori believed that, rather than trust to Fortune (as Niccolò had argued), Leo should adopt a completely different policy. With uncharacteristic forcefulness, Vettori contended that he should stop spending, keep the Swiss happy, obstruct a treaty between Louis and Ferdinand, and refuse to sign any peace unless it reconciled the interests of *all* the Italian powers.

When no reply was forthcoming, Vettori began to suspect that he may have disagreed a little too harshly with Niccolò's prognostications. Surrounded by the hustle and bustle of the papal court, he had perhaps forgotten that he was addressing a friend in need, rather than just another diplomatic colleague. On 12 July, he wrote again – still with the peace in mind, but this time in a friendlier manner.[47] 'I wish I could be with you,' he began, 'and see whether we could organize this world, and if not the world, at least this part here . . .' Playfully, he then set out the interests of the different Italian powers, as if laying out the pieces on a chess board, and invited Niccolò to 'organise peace terms for [him] with [his] pen'. It was a bit of fun, and it should have been just the thing to tickle Niccolò's fancy.

But sorrow intervened. On 4 August, Niccolò wrote to his nephew, Giovanni Vernacci, with the heart-breaking news that Marietta had given birth to a baby girl, who had died after three days.[48] As his matter-of-fact tone suggests, he was trying to bear the loss as philosophically as he could. It was, after all, not wholly unexpected. In sixteenth-century Tuscany, infant mortality rates were still remarkably high, and it was not uncommon for parents to lose a child soon after birth – especially in the countryside.[49] But his daughter's death hit him and Marietta hard. On top of all that they had suffered in recent months, this latest blow must have been almost too much for them to bear.

It was more than a week before Niccolò could bring himself to reply to Vettori.[50] It was a long and detailed letter, carefully evaluating the motivations of each of the different actors and offering a balanced assessment of what forms the peace might take. But it was peculiarly joyless. His prose, usually so elegant and flowing, was dry, turgid, even slightly bitter. There were no flashes of wit; there was no irony; indeed, there was scarcely any warmth to it at all.

Throughout the second half of August, Vettori tried valiantly to keep the discussion going – evidently hoping that it might cheer his friend up.[51] But it had run its course. Coupled with the death of his daughter, the parlous state of Italian affairs had destroyed any hope Niccolò might have had for the future. Peace – of any sort – was now an impossibility. Spanish and imperial troops were already flooding into the Veneto,[52] and it was only a matter of time before the whole peninsula was once again plunged into conflict. The suffering that would surely follow didn't even bear thinking about. On 26 August, Niccolò told Vettori that he was ready to start weeping over the 'ruin and servitude which, if it does not come today or tomorrow, will [certainly] come in our lifetimes.'[53] It was clear from his tone that he would rather not talk about such things anymore. Reluctant to cause him further grief, Vettori let the matter drop.

*

It was not until late November that Vettori wrote again. Pretending to have lost Niccolò's last letter, he deftly brushed the question of peace under the carpet and, having grown heartily sick of his work over the autumn, tried instead to raise his friend's spirits with an amusingly self-deprecating portrait of his life in Rome.[54]

For some time, Vettori had been living in a secluded little house near the Vatican, most probably somewhere along the modern Borgo Santo Spirito. Just across the road was the church of Santi Michele e Magno, and, behind it, there were some gardens, 'now largely abandoned'. From there, you could go up the Janiculum Hill, which was said to have been the site of Nero's gardens, and which afforded splendid views across the city. Being rather more religious than Niccolò, he enjoyed being close to so many churches. He often heard Mass, and made a particular point of doing so on feast days.

His daily routine was hardly glamorous. Rising at around ten o'clock in the morning, he got dressed, and – one day in two or three – sauntered over to the Apostolic Palace. There, if he was lucky, he exchanged 'twenty words with the pope, ten with Cardinal [Giulio] de' Medici, six with the Magnificent Giuliano', or, if he was not available, with the pope's secretary, Piero Ardinghelli. He then chatted with the other ambassadors, as much to pass the time of day as to pick up information. Lunch he usually ate with his household and, occasionally, the odd guest. Then, he played cards, walked in the gardens, or – if the weather was fine – went for a ride outside Rome. At night, he returned home and read the ancient historians – Livy, Sallust, Plutarch, Appian, Tacitus and Suetonius being among his favourites. Every few days, he scribbled a note to the Florentine government, but, since he usually had nothing important to say, trotted out 'some tired and irrelevant news'.

His amusements were few. Being short of money, he didn't entertain much, and he scarcely talked to anyone. He was, however, an inveterate womanizer. When he had first arrived in Rome, he told Niccolò, he had kept several courtesans, but, 'frightened by the summer air' – that is, by venereal disease – he had abstained. But there was one girl – 'reasonably pretty and pleasant in speech' – who he still saw regularly. He also had a neighbour whom Niccolò would probably not find unattractive; and, though she was from a noble family, she still 'carrie[d] on some business'.

Niccolò was thrilled to hear from his friend again. He had been worried that Vettori might have been angry with him, but the charming, witty letter reassured him no end. It left him in no doubt of the warmth of Vettori's friendship, and rekindled his old love of light-hearted badinage. Only too happy to reciprocate in kind, now that he had been stirred from depression, he replied with an equally humorous description of his own life at Sant'Andrea in Percussina, on 10 December.[55]

It was rich in literary allusions. Behind Niccolò's contrast between the simplicity of country living and the rich grandeur of the metropolis may lie Horace's tale of the town mouse and the country mouse

(*Sat.* 2.6). Describing his own, rather barren, love life – a far cry from Vettori's carryings-on with courtesans – he turned to the works of the lyric poets. There is also a comical comparison between his hunting methods and a character from a well-known elegy by Vitalis of Blois that is perhaps designed to highlight how ill-suited he was to such rustic pursuits. Throughout, there are countless other little *clins d'oeil*, all designed to flatter the intellect and raise a smile. But, despite its literary qualities, it was no artifice. Enlivened with telling vignettes, it was doubtless taken from life, and its naturalism makes the contrast between Vettori's luxurious, but unsatisfying, existence in Rome and Niccolò's humble, yet profoundly human, experiences all the more striking.

*

Until recently, Niccolò had devoted much of his time to catching thrushes.[56] Getting up before daybreak, he would prepare his birdlime and go out with so many birdcages on his back that he looked like the hapless Geta, coming back from the harbour with a huge stack of his master Amphitryon's books. He would catch at least two, at most six, birds; not exactly a lavish haul, but enough to keep hunger at bay.

Now the thrushes had left for warmer climes, however, Niccolò's routine had changed. Rising with the dawn, he went into one of the woods that he was having cut down and there spent a couple of hours with the woodsmen, who were always quarrelling among themselves or with some neighbour. He could tell Vettori 'a thousand tales about these woods' – and about the trouble he had with the men who wanted to buy some of his logs. A little while ago, Frosino da Panzano had sent for a few cartloads of wood, without so much as saying a word to Niccolò, but, when the time came to pay up, he wanted to keep back ten *lire* that he said he had won off Niccolò four years earlier, when he had beaten him at cards at Antonio Guicciardini's house. Niccolò, of course, had started to 'raise hell', and was on the point of calling the wagoner who had delivered the wood a thief. Thankfully, Giovanni Machiavelli had stepped in at the last minute and persuaded the two to patch up their differences. But it had left such a bitter taste in Niccolò's mouth that, when Battista Guicciaridini, Tommaso del Bene and a few other friends had asked to buy some wood at the start of winter, he had demurred – much to their annoyance.

After leaving the woods, Niccolò walked to a nearby spring, and thence to one of the places where he caught thrushes. Stretching out on the grass or sitting on a mossy tree stump, he pulled out a volume of poems that he had brought from home that morning – Dante, Petrarch, or one of the Latin poets like Ovid or Tibullus – and, for a few hours, lost himself in reading about their 'amorous passions and their loves'. Perhaps inevitably, these reminded him of his own, and, for a while, his recollections made him happy.

By mid-morning, he was hungry. Tucking his book under his arm, he made his way home, chatting with passers-by as he went. With the same insatiable curiosity he had displayed on diplomatic missions past, he asked for news of their homelands. Thus, he learned about all manner of unexpected things and saw mankind in the raw: 'the variety of its tastes, the diversity of its fancies'. Arriving at the *albergaccio*, he then sat down to lunch with the rest of his household – Marietta, the children and perhaps a trusted servant or two. Their meals were simple. As Niccolò noted, they ate only 'what food this poor farm and my minuscule patrimony yield.' But it was good, honest fare all the same.

When he had finished eating, Niccolò went to the tavern, where he usually found the innkeeper, a butcher, a miller and a couple of kiln workers. The rest of his day was spent 'slumming around' with these birds of a feather, playing cards and backgammon. Helped along by wine and beer, these games frequently led to arguments – or even fights. 'More often than not,' Niccolò noted, 'we are wrangling over a penny; be that as it may, people can hear us yelling even in San Casciano.' But he enjoyed it nonetheless. It was cathartic, even reassuring. 'Thus, having been cooped up among the lice,' he wrote, 'I get the mould out of my brain and let out the malice of my fate, content to be ridden over roughshod in this fashion, if only to discover whether or not my fate is ashamed of treating me so.'

But, although Niccolò claimed he had become a true *gaglioffo* – a loutish good-for-nothing – he was unable to forget, or forsake, his former life entirely. Despite the agonies of spring and the disappointments of summer, he still had politics in his blood. He was still a literate and cultured man, with a passion for ancient history and a lively interest in applying the lessons of the past to his own day. Most of all, he was still poor. Unless he could find employment, or secure the patronage of a powerful man, his pos... would soon be wretched. 'I am wasting away,' he told Vettori, 'an... cannot carry on like this much longer without becoming contemptible in my poverty.'[57]

He turned to the pen. Returning to the *albergaccio* late at night, he would enter his study, take off his workday clothes and, as if reliving the dramas of his previous existence, 'put on the garments of court and palace'. Thus 'fitted out appropriately', he settled himself in his chair and, by the flickering light of the fire, embarked on what would prove to be his most ambitious and imaginative project to date.

20

rincely Aspirations

December 1513–August 1514)

Seated at his desk, beneath the vaulted ceiling of his study, Niccolò immersed himself in reading. As ever, his first love was for the ancient historians, especially Livy, but he also found time for Homer and Virgil, as well as for works of moral and political philosophy, such as Aristotle's *Politics*, Cicero's *De officiis* and Seneca's *Epistulae morales*.[1] This, he told Vettori, was what he had been born for. It delighted him to 'converse' with these long-dead figures, to question the motives for their actions and to nourish himself on their wisdom.[2] For up to four hours at a time, he felt completely happy. Pausing only to replace a guttering candle or to throw a log on the dying embers of the fire, he forgot his worries, his poverty – even his own mortality.

Yet it was no idle pleasure. Jotting down notes as he went, he had been gathering material for a new book. It was, admittedly, only a 'short study' (*opuscolo*) – barely more than a pamphlet – but it was unlike anything he had written before; and by the beginning of Advent, it was already nearing completion. Now known as *Il principe* (*The Prince*) – but originally entitled *De principatibus* (*On principalities*) – it was an attempt to delve as deeply as possible into the nature of princely government.[3] In twenty-six short chapters, illustrated with examples from ancient and modern history, it set out to explain 'what a principality is, of what varieties they are, how they are acquired, how they are maintained, [and] why they are lost.'[4] It was, however, unmistakably a book of advice, intended to show a prince how he could secure his rule – and, though Florence was seldom mentioned, its counsel was plainly intended for the Medici alone.

Niccolò's hope was that *Il principe* would restore him to favour. Although he was aware the Medici still viewed him with suspicion, that he was confident that, were they to read his book, they would see he had not been idle during his years in the chancellery, and that, given the chance, he could still be of service to them. Indeed, he told Vettori that 'anyone ought to be happy to be served by someone who, at others' expense, has had so much experience.'[5] Of course, he knew they would probably have some reservations – and may even be tempted to view his advice with scepticism – but his poverty was a witness to his honesty and loyalty. And, as he would go on to demonstrate, it was often those whom a prince spurned at first who ultimately proved to be the most faithful servants.[6]

*

So as not to appear too fawning – or too critical – Niccolò knew he would have to avoid addressing the Medici's situation openly. He therefore settled on a more discreet approach. Under the pretence of scholarly objectivity, he would begin by categorizing the various types of principalities – listing their characteristics, their strengths and weaknesses with as much precision as he could muster. He would then subtly steer the discussion round to whichever most closely resembled the Medici's position in Florence. Having thus introduced his subject through the back door, as it were, he could dissect the Medici's regime to his heart's content – without ever having to mention their name.

All states, Niccolò began, are either republics or principalities.[7] Having already discussed republics at length in his previous works, however, he did not propose to waste any more time on them, instead passing straight on to principalities.[8] Of these, he briefly discussed the hereditary[9] and the composite (that is, those, like the kingdom of Naples, which had been annexed to another state);[10] but what really interested him were completely new principalities. These, however, existed in two forms: those won by one's own arms and *virtù*, and those won with another's arms and the help of *fortuna*.[11]

The former certainly piqued Niccolò's imagination. As he was the first to admit, the history books were filled with tales of extraordinary men who had acquired their states through their own arms and *virtù*.[12] His own days had produced their fair share of outstanding figures, too – the most notable of which was undoubtedly Francesco Sforza, who 'with tremendous effort, and by his own great prowess, from being a private citizen, became duke of Milan.'[13] Yet, precisely because these princes possessed such exceptional prowess and received from fortune nothing beyond the opportunity to succeed, they were generally secure in their rule. Though they might encounter some objections from the people, they could use their own arms to override any opposition and institute whatever changes they desired in a state's constitution.

Far more interesting were those princes who had won their states with another's arms and with the help of *fortuna*. Although he was careful not to say so openly, this perfectly described how the Medici had come to power. They had, of course, been helped by the fragility of Soderini's regime and the support of leading *ottimati*, but they owed their return above all to the brutality of Cardona's Spanish troops and the unexpected collapse of the French army in Lombardy. After all, as even they would have admitted, they had enjoyed little popular support. Had the *popolo* not been robbed of Louis XII's support and frightened into submission by the massacre at Prato, the Medici might never have been able to force their way back into the city.

Precisely because of how they came to power, princes like the Medici were faced with particular difficulties. Though they might have acquired their states with little effort – indeed, almost by accident – they could only maintain their position with great effort. From the moment they took up the reins of power, they were the prisoners of fortune. At any moment, those upon whose arms they had depended might either abandon them or suffer a crushing defeat; while their governments, lacking strong roots, could easily be swept away in a political storm. There were, of course, a few princes who had managed to overcome such dangers. Of these, the most striking example was Cesare Borgia, who, despite 'acquiring his state through the fortune of his father', had successfully consolidated his power in the Romagna within only a short space of time.[14] But Cesare was an exception. Few, if any, could match his 'talent and prowess'. All too often, princes had no idea how to defend themselves without recourse to foreign arms, or how to gain a secure hold over their people. As such, Niccolò took it upon himself to explain how they could 'preserve what fortune [had] suddenly tossed in their laps'.

Niccolò was, of course, aware that he was not the first to write about this subject.[15] As far back as classical antiquity, learned men had been advising princes about the qualities they needed (e.g. Seneca, *De clementia*, *De ira*) and the nature of good government (e.g. Xenophon, *Cyropaedia*, Philodemus, *De bono rege secundum Homerum*). Adapted to a Christian context by the Church Fathers – especially Augustine and Ambrose – these ad hoc works of advice had later evolved into a 'complete and compact literary form, that of the "mirror of princes"';[16] and by the late thirteenth century, several hundred *specula principum* had been produced for rulers to choose from, including John of Salisbury's *Policraticus* (*c.* 1159), St Thomas Aquinas's *De regimine principum* (*c.* 1265) and Egidio Colonna's treatise of the same name (*c.* 1277–9). Naturally, these had varied in emphasis and tone, but they had all argued the prince could master fortune by embodying the life of Christian virtue.[17]

In recent years, there had been a revival of interest in *specula principum*. At first, the genre had found expression primarily in letters, such as Petrarch's lengthy epistle to Francesco 'il Vecchio' da Carrara[18] and Coluccio Saltutati's panegyric of Charles of Durazzo,[19] but, by the end of the fifteenth century, longer and more fully-developed treatises had begun to appear. Of these, the most ambitious were Bartolomeo Platina's *De vero principe* (*c.* 1478)[20] and Francesco Patrizi's *De regno et regis institutionis* (*c.* 1481–4),[21] but there were plenty of other, lesser works, such as Giuniano Maio's fawning *De maiestate* (1492)[22] and Giovanni Pontano's *De principe liber* (scr. 1465; publ. *c.* 1503).[23] Though they owed a greater stylistic debt to Cicero and Seneca than to the Church Fathers, and tended to argue more from example than from abstract principle, they too portrayed virtue as the surest weapon against the vicissitudes of Fortune, and, while they sometimes glossed this in different ways, they generally agreed that it was just an exaggerated form of those moral qualities to which all Christians should aspire – namely, prudence, fortitude, temperance, and, above all, justice.

Niccolò, however, regarded all that as hogwash. In seeking to describe the characteristics of an 'ideal' prince, he argued, contemporary humanists had confined themselves to a world of theoretical fancy, far removed from the often harsh realities of politics.[24] As such, any ruler who attempted to follow their advice would find himself woefully unprepared not only to deal with the practical problems of government, but also – and more importantly – to withstand the blows of Fortune. As Niccolò had suggested in the *Ghiribizzi* and the *Capitolo di Fortuna*, Fortune was blind to human merit. Though there were undoubtedly ways of gaining her favour, she exercised her power without any regard for virtue or vice, so that a prince who tried to 'act virtuously in every way' would almost inevitably come to grief. It was this deficiency that Niccolò meant to address. Rather than waste time expounding fine principles that would be of no value in the real world, he set out to demonstrate that, if the Medici wished to maintain their state, they would have to learn 'how *not* to be virtuous'.[25]

In explaining what he meant by this, Niccolò returned to the rather misogynistic image of Fortune as a woman, which he had previously employed in both the *Ghiribizzi* and the *Capitolo di Fortuna*.[26] Just like a coquettish young girl, he argued, Fortune was capricious with men who were either stuck in their ways or too weak willed to stand up to her. Only a man who was circumspect, who could adapt himself to her wiles and who, if necessary, was prepared to 'beat and coerce her' would receive her favour. What a prince required, therefore, was not 'virtue' in the traditional Christian sense, but *virtù* – the quality of being a *vir* (man).[27] He needed to be bold, daring and audacious; he needed to rise above the base and unworthy pursuit of riches; and, above all, he needed to govern in such a way that it would bring him glory and honour.[28]

To do this, Niccolò argued, a prince needed two things. The first was a means of defending himself against 'external aggression by foreign powers' *without* relying on another's help.[29] Now, you didn't have to be a genius to see that by far the best option was to raise an army. But what sort of troops should it comprise? Mercenaries were clearly a bad idea. Remembering how greatly Florence had been harmed by the misconduct of Paolo Vitelli during his early days in the chancellery, Niccolò described them in the most disparaging terms. Echoing the opening paragraphs of the *Provisione della ordinanza*, he opined that they are disunited, ambitious, undisciplined, [and] disloyal; [they are] brave among their friends and among the enemy, cowards; [they have] no fear of God, [they] do not keep faith with men; [they] avoid defeat, only as long as [they] avoid battle; and in peacetime you are despoiled by them, in wartime by the enemy.[30]

Indeed, if Italy's ruinous condition was to be attributed to a single cause, it was undoubtedly the 'reliance placed [by various states] for so many years on mercenary troops.' Auxiliaries were not much better. In themselves, they were sometimes useful and reliable, but 'to him who calls them in, they are almost always detrimental.'[31] If they were defeated, you were left in the lurch (as Florence had found when it had employed 10,000 Frenchmen to recapture Pisa), but if they were victorious, you immediately found yourself in their power (as the Byzantine Emperor John VI Cantacuzene had discovered when he had hired a Turkish army to fight on his behalf in a civil war). It was for these reasons, Niccolò concluded, that 'wise princes' had relied instead on troops drawn from their own people – that is to say, on a citizen militia similar to that which he had helped establish in Florence in 1506. As he knew from first-hand experience, militiamen were far from perfect, but the loyalty and valour with which they were prepared to defend their homeland offered a prince the best means of securing his state.

The second thing that a prince needed, after a citizen militia, was an understanding of how to 'conduct himself with his subjects or his friends' to avoid provoking 'internal subversion from his subjects'.[32] From the Medici's perspective, this was a particularly important concern. Though Niccolò was careful not to say so openly, Florence remained bitterly divided. Rival factions continued to eye each other mistrustfully; and, despite the brutal suppression of Boscoli's conspiracy, revolt was still in the air. If the Medici were to maintain their power, they needed to know what sort of behaviour was most likely to bind the city together – and to themselves.

Having already dismissed both the humanist authors of *specula principum* and the classical sources on which they had drawn, Niccolò saw no need to waste any time discussing either the four cardinal virtues (justice, fortitude, temperance and wisdom) or the three 'theological' virtues (faith, hope and charity). He did, however, think it useful to say something about three closely allied qualities that had come to be viewed as essential to princely government: generosity, compassion and honesty.[33] Each of these was, of course, all very well and good in an ideal world, but, giving free rein to his love of paradox, Niccolò set out to demonstrate that, in reality, a prince who wanted to preserve his state might be better advised to ignore them.[34]

Beginning with the first of the 'princely' qualities he had named, Niccolò observed that, while it would be splendid if a prince had a reputation for generosity, such a reputation would undoubtedly bring him to grief.[35] It was not hard to see why. If a prince wanted to be known for his generosity, Niccolò argued, he had to be 'ostentatiously lavish'; and in this way, he would quickly squander all his own resources. In order to maintain his standing, he would then be forced to impose burdensome taxes on his people – which would inevitably make them hate him. By contrast, if he cultivated a reputation for miserliness, he would easily earn their respect. Everyone would see that 'because of his parsimony, his own income is enough for him, [and] he can defend himself from those who make war on him, and he can embark on ventures without burdening the people.' Thus, he would show himself to be generous towards those from whom he took nothing, thereby earning the admiration, rather than the enmity, of his subjects.

It was much the same with compassion. While it was only natural for a prince 'to want to be thought merciful rather than cruel', he must take care 'not to use [his] mercifulness badly'.[36] Sometimes, Niccolò contended, one can come to harm in trying to be too compassionate. For example, if a rebellious people are allowed to believe that they can rise in rebellion without suffering any adverse consequences, it will be impossible to keep order. Florence had found this to its cost in Pistoia, in 1501–2. Rather than punish the warring factions, the Signoria had chosen to be compassionate, allowing the city to be torn apart by civil strife. It would thus be far better for a prince to acquire a reputation for cruelty, Niccolò argued. Again, Cesare Borgia provided a salutary example. Although he was thought cruel, his cruelty nevertheless 'reformed the Romagna, unified it, and reduced it to peace and obedience.'

This, however, raised an interesting question – one which Niccolò had been toying with in one form or another since writing his first official report on Pisan affairs, almost fifteen years earlier: is it better for a prince to be loved or feared? Niccolò imagined that most of us would want him to be both, but, since it would be difficult to combine the two, it would be better to be feared than loved. Underlying this was an uncompromisingly 'realistic' assessment of human nature. Men were, Niccolò claimed, 'ungrateful, changeable, liars and dissimulators, fugitives from danger, and greedy for profit; while you treat them well, they are all yours . . . but when you are in danger, they revolt.'[37] A prince who relied on their affections, therefore, built his government on sand. Julius Caesar was a case in point. As Petrarch had noted in his famous letter to Francesco 'il Vecchio' da Carrara, Caesar had done 'everything to be loved rather than feared',[38] but, as Niccolò no doubt recalled, he had ended up being brutally murdered by his former friends. Fear provided a far more solid foundation. Even fear needed careful handling, though. Perhaps recalling Seneca's critique of the tyrant's adage *'oderint dum metuant'* ('let them hate, so long as they fear'), Niccolò pointed out that, if a prince were too harsh, he would make himself hated and, in time, the people's hatred could easily come to outweigh their fear.[39] As such, he should take care to 'make himself feared in such a way that, if he is not loved, he [at least] avoids being hated'. This he could do by ensuring that his cruelty was limited by necessity. If he had to execute someone, he must be sure that he is fully justified in doing so; and he must, at all costs, avoid seizing his subjects' property unless he has good cause. For, as Niccolò had previously argued in his memorandum to the then-Cardinal Giovanni de' Medici in the autumn of 1512, 'men sooner forget the death of a father than the loss of their patrimony.'

Honesty need not trouble the prince too greatly, either. It would, of course, be nice if he were honest, Niccolò argued, but, since very few men were, it would be madness for the prince to stand by his word on principle.[40] Sometimes, he had to be ready to act not like a human being, but like an animal. The lion was an obvious creature to emulate. It was, after all, strong, courageous and famously regal. It could easily scare off wolves. But it was nevertheless unable to recognize traps, and often blundered unthinkingly into the hunter's snare. A prince should therefore emulate the fox, as well. Though it might not be any good at scaring off other predators, it was tremendously cunning – and it was this quality which the prince would have to cultivate if he was to survive in the cut-throat world of politics. He must know not only how to sniff out danger, but also how to avoid it without compromising himself. He 'cannot, and must not, honour his word when doing so puts him at a disadvantage, and when the reasons for which he made his promise have disappeared.' In short, he must know how to be a 'great liar and dissimulator'.

This, in fact, was the most important lesson a prince could learn. If he was to avoid the contempt of his people, he must *never* allow them to know that he was following Niccolò's advice. Indeed, he should take great care to appear to be exactly like the ideal princes portrayed in *specula principum* – that is, as a man of compassion, good faith, integrity, humanity and religion.[41] But this was not to say that he could do whatever he liked, under cover of being a model ruler. Niccolò recognized that, if he wanted to escape being hated, he must never be rapacious or aggressive; he must never seem indecisive, effeminate, cowardly or irresolute.[42] Provided he followed this advice, Niccolò believed, he should be able to keep the goodwill of his people; provided he had that, he could sleep easy at night, secure in the knowledge that no conspiracies would haunt him.

There was, admittedly, little that was new about the advice Niccolò had offered. Most of it he had either voiced in earlier works, or – in the case of the militia – actually put into action. But *Il principe* was much more than the sum of its parts. In bringing together the lessons he had learned during fifteen years in the chancellery and placing them at the service of a *signore*, rather than a republic, Niccolò succeeded in producing a truly original work, which broke with the long-established tradition of *specula principum*, and which offered a profoundly 'realistic' solution to the challenges then facing the Medici.

*

Niccolò had originally planned to dedicate *Il principe* to Giuliano de' Medici, but, by the time he wrote to Vettori on 10 December 1513, he had begun to have second thoughts. Having discussed the matter with Filippo Casavecchia, he had come to feel that it might be risky to send a copy to Rome. If he did, Giuliano might not even read it, or – worse – the papal secretary, Piero Ardinghelli, might take credit for the book himself. Then again, Niccolò could hardly afford *not* to present Giuliano with a copy. His situation was already desperate. He *needed* Giuliano to read it and – if possible – to employ him. But he couldn't seem to make up his mind.

Intrigued by Niccolò's brief description of *Il principe*, Vettori offered to help. 'I shall be grateful if you send it to me,' he wrote on Christmas Eve, 'and although I am not an authority, I judge it proper that I should judge your thing; so far as knowledge and judgement are lacking, affection and trust will make up for them.'[43] When he had read it, he would tell Niccolò whether he thought it should be presented to 'the Magnificent Giuliano' or not.

Niccolò was thankful for the offer. A few days later, he despatched a manuscript copy of the unfinished treatise, comprising at least the first eleven, and perhaps as many as nineteen, chapters. Vettori was impressed. On 18 January 1514, he told Niccolò, 'I have seen the chapters of your work, and I like them immeasurably.'[44] That said, given its incomplete state, he did not feel able to pass a definite opinion – least of all about whether Niccolò should present it to Giuliano. Nevertheless, it was shaping up to be a splendid piece.

Eminently reassured, Niccolò's spirits appear to have improved. Bursting with energy and excitement, he worked diligently at *Il principe* over the next few months, reworking passages here and there, and continually adding to the text in response to political developments. On learning of a proposal to decommission some of Florence's fortresses in the *contado*,[45] for example, he added a new – and unusually balanced – chapter on the utility of fortifications.[46] Perhaps prompted by the selection of a *Signoria* stacked with Medici partisans,[47] he also penned two more on the composition of the prince's staff and the need to avoid flatterers.[48] Now full of confidence, he wove into these chapters some overt self-promotion. Though he never went so far as to recommend himself by name, he made it quite clear that he was exactly the sort of person a prince should want running his affairs. '[T]he man who is entrusted with the task of government,' he wrote, with an obvious nod to *Il principe* itself, 'ought never to think of himself, but always of the prince, and should never concern himself with anything that does not pertain to the prince's affairs.'[49] Indeed, the Medici had a *duty* to employ people like him. 'A prince ought to show his regard for talent,' he noted, 'recognising able men, and honouring those who excel in their chosen profession (*arte*).'[50]

*

As *Il principe* neared completion, Niccolò found the time to try out other literary projects. At some point, most likely in the early spring, he began work on the *Decennale secondo*.[51] Picking up where the *Decennale primo* had left off, this was intended to be a poetical history of the period 1504–14.[52] Yet, while it was billed as a sequel, it was stylistically very different from its predecessor. Perhaps influenced by Niccolò's reading of the classical poets, its tone was more self-consciously 'epic'. The opening invocation was not to the intended dedicatee (which appears to have been Florence), but to Niccolò's 'Muse', whom he asked to favour him with inspiration; its scenes are populated not by small, imperfect men, but by heroes, kingdoms and empires; and its drama is a sweeping tale of tragedy, triumph and thwarted ambition. Particularly in that it looks back on ten years of almost unceasing war – in which the recapture of Pisa played a star-ring role – it even feels rather Homeric at times. But its themes were nevertheless similar to those of the *Decennale primo*, and there are notable continuities with *Il principe*, too. At its heart stands the figure of Fortune – cruel, capricious and blind to merit, but still working in harmony with God's providential plan for humanity. It was she, Niccolò claimed, who cast down his friend, Antonio Giacomini, who, despite defeating Bartolomeo d'Alviano's forces at the Battle of San Vicenzo, 'now, neglected and vilified lies | in his house, poor, old, and blind'.[53] Most crucially, it was Fortune, too, who destroyed Venice's hopes after the Battle of Agnadello. Reflecting on this unforeseen reversal, Niccolò was moved to offer a prophetic lament that would not have been out of place in either the *Decennale primo*, or, indeed, *Il principe*:

> O proud men, ever with a haughty face
> you who hold the sceptre and the crown
> and of the future you know not one truth!
>   So completely are you blinded by your present yearning
> which holds a heavy veil over your eyes,
> that you cannot see remote things.
>   From this it follows that heaven, shifting
> from this to that, changes your states
> more often than the heat and frost,
>   because if your prudence were turned
> to diagnosing the ill and [finding its] remedy,
> such power from heaven would be taken.[54]

The implied promise that Niccolò would go on to reveal how princes could learn to master Fortune – as he had done in *Il principe* – is palpable; but it was never to be fulfilled. Whether out of uncertainty about how to handle the Medici's return, or out of concern for how he would portray his own role in Florence's recent history, he broke off the narrative shortly after describing Maximilian's descent into Italy, never to resume it.

*

There was still plenty else to keep him busy. He kept up a lively correspondence with Vettori, their letters once again chatty, cheerful and amusing, full of scurrilous gossip and self-deprecatory humour. Back in January, Vettori had delighted Niccolò with tell of an unexpected love affair. Vettori had, it appears, been chided by his friends for not asking his neighbour – a widowed noblewoman who still 'played around a bit' – to dinner. After much badgering, he eventually sent one of his servants round with an invitation one afternoon, expecting her to come one night later in the week. To his surprise, however, she came over that very evening, accompanied by her fourteen-year-old son and her twenty-two-year-old daughter, Costanza. After some initial awkwardness, they passed an enjoyable evening together, and Vettori could not help noticing that Costanza 'was supremely beautiful'. By the end of dinner, he had fallen head over heels in love with her. 'I have become almost a prisoner of this Costanza,' he told Niccolò on 18 January; 'you never set eyes on a more beautiful woman, nor a more seductive one.'[55] She was 'plump rather than thin, white, with a bright complexion, a face that I do not know whether it is sharp or rounded . . . Graceful, pleasant, bantering . . . always laughing.'[56] It was foolish of him, he knew. He was already forty years old, he had a wife and he had married and marriageable daughters. But he was almost obsessed with Costanza. He was jealous if she saw anyone else, and, when they were together, he spent money like water – even though he knew that he was robbing his family in the process. He even made himself laugh at the ridiculousness of it all.

Niccolò had his own tales to tell, too. Having recovered his spirits, he had plucked up the courage to return to Florence at the beginning of February, and – while continuing to add to *Il principe* – had eagerly returned to his old ways. He divided his time between his long-term mistress, La Riccia, and Donato del Corno's shop, which appears to have doubled as a male brothel.[57] He spent so much time with them, in fact, that he was worried he was getting on their nerves. Donato called him 'Shop Pest' and La Riccia called him 'House Pest'. Each seemed to know about the other, and La Riccia, at least, was getting jealous. She had even mocked him for two-timing her, poking fun at the 'wisdom' of which he was so proud. This had left Niccolò with a problem. He wanted to keep seeing them both ('as friends', he claimed), but he didn't know how he could. Vettori's advice was, however, sanguine.[58] He didn't think La Riccia would throw Niccolò over. Indeed, he was fairly confident that she still loved him, and would not shut the door in his face. But, if she really was that angry, Niccolò shouldn't waste time trying to appease her. Instead, he should stick to a boy named Riccio – who seems to have been his regular squeeze at Donato's shop.

What Niccolò made of this is not known, but his predicament certainly doesn't seem to have stopped him indulging his passions. On 25 February, he sent Vettori a lively account of one of his most recent adventures, presented in the form of a *fabula*.[59] Whether for comic effect, or simply out of good taste, however, he hid his identity behind a false name and papered over some of the most graphic sexual details with a rather clumsy metaphor.

One night, the tale began, 'Giuliano Brancacci' (that is to say, Niccolò)[60] had gone out in the hope of catching a 'bird' – a rent boy.[61] Finding no 'birds on the lookout for him' in the Borgo Sant[i] Apostol[i], a well-known sink of vice, he walked on, taking refuge from the rain 'under the Tetto de' Pisani' at the western end of the Piazza della Signoria. There, he scoured 'every nook and cranny one by one,' until, eventually, he happened upon a likely-looking 'young thrush'. After satisfying himself that the bird's 'disposition was generous', Niccolò started kissing it, and then 'ministered to several of its hind feathers.'

This, however, was just the beginning. Setting the metaphor aside, Niccolò explained that, once he had finished his business, he had asked his companion's name. 'Michele,' the boy had replied, the nephew of Consiglio Costi. At this, Niccolò sprung a trick. Realizing that Michele could not see his face in the darkness, he introduced himself as Filippo Casavecchia, and, on the pretence that he did not have any money on him, told Michele to come to Filippo's shop the following day to collect his payment. Michele, of course, suspected nothing. The next morning, he duly trotted round to Filippo's shop and demanded his cash. Naturally, Filippo had no idea who he was and refused to pay up. But Michele – 'who was more sly than stupid' – then began 'berating him for the favours he had received, and ended up saying that if Filippo had no scruples about cheating him, he would have none about denouncing Filippo' for sodomy. This was serious stuff. Realizing what must have happened, Filippo told Michele that he had been tricked, and assured him that, if he returned the next day, everything would be sorted out. By now, Michele was thoroughly confused; but, still hopeful of receiving his money, he agreed to come back. Filippo, however, was at a loss to know what to do. He knew that, if he paid Michele a florin or two, just to keep him quiet, he would effectively be admitting to a sin he hadn't committed, and would risk being pumped for more money in future. But he also knew that, if he *didn't* pay, and denied everything, he would have to prove his innocence both to Michele and to the world. And, to do this, he'd have to accuse someone else of carrying on with the boy instead of him. If he accused the wrong person, however, he'd be in an even bigger mess than before. After much reflection, he decided that the latter course might be safer. Luckily, Filippo guessed that 'Brancacci' – that is to say, Niccolò – must be behind this, and, after enlisting the help of a friend 'Alberto Lotti' – who also happened to be one of Michele's kinsmen – hatched a plan to shame him into paying up.

Summoning Michele back to the shop, Alberto asked him whether he would recognize the voice of the man who had claimed to be Filippo if he heard him talk. When the boy said 'yes', Alberto took him off to Sant' Ilario a Colombaia, just outside the Porta Romana, where Niccolò was known to hang out. It was a fitting spot. Although the church was dedicated to Saint Hiliary of Poitiers, its name could also mean 'Saint Hilarious' – and there was no shortage of laughter to come. When Alberto and Michele arrived, they found Niccolò sitting down on a bench, 'spinning a yarn to his cronies'. Taking care to approach him from behind, Alberto managed to get Michele close enough to hear his voice. Just then,

Niccolò turned around. As soon as he saw Michele, he realized that he had been found out, and ran off, thus revealing his guilt and completely exonerating Filippo. Word of the affair soon spread, however, and, for the whole of the carnival season, people in Florence jokingly asked each other, 'Are you Brancacci or are you Casa?'

Of course, not all of this may have been true, but it made for a good story – and, for Niccolò, that was all that mattered. While he was cavorting with rent boys and prostitutes, he was happy to embellish his adventures a little here and there for the sake of raising a smile – even at his own expense. Swept along by love and laughter, he even turned his hand to writing a couple of carnival songs – something he hadn't done in a long time. No doubt inspired by the high time he and Vettori were having with their lovers, each of these took for its theme *amore*, or rather, *passione*, and each was bursting with the ribald wit which Niccolò's friends had come to appreciate so much. The first – 'De' romiti' ('The Hermits') – took its cue from the predictions of severe floods made by Fra Francesco da Montepulciano a few weeks earlier.[62] Having learned of the distress caused by these absurd prognostications, Niccolò and his friends – in the guise of randy old hermits – come down to the city from their home in the Apennines, and, taking advantage of the religious hysteria, try to persuade its womenfolk to take refuge with them in the mountains:

> The [rising] waters will be the tears of those who die for you,
> O chosen ladies,
> the earthquakes, avalanches, and their grief,
> shall be the tempests and the wars of love:
> the lightning and the thunderbolts
> shall be your eyes, which will make them die.
> Do not fear any other harm,
> for that will be which it is accustomed to be.
> Heaven wishes to save us:
> and in any case, who really sees the devil
> sees him with smaller horns and not so black.[63]

The hermits are, of course, not so naive as to believe these predictions themselves, but, if the ladies put any faith in them at all, they should not hesitate to come along with them 'to the summit of [their] high rocks'.[64] There, they will make their hermitages, and, when the rain begins to fall, they will scarcely even notice. For, as the lascivious hermits gleefully insinuate, they will be too busy making love to worry about the waters below.

The second of Niccolò's carnival songs – 'Di amanti e donne disperati' ('Lovers and ladies without hope') – was rather more subtle.[65] Taking the form of a dialogue between a group of young women and their beaux, it turned the familiar poetic trope of unrequited love into a plea for lovers not to wait before consummating their passions. The men are the first to speak. Confined to the 'deep centre of Hell', they are without hope, frightened and dirty.[66] They are, however, there by choice. When they had been in love with these ladies, they had been so tormented by pain that they had given themselves to the 'infernal powers' in order to escape their suffering.[67] Their prayers, tears and sobs had been to no avail, because their beloveds had appeared to desire only their agony. Even in Hell, such cruelty could not be found. When the ladies' turn comes, they protest that they had never meant to hurt their lovers so deeply. They had, in fact, loved the men deeply, but honour had forbidden them to voice it openly. Only someone with 'more fury than patience' could think that the lovers' injuries were their fault. Since it would be too great a sorrow to lose their suitors, however, the ladies continued to follow them,

> with music and songs and sweet words
> calming the spirits,
> so that, releasing you from the hellish path,
> to our liberty they will restore you,
> or of both you and us they will make prey.[68]

Yet it was in vain. Having found some solace in the pains of Hell, the men would neither listen nor speak to them. It was, in any case, too late. The ladies should have acted when they had the chance; there was no point in them repenting their cruelty now. It was a brilliant turning of the tables – and it had a clear 'moral' to it. In the final stanza, the ladies offer female readers (or listeners) the following advice:

> when you have some lover
> bound to your love,
> in order not to be wanderers like us,
> avoid all bashfulness;
> do not send them to the cursed Kingdom;
> because one who brings damnation on another,
> is condemned by Heaven to the same punishment.[69]

It was typical of Niccolò's bawdy, misogynistic humour. Only he could have used the poetry of unrequited love to persuade young women that Christian charity obliged them to accept their lovers' sexual advances.

*

Towards the middle of April – just as Niccolò was putting the finishing touches to *Il principe* – his thoughts turned from amorous pursuits to politics. Not for the first time, it was the actions of Ferdinand of Aragon which had caught his attention. Still resentful at being short-changed after the Battle of Novara, and fearing the kingdom of Naples would be dangerously exposed unless he controlled the north, Ferdinand had set his sights on acquiring either the duchy of Milan or a sizeable part of the Veneto for his grandson, Archduke Ferdinand of Austria.[70] To achieve this aim, he had kept an army in western Lombardy to support Maximilian's struggle against the Venetians. But he had also taken the rather more surprising step of opening negotiations for a marriage alliance between his grandson, Ferdinand, and Renée, the youngest daughter of Louis XII, in the hope of securing French support for an attack on Milan. This had thrown the papacy into a panic. Fearing Spanish domination every bit as much as a French presence in Italy, Leo X had scrambled to reconcile France and England, in the belief that, if Louis' domestic position were strengthened, he might be less willing to strike a deal with Ferdinand over Lombardy. Niccolò, however, did not share the pope's alarm. As he admitted to Vettori on 16 April, he could not help feeling that Ferdinand's strategy was self-defeating.[71] While the king had correctly recognized that he would never be able to expel the Swiss from Milan without French help, he had failed to realize that Louis would never agree to enter Italy unless it was to take

Milan for himself. What was more, Niccolò argued, it was highly doubtful that Louis would consent to hand the duchy over to Ferdinand of Austria. Nor, indeed, would he allow it to be given to anyone else, least of all the pope or the emperor. Even if Ferdinand of Aragon somehow managed to seize the duchy of Milan on his own, however, he would still be left with the same problem. To hold it, Niccolò estimated that he would need at least 20,000 infantry and 6,000 cavalry; and since neither he nor the emperor could muster so many men, he would have to call on the French for help. But it was hard to believe that Louis would consent to defend a duchy which had been won for someone other than himself. Either way, Niccolò felt that Ferdinand was on a hiding to nothing. He was, however, keen to have Vettori's thoughts on the matter, especially as the ambassador was much better informed about what was going on than him.

It was a month before Vettori replied.[72] Swamped with work and still head-over-heels in love with Costanza, he had not had the time to write sooner.[73] He was, however, broadly in sympathy with Niccolò's assessment of the situation. With his usual prolixity, he agreed that the proposed marriage was not in Ferdinand of Aragon's interest. He queried whether it was in Louis XII's interest, either – but, on this score, he was reluctant to commit himself, at least for the time being.

As it turned out, the marriage negotiations quickly petered out – due largely to diplomatic representations made by the pope – and a new match between Louis XII and Henry VIII's sister, Mary Tudor, was soon in the offing.[74] It is impossible to know for sure whether Niccolò and Vettori discussed this, as a number of their letters appear to have been lost. It is, however, easy to picture them carefully weighing each party's prospects and trying to second guess the effect the new configuration would have on the fragile balance of power in Italy.

*

By the middle of May, *Il principe* was at last finished – at least in its earliest form.[75] Buoyed by Vettori's praise of the first few chapters, and further encouraged by their recent discussion of political affairs, Niccolò had made up his mind not only to dedicate the work to Giuliano de' Medici, but also to present it to him in person. Towards the end of the month, he began making arrangements to visit Vettori in Rome, and, with his friend's help, to secure an audience with 'the Magnificent Giuliano'. From these heady days, no letters have survived, but his excitement can readily be imagined. Confident that *Il principe* would be warmly received, he must have been looking forward to being restored to favour – and perhaps even to being given a job.

But it was not to be. At some point in early June, he received a letter from Vettori telling him not to come. Although the text has since been lost, it evidently warned Niccolò that he was still a persona non grata, and that neither his presence, nor his book, would be welcome. Niccolò was devastated. Taking up his pen, he wrote a brief, but emotionally-charged note to Vettori which shows him plunging headlong into depression.[76] Seeing that there was no one who remembered his years of service to the Florentine Republic, or who believed he was good for anything, he resolved to stay where he was, among the 'lice' in Sant'Andrea in Percussina. But he knew that even this was unsustainable. '[I]f God does not show me a more favourable face,' he wrote, in despair, 'I shall soon be forced to leave home and place myself as a tutor or secretary to a governor, if I cannot do otherwise, or to stick myself in some deserted spot to teach reading to children, and leave my family here to count me dead[.]'[77] Marietta and the children would be better off without him, he thought.

Vettori sympathized with Niccolò's plight. On 27 July, he promised to do whatever he could to help.[78] But both men knew there was no point in him even trying. Niccolò's situation was hopeless. Regretting ever having wasted his time on *Il principe*, he gave himself over to sorrow and self-pity. For almost two months, he wrote not a single line – either to Vettori, or to anyone else.

*

Then heavily pregnant, Marietta no doubt tried to console him. But her loving kindness was evidently not to his taste. Perhaps her tenderness made his sense of guilt and failure more acute; or perhaps the rejection had simply made him selfish and ungrateful. Turning his back on family life, he sought solace in the arms of others. More likely than not, he took himself off to Florence to see La Riccia, or to spend a night with one of the boys at Donato del Corno's shop whenever he could; but it was in Sant'Andrea in Percussina that he eventually found the relief he needed. On 3 August, he confessed to having fallen in love with a woman named 'La Tafani', who was most probably the widowed sister of Niccolò Tafani.[79] She was, by all accounts, a beauty, and his affection for her no mere passing fancy. As he told Vettori, she was 'so gracious, so refined, so noble – both in nature and in circumstance – that never could my praise or my love for her be as much as she deserves'.[80] When he was with her, nothing else seemed to matter. '[A]lthough I am approaching my fiftieth year,' he claimed, with a touch of exaggeration, 'neither does the heat of the sun distress me, nor do rough roads wear me out, nor do the dark hours of the night terrify me. Everything seems easy to me: I adapt to her every whim, even to those that seem different and contrary to what my own ought to be . . .' Most importantly, she helped him forget the bitter taste of disappointment. 'I have laid aside all memory of my sorrows,' he confided to Vettori. 'I have renounced . . . thoughts about matters great and grave. No longer do I delight in reading about the deeds of the ancients, or in discussing those of the ancients', as he had done while writing *Il principe*. And now that all that was behind him, everything had been 'transformed into tender thoughts.' It was like living in a beautiful dream, and he begged Vettori not to wake him.

21

The Garden of Delights

(August 1514–March 1519)

The autumn passed, quite unhurriedly. The sun – still hot, but no longer fierce – would have spread a golden languor over Sant'Andrea in Percussina. Between the hours of terce and none, its single street would have been all but deserted, save for the occasional cart, rumbling towards Florence. The mills turned slowly, if at all; the kilns stood idle; even the inn – usually thronged with *gaglioffi* – would have been half-empty. In the fields nearby, the vines grew heavy and the corn bowed its head in sleep. No breeze disturbed the cypress trees; no hunters stirred the thrushes. Only the sound of gently running streams would have broken the stillness.

Lulled into an agreeable torpor, Niccolò put the past behind him. Ignoring Marietta's reproaches, he continued to spend his days in La Tafani's willing embrace. Enchanted by her beauty and bewitched by her pleasures, he succeeded in pushing all thought of politics from his mind. He barely wrote. He scarcely even looked at a book. For a time, he was almost content.

Yet, no sooner had the harvest been gathered in than sorrow returned to haunt him once again. Perhaps the crops were poorer than he had hoped; perhaps his tenants had not been able to pay their rents; or perhaps it was simply that La Tafani's affections had begun to cool.[1] Whatever the case, the misery of his condition gnawed at him. As the nights drew in and the north wind began to blow, he brooded darkly on the position he had lost and the forgiveness he had been denied. It galled him that, while the Medici feasted on Florence's prosperity, they could not spare him so much as the crumbs from the table. By the time winter came, he could bear it no longer. On 4 December, he sent Vettori a tear-stained note, bemoaning his fate.

'[I]f you love me now as once you did,' he wrote bitterly, 'you will perceive – not without indignation – how sordid and ignominious my life is.'[2]

By a happy coincidence, Vettori had sent him a letter from Rome only the day before.[3] Then making its way across country in a courier's saddlebag, this would rekindle not only his interest in politics, but also his hopes for rehabilitation. As so often in the past, Vettori wanted Niccolò's help with a thorny diplomatic problem. Given that Louis XII was determined to recover the duchy of Milan, Vettori asked, what should the pope do to 'keep the Church in the same spiritual and temporal dignity that he found it in'?[4] Should he join an alliance with the emperor, the king of Spain and the Swiss against the king of France; should he ally with Louis XII against the others; or should he remain neutral? It would be a difficult task, but Vettori had no doubt that Niccolò was up to the challenge: 'although two years have passed since you left the workshop,' he noted, with an affectionate smile, 'I don't believe you have forgotten [your] craft.'[5] Almost casually, he suggested that Niccolò frame his reply as if it was going to be read by the pope. This was, of course, just the sort of playful device they had used to give focus to their discussions in the past. But, this time, it was nothing of the kind. What Vettori was not telling Niccolò was that he was, in fact, writing at the request of Cardinal Giulio de' Medici, who would almost *certainly* share Niccolò's advice with the pontiff.

Niccolò did not need to be asked twice. Within a matter of days, he had produced a long and thoughtful response.[6] He felt that, despite the Medici's debt to Ferdinand of Aragon, an alliance with France's enemies would probably not be in the pope's best interests. Their chances were slim at best. Compared to Louis XII, the emperor, the king of Spain and the Swiss could muster only a paltry number of troops. Even with Leo's support, they would be unlikely to win; and, if they lost, a vengeful Louis would surely waste no time in convening a Church Council to censure – or possibly even depose – the defeated pontiff. If, by some miracle, they *did* manage to beat the French, however, it would spell ruin, both for the Church and for Italy. While the Swiss would probably let Leo keep his territory, they would subject his prelates to untold abuses, and, as soon as they took either Ferrara or Lucca under their protection – as they surely would – it would be 'all over for Italy's freedom'.[7] Far better, Niccolò argued, that the pope ally with France. With his support,

Louis' victory would be assured. While the French advanced on Lombardy from the west, he could use his fleet to move a large army to Tuscany and launch a coordinated attack with the Venetians from the south-east. Forced to fight on two fronts, the Swiss and the Spanish could not possibly hold out for long – especially if the people of Milan rose in rebellion at the same time. Once the duchy was taken, Louis – whose honesty was unimpeachable – would no doubt stand by whatever terms he had agreed. Niccolò believed that he would refrain from taxing the Church, and would be at pains to keep on good terms with the pope to guard against any future danger. Since neutrality was out of the question, Niccolò thus had no hesitation in recommending that Leo side with France.

Vettori could not fail to be impressed. He was, however, wary of raising Niccolò's hopes too high. Although he, like many Florentines, may have sympathized with his friend's advice, he was aware that opinion in Rome was already turning against a French alliance. The previous month, it had been revealed that the pope had purchased Modena from the emperor, and this, together with Lorenzo's attempts to secure a Spanish bride for himself, was construed as the mark of growing antipathy towards Louis XII's ambitions.[8] Before showing Niccolò's letter to Cardinal Giulio, therefore, Vettori thought it wise to remind Niccolò of how fickle fate could be. He was, as ever, the model of tact. Over the past few days, he wrote on 15 December, he had been reading Pontano's *De fortuna*, which had been published by Sigismund Mayr some two years earlier.[9] In this book, Pontano had shown that 'neither talent, nor foresight, nor fortitude, nor the other virtues avail at all when Fortune is absent.' Proof of this could be seen every day in Rome, Vettori claimed. The low-born, the talentless and the unlettered occupied 'positions of the highest authority', while the noble and the learned seldom, if ever, received the recognition they deserved.[10] It was painful, to be sure, but it had to be accepted – especially by Niccolò. Though he had already suffered greatly, Vettori intimated, he should not take it too badly if his efforts were not rewarded on this occasion. It would be no reflection on his ability, and he could take some comfort from the knowledge that, sooner or later, God would bring an end to his hardship.

Niccolò already suspected that he might have said the wrong thing. On 20 December, he sent Vettori another letter, examining the prospects for neutrality at greater length.[11] His conclusion was, however, the same. Although he knew that many people were urging the pope to steer a middle course, he could not bring himself to look favourably on it. He could not recall any occasion in the past when neutrality had been a good thing; indeed, 'it has always been an extremely destructive policy because it is certain to lose.'[12] The reason was simple. When you tried to adopt a neutral stance between two belligerents, Niccolò explained, rehashing an argument he had used in *Il principe*, you were asking to be hated and despised.[13] One of them will always believe that, 'as a result either of the services he has rendered or of some other long-standing alliance you have with [him], you are obliged to follow his fortune; [and] if you do not side with him, he conceives a hatred for you.'[14] Meanwhile, the other belligerent 'despises you because he views you as timid and uncertain and you are immediately taken to be an ineffective ally and an enemy not to be feared; consequently, whoever wins has no scruples about attacking you.'[15] This being so, Niccolò reiterated his belief that the pope should side with France.

Moments after writing this, Niccolò received Vettori's letter of 15 December. As he read it, his heart sank. He could see what Vettori was trying to tell him, and bitterly regretted compounding the error of his first letter with the second. Scribbling Vettori a hasty note, he admitted that Pontano had been right: those whom Fortune wished to torment, she harassed with obstacles, or tempted with opportunities – or, in his own case, both at the same time.[16] Had she willed that the Medici might once have employed him – 'whether for affairs in Florence or abroad . . . for their private concerns, or their public ones' – he would have been content, but she clearly had other things in mind for him. He had not given up hope just yet, though. Bleak as things seemed, he told himself, there was still a faint chance they might change for the better.

On 30 December, Vettori wrote with good news.[17] Despite the anti-French feeling in Rome, Niccolò's advice had been well received. 'Both your letters . . . have been seen by the pope and Cardinals Bibbiena and de' Medici,' Vettori explained, 'and all were astonished at their wit and praised their judgement.' They had not, admittedly, made any offer of employment, but still, 'being in the good opinion of great men' would doubtless serve Niccolò well in future.

*

Niccolò did not have to wait long before putting this to the test. On
1 January 1515, Louis XII died after a prolonged attack of gout, and
was succeeded by his cousin, Francis I.[18] Though only twenty years
old, Francis quickly proved that he was every bit as ambitious for the
recovery of Milan as his predecessor. After entering into an alliance
with Charles of Habsburg, he announced his intention of mounting
an expedition to Lombardy.[19] He was, of course, opposed by Maximilian,
Ferdinand of Aragon and the Swiss. But the pope was still trying to
play both sides. While publicly expressing his support for the anti-
French league, he secretly opened negotiations with Francis, offering
to change his allegiance in return for recognition of papal sovereignty
over Parma, Reggio, Modena and Piacenza. Having by now returned
to Florence, Niccolò had heard that Leo was planning to entrust these
cities to Giuliano, and that, in turn, Giuliano had promised to make
Paolo Vettori one of his governors.[20]

Niccolò could hardly have wished for a better opportunity. Without
wasting a moment, he set about offering Paolo advice about how
Giuliano should rule his new dominions – evidently in the hope that
one of them would reward him with a position in the new Medici
administration.[21] Much as in *Il principe*, Niccolò argued that Giuliano's
principal concern should be for the unity of his cities. As long as
each retained its own sense of civic identity and its own organs of
government, Niccolò observed, Giuliano would be unable to count
on his subjects' loyalty; but, if he were to unify them and train them
'to think of themselves as a single body', his authority would be
unquestioned. This he could accomplish in one of two ways: either
he could live there in person, or he could appoint one of his lieutenants to govern them all on his behalf. The latter had been Cesare
Borgia's preferred option. After conquering the Romagna, Niccolò
recalled, he had appointed Ramiro de Lorqua as his governor-general,
a decision which 'united those peoples and made them afraid of his
authority, fond of his power, and trusting in it'. Omitting to mention
either Ramiro's corruption or the brutal death he met at Cesare's
hands, Niccolò added that 'all the love they felt for [Cesare] resulted
from this decision.'[22] Paolo Vettori would, of course, be the obvious
choice for such a role. Were he to be chosen, Niccolò observed, he
would not only bring honour to Giuliano, but would also see his
fame spread throughout Italy. Naturally, Paolo was delighted.

For a week or two, Niccolò seems to have believed that his

political rehabilitation was at hand. Although Giuliano does not appear to have given him any assurances, rumours soon spread that he was to be taken into the Medici's service – fuelled, it seems, by Paolo Vettori. Niccolò could hardly contain his excitement. His letters, long overshadowed by self-pity, abounded once again with bawdy jokes and clever puns. Inspired by tales of Francesco Vettori's amorous adventures, he even wrote a poem describing his own (unrequited?) love for La Tafani in terms borrowed from Ovid and Petrarch:

> The youthful archer [i.e. Cupid] many times has tried,
> To wound me in the breast with his arrows;
> He takes his pleasure thus – spite for all
> And harm to everyone is his delight.
>
> Though no diamond exists that might withstand
> His arrowheads piercing and keen,
> Yet now they've struck an object so strong
> It took little account of their power.
>
> So, full of rage and anger, in order
> To demonstrate his consummate skill,
> He made a change of quiver, bow, and shaft;
>
> With such force he let one fly,
> That I feel its painful wound still; thus I
> Confess and acknowledge his power.[23]

But, just as success seemed to be within Niccolò's grasp, it was cruelly snatched away. On 14 February, the papal secretary, Piero Ardinghelli, warned Giuliano against employing him:

> Yesterday, Cardinal [Giulio] de' Medici questioned me very closely about whether I knew if Your Excellency had taken Niccolò Machiavelli into your service; since I answered that I had no knowledge of it or belief in it, His Most Reverend Lordship said precisely these words to me: 'I do not believe it either; since there is no report from Florence about it, I would remind him that it is neither to his advantage nor ours. This must be something fabricated by Paolo Vettori . . . write him that, for my part I counsel him not to get

involved with Niccolò; I do not say this in order to instruct him about what he ought to do, but because I am prompted out of love from him.[24]

Niccolò's disappointment can well be imagined. But he did not despair. If Giuliano and the pope would not take him on, their young kinsman Lorenzo might still be willing to give him a chance. Since taking charge of Florentine affairs in late 1513, Lorenzo had shown a growing tendency to act independently of his relatives in Rome. Having failed to secure a Spanish bride, he had shown a marked preference for an alliance with France – partly in recognition that this was what many of the Florentines were also hankering after. Just recently, he had also contrived to have himself appointed captain-general of the Florentine militia. Seeing that private citizens were technically forbidden from serving in such a role, this had required some ingenuity.[25] After persuading the Seventy to authorize the *Otto di Pratica* – which had replaced the *Dieci* – to hire an additional 500 men-at-arms, he had then strong-armed the *Otto* into employing him as their captain. It had then been a simple matter to have his command enlarged to cover the whole militia. His appointment had, admittedly, aroused a good deal of opposition. Many feared that Lorenzo was planning to use the militia to set himself up as a tyrant. But, for Niccolò, it was a golden opportunity. Since the legislation re-establishing the militia had been modelled after the bill he had drafted almost a decade before, it was only natural that he should now be invited to advise Lorenzo on how to organize his troops. He threw himself into the task with gusto. By the beginning of July, he had produced a briefing note, now known as the *Ghiribizzi d'ordinanza*.[26] This was every bit as thorough and detailed as his earlier writings on the militia. Though it has survived only in part, the surviving fragments explain exactly how many men would be needed for various purposes, how they should be divided into battalions, and where they should be concentrated. What Lorenzo made of it cannot be known with any certainty, but it seems likely that his response was encouraging, at the very least.[27]

*

Before Niccolò could capitalize on this new-found favour, however, Francis I launched his long-awaited invasion of Lombardy. Travelling by the treacherous Col de Montgenèvre, he caught a Milanese army under Prospero Colonna unaware at Villafranca, 15 kilometres from Saluzzo.[28] In the ensuing rout, Colonna was taken prisoner and most of his cavalry captured. Horrified, the Swiss fell back on Milan. Francis, meanwhile, continued to advance. After a short siege, Novara was captured and, a few days later, a French detachment was sent along the banks of the Ticino to encircle Milan from the south.

Having been denied the territories he had demanded, Leo X had joined the anti-French league in July; and now that Francis' troops were looming dangerously close, he immediately sent the papal army north to defend Piacenza against a possible attack.[29] The Florentine militia was ordered to follow, and Lorenzo naturally expected to be at its head. But Leo gave him strict instructions to remain in Tuscany – fearing that, if he were allowed to join his troops, he might be tempted to turn traitor. Only a few weeks earlier, Lorenzo had sent a message to Francis, assuring the French king of his loyalty and *servitù*. Suspecting that Lorenzo might be planning to negotiate a separate peace with France, Leo had forbidden his ambassadors to leave Florence.[30] Now that the war had begun, the pope did not want to take any chances. Lorenzo was, of course, furious. In retaliation, Brea refused to allow Giuliano – who had been appointed captain-general of the Church – to use Florentine troops for the defence of Parma and Piacenza. When Giuliano suddenly fell ill, the dispute reached a head. Although Lorenzo was the obvious candidate to replace him, the pope made it clear that he wanted to send Cardinal Giulio instead. Not until the beginning of August was Leo finally persuaded to appoint Lorenzo commander of the papal army.[31] Even then, however, he had serious misgivings.

By the time Lorenzo reached Piacenza, the papal forces had been joined by a Spanish army under Cardona.[32] This greatly strengthened his hand, but, not long afterwards, a Venetian army under Florence's old bête noire, Bartolomeo d'Alviano, arrived to rendezvous with the French, and – in preparation for a combined attack on Piacenza – took up position at Lodi, just fifteen kilometres away from Francis' camp at Marignano. Even with Cardona's help, Lorenzo knew he would stand little chance against such a force. But, before the two armies could link up, the Swiss intervened. As Francis was trying on a new suit of armour on the morning of 13 September, a scout ran into his tent with news that they were marching towards

Marignano. Within a matter of hours, they would be upon him. Francis was horrified. Snatching up his sword, he immediately gave orders for his troops to be made ready.

The Swiss presented a formidable sight. Though they were outnumbered, poorly clothed and in some cases barefoot, their self-confidence struck fear into the hearts of the French. They did not seem to care that they had little in the way of artillery and almost no horsemen. Lowering their halberds, they charged straight at Francis' vanguard. A fierce struggle ensued. Surprised by the force of the assault, and finding their guns of little use against so rapid an advance, the French started to fall back. Only a timely cavalry charge by the dashing twenty-six-year-old duc de Bourbon stopped it turning into a rout.

The fighting continued until nightfall. Exhausted, the opposing forces made their beds on the field, amid the dead and wounded. At dawn, the sound of trumpets called them to arms once more. The Swiss again seized the initiative, hurling themselves at the French lines, seemingly oblivious to the cannonballs falling in their midst. Finding it impossible to resist the ferocity of this ragtag army, Francis' men began to lose faith. Even the king was unsure how much of this he could take. But, just as the battle seemed lost, Francis' Venetian allies suddenly appeared on the field. Throwing themselves into the fray, they tipped the balance in France's favour. Overwhelmed, the Swiss took flight.

Francis had won a great victory – albeit by the skin of his teeth. After riding into Milan in triumph, a few weeks later, he had a medal struck with the legend *Vici ab uno Caesare victos* ('I have vanquished those defeated by Caesar alone').[33] With the Spanish and papal armies now in retreat, it seemed as if he might even sweep southwards towards Tuscany and oust the Medici from Florence.[34] But Francis, who had now accomplished his primary objective, had no wish to overstretch himself. In October, he offered the pope terms. In return for Parma, Piacenza and recognition of his rule over the duchy of Milan, Francis would take the Papal States, Florence and the Medici under his protection. Leo was enough of a realist not to quibble. If Italy had to be dominated by someone, he reasoned, better it was Francis than Ferdinand or Maximilian. As Niccolò had astutely pointed out in December, he could at least count on Francis not to harass the Church too severely. Signalling his acceptance of Francis' offer, he agreed to meet the king in Bologna shortly before Christmas.

On his way northwards, Leo stopped off at Florence for a brief visit, entering the city in truly magnificent style.[35] Grand triumphal arches had been erected along his route, complete with allegorical depictions of the pope's supposed virtues; specially composed pieces of music were played; and humanist orators delivered fine speeches in his honour. As a piece of pageantry, it was unequalled in Florence's history. But it was also hollow. It belied both the devastating blow that had been dealt to Leo's ambitions at Marignano and the erosion of his position in Florence. Had the pope troubled to look past the pomp and circumstance on his way through the city, he would have seen anti-Medicean graffiti on every wall and heard shouts of derision from the many who were tired of financing ill-fated military adventures.

Of all the Medici, only Lorenzo came out of the conflict with his standing enhanced. Having taken care to assure Francis of his loyalty, and having played almost no role in the actual prosecution of the war, he now tasted the fruits of royal favour. When he went to pay his respects to Francis at Pavia, 'he was honoured and feted',[36] and, at the many celebrations that were later held in Milan, he succeeded in setting himself up as an unofficial intermediary between the king and the pope. Tactfully, he asked for nothing for himself – not even a pension – but, by flattery and persuasion, convinced the king to acquiesce both in the reconsolidation of Medici power in the Papal States, and, more surprisingly, in the pope's plan to oust Francesco Maria della Rovere from Urbino and invest him – that is, Lorenzo – with the duchy instead.

*

Niccolò was no doubt hoping to share in Lorenzo's good fortune. In the weeks after the Battle of Marignano, he waited patiently in Florence for some token of appreciation, some mark of friendship. But nothing came. He was, at first, bitter. On 19 November, he complained to Giovanni Vernacci that Fortune had left him 'nothing but his family and friends'.[37] But he soon took heart. Lorenzo was, after all, weighed down by affairs of state just then; he could hardly be blamed if he had more important things to think about than the fallen second chancellor. All Niccolò needed to do was remind Lorenzo of how valuable his advice had been in the past – and how useful he could be in future.

Thankfully, Niccolò had just the thing. In early January 1516, he rededicated *Il principe* to Lorenzo. Although the bulk of the text was unchanged, he may already have added an extra chapter during the Marignano campaign and, in the hope of recommending himself more clearly, he now appended an elegant prefatory letter, as well. Richly embroidered with flattering blandishments, this was a masterpiece of supplicatory prose that bears quoting at length:

> I am anxious to offer myself to Your Magnificence with some token of my devotion to you, and I have not found among my belongings as dear to me or that I value as much as my understanding of the deeds of great men, won by me from a long acquaintance with contemporary affairs and a continuous study of the ancient world; these matters I have very diligently analysed and pondered for a long time, and now, having summarized them in a little book, I am sending them to Your Magnificence . . . I have not embellished or crammed this book with rounded periods or big, impressive words, or with any blandishment or superfluous decoration of the kind which many are in the habit of using to describe or adorn what they have produced; for my ambition has been either that nothing should distinguish my book, or that it should find favour solely through the variety of its contents and the seriousness of its subject matter. Nor I hope will it be considered presumptuous for a man of low and humble status to dare discuss . . . how princes should rule, because, just as men who are sketching the landscape put themselves down in the plain to study the nature of the mountains and the highlands, and to study the low-lying land they put themselves high on the mountains, so, to comprehend fully the nature of the people, one must be a prince, and to comprehend fully the nature of princes, one must be an ordinary citizen.
>
> So, Your Magnificence, take this little gift in the spirit in which I send it; and if you read and consider it diligently, you will discover in it my urgent wish that you reach the eminence that fortune and your other qualities promise you. And if, from your lofty peak, Your Magnificence will sometimes glance down to these low-lying regions, you will realise the extent to which, undeservedly, I have to endure the great and unremitting malice of fortune.[38]

Confident that this would do the trick, Niccolò settled down to wait for an opportune moment to make a gift of his book. Writing to Vernacci on 15 February, he again bemoaned how useless he had become to his family and friends; but, in a telling aside, he added, 'I bide my time so that I may be ready to seize good Fortune should she come . . .'[39]

But Niccolò's hopes were dashed – this time for good. Writing some decades later, the historian Riccardo Riccardi reported that, when Niccolò went to present Lorenzo with a copy of *Il principe*, he had the misfortune to arrive at the Palazzo Medici just as someone else was giving the young *signore* a pair of dogs.[40] A keen huntsman, Lorenzo was so captivated by the hounds that he scarcely even glanced at Niccolò's book. The humiliation was too much for Niccolò to bear. Storming out in a fury, he swore never to have anything to do with the Medici again. They could go hang, for all he cared. As he told his friends, later that evening, he wasn't the sort to foment rebellion, but he wouldn't be surprised if, having rejected his advice, the Medici found themselves engulfed by conspiracies. As Riccardi noted, it was almost as if he wanted *Il principe* to be his revenge.

There were many in Florence who shared Niccolò's sense of alarm, if not his sense of disappointment. Among them was Francesco Guicciardini. He, too, was troubled by Medici's apparent reluctance to strengthen their position in Florence. In his *Del modo di assicurare lo stato ai Medici*, he reproved Lorenzo, in particular, for holding the city in contempt, for failing to appease the *popolo* and, most of all, for refusing to trust loyal bureaucrats like Niccolò.[41] Although the remedies Guicciardini suggested were far removed from the advice Niccolò had offered in *Il principe*, he, too, seems to have believed that, unless Lorenzo changed his ways, the Medici might find themselves in jeopardy.

To Niccolò's dismay, however, these dire predictions were wide of the mark. Over the months that followed, Lorenzo went from strength to strength. In March, Leo X formally deprived Francesco Maria della Rovere of his possessions in the Papal States, and preparations for a military campaign were soon underway. Helped by Maximilian's invasion of Northern Italy later that month, the Medici's forces advanced swiftly; and by early June, Lorenzo was master of Urbino. On 18 August, he was solemnly invested with the title of duke. According to Paolo Giovio, it was rumoured that he also wanted to conquer Lucca and Siena, so that his territories would reach from the Adriatic to the Mediterranean;[42] while the German scholar and adventurer, Ulrich von Hutten, feared that he might even try to have himself crowned king of Tuscany.[43]

Lavish *ferie* were held to celebrate Lorenzo's triumph, but, like many Florentines, Niccolò probably stayed away.[44] Retreating to Sant'Andrea in Percussina, he was consumed by bitterness and despair. He had put all his hopes in Lorenzo, but all he had now were shattered dreams. Even he could see that his political career was finally over. He hardly knew what to do with himself. Wandering listlessly about the countryside, without direction or purpose, he was a man adrift. Usually fastidious about his appearance, he stopped caring how he looked. He scarcely ever read, and, when letters came, he left them unanswered, often for weeks at a time. As he later admitted to Giovanni Vernacci, he sometimes went a month without thinking of himself – let alone about others.[45]

Seeing his anguish, Niccolò's friends tried to lift his spirits by finding things for him to do. In October, Paolo Vettori – who had recently been appointed commander of the papal galleys – asked him to undertake a mission to Livorno. Behind it lay a matter of the highest importance. Some months earlier, Egypt had fallen to the Ottoman Empire, and the sighting of Turkish ships between Corsica and Sardinia had raised fears of Muslim expansion in the Western Mediterranean.[46] While Leo X rallied support for a new crusade against the Ottomans, it fell to Vettori to ready the fleet. In this great drama, Niccolò's role was, admittedly, only small. Judging by the one letter that has survived, he was asked to do nothing more than prepare for Vettori's arrival and to enquire whether there had been any further sightings of Ottoman ships in the Tyrrhenian Sea.[47] But Vettori probably hoped that it would make Niccolò feel useful again – and perhaps even remind him a little of his former life.

No doubt Niccolò appreciated the gesture. But it does not seem to have helped. Now that he had given up hope of ever returning to the chancellery, he no longer wanted to waste his time chasing ghosts of the past. Turning his back on the Medici's increasingly mistrustful court, he sought new outlets for his restless spirit – far removed from the thankless world of politics.

*

It was in the Orti Oricellari that Niccolò found what he was looking for. Tucked away behind the Palazzo Rucellai, halfway between the church of Santa Maria Novella and the Porta al Prato, this secluded little garden, surrounded by high walls, was an oasis of calm amid a world of troubles.[48] Shielded from the sun by countless trees, it was pleasantly cool even on the hottest of days. Rare plants had been imported from far-off lands so that 'all the species mentioned in classical literature' would be represented, and busts of ancient heroes – many of them recovered from excavations in Rome – lined the gravelled paths.[49] Peace and tranquillity reigned. Besides the murmuring of fountains and the rustling of leaves in the breeze, scarcely a sound could be heard.

For those seeking repose, it was a paradise. As Pietro Crinito recalled, there, seated 'beneath the ancient ilex, free from jealous striving,' a man could immerse himself 'in the sacred gift of the poets,' or devote his days to 'leisurely learning, unhindered by cares'.[50] But it was more than just a bucolic retreat. Since 1514, it had also played host to an informal conversation group that had gathered around the young and aristocratic Cosimo Rucellai.[51] Having grown out of a similar *cenacolo* hosted by Cosimo's father, Bernardo, almost a decade earlier, this had become one of the focal points of Florentine cultural life, and a haven for those of a political disposition. Its membership was diverse.[52] Far from being frequented simply by opponents of the Medici regime, as has sometimes been suggested, it welcomed men of all persuasions. Ardent republicans rubbed shoulders with friends – and even relatives – of the Medici, without the least difficulty, and their interests reflected the range of their social backgrounds. Besides the Neo-Platonic philosopher Francesco Cattani da Diacceto and his kinsmen Jacopo and Francesco ('Nero'), there were the poet Luigi Alamanni, the would-be historian Zanobi Buondelmonti, the translator and moralist Antonio Brucioli, the *littérateur* Giovanbattista Gelli, the philologist Giangiorgio Trissino, the aristocratic sophisticate Francesco Guidetti, and the Greek scholar Giovanni Lascaris.[53]

Exactly when Niccolò joined the Orti Oricellari group is unclear. Although it is possible that he began taking part in their gatherings as early as 1514, it was only after his mission to Livorno that his attendance became regular. How he became a member is equally uncertain. Other than Nero da Diacceto – whom he knew through Filippo Casavecchia[54] – he did not mention any of the Orti Oricellari's habitués in his letters until the autumn of 1516. This is not, of course, to say that he was a complete stranger to them – especially to some of the older members. He had probably bumped into Lascaris once or twice during his time at the *Studio*, many years before, and it is likely that he gained at least a nodding acquaintance with Francesco Cattani da Diacceto during the latter's term as a magistrate in 1498 and 1510.[55] But they could hardly be described as friends, and many of the others were too young to have entered his ambit before mid-1516 at the very earliest. Yet, adversity often makes for unlikely friendships, and once Niccolò had been welcomed into the fold, differences of age and background were quickly forgotten.

Stretched out on the grass in the autumn sun, Niccolò and his friends would lose themselves in ardent, humorous discussions of classical history or philosophy, or listen, enraptured, as one of their number recited his latest poems. Sometimes, they would even arrange for one of their plays to be performed. The effect on Niccolò was dramatic. Shaking off his sorrow, he found in that heady atmosphere of scholarly sophistication and youthful exuberance not only a new sense of literary purpose, but also a long-sought opportunity for catharsis.

*

Though Niccolò may have been a little befuddled by some of his companions' more esoteric philosophical concerns, he was intrigued by what they had to say about fate and change, humanity and 'virtue'. These were, of course, topics with which he had grappled in the past, but now he seemed to see them through new eyes – and recognized in them a means of coming to terms with the frustrations of recent years.

Taking up his pen for the first time in many months, Niccolò began work on a long and ambitious poem called *L'asino* ('The Ass').[56] Inspired by Lucius Apuleius's *Metamorphoses*, this unfinished epic, written in terza rima, wove these themes into a gloriously vulgar mythological romp. After a brief prologue, the anonymous narrator relates how, on finding himself unexpectedly stranded on a mysterious isle, he had been rescued by one of Circe's handmaidens and whisked off to her mistress's enchanted domain. After passing a night of passion with the nameless girl, he is then introduced to the animals into which Circe had transformed the men who had chanced upon her realm in the past. There was a cat, which, 'through too much patience', had lost her prey;

> . . . a dragon, deeply troubled,
> turning himself over, without ever resting,
> now onto his right, now onto the other side.
> . . . a fox, malicious and importunate,
> that had still not found a net that could catch him;
> and a dog from Corsica baying at the moon.[57]

There was even a lion 'that had cut his own claws' and 'pulled his own teeth'; and a 'tiny mouse that grieved at being so small'. By far the most poignant, however, was a pig, with its snout 'all smeared with shit and mud', which bluntly refused the handmaiden's offer to be turned back into human form.[58] The stage is then set for the narrator to recount his own transformation into an ass, but, before he can begin, the poem breaks off.[59]

In literary terms, it is remarkably rich. Though the plot is loosely based on that of Apuleius's original, much of the comedy derives from Niccolò's topsy-turvy allusions to characters and tropes familiar to other works of classical and vernacular poetry.[60] That it was set on Circe's isle was, for example, a clear reference to Homer's *Odyssey*, and Niccolò's friends in the Orti Oricellari would doubtless have spotted the many verbal echoes of Ariosto's *Orlando furioso*,[61] but, much to their amusement, his narrator was neither brave nor noble. Cowardly, lustful and crude, he is, in fact, the very opposite of what an epic hero should be, and his adventures (or, rather, misadventures) are far from edifying. Much the same could be said of the hand-maiden. Despite some playful borrowings from Dante's *Commedia* and Petrarch's *Canzoniere*, she is as different from Beatrice and Laura as could be imagined. Rather than being pure and chaste, she is gloriously saucy and wanton. And though Niccolò's language consciously imitates the sophistication of his models at times, it serves only to emphasize the humour of the crude argot that follows.

But *L'asino* was also a biting critique of Florentine politics and society. Barely thirty lines into the poem, Niccolò interrupted the prologue with a tale allegorizing his own recent suffering at the hands of the Medici.[62] Written in much the same style as Boccaccio's *Decameron*, this told of a young man 'right here in Florence' who could not stop running – just as Niccolò himself had chased madly after political office. His father had tried everything to cure him, but nothing had helped. At last, a quack doctor promised to make him well; and since those, like doctors (*medici*), who promise benefit are always believed, his father gladly 'put the case in the fellow's hands'. After holding perfumes to his nose and taking blood from his head, the doctor pronounced the young man better, perhaps reflecting Niccolò's ejection from the chancellery and imprisonment. For four months, all had seemed well. But on coming into the Via de' Martelli, 'from which he could see the via Larga' – where the Palazzo Medici stood – the poor chap started running like never before, just as Niccolò himself had started pursuing office with renewed vigour the moment he thought there might be a chance the Medici would employ him again. The narrator's awakening on Circe's isle, in the next section, mirrors his 'coming to' after Lorenzo de' Medici's rejection of *Il principe*. Though the world in which he finds himself seems strange, Niccolò – like the narrator – soon begins to see men's characters more clearly. As the reader quickly realizes, the animals into which Circe has transformed visitors to her realm represent members of Florence's political elite, and their strange behaviour reflects the corrupt and vicious practices on which the Medici's regime had thrived.[63] A more savage satire can hardly be imagined. But its real power is revealed only at the very end. As the pig explains, a reasonable person would rather live as a filthy beast, covered in shit, than experience again the jealousy and fear by which Florentine politics were marked. And, by implication, the narrator's transformation into an ass not only reflects Niccolò's renunciation of his former life, but also testifies to how foolish he had been in the past. Now, however, he was a changed man. By escaping from the 'prison' of political office and setting aside all ambition, he had gained 'both glory and liberty' in his new guise as a poet.[64]

*

Given Niccolò's amorous nature, it is unsurprising that he also succumbed to the fascination which the theme of love held for the Orti Oricellari group. Perhaps inspired by Francesco Cattani da Diacceto's readings from his *Panegyricus in amorem* ('Panegyric on love'),[65] or by the bawdy jokes which Luigi Alamanni would later include in his *Flora*,[66] Niccolò put his passions to literary use in a series of lively comedies that made his friends roar with laughter. His first effort was perhaps a revised translation of Terence's *Andria*.[67]

Though the chronology is somewhat difficult to establish, it seems likely that he followed this with two further works of classical imitation, each of which has since been lost. The first of these may have been *La sporta* ('The Purse').[68] Said to have been based on Plautus's incomplete *Aulularia*,[69] this was, in all probability, a typical romp, replete with a cast of stock characters. In Plautus's original, the miserly Eulio attempted to marry off his daughter to a wealthy neighbour named Megadorus, unaware that she is already pregnant by Megadorus's impecunious young nephew, Lyconides. In Niccolò's hands, however, even lusty comedies could be turned into a critique of Florentine politics and society. The second of his 'lost' plays, *Le maschere* ('The Masks'), was notionally a lascivious retelling of Aristophanes' *Clouds*, but ridiculed the intellectual pretensions of Florence's leading men so viciously that it bordered on the libellous.[70] The most striking of the comedies Niccolò wrote in this period, however, is *Mandragola*.[71]

This five-act play tells a delightfully silly story of lust, trickery and superstition. Callimaco Guadagni, a young Florentine recently returned from Paris, has been told about the extraordinary beauty of Lucrezia, the childless wife of Nicia Calfucci, a wealthy, if thick-skulled, lawyer, and contrives to see her for himself. To his amazement, she is even more gorgeous than he had been led to believe. '[O]n fire with . . . longing to be with her',[72] he enlists the help of Ligurio, a thoroughly unscrupulous trickster, who also happens to be a friend of Nicia. After some to-ing and fro-ing, the two of them eventually hit upon a winning plan to inveigle Callimaco into her bed. Disguising himself as a doctor, Callimaco offers to help Lucrezia and Nicia conceive a child by cooking up a potion made from a mandrake root – a traditional remedy for infertility. The only catch is that the first person to sleep with Lucrezia after she drinks it will die (or so Callimaco claims). As such, they need to find an unsuspecting dupe to take Nicia's place. Being an upright matron, Lucrezia naturally objects to the idea of committing adultery, especially with a stranger, but under pressure from her mother, she is eventually talked round. Disguising himself once again as a hapless youth, Callimaco then allows himself to be kidnapped and 'dragged' into bed with Lucrezia. So delighted is she by his sexual prowess that, when he reveals his true identity in a fit of remorse, she proposes that they become lovers. Nicia, of course, suspects nothing. Indeed, he is so grateful for Callimaco's 'sacrifice', that he even gives him the key to his house, so that the young man can come and go as he pleases. At the play's close, Lucrezia – eagerly looking forward to having a child – receives her confessor's blessing in church, in return for a hefty donation.

At one level, it was a cutting satire on the hypocrisy of contemporary morality.[73] Convinced that even the most honest and upright people will sacrifice their virtue to self-interest, Niccolò used his characters to mock the social tropes Florentines had invented for themselves. He first sets his sights on the respectable lawyer – a favourite of the city's bourgeois elite. When Callimaco, disguised as a doctor, first offers the potion to Nicia, the lawyer, jealous of his respectability, is reluctant to prostitute his wife; but he is so desperate for a son, and so fearful of losing his own life, that he soon agrees to pimp her out. Even more shockingly, he shows no concern for the life of the young man they are going to kidnap. The myth of the faithful wife is the next to be skewered. Despite Lucrezia's reluctance, she, too, is willing to disregard her marriage vows for the sake of a child, and no sooner has she passed a night of pleasure in Callimaco's arms than she throws over her husband for good. In much the same way, the prudent mother is shown to be gullible, and the conscientious priest is unmasked as a cunning fox, who is willing to forgo his religious scruples in return for a handful of coins. Only the young student has a shred of decency about him, but even this is nothing to write home about. His pangs of conscience come too late and are quickly smothered in love's embrace.

At another level, *Mandragola* was also a political allegory. Pointing to a number of similarities with *Il principe*, some scholars have argued that it can be read as a call for Lorenzo de' Medici (Callimaco) to 'take Florence (Lucrezia) in hand, and give her, so to speak, the government she needs.'[74] But it is perhaps more convincing to read the play as a covert attack on the growing tyranny of the Medici regime. Among Niccolò's friends in the Orti Oricellari, the character of Lucrezia would have immediately called to mind the Roman matron Lucretia, whose rape by Sextus Tarquinius – the youngest son of the king, Tarquinius Superbus – had provoked Lucius Junius Brutus to overthrow the monarchy and establish the Roman Republic.[75] Although Niccolò may have inverted the sexual roles, the

symbolic meaning of *Mandragola* was essentially the same. W[...]
Lucrezia's sterile marriage to Nicia symbolized Florence's subjection
to the tyranny of the Medici,[76] her subjection by Callimaco allegor-
ically justified any conspiracy which aimed to restore the city's liberty.
And that Callimaco was almost certainly named after the Greek
poet Callimachus suggests Niccolò wanted the literary-minded
habitués of the Orti Oricellari to take the initiative.

*

Whether or not Niccolò intended these seditious insinuations to be
taken seriously, it did him good to vent his frustrations. He was still
prone to bouts of depression. In a letter to Giovanni Vernacci on 25
January 1518, he lamented that he had been reduced to such a condition that he could do little good for himself and less for others.[77]
But he had nevertheless reconciled himself to his political failures
and embarked on a new career as a poet and dramatist. What was
more, he had found some true friends in the Orti Oricellari. They
shared not only his disdain for the Medici regime, but also his taste
for classical literature, his fondness for amorous adventures and his
wicked sense of humour. Most of all, they gave him hope – and he
loved them for it.

For the first time in years, he wanted to travel again. On 17
December 1517 – during a lull in meetings – he wrote to Luigi
Alamanni about a trip to Flanders he was planning to make with a
few of the others.[78] Sometimes, he wrote, they got together and
discussed it with so much enthusiasm that they fancied they were
already on their way there.

He was even ready to undertake little missions again – albeit of
a commercial, rather than diplomatic, nature. On 1 March 1518, he
travelled to Genoa with Giuliano Brancacci and Niccolò degli Agli
to resolve a quarrel over payment on behalf of a wool merchant
named Niccolò Salvetti.[79] It was a far cry from the embassies of the
past, but it would have brought him some money and it would have
been good to be back in the saddle. Brimming over with enthusiasm
as they rode along, he chatted away happily with his companions,
even telling them about his work on *L'asino*.

He was, if not happy, then at least contented – and at long last,
he had his eyes fixed not on the past, but on the future.

22

...e Radical Conservative

While Niccolò's literary and dramatic works from this period abound in social satire and biting political criticism, the rarefied intellectual atmosphere of the Orti Oricellari offered him more than the opportunity to vent his frustrations. As he quickly came to appreciate, the men who gathered there were united more by a passion for political debate than by anything else. And while some – like Zanobi Buondelmonti and Luigi Alamanni – were more radical than others, Antonio Brucioli spoke nothing less than the truth when he later noted that scarcely a day went by without their discussing the character, fortune, and future of the *res publica*.[1]

Niccolò was in his element. He had always loved the cut and thrust of debate, and, in the company of his young friends, he recovered his old fascination with the problems of the day. Like them, he lamented the pitiable condition of government – both in Florence and in states throughout Italy. He agreed civil society was coming apart at the seams. Yet, the more time he spent in the Orti Oricellari, the more he began to attribute the 'corruption' of the present to a disregard for the past.

It had struck Niccolò that, while some men were willing to pay huge sums for small fragments of ancient statues, the same veneration for classical antiquity did not extend to the political arena.[2] The illustrious deeds of great men were seldom, if ever, imitated, while, 'in setting up states, in maintaining governments, in ruling kingdoms, in organising armies and in managing war, in executing laws among subjects, in expanding an empire, not a single prince or republic now resorts to the example of the ancients.'[3] According to

Niccolò, this, and this alone, was why citizens everywhere had become corrupted, states were prey to foreign invaders and any trace of 'greatness' had been lost.

It was not, of course, that people had forgotten the ancient past altogether. Quite the opposite. Not since before the 'fall' of the Western Roman Empire had the works of classical historians enjoyed such wide circulation or been read so avidly by so many. Rather, it was that no one *understood* what they were reading. Lacking even the most basic grasp of Roman politics, Niccolò believed, they could not appreciate the significance of the events described, let alone appreciate what lessons the past could teach the present.[4]

Niccolò resolved to rectify this deficiency. At the suggestion of Cosimo Rucellai and Zanobi Buondelmonti, he began writing what would prove to be his longest and most daring work – the *Discorsi sopra la prima deca di Tito Livio*.[5] Framed as a loose commentary on the first ten books of Livy's history of Rome, its ostensible purpose was simply to explain what was needed to understand the broad thrust of Livy's narrative. But it was also much more than that. As Niccolò admitted, his intention was to derive from the ancient past a set of general rules for governing states in the present, reinforced with examples from other periods and observations from his time in the chancellery.[6]

In many respects, its method was quite similar to that of *Il principe*. As even the most cursory reading reveals, Niccolò's analysis still prioritized the realistic over the idealistic, and his central concern remained the art of government. But the *Discorsi* was nevertheless a very different work. Niccolò was no longer writing with an eye to currying favour. Dedicating the *Discorsi* to Cosimo and Zanobi, rather than to some prince, he intended his work to serve a primarily didactic purpose.[7] As such, he eschewed the praise of a would-be courtier for the frankness of an older friend, and even allowed himself to take the Medici to task where it served to prove his point. Most importantly, the scope of his work was broader. Whereas, in *Il principe*, he had considered only how certain types of principality could be won and maintained, he now set out to enquire into how states of *all* kinds should be established, governed, and enlarged, how social tensions could be harnessed to strengthen, rather than weaken, the body politic, and how lasting glory might be won. And in outlining his vision, Niccolò revealed himself to be neither a revolutionary nor a reactionary, but that rarest of things – a radical conservative.

*

As Quentin Skinner has rightly pointed out, a single overriding concern runs through the *Discorsi*: 'to discover what "made possible the dominant position to which [the Roman R]epublic rose"'[8] – and, by extension, how *other* states could rise to similar greatness.

As it turned out, the answer was relatively straightforward. If history taught anything, Niccolò argued at the beginning of the second book, it was 'that cities have never achieved anything except when they have been at liberty'.[9] As long as they are free, they 'increase in power and riches', but, as soon as they succumb to tyranny, they start 'to go backwards'. Liberty, in short, was all that mattered.[10]

Niccolò was not the first to notice this. More than a century earlier, the Florentine chancellor, Coluccio Salutati, had made exactly the same point – also in relation to Roman history. In a letter dated 6 November 1377, Salutati had noted that 'the zeal for liberty alone created for the Romans empire, glory, and all their dignity.'[11] But it raised an important question, which earlier writers had sometimes struggled to answer: what *was* liberty – and on what did it depend?

As Niccolò's readers were no doubt aware, liberty was most commonly understood in a negative sense – as a freedom from tyranny and oppression.[12] That this was essential to greatness hardly needed saying. Even a fool could see that no city could hope to equal Rome's might unless it enjoyed political autonomy and lived according to its own law. And to be assured of this, a city needed to be able to defend itself with arms. But as Niccolò appears to have recognized, this was intimately intertwined with another, more positive form of liberty. If citizens were to come together to serve their city – in war and in peace – they needed to be free to live on an equal footing with one another. This was only logical. After all, why would anyone risk their life in defence of their homeland unless they could be sure of enjoying the same rights as everyone else? This required everyone to embrace the ideals of equity and justice, and to subordinate their private interests to the common good.[13] For as Niccolò explained at the beginning of the second book, it is 'not individual good, but common good' which made cities great and free.[14]

As such, liberty relied more on virtue than on anything else.[15] It was *virtù* – and *virtù* alone – which made people choose the good of the social whole over their own advancement, or take up arms in defence of their city's independence. As long as a city remained virtuous, it would be free and great.[16] But, as soon as it wavered, even slightly, there would be nothing to stop it sliding into tyranny, servitude and obscurity.

There was nothing particularly novel about this observation. It had been a commonplace of classical literature. Livy, Sallust and Lucan, to name but a few, had all attributed Rome's rise to greatness (at least in part) to her steadfast virtue, and the decline of her liberty to the corruption of her citizenry. It had also become a familiar feature of humanistic political thought. In the early fourteenth century, Albertino Mussato had argued that, while the Paduan citizenry's upright nature had allowed them to dominate the Marches, their prosperity had bred injurious vices. Whipped on by greed and ambition, Mussato argued, they had divided against themselves, thereby paving the way for Padua to fall under the tyranny of Ezzelino da Romano.[17] Similar views were later expressed by Ferreto de' Ferreti in tracing the origin of Verona's woes,[18] and by Niccolò's beloved Petrarch in describing the demise of Rome.[19]

Where Niccolò differed, however, was in the meaning he attached to *virtù*. For most fourteenth- and fifteenth-century humanists, the *virtù* necessary to political life should be viewed in rigidly moralistic terms. They did not, to be sure, always agree about its constituent elements. Some – influenced by Christianized readings of Cicero's *De officiis* and the *Tusculan Disputations* – identified it with the 'contemplative' virtues of faith, hope and charity, and the 'active' virtues of prudence, justice, magnanimity and temperance.[20] Others – inspired more by Macrobius's commentary on Cicero's *Somnium Scipionis* – associated it more with piety, justice and duty.[21] But, as in *Il principe*, Niccolò had no truck with such moralistic cant. To his mind, the possession of *virtù* entailed nothing more than the willingness 'to do whatever may be necessary for the attainment of civic glory and greatness', regardless of 'whether the actions involved happened to be intrinsically good or evil'.[22] No matter what his station in life, a virtuous man should, Niccolò believed, always place the good of the community not only above his personal interests, but also over all the usual moral considerations. There were, in fact, many situations in which he should be prepared to act in a manner which conflicted with the dictates of morality. 'When it is absolutely a question of the safety of one's country,' he wrote, 'there must be no consideration of just or unjust, of merciful or cruel, of praiseworthy or disgraceful; instead, setting aside every scruple, one must follow to the utmost any plan that will save her life and keep her liberty.'[23] Violence, cruelty, torture, rape, murder – all were justified if they upheld freedom and the common good.

The only problem was that men were seldom virtuous. As Niccolò observed at the beginning of the first book, and as he had also argued in *Il principe*, it was generally wise to assume that, at heart, 'all men are evil and that they are always going to act according to the wickedness of their spirits whenever they have free scope.'[24] At first, they might seem decent enough, but most would cut their own neighbour's throat if they thought they would profit by it. And the more prosperous and secure they were, the more corrupt and ruthless they became.

*

So, how had Rome gained and preserved its liberty? How had she nurtured *virtù* for so long? And how could other cities do the same?

Beginnings were clearly important.[25] If a city was founded in freedom, without any ties of dependence, it stood a good chance of staying free. A fertile, easily defensible location could be chosen and sound laws could be put in place, while the people, having been accustomed to liberty from the outset, would be ready to protect it with their lives. If, by contrast, a city was founded by foreigners, or in a state of servitude, then it would struggle ever to enjoy the fruits of liberty.[26] A barren or vulnerable site and the want of decent legislation would make freedom almost impossible to attain. Besides, those born in chains could not easily be persuaded to risk their necks for something they had never known. Rome was a good illustration of this. Though some claimed it was founded by Aeneas – a foreigner – Niccolò preferred to believe the credit belonged to Romulus – a native. Thanks to his *virtù*, Rome had been established on a site which naturally fostered unity, endowed with good laws which kept it free, and trained to value liberty and greatness from its birth.

But beginnings alone were not enough. Whether a city was founded in liberty or servitude was largely a matter of luck. As Niccolò had often warned in the past, Fortune could be fickle: that she had smiled on a city's birth was no guarantee that she would not turn on it in future. If a city born in freedom was to defend its liberty and guard against the rise of tyranny, it needed to ensure that, as its population grew, it was equipped with robust constitutional structures, capable of keeping the body politic united and fostering *virtù*.

This was, however, more difficult than it seemed. Whereas the earliest inhabitants of a free city were generally virtuous figures, dedicated to making a success of their new endeavour, later generations were seldom as upstanding. Indeed, the more time went by after a city's foundation, the more liberty was taken for granted, and the more *virtù* was corrupted by prosperity. Greed, envy and ambition crept into men's hearts; disparities of wealth widened; rivalries between social classes sprang up; and self-interest became the watchword of whoever happened to hold the reins of power. This meant that, whichever of Aristotle's three 'good' constitutions a city chose (monarchy, aristocracy or popular government), it almost invariably degenerated into one of the three correspondingly 'bad' forms (tyranny, 'government by a few' or anarchy).[27]

Generally speaking, free states like Rome went through a cycle. They usually started out as princedoms.[28] Their first rulers – strong, upright men[29] – gave them laws and an understanding of justice. But their successors were soon corrupted by luxury. As tyranny took hold, hatred grew – so much so that, eventually, the nobility rose up and overthrew their prince. An aristocracy was then established. But, in time, this, too, was corrupted, and a narrow oligarchy usurped the state for its own ends. More often than not, another revolt ensued, and, in its wake, a popular government was set up. Though this was ardent in its defence of liberty at first, such high ideals were forgotten as soon as its founders died. As the next generation took up the reins of power, liberty gave way to licence, and each did as he pleased, without regard for justice.

Given how painful this cycle generally proved, Niccolò argued, most states often ended up trying to break free of it altogether. In the recognition that each of the three 'good' constitutions was unsuitable on its own, they chose 'one which partakes of them all, judging it more solid and stable,' because, in such a 'mixed' government, each of the three principal elements – the monarchical, the aristocratic and the popular – would keep the others in check.

That, at least, was the theory. But, in practice, it could be difficult to maintain the requisite equilibrium – as the example of Rome went to show. Like many other cities, Rome had found it almost impossible to heal the bitter, often violent, rivalry between the *popolo* and the *grandi*. As Niccolò had already observed in *Il principe*, the ends of these two groups were hopelessly, irreconcilably, opposed.[30] Whereas the *popolo* wished only not to be oppressed, the *grandi* strove constantly to achieve dominance over the people. And as time went on, their enmity only grew worse.

Though bloodshed was rare, the unrest eventually became so severe that it threatened to tear the tripartite system of government apart. To avert disaster, and to balance the popular and aristocratic elements, it was decided to establish the Tribunes of the Plebs. Invested with the power to veto any legislation proposed by the Senate that might be harmful to the *popolo*, the tribunes were intended to act as a restraint on the power of the *grandi*. It was, from the beginning, a fragile arrangement. Their appetite for power having been whetted, the people soon began agitating for a greater share of power, while the nobles, whose vanity had been severely wounded by the plebs' growing influence, strove to override the tribunes' decisions and reverse legislation that threatened their interests. Tempers often frayed; so persistent did the tensions between the two classes become that they seemed to have been enshrined as a permanent, even 'institutionalized', feature of Roman politics.[31] Nevertheless, Niccolò could not help feeling that such continual discord might actually have been why, despite the corruption of civic morality, Rome had succeeded in preserving her liberty and greatness for so long.[32]

*

For many of Niccolò's contemporaries, this was an absurd claim. Such tension was, they believed, far too chaotic to be productive of liberty, let alone of greatness. Pouring scorn on the 'inadequacy' of the Roman polity, they instead pointed to the constitutions of Sparta and Venice as models of how a city *should* be organized. Despite their differences, some argued, these two cities had succeeded in balancing the interests of competing classes and preserving their liberty *without* provoking unrest and disunity. But, for Niccolò, this was muddle-headed nonsense which missed the point of what he was trying to say.

While Sparta and Venice may indeed have enjoyed more domestic peace, he explained, they had not actually balanced the two classes at all. Instead, they had denied the people any role in government and had placed themselves entirely in the hands of the nobles. That they had managed to avoid social tensions was due more to the skill with which they had persuaded the people to acquiesce in their political exclusion than to the supposed 'perfection' of their constitutions. Venice had achieved this by making nobility a matter of historic residency. When the Republic had been founded, all those who lived in the lagoon had attended council meetings. Finding that this worked perfectly well, they had then 'closed the road to any share in their government against all those who might later come there to live' – thus creating the distinction between nobles (or 'gentlemen') and people. Newcomers had neither reason nor opportunity to rebel. 'Reason there was not, because from them nothing had been taken. Opportunity there was not, because those who ruled held them in check and did not employ them in things through which they could seize authority.'[33] Sparta, by contrast, had far more starkly defined social classes, but had taken care to ensure they were defined by status rather than property. Though office-holding was restricted to very few citizens, all were equally poor, with the result that the common people felt less excluded; and since the nobles never treated them badly, they never felt any desire to share in the business of government. Nor was there ever any need to expand the administration. Since Sparta refused 'to receive foreigners into the state', its inhabitants remained few in number, 'and for this reason, they could be governed by a few'.[34]

But, while Venice and Sparta were both 'free', in the sense that neither had succumbed to tyranny, Niccolò could not help observing that their internal harmony had been purchased at the price of territorial expansion. Being instinctively fearful of loss, the nobles who governed these two cities were resistant to change and reluctant to take risks. And since they were unwilling either to arm the common people or to open their doors to foreigners, they struggled to acquire and maintain an empire. Such paltry gains as Sparta had made were quickly taken from her; and, as Niccolò had already remarked in *Il principe*, Venice had lost all that she had gained in Italy in a single afternoon at the Battle of Agnadello.[35] He thus concluded that liberty without tension could never lead to greatness.

It was a different story with Rome. Though the Republic had never enjoyed domestic peace, Niccolò argued, the conflict between *popolo* and *grandi* had allowed it to achieve what had eluded Sparta and Venice. Not only had the tension led to the creation of the tribunes, but it had also forced the people to be always on their guard against the subversion of their prerogatives by the nobles. As such, it had facilitated their emergence as the 'guardians of liberty'.[36] At the same time, this tension had allowed the people to take up arms and counterbalance the nobles' instinctive aversion to risk, thereby opening the doors to territorial expansion, as well. So long as social tensions had existed, therefore, Rome's liberty had been crowned with greatness.

*

This, however, required some qualification. As Niccolò was at pains to stress, tension was only productive if the fragile balance between nobles and people was preserved. Provided they were struggling against each other, he argued, all would be well;[37] but were one to succeed in triumphing over the other, liberty would quickly collapse into tyranny. Seeing that the Roman nobility already had ample means to keep the people in check, it was therefore necessary to counterbalance this by giving the people a way to prevent the nobles from gaining the upper hand. Two measures were hence introduced. The first gave the tribunes the power to bring charges against anyone who 'in any way sin[ned] against free government.'[38] Such formal indictments, Niccolò argued, made it possible to prevent the nobles from harming or otherwise acting against the interests of the *popolo*. A good illustration of how effective it could be was provided by Coriolanus. An avowed 'enemy of the popular party', Coriolanus had withheld grain from the plebs to punish them for instituting the tribunes, and would surely have been killed by the people outside the Senate House had he not been charged.[39] The second measure allowed for indictments to be brought against slanderers. Though less dramatic, slander was no less insidious, and, in some ways, even more dangerous to liberty than hostile actions. Where slander is allowed to spread unchecked, Niccolò argued, there arises in the victims a desire for vengeance; and if this cannot be sated by public redress, they resort to private means, often turning to clients and friends for help. This quickly leads to the formation of factions, and ultimately ruins states – as Florentines had seen for themselves in the case of Francesco Valori and Piero Soderini, who had unjustly been killed and exiled, Niccolò claimed, because liberty had been eroded by untruth. By forcing slanderers to prove their calumnies in court, Niccolò argued, this could be prevented.

*

Yet, even Niccolò had to admit that such measures were often insufficient. While the Roman *popolo* may have held the nobles in check for a long time, the persistence of social tensions could sometimes lead to the emergence of a despotic individual whom they were powerless to resist. As Niccolò argued, this could happen in two ways. On the one hand, people and nobles could be seduced by charisma. Every now and again, Niccolò argued, there appears a man so extraordinary that citizens and nobles alike 'turn their eyes toward him and agree, without reservation, in honouring him, so that, if he has a bit of ambition . . . he soon gets to such a place that, when the citizens realize their mistake, they have few means of stopping him, and if they try to make use of those they have, they only hasten his rise to power.'[40] From Roman history, the most obvious example was Julius Caesar. But a more recent, and telling, case in point was provided by Cosimo de' Medici. '[A]s a result of his prudence and the ignorance of his fellow citizens,' Cosimo had arrived at so high a reputation that he 'frightened the government'. When Cosimo's opponents drove him out of the Florence, however, they succeeded only in inflaming his supporters further, with the result that, a little later, they called him back 'and made him prince of the republic – a rank to which without that open opposition he never could have risen.'[41]

On the other hand, social tensions could reach such a pitch that it was impossible to prevent factionalism occurring. Shortly after the establishment of the tribunate, Niccolò noted, new quarrels had begun to emerge in Rome, provoked in the first instance by the charges brought against the *decemvir* Appius Claudius Crassus.[42]

Though such quarrels were usually positive – as Niccolò had argued earlier – they here began to assume a more dangerous form. Believing that the tribunes had gone too far, the nobles had immediately set about defending themselves. Quite reasonably, the more ambitious among them formed friendships with well-placed individuals 'in ways apparently honourable, either by aiding [them] with money or by protecting them from the powerful.' So reasonable had this seemed, indeed, that no one had thought badly of it – much less sought to curtail it. But the effect was to foment factions – and hence pave the way to tyranny. Supported by vast networks of supporters, factional leaders soon became so powerful that private citizens were afraid of them, and even magistrates treated them with deference. The only way of stopping this would have been for the people who were still desirous of protecting liberty to try beating the nobles at their own game – that is, by forming 'friendships' of their own and thereby robbing their enemies of their support.[43] But, by the time things had reached such a pass, the people were rarely able to save themselves. Though they were strong when united, fear had divided them, and, on his own, each man was craven, self-interested and weak.[44] Frightened and confused, they were easily tricked into accepting the loss of their liberty either by 'mighty promises' or by a haughty display of courage.[45]

To guard against such eventualities, Niccolò believed, it was essential for the people to remain ever watchful.[46] They must train themselves to recognize how factions grow and how individuals acquire 'more power than is safe', and keep their eyes open for any warning signs. They must also include among their *ordini* (a term Niccolò used to describe all 'the public institutions, laws, and customs that sustain healthy states'[47]) a provision for citizens to be watched 'so that they cannot under cover of good do evil and so that they gain only such popularity as advances and does not harm liberty.'[48] Perhaps most importantly, they must be ready to act as soon as they perceive a threat to liberty, using the full force of law to eradicate any danger before it is too late.[49] They must even be prepared to appoint a dictator, if necessary. Indeed, Niccolò opined that 'those republics that cannot against impending danger take refuge under a dictator or some such authority will in serious emergencies always be ruined.'[50] Though it was true that the extension (and expansion) of military commands often accelerated the slide into despotism,[51] the risk could be averted by limiting his term of office and granting him only such powers as were needed to deal with the current crisis.[52]

But Niccolò was forced to concede that even these measures might not be enough. No matter how stringent the legislation, how vigilant the people or how resolute the city, nothing would be sufficient to counterbalance the corruption of the citizenry. The longer Rome had held on to its liberty, the larger its empire had grown and the more staggeringly wealthy it had become. So greatly had this accelerated the decline in civic morality that, eventually, *virtù* all but vanished – and any hope of achieving a stable balance between the classes evaporated. Pursuing wealth, glory and honour with ever greater fervour, the citizenry lost sight of what had made the city great, and put their own profit before all else. As such, they were divided by faction as easily as they were seduced by the promises of extraordinary individuals. In each case, they had no hesitation in choosing their private interests over the common good, and injustice over equity – regardless of the effects it would have on the city as a whole. They could not remain on their guard against the threat, because they *were* the threat; nor, for the same reasons, could they take decisive action against it. Thus, Niccolò argued, liberty was destroyed by the very people who were supposed to protect it.

*

This brought Niccolò to an uncomfortable conclusion. Though 'free' origins, social tensions, *ordini* and the empowerment of the *popolo* all played an important role, none of them would ever be able to safeguard freedom. Instead, the liberty of a city would depend on its taking more active measures to cultivate *virtù* – and, as far as possible, return the citizen body to the upright morality of its earliest days.[53] Granted, this would not be easy. If, as Niccolò maintained, men were naturally inclined to vice, and prosperity brought out all their worst instincts, it would be like trying to make a silk purse out of a sow's ear. Yet Niccolò still thought it might be possible.

There were, he suggested, four means of making men virtuous. The first was to eliminate, or at least minimize, the disparities of wealth on which class divisions were based, and from which corruption inevitably sprang. This was best achieved by keeping 'the citizens poor'.[54] Even if they lacked 'goodness and wisdom', he argued, they would not be able to 'corrupt themselves or others with riches'. In practice, however, such equality could only be achieved by clamping down on the nobility – that is to say, on those 'who without working live in luxury on the returns from their landed possessions, without paying any attention either to agriculture or to any other occupation necessary for making a living.'[55] Remembering the admirable simplicity of life that he had seen in the German lands, he pointed out that 'those republics where government has been kept orderly and uncorrupted do not allow any citizen of theirs to be a nobleman or to live in the fashion of one, but . . . preserve among themselves a complete *equalità*.' To some extent, this already existed in Tuscany. Since the late thirteenth century, Florence, Siena and Lucca had all enjoyed equality of a sort. So far, however, no one had yet managed to turn it into the basis of a 'well-regulated' government.

The second method was to enforce the law. On the face of it, this was rather surprising. Niccolò had, after all, just devoted a lot of time to showing how inadequate laws were to prevent the slide into tyranny. But, here, he was thinking of law more as the root of education. As he knew only too well, 'men never do anything good except by necessity'. If they are left to their own devices, they will inevitably indulge their baser appetites and 'everything is at once filled with confusion and disorder'; but, if their licence is restricted and a positive incentive towards *virtù* extended, Niccolò argued, they can be induced to change their ways. Before the Tarquins had been expelled, the Roman Senate had understood this. United by their hatred of the kings, the nobles were then lacking in pride, and generally 'democratic in spirit'. As such, they used the law to instil *virtù* in the people in precisely this manner. In punishing those who harm the state and rewarding those who enhance its glory, therefore, the law can indeed make men good – whether they like it or not.[56]

A third method was to foster the institutions of religious worship.[57] If anything, these were more effective even than laws in moderating the habits of a people. For, whereas laws constrain men to love the common good and equity through fear of earthly punishment or hope of material reward, the practice of religion can instil the same through fear of divine retribution or the hope for heavenly favour.[58] As such, Niccolò viewed it as the foundation of a state's prosperity. Where the institutions of religion were well respected, he argued, a city would have good laws, good fortune and, most importantly, liberty.[59] By contrast, 'one can have no better indication of the ruin of a country than to see divine worship little valued.'[60] Indeed, 'as the observance of religious teaching brings about the greatness of states, so contempt for it brings about their destruction.'[61]

The Romans had, of course, grasped this at an early stage in their history. Shortly after succeeding Romulus, the second king of Rome, Numa Pompilius, had found himself faced with the task of governing 'a very savage people', and had realized that religion was 'something altogether necessary if he wished to maintain a well-ordered state.'[62] So successfully did he do this that 'for many ages there was never so much fear of God as in that republic'; and this, in turn, 'facilitated whatever undertaking the Senate or those great men of Rome planned to carry on.' The Romans were, however, not alone. The Etruscans, too, had also recognized the need for religion. Though they had never acquired 'an empire like that of Rome', they had nevertheless enjoyed many long years of security, 'with the utmost glory of authority and of arms, and with the highest reputation in manners and religion.'[63] The same was true of the Samnites. Despite being defeated by the Romans many times, the Samnites had the resolve to make one last attempt to defend their liberty. Knowing that, if they were to succeed, they would need to 'put determination into the minds of their soldiers', they therefore turned to religion to restore their lost virtue.[64]

Had the rulers of contemporary Italy followed these examples, Niccolò argued, they would surely have been united and happy.[65] But they had singularly failed to appreciate how closely their liberty depended upon the health of their religious institutions – that is to say, of the Catholic Church. As it was, the Italian people had, 'through the bad example of [the Roman] court . . . lost all piety and religion'.[66] With nothing to sustain their virtù, they had soon succumbed to an excess of internecine violence, which had prevented them from ever uniting under a single leader, and which had left them divided and enfeebled. It was for this reason that, in Niccolò's own day, the Italian people had become 'not merely the prey of powerful barbarians, but of whoever assails her'; and it was hence for this reason, too, that he laid the blame for the loss of Italy's liberty squarely on the Church's shoulders.[67]

Niccolò was, of course, not the first to suggest that religion should make a people love equity and the common good. During the late thirteenth and early fourteenth centuries, scholastic philosophers – from Albertus Magnus and Thomas Aquinas to John of Paris and Remigio dei Girolami – had consistently made this case, albeit in a variety different ways.[68] In the decades that followed, it underpinned the great 'festivals of peace' that were orchestrated by the mendicant orders and the various revivalist movements that made their way around Northern Italy; and later, it was even voiced by several of the humanists. It was, for example, implicit in the works of Ferreto de' Ferreti, Petrarch and Cola di Rienzo, to name just a few.[69]

But where Niccolò differed from these figures was in his refusal to believe that religion needed to be 'true'. Insofar as liberty was concerned, he pointed out, the ontological underpinnings of a religion hardly mattered; only its practical *effects* were of any concern. As Maurizio Viroli has rightly observed, what he wanted was a religion based on 'faith and the fear of God' that could arouse sincere devotion, train the faithful to value the common good above themselves, teach 'its adherents to love liberty', and help 'men to find within themselves the moral strength to defend the free way of life.'[70] Provided it did this, Niccolò argued, the leaders of a community had an obligation to further it, 'even [if] they think it false'.[71]

What a religion must *not* do, by contrast, is to become nothing more than a collection of hollow rites, repeated without faith for the absolution of the wicked. Nor, for that matter, should it encourage men to be withdrawn and cowardly. That way led, at best, to the erosion of public faith and an unwillingness to take up arms in defence of the state, or, at worst, to the primacy of self-interest over the common good, and the ultimate demise of liberty. Even if it was based on the most undeniable truths, the institutions of such a religion would be a pernicious menace which the leaders of a city had a duty to correct.

It was for this reason that Niccolò spoke so highly of Roman religion, and so badly of Christianity in contemporary Italy. Whereas Roman religion had served to strengthen *virtù*, the Christian faith had done the exact opposite. Despite being undeniably true, it had been interpreted in such a way (that is, 'according to sloth'[72]) that it actually undermined the people's commitment to the common good. Its teachings glorified 'humility, abjectness, and contempt for human things', and its rites, though often celebrated with some pomp, lacked the magnificent ferocity that stirred men to great deeds. It had, in short, made the people weak and craven.[73] This was bad enough; but to make matters even worse, the Church's conduct had destroyed what little piety there was in Italy, as well. Not only did the 'evil habits' of the Roman Curia set a 'bad example'; but the temporal ambitions of the papacy had also caused such suffering across Italy that it was difficult for ordinary believers to hold the Church in any respect.[74]

If the Christian faith was to serve any useful purpose, therefore, it must become more like Roman paganism. While holding fast to its essential truths, the leaders of the Italian states should ensure that it interprets them in a more vigorous manner, and articulates them through glorious, fierce and even bloody rites. At the same time, they should cleanse the Roman Curia of its corruption and oblige the popes to cease their meddling in worldly affairs.

The fourth and perhaps most provocative means of fostering *virtù* in a people was, however, leadership.[75] Despite having asserted that the *popolo* were the true 'guardians of liberty', Niccolò was firmly convinced that they could not be expected to display much virtue unless they were fortunate enough to have a leader who displayed *virtù* to an extraordinary degree.[76]

As Skinner has stressed, such figures were crucial to the liberty and greatness of a city – more so, indeed, than laws or even religion.[77] It was due largely to the 'extraordinary and noble examples' of Horatius Cocles, Mucius Scaevola, Gaius Fabricius, the two Decii, Atilius Regulus and some others that Rome had clung to *virtù* so assiduously in the centuries after its foundation. Had similar such *virtuosi* appeared at least once every ten years thereafter, Niccolò opined, the city 'would never have become corrupt.'[78] In fact, they need not appear even that often. Towards the end of the third book, Niccolò noted that, if one truly exceptional individual – equal in stature and severity to Manlius Torquatus – emerged only occasionally, it would be enough to return the laws 'to their ancient vigour', keep the people from corruption and build a republic which flourished eternally in liberty.[79]

Where a suitably remarkable figure led, Niccolò argued, others would follow. Sometimes, this was achieved by inspiring those with a natural inclination towards *virtù* to follow their instincts. Leaders like Cocles, Scaevola and Fabricius are, he suggested, 'of such reputation and their example is so powerful that good men wish to imitate them, and the wicked are ashamed to live a life contrary to theirs.'[80] Indeed, the effect of such extraordinary leaders is so strong that it is almost equal to the power of 'laws and customs'. More often, however, it was achieved by means of charismatic compulsion. If a leader was sufficiently strong-willed and strict, he could simply impose his virtue on the people, whether they wanted him to or not. One way he could do this was by cultivating a reputation for severity, even bordering on cruelty. It had been thus with Hannibal. As in the *Ghiribizzi*, Niccolò heaped praise on him for frightening his troops into remaining 'united and quiet' on the long march into Italy.[81] It had been the same with Manlius Torquatus, who had famously executed his own son for disobeying his orders during the Latin War, and who thereby restored the resolve of his wavering army.[82] But another method was to compel with kindness. This was illustrated by Marcus Valerius Corvus, who was 'in every way and manner kind and full of familiar intimacy', and who thereby succeeded in rallying his soldiers behind him.[83] Which of these two methods was the safer, Niccolò could not say. Although he repeated the claim – made originally in *Il principe* – that 'the leader who makes himself feared is better followed and better obeyed than he who makes himself loved',[84] he admitted that he now found it rather difficult to decide between them.[85] While he had little doubt that a citizen general should employ fear, he was inclined to think that a prince might be wiser to use kindness, after all.[86]

Outstanding leaders could also foster *virtù* in people more directly – in the way they handled the business of government. As the example of Camillus illustrated, they were able to weed out corruption before it took root, and drive men on to virtuous action.[87] If they aroused envy, they knew how to assuage it;[88] if they were faced with conspiracies or plots, they were sufficiently circumspect and wary to diffuse them without arousing further unrest;[89] and if called upon to take command of an army, they were courageous enough to lead their men into 'the thickest press of battle'.[90]

This, however, led Niccolò to a sorrowful observation. Unlike Rome, Florence had never had a leader of such quality. More than anything else, this helped to explain the slow demise of the Florentine Republic. Had Savonarola and Piero Soderini displayed even a fraction of the *virtuoso* qualities of Rome's early heroes, Niccolò argued, her liberty might well have been preserved. But they had not been sufficiently severe or kindly to inspire virtue in their people;[91] they were incapable of stemming the tide of envy;[92] they were easily deceived; and they were utterly lacking in good sense. As such, the Florentines had become corrupt, venal and credulous;[93] they had succumbed to foreign invaders and, as a result, they had lost both their liberty and their chance of greatness.

Niccolò was, however, hopeful. Although he was forced to admit that leaders of quality were not always able to correct the faults of a people already well down the road of corruption – especially if a long time had elapsed since the last such individual had appeared – he nevertheless seems to have believed that, if a *virtuoso* figure *were* to emerge, there was still a chance that Florence's ills could be righted, its social tensions eased (or at least harnessed) and its liberty restored.[94] The only question was: where could such a leader be found? Given the book's dedication, it is possible that Niccolò hoped such a figure might arise from among the younger members of the Orti Oricellari group, but he was wise enough not to exclude the possibility that Florence's salvation might still lie with one of the Medici. And, with that, he brought the *Discorsi* to a close.

*

Although celebrated within the Orti Oricellari group, the *Discorsi* was met with mixed reactions from other quarters. Francesco Guicciardini, for example, was horrified by Niccolò's suggestion that dissent should be tolerated.[95] But, while this may perhaps give the impression that it was a work designed to arouse 'shock and awe', it is arguable that its radical conservatism actually had precisely the opposite effect. While it was critical of many aspects of Medici rule, it was more a book of dispassionate theory than a work of opposition – devoted more to restoring balance to Florence's still bitterly divided political society than to revivifying 'republican' liberty. What was more, since it was not written with the intention of currying favour, and betrayed a sense of calm, mature assurance, it came across as a balanced and sensible study recommending changes that many would doubtless have seen as both necessary and desirable. Given the tumultuous events which were soon to be unleashed, nothing could have been better for Niccolò.

PART VII

The Prodigal Son

(1519–27)

23

Deaths and Resurrection

(March 1519–April 1520)

While Niccolò had resigned himself to life as a political outsider and carved out a new career for himself as a dramatist, a poet, and a classically-inspired theorist of liberty, this had done nothing to improve his dire financial situation. Apart from occasional handouts from wealthy friends, his only income came from his little farm in Sant'Andrea in Percussina; and, though his two eldest sons, Bernardo and Lodovico, would soon be embarking on careers of their own, this can scarcely have been enough to support his ever-growing family. But he seems to have been happy, nonetheless. His letters bubble over with cheery good humour, now sharing literary gossip with unabashed delight, now offering warm-hearted advice to a young kinsman.

Yet Niccolò could not afford to be complacent. From at least the fourteenth century onwards, humanists of all complexions had warned that nothing in life is immune to change. With time, strength fades, beauty withers and even the sharpest minds grow dim. Inevitable and irresistible, such change cautioned against contentment; and since no change was more dramatic, inevitable or irresistible than dying, many humanists had regarded death as its most potent symbol. As Niccolò's beloved Petrarch had noted, it was a reminder that all worldly things must come to an end, and that the high prizes men seek after are ultimately lost.[1] But death could also be viewed more positively – as an emblem of transformation. In the Christian mind, after all, it was a departure from suffering, a transition to greater happiness, and – for some – a prelude to resurrection.

During the spring of 1519, this image can hardly have failed to have been on Niccolò's mind. Shortly after Easter, Lorenzo de'Medici died. Though only twenty-six years old, his health had been ruined by syphilis and self-indulgence. Few mourned his passing.[2] As Francesco Guicciardini's nephew had complained only a few weeks earlier, his financial irresponsibility, his disregard for counsel and his lordly pretentions had alienated all but the most blinkered of partisans.[3] But his death gave Florence new hope.

Even before Lorenzo was buried, the pope appointed his cousin, Cardinal Giulio de'Medici, to take charge of the city until a suitable successor could be found. Giulio could not have been more different from his kinsman. Then just a few days short of his forty-first birthday, he had been born barely a month after his father, Giuliano, had been murdered in the Pazzi conspiracy, and had been haunted by fears of conspiracy all his life. Though occasionally prone to indecision – for which later biographers would often reprove him – he had gained a reputation for learning and serious-mindedness.[4] He was keenly aware of how badly Lorenzo had jeopardized the Medici's position in Florence, and immediately set about repairing the damage. Within a matter of weeks, he had appeased the *ottimati* by abolishing an unpopular law limiting the size of dowries and by welcoming a number of former *frateschi* back into the political fold.[5] He then pared down the Medici household, and, at the beginning of June, delighted the *popolo* with an 'ambitious programme of public works.'[6] Most importantly, he also began reforming the city's constitution. While taking care to reserve as much authority for himself as possible, he took steps to broaden participation in government. He first asked the Medici's leading supporters to draw up lists of men who should be restored to favour, and allowed a number of lesser offices to be filled once again by election. He then enlarged the Seventy and the Hundred, which had been revived shortly after the Medici's return to oversee taxation and scrutiny,[7] and hinted that further, more wide-ranging, reforms would follow.

In the Orti Oricellari, this sparked much excitement. It was widely expected that, before long, the cardinal would restore 'traditional republican government' – although what that might entail was still somewhat unclear.[8] While those who already enjoyed friendly relations with the Medici – such as Lorenzo di Filippo Strozzi and Battista della Palla – confidently anticipated the establishment of a broadly oligarchic regime, not dissimilar to that of Lorenzo the

Magnificent, those of a republican temperament looked forward to a return to a more popular form of government.

Despite their differences of opinion, however, they all agreed that, whatever shape the constitution ultimately took, Florence could not have been in better hands. Though somewhat wary of the Medici's ambitions, even the fiercely republican historian Jacopo Nardi could not help admiring the cardinal's humanity and justice. Comparing Giulio to Piero Soderini, Nardi praised him for settling disputes equitably, for setting aside favouritism and – most importantly – for distributing honours 'according to the merits of the worthy, rather than according to the tiresomeness of the petitioner.'[9]

Niccolò's delight can well be imagined. For the first time, he must have felt there was a real chance of returning to political favour.[10] Learned, liberal and conciliatory, the cardinal seemed to be willing to forgive talented men their offences, if it meant the Medici regime would thereby be strengthened.

If Niccolò could somehow impress the cardinal – or those close to him – with his acumen, the political rehabilitation he had so long been denied might be within his grasp. The only problem was how to do so. Clearly, he could not dedicate *Il principe* for a third time. Nor was there any point in writing a risky letter of advice like the *Ai Palleschi*. Instead, he needed to offer the cardinal something that reflected the Medici's domestic security and played to his own strengths. But what?

*

It was the death of the Emperor Maximilian on 12 January 1519 that appears to have suggested an idea. Having been in bad health for some time, Maximilian's demise had not come as a surprise to anyone – least of all to him. During the last years of his life, he had devoted much effort to ensuring that he would be succeeded by his nineteen-year-old grandson, Charles of Ghent.[11] There were, of course, plenty of others who coveted his throne. But so carefully had Maximilian made his preparations that, when the election was held in Frankfurt on 28 June, Charles was elected unopposed.

To the casual observer, the new king of the Romans may have appeared unprepossessing. Though cultured and discerning, he was still young and would not take up the reins of government for at least another year or two. What was more, he was beset by serious unrest in Friesland, and was struggling to assert his rule in Aragon and Castile. Yet his election nevertheless sent shock waves through Italy. Having inherited not only the Habsburg possessions in the Iberian peninsula, Austria and the Low Countries, but also the Valois duchy of Burgundy and the kingdoms of Naples and Sicily, he had the means to reshape the map of Italy, if he chose – and was perhaps already thinking about pressing his claims to Milan.[12] This naturally alarmed Francis I, who was then in possession of the duchy and who also desired the kingdom of Naples for himself. But the pope was equally disturbed. Already unsettled by the presence of imperial troops less than sixty-five kilometres from Rome, he was afraid that, if Charles ventured into Italy, he might easily find himself encircled by Habsburg territories and prevented from enlarging the Papal States any further. Over the summer, Leo X tried desperately to forestall the danger. After swiftly capturing Pesaro, his first thought was to secure an alliance with France.[13] But, though a treaty was signed in October, Francis I's stubborn refusal to allow him to annexe the duchy of Ferrara persuaded the pope that his ambitions might be better served by expelling the French from Italy with imperial help. While taking care not to disclose his intentions, he therefore began seeking an agreement with Charles. Whether or not he succeeded, however, it was clear that war would soon be declared – and that Florence would inevitably be drawn into the fray.

It had already been decided that Cardinal Giulio de' Medici would play a decisive role in the coming hostilities. Having recently been appointed apostolic legate to the papal army, he was expected to oversee preparations. Accordingly, in late October, he set off for Lombardy, where the pope's forces were to muster, leaving Florence in the charge of Silvio Passerini, cardinal of Cortona, and Goro Gheri, the bishop of Pistoia.[14] In his absence, however, the city's mood grew ugly. The Florentines bitterly resented the pope's anti-French policy and, for a brief moment, there were displays of open resistance.[15] But even those who opposed the imperial alliance recognized they had little choice in the matter. Like it or not, the city needed to prepare itself for war. Its forces were, however, not in the best shape. Since Lorenzo's death, little effort had been made to find a new commander, and as yet, no decision seemed to have been taken about whether to hire more mercenaries or to strengthen the militia. Organization, supplies, arms and training were all lacking, and no one seemed to have much idea how to remedy the situation.

But it was in this that Niccolò spied his opportunity. Seeing Florence scramble to ready itself, he conceived the idea of writing a treatise on the theory and practice of war. It was the perfect subject. As the original architect of the revived militia, he was uniquely well informed about military matters – so much so that even Lorenzo de' Medici had sought his advice. As such, it was perfectly natural for him to offer the cardinal – or someone in his circle – the benefit of his experience. In doing so, he could be sure not only of displaying his abilities to greatest effect, but also of recommending his services as a counsellor.

*

Yet it was not until a few weeks later that Niccolò took up his pen. He may perhaps have been unnerved by the unpopularity of the cardinal's deputies, who, being from subject territories, had found little sympathy among the snobbish Florentine elite. But, more likely, he was simply hesitant about returning to the cold and hostile world of Florentine politics after so long in the warm embrace of the Orti Oricellari.

Once again, however, death intervened to change his mind. On 2 November, Cosimo Rucellai died, little more than a month after his twenty-fourth birthday. As Filippo de' Nerli indicated in his *Commentari*, his loss came as a heavy blow – especially to Niccolò.[16] Not only was Cosimo one of Niccolò's closest friends, but he was also the patron and guiding light of the Orti Oricellari group. Without him, the little band quickly began to lose its way. Though they continued to meet, their gatherings took on an altogether more sombre tone. For Niccolò, it must have seemed as if a curtain had come down on the life he had built for himself since leaving the chancellery. Yet his grief impelled him to begin writing the work which would later become known as *L'arte della guerra* (*The Art of War*).

*

Dedicated to Lorenzo di Filippo Strozzi, the *Arte della guerra* is set in the autumn of 1516, when its principal character, the *condottiere*

Fabrizio Colonna, passed through Florence on his way back from Lombardy, where he had been campaigning for Charles V's maternal grandfather, Ferdinand of Aragon.[17] During his stay, Niccolò tells us at the beginning of book one, Cosimo Rucellai invited him to discuss ancient and modern warfare over dinner in the Orti Oricellari, and asked others to join them. Niccolò was also present, but in what followed, he remained uncharacteristically silent.

Though Niccolò's account of the ensuing discussion is ostensibly given in the form of a Ciceronian dialogue, the Swedish historian Mikhael Hörnqvist has recently observed that it lacks some of the 'dramatic qualities and multivocal charm' typical of the genre.[18] Whereas other Renaissance dialogues – such as Leonardo Bruni's *Dialogi ad Petrum Histrum*, Lorenzo Valla's *De voluptate* and Francesco Guicciardini's *Dialogo del reggimento di Firenze* – were characterized by a lively exchange of ideas between equals, the *Arte della guerra* is dominated by the voice of Fabrizio Colonna. The other characters might ask the odd question now and again, but they are rarely, if ever, given the opportunity to express opinions of their own. Ciceronian purists might, of course, have turned their noses up at this, but it was less of a fault than it might seem. By casting Fabrizio in the role of a sage enlightening younger and more inexperienced friends, Niccolò allowed himself the freedom to develop complex ideas at length, while still keeping things lively – or at least livelier than they might have been in a more conventional treatise.[19]

As Niccolò explains in the preface, his purpose in the *Arte della guerra* is to 'bring military practice back to ancient methods and to restore some of the forms of earlier excellence'.[20] In doing so, he also explains how a state desirous of preserving its liberty should be organized for war – a topic he had already addressed at length not only in his writings on the militia but also in *Il principe* and the *Discorsi*. In the first book, Fabrizio Colonna sets the tone by demonstrating that it is not only possible, but even necessary to emulate the ancients, both in their vigour and in their techniques of war. Drawing on a number of examples from classical history, he then shows that a citizen militia is to be preferred to a mercenary army, and that the former should, if possible, be recruited from the countryside rather than from the town. In the second book, Fabrizio, goaded by Cosimo's questioning, discusses organization and armaments. Showing a clear preference for infantry over cavalry, he argues that the swords and shields favoured by the Romans are far better than the pikes and halberds used by the Swiss. After extolling the merits of regular training, he then goes on to claim that an army should be divided into brigades of 6,000 troops, each consisting of ten battalions, kept in order using insignia, flags and music. The third book examines how these units should be used in battle. Following a detailed description of how different troops should be arrayed, Fabrizio explains that each battle should begin with an artillery barrage, and that, thereafter, the front line should regularly be replaced by fresher troops in the rear. These general principles are then developed further in the fourth book. While discussing famous battles from the classical past, Fabrizio suggests ways in which a general could turn a battle to his advantage. These range from the choice of an advantageous position and the use of confusion and surprise, to bolstering the troops' fighting spirit with religious faith, oratory and music. In the fifth book, Fabrizio considers how the army should be managed when it is either marching through a hostile region or surprised by an enemy attack. He lays particular emphasis on the ordering of a column and the need for constant vigilance, but also touches upon questions of pay, provisioning and the distribution of booty. Making and breaking camp are addressed in the sixth book, in the course of which Fabrizio provides a detailed description of the layout of Roman camps. He also stresses the importance of discipline and advises commanders to prohibit both prostitution and gambling. Finally, in the seventh book, Fabrizio tackles fortresses and siege techniques. Though rather dismissive of artillery as a siege weapon, he emphasizes that deception and surprise can be particularly effective in taking a citadel or town. He then adduces twenty-four general rules of warfare ('What helps your enemy hurts you, and what helps you hurts the enemy'; '[d]iscipline does more in war than enthusiasm'; etc.[21]). By way of conclusion, Fabrizio launches a scathing attack on Italy's divided rulers, whose incompetence has, he believes, left it prey to foreign invaders.

There was much in the *Arte della guerra* that was already familiar to Niccolò's works – particularly with respect to the organization of an army and the role of war in civil society. His claim, at the very beginning of the dialogue, that arms were the foundation of a state's liberty and greatness had, for example, already appeared in both *Il principe* and the *Discorsi*.[22] So too, his insistence on the superiority of citizen soldiers over mercenaries, the importance of discipline and the need for regular provisioning had all been central pillars of *La cagione dell'ordinanza*, the *Provisione della ordinanza* and even some of his more recent writings on the militia. The same is also true of his preference for infantry over cavalry, his invectives against corruption in the ranks and his belief that captains should be chosen from a different region than the troops they were to lead.

Underlying many of these similarities was a desire for self-justification. As Robert Black has noted, Niccolò had evidently realized that, if he was to be taken seriously as a military expert, he needed not only to 'retain key features of earlier schemes', but also to vindicate 'his militia against its many critics'.[23] Thus, while repeating some of the arguments he had used in the past, he also went to great pains to rebut the charge that too many recruits had been enlisted in the years before Soderini's fall,[24] and to counter the accusation that the militia had been to blame for the sack of Prato in 1512 – albeit rather discreetly.[25] He was especially concerned to demonstrate that the militia was not an instrument of tyranny, as some had feared.[26] Quite the reverse was the case. Without a militia, he argued, it was almost impossible to *avoid* sliding into tyranny. On the whole, cities which relied on foreign mercenaries rather than their own people were seldom able to preserve their liberty for very long. As he went on to explain, this was because a city which did not arm herself had to fear two enemies rather than one: the un-reliable foreigners she hired, and a restive citizenry, resentful of paying exorbitant amounts for nothing.

No more original was Niccolò's depiction of war's moral founda-tions. Although it has sometimes been suggested that, in comparison with the *Discorsi*, the *Arte della guerra* rested on a far more conven-tional view of morality,[27] the two works display a marked continuity. Despite employing a more traditional vocabulary in describing the moral qualities he wished commanders to cultivate, Niccolò's view of military leadership in the *Arte della guerra* nevertheless rests on the same general precepts as in the earlier work. Much as in the *Discorsi*, Niccolò maintains that no army can be effective unless its soldiers place a higher value on their country's good than on their own safety. A good general can instil this patriotism – this *virtù* – partly through harsh discipline. By dispensing punishments and rewards, Niccolò argues that he can simultaneously uphold the law and inculcate respect for the common good and justice.[28] He can also inspire patriotism in his troops by example. After all, where he leads, they will follow – both literally and metaphorically. Most strikingly of all, however, Niccolò suggests that the ideal general should also foster a vigorous fighting spirit by nurturing religious faith.[29] Not, admittedly, the Christian faith as it was currently constituted – as in the *Discorsi*, Niccolò reproves contemporary Christianity for making men weak, albeit in slightly different terms – but rather, a more vigorous and bloodthirsty version, similar in many ways to the religion practised by the Romans.

That there should have been some continuity between the *Discorsi* and the *Arte della guerra* was, of course, only to be expected; but that Niccolò chose to articulate so many of the same arguments using a different lexicon – and with fewer overt references to liberty – is indicative of a desire to 'soften' his image. Though the *Discorsi* had been written more as an enquiry into the liberty and greatness of states than as a work of political opposition, it had provoked sufficient surprise among his friends that he appears to have thought it wise to protect himself against any suspicion that he might be harbouring republican sentiments. Needless to say, he could not repudiate the *Discorsi* entirely, but he seems to have realized he could nevertheless achieve the desired effect simply by transposing the substance of the text into a setting more attuned to the Medici's concerns, and by cloaking it in more familiar language.

Where the *Arte della guerra* did break new ground, however, was with regard to its treatment of weapons and fortifications. Although Niccolò had declared that he wanted to 'bring military practice back to ancient methods', he was not nearly as slavish in his admiration of the classical past as he claimed, and it was in arguing for the superiority of modern innovations that he went far beyond anything he had written before.[30] Whereas Niccolò had expressly condemned those who put their faith in fortresses in *Il principe*,[31] for example, he now extolled their merits, and devoted considerable effort to describing how walls should be built, the relative merits of moats and ditches, the design of castles and the fortification of gatehouses, in terms redolent of the very

latest developments in military architecture. Perhaps most strikingly, he also expressed considerable admiration for artillery.
Though he was prepared to admit that cannons had their limitations, especially in sieges, he recognized that, if they were used
properly, they could win or lose a battle, and he devoted much
time to explaining how they could best be deployed and protected.[32]
He was even more enamoured of guns – especially arquebuses,
the accuracy of which had only recently been improved. Recognizing
that they could be every bit as effective as crossbows, if not more
so, he called for all citizens to be trained in their use.[33] This was
a truly revolutionary suggestion. As Christopher Lynch has noted,
Niccolò may actually have been the first person ever to advocate
compulsory weapons training.[34]

Of course, Fabrizio Colonna has to admit that he has never
actually put any of these theories into practice.[35] This was not for
want of trying. At the very beginning of the dialogue, Fabrizio tells
Cosimo Rucellai that anyone wishing to accomplish anything of
importance must first prepare themselves diligently and, as far as
possible, in secret, so that when a suitable opportunity presents itself,
he will be ready to put his plans into action.[36] But Fabrizio has never
had such an opportunity; and as such, he has never been able to
show the preparations he has made for 'bringing the soldiers back
into their ancient course.' For this, he could hardly be censured –
either by Cosimo or by anyone else. But he nevertheless hopes that
the lesson of his failure will inspire others to achieve what he never
could. As he tells his young friends towards the end of the dialogue,
whichever state first adopts the methods he has described will become
the master of Italy, just as the Macedonians, having perfected their
military techniques while their neighbours wasted their time in
theatres, had become masters of the world.[37]

*

No documentary evidence has survived to indicate what Lorenzo di
Filippo Strozzi made of the *Arte della guerra*, but his impressions can
only have been positive. Aware of how greatly the Medici needed
talented men with a gift for military matters just then, Lorenzo
appears to have told the cardinal that, despite Niccolò's questionable
past, he might be someone they could use. When the cardinal returned

to Florence at the beginning of March 1520, Lorenzo and a few friends from the Orti Oricellari therefore arranged for Niccolò to be introduced to him. What they talked about cannot be known with any certainty, but, based on Battista della Palla's remarks a few weeks later, it seems likely that they discussed both the *Arte della guerra* and Niccolò's plans for future works.[38] Whatever the case, however, there was soon talk of an imminent return to favour. A few days later, Lorenzo received a letter from his brother, Filippo, congratulating him on having arranged the meeting. 'I am quite pleased that you presented Machiavelli to the Medici,' Filippo wrote, 'because, should he gain the confidence of [our] masters, he is a person on the rise.'[39]

Niccolò does not appear to have shared Filippo's optimism. Although his meeting with the cardinal seems to have gone well, the Medici had disappointed him so many times that he was probably wary of getting his hopes up. On 15 April, he wrote to his nephew, Giovanni Vernacci, in a decidedly morose frame of mind. Though deeply concerned with Giovanni's mounting legal troubles, he regretted that there was little point in him trying to help: 'because I would do you harm and not good, as a result of the conditions under which I exist.'[40]

Behind the scenes, however, things were changing for the better. Having evidently been taken with Niccolò's acuity, the cardinal had appealed to the pope on his behalf. Leo X was, perhaps, reluctant to abandon his previous antipathy at first, but the cardinal's praise, coupled with the looming threat of war and a sell-out performance of *Mandragola* in Rome, seems to have persuaded him that the fallen chancellor deserved a second chance. On 26 April, Battista della Palla wrote to him with good news. After speaking at length to the pope, he had been 'asked to tell Cardinal de' Medici on His Holiness' behalf ... that he will be very pleased if the goodwill that His Reverend Lordship [had] towards [Niccolò] should henceforth be put into effect.'[41]

What this entailed was explained only in the most general terms. In his usual, clumsy way, Battista suggests that Niccolò would be commissioned to write a new work on Florentine history, and intimates that this had been discussed a few days earlier. Battista did not, however, specify what its scope would be, how long it would be or what remuneration Niccolò would receive in return. But the details can hardly have mattered to Niccolò just then. Having only recently mourned the death of his political career, he was now rising from the grave – a man reborn.

24

A Second Apprenticeship

(April–December 1520)

Excited though Niccolò was, he knew better than to expect a contract to be signed any time soon. His long years in the wilderness had taught him that, while the Medici were quick with their promises, they could often be slow to keep their word – and this would be no exception. Though Leo X had been persuaded to swallow his bitterness, neither he nor Cardinal Giulio could trust Niccolò completely, and given how sensitive the political situation was just then, they would not want to commit themselves without first making sure of him. Whether Niccolò liked it or not, therefore, he would have to serve a second apprenticeship. How far and how fast he earned the Medici's confidence would be up to him.

After two months of waiting, Niccolò was put to the test. On 7 July 1520, he was sent to Lucca to deal with the bankruptcy of a certain Michele Guinigi. It was, on the surface, an unremarkable case.[1] The dissolute son of an illustrious family, Michele had been disinherited for his wayward conduct, but his father had been unable to deny him the capital to establish a business of his own in the Lucchese *contado*. For a time, this had flourished. Michele entered into partnership with a number of other merchants and, thanks to the prestige of his family name, was given credit whenever he asked. But old habits die hard, and before long, Michele had run up large gambling debts, for which his partners were understandably reluctant to share responsibility. His creditors, many of them Florentines, were horrified. So carefully had Michele disguised his gambling debts that they took priority over everything else; once they had been satisfied, there would be almost nothing left to pay his commercial obligations. His creditors could, of course, have fought him in the courts, but, before judicial proceedings could get underway, the Florentine Signoria intervened. Ordinarily, they would have had nothing to do with matters such as this, but since Michele's creditors included Jacopo Salviati – the brother-in-law of Pope Leo X, and the father of a cardinal – his bankruptcy had political implications. At Cardinal Giulio de' Medici's insistence, the Signoria had therefore urged the Anziani of Lucca simply to set aside Michele's gambling debts on their own authority and force him to settle his mercantile dues. This had put the Anziani in a difficult position. Though they would have been happy to oblige the Medici, they were nevertheless wary of antagonizing the Guinigi, who, despite Michele's recent stupidity, were still one of the city's most powerful families. Not wishing to offend either, they prevaricated, in the hope that the whole affair could be settled in the courts. But the cardinal could not be brushed off so lightly. Seeing that there was no point repeating their earlier demands, he instead decided to despatch an emissary to secure the appointment of an independent arbitration committee, before whom the whole dispute could be placed. It was for this task that Niccolò had been chosen.

Niccolò's friends could not help feeling it was a little beneath him. Even though he had undertaken a similar mission to Genoa two years before, Giovambattista Bracci thought it was a matter more for 'an accountant or a pen-pusher' than for someone of his experience.[2] But Niccolò was happy to take the job. The extra money would come in handy and, besides, he was glad to have the opportunity to prove himself.

With a smile on his face and a spring in his step, he began packing his saddle bag. Before he had finished, however, he received an additional commission. Evidently realizing that he was more than capable of dealing with Michele Guinigi's bankruptcy, the cardinal asked him to take the Anziani of Lucca to task for minting too many silver coins of inferior purity and weight, an infringement of currency agreements which had already caused serious problems for Florentine merchants.[3] No doubt in a cheerful frame of mind, Niccolò then set off. Barely three weeks after his arrival, however, he received yet another commission from the cardinal – this time to request the extradition of three Sicilian students responsible for causing a disturbance in Pisa.[4]

The cardinal's letter was written in a stiff chancellery style. Though courteous, his greeting (*Spectabilis vir, amice mi carissime*; 'Dear man, my most dear friend') was a well-worn formula, devoid of any real warmth; his instructions were succinct to the point of terseness; and his manner haughty.[5] Yet, beneath this cold and forbidding surface lay a sincere respect for Niccolò's abilities. In the opening sentence, the cardinal acknowledged the former secretary's 'prudence'; while, in his closing remarks, he expressed his certainty that Niccolò would carry out his duties with 'all diligence and circumspection'.[6] This was a far cry from the praise that Niccolò had been accustomed to receiving during his time in office, but it would have been enough to bolster his confidence.

He did not get the chance to savour the cardinal's words for long. The very next day, Filippo de' Nerli sent him a letter that must have made his heart sink.[7] Though Filippo was happy to report that life in Florence had become a little freer of late, he had grave misgivings about Niccolò's future. The former chancellor's recent return to favour could not possibly last. As his brush with Giuliano and Lorenzo de' Medici had shown, he always made 'a stupid mess of these affairs'.[8] Besides, his enemies would be queuing up to cut him down, and it would be difficult, if not impossible, for him to parry their attacks. Even if he somehow managed to keep Michele Guinigi's bankruptcy case out of the courts, he would struggle to defend himself against a timely accusation whispered into the cardinal's ear. This being so, Filippo could not help feeling that Niccolò's stay in Lucca was going to be his 'last hurrah'. And the sooner Niccolò accepted this, the better.

So as not to seem too negative, Filippo was careful to round his letter out with a healthy dose of banter – including some gentle raillery about Niccolò's preference for writing in Italian, rather than in Latin, and a light-hearted reminder that Donato del Corno was still moaning about Niccolò's failure to pay an old debt. But Niccolò had no time for tittle-tattle. Now that his political rehabilitation was almost within reach, he was damned if he was going to let his enemies snatch it away from him again. Ignoring Filippo's advice, he decided he would have to do something special to remind the Medici's friends of his abilities – both as a political adviser and as an historian.

*

While the negotiations over Michele Guinigi's bankruptcy dragged on, Niccolò busied himself writing the *Vita di Castruccio Castracani* ('Life of Castruccio Castracani').[9] Dedicated to Luigi Alamanni and Zanobi Buondelmonti, this purported to be a biography of a four-teenth-century *condottiere* who had risen to prominence as leader of the Tuscan Ghibellines and who had ruled Lucca – first as *capitano delle milizie*, then as duke – for more than a decade.[10] But it was not a history in the modern sense of the word. Despite offering a vivid portrait of its subject, it had scant regard for the truth. Drawing on the fantastical tales of Bartolomeo Cennami and on figments of his own imagination, Niccolò twisted great portions of Castruccio's life out of all recognition.[11] Whereas Castruccio had, in reality, been born into one of Lucca's most illustrious noble families, Niccolò concocted a cock-and-bull story about him being abandoned by his mother while still an infant, and found under some vines in the garden of a priest called Antonio Castracani.[12] It was the same story with Castruccio's youth. Although Niccolò must have known from his reading of Niccolò Tegrimi's recently published biography that Castruccio had spent his formative years in England before entering the service of Philip IV of France,[13] he instead claimed that the *condottiere* was taken into the household of an imaginary *signore* of Lucca named Francesco Guinigi while still a boy.[14] And so it went on. With an almost total disregard for the facts, Niccolò systemat-ically misrepresented Castruccio's rise to power, distorted his military exploits, exaggerated his triumphs, and ignored his shortcomings. Not even the condottiere's private life was safe. Glossing over Castruccio's wife, mistress, and children, Niccolò instead portrayed him as a lifelong bachelor, untouched by sexual desires and untrou-bled by the burdens of family. Most peculiarly of all, Niccolò also attributed to Castruccio a series of witty sayings that he had lifted from other sources.[15]

Yet truth was never Niccolò's aim. Like many other Renaissance historians, he had little interest in discovering what had actually happened, let alone in providing a faithful account of the past. Instead, he set out to craft a version of Castruccio's life which, given the *appearance* of truth, could illustrate his conception of *virtù* and inspire his readers to emulate the ideals of military and political leadership he had expounded in his earlier works – especially the *Arte della guerra* and *Il principe*.

Underlying Niccolò's narrative was the by now familiar opposition between greatness and fortune. Much as in *Il principe* and the *Arte della guerra*, he began by explaining that few of those who had achieved great things in history had enjoyed illustrious origins or the blessings of fortune.[16] Rather, it had only been by overcoming adversity – through courage, ruthlessness or cunning – that they had succeeded in making themselves the equal of the gods. There was, Niccolò believed, no better example of this than Castruccio Castracani – who, from being an unwanted foundling, had risen to the pinnacle of earthly glory.

In his youth, Castruccio had already displayed the virtues suited to making a man (or rather, a prince) loved and respected. Whenever he played with his friends in the piazza outside the church of San Michele, he distinguished himself not only by his superiority to the other boys, but also by his 'kingly authority',[17] and it had been this which had first brought him to the attention of Francesco Guinigi. Welcomed into the *signore*'s household, he then swiftly mastered 'all those capabilities and habits that are expected of a true gentleman': 'First of all, he made himself an excellent rider, managing even the most fiery horse with the greatest skill; and in jousts and tournaments, though he was a mere boy, he was more notable than anyone else, so that in every feat, whether of strength or skill, no man could be found who surpassed him.'[18]

Most striking of all, however, were his social graces. Just as Niccolò had recommended that a prince should always appear to be kind, faithful and honest in *Il principe*, so he praised the young Castruccio for being 'respectful to his betters, modest with his equals, and gracious with his inferiors.'[19] It was hardly surprising that, in Niccolò's version of events, Castruccio had earned the admiration of everyone in Lucca before he had even begun to shave his beard.

When Castruccio came of age, he began to manifest virtues of a different kind. The first of these were military. Naturally, his bravery was apparent from the beginning. Fighting against the Guelphs of Pavia, shortly after his eighteenth birthday, he showed such courage that, by the time he returned to Lucca, his fame had already spread throughout Lombardy.[20] But, following Francesco Guinigi's death, his skill as a general came to the fore. As Niccolò would have it, his conduct mirrored the advice Fabrizio Colonna had given in the *Arte della guerra*, and, to a lesser extent, Niccolò's description of military leadership in the *Discorsi*. Aware that a few well-motivated soldiers could be more formidable than a large but weak-willed army, he took care to foster a vigorous fighting spirit among his men. Not only did he deliver rousing speeches before every battle (cf. *Arte della guerra*, 4), but he also made sure that he led by example (cf. *Discorsi*, 3.1). He was always the first onto the field of battle and the last to leave. No less inspiring was his daring. 'Nobody,' Niccolò claimed, 'was ever bolder about entering into dangers, or more wary in getting out of them.'[21] What was more, he was also a skilled tactician. He placed a high value on intelligence, knew the importance of choosing an advantageous position, and exploited his enemy's weaknesses better than any man alive (cf. *Arte della guerra*, 4, 6). Most importantly of all, he was cunning. 'Never when he could win by fraud did he attempt to win by force,' Niccolò explained, 'because he used to say that the victory, not the manner of victory, would bring you renown' (cf. *Arte della guerra*, 6).[22]

His brilliance was never more evident than in his victory over the Florentines at the Battle of Serravalle.[23] As was his habit, Castruccio had chosen his ground carefully. The narrow pass which lay beneath the town would negate the Florentines' numerical advantage, while the hill on which Serravalle was situated would provide him with the cover he needed to manoeuvre himself into position without being seen. But it was through subterfuge and trickery that he turned a likely victory into a complete rout. By keeping the bulk of his army in Montecarlo, some ten kilometres away, he lulled the Florentines into a false sense of security. Thus reassured, they decided to camp outside Serravalle and cross the hill the next day. Under cover of darkness, however, Castruccio captured the town with a small force without making a sound, and, at around midnight, set out from Montecarlo with the rest of his army, taking up position outside Serravalle in silence a few hours later. The next morning, when the Florentines began to climb the hill from one side, Castruccio's army advanced towards them from the other. This caught the Florentines by surprise and, in a matter of minutes, they were in the grip of confusion. Before they could recover themselves, Castruccio had sent 1,000 cavalrymen through the town, 'and struck the enemy on the flank with such fury that the Florentine soldiers, unable to resist their charge, and defeated as much by the place as by their enemies, fled.'

Castruccio was, however, also blessed with political virtues. While still a young man, he had known how to make himself loved, but upon succeeding Francesco Guinigi as *signore* of Lucca, he had learned how to make himself feared, as well. Faced with unrest on two separate occasions, he responded in precisely the way Niccolò had recommended in *Il principe*. The first was, perhaps, the least serious. Among the few who disliked Castruccio at the beginning of his rule was a certain Giorgio degli Opizi, the leader of the Guelph faction, who had hoped that he – rather than Castruccio – would succeed Francesco Guinigi.[24] Consumed by jealousy, Giorgio started spreading malign gossip about Castruccio and threatened to put him into disfavour with Robert of Naples, who could easily drive him from Lucca. Not wanting to take any risks, Castruccio therefore secured the support of the *condottiere* Uguccione della Faggiuola, smuggled his troops into the city by stealth and killed Giorgio and his family. Realizing it was foolish to depend on foreign arms (cf. *Il principe*, 7), however, he avoided placing too much trust in Uguccione and fully anticipated a rupture. When they eventually came to blows, therefore, Castruccio had no difficulty in defeating his erstwhile ally and securing his position both as *signore* of Lucca and as the champion of the Tuscan Ghibellines.[25]

The second outbreak of unrest was more dangerous. The Poggio family, who had long supported Castruccio against his enemies, felt they had been poorly rewarded for their services, and, uniting with the other Lucchese families, rose in rebellion against him.[26] After an initial assault in which a magistrate was killed, Stefano di Poggio – 'an old and peaceful man' – offered to mediate, and asked the rebels to lay down their arms while he parleyed with Castruccio. Out of sheer naivety, they did so. This gave Castruccio his opening. After listening to Stefano's plaint, he sprang a trap similar to that used by Cesare Borgia at Sinigaglia (cf. *Il principe*, 7). Making a great show of clemency and kindness, he invited the Poggio family to join him for talks. When they arrived in his camp, however, he took them prisoner and had them put to death – along with the unfortunate Stefano.

In Niccolò's eyes, Castruccio was the perfect prince. A paragon of *virtù*, he had succeeded in securing his rule at home and enlarging his domains abroad. He had been loved by his soldiers, respected by his subjects and feared by his enemies. He was, indeed, a man worthy not merely of admiration, but also of emulation. Yet Niccolò nevertheless felt obliged to add a note of caution – and, in doing so, departed from his earlier works. Whereas, in the *Arte della guerra* and *Il principe*, he had maintained that the mastery of fortune would lead to everlasting glory, he now observed that fortune could never truly be overcome, and that glory would always fade. For all his merits, Niccolò explained, even Castruccio had succumbed to fortune in the end. After his last victory over the Florentines, he had stood at the gates of Fucecchio, waiting to welcome his soldiers back.[27] He was still drenched in sweat from the fighting, and, in the breeze which was blowing from the river, he caught a chill. Within hours, he was mortally ill. Realizing that he was dying, he called Francesco Guinigi's son, Paolo, to his side, and delivered a stirring speech, tinged with bitterness and remorse. Had he known that fortune would cut him down in the middle of his journey, he would have striven less and bequeathed to Paolo a smaller, but more secure state. For, though the extent of his territories was a source of some pride, it grieved him that they were 'weak and insecure'. Lucca was unstable, Pisa 'fickle and full of deceit' and Pistoia disloyal.[28] The Florentines were 'embittered and in a thousand ways injured, but not destroyed'; and neither the Visconti of Milan nor the Holy Roman Emperor could be trusted.[29] With his dying breath, he therefore urged Paolo to rely on nothing but his own wit and the memory of his ability, and, above all, to know himself. If he felt he was not cut out for war, he should endeavour to reign instead 'by means of the arts of peace'. But his advice was of no avail. After Castruccio's death, Paolo – to whom '[a]bility and fortune were not so friendly' – soon 'lost Pistoia, then Pisa,' and only 'with difficulty kept the sovereignty of Lucca.'[30] Though Castruccio's memory lived on, therefore, the glory of his conquests had gone forever.

This had clear implications for the Medici. Though they should strive to emulate Castruccio's *virtù*, they should also weigh carefully the merits of pursuing further territorial expansion. If Cardinal Giulio and the pope persisted with their plan to ally with Charles V and drive the French out of Italy, they might well succeed in enlarging the Papal States and covering themselves in glory. But it was equally possible that they would be defeated by Francis I. Were this to happen, they would be forced to cede the duchy of Ferrara to France, and might even find their hold on Florence weakened. Of course, only they could decide which course was wisest. But, if they felt they were not quite as strong as they had supposed, no one – least of all Niccolò – would think ill of them for preferring a small but stable state, to a large but 'weak and insecure' one.

*

Niccolò finished the *Vita di Castruccio Castracani* by the end of August, and immediately sent it to Zanobi Buondelmonti and Luigi Alamanni in Florence. On 6 September, Zanobi replied with fulsome praise. Writing on behalf of everyone in the Orti Oricellari, he confessed that the *Vita* was 'as dear to us as anything in the world . . . We read it and considered it thus together a while, Luigi [Alamanni], [Francesco] Guidetti, [Jacopo da] Diaceto, Antonio Francesco [degli Albizzi], and I. We all decided that it was a good thing, and well written . . . Jacopo Nardi and Battista della Palla . . . have seen it and read it, and they praise it highly. Pierfrancesco Portinari and Alessandro also . . . have universally commended it . . .'[31]

Of course, this was not to say that the *Vita* was perfect. Here and there, there were passages that could be improved. The catalogue of 'Castruccio's' apophthegms, for example, would 'turn out better if it was shortened, because in addition to these sayings or witticisms of his being too numerous, there are some of them that are attributed to other sages, both ancient and modern.'[32] But these were just trivial concerns. On the whole, Zanobi and his companions thought it a magnificent achievement – in the best traditions of humanist historiography. They thought Castruccio's deathbed speech, in particular, exceptional. There, Zanobi explained, Niccolò had risen higher in his style than anywhere else, 'just as the material deserves.'[33]

It seemed to everyone in the Orti Oricellari that Niccolò ought to start work on his history of Florence as soon as possible. Zanobi himself desired it 'above all things',[34] and it is more than likely the others felt the same. Whether or not any of them said anything of this kind to Cardinal Giulio cannot be known, but Niccolò was sufficiently encouraged to think a contract would not be long in coming. At some point after 10 September, he even sent his brother-in-law Francesco del Nero a draft of the conditions under which he wanted the Studio Fiorentino to commission him to write his proposed history.[35] Tactfully, he avoided specifying what his salary would be, but he took care to give himself as much freedom as possible. Bubbling over with self-confidence, he stipulated that he should be allowed to 'write the annals or else the history of the things done by the state and the city of Florence, from whatever time may seem to him most appropriate, and in whatever language – either Latin or Tuscan – may seem best to him.'

*

By mid-September, Niccolò's mission was drawing to a close. Despite some difficulties,[36] he had at last succeeded in persuading the Anziani of Lucca to set up an arbitration committee to settle the dispute over Michele Guinigi's bankruptcy.[37] With nothing else to keep him there, he packed up his bags and returned to Florence, no doubt feeling quite pleased with himself.

But, if he expected Cardinal Giulio de' Medici to welcome him with open arms, he was disappointed. There were no official thanks – and no contract. This should not, in itself, have caused him too much alarm. After all, he had never been congratulated for carrying out missions in the past, and he knew only too well how slowly the wheels of the Medici's bureaucracy could turn. But it must have made him nervous, nonetheless.

Not wishing to leave anything to chance, Niccolò began writing a detailed report on his mission, now known as the *Sommario delle cose della città di Lucca* ('Summary of the affairs of the city of Lucca').[38] There was, in principle, nothing unusual about this. As has recently been pointed out, it was standard practice for diplomats to write such reports at the end of an embassy, detailing not merely the course of the mission, but also reflections on the country, on its political affairs and its institutions.[39] Niccolò had already written several in the past: the *Rapporto di cose della Magna* (1508), the *Ritratto di cose di Francia* (1511) and the *Ritratto delle cose della Magna* (1514). But the *Sommario delle cose della città di Lucca* was not a report in the usual sense. It gave no clues as to what Niccolò's task had been; it said nothing about his negotiations with the Anziani; and it did not so much as mention Michele Guinigi. Nor, indeed, did it say much about Lucca and its countryside. Instead, it concentrated exclusively on Lucca's constitution. Such a narrow focus had not been chosen lightly. Although no addressee is named, the *Sommario* seems to have been intended either for the Signoria or – more likely – for the cardinal, who was then debating whether to continue with the reform of the Florentine government. Needless to say, Niccolò did not want to risk causing offence by offering unsolicited advice, but he seems to have realized that, by describing a very different form of constitution under the guise of a diplomatic report, he could provide a more subtle form of counsel – and thereby reaffirm his utility as a political adviser.

The *Sommario* was divided into three unequal sections. In the first, Niccolò described the organs of Lucchese government: the *Nove* – the supreme executive council – of which three members were chosen from each of the city's three quarters; the *gonfaloniere di giustizia*, who served for a mere two months, and who, with the *Nove*, made up the Anziani; the Council of Thirty-Six, elected for a term of six months; and the General Council, which Niccolò mistakenly believed consisted of seventy-two citizens. The second section then turned to examine the relationship between these bodies. To Florentines, who were used to a strong Signoria, the division of powers, in particular, must have seemed quite strange. While the Anziani convened the other magistracies and tabled motions for debate, their principal function was to supervise elections to civic offices in collaboration with the Council of Thirty-Six. Meanwhile, the General Council 'makes and unmakes laws, treaties [and] pacts, [and] imprisons and executes citizens.'[40] These peculiarities having been noted, Niccolò went on, in the third and final section, to offer a critical assessment of the Lucchese constitution.[41]

One of the most positive features was that the Anziani of Lucca had no authority over ordinary citizens – thus limiting the opportunities for abuse. But, unfortunately, they also lacked stature. After the expiry of their terms, members of the Anziani had to wait many years before they were eligible to stand again. Since this made it difficult to achieve anything particularly remarkable in office, only members of the lower classes tended to serve. Paradoxically, the effect of this was to concentrate *real* power in the hands of wealthy aristocrats. Rather than hold office themselves, they used patronage and family networks to control those who did. Since the Anziani administered elections, this gave the *grandi* a stranglehold on government. To Niccolò's eyes, this was a perversion of the natural order of things. Whereas in Rome and Venice, the common people administered elections to office, the *grandi* advised and the executive ruled, in Lucca exactly the opposite was the case. This had some advantages. It encouraged the common people to aspire to office; it allowed legislation to be passed reasonably quickly; and it arguably protected the city from corruption and overweening ambition. But it was nevertheless seriously flawed. Since the *grandi* exercised such enormous influence, they could easily prevent the General Council from punishing someone who threatened the state if they so wished. Were the *grandi*'s interests to intersect with those of a rebellious populace, or of intemperate youths – the two most dangerous groups in any polity – Lucca would thus find itself without any means of defending itself. As such, Niccolò suggested that an additional magistracy – of four or six citizens – should be established specifically to punish any transgressions by these two groups. But, even with this qualification, he could not recommend Lucca's constitution as a model for imitation. While the Medici had always shown a marked fondness for ruling Florence through the ties of blood and patronage, he discreetly warned the cardinal that it might be better to look to Rome and Venice for inspiration.

*

There is no way of knowing whether the cardinal ever read the *Sommario delle cose della città di Lucca*, but he was nevertheless sufficiently impressed with Niccolò's conduct that, on 8 November, the former chancellor was finally awarded the contract he had been hoping for. Over the next two years, he was to write 'the annals or history of Florence', and to carry out any other tasks which the officials of the Studio Fiorentino might think necessary.[42] In return, he was to receive a salary of a hundred *fiorini di studio* – about half what he had been paid in the chancellery, but still infinitely more than he had earned since leaving.

Even if he had not been returned to office, this was a great honour. By the early sixteenth century, the writing of 'official' histories had become integral to Florence's sense of civic pride.[43] Often paid for by the Florentine government, works like Leonardo Bruni's *Historiarum Florentinarum libri XII*, Poggio Bracciolini's *Historiae Florentini populi* and Bartolomeo Scala's *Historia Florentinorum* had served not only to memorialize the city's past, but also to shape its identity in the present.[44] They had defined *who* its people were; they had explained what political values they stood for; and, more often than not, they had provided a justification of its system of government, as well. As such, the writing of 'official' history could not be entrusted to just anyone. It required an elegant style of writing, a searching eye for detail and – most importantly – the 'right' political outlook. That Niccolò had been commissioned to write a new history of Florence was thus a mark both of his literary talent and of the confidence reposed in him by the cardinal.

*

Yet, as the terms of Niccolò's contract suggested, the cardinal was interested in more than just his talent as a historian. On 17 November, Filippo de' Nerli wrote to tell Niccolò that the cardinal had requested a copy of the *Arte della guerra*.[45] What the cardinal made of it has not been recorded, but his impressions can only have been positive. At some point over the next few months, he gave Niccolò another, more pressing, commission – to draw up a set of proposals for how Florence's government could be remodelled.

Niccolò jumped at the chance, and, by the following Candlemas, his report was finished. Now known as the *Discorso delle cose fiorentine dopo la morte di Lorenzo* ('Discourse on Florentine affairs after the death of Lorenzo'), this was by far the longest of his political memoranda.[46] Dedicated to Pope Leo X and illustrated with frequent references to Florentine history, it set out to explain how the ideas he had outlined in the *Discorsi* and the *Sommario delle cose della città di Lucca* could be used not only to rectify the deficiencies of Lorenzo's regime, but also to safeguard the Medici's position in the longer term.

Niccolò was, however, conscious that he had to tread carefully. While the cardinal's highest priority was to secure his family's future, Niccolò knew that he was wary of tinkering with the Florentine constitution – and it was not hard to see why. In the past, Florence had often changed her system of government. Between 1393 and 1512, the city had been ruled by three different '*stati*' – that of the *ottimati* (1393–1434), that of Cosimo de' Medici and his heirs (1434–94) and the popular republic of Savonarola and Piero Soderini (1494–1512).[47]

But none of them had lasted for long. Though very different, each had collapsed in turn, forcing its leaders to escape into exile and plunging the city into yet another bout of violent unrest. This being so, it was only natural for the cardinal to be wary of reform.[48] If he started fiddling with the constitution now, there was no guarantee that he would leave his family any stronger than before. Indeed, if the past was anything to go by, he might inadvertently end up sowing the seeds of its demise.

Niccolò's first task was thus to expose the fallacy of the cardinal's reasoning. That Florence had experienced such instability in the past was, he explained, the result not of constitutional reform per se, but of the inadequacy of the governments that had been established. Although each of the three *stati* resembled one of the three 'true' constitutions described by Aristotle, none of them had actually been endowed with the qualities of either a principality or a republic (whether aristocratic or popular).[49] Rather than being directed towards the common good – as Aristotle had recommended in the *Politics* (3.6, 1279a17–18), as Cicero had urged repeatedly in the *De officiis* and as Niccolò himself had suggested in the *Discorsi* – they had each been established solely for the sake of strengthening and safeguarding an individual faction or party. Yet this they had never been able to achieve. Precisely because they had excluded others from sharing in the business of government, they had inevitably fuelled the growth of discontent – and thereby created the conditions for revolution. According to Niccolò, the *ottimati*-led regime founded by Maso degli Albizzi had drawn up lists of people eligible for office too far in advance, had created untold opportunities for corruption, had done nothing to stop the growth of factions and had concentrated too much power – but too little prestige – in the Signoria's hands. That it lasted for forty years was nothing short of a miracle. Had the Visconti Wars not kept it united, it would surely have collapsed long before it did. '[T]ending more towards a princedom than a republic,' the government of Cosimo de' Medici had lasted a little longer – partly because it was established with the help of the *popolo*, and partly because authority was concentrated in the hands of a remarkable man. But the marriage between popular and signorial elements ultimately proved its undoing. Since everything was done 'according to the will of one man, yet . . . decided with the approval of many,' it was slow to act and vulnerable to external shocks. Even more flawed was the popular republic of Savonarola and Piero Soderini. Despite its pretentions, this had not really been a republic at all. It failed to satisfy the *popolo*, it lacked coercive power and it had proved so fragile that it had been necessary to appoint a pseudo-signorial *gonfaloniere a vita*, who 'if he was intelligent and wicked, could easily make himself a prince; [but who,] if he was good and weak ... could easily be driven out, to the ruin of the whole government.'

Wisely, Niccolò avoided discussing the government Florence had had since 1512 in too much detail. But even the cardinal would agree that Lorenzo's death had 'brought things to a point where new types of government must be considered.' Since it was evident that reform was necessary, the challenge was therefore to determine *how* the constitution could be remodelled to ensure lasting stability for the Medici regime. There had, of course, been plenty of proposals, but they had all simply repeated the same old mistakes. Those who said Florence should return to how it had been governed under Cosimo and Lorenzo 'il Magnifico' de' Medici, for example, failed to realize that this had been an inherently unstable system of government, and would surely suffer the same fate if it were revived. Nor were calls for the establishment of a truly 'popular' republic any more convincing. The proponents of this scheme spoke only in generalities and seemed to have no idea how to overcome the weaknesses of the previous republic. Clearly, if Florence's constitution was to be reformed, it would have to be modelled on completely different lines. But what?

Niccolò's answer was comparatively simple. Since Florence's *stati* had failed because they had been defective constitutional hybrids, it followed that only a government which was 'either a true princedom or a true republic' would succeed. For, whereas a hybrid could easily collapse into tyranny or mob-rule, a princedom could only degenerate into a republic, and a republic collapse into a princedom. Having only 'one path to dissolution', rather than two, 'true' republics and 'true' princedoms were hence stronger and more stable than anything in between.

As in the *Discorsi*, Niccolò did not propose to say much about true principalities other than that they could not easily be set up where a people were accustomed to equality. In Florence, for example, 'where equality is great, the establishment of inequality would be necessary; [while] in walled towns, noble lords would have to be installed, who in support of their prince would with their arms and their followers stifle the city and the whole province.'

Instead, Niccolò concentrated on 'true' republics. This was, he argued, a system of government to which Florence was particularly suited. He also knew the cardinal was 'much inclined towards' such a constitution. In fact, he suspected the only reason the cardinal had put off establishing it was because he had not yet discovered a means of retaining his authority and safeguarding his friends. Thankfully, however, Niccolò had found a solution, and he begged the cardinal's indulgence while he outlined his scheme.

In every city, Niccolò explained, there existed three different sorts of men: the *primi* (the most important citizens), the *mezzani* (the middling bourgeoisie) and the *universalità dei cittadini* (the rest of the citizen body).[50] If a republic was to be firmly established, *all* of these must be satisfied. In Florence, this required several key changes to be made. To satisfy the ambition of the *primi*, it was necessary for them to be confirmed in their 'status as a governing elite', and accorded the 'grandeur' of which he had spoken in the *Sommario delle cose della città di Lucca*. Since the current Signoria and colleges were so lacking in dignity that 'the most important and influential men sit in them only rarely',[51] Niccolò therefore recommended that the Signoria, the *Otto di Pratica*, and the *Dodici Buon' Uomini* be abolished.[52] In their place, the pope should appoint sixty-five 'friends and confidants' to conduct the business of government for life. Of them, one should be chosen to serve as *gonfaloniere di giustizia* for two or three years. The remaining sixty-four should be divided into two groups of thirty-two. One of these was to govern one year, the other the next. When in office, each group of thirty-two was to be subdivided into four groups of eight, which would each reside with the *gonfaloniere* in the Palazzo della Signoria and carry out the functions of the current Signoria for a period of three months. Meanwhile, the thirty-two *not* in office in a given year would act as advisers, replacing the now-defunct *pratiche*. To satisfy the *mezzani*, Niccolò suggested doing away with the Seventy, the Hundred and the Council of the People, and replacing them with a council of 200 citizens, to be appointed by the pope for life, and known as the *Consiglio dei Scelti* ('Council of the Chosen').

Thus far, Niccolò's proposals were comparatively uncontentious. Not only did they reflect ideas he had previously voiced in the *Sommario delle cose della città di Lucca*, but they also chimed neatly with the reforms which the cardinal had already enacted. When he turned to address the *universalità dei cittadini*, however, Niccolò ventured into more dangerous territory. This group, he explained, would never be satisfied unless their power was restored.[53] As such, the Medici had little choice but to reopen the Great Council with 1,000, or at least 600 members. This could, of course, be done gradually over a period of many years, but Niccolò envisaged that, in time, the Council 'would allot, just as they formerly did, all the offices and magistracies', except those appointed by the pope and the cardinal.

This, of course, would guarantee that all three sections of Florentine society were appeased. Yet it ran counter to the Medici's most cherished beliefs. At least since the expulsion of Piero de' Medici in 1494, they had regarded the Great Council as antithetical to the sort of regime they wished to re-establish. It was too large, it was too unwieldy and, crucially, it was too much of a threat. However wide their network of clients and friends, they could never be sure of bending a majority to their will. There was always a risk the Council might appoint their enemies to key posts and thereby undermine the stability of their regime.

Niccolò was, of course, at pains to point out that this really was the *only* way to placate the people, and that it would be safer for the Medici to reopen the Great Council on their own terms than be forced to do so by their enemies at a later date. But he evidently realized that, if the Medici's position in the new republic was to be secure, they needed a way of keeping the *popolo* in check. Rather than giving the Great Council the freedom to appoint who it wanted to offices and magistracies, for example, Niccolò suggested the Medici be given the right to appoint eight *accoppiatori*, who, 'remaining in secrecy, [could] declare elected whom they wish[ed], and [could] deny election to anybody.'[54]

But, while control over elections was all very well and good, Niccolò recognized that it was not enough to secure the Medici's position on its own. After all, Cosimo and Lorenzo 'il Magnifico' had each exercised a more informal right to appoint chosen candidates to offices and magistracies in the past, yet it had proved insufficient either to safeguard them against plots, or to prevent Lorenzo's son, Piero, from being driven into exile. In order to keep the Signoria, the Two Hundred and the Great Council in check, Niccolò therefore suggested that the pope and the cardinal be given 'as much authority during the lives of both as is held by the entire people of Florence.'[55] They alone should have the right to appoint the *Otto di Guardia* – which maintained law and order – while the militia should be divided into two brigades, each headed by a commissioner of their choosing. This would give them absolute control over the armed forces, over criminal judges and over the laws – in short, over everything they needed to maintain constitutional balance, to keep all sections of the populace happy and to assure their own position.[56]

What Niccolò had described was, in essence, a modified version of a 'mixed' constitution. The Great Council would constitute the 'popular' component; the Signoria and the Two Hundred the 'oligarchic'; and the Medici the 'royal'. Each would keep the others in check and, together, they would ensure all elements of Florentine society were satisfied, while simultaneously securing the Medici's government. But Niccolò was under no illusions about it. He knew it would only work as long as the pope and the cardinal were alive. Since they were both churchmen, they had no heirs to take their place when they died; and without heirs, there would be nothing to maintain the delicate balance between the Signoria, the Two Hundred and the Great Council. As such, one further reform would be necessary to ensure the lasting stability of the republic: the transformation of the sixteen *gonfaloniere* into latter-day tribunes of the people.[57] Of the sixteen – who were to be elected as they always had been – four were to be chosen to serve as 'provosts' for a period of one month. Each week, one of these four was to stay in the Palazzo della Signoria. During this time, the Signoria was not to do anything unless the provost was present. Needless to say, he would not have the right to vote, or even to speak at meetings, but he would nevertheless have the power to veto any of the Signoria's decisions, or to appeal to the Thirty-Two if no decision could be reached. In much the same way, provosts were also to be present at meetings of the Thirty-Two, the Two Hundred and the Great Council – exercising in each case a power either of deferment or of appeal, but not of veto. This would, of course, ensure that each organ of the republic would be subject to oversight, and – crucially – accountable to all the others. It would also prevent public business from getting held up, and would go some way towards compensating the *popolo* for being excluded from the Signoria.

Niccolò was in no doubt that, when taken together, his proposals were nothing short of revolutionary. He knew perfectly well that, even with his qualifications, the cardinal would have difficulty accepting them. But it was impossible simply to sit by and do nothing. If the Florentine government remained as it was, Niccolò warned, the Medici would suffer 'a thousand vexations'.[58] Some citizens were already behaving too arrogantly, while others, because they felt unsafe, were demanding that order be restored – even though everyone had a different idea of how that should be done. The fragile peace that had reigned since Lorenzo's death was fracturing by the day. Unless reform were enacted soon, dire consequences would surely follow. Either 'in riot and haste a [new] leader will be set up who with arms and violence will defend the government', or the *popolo* would forcibly reinstitute the Great Council and take harsh measures against the patricians.[59] In either case, there would be much bloodshed, many exiles and, more likely than not, an end to Medici rule. If Niccolò's constitution was adopted, by contrast, Florence would 'lack nothing necessary to a free government'; its people would be satisfied; and the Medici would be safer than they had ever been before. Indeed, if the cardinal followed his advice, he would acquire the 'power and material for making [his family] immortal, and for surpassing by far . . . [his] father's and [his] grandfather's glory.'[60]

*

Niccolò's proposals were not greeted with enthusiasm. Far too radical for the cardinal's tastes, his report was quietly shelved. Yet Niccolò had not done himself a disservice. While he may not have been completely attuned to the Medici's thinking, he could reassure himself that his opinion had still been sought. With the sweat of his brow and the power of his mind, he had earned both their confidence and their respect. No longer the political outsider, he had been restored, if not to office, then at least to a certain dignity, and, as he embarked on the *Istorie fiorentine*, he could look forward to even happier days ahead.

25

The Republic of Clogs

(January–December 1521)

As 1521 dawned, the fears and frustrations of recent years having been swept away, Niccolò seemed at last to be at ease with himself. Any 'unfinished business' left over from his chancellery days had been settled, and he had been given a commission which was not only to his taste as a man of learning, but which also flattered what little vanity remained to him. He had nothing left to prove. With all political ambition now stripped away, he settled down to write what he hoped would be his own memorial.

Nothing, it seemed, could disturb his newfound contentment. Though, in the past, Giovanni Vernacci's financial troubles had caused him to tear his hair out with worry, his nephew's wayward habits now elicited nothing more than sober good sense, and he did what he could to put Giovanni's affairs in order. On 15 February 1521, Niccolò asked him for power of attorney, promised to deal with the *Monte* on his behalf and proposed to invest a legacy he had received from 'Madonna Vaggia' at a preferential rate of interest.[1] There were, admittedly, some trifling matters still to attend to, but in the meantime, Giovanni's debts had at least been settled.

Not even a letter from Piero Soderini could shake Niccolò from his serenity. Having recently failed to persuade Niccolò to accept the chancellorship of the tiny Adriatic republic of Ragusa (Dubrovnik), Soderini now tried to tempt him with an even more attractive proposition.[2] On learning that the aristocratic *condottiere*, Prospero Colonna, was looking for a secretary, Soderini had taken the liberty of suggesting Niccolò's name. Perhaps aware of how flatteringly his cousin, Fabrizio Colonna, had been depicted in the *Arte della guerra*, Prospero had welcomed the idea and had given Soderini permission to offer Niccolò the job.[3] The work would be demanding and would no doubt require a good deal of travelling, but the stipend was generous: 200 gold ducats, plus expenses – more than four times what Niccolò was being paid under his current contract. Of course, Soderini knew he would want to think it over, but the former *gonfaloniere* advised him to take it. 'I know of no better prospect at present,' Soderini wrote, 'and I judge it much better than to stay [in Florence] and write histories for *fiorini di sugello*.'[4] He was, perhaps, right. But Niccolò turned him down flat. Having at last found peace in Florence, he was not going to sell it, even for all the gold in Christendom.

To be sure, Niccolò could not pretend that his freedom was complete. According to the terms of his contract, he could still be called upon to perform duties which would take him away from the *Istorie fiorentine*, and which might not always be to his taste. Yet, as he was drawn into the maelstrom of Florentine affairs in the months that followed, he proved that he could face these, too, with smiling equanimity.

*

Not long after Niccolò had rejected Soderini's offers, the long-awaited conflict between Charles V and Francis I of France at last broke out.[5] Charles had done his best to avoid it. Prior to his election, he had signed a treaty with Francis which he had hoped would reduce the tension between them. Though Charles refused to surrender the kingdom of Naples, he had acknowledged the French king's rival claim, and had offered him a large annual subvention by way of compensation. In return, Francis promised to recognize Charles as king of the Romans once his election had been confirmed, and to resolve any remaining territorial disputes in the north. At the time, Francis had been happy to agree to this – especially as Charles, then still a political novice, was not yet firmly established in his realms, and hence in no position to threaten him. But, by January 1521, Francis had changed his mind. Having been crowned king of the Romans in Aachen the previous October, Charles was growing in confidence and looked set to be every bit as ambitious as his grandfather. It seemed quite possible that, in the not too distant future, he would cross the Alps and conquer the duchy of Milan while en route to Rome for an imperial coronation. Horrified, Francis decided to strike first. While Charles was mired in religious dissent in Germany and beset by rebellion in Castile, the king launched a series of coordinated attacks against Luxembourg and Navarre, in the hope of keeping him busy, as far from Milan as possible.[6]

Francis had, however, underestimated the young king of the Romans. Though barely twenty-one years old, Charles was determined to repel the French attacks and punish Francis for his temerity. After condemning Martin Luther at the Diet of Worms, he crushed the Castilian revolt, raised a new army and drove the French forces from both Navarre and Luxembourg. His frontiers thus secure, he set about tilting the balance of power in Italy in his favour. In May, he concluded an alliance with the pope.[7] For his part, Charles agreed to expel Francis from Milan, to restore the Sforza to their former duchy and to guarantee the Medici's position in Florence. In return, Leo agreed to send troops to the *Regno* in the event of a French invasion, and even to take the field against Venice, should it prove necessary. In a matter of weeks, preparations for an attack on French-held Milan had begun.

Though busy with his writing, Niccolò followed these developments with interest. Eagerly seizing on whatever scraps of information he could pick up from his correspondents, he would have speculated feverishly about how Florence might fare in the conflict ahead.[8] But if he expected the Medici to call on him for advice or to ask him to act as an emissary, he was mistaken.

*

He was, however, asked to help with another – very different – matter.[9] For some time, the Florentine government had been exercised by the peculiar status of the Franciscan Order in its territories. The Friars Minor, as they were often known, were everywhere. Reputedly founded by St Francis of Assisi himself, the Basilica of Santa Croce was by far the largest Franciscan church in Europe, and the Order had countless smaller friaries scattered throughout Florentine territory. Thanks in no small part to the vows of poverty by which all friars were bound, the Franciscans were tremendously popular with the common people.[10] They were also highly regarded as preachers. Taken together, this gave them considerable political influence – especially in times of crisis. Owing to a peculiarity of ecclesiastical organization, however, the Franciscans of Florence belonged to the much larger 'province' of Tuscany, of which Siena was also a part. This meant that whenever a Sienese subject was elected provincial minister – which happened more often than not – a foreign power was able to interfere in Florence's religious affairs, as and when it wanted. This had rankled with the Signoria for some time, but when it was discovered that, at the forthcoming general chapter of the Franciscan Order in Carpi, some 120 kilometres to the north, the provincial minister, a Sienese friar named Bernardino Tolomei, was planning to have another Sienese subject, Bernardino Ochino, elected as his successor, Cardinal de' Medici decided the time had come to act.[11] Unwilling to tolerate the subordination of their friars to Siena any longer, the Signoria wanted the province of Tuscany to be divided into two parts – one Florentine, the other Sienese. To achieve this, the Signora threw its weight behind Fra Ilarione Sacchetti, who intended to unseat Tolomei, exclude him from the chapter and install the procurator general, Francesco da Potenza – who was thought favourable to a split – as the new provincial minister. Perhaps realizing that Ilarione was a bit of a hothead, however, the *Otto di Pratica* also decided to send a secular ambassador to present their request more formally. For this task, they chose Niccolò.

On 11 May, Niccolò was ordered to proceed to Carpi, where the Franciscans' chapter was due to be held.[12] As his instructions explained, he was to seek out the minister general as soon as he got there and present the Florentines' request. Rather than complain about Sienese interference in their affairs – which would only cause unnecessary offence – he was to claim that they were instead motivated by a genuine concern for the Franciscans' spiritual wellbeing. In recent years, he was to point out, Florence's friars had seemed to lack the 'spirit' of holiness for which they had always been famous,[13] and that, as a consequence, donations from the laity had dropped off. The reason for this was a relaxation of discipline in Franciscan houses. Naturally, the Signoria had searched for a remedy, but they had come to the conclusion that it was impossible for them to restore the Order to its 'ancient reputation' unless the friaries in Florentine territory belonged to a 'separate and distinct' province.[14] It was a neat argument, calculated to appeal to the Franciscans' better instincts. But Fra Ilarione, ever the firebrand, thought it should be backed up with threats, just in case.[15] In a separate letter, he suggested Niccolò should intimate that the Signoria would very much like it if the friars were to adopt the Florentine proposal of their own free will, but that, if they did not, the cardinal would use his ecclesiastical authority to force them to do so.

Shortly after Niccolò left Florence, he received a second commission from the consuls of the *Arte della Lana* (wool guild).[16] Responsible for finding a preacher to deliver the Lenten sermons in the *Duomo* next year, they had settled on a Franciscan – Fra Giovanni Gualberto da Firenze, known as 'il Rovaio'. But, since their letters had so far gone unanswered, they asked Niccolò to do his best, while he was in Carpi, to secure Fra Giovanni's services for them.

Such a mission was, by any standards, beneath his dignity. Given that he had been used to dealing with kings, popes and emperors in the past, it was almost insulting for him to be sent to discuss such trifles with friars, especially when more momentous things were afoot. When his old friend, Francesco Guicciardini, heard what he had been asked to do, he was put in mind of the Spartan general, Lysander, 'to whom, after so many victories and trophies, was given the task of distributing meat to those very same soldiers whom he had so gloriously commanded.'[17] But, far from being upset, Niccolò seems to have accepted the commission with perfect good humour.

*

Pausing briefly to visit Guicciardini – then acting as the pope's commissioner in Modena[18] – Niccolò travelled over the Apennines at a leisurely pace and arrived in Carpi shortly before vespers on 16 May.[19] A plain, uninspiring little town, famed for its dishonesty,[20] it cannot have inspired confidence in him. But, as he stepped across the threshold of the recently-completed church of San Nicolò, he was surprised to find a gathering of friars that was more riven with petty concerns and backbiting than anything he had ever seen. It was, indeed, so fiercely politicized that, when he told Guicciardini about it, his friend derisively dubbed it the 'Republic of Clogs', after the footwear which the mendicants wore – and which they were not averse to using as weapons when their disputes became heated.[21]

No doubt hoping to get things over with quickly, Niccolò looked about for the minister general.[22] To his dismay, however, he found that the friars hadn't got around to electing one yet – and, until they did, he couldn't present the Signoria's request. It was almost too absurd for words, but, since there was nothing he could do about it, he would just have to bide his time. He still had the matter of the preacher to attend to, and he could always find ways of keeping himself amused.

Striding out of the church, Niccolò headed to the house of Sigismondo Santi, where he was to lodge for the duration of his mission.[23] A great friend of Guicciardini's, Santi was the chancellor of Count Alberto Pio, and was said to be 'a skilful man . . . greatly trusted by the pope'.[24] But he had a fondness for malicious gossip, and a taste for playing tricks on people.[25] He was certainly not Niccolò's cup of tea, but Niccolò was still grateful for his hospitality[26] and didn't want to ruffle any feathers. Heading sleepily to bed later that night, Niccolò seems to have decided to keep himself to himself, at least for the time being.

The next morning, 18 May, Niccolò was sitting on the toilet, mulling over his commission from the *Arte della Lana*, when a crossbowman arrived with a letter from Guicciardini, filled with amusing badinage.[27] Remembering Niccolò's distaste for contemporary religion, Guicciardini mocked the wool guild for entrusting the choice of a Lenten preacher to someone who had never given a hoot about salvation. He likened it to asking Pachierotto or Ser Saro – two notorious Florentine homosexuals – to 'find a beautiful and grateful wife for a friend.'[28] Nevertheless, he was sure Niccolò would carry out his task to the guild's satisfaction – not because he expected Niccolò suddenly to start caring about his soul (which, at his age, people would attribute to senility rather than to goodness), but because he knew this was what Niccolò's honour required.

In his reply, written later the same day, Niccolò reassured Guicciardini that he had no intention of letting Florence down,[29] but he preferred to choose a preacher who reflected his own ideas, rather than those of his fellow citizens. In this, as in so many other matters, Niccolò knew that he was at odds with them. Whereas they longed for a 'prudent, honest, and genuine' preacher to show them the way to Paradise, he wanted someone 'madder than [Fra Domenico da] Ponzo, wilier than Fra Giovanni [Savonarola], and more hypocritical than [Boccaccio's] Frate Alberto', who could 'teach them the way to go to the Devil'.[30] For it was only by learning the way to

Hell, he explained, that they would find out how to steer clear of it and follow the road to Paradise instead. Besides, it was easier to believe an honest crook than a deceitful saint. With a wry smile, he noted that, for this reason, he would probably choose 'il Rovaio', after all. If he was like everyone else in the Franciscan Order, Niccolò chuckled, he'd be just right.

Even so, Niccolò had to admit that he wasn't particularly enjoying his stay. He had never been one to idle about, and his enforced languor was already beginning to frustrate him. Needing something to keep him entertained, he had been looking for a way of playing a trick on the friars – and Guicciardini's letter had given him an idea. When the crossbowman had arrived that morning, Niccolò explained, it had caused a huge stir. In the mistaken belief that he must have come on urgent state business, the friars had immediately jumped to their feet in excitement and caused 'such a hubbub that everything was turned topsy-turvy'.[31] They all wanted to know what the news was – and, of course, Niccolò was happy to play along. Seizing the opportunity to heighten his prestige, he told them that 'the emperor was expected at Trent, that the Swiss had called fresh assemblies, [and] that the king of France wanted to go and confer with [Charles V], but his counsellors were advising him against going.'[32] Stunned, the hapless friars had 'stood around with their mouths hanging open and their caps in hand.' Even as Niccolò was writing, he was surrounded by a gaggle of them, gazing at him with awe and wonder. Needless to say, he found all this tremendously funny, and he couldn't help thinking that it'd be a good wheeze to keep the pretence going. To do this, Niccolò needed Guicciardini to keep sending him letters, ideally by means of impressive-looking couriers – and the more, the better!

Guicciardini was, of course, only too glad to oblige. The next morning, he scribbled a quick note and told the crossbowman who was delivering it to ride 'with the greatest dispatch . . . so that he [would] come with his shirt flying out behind his hips.'[33] This way, Guicciardini was sure everyone would believe that Niccolò was an extremely important person, and that his mission to Carpi had to do 'with more than just friars.' Just to be sure, however, he had taken the precaution of including with his letter a bundle of notices which had recently arrived from Zurich. Niccolò could either show them to the friars, or simply hold them portentously in his hands, just as he liked. Nevertheless, Guicciardini warned Niccolò not to take the prank too far. The previous afternoon, Guicciardini had written to Sigismondo Santi, explaining that Niccolò was a 'very exceptional person,' but without giving any further details. His curiosity piqued, Santi immediately wrote back, begging to be told what made Niccolò so exceptional. Naturally, Guicciardini had not bothered to reply, knowing this would keep him in suspense. But he advised Niccolò not to squander his renown too easily. He would not always be among hapless friars and naive bureaucrats, and, if his trick was uncovered, the opprobrium that would be heaped upon him might be hard to shake off.

Niccolò was, however, too excited to pay much attention to such warnings. Coupled with the breathlessness of the crossbowman, the huge bundle of letters that Guicciardini had sent caused such a stir that there was scarcely a person in Carpi who was not excited. Delighted, Niccolò had even decided to try tricking Sigismondo Santi, as well. Given how incurably nosy Santi was, it was easily done. When Niccolò showed him a few despatches about the Swiss and the king of France, and told him about Charles V's recent illness, Santi had been left 'drooling'.[34]

But Santi was not as gullible as the friars. Writing to Guicciardini later that afternoon, Niccolò expressed his fear that his host might soon cotton on to the trick. He was already asking himself 'why such Bible-length letters' needed to be written to those 'Arabian deserts', where there was nothing but friars; and, because Niccolò spent all day sleeping and reading indoors, he probably also suspected that the Florentine might not be the 'extraordinary man' Guicciardini had made him out to be.[35] It certainly didn't help that Niccolò kept shooting his mouth off, either. Whenever Santi pestered him for more details, he told Guicciardini, he would reply with 'a few ill-chosen words' about the coming war, 'or the Turk, who is bound to invade, or the advisability of having a crusade during these times,' and all manner of other nonsense.[36] There was a good chance that, before long, Santi would write to Guicciardini, asking what he and Niccolò were up to . . .

Il Rovaio was also proving to be a pain.[37] Despite Niccolò's entreaties, he kept inventing all kinds of excuses. One moment, he wasn't sure whether he could come; the next, he was undecided about what preaching methods to use; and, the next, he was complaining that, since his last visit to Florence, the city's moral standards seemed to have become even more lax. Niccolò assured Guicciardini that he would keep trying, but it is evident he did not hold out much hope.

Still, his dealings with the Franciscans were looking up. That morning, the friars had elected as their minister general Paolo da Sonchio, a humane and good man, who was also not ill-disposed towards the Florentines' case.[38] Later that evening, Niccolò would go to see him. With a bit of luck, Niccolò told Guicciardini, he would be finished by the next day.

Perhaps realizing that his last letter might have sounded a little patronizing, especially given that Niccolò was fourteen years older than him, Guicciardini greeted this news with warm congratulations. Scribbling a quick note later that evening, he reassured Niccolò that his time in Carpi had not been wasted. During his three days of enforced idleness, Niccolò had probably learned everything there was to know about the 'Republic of Clogs' – and he would no doubt find some way of putting this to good use in the *Istorie fiorentine*.[39] Even if the Franciscans didn't feature that much in his narrative, he could always use the friars' peculiar ways to illustrate some point or other – and Niccolò was inclined to agree.[40]

Nevertheless, Guicciardini felt obliged to repeat his warning. Although he would continue to send couriers to Carpi, he urged Niccolò not to take their prank too far, especially with the mean-spirited Santi. If he was not careful, Santi would easily turn the tables on them – with who knew what consequences.[41]

Too late, Niccolò realized the wisdom of Guicciardini's words. On the morning of 19 May, he wrote back in a state of some agitation.[42] Santi was already catching on. When Guicciardini's last letter had arrived, he turned to Niccolò and said, 'Look here, there must be something big going on; the messengers are coming thick and fast.'[43] Hoping to defuse the situation, Niccolò passed him a note from Guicciardini. But this only made things worse. After reading it, Santi sneered that Guicciardini must be playing some sort of trick – perhaps on both of them. Rattled, Niccolò feigned innocence. The reason he was receiving so much correspondence, he claimed, was that he had 'left some dealings in Florence up in the air', and had asked Guicciardini to keep him informed about them.[44] But Santi didn't seem persuaded. Niccolò was 'scared shitless'. Living in 'constant fear' that Santi would 'take a broom and pack [him] off to the inn', he asked Guicciardini to take the next day off, so that the joke wouldn't deprive him of the 'solid meals' and 'splendid beds' he had been enjoying up to then.[45]

It didn't help that 'il Rovaio' was still hemming and hawing, unable to make up his mind one way or the other. Niccolò was beginning to lose hope. 'I think I am going to return in disgrace,' he told Guicciardini. [46] The *Arte della Lana* would be furious. He didn't even want to imagine how he'd appear to Francesco Vettori and Filippo Strozzi, who had written to him privately about this matter, begging him to do his 'utmost so that during this Lenten season they might dine on some spiritual food that would be to their advantage.'[47] It didn't help that he'd already disappointed them once before. One Saturday evening the previous winter, they'd asked him to find someone to preach the sermon at Mass on Sunday, but the priest he'd chosen hadn't turned up until after lunch. The whole day had been turned upside-down, and his friends had rightly given him hell for it. He didn't want to risk their ire by making a mess of things again, but it was starting to look increasingly likely.

Fortunately, his dealings with the friars had gone much more smoothly. As Niccolò explained in a letter to Cardinal Giulio de' Medici, he had been granted an audience with the minister general that morning, and had taken care to present the Florentines' request exactly as he had been asked.[48] The minister's initial response had been a little discouraging. Though he was anxious to please the Florentines, he thought it only right to place such an important matter before the chapter. He hoped the friars would reach a decision in a few days, but it was such a thorny issue that it might not be possible to consider it carefully enough before the end of the session. Needless to say, this was as good as a refusal. But Niccolò was too experienced a diplomat to be brushed off quite so easily. Assuming his sternest countenance, he reminded the minister general that he had not been sent to quibble over details, but simply to ask the friars to comply with the *Otto di Pratica*'s wishes. Had they done so, they would doubtless have won the Florentines' undying gratitude. But that the minister general was now trying to fob them off with stupid excuses would only cause offence. As the minister knew perfectly well, there was no need to involve the chapter at all, given that the pope had already empowered him to effect the desired separation on his own. Still, now that everything was out in the open, Niccolò was sure the Franciscan Order would do all it could to please the *Otto*, the cardinal and – by implication – the pope.

So menacing was the unspoken threat that the minister general must have been quaking in his boots. But Niccolò did not want to leave anything to chance. After taking his leave, he sought out Francesco da Potenza and a few others, and strong-armed them into supporting the Florentines' demands. Should the minister general try to pass the buck again, Niccolò was fairly confident the chapter would place the whole matter back in his hands – thus obliging him to come to Tuscany and sort it out in person. It would be messy, but Niccolò and Fra Ilarione felt sure that, if this course of action was taken, the *Otto* would not be disappointed. All that remained was for the *Otto* to write an angry letter, complaining about the delay and demanding the chapter's immediate acquiescence.

His meetings concluded, Niccolò decided the time had come for him to leave. Bidding a hasty farewell to Sigismondo Santi, he mounted his horse and made for Modena, where he was welcomed by Guicciardini. He had probably intended to leave the next morning; but, finding that the ride had disagreed with him, resolved to stay in Modena until he felt well enough to travel again.

For a day or two, Niccolò passed an agreeable time in Guicciardini's company – drinking, joking and swapping gossip. But eventually, he had to leave. Probably still feeling a little stiff in the saddle, he wended his way slowly across the Apennines, arriving in Florence on or around 22 May.[49]

*

For perhaps the first time in his life, Niccolò returned home with a smile on his face. Apart from the question of 'il Rovaio' – which may have been left hanging – he had accomplished his mission to everyone's satisfaction. What was more, he had enjoyed himself. Not only had he had some fun at the friars' expense, but, in pretending to be more important than he really was, he had also laughed heartily at his own insignificance.

Yet, if he was happy to remain on the fringes of Florentine politics, he had lost none of his fascination for Italian affairs. Despite the self-mocking tone of his letters to Guicciardini, he had evidently been following the preparations for war carefully during his stay in Carpi. Now that he was back in Florence, his interest only intensified.

From his study in the Via Romana, Niccolò watched as Charles V gathered his forces.[50] Overall command had been given to Prospero Colonna, whose secretary Niccolò could so easily have been, and under his gaze, troops from all quarters began assembling in the Romagna.[51] Among the first to arrive was Federico II Gonzaga, the dashing young marquis of Mantua, at the head of the papal army. Next came Fernando Francesco d'Ávalos, the marquis of Pescara, with some 2,000 Spanish infantrymen. These were then joined by 4,000 German men-at-arms, 2,000 Grignon foot soldiers and a further 6,000 Swiss mercenaries. The numbers were not to be sniffed at. By mid-July, when Guicciardini was appointed commissioner-general of the papal army, no fewer than 23,000 men were ready to take the field.[52]

While he waited for the last few commanders to arrive, Colonna took up position at San Lazzaro, just outside Parma. There, he faced all the usual problems: the Germans started quibbling over money; the Venetians refused to fight outside their own territory; and the Swiss revealed that their Confederation had also supplied France with soldiers. Eventually, however, Colonna felt ready to launch his campaign. But his captains could not agree how to proceed.[53] Some argued that he should attack Parma straight away, on the grounds that he could not advance any further with an enemy city in his rear. Others thought this too dangerous. Parma was too well fortified and too well defended to be taken with a frontal assault. Colonna would do much better to press on towards Piacenza, while a smaller force stayed behind to lay waste to the countryside and starve the city into submission.

Wary of making the wrong decision, Colonna hesitated. While he agonized, however, the French governor of Milan – Odet de Foix, vicomte de Lautrec – was preparing to march against him. Colonna needed to make up his mind soon, or else his whole campaign would be put in jeopardy.

For a few tense weeks, Italy's fate hung in the balance. To Niccolò, the uncertainty must have been excruciating. Perhaps realizing how readily the *Arte della guerra* could be applied to the present situation, he arranged to have it printed by the Giunti press – the first time he had done anything of the kind since his unfortunate experience with the *Decennale primo*.

Published on 16 August 1521, it was a handsome octavo volume, with a clear typeface and wide margins.[54] It was also lavishly illustrated. So that the reader might better understand 'the arrangement of the battalions and of the armies and of the encampments' described in the text, Niccolò had taken care to include a diagram for each of them. These were quite remarkably detailed. Using an array of symbols, they indicated exactly where the men-at-arms, light cavalry, regular and irregular light infantry, pikemen, shield-bearers and cannon should be placed. He even marked where the captain general should stand, where the standard should be set up and where the band should play.

The edition had clearly been designed to reflect the tastes of the powerful, and Niccolò lost no time in sending copies to some of the leading men of the day. Although there is no way of identifying all of those he so honoured, it is at least certain that among them was Cardinal Giovanni Salviati, the son of Jacopo Salviati and the nephew of Pope Leo X.[55] On 6 September, Salviati sent a note of thanks, brimming with compliments:

> Following my custom, [I] have looked diligently at your book, and the more I have considered it, the more I like it, for it seems to me that you have coupled to the most perfect manner of warfare in antiquity everything that is good in modern warfare and compounded an invincible army. To this opinion of mine has been added some small experience from those wars that there are at present, since I have seen that all the disorders that have arisen today or in the French armies or in those of the emperor or of the Church or of the Turk come about for no other reason than for the lack of organisation that is described in your book. I therefore thank you deeply for having published this book, for the common welfare of all Italians . . . I urge to you continue thinking and writing things, and to adorn our country with your talents.[56]

It was high praise indeed – and, in years gone by, Niccolò would have been rubbing his hands with joy at the thought of the rewards that might soon be coming his way. But he had evidently not published the *Arte della guerra* simply to further his career. After all, manuscript copies had already been given to Cardinal de' Medici and his circle,[57] and, as we have seen, it seems likely that the text had also been made available to Prospero Colonna. All those from whom he might reasonably have expected some reward had, in other words, already been tapped. Besides, his political ambitions had long since dried up. He no longer hankered after office, and he had ceased to expect further advancement from the Medici. Instead, his primary concern had been to help stave off military disaster. As Salviati's letter suggests, he appears to have believed that, by making his treatise available to a wider audience, he might help foster better military practice among the Papal–Imperial forces, and thereby safe-guard 'the common welfare of all Italians'.

Whether or not the *Arte della guerra* had any effect on the conduct of the war, his hopes for Italy were not disappointed.[58] After much equivocation, Colonna had besieged Parma. But he had left it too late. Hurriedly breaking camp, he despatched a small force to guard his rear, and advanced towards Cremona, no doubt fearing the worst. But it was there that the tables began to turn. While Colonna was strengthened by the arrival of reinforcements from north of the Alps, Lautrec's army suddenly started haemorrhaging troops. Having not been paid, his Swiss mercenaries deserted him, and he was so short of money that he had to dismiss more of his own men. Heavily outnumbered, he retreated to Milan and began preparing for a siege – in the most incompetent way imaginable. He alienated the already hostile citizenry by setting fire to the outlying suburbs, and wasted huge amounts of time building useless earthworks. As soon as Colonna's army arrived outside the city on 20 November, Lautrec saw how futile it would be to go on. That night, as the Milanese rose in rebellion, he fled, taking his remaining troops with him. Over the next few weeks, all the other cities in the duchy, except Cremona, surrendered. And, just like that, the French were gone.

For Niccolò – calm, happy and contented – it was perhaps reward enough.

26

Love, Labour, Loss

(December 1521–March 1525)

As the winter drew close and an icy wind began to blow off the Arno, Niccolò left Florence for Sant'Andrea in Percussina.[1] Settling down in his study, with a roaring fire crackling in the grate, he resumed work on the *Istorie fiorentine*. In truth, he was glad to be getting back to it. Now entering the twilight of his life, he was content to remain on the fringes of political life – offering advice when asked, acting as an emissary when required, but otherwise keeping himself very much to himself. His life was simple, but he was as free from worry as he had ever been. He had no enemies to speak of, he could rely on his friends, many of whom had risen to high office, and, now that the French had been driven out of Italy, he could reassure himself that Florence was safe. Able at last to breathe easy, he could have asked for nothing better than the freedom to read and write about the city he loved so dearly. Sadly, he was not to enjoy it for long.

While celebrating the fall of Milan at Magliana towards the end of November, Pope Leo X had caught a chill. By the time he had been carried back to Rome, pneumonia had set in; and, before his doctors could do anything, he was dead.[2] Those who knew him well were not surprised. Though just ten days shy of his forty-sixth birthday, the pleasure-loving pontiff had been grossly overweight, and, having never enjoyed the best of health, had always been coughing.[3] But so sudden was his demise that others suspected foul play.[4]

As rumours of poisoning spread throughout Rome, the war in Lombardy was plunged into confusion. With the Papal–Imperial alliance now in doubt, Prospero Colonna's army fragmented.[5] The Swiss deserted him, and, deprived of the Church's money, he had no choice but to dismiss many of his own men. He tried valiantly to make do with what he had, but his remaining troops were hopelessly overstretched. His weakness was palpable – and his enemies would not be slow to take advantage of it.

Meanwhile, in Florence, the Signoria scrambled to prevent civil unrest. Having learned of the pope's death a few hours before it became common knowledge, the priors immediately put Medici partisans throughout Tuscany on their guard. Two days later, seventeen leading supporters of popular government – including Niccolò's friend, Niccolò Valori – were thrown in gaol. A vicious clampdown then began. On 21 December, an Augustinian friar was arrested for running through the streets shouting, '*Popolo e libertà!*' – the traditional rallying cry of popular revolts. Under interrogation, he acted so bizarrely that anyone could see he was just a harmless madman, but the regime had him tortured to death all the same.[6]

*

By the beginning of January, the Medici's position in Florence was starting to look precarious. Despite the government's clampdown, the citizenry was growing restive. In Rome, Cardinal Francesco Soderini was already calling for the Medici 'tyrants' to be expelled, and though he had little support in the Sacred College, he and his sympathizers in Florence would not have had much difficulty finding allies elsewhere.[7] Across Northern Italy, the Medici's enemies were on the march. With Prospero Colonna's forces in disarray, Francesco Maria della Rovere had recaptured the duchy of Urbino; Orazio and Malatesta Baglioni had returned to Perugia; and Francis I, with whom the Soderini had long enjoyed good relations, was preparing to mount a fresh campaign against Milan.[8]

The election of Adrian of Utrecht as Pope Adrian VI seemed to offer the Medici some hope. Though relatively little known in Italy, this unprepossessing Dutchman had spent his entire career in the service of the Habsburgs. Starting out as Charles V's tutor, he had risen to become inquisitor general of Aragon, and – eventually – regent of Spain. As such, everyone, especially Cardinal de' Medici, expected him to renew the Papal–Imperial alliance and prosecute the war against France with the vigour that Charles V demanded.

But Adrian had other ideas. To his uncluttered mind, the Ottoman

Turks were of much greater concern than the French. The previous summer, the Sultan, Suleiman the Magnificent, had invaded the Balkans with a large and well-supplied army. In late August, Belgrade fell and it was feared that, before the winter was out, he would conquer Hungary as well.[9] As Marino Sanudo noted, this posed a grave threat. If, having taken Hungary, Suleiman were then to sweep down through Dalmatia, nothing would stand between him and Italy.[10]

Convinced that Christendom needed to unite against the infidel, Adrian stubbornly refused to continue the war against France.[11] Though he would allow papal troops to remain in Lombardy for the time being, he made it clear that, as soon as a suitable opportunity presented itself, he would make peace with Francis I – and expected Charles V to do the same.

Yet Adrian's naive attempt to end the war only exacerbated it further. Encouraged by Charles V's apparent isolation, Francis I now sent an army under Odet de Foix to invade Lombardy.[12] A first attempt on Milan had to be abandoned when Francesco Sforza succeeded in slipping past the Venetians with reinforcements, but, by the end of February, de Foix was ready to turn the tables. While Prospero Colonna was still holed up in Milan, de Foix had been joined by thousands of reinforcements; and, with this advantage, he proceeded to lay siege to Novara and Pavia, in the hope of drawing Colonna out into the open, where he could more easily be defeated.

*

At this, Cardinal Soderini's resolve was strengthened. Shortly after de Foix had crossed into Italy, Soderini was reported to be plotting with the captain Renzo da Ceri to oust the Petrucci from Siena and return his brother to power in Florence.[13] He had already been promised financial support by Francis I, and a host of disgruntled exiles stood ready to join him. Preparations were soon underway. On 23 February, the *Otto di Pratica* were informed that Renzo had already brought his men-at-arms to Rome; before long, contact would be made with republican sympathizers in Florence.[14] It was only a matter of time before they struck.

Alarmed, Cardinal de' Medici raced to secure Florence's borders. With a pragmatism of which Niccolò would have been proud, he drew his erstwhile enemy, Francesco Maria della Rovere, into an alliance by holding out the prospect of a marriage with the Salviati.[15] He then extended the hand of friendship to the Baglioni,[16] and hired a number of new mercenary captains.[17]

The cardinal's greatest worry was, however, domestic. Talk of Soderini's plot had fuelled growth of dissent. Though members of the *reggimento* maintained a show of confidence,[18] Cerretani estimated that three quarters of the city were now hostile to the Medici's rule.[19] Fearing that civil strife might break out even before Renzo da Ceri left Rome, the cardinal hastily tried to win back the people's favour by promising that the constitution would soon be reformed.[20] Whether it would be enough, however, remained to be seen.

*

For a moment, Niccolò's loyalties must have been torn. He could not have helped feeling drawn to the Soderini. After all, Piero and Francesco were more than just patrons: they were also friends. They had taken him under their wing when he was still an inexperienced youth, and they had remained true to him, even when their own fortunes had taken a turn for the worse. Even though they had drifted apart a little in recent years, Niccolò could be sure that, if Piero were returned to power, he would find his protégé some role. It was certainly an attractive prospect, and, in years gone by, he might have been tempted to throw his lot in with them. But age and bitter experience had taught him to be more circumspect. Having worked so hard to earn the Medici's favour, Niccolò did not want to risk losing everything now – especially given how uncertain and undignified coups could be.[21] Though he would prefer to stay out of the political fray as far as possible, he was ready to serve the Medici however they saw fit, and they, in turn, were glad to have the benefit of his advice.

In early April, Niccolò was one of five leading figures invited to submit proposals for the reform of the government.[22] Of these, only two others are known. The first, by Niccolò's republican-minded friend, Zanobi Buondelmonti, has unfortunately been lost,[23] but the second, by Alessandro de' Pazzi, has survived.[24] Though only lightly sketched, this 'aristocratic' work articulated the same demands which the *ottimati* had been making for the past twenty years. At root,

Pazzi wanted a Venetian-style constitution, with a *gonfaloniere a vita* and a Great Council. So as to protect the interests of the elite, however, he also called for the creation of an all-powerful Senate. Composed of one hundred citizens, appointed for life, this would elect all the most important magistrates, control taxation and finance, and dictate Florence's foreign policy.

Niccolò's proposals could hardly have been more different. Although the greater part of the text has been lost, what remains is broadly in line with the suggestions he had made in the *Discorso delle cose fiorentine dopo la morte di Lorenzo*, two years earlier.[25] His tone was, however, much more direct. Having long meditated on the question of constitutional reform, he knew his own mind; and given the gravity of the current crisis, he saw no need to mince his words.

All those who loved the common good, Niccolò began, would agree that Florence needed a *gonfaloniere di giustizia* and a Great Council. As in the *Discorso*, he appears to have seen each of these as a response to the conflicting desires of different social classes. The Great Council was designed to appease the *popolo*. Whether it had 1,000 members (as before) or fewer did not matter all that much, but it should be large enough that all citizens could aspire to it. The *gonfaloniere di giustizia*, meanwhile, was meant to appease the elite. Serving for several years at a time, the *gonfaloniere* would provide government with a measure of continuity, and would consequently be invested with considerable dignity. He could either be chosen using a complicated system of 'sortition, nomination, and election in the Council' or 'directly, in the first instance, by Cardinal Giulio'.[26] Many of Florence's other institutions – such as the Council of the People and the Cento – were also to be done away with and their roles assumed by the Great Council, but whether Niccolò later went on to call for an elaborate system of checks and balances to prevent the Great Council abusing its power – as in the *Discorso* – cannot be known.

Niccolò's proposals were every bit as radical as they had been two years before, but so dramatically had the political landscape changed that what the cardinal had once dismissed as unrealistic, he now regarded as a panacea. He did not agree with Niccolò on every point, but he was sufficiently impressed that, in late April, he asked Niccolò to help draft a law to reform the Florentine government.[27]

The resulting '*Minuta*' ('Draft') attempted to strike a compromise between the different proposals, and was revised several times.[28] The earliest version was based largely on Niccolò's recommendations. A Great Council was to be re-established, initially with 800 members; the *gonfaloniere di giustizia* was henceforth to serve for three years; and the Council of the People and the Cento were to be abolished. In a later version, however, a number of more 'aristocratic' reforms were added. Much as Alessandro de' Pazzi had proposed, a new 'Council of the Middle' (*Consiglio di Mezzo*) was also to be established to function as a sort of Senate. Membership would be for life, and, in the first instance, it would comprise the current Council of Seventy, plus thirty additional members. Should any of its members die, or prove unable to discharge their duties, they were to be replaced using a complicated method of election. Its powers were, however, not quite as expansive as Pazzi had wanted. Though it was to have responsibility for the levying of taxes and the 'reform of the *Monte*', it was to have no role either in appointing magistrates, or in conducting foreign policy.

Niccolò and his colleagues were, however, in no doubt that these reforms were only meant to be a stopgap. Their role was simply to pacify the citizenry enough for the Medici to cling to power. As soon as the danger had passed, the cardinal intended to consolidate his family's authority once again; and for this, he would need some constitutional means of remaking the government – at least in part. As such, the '*Minuta*' called for a committee of twelve citizens to be appointed by the Medici for a period of twelve months, during which time it would be empowered 'to reform and reorder whatever they judge [necessary] for the good and the peace of the city'. Together with the cardinal, it could remodel the chancellery, the *Otto di Pratica* or the *Dieci di Guerra*. If it suspected corruption or factional bias, it could even dismiss the Signoria and call fresh elections. Only the Great Council was to be beyond its remit.

*

The cardinal had planned for these reforms to come into effect on 1 May.[29] But before the '*Minuta*' could be passed into law, the war in Lombardy took an unexpected turn.

Although Odet de Foix's strategy had been sound, his luck had quickly begun to run out.[30] Not long after de Foix took Novara, Prospero Colonna had at last ventured out of Milan. But, rather than taking the field, as de Foix had hoped, he holed himself up in the impregnable Certosa di Pavia. From there, he could protect Pavia – then still being besieged by the French – without exposing himself to danger. This enraged de Foix's Swiss mercenaries. Having not been paid since crossing the Alps, they did not want to waste any more time trying to trick Colonna out into the open. They told de Foix that, unless he attacked immediately, they would leave. Grudgingly, de Foix agreed. By the time his army had set off for Certosa di Pavia, however, Colonna had already taken up a new position at Bicocca. Lying about six kilometres north of Milan, it was a formidable site. A thin strip of land, sandwiched between an impassable marsh and a deep ditch, it would completely negate de Foix's numerical advantage. But Colonna was not content simply to rely on the existing topography. Alert to the potential of modern artillery, he also built a large mound along the edge of a sunken road running across the plain. From wooden platforms on top of this, his cannon would have a commanding view of the field, while, from behind it, his arquebusiers could fire at the enemy in almost complete safety.

It did not take de Foix long to realize how unfavourable his position was. But the Swiss were determined to fight. On 27 April, a reluctant de Foix ordered the attack. Oblivious to the danger, the Swiss charged straight at Colonna's lines. Before they were even halfway across the plain, more than half had been cut down in a hail of cannon fire. The few who made it to the earthworks were easily picked off by the arquebusiers. Within minutes, 3,000 of them were lying dead on the field. Terrified by the scale of the slaughter, the rest of de Foix's army turned and fled.

Falling back on Monza, de Foix watched helplessly as his remaining forces melted away. The surviving Swiss limped back across the Alps, while the Venetians, fearful of provoking another attack, hastily withdrew across the River Adige. His campaign now in tatters, de Foix returned to face his master's wrath in France, leaving his brother to negotiate the terms of surrender.

*

For Cardinal Soderini, the French defeat at Bicocca came as a heavy blow, but he had gone too far to back out now. Three days before the battle, Renzo da Ceri had set off for Tuscany with between 10,000 and 12,000 men, intending to strike Siena first.[31] It had been agreed that, once the city had been captured, he would then head on to Florence, where a coup would be launched against the Medici. Led by Niccolò's old friends, Zanobi Buondelmonti, Luigi Alamanni, and Jacopo da Diacetto, a group of radical republicans would assassinate Cardinal Giulio, seize control of the Palazzo della Signoria and open the gates to Renzo's troops.

Had Renzo been quicker and Soderini more discreet, it might yet have worked. But having long ago learned of their intentions, Cardinal de' Medici was ready for them. Some weeks earlier, he had despatched a large number of troops to Siena, making it virtually impossible for the city to be taken by force. Taken aback, Renzo roamed the countryside aimlessly, in the vague hope of finding some sort of weakness, but after ten days without food, his men began to desert. He had no choice but to return to Rome.

Meanwhile, the plot in Florence had been uncovered. A French courier had been captured and, under torture, had revealed everything.[32] The ringleaders, Luigi Alamanni and Jacopo Cattani da Diacceto, were executed; Zanobi Buondelmonti and the others managed to flee. Whether they were simply lucky, or the cardinal – who had a horror of bloodshed – allowed them to escape, is unclear,[33] but they all had a price put on their heads. Most took refuge in France; many never saw Florence again.

*

Cardinal de' Medici was triumphant. He had emerged from the plot stronger than ever before. The French had been routed, his enemies crushed and his critics silenced. Not only was Cardinal Soderini in disgrace, but his brother Piero had also died just weeks after the coup had been discovered.[34] There was no one left to challenge the Medici, either at home or abroad. As Jacopo Pitti recalled, the once restive citizenry now hurried to renew their allegiance, and, though steps were taken to broaden the regime, 'all talk . . . of constitutional reform' ceased.[35]

For Niccolò, however, the cardinal's glory was tinged with sadness. Although doubtless relieved that Florence had been spared, he took little comfort from the security he now enjoyed. A curtain seemed to have come down on his earlier life. Piero Soderini's death grieved him particularly. However much their paths had diverged in recent years, he had always respected and even admired Soderini's principles, never wavering in his belief that Soderini had placed his republican ideals before personal ambition. It revolted Niccolò that this elder statesman, who, by rights, should have passed his final days in quiet dignity, should instead have allowed himself to be swept up in such a grubby ploy – and for the sake of nothing more than his own vanity. It was pathetic. Feeling ashamed, Niccolò penned a bitter epigram, ridiculing Soderini's childish stupidity:

> The night Piero Soderini died,
> his soul went up to the mouth of Hell;
> roared Pluto: 'Why to Hell? Stupid soul,
> go up to Limbo with all the other babies.'[36]

No less painful – if perhaps less bitter – was the loss of his friends from the Orti Oricellari. Since the death of Cosimo Rucellai, the meetings in the garden had, admittedly, become a little less frequent, but the friendships he had made there had sustained him through the most difficult years of his life. Though he had not always agreed with the conspirators' more radical views, he had nevertheless been invigorated and even inspired by their passion for ancient history, philosophy and, of course, politics. To them, he had dedicated two of his most important and brilliant works: the *Discorsi* and the *Vita di Castruccio Castracani*. Yet, now, they were gone. He could not, of course, blame them – as he did Soderini – for their involvement in the plot against the Medici. It was, after all, the nature of young men to do such impetuous things. But the price they had paid had been a heavy one, and Niccolò would never get over their loss.

*

Even greater sorrow was to come. Towards the end of May, Niccolò's brother Totto was suddenly taken ill in Rome.[37] Whether he returned home to Florence or not is unclear, but, by the following month, his condition had become grave. On 8 June, Roberto Pucci – then the *gonfaloniere di giustizia* – sent Niccolò a letter of comfort.[38] Having heard that Totto's life was now in danger, Pucci was beside himself with sadness. Stifling his tears, he urged Niccolò not to despair. After all, there was still a chance that Totto might recover. But it was not to be. Before the end of the month, Totto was dead.

Having already lost so much, Niccolò must have found Totto's death almost too much to bear. Wandering disconsolately through the Tuscan countryside in the weeks that followed, he would probably have felt more alone – and more cursed by fate – than at any other point in his life.

Work had always been his solace, but even this proved elusive. Throughout the summer and autumn, he was besieged with petty problems, each more frustrating than the last. The chaplain at one of Totto's old benefices was causing trouble. One minute, he was quibbling about grain,[39] and the next he was asking for money – which Niccolò plainly didn't have.[40] Then there were his servants. When one of them was beaten up, he had to ask for Francesco del Nero's help in persuading the perpetrator's employer to punish the man.[41] And so it went on ... His head, still heavy with sadness, must have been spinning.

Not until October did Niccolò begin to recover some of his spirits. Midway through the month, his friend, Raffaello Girolami, was chosen to serve as an ambassador to Charles V, in Spain.[42] It was a fairly trivial mission. All he had to do was to offer Florence's belated congratulations to Charles on his election as king of the Romans three years earlier, and, presumably, to gain an idea of Charles's plans for Italy. Even then, he wouldn't be going alone. Also taking part in the embassy were Giovanni Corsi and Raffaello de' Medici. But Girolami was still nervous. Though he had undertaken a few 'domestic' missions in the past – carrying messages to various members of the Medici family, or overseeing defences in the dominions – he had never been on an embassy to a foreign court. Frightened of making some terrible mistake, he therefore turned to Niccolò for advice on how to conduct himself.

Niccolò could not have asked for a more congenial diversion. Setting aside both the *Istorie fiorentine* and his worries, he threw himself into the task with gusto and within just over a week, he had produced a lengthy memorandum – the so-called *Memoriale a Raffaello Girolami*.[43] While the style was clumsy and the argument frequently repetitive, it was powerful, nevertheless. Drawing on many years of experience as an emissary, Niccolò succeeded in producing what is perhaps the most detailed portrait of diplomatic practice of his time.[44]

Any reasonably talented person could be an ambassador, Niccolò began, but not everyone could do it well. If Raffaello wanted to make a success of his mission, there were a few things he should do. After presenting his credentials, he should first make a careful study of Charles's nature, and of his principal advisers. This would ensure that, if any difficult business arose, he would find it easy to gain an audience. Raffaello should then try to win the respect and friendship of the court. To this end, he should cultivate a reputation for liberality by throwing banquets, laying on all manner of entertainments and gambling as often as necessary. He should also be known for his honesty. This was not, of course, to say that he always had to tell the truth. Now and then, some deception would be necessary. But if he had to lie, he should either know how to conceal his lies, or else have a plausible excuse to hand. With any luck, these qualities should allow him to gather information relatively easily, but, to be sure of getting others to tell him what they knew, he should always take care to have plenty of titbits to give them in return.

Most importantly, Raffaello should write the Florentine government regular reports. Needless to say, these should be concerned principally with how the mission was going. But they should also contain an account of what was happening at court – and some sense of what Charles and his advisers might do in future. No doubt, the Florentine government would be particularly anxious to know what Charles's plans were, how well he understood Italian affairs, whether he coveted Milan for himself or intended to let the Sforzas enjoy it, whether he still wanted to come to Rome and when, how he felt about the Church, how much he trusted the pope and, if he came to Italy in person, what good or ill Florence could expect.[45] It was not always easy to predict such matters, or to venture opinions in writing. Niccolò had often been chided for speculating too freely. Rather than offer views as his own, therefore, Raffaello should instead say something like: 'prudent men here judge that the outcome will be such and such.'[46]

Of course, Raffaello need not write a report every day. Sometimes, he would have nothing of importance to say. Niccolò had often seen ambassadors keep a note of what they had learned and distil the most important points into a letter every eight or ten days. But, after a little while, Raffaello would probably get a feeling for how often he should be writing. If he was going to be away for a long time, however, Niccolò suggested that, every couple of months, he might like to send the Florentine government a description of the 'condition and situation' of the Spanish kingdoms, just to give them a sense of how things stood.[47]

Niccolò clearly relished writing the *Memoriale*. His vigorous – if inelegant – prose is positively bursting with enthusiasm, and, at times, there are flashes of his old self. But no sooner had he waved Raffaello off than the sorrows of recent months returned to haunt him. Still oppressed by thoughts of death, he went to Florence to draw up a new will on 27 November.[48] This done, he then hurried back to the countryside and buried himself in his work, hoping no doubt to forget; for the next five months, nothing more was heard from him.

*

The following spring, Niccolò emerged from the shadows. But while the pain of Totto's death may have faded a little, he was beset by worries. Among the most pressing concerned his nineteen-year-old son, Lodovico, who had recently been spending a lot of time in the countryside with a young boy.[49] They were, by all accounts, very close. They played together, they sported about, they whispered in each other's ears – and they even shared the same bed. Of course, it might all have been perfectly innocent. After all, it was not uncommon for high-spirited young men to enjoy close, even intimate friendships. But it was more likely that it was a sexual relationship.

Niccolò had no problem with this per se. As Francesco Vettori reminded him on 16 April, they both had strong homosexual tendencies – so strong, in fact, that if they had had their own way when they had been Lodovico's age, they would probably not have married at all. But what *did* bother Niccolò was that his brother-in-law, Francesco del Nero, had found out about it and was already spreading malicious gossip. This could have landed Lodovico in real trouble. Although legislation had recently been relaxed, homosexuality was still illegal and a conviction could lead to a heavy fine – or worse. Good friend that he was, Vettori told Niccolò not to worry too much. Francesco was just a blabbermouth. He was more likely to harm himself than Lodovico.

Niccolò was also having money troubles.[50] He had heard that a new set of tax collectors were to be appointed, and was frightened that, if they were 'too vigorous in exacting tribute', he would be unable to pay. Once again, he turned to Vettori for help. But, though Vettori reassured him that the tax collectors would probably not be appointed any time soon, the relief was temporary, at best. Even without a tax bill to cover, he would struggle to make ends meet. Over the summer, things got so bad that, on 26 September, he was even forced to write to the troublesome Francesco del Nero – who, as the administrator of the Studio Fiorentino, was responsible for his salary, then evidently in arrears. Unless he was paid soon, he wailed, he might have to have his chimney bricked up again.

Perhaps most disturbing of all, however, was the renewal of war. In the months after the French defeat at the Battle of Bicocca, Francis I's position had looked dire. Though he had despatched a second army to Italy shortly after de Foix's return, the fall of Genoa on 30 May 1522 had forced it to beat a hasty retreat, apparently depriving him 'of any hope of being able to alter the affairs of Lombardy'.[51] But the suspicion remained that he might soon try again – with a stronger and better supplied army.[52] Were he to do so, the imperial army would be ill-prepared to meet the challenge.[53] Although Charles V had managed to talk the Venetians into switching sides in July 1523, Prospero Colonna was once again struggling to pay his troops, and the people of Milan – exhausted by war – were growing restive. If he was to hold the city, the emperor would need new allies.

On 23 August, Charles succeeded in persuading Adrian VI to join a league, with Henry VIII of England, Ferdinand of Austria, Francesco Sforza, Florence, Siena, Lucca and Genoa. This was notion-ally defensive, but Charles soon convinced the other powers to go on the attack. Before Francis had a chance to regroup, the English would invade Picardy, a Spanish army would pour across the Pyrenees, and Prospero Colonna would march into Provence, where Charles de Bourbon would already have risen in rebellion. It was an ambitious plan. But Charles had underestimated Francis' readiness. While Colonna was still in Lombardy, a French army under Guillaume Gouffier crossed the River Ticino and marched on Milan. Despite

Colonna's pleas for help, the Venetians failed to come to his aid and for a time, it looked as if Gouffier might besiege the city. But even worse was to come.

On 14 September, Adrian VI died, putting the papacy's position again in doubt. When the Sacred College convened to elect a successor, a little over two weeks later, the conclave was divided between French and imperial camps.[54] The French initially had the advantage. After a few rounds of voting, one of Francis I's preferred candidates, Niccolò Fieschi, had emerged in the lead. Meanwhile, the imperial vote splintered. Although Charles V would have been happy with either Giulio de' Medici or Pompeo Colonna, the two candidates hated each other so much that neither was willing to let the other win.

With deadlock threatening to set in, Charles V's league teetered on the brink of collapse. As Prospero Colonna retreated, the French first occupied Lodi, then pushed on towards Cremona.[55] At the same time, the Papal States were fragmenting. Reggio Emilia fell to Alfonso I d'Este and, by the beginning of November, Modena, too, was under threat.[56]

Niccolò could not have helped being unnerved. Although Florence was less politically volatile than it had been after the death of Leo X, the city was far from stable – and was in no position to resist threats from without. A pro-French pope like Fieschi would spell disaster. With Charles V's league in tatters, and the balance of power in Italy tilted firmly against the Medici, Florence would soon be assailed by its enemies. Yet the election of Cardinal Giulio might not be much better.[57] While Leo X had been alive, the Florentines had bitterly resented having to bankroll his wars and they would surely not welcome the prospect of having to pay for another pope's campaigns – especially if it meant they might end up on the losing side. There was also the thorny question of how Florence would be governed. Given that the only other Medici males were not only illegitimate, but also underage, the citizenry would doubtless expect to govern themselves, but this the cardinal would never countenance. Though there were no coups in the offing, it would not take much for the Florentines to rebel. And, if the Medici regime faltered, Niccolò could easily find himself in difficulties.

Any fears that Niccolò may have had were quickly dispelled, however. Following a series of tactical blunders, Fieschi's support melted away and Pompeo Colonna withdrew, leaving Giulio de' Medici as the only viable candidate. Elected Pope Clement VII on 19 November, he immediately assuaged the Florentines' fears about the war. Despite having been an enthusiastic supporter of Charles V only a few months before, he now realized the costs of such an endeavour would be prohibitive. The papal treasury was bare, and he knew that Florence could not be expected to shoulder the burden.[58] When the Spanish ambassador arrogantly demanded that he honour his predecessor's obligations, therefore, he bluntly refused. Citing the Ottoman Turk's advance across the Mediterranean, he instead called upon the warring parties to make peace.

The ambassador was, of course, furious, but, fortunately for Clement, the war in Lombardy had already begun to turn against Francis I.[59] Caution had got the better of the French commander. Instead of attacking Milan when he had the advantage, he instead decided to go into winter quarters – thus giving the league's forces time to recover their strength. On 28 December, the new viceroy of Naples, Charles de Lannoy, arrived with fresh troops. Assuming command of the imperial army, following the death of Prospero Colonna, two days later, he quickly spied a means of turning the situation to his advantage.[60] Since it would be foolhardy to seek battle at such an early stage, he instead set about weakening the French by attrition. With winter snows still lying thick on the ground, he drew them into countless skirmishes, disrupted their supply lines and lost no opportunity to weaken their morale. Such a strategy was not without its risks – especially given that Lannoy was painfully short of money. But it worked beautifully. By early February, the French had been ravaged by starvation and disease. Helped by the Venetians, Lannoy had no difficulty pushing them back across the River Ticino and towards the Alps. There, Gouffier was abandoned by his Swiss mercenaries. Having no option but to retreat further, he tried to cross the Sesia, near Romagnano.[61] As his men waded through the water, however, they were cut to pieces by the imperial forces. Badly wounded, Gouffier fled, taking the shattered remains of his once proud army with him. Before long, the towns he had captured – including Lodi and Novara – were once again in imperial hands, and Bourbon, who had recently joined Lannoy in Lombardy, was ordered to launch an invasion of Provence.

Meanwhile, Clement turned to settle the question of Florence's political future. He did so with typical cunning. When, in early February 1524, a large Florentine embassy came to congratulate him on his election, he meekly asked them for their advice on how the city should be governed.[62] As was only to be expected, some of them – including Jacopo Salviati, Francesco Vettori and Lorenzo Strozzi – favoured a republican settlement, which would allow Florence essentially to govern itself. But, with a little prompting from one of Clement's intimates, others claimed they would prefer for the pope to send his illegitimate kinsmen, Alessandro and Ippolito, to Florence in his stead. This was all Clement needed to hear. Ignoring cries of protest from the dissenters, he swiftly began building a new regime in his own image. In May, Cardinal Silvio Passerini was appointed governor, and, in August, the two Medici bastards made their entrance. Being the eldest, Ippolito was to rule the city under Passerini's guidance, while Alessandro went to complete his education at the family's villa in Careggi. It had all been managed so well, and so quickly, that there was scarcely even a whisper of opposition. By the autumn, the city was at peace with itself – and, for a time, with the world.

*

A weight seemed to lift from Niccolò's shoulders. Putting the fear and sorrow of recent months behind him, he shook off his rustic malaise and began to spend more time in Florence. It was much changed. The Orti Oricellari had closed; many of his dearest friends were either dead or abroad; and the house in the Via Romana must have seemed strange and unfamiliar. But, in the gardens of Jacopo Falconetti, just outside the Porta San Frediano, he found a new source of inspiration and delight. Known as 'il Fornaciaio' ('the kiln-owner'), because of his background in the pottery trade, Falconetti had fallen victim to the political rivalries by which Florence was still beset, and had been banished from the city for a period of five years.[63] He was no Cosimo Rucellai, but, beneath the spreading laurel trees, the wine flowed freely, the talk was uninhibited, and laughter was always in the air. Towards evening, there would often be music or song, and, from time to time, Falconetti even arranged for plays to be performed – complete with richly decorated sets and lavish costumes.

Of all the delights of Falconetti's gardens, however, none was

20. Leonardo da Vinci, *Portrait of Isabella d'Este* (*c.* 1499–1500).

21. German landsknechts by Daniel Hopfer (*c.* 1530).

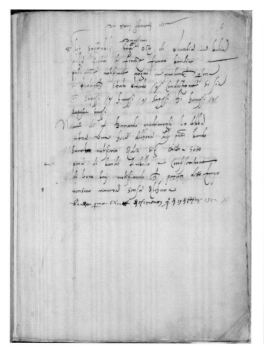
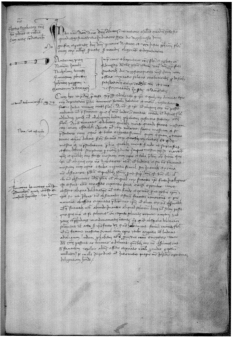

22. The warrant for Machiavelli's arrest and terms of employment of the *banditori* appointed to read out the notice. (ASFi, Ufficiali della condotta, 2, fol. 72 / ASFi, Otto di guardia, 223, bando, 6, 19 febbraio 1512)

23. The *albergaccio* in Sant'Andrea in Percussina today.

24. Machiavelli's study in Sant'Andrea in Percussina, where he wrote *Il principe*.

25. After Raphael, *Portrait of Giuliano de' Medici, Duke of Nemours* (c. 1515).

26. Sebastiano del Piombo, *Portrait of Pope Clement VII* (*c.* 1531).

27. The Orti Oricellari today.

28. Bernard van Orley, *Portrait of Charles V* (*c.* 1516).

29. Jean Clouet (*attr.*), *Portrait of Francis I* (*c.* 1515–20).

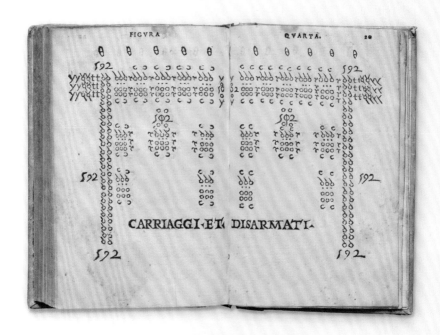

30. Diagram of how an army should be drawn up for battle, from the first edition of Machiavelli's *Arte della guerra* (1521).

31. An anonymous depiction of Francesco Guicciardini in his prime (sixteenth century).

32. Gian Paolo Pace, *Portrait of Giovanni delle Bande Nere* (*c.* 1545). Giovanni showed Machiavelli that, in war, theory is no match for experience, but died after being hit by a cannonball at the Battle of Governolo.

33. Depiction of the Battle of Pavia (*c.* 1521–5).

1527.

BORBONE OCCISO, ROMANA IN MOENIA MILES
CÆSAREVS RVIT, ET MISERANDAM DIRIPIT VRBEM.

Aqui fue Borbon muerto, y derribado	Soudain apres que Bourbon fut occis
Por los muros de Roma: pero entraron	Le tresvaillant Empereur feit emprife
Los Soldados con animo efforçado,	D'affaillir Romme, & de fens trefraftis
Y ellos la ciudad toda faquearon.	En combatant en peu de tempz l'eut prinfe.
III	

34. Engraving of the Sack of Rome, showing the death of Charles,
duc de Bourbon, after Maarten van Heemskerck (1556).

35. Death at the door of a sick man, from Girolamo Savonarola,
Predica del arte del bene morire (*c.* 1496).

more bewitching than Barbera Raffacani Salutati. Not yet thirty years old, she was quite exceptionally talented.[64] Although best known for her acting abilities, she was an accomplished musician, who – according to Vasari – 'sang divinely'.[65] She wrote poetry, too.[66] She was also ravishingly beautiful, with long, strawberry-blonde hair and gentle, almost pleading eyes.[67]

When Niccolò first met Barbera is not known, but, by the beginning of 1524, he was already head over heels in love with her. He does not seem to have cared that she had scores of men chasing after her, or that she was the mistress of several others.[68] As he later told Francesco Guicciardini, she had enough grace and charm to spare; all that he asked was to share in her favours.[69]

Seeking out every opportunity to be with her, he let his social obligations slip and paid scant attention to his friends. Then serving as one of the ambassadors sent to congratulate Clement VII, Francesco Vettori was positively jealous. In a letter written on 5 February 1524, Vettori told Francesco del Nero 'that it must be much more pleasant to dine occasionally with Barbera at Fornaciaio's expense than to have to spend every evening outside a door that never opens, even after hours of waiting.'[70]

Niccolò knew it was wrong. It wasn't just that he was old enough to be her father; he was also a married man, and, by the end of the summer, Marietta was pregnant once more – this time with twins. But he couldn't help himself. The fires of passion, once rekindled, burned too fiercely to be quenched. His only regret was that, at the age of fifty-five, he did not always have the stamina to satisfy a young woman's urges. In the madrigal, 'S'a la mia immensa voglia' ('If to my immense desire') – also known as 'A Barbera' ('To Barbera') – he borrowed tropes from Petrarch both to reaffirm his love and to excuse his sexual performance.[71] He admitted that, if his 'valour' had been as strong as his desire, his 'devotion' would not now be slumbering. But, since his strength was not equal to his lust, he was bound to suffer. It was his fault – not hers, of course. Such beauty, he could see, needed someone of 'greener age'. His tone was, however, jocular, and, though he might have been a bit of a disappointment at times, it seems clear that Barbera was ready to forgive him.

It was not always an easy relationship, and occasionally they even came close to throwing in the towel. But they always made up in the end. One such reconciliation was depicted in Niccolò's madrigal,

'Amor, io sento l'alma' ('Love, I feel my soul'). Also known as 'A Stanza della Barbera', this was written as if Barbera were speaking, and was the only occasion on which Niccolò ever adopted a female voice in his poetry. Cast as a prayer to Love, it is at once arrogant, wheedling and light-hearted:

> Love, I feel my soul
> burning in the fire, where I
> happily burned and more than ever I long to burn.
>
> If you set my heart on fire once again
> and I am happy with it,
> and humbly return to the ancient yoke,
> make it that my master
> feels that fire as well
> where I burn entirely and nourish my thoughts;
> make it that he forgets
> my escape, and tell him of my new desire.
>
> If with your holy valour,
> you, Love, can make it that always
> seeing him in that fire,
> I will be happy
> that, even in the most difficult circumstances,
> living will be a joy to me, and death a joke;
> and always shall my song
> call him lord and you my god.[72]

Basking in the warmth of Barbera's love, Niccolò returned to his work with renewed delight. Now nearing completion, the *Istorie fiorentine* seemed to fly along. From time to time, of course, he came across the odd difficulty. Since he was dealing with more recent periods of Florence's history, there was a danger that his presentation of certain events might offend some people – especially the Medici. But he took these in his stride and greeted each with cheery optimism. Even when he felt the need to ask his friends for advice, he was confident that he would somehow manage to tailor the facts to suit his audience's tastes. 'I would pay ten soldi,' he wrote to Francesco Guicciardini on 30 August 1524, 'to have you by my side so that I could show you where I am, because, since I am about to come to certain details, I would need to learn from you whether or not I am being too offensive in my exaggerating or understanding of the facts. Nevertheless, I shall continue to seek advice from myself, and I shall try to do my best to arrange it so that – still telling the truth – no one will have anything to complain about.'[73]

From Barbera's love also came a renewed sense of intellectual purpose; and, as summer gave way to autumn, Niccolò threw himself once again into those debates which had so delighted him in the past. Uppermost in his mind was the so-called *questione della lingua* ('question of language'). An age-old problem, the roots of which could be traced back at least to the mid-thirteenth century, this was the ground on which the battle for the soul of Italian literature was then being fought.[74] It was primarily concerned with whether Latin or the vernacular was more fitting for literary composition, and, as such, tended to revolve around issues of style, 'naturalness' and comprehension. But at its heart was a profoundly historical conundrum: had Italy's vernacular languages emerged simply as the debased offshoots of the Latin tongue, or had Latin evolved *alongside* the vernacular? Who, for that matter, had spoken Latin in the first place? And what did the development of Italian poetry say about the quality of different vernaculars?

The first serious attempt to grapple with this had been made by Dante Alighieri. In his *De vulgari eloquentia*, Dante argued that men had originally spoken a single language, but that, as punishment for building the Tower of Babel, God had confounded their speech and scattered them across the earth, so that they could no longer understand each other.[75] It had been to compensate for this linguistic confusion that Latin had later been developed. A synthetic language created by scholars, it was governed by a series of carefully-defined rules. This ensured not only that it was consistent, but also that it was immutable. It was the same for everyone, everywhere – and forever. A Latin poem written in Calabria in the first century BC, for example, could be read with perfect ease by someone in Kraków fourteen hundred years later. But Latin's great flaw was that it was an artificial creation, developed in isolation from everyday life and speech. And it was for precisely this reason that Dante preferred the vernacular as a medium for literary composition. To be sure, vernacular languages had none of Latin's coherence and stability.

As Dante readily admitted, they were as mutable and disorderly as they were numerous. In the eastern Mediterranean, Greek was spoken; in the north, there were the Germanic tongues – including Hungarian, Slavic and English; while, in the rest of Europe, there were the three Romance languages, distinguished by their word for 'yes' – the *langue d'oc*, the *langue d'oïl* and Italian. What was worse, each of these existed in a dizzying number of dialects. Italian alone had at least fourteen different varieties, none of which was any better than the others. Yet Dante nevertheless believed that, underlying Italy's many dialects, there was a 'common' form of the Italian vernacular which, though spoken by none, could be understood by all. Not only was this 'illustrious vernacular' nobler than Latin, but, by virtue of its proximity to everyday speech, it was also far more suited to modern poetry. What its characteristics might be, however, Dante never explained.

In years gone by, Niccolò had often discussed the *questione della lingua* in the Orti Oricellari. In contrast to his friends – most of whom were avowed Latinists – he appears to have expressed a preference for his native tongue. Whatever his reasons were, however, they cannot have been very compelling. In a letter written on 1 August 1520, Filippo de' Nerli jokingly suggested that, rather than waste time arguing, his chums should simply hire a good Latin teacher to put him straight when he was next in the city.[76] Since then, however, his thinking had matured. Not only had he a better grasp of the historical underpinnings of the debate, but he was also more highly attuned to its political implications. And, though he remained a passionate advocate of the Florentine dialect, he had become increasingly sceptical of Dante's arguments. All he needed was the occasion to set out his views in full.

The publication of Giangiorgio Trissino's *Epistola de le Lettere Nuovamente Aggiunte ne la Lingua Italiana* ('Epistle on the letters newly added to the Italian language') in October 1524 gave him the excuse he was looking for.[77] Inspired by a close reading of Dante's *De vulgari eloquentia*, this curious little treatise called on Pope Clement VII to introduce a series of spelling reforms which, it was hoped, would transcend the political divisions of the Italian peninsula and create a more unified 'Italian' language – modelled on the Florentine dialect. Despite its eccentricity, it was the sort of book that Niccolò might have been expected to welcome, especially as the ideas it contained had been avidly discussed in the Orti Oricellari some years before. But, far from applauding Trissino's proposals, Niccolò was so offended that he felt moved to write a rebuttal. Known as the *Discorso intorno alla nostra lingua* ('Discourse about our language'), this lively little treatise was a masterpiece of counter-intuitive reasoning.[78] Using Trissino's *Epistola* as an excuse to attack Dante, it set out to prove that, while Florentine was the perfect medium for literary composition in Florence, it was not, and could never be, a language for all Italians.

While writing the early sections of the *Istorie fiorentine*, Niccolò had noticed that Italy's linguistic development had been inexorably bound up with its political history. For as long as the Roman Empire had fought to defend its liberty and enlarge its dominions, he argued, virtue had flourished, justice had reigned, and Latin had been a simple, practical language, common to all. But no sooner had peace been established than leisure and prosperity had begun to eat away at Rome's vitals. As greed and envy took hold, law became partial and Latin became decadent. When the barbarians came, Rome was unable to defend herself – militarily, politically or culturally. First the Goths, then the Lombards began to carve up the Western Empire into separate fiefdoms, and, as they did so, they gave their own names to places and institutions. Encouraged by the Church (which adopted Latin as its own), this political fragmentation gradually led to the emergence of different dialects – until, eventually, the Italian peninsula had become a second Babel.[79] Generally speaking of course, the history of states followed a cycle. Just as order usually collapsed into disorder, so confusion was often succeeded by harmony. But, in Italy, this had never happened. The 'ordinary cycle had been stopped by an extraordinary force – an unnatural stasis and stifling of vital impulse.'[80] Riddled with corruption and harassed by constant foreign invasions, the peninsula had remained a patchwork quilt of petty statelets, each speaking its own form of the vernacular.[81]

None of these was any better – or 'purer' – than the others. Like all languages, they were a crude mixture of different linguistic elements. Words were borrowed from neighbouring towns, foreign expressions were adopted, and even the most unfamiliar idioms were sometimes assimilated. And the more powerful a city was – that is to say, the more contact it had with other societies – the more 'alien' elements it contained. As a consequence, a vernacular could only be said to *belong* to a particular city when it succeeded in adapting these borrowed lexemes to its own use, rather than being swamped by them.

This did not, however, mean that Latin should enjoy a special status. Niccolò refused to believe that Latin was any better or any worse than the vernacular. That the latter had descended from the former was, to his mind, not a form of debasement, but a natural progression. In linguistics, as in all else, change was inevitable; it was only to be expected that cultural shifts should follow political developments.

But nor did the mixing of Italy's vernaculars mean that a 'common language' could be stitched together out of the elements they all shared, as some of Dante's more recent adherents might have been tempted to argue. Quite the opposite. That the various dialects were, to a certain extent, mutually intelligible was, he claimed, merely a testimony to their shared Roman heritage. Dig a little deeper and you would soon see they had much less in common than first appeared. Some of their shared 'similarities' were not unique to Italy at all. Take the word *sì* – which Dante had seen as proof of Italy's distinctive linguistic identity. Although the Italian peoples did indeed use *sì* to mean 'yes', they were not the only ones to do so.[82] The Spanish and the Sicilians had long ago abandoned their native *oc*, and had taken to using *sì* instead. Other 'similarities', by contrast, were far outweighed by the many differences which had resulted from barbarian influences in different regions. This was particularly true of nouns and verbs, which together made up the 'sinews and nerve' of a language. While all Italians said *amare* (to love), *stare* (to stay) and *leggere* (to read), for example, only Florentines used the words *deschetto* (desk), *tavola* (table) and *quastada* (jug or cruet).[83] But the same could also be seen in personal pronouns, too. Whereas, in most places, *io* and *tu* were used to mean 'I' and 'you', *mi* and *ti* were used in others.

Nor, indeed, could Niccolò accept Trissino's suggestion that a single dialect could be made to serve as a language for all. In the absence of political unity, this was quite simply impossible. For, whereas a dialect consisted principally of usages specific to an individual city or region, a common language should, in theory, contain more of the shared than of the particular.[84] Put another way, Florentine could not become Italian without ceasing to be Florentine, and no spelling reforms could make it otherwise.

Of course, Niccolò was aware that there were those – like Dante and Cristoforo Landino – who argued that poetry was the clearest proof of the existence of a common 'Italian' language, and it was to this problem that he now turned. Going straight to the heart of the matter, he flatly denied that any of the great poets of the past had written in Italian. With the exception of Guido Guinizelli, Guittone d'Arezzo and Cino da Pistoia – who had, in any case, written so little as to be scarcely worth mentioning – they had all written in Florentine. Of these, the three most famous were Dante, Petrarch and Boccaccio. To the best of Niccolò's knowledge, Petrarch had, admittedly, never discussed language explicitly, but Boccaccio had quite openly admitted that he wrote in *volgar fiorentino*. Only Dante had denied that he had written in Florentine – purporting instead to have written the *Commedia* in a 'courtly language' common to all Italy.

The better to examine this claim, Niccolò then summoned up Dante's ghost and quizzed him about the language he had used in his magnum opus. After some prodding, Dante admitted that he borrowed Latin words, appropriated Lombard terms and even invented a number of neologisms, but he stubbornly maintained that, in doing so, he had created a *different* poetic language – more 'Italian' than Florentine. Niccolò pounced on this immediately. Since all languages are mixtures, he observed, such linguistic borrowing was only to be expected, and in no way changed the fact that he was adapting his loan-words to Florentine usage. It was no use his trying to dress the *Commedia* up as a 'courtly' work, either. As everyone knew only too well, the courts of Italy – Mantua, Naples, etc. – all spoke in the local dialect. And, besides, in an unguarded moment in the *Inferno*, Dante had actually let it slip that he was writing in Florentine!

Had the real Dante actually been able to speak, he would no doubt have protested that, even if this were true, it misrepresented his aims. What he had been trying to do in the *Commedia* was to reach beyond the particular, to 'transcend the parochial dialect of his native city' – albeit unsuccessfully.[85] But Niccolò refused to allow his ghost such liberty. That Dante had persisted in denying his own tongue was, for Niccolò, tantamount to denying Florence itself. It was, in fact, treasonous – and it was pathetic, to boot. Still seething with fury at his own exile, Dante had allowed himself to become vengeful and cruel – exactly like the factional rivals he claimed to despise. In doing so, he had lost all 'gravity, doctrine, and judgement.' It would have been far better, far more patriotic and far more dignified had he simply admitted to writing in his native tongue.

Needless to say, there were still plenty of people throughout Italy who tried to imitate Dante, but, as Niccolò pointed out, his imitators rarely succeeded – least of all when they tried to write comedy. In its truest form, Niccolò noted, comedy should be a mirror of everyday life. If it was to be compelling and amusing, the audience needed to be able to relate to it. It was hence necessary to give the script some local flavour – and, more importantly, to use the local dialect. Niccolò had done this in his own comedies, and he urged anyone who wished to write comedies to do the same.

For reasons both patriotic and dramatic, therefore, he felt bound to defend Florentine as the best language for poetic composition *in Florence*. Since there was no such thing as a common language – and never would be, so long as Italy remained divided – each city had to content itself with its own unique dialect. To write in the local vernacular was hence not only to be understood by local people, but also to take pride in the city itself. And the result would be better poems, plays and treatises. It was, perhaps, a rather parochial stance to take, but it was characteristically realistic – and in one fell swoop, it succeeded in turning the *questione della lingua* on its head.

*

Niccolò was not always so serious, however. As his repeated references to comedy suggest, Barbera had also reawakened his fondness for humorous tales. According to Michele Bandello, he was well known as a fine storyteller, and was often called upon to liven up evenings with ribald tales.[86] At some point in the winter of 1524, however, he took the unusual step of writing one of these down. Now known as *Belfagor archidiavolo* ('Belfagor the archdevil'), this darkly satirical tale was a classic Florentine *novelle*.[87] Much like Boccaccio's *Decameron* and Franco Saccheti's *Trecentonovelle*, it was littered with blue jokes, anticlerical jibes and local details.[88] Yet its inspiration came from closer to home. Having no doubt caught hell from Marietta for carrying on with Barbera, he may perhaps have decided to get his own back by taking aim at the hectoring ways of Florentine wives.

Back in the days of yore, Niccolò began, there was a very holy man, who, in the ecstasy of his prayers, learned that, of the countless wretched souls in Hell, all or most 'complained that they were brought to such great misfortune by nothing else than by getting married.'[89] When word of this reached the underworld itself, however, the judges of Hell were astonished. They could not believe that what the damned were saying about the fairer sex was true; but, since new reports were flooding in every day, Pluto felt obliged to summon a council of devils. After much debate, it was decided that the archdevil Belfagor should settle the matter by assuming human form, taking a wife, and living with her for a period of ten years.

Taking the name Roderigo of Castile, Belfagor sets himself up in Florence as a prosperous moneylender. He rents a fine house in the Borgo Ognissanti – not far from the Orti Oricellari – and provides himself with horses, servants and all the other accoutrements which befitted an eligible bachelor. After spending a few days making a show of his wealth and generosity, he receives a number of proposals from noble citizens, who have plenty of unmarried daughters, but little money. From among these, he chooses 'a very beautiful girl named Onesta ['Honesty'], daughter of Amerigo Donati', and soon afterwards, they are married in a spectacularly lavish ceremony.[90]

But Onesta soon shows her true colours. Along with her beauty and nobility, she brings to Belfagor's household 'such great pride that Lucifer's was never so great'. As soon as she realizes her husband's love for her, she begins to 'lord it over him'.[91] She makes demands of him 'without mercy and consideration', and, if he dares to refuse her anything, she gives him such a scolding that he hardly knows whether he is coming or going. Forced to provide her unmarried sisters with 'huge' dowries, set her brothers up in business and 'dress her in the latest fashions', Belfagor is soon completely bankrupt.

Rather than face his creditors, Belfagor decides to flee. Early one morning, he mounts his horse, rides out of the Porta al Prato and heads into the countryside. Near Peretola – where the Vespucci family were said to have originated – he comes across one of Giovanni del Bene's tenants, Gianmatteo del Brica, and promises that, if the farmer will help him, he will make him rich in return. Gianmatteo readily agrees and, once Belfagor has revealed his true identity, they devise a cunning plan together. Taking on his devilish form once again, Belfagor would possess a series of well-to-do women. In the guise of an exorcist, Gianmatteo would then 'cure' them, and the two con-artists would rake in huge rewards from their grateful relatives.[92]

The ruse works like a dream. A few days later, Gianmatteo 'cures' the daughter of Ambrogio Amadei, and is duly paid 500 florins. Not long afterwards, he does the same with the daughter of King Charles of Naples. For this, he receives the princely sum of 50,000 ducats in return. Feeling that he has now discharged his obligations, Belfagor tells the farmer not to bother him again and heads off to have some fun. Gianmatteo is happy enough to oblige. Returning to Florence a rich man, he plans to settle down to enjoy the rest of his life in comfortable retirement.

But Gianmatteo's success soon threatens to be his undoing. When Belfagor decides to possess the king of France's daughter, Gianmattero is dragged unwillingly to Paris and threatened with execution if he does not cure her. Sweating profusely, he pleads with Belfagor to let the girl go, but the archdevil – who, having failed in his mission, has no desire to face the fury of Pluto in Hell – refuses to listen. Gianmatteo has no choice but to resort to trickery. At a vast spectacle in front of Notre Dame, he causes a huge noise to be made – and leads Belfagor to believe that it is the sound of his wife arriving from Florence. More frightened of Onesta's hectoring than Pluto's vengeful anger, the demon immediately scarpers. 'Thus,' Niccolò concluded, 'Belfagor bore witness in Hell to the ills a wife can bring into a house. And Gianmatteo, who was shrewder than the devil, returned home in complete happiness.'[93]

*

Deep down, however, Niccolò must have known that Marietta was right to shout at him. Though he was still hopelessly in love with Barbera, he was doing his family wrong – and was making himself look ridiculous in the process. He did not feel so bad that he was ready to break things off just yet, but he nevertheless seems to have felt that, if he was going to laugh at Marietta, he should at least have the decency to laugh at himself, too. Happily, he did not have to wait long for a suitable opportunity.

By early 1525, Falconetti's period of exile was coming to an end. Wanting to celebrate it in style, he asked Niccolò to stage a production of *Mandragola*, which had been performed to great acclaim only the year before.[94] To gratify his host, however, Niccolò instead offered to write a new play – the *Clizia*.[95] Based on Plautus's *Casina*, this ribald farce was in the best tradition of Roman comedy. Featuring the usual array of stock characters, it ridiculed social conventions and poked fun at just about everyone. But the real butt of its humour was Niccolò himself.

As the prologue makes clear, the *Clizia* is a tale of love and old age. The 'hero', Cleandro, is in love with Clizia, a seventeen-year-old foundling, who was entrusted to his family's care by a French soldier shortly after the fall of Naples in 1494, and who has been living with them ever since. Much to Cleandro's consternation, however, his seventy-year-old father Nicomaco – who has lived a blameless life up until now – has also fallen for her charms. Since Nicomaco is already married, he knows that he has no chance of enjoying her favours openly, but, being a wily old fox, he reasons that, if he marries Clizia to his rascally servant, Pirro, he will be able to block his son's plans and conduct an affair with her without anyone suspecting. But Nicomaco's cunning wife, Sofronia, soon guesses what he is up to and plots to thwart his plans by marrying Clizia to their foreman, Eustachio, instead. With three (or rather, four) suitors now competing for the poor girl's hand, a tremendous argument erupts – and things soon threaten to turn violent. At Nicomaco's suggestion, the rivals eventually agree to settle the matter by drawing names out of a hat. When Pirro emerges as the victor, Nicomaco – impatient to enjoy his winnings – insists on celebrating the marriage straight away, and hastily rents the house of his neighbour, Damone, for the nuptials. Sofronia, however, has one more trick up her sleeve. Guessing what Nicomaco has in mind, she arranges for a servant, Siro, to disguise himself as Clizia and take her place in the marriage bed. When the lusty Nicomaco slides between the sheets later that night, Siro gives him a sound beating, before poking him in the back with 'something hard and sharp'. Believing that 'Clizia' was about to stab him with a 'dagger', Nicomaco jumps out of bed with a start and calls for a light – whereupon he realizes not only the trick which has been played upon him, but also the shame with which he has inadvertently covered himself. The next day, a chastened Nicomaco tells Damone all about his misfortunes; and, after receiving a suitable telling-off from his wife, promises not to chase after young girls ever again. No sooner has he done so than a Neapolitan gentleman named Ramondo arrives out of the blue, and reveals himself to be Clizia's father. Much to Sofronia's delight, he then agrees to Damone's suggestion that Clizia should marry Cleandro, and they all live happily ever after.

It was, in many ways, Niccolò's most accomplished piece of theatre.[96] Unlike *Mandragola*, it is a cleanly written and linear narrative, sustained by its own comic momentum and free from fruitless digressions. The action is, moreover, tightly choreographed. As Robert Black has rightly emphasized, everything happens in the street outside Nicomaco's house, and takes place over a single day. At no point is the stage either empty or crowded, and care is taken to prevent the dialogue from becoming unwieldy. Perhaps most importantly, however, the characters are all realistically drawn – none more so that Nicomaco and Sofronia. Though a familiar dramatic 'type', the dirty old man who makes a fool of himself chasing after a younger woman is clearly recognizable as Niccolò himself, while his cunning, shrewish wife, who rightly upbraids him for flouting moral norms, is unmistakably Marietta.

The *Clizia* received its first performance in Falconetti's gardens on 13 January 1525.[97] Almost the whole city was there – from the young Alessandro and Ippolito de' Medici and their court, to *popolani* and pedlars – all clamouring to see the spectacle.[98] It was a lavish affair. The artist Bastiano da Sangallo had designed the sets – which, according to Vasari, were universally admired[99] – and, for the first time in the history of theatre, a composer – Philippe Verdelot – had been commissioned to write the music for the madrigals which were to be sung between each act, most likely by Barbera herself.[100]

It was an instant hit. Before long, people everywhere were singing its praises. On 22 February, Filippo de' Nerli joined the chorus. Writing from Modena – where he was then serving as the pope's governor – he congratulated Niccolò on his triumph. 'The fame of your comedy has flown all over,' Nerli exclaimed, 'and you should not think that I have heard this from friends' letters [alone], but I have also heard it from wayfarers who wander along the roads preaching about 'the glorious celebrations and praiseworthy spectacles of the Porta San Frediano.'[101]

No doubt Niccolò was delighted, but he did not let success go to his head. His focus remained on the *Istorie fiorentine*. Working harder than he is often given credit for, he had completed the work by March 1525, and, with Barbera at his side, he was content to remain an esteemed – if now purely literary – elder statesman.

27

'This Ruined World'

The *Istorie fiorentine* was a fitting culmination to Niccolò's literary career.[1] Covering more than a thousand years of Florentine history – from the decline of the Roman Empire in the west, to the death of Lorenzo 'il Magnifico' de' Medici – it was a towering monument to the historian's craft. While lavishing attention on Florence's often fraught political evolution, in all eight books, Niccolò never failed to place the city's travails in the wider context of Italian – and European – affairs. For a lesser writer, such an abundance of material would no doubt have been daunting, but Niccolò succeeded in weaving together the disparate strands of his story to produce a seamless narrative of unparalleled elegance. His language was clear and direct, his style rich and flowing, and his tone as much that of a seasoned diplomat as that of a disinterested scholar.[2]

Of its many virtues, Niccolò was most anxious to emphasize its fidelity. When he had received his commission, he had been charged with writing in such a way that he would always be 'far from flattery',[3] and this he had taken to heart, striving to remain faithful to the truth, even when his narration of events was likely to cause offence to the descendants of those involved.[4] His research had, accordingly, been thorough. Though he had not consulted the communal archives, he had made a careful study of fourteenth- and fifteenth-century chronicles, and, of more recent histories, there was scarcely a volume which he had not read.[5]

Yet the *Istorie fiorentine* was never meant to present an 'objective' view of the past. Much like the *Vita di Castruccio Castracani*, it had been written in the classical tradition beloved of Renaissance humanists.[6] Though often exacting in his use of detail, Niccolò set out to craft a *version* of Florence's past, which – enlivened with invented speeches and dramatic, if imaginary, battle scenes – could impart moral and political lessons to the present. This not only entailed using the lives and deeds of great men to exemplify the *virtù* on which the health of a republic depended, but also required the city's constitutional development to be presented in such a way as to illustrate the manner in which it should be governed.

Niccolò was not the first to write with such a purpose in mind. A century before, Leonardo Bruni and Poggio Bracciolini had each been animated by a similar understanding of history. In the preface to his *Historiarum Florentinarum libri XII*, for example, Bruni had affirmed that, from his pages, readers would 'learn with ease what behaviour we should imitate and avoid, while the glory of great men, as therein recorded,' would inspire them 'to perform acts of virtue.'[7] At the same time, he hoped that his depiction of the city's politics would provide, if not a prospectus for its future, then at least some justification for its present form of government.[8] But what set Niccolò apart was his selection of material. As he explained in the proem, he had initially intended to begin his narrative in 1434, in the belief that Bruni and Bracciolini had already covered the period before that date in sufficient detail. When he had gone back over their works, however, he had found that, while they had carefully described Florence's wars with foreign princes and peoples, they had said little about the 'civil strife and internal hostilities' by which the city had been afflicted, and nothing whatsoever about the effects those divisions had produced.[9] Perhaps, Niccolò speculated, they had thought such matters 'unworthy of preserving in writing', or perhaps they had simply been afraid of offending the families of those whom, 'in such narratives, they would have to calumniate.' But there was no doubt that their omission had fatally weakened their ability to impart meaningful advice to the present. For, without exploring the 'causes of hatreds and factional struggles within a city,' Niccolò explained, it was impossible to show those who governed how civil discord could be avoided.[10] Yet this, he believed, was the most important question facing any republic. Determined not to make the same mistake, he had therefore decided to concentrate expressly on the bitter divisions by which Florence had been afflicted since its foundation, in the belief that, in so doing, he would be able to show the Medici how best to keep the city united.

Now, all cities experienced divisions of one sort or another. In ancient Rome, for example, the nobles and the people had fought each other for centuries after the expulsion of the kings. It had been the same story in Athens – and, indeed, in almost every city in the classical world. But Florence was unusual in that it had experienced several divisions: first between the nobles, then between the nobles and the *popolo*, and finally between wealthier members of the *popolo* and the disenfranchised masses (*plebe*).

Such divisions were not necessarily bad in themselves, of course.[11] As in the *Discorsi*, Niccolò pointed out that, while some divisions could be harmful, others could be tremendously beneficial. 'Those that do harm,' he wrote at the beginning of the seventh book, 'are accompanied by factions (*sette*) and partisans; those bring benefit that are kept up without factions and partisans.'[12] This being so, there was no point in trying to stop enmities arising; all that any government could do was to prevent factions from forming.

In the Roman Republic, Niccolò argued, divisions had been so managed as to benefit the state. Though the nobles and the people had fought each other for centuries, neither had ever sought more than a share in government. As such, their struggles had led to debate, rather than violence, had resulted in new laws, rather than in exile or death, and had held them in a finely-balanced equilibrium.[13] Needless to say, there were always tensions. But, since each had constantly been on its guard against the other, nobles and people alike had been obliged to maintain their cohesion. While this may have perpetuated social inequalities, it had also prevented factions from forming. And, as long as the two social classes had kept each other in check, their rivalry had safeguarded Rome's liberty and enhanced its military *virtù*.

In Florence, by contrast, divisions had never been anything but destructive. Rather than merely seeking an equal share of public offices, each social group – nobles, *popolo* and *plebe* – had sought to exclude the others from government entirely. Their conflicts had, accordingly, been bloody and merciless, and had only ever ended in banishment or murder. Had any of these groups remained united, there might still have been some glimmer of hope. Perhaps, in time, worn down by long years of strife, they might have been persuaded to seek some manner of accord. But, whenever one group emerged victorious, it only remained united so long as its opponents continued to pose a threat.[14] Once they were crushed, the group in power, having nothing more to fear and no law to restrain it, quickly divided. From this, factions had emerged. Whether by rising to prominence through some great act of public service or by using nefarious means to build up a network of clients, ambitious men soon attracted partisans seeking protection or favour – and, before long, a new cycle of conflict had begun.

Doomed to undergo frequent, violent changes of regime, Florence had swung wildly between political antipodes, often accompanied by the spilling of much blood.[15] At the beginning of the thirteenth century, Niccolò explained, the nobles had been in the ascendant and, as was their wont, they had striven to dominate the common people. A broken engagement, however, had led to factionalism, and, ultimately, to the bloody struggle between the Guelphs and the Ghibellines.[16] This had resulted, in the mid-fourteenth century, in the tyranny of Walter of Brienne, duke of Athens.[17] Appalled by his disregard for the rule of law, however, the *popolo* had risen in rebellion, and, after expelling the duke, had established the first 'popular' regime.[18] Yet this had only served to awaken the ambition of the disenfranchised *plebe*. Demanding to share not only in the city's government, but also in its wealth, they had themselves revolted, and, while the *popolo* had been busying themselves with another bout of factionalism, the 'Ciompi' had succeeded in seizing control of the republic for themselves.[19] Needless to say, this had met with strong opposition – especially from the wealthier *popolani*. Rallying their forces, they ousted the *plebe*, and, after a brief period of compromise, succeeded in establishing a new constitution which concentrated power in their own hands and dramatically reduced the common people's access to public office.[20]

Such travails would have ruined a lesser city, but not Florence. At least during her early history, she had grown ever stronger.[21] Though she was a shadow of what she *could* have been, she had, by the end of the thirteenth century, achieved a measure of 'greatness'. As Niccolò noted, '[a]ll Tuscany, partly as subject, partly as ally obeyed her.'[22] Had she somehow managed to free herself from divisions, there would have been no republic, ancient or modern, to equal her.[23] But, since then, the steady growth of factionalism had robbed her of her glory. While she had continued to play a role in the drama of Italian affairs, her liberty had gradually been eroded, until, by the late fifteenth century, hardly a trace of it had remained.

Part of the reason for this was that the exclusion of the nobles had so diminished Florence's military *virtù* that she was scarcely able to defend herself. More concerned with private matters than with the common good, her citizens were loath to fight foreign enemies; her leaders, preoccupied with domestic rivalries, were disorganized and short sighted; and her captains, who were often hired mercenaries, were unprincipled scoundrels. The resulting blunders were so numerous that Niccolò did not have time to examine them all. But there were a few battles which nevertheless illustrated Florence's diminished military strength particularly clearly. As Quentin Skinner has pointed out, Niccolò's descriptions deliberately parodied the set-piece battles common to humanistic histories.[24] Rather than extolling the courage or martial spirit of the combatants, he paints the Florentines as ridiculous fools. Take the Battle of Zagonara (1424). Hopelessly outmatched by the Milanese commander, Agnolo della Pergola, Niccolò noted that the Florentines had marched straight into a trap, and, in heavy rain, were easily vanquished.[25] It was a catastrophic defeat, which was soon 'reported everywhere in Italy' – but what made it all the more humiliating, according to Niccolò, was that it had been almost bloodless. Other than Lodovico degli Obizzi and his two followers, who fell from their horses and were drowned in the mud, no one lost their lives. The Battle of Anghiari (1440) was another good example. Though this famous victory had long been regarded as one of the proudest moments in Florentine history, Niccolò portrayed it as little more than an unseemly scrum. Decked out in heavy armour, none of the horsemen who had taken part had ever been in danger of harm. Indeed, in 'this great and long fight lasting from two until six o'clock,' Niccolò wryly observed, 'not more than one man died, and he perished not from wounds or any honourable blow, but by falling from his horse and being trampled on.'[26]

Yet, a far more important reason for the demise of Florentine liberty was that civil strife paved the way for the Medici to seize control of the state. It was not that Niccolò had any problems with the Medici per se. Although Donato Giannotti later claimed that Niccolò had concealed his *true* opinion of them, there is little doubt in the *Istorie fiorentine* that, as individuals, they were no worse than anyone else.[27] Indeed, in most respects, they were much better. Giovanni di Bicci – the founder of the family's fortunes – had been modest, kind and peace-loving;[28] his son, Cosimo, had 'surpassed every other in his time', not only 'in influence and wealth, but also in liberality and prudence';[29] while his great-grandson, Lorenzo 'Il Magnifico', had been 'eloquent and penetrating' in discussing affairs, wise in settling them and 'prompt and courageous' in carrying them out.[30] Rather, it was that the Medici had risen to power, not as unifying figures, but as factional leaders – and, as such, had corrupted the republic from within.

At first, they had merely been on an equal footing with the other great families. Though they might have disagreed with their rivals – sometimes vehemently so – they were just one faction among many. As a consequence, it had still been possible for dissenting opinions to be heard. But, like all other factions, they had craved dominance, and, little by little, they had used their immense wealth to crowd out their rivals. With loans and gifts, they acquired partisans, more interested in personal profit than the common good; through their trusted lieutenants, they slandered their opponents;[31] and, by bankrolling the public debt, they made themselves indispensable to the conduct of foreign and domestic policy. By 1466, they had gained a stranglehold on government. They saw no need to reform the constitution – except in their favour – and had no intention of admitting any but their allies to office. Opposition was stifled and, as Niccolò noted, 'the discontented were forced either with patience to bear that kind of government, or, if they did attempt to destroy it, to do so with conspiracies and secretly.'[32] But such desperate measures were already doomed to failure. In his account of the Pazzi conspiracy, he depicts Jacopo de' Pazzi trying desperately to save the failing coup by riding to the Piazza della Signoria and raising the old cry: '*Popolo e libertà!*' But it was to no avail. By then, the Medici had so debased civil life that 'the people had been made deaf' to such appeals.[33] And liberty had become no more than a memory.

*

In history, as in fiction, suffering is generally followed by redemption. As Niccolò noted at the beginning of book five, states like Florence 'generally go from order to disorder and then from disorder move back to order, because . . . when they have come to their utmost perfection and have no further possibility for rising, they must go down. Likewise, when they have gone down and through their defects have reached the lowest depths, they necessarily rise, since they cannot go lower.'[34]

But Florence's was not such a happy fate. Corruption had put redemption out of reach, and cowardice had opened a new path to the 'barbarian' foe. Though Niccolò's narrative ended with the death of Lorenzo 'il Magnifico' in 1492, his readers would have recalled that, just two years later, the French had invaded. Florence had been overrun and the Medici expelled. When the chips had been down, they had been powerless to resist the invader, and their partisans – whose loyalty had only ever been conditional – had abandoned them to their fate. Rather than being restored to liberty, however, Florence had succumbed first to tyranny, and then to licence once again. It went to show that, in 'this ruined world' (*questo guasto mondo*), nothing could be taken for granted.[35] As long as a city remained divided, it seemed, servitude was not always followed by freedom, and even the strongest tyranny was fragile.

Given that the *Istorie fiorentine* had been commissioned by the current head of the Medici family, this might well have seemed a bold, even foolhardy, position for Niccolò to have taken. But his depiction of the Medici was intended more as advice than criticism.[36] In showing how greatly they had eroded Florence's liberty and their own security in the past, he was also discreetly revealing how Clement VII could avoid repeating the same mistakes in the future. If the Medici bastards, Ippolito and Alessandro, were to stand any chance of establishing a stable regime, he implied, they must do everything they could to unify the city. Rather than rely on partisans alone, they should open up government to everyone, including their enemies; they should tolerate dissent, within reason; they should restrain their generosity and prefer modesty to liberality; they should hold law in the utmost respect; and they should strive always to balance the interests of nobles, *popolo* and *plebe*. If they could do this, they would avoid the divisions which had proved so ruinous in the past. In doing so, they would not only safeguard the city against its enemies, but also restore Florence's lost liberty – and secure their power for generations to come.

There was not much about this which was new. Barring a slight difference of emphasis and a handful of technical revisions, the advice Niccolò offered was similar in spirit to that contained both in the *Discorsi* and in his various proposals for the reform of the Florentine government. But what set the *Istorie fiorentine* apart was its underlying sense of optimism. Whereas, in the *Discorsi*, Niccolò had been forced to admit that, after many centuries of 'balanced' liberty, Rome had succumbed to tyranny and dictatorship, in the *Istorie fiorentine*, he held out the hope that, after many centuries of tyranny and civil strife, Florence could still be refounded as a 'true' republic – provided, of course, the Medici followed his advice.

It was an exhilarating prospect. But, as the years to come would show, Niccolò's optimism could hardly have been more misplaced.

28

An Old Man in a Hurry

(March 1525–September 1526)

Niccolò was eager to present the pope with a copy of the *Istorie fiorentine*. It was, as he well knew, his finest work. Despite all the heartache of recent years, he had succeeded in producing a history of surpassing beauty. It was a splendid monument to the city he loved, and a worthy offering for any patron. Within weeks of the *Clizia*'s first, triumphant performance in Jacopo Falconetti's gardens, he was already talking about travelling to Rome.

But experience had taught him that, no matter how good a book might be, timing was everything, and he couldn't be sure if now was the right moment. Wracked by doubt, he therefore asked the advice of Francesco Vettori, who had recently been sent to Rome to lobby the pope on behalf of the *Otto di Pratica*.[1] Being cautious by nature, Vettori had, at first, not known what to say.[2] When the pope had heard that Niccolò's history had reached the death of Lorenzo, 'and that it was something that would give satisfaction,' however, he had rebuked Vettori for being so chary. Of course Niccolò should come to Rome, Clement exclaimed; his book was sure to be a treat!

Nevertheless, Vettori warned Niccolò not to get his hopes up too much. The times were, he pointed out, 'opposed to reading and to gifts'. Beset by grave political concerns, the pope was constantly changing his mind about everything and Vettori did not want Niccolò coming all the way to Rome, only to leave empty-handed.

*

For once, Vettori was right. While Niccolò had been busy finishing the *Istorie fiorentine*, the tides of war had turned once again – this time for the worse. Late the year before, Bourbon's invasion of Provence had ground to a halt.[3] Despite a lengthy siege, Marseilles had remained defiant, and Charles V, disappointed by the whole affair, had refused to supply Bourbon with more money. Spying a golden opportunity, Francis I assembled a fresh army at Avignon and marched on Marseilles. Within days, the siege of Marseilles had been lifted and Bourbon's troops put to flight. Pursuing them across the Alps, Francis then marched into Lombardy, intent on reclaiming his lost possessions. By late October, he had taken Milan and a few weeks later, he laid siege to Pavia.[4] One by one, Charles's Italian allies deserted him: Venice, timorous as ever, signed a non-aggression pact with France; and the duke of Ferrara placed himself under Francis' protection. It looked to all the world as if the shattered remnants of the imperial army might soon be swept out of Italy.

Standing by his earlier position, Clement VII initially refused to support either side, hoping to keep both Florence and the papacy out of the fray.[5] But when Francis sent a *second* army, under the duke of Albany, against the kingdom of Naples, the pope could no longer afford to remain neutral.[6] Terrified of what might happen to his states as this army marched southwards, he hastily agreed to allow Albany safe passage in return for an assurance that Florence would be left in peace, and for an acknowledgement of his rights over Parma and Piacenza.[7]

It was to prove a grave mistake. While Francis had been laying siege to Pavia over the winter, the new imperial commander, Charles de Lannoy, had been busy rallying his forces. By late January, he was ready to launch a counter-attack. Marching out from Lodi, he soon reached Pavia, where he found Francis firmly entrenched behind a defensive wall. After several weeks spent trying to draw the king out into battle, Lannoy's forces succeeded in breaking through the French lines on the night of 23 February. By the following morning, Francis' once proud army had been annihilated.[8] Some of France's most distinguished commanders had been killed, and – most devastatingly of all – the king himself had been taken prisoner.

Clement VII was now dangerously exposed. With both Milan and Naples in imperial hands, the Papal States were effectively surrounded. If he had wanted, Charles could have punished the pope for his recent dalliance with the French by imposing the most humiliating conditions on him. But, for whatever reason, his representatives in Italy chose to make only the most modest demands. Clement, of course, jumped at the opportunity. On 1 April, he entered into a 'perpetual alliance' with the emperor. As part of this, he agreed to recognize Francesco Sforza as duke of Milan. In return, however, he asked for the Medici to be taken under imperial protection, the imperial army to be withdrawn from his territory, and the duke of Ferrara to return Reggio and Rubiera to the Church.[9]

Had Charles agreed to these terms, he would have handed the pope a great victory. At last, however, the emperor came to his senses. On Lannoy's advice, he refused to ratify Clement's terms – especially those concerning the withdrawal of imperial troops from the Papal States, and the return of Reggio.[10] Instead, he made some demands of his own: he wanted Modena to be handed back to the duke of Ferrara; Bologna to be returned to the Bentivoglio; and, most gallingly of all, Siena, Lucca and Florence to be placed under imperial suzerainty.

Clement was horrified. He could never agree to such terms – and Charles knew it. Realizing the 'perpetual alliance' had been a sham all along, the pope saw that war with the emperor was now virtually inevitable. He was, however, in no position to fight. He had no army, no money and no allies. To buy himself time, he decided to send Cardinal Giovanni Salviati to 'negotiate' with Charles in Madrid. Seeing that it would be a mission of the utmost difficulty, however, he thought it might be a good idea to send Niccolò, too.

From Cardinal Salviati's point of view, Niccolò would have made a splendid companion. Back in 1521, the cardinal had received a copy of the *Arte della guerra*, and had immediately recognized the subtlety of Niccolò's mind. His father, Jacopo, was also an admirer. Having witnessed Niccolò's diplomatic skills at first hand, he would have liked nothing more than to see him appointed. 'As a secretary', he told his son on 13 May, 'Niccolò Machiavelli would please me above all others.'[11] He had already spoken to the pope about him, and, though no decision had yet been taken, he would see what could be done.

It was more than Niccolò had dared hope for. A diplomatic mission to Spain would not just have revived his political career – it would have catapulted him to the forefront of European affairs. But it was not to be. Within days, the pope, anxious and irresolute, had begun to have second thoughts and on 24 May, Jacopo Salviati dolefully informed his son that Niccolò would not be accompanying him, after all.[12]

It was disappointing, but Niccolò had no reason to be downhearted. That he had been considered for such an important mission at all was something of an achievement. It testified not only to the esteem in which his diplomatic expertise was held at the papal court, but also to Pope Clement VII's faith in him. If nothing else, it boded well for the future.

*

Despite Vettori's warnings, Niccolò felt the time had come to deliver the *Istorie fiorentine*. With a spring in his step, he set off from Florence towards the end of May. Within a matter of days, he was in Rome.[13] Kneeling before the papal throne, he handed the finished manuscript to the Holy Father. What passed between them has not been recorded, but, of the pope's delight, there can be no doubt. In recognition of the brilliance of his achievement, Clement arranged for him to be given the handsome sum of 120 gold ducats out of his privy purse.[14]

It was a crowning success. Not only had Niccolò's hard work received the recognition it deserved, but he had finally been accepted into the Medici fold. An outsider no longer, he had become a tried and tested intimate, worthy of respect and admiration. Had he so wished, he could have settled down to a quiet retirement, secure in the knowledge that he could at last rest easy on his laurels.

But Niccolò had no intention of retiring just yet. Along with his book, he had brought a proposal which, he believed, would save the Church from its current peril – and, at the same time, restore him to political office. Whatever the outcome of Cardinal Salviati's mission to Spain, he argued, the imperial forces then encamped in the Paduan plain would soon cross the River Po and invade the Papal States. Seeing that the pope had neither the money with which to hire fresh mercenaries, nor allies upon whom to call for help, his only hope of resisting the onslaught was to raise a militia of his own in the Romagna. It was, of course, not the first time Niccolò had suggested such a scheme. He had, after all, been instrumental in re-establishing a Florentine militia in both 1506 and 1514 – and, on each occasion, it had not been short of critics. But the pope immediately recognized its potential. Brimming over with enthusiasm, he immediately sent Niccolò to Faenza to discuss his plan with Francesco

Guicciardini, who, as president of the Romagna, was in the best position to know how it might be set in motion.

Setting out from Rome on 10 or 11 June, Niccolò travelled northwards, through Terni and across the Apennines. With him, he was carrying a brief, written by the papal secretary, Jacopo Sadoleto, which testified both to the far-reaching consequences of his mission, and to the extraordinary favour in which he now stood. In it, Sadoleto exhorted Guicciardini to listen carefully to what Niccolò had to say, and to report back on the feasibility of his plan as soon as possible[15] – for it was, Sadoleto explained, a matter of the greatest importance, upon which depended the wellbeing not just of the Church, but of Italy as a whole, and of virtually all Christendom.

On 21 June, Niccolò arrived in Faenza. Guicciardini, of course, greeted him with open arms – but, if Niccolò was expecting the *ordinanza* to be met with the same warmth, he was cruelly disappointed. Guicciardini had already heard rumours about Niccolò's scheme, and, on 18 June, had written to his agent in Rome, Cesare Colombo, expressing his doubts about its feasibility. Now he had the opportunity to learn more about it from Niccolò himself, his scepticism only grew. On 23 June, he wrote to Colombo once again, setting out his objections.[16] The Romagna, he explained, was no longer the proud and unified province it had once been. Ravaged by long years of war, and rent by factional strife, it was now divided, hostile and restive. The Church enjoyed little respect, and papal government was pitifully weak. Since few people expected the pope's rule to last much longer, no one paid any attention to the law; most simply laughed when threatened with punishment. Even if men were pressed into service, a militia would be unreliable at best, and disloyal at worst.

Nor was there much chance of raising the money to pay for a militia, either. Over recent years, the Romagna had been so heavily taxed that there was scarcely a *soldo* left to be had. Imola, Forlí and Rimini, in particular, were virtually penniless. Only 'with force' could the people be compelled to hand over what little remained to them – and then only at the risk of provoking open unrest. This was, of course, not to say that a militia was completely out of the question, but, if it was to have any chance, the pope would have to commit to it fully, and in the knowledge that it might first have to be used against the Romagna itself.

At Guicciardini's request, Colombo showed this letter to the pope.

As the president no doubt hoped, Clement's enthusiasm for the militia quickly withered in the pitiless glare of his criticism. Though only dimly aware of what Guicciardini had said, Niccolò tried valiantly to defend himself in a (now lost) letter to Sadoleto towards the end of the month. But it was to no avail. Replying on 6 July, Sadoleto informed him that, while the pope had 'looked with favour on everything' he had said, he wanted to think about his proposals a little more before making a final decision.[17]

Over the next few weeks, Niccolò hung around in Faenza, waiting for news. Despite their disagreements over the militia, he and Guicciardini probably met for dinner fairly often. Over lavish dishes served on local maiolica, they would have talked gaily of politics and literature until well into the night. Though he was still carrying on with Barbera, Niccolò also began an affair with a courtesan named Mariscotta, who – as Guicciardini later recalled – was captivated by his witty conversation and graceful manners.[18]

Eventually, however, he grew tired of waiting. It was obvious the pope had given up on the idea of raising a militia. On 26 July, he left Faenza for Florence, ostensibly to 'attend to his affairs'.[19] He could not have helped feeling disheartened. It was, of course, Guicciardini's doing. Had he not scared the pope off, things might have been very different. Yet Niccolò could not bear his friend any ill will. Deep down, he probably knew Guicciardini was right. Besides, their friendship was too strong for politics ever to come between them. Sharing the same tastes, the same ribald sense of humour and the same easy-going nature, they would always be birds of a feather. Indeed, if anything, adversity had made them fonder of each other than ever before.

*

On returning to Florence, Niccolò was gratified to find that, though his proposals for a militia had come to nothing, he nevertheless continued to enjoy the pope's favour. As Francesco del Nero explained in a letter written shortly after Niccolò's departure from Faenza, Filippo Strozzi had asked the pope to increase Niccolò's salary, and had found him 'very well disposed'.[20] Now that Niccolò was back home, all he had to do was to write Filippo a quick note and everything would be arranged. It was just as well, too. Niccolò's daughter, Bartolomea ('Baccina'), was getting married to Giovanni de' Ricci, and he needed the extra money to pay for her dowry.[21]

After an absence of almost three months, Niccolò would have enjoyed catching up with his friends. But it was Guicciardini's friendship which he appears to have cherished the most. Not long after Niccolò had set out for Florence, Guicciardini had sent him a short, but affectionate letter, which marked the opening of a new phase in their relationship.[22] It contained little news. In fact, the only thing Guicciardini had to report was that, since Niccolò's departure, Mariscotta had been speaking of him 'very flatteringly'. He knew how much Mariscotta's words would mean to Niccolò, and it warmed his heart to pass them on – not because he particularly enjoyed being a middle-man, but, as he explained, 'because I desire everything that makes you happy'.

Niccolò felt the same way. While he had been in Faenza, he had promised to visit two properties which Guicciardini had bought sight unseen, and to report back to him on their condition. Having made good on his word within days of his return, Niccolò wrote to Guicciardini on 3 August.[23] His letter was characteristically detailed. With painstaking care, he described the location of each house, the crops grown on their farms, the arrangement of their rooms, the state of their roofs and the likely cost of repairs. But he also allowed himself the odd flash of humour. Finocchietto – the first of the two properties he had visited – was, he claimed, so isolated that it reminded him of 'rocky Arabia'; the house was like 'a dungeon'; and, if Guicciardini didn't make the necessary improvements, he would have no chance of selling it on, except to some poor sap like him, who hadn't seen it.

Niccolò's wry humour pleased Guicciardini no end. After begging his friend not to address him by his title anymore,[24] he replied with a deliciously funny letter, purporting to be from 'Milady Property of Finocchietto.'[25] In this guise, Guicciardini chided Niccolò for his unkind remarks about his farm. He ought to have known better than to judge by appearances, 'Milady Finocchietto' screeched. Had he not been so quick to jump to conclusions, he would have seen that, 'under the rigidity and harshness that were apparent in me at first glance', there were many good features, which deserved praise, rather than blame. Rather cattily, 'Milady' then pointed out that he should have learned this from Barbera, who, though her name suggested a cruel and ferocious nature, was actually gentle and kind. Next time, 'she' warned him, he should think more carefully before opening his big mouth, because a mistake for which another person could be forgiven could not be forgiven when it was made by someone of his 'wisdom and experience'.

It was just the sort of light-hearted raillery that Niccolò enjoyed, and, by way of return, he sent Guicciardini a copy of the *Mandragola*.[26] Had he had the time, he would probably have been glad to continue their correspondence in a similar vein, but, on 17 August, he revealed that the superintendents of Levantine affairs were planning to send him to Venice to secure the release of some Florentine merchants, whose boat had been captured by an aristocratic adventurer named Giovanni Battista Donà (or Donato).[27] It was a relatively unexciting mission – scarcely any more diverting than the wearisome commercial disputes that had taken him to Genoa and Lucca a few years before. But he was grateful for the chance to travel again – especially as, on his return trip, it would give him an excuse to drop in on Guicciardini and his friends – who were now in Modena.

Setting off from Florence in the third week of August, he arrived in Venice five or six days later. It was the first time he had visited the Serene Republic, and he was immediately seduced by its charms – far more, in fact, than he should have been. After presenting his credentials to the doge, and making contact with the apostolic nuncio, Tommaso Campeggi, and the French ambassador, Ludovico Canossa – who had both taken an interest in the matter – he threw himself into the city's cultural life with such enthusiasm that he lost all track of time. On 6 September, Filippo de' Nerli wrote from Florence urging him to 'take care of things quickly, because here there is a lot of gossip among these merchants that you are passing your time at their expense entertaining literary people there'.[28] There was also a rumour going around that Niccolò had won two or three thousand ducats in the Venetian lottery. Though this ultimately proved to be false, the fact that he hadn't said anything to his friends had caused some offence – and may have led them to believe that he was planning to stay in the lagoon indefinitely.

*

On 16 September, Niccolò finally left Venice.[29] After passing through Padua – the birthplace of his beloved Livy – he arrived in Modena, where he spent a few happy days with Guicciardini, sharing jokes, exchanging gossip and catching up on news. When he eventually set out again, he was in no hurry. Travelling at a leisurely pace, he did not reach Florence until the end of the month.

In the event, it hardly mattered that he was late. While he had been away, he had been declared eligible for public office – for the first time in his life. His friends were surprised, to say the least. As the son of a public debtor, his status had always been rather questionable. With characteristic humour, Nerli joked that the *accoppiatori* must have had their eyes closed when they read out his name.[30] But there could be no doubt that it was the work of the Medici. Having now accepted Niccolò as one of their own, they had marked him for greater things.

For the moment, however, Niccolò was content to return to his literary pursuits. Chief among them was the *Mandragola*. Having greatly enjoyed reading the copy Niccolò had sent him earlier in the summer, Guicciardini had suggested putting on a performance of the play in Faenza – whence he had since returned – at the next carnival.[31] Niccolò jumped at the chance – not least because it would give him an opportunity to revise the script. Towards the end of October, he wrote to Guicciardini with news of his progress:

> Ludovico Alamanni and I have been dining these last few evenings with Barbera and discussing the play; hence, she has offered to come with her singers and sing the songs between the acts. I have offered to write lyrics consistent with the action, and Ludovico had offered to provide her and her singers with lodging at the Buosi's house. So you see we are applying ourselves diligently so that this celebration will have all it needs to perfection.[32]

This was, of course, all very encouraging. But Guicciardini had begun to worry that the comedy's Florentine allusions might be lost on the people of Faenza. In a letter written on 26 December, he explained that the prologue was a particular concern. Believing it would not be understood, the actors had substituted their own text, but Guicciardini, who did not want to see it 'watered down', asked Niccolò to write another one of his own, 'suited to the low intelligence of the audience, and in which they would be depicted rather than you.'[33]

By the New Year, Niccolò had finished. Writing to Guicciardini on 3 January, he proudly announced that he had written 'five new songs, appropriate to the play, which have been set to music and which are to be sung between the acts.' This was something of an untruth. Of the five songs he had boasted about, only two were actually 'new'. The others had been taken from the *Clizia*. But the effect was nevertheless dramatic. With just a few small changes, the whole play had become lighter, more carefree and cheerful. It was less a brooding satire than a gleeful invocation to make merry while there was still time. The new prologue set the tone:

> Because life is short,
> and many are the pains
> that every man bears who lives and stints himself,
> let us go on spending and wasting the years as we will,
> for he who deprives himself of pleasure
> only to live with labour and toil
> does not understand the world's deceits,
> and what ills and what strange events
> crush almost all mortals.[34]

But, despite Niccolò's light-hearted optimism, politics had already begun to catch up with him. While he had been rewriting the *Mandragola*, the uneasy peace which had reigned in Italy since the Battle of Pavia had begun to fracture. There had, for a time, been some hope. Shortly after Cardinal Salviati's departure for Madrid, fate had handed the pope an unexpected bargaining chip. Since coming to the Spanish throne, Charles V had been under pressure from his nobles to marry and, now that his star seemed to be on the rise, he could no longer put it off. For his bride, he selected Isabella, the daughter of King Manuel I of Portugal. She was, in many ways, a perfect choice: she was close to him in age; she spoke fluent Spanish; and she would bring with her a dowry of 900,000 ducats. At a stroke, Charles's financial woes would be solved. The only problem, however, was that Isabella was his first cousin. In order to marry her, Charles would need papal dispensation.[35] For Clement VII, this was a golden opportunity. Given how vital this marriage was to Charles, he could have demanded whatever concessions he liked – or, at the very least, he could have strung the negotiations out for long enough for him to prepare for war. But it was an opportunity squandered. '[A]s nervous and inconstant as his master,' Cardinal Salviati had no idea how to take advantage of Charles's need.[36] After hemming and hawing for months, he ended up handing over the dispensation without securing anything in return.

Niccolò could not help being alarmed. When Guicciardini asked him to clarify some rather obscure parts of the *Mandragola* in mid-October, he used it as an excuse to pour scorn on the cardinal for returning to Rome empty-handed.[37] Of the many Florentine proverbs he had included in the script, perhaps the most perplexing occurred in the middle of the third act. On hearing some apparently bad news, Ligurio and Frate Timoteo leave for a private chat in the church, promising Messer Nicia that they will return soon. In reply, Messer Nicia mutters, 'As the toad said to the harrow.'[38] It was, Niccolò conceded, not an easy expression to explain. He had trawled through a great many books to find out where it had come from, but had at last traced its roots back to a folk tale. One day, long ago – the tale went – a peasant was breaking up the soil on his land with a harrow – which, according to Livy, had been invented in Fiesole. While he was doing so, a toad,

> unaccustomed to seeing such a big implement, watched in amazement and amusement what was going on; the harrow ran over the toad and scraped its back severely, and the toad rubbed the spot with its foot more than once. So, after the toad felt itself scraped hard by it, the toad said to the harrow as it passed over its back, 'Don't bother to come back!' This gave rise to the expression that goes 'as the toad said to the harrow' – used whenever you do not want someone to return.[39]

While Niccolò had been looking for this story, however, he had also come across a verse by the fifteenth-century poet 'Burchiello' which alluded to the same idiom, and which had struck him as peculiarly apposite:

> Fearing that the empire might invade
> A linen kettle was sent as ambassador,
> The tongs and the paddle were given the chase,
> For four skeins were found missing,
> But the harrow of Fiesole dragged there . . .[40]

It was, to be sure, a fairly mysterious verse, but Niccolò was sure that anyone who scrutinized it carefully would see how well it appeared to poke fun at the current situation. Much as in Burchiello's day, Florence was quivering with fear at the prospect of an imperial invasion, but no one wanted the ambassador, who had been sent to stay the danger, to return. The only difference, Niccolò claimed, was that 'whereas once we sent a *linen kettle*, the linen has now become a *noodle*.'[41]

Strengthened by Cardinal Salviati's failure, Charles V began casting about for an excuse to flex his muscles. He did not have to wait long.[42] Towards the end of the summer, Francesco Sforza's chancellor, Girolamo Morone, had grown alarmed at the continued presence of imperial troops in Lombardy. Fearing some threat to his master, Morone had tried to tempt the commander of the Spanish forces, Francesco d'Avalos, into swapping sides – even going so far as to promise d'Avalos the crown of Naples on the pope's behalf if he agreed. It was, however, a fatal miscalculation. Though d'Avalos had feigned interest for a time, he had kept Charles V informed about the plot all along, and the emperor had empowered him to deal with it as he thought fit. On 15 October, Morone was arrested – and, under questioning, insinuated that it had all been Francesco Sforza's idea.[43] It was exactly what d'Avalos had been hoping for. Without bothering to establish whether Morone was telling the truth or not, he charged Sforza with treason, and – in the emperor's name – began seizing control of the duchy. Soon, imperial troops had occupied almost every major castle and town, and the fortresses of Cremona and Milan – which alone remained in Sforza's hands – were placed under siege.

Niccolò was horrified. '[T]he duchy of Milan is lost,' he wailed. There was no doubt of what would happen next. Just as Francesco Sforza had been brought low, 'so too will all the other princes' – and there was nothing they could do to save themselves. More vulnerable than any, however, was the pope. Recalling a line from Dante's *Purgatorio*, Niccolò predicted that, much as Boniface VIII had been taken captive by the forces of Philip IV of France in 1303, so Clement VII would soon find himself the prisoner of Charles V.[44]

The unexpected death of Francesco d'Avalos on 3 December dealt a heavy blow to the emperor's plans.[45] Until his replacement – Charles de Bourbon – arrived from Spain with money and reinforcements, the imperial forces could advance no further. The pope – who had been discussing a rapprochement only a few weeks earlier – breathed a heavy sigh of relief. Though the threat might not have passed, he believed he now had time to prepare for the onslaught. Putting all thought of Lombardy from his mind, he therefore settled down to build a new anti-imperial alliance.

To Niccolò's mind, however, the pope was making a grave mistake. What Clement had failed to realize was that, in the wake of d'Avalos's death, the imperial captains had been struggling to hold their army together.[46] Had the pope chosen to launch an attack at that moment – especially in concert with the Venetians – he would have stood a good chance of driving Charles back across the Adda. By holding back, however, he was only harming himself. Convinced that he had time, he was actually giving the emperor's men the time they needed to recover their strength – and launch an attack of their own.[47] It was almost too bewildering for words. Sadly, the Florentines were no bolder. '[T]his gang will never do anything honourable and bold worth living or dying for,' Niccolò complained.[48] They were so timorous that they would rather allow themselves to be devoured by their enemy than take up arms in their defence. More even than before, he saw disaster ahead – both for Clement, and for Florence.

Guicciardini hardly knew what to say. As he admitted, he had lost his bearings.[49] Given the circumstances, the pope's plans for an anti-imperial alliance seemed to offer the only hope, but he had heard plenty of people arguing against it. Even the pope seemed to be having his doubts.[50] As to what might happen, he did not dare speculate. Though he had been summoned to Rome to participate in negotiations, he could not guess what the other Italian powers might do. The Italians were, after all, the only people in the world who, when they saw bad times coming, preferred 'to await them unprotected in the middle of the road' instead of trying to defend themselves.[51]

For a brief moment, there was a glimmer of hope. On 31 December, Niccolò received word that the 'Italians' – that is to say, the pope and Venice – might be on the brink of forming a league with France, then being ruled on Francis I's behalf by his mother, Louise of Savoy.[52] Nothing had yet been signed, but, since it was in everybody's interests to unite against the emperor, Niccolò had no reason to doubt that it soon would be.

Before he could celebrate, however, his hopes were dashed. Just days later, news came that Francis I had signed a treaty with Charles V in Madrid. Under intense pressure, the king agreed to surrender the duchy of Burgundy, renounce his claims to Milan and Naples, marry the emperor's sister, provide her with a dowry of 400,000 ducats and hand over one of his sons as a hostage.[53] Niccolò was quick to grasp what this meant. Writing to Guicciardini on 3 January 1526, he pointed out that, as long as Francis was bound by these terms, France would find it impossible to join the pope's league – and that, without France, the alliance would be rendered worthless.[54]

*

Some small consolation was provided by the *Mandragola*. Although Guicciardini's departure for Rome had obliged him to cancel the performance in Faenza, Niccolò's play was enjoying great success in Venice. It had been performed twice during the carnival of 1522, each time to tremendous acclaim. In fact, so many people had crowded into the theatre for the first performance that the actors had been unable to get through the final act.[55] Not long afterwards, the printer Alessandro Bindoni had brought out a second edition of the text – most likely without Niccolò's approval.[56] Now, it was being revived once again. As Giovanni Manetti related in a letter written on 28 February, it had been performed alongside Plautus's *Menaechmi*, which had been staged at great expense in a new translation by a group of Venetian noblemen.[57] So well was the *Mandragola* received, however, that the *Menaechmi* – though 'performed by good actors' – was put to shame. Indeed, such was the praise heaped upon Niccolò's play that the nobles who had translated the *Menaechmi* even asked the actors to perform it in their own house a few days later. There, it received a similarly rapturous welcome. As Manetti noted, 'applause was given abundantly, first of all to the writer, and then to all the rest, who had gone to the trouble of putting it on.' Already considerable, Niccolò's fame as a comic writer only grew – especially among the Florentine community in Venice. They begged him to send them another play, and promised that, if he did, they would have it performed on 1 May, provided it arrived in time. It didn't matter if it was something he had already written, or something completely new; as long as it was his work, Manetti observed, they would be happy.

*

It was the greatest triumph of Niccolò's theatrical career, but even the radiance of his glory could not dispel the storm clouds which were then gathering. Since the signing of the Treaty of Madrid, Italy's fate had hung in the balance. Everything depended on whether Francis I was released or not. As Niccolò explained in a letter to Guicciardini on 15 March, he did not think it likely.[58] There was, after all, no reason for Charles V to let the king go. As long as he had Francis in his grasp, he could be sure of holding him to his promises, stymying the pope's league and keeping the duchy of Milan safe from attack. But, the moment he let Francis go, all certainty would be lost.

Charles would be 'crazy' to set Francis free,[59] but, even if he *did*, Niccolò thought it likely the king still would respect the terms of the Treaty of Madrid. For, if he did not, there was always a chance that, in the ensuing war, he would not only fail to recover his Italian possessions, but would also lose his kingdom into the bargain. To his 'French brain', Niccolò argued, the possibility would be too appalling to contemplate.[60]

Niccolò was, however, careful to stress that he was only speaking about what he thought *would* happen – not what he thought *should* happen. From a Florentine perspective, by far the best thing would be for Charles to set Francis free, and for Francis to join the pope's league. This would only hasten the rush to war, but it was nevertheless the pope's only real chance of saving himself from the imperial yoke. It was just a pity, Niccolò sighed, that the odds of it happening were so slight.

Whatever happened, Niccolò argued, the pope should prepare for war in earnest. He had heard it said in Florence that the *condottiere* Giovanni delle Bande Nere was 'raising a company of mercenaries in order to fight wherever he saw the best opportunity' and Niccolò had quickly come to the conclusion that Clement should hire him, no matter what the cost.[61] After all, among the Italians, there was no leader whom soldiers were more willing to follow, or whom the Spanish feared more. He – and he alone – could stop the imperial forces 'demolishing Tuscany and the Church'.[62] And if, by any chance, the king of France *was* released, the presence of such a noted commander in the papal army might be enough to persuade him to abandon the Treaty of Madrid and join the league.

Niccolò had expressed a similar assessment of the situation in an earlier (but now lost) letter to Filippo Strozzi in Rome. On 31 March, Strozzi at last replied.[63] After apologizing profusely for not having written sooner, he revealed that, after glancing through Niccolò's letter, he had taken it to the pope and read it out loud. The pope had listened to it with 'great attention', and had even praised certain passages. It seemed to him that Niccolò had 'touched on everything that could come to the mind of anyone who, without specific reports or notices, discussed such matters'.[64] Nevertheless, the pope felt bound to disagree. He was sure that Francis *would* be set free. That this had not yet come to pass was, in itself, not a reason to doubt that it soon would. Charles was probably delaying the king's release either to buy himself more time to prepare his forces, or to further humiliate his captive. Once free, however, Francis would almost certainly renege on the treaty and join the struggle against the emperor in Italy. As for Niccolò's suggestion that the pope should hire Giovanni delle Bande Nere, it was out of the question. Guicciardini had discussed it with Strozzi, and they had both agreed that, without sufficient funds, 'such a captain of fortune would not be effective, if he should find opposition in Lombardy', but that, if Giovanni were to be given more money, 'the venture would become his,' and he would go about 'with banners unfurled', wreaking all sorts of havoc, rather than defending the pope's territories.[65] Besides, there was always a chance that Charles might still hold back from advancing further.

This was, of course, wishful thinking – but, about the king of France, Clement was proved right. News soon arrived that Francis had been freed, and, with the pope's approval, he immediately announced his intention of abandoning the Treaty of Madrid.[66] Niccolò could scarcely believe it. None of it seemed to make any sense. Charles V had gained nothing by releasing the king. Indeed, given Francis' repudiation of his promises, the emperor had only succeeded in making things more difficult for himself. Niccolò expressed his bewilderment in a sardonic epigram. Apparently writing in the pope's voice, this drew on the myth of Argus – an ever-watchful giant with a hundred eyes – to mock the emperor's blindness:

Know that I am not Argus, as I seem,
nor have these eyes of mine ever belonged to Argus,
but they are truly the many eyes
that from Christian princes everywhere I have taken;
and so it happens that the idiotic
Charles, king of the Romans, and the Viceroy [Charles de Lannoy],
because they cannot see, have released the king.[67]

War was now inevitable. Realizing that Charles might, at any moment, launch a campaign against Rome, Clement raced to strengthen his defences as much as possible. His first thought was, naturally, of the league. As soon as Francis' release had been confirmed, he sent ambassadors to France, to Venice, to England and beyond, in the desperate hope that at least some might be willing to join him against the emperor.[68] Florence was, however, an equally pressing concern. It now stood in serious danger. If Charles did indeed drive southwards from Milan, it would be his first target. It was, however, woefully ill-equipped to withstand a siege. Not only was it poorly supplied with troops, but – more worryingly – its walls were also in a parlous state. In early April, Clement therefore ordered an urgent review of the city's fortifications, and sent Count Pietro Navarra, a Spanish exile famed for his skill as a military engineer, to oversee the repairs. Having been deeply taken with *Arte della guerra*, he asked Niccolò to play a part, as well.

Niccolò went straight to work. On receiving a letter from Guicciardini confirming the pope's instructions, he went directly to discuss Navarra's progress with Cardinal Silvio Passerini, who was still governing the city on the Medici's behalf.[69] Almost immediately, however, it became apparent that the repairs were going to be more difficult than they had imagined. The following day – 5 April – Niccolò and Navarra made a tour of the walls. Beginning at Monte Oliveto, they traipsed through fields and gardens, checking for weaknesses, weighing likely points of attack, and assessing what changes would be most effective. On the basis of what they found, Niccolò then wrote a report summarizing their recommendations, the *Relazione di una visita fatta per fortificare Firenze* ('Account of a visit made to fortify Florence').[70] He did not mince his words. Having been built almost two centuries earlier, the city's present walls were ill-suited to modern artillery. They needed to be strengthened, reduced in height and equipped with as many gun emplacements as possible. Only then would the Florentines be able to maintain heavy enough fire to hold the enemy back – or, if the worst happened, to withstand a sustained bombardment. The only real worry was the quarter of Santo Spirito, where Niccolò himself lived.[71] Extending from the Arno up into the hills, it was unusually difficult to defend. Even if the existing walls were reinforced as Niccolò and Navarra had suggested, they would have to be manned by a huge number of men if the enemy were to be prevented from bringing down a section hidden away in some gully or other. Since the only alternative was to demolish the entire quarter, however, Niccolò felt they had no option but to try to fortify it as best they could.

Impressed by the thoroughness of Niccolò's report, Clement VII summoned him to Rome, where he remained until around 27 April.[72] During the three weeks or so he was there, he explained his recommendations at greater length, and persuaded the pope to set up a new magistracy to oversee the city's fortifications – the *Cinque Procuratori delle Mura* (Five Procurators of the Walls). This alone was something of a triumph, but, to make it all the sweeter, he was to be appointed its chancellor, and his son, Bernardo, an assistant.[73]

Riding back to Florence as quickly as he could, Niccolò hastily began drafting the legislation needed to establish the new magistracy – and to return him to political office.[74] His delight can well be imagined. After so many years in the wilderness or on the fringes of the Medici regime, he was now definitely 'back'.

As he stepped into the Palazzo della Signoria for the first time in more than a decade, however, the enormity of his new role dawned on him. All sorts of worrying rumours were flying about. He had heard it said that a last-ditch attempt by the emperor's ambassador to reach an accommodation with the pope had failed, and that, in Milan, the intemperate behaviour of the Spanish captains had sparked off anti-Spanish riots.[75] Fearing that war might break out any day, Niccolò rushed to get the repairs done before it was too late. As he told Guicciardini on 17 May, his head was 'so full of ramparts' that he could scarcely think of anything else,[76] but with every passing moment, more – and more pressing – demands came crashing in on him. Twenty years ago, he would have had no trouble in tackling such demanding obligations, but, now, he found it much more difficult to keep up with the frenetic pace of politics and war. He was an old man in a hurry.

*

On 22 May, Clement VII's anti-imperial league was at last concluded.[77] Known as the League of Cognac, its principal signatories were, naturally, Francis I of France, the Republic of Venice and the papacy, but among its other members were Francesco Sforza and – of course – Florence. As its articles made clear, its purpose was first to expel Charles V's forces from Northern Italy. This, it was hoped, would force the emperor to come to terms, but, if he did not, the League would then seize the kingdom of Naples and bestow it on whomever the pope thought best.

Without waiting for the French army to arrive, Clement and the Venetians immediately went on the offensive. Under the command of Francesco Maria della Rovere, the Venetian forces set off first, intending to make for Chiari, just outside Brescia. A few days later, the pope's men began gathering at Piacenza. Guido Rangoni was given overall command; Giovanni delle Bande Nere was made 'captain general' of the infantry; and Vitello Vitelli was placed at the head of the Florentine contingent. Francesco Guicciardini was to serve as lieutenant general, 'with full and virtually absolute authority'.[78]

The campaign began well. On 24 June, the Venetians succeeded in taking Lodi by stealth. Lying on the River Adda, a little over thirty kilometres south-east of Milan, this heavily-fortified city had been central to the imperial army's defensive strategy. Indeed, such was its importance that 'the emperor's men had always sworn to defend until the last.'[79] With it in della Rovere's hands, the League's armies were now able to march 'unopposed right up to the gates of Milan.' There, however, their luck began to turn. Although Milan had recently been convulsed by yet another bout of anti-Spanish rioting, Bourbon had secretly arrived with reinforcements just a few days before. This shook della Rovere's confidence. Unwilling to tie himself down to a lengthy – and potentially fruitless – siege, he withdrew after a single night, setting up camp at Marignano instead. It was, perhaps, a sound decision. But, not having been consulted,

Guicciardini was furious. To his mind, della Rovere's decision was not just wrong, it was cowardly and dishonourable, to boot.[80]

*

When the campaign had begun, Niccolò had been busily attending to Florence's defences. His greatest concern had been the area around San Miniato. Lying in the south-east of the city, this sparsely populated quarter sat atop a steep hill, surrounded by deep, irregular valleys. For centuries, it had remained outside the city's fortifications, but, given that it offered a tempting prospect for enemy guns, the pope had suggested it should now be enclosed within the walls. Niccolò's colleague, Giuliano del Bene, was all in favour of the plan. It would, he claimed, provide greater security at little cost. But Niccolò was adamantly opposed. As he explained to Guicciardini in two angry letters written on 2 June, it would not only be hugely expensive to build ramparts along such precipitous slopes, but it would actually make the city more vulnerable, too.[81] What the pope's plan would actually do, he argued, would be to create a large, open area, surrounded by a wall which – because of its length and irregularity – would be difficult, if not impossible, to defend. Were the enemy to descend on the city in force, they could easily break through the ramparts and turn the area between the new wall and the old into a fortress from which to press their attack in safety. He had a point, of course. But it was hard work arguing against the pope's plans; Niccolò must have been tearing his hair out with frustration and worry.

At some point in late June or early July, however, Niccolò was ordered to leave Florence and join the League's forces in Lombardy. Who sent him is something of mystery. Uniquely among his missions, neither patent nor instructions were issued to him by the *Otto di Pratica*, and, as Ridolfi noted, it seems unlikely that he would have been given such a task by Cardinal Silvio Passerini. Perhaps the most likely possibility is that he was summoned by Guicciardini, but, since no letter or brief has survived, this, too, must remain speculative.[82] Of his task, however, there is no doubt. Writing to Roberto Acciaiuoli some weeks later, Guicciardini made it abundantly clear that Niccolò had been charged with restoring order and discipline to a demoralized and increasingly chaotic army.[83]

Exactly when Niccolò arrived in the field is not known. Some of his later comments suggest that he may have joined della Rovere's forces before the attempt on Milan.[84] His wording is, however, frustratingly imprecise and, since none of the letters which he is known to have written at the time have come down to us, there is no way of judging one way or the other. All that can be said with any certainty is that he was in camp at Marignano no later than 13 July.[85]

Niccolò found the army in a worse state than Guicciardini had suggested. Even della Rovere was dispirited; he mistrusted his men and, having received no clear orders from either Venice or the pope, had begun to lose faith in the enterprise as a whole. Reluctant to take any risks, he resolved not to do anything until either the French forces or the League's Swiss mercenaries arrived. Even then, he did not hold out much hope. Niccolò, however, was surprisingly optimistic. Writing to Bartolomeo Cavalcanti – a young friend from the Orti Oricellari[86] – he confided that, provided he could keep the men in order until reinforcements appeared, he did not see any way the League could possibly lose.[87] If the French and the Swiss arrived *before* additional imperial troops reached Milan, 'this war will be over in two days.' If, by contrast, the two armies should be reinforced at the same time, the League could easily confine Charles's forces within a relatively narrow area. As soon as shortages began to bite, he argued, 'the German troops will be disbanded and victory will fall into our hands.'

Such optimism was, however, badly misplaced. Emboldened by the arrival of the Swiss, della Rovere ordered his army to take up position just outside Milan, between the abbey of Casoretto and the River Lambro, on 22 July.[88] But no sooner had he done so than he faltered. With growing urgency, his captains urged him to attack the walls at once; but, afflicted by nerves, he kept finding reasons why it could not be done.[89] Nothing could change his mind. He did not seem to care that his reserves were dwindling, or that, by delaying, he was putting Francesco Sforza – who had been holed up in Milan's *castello* for more than ten months – in mortal danger. Forbidden to advance, yet unable to retreat, the army ground to a miserable halt.

With little else to do, Niccolò fell to talking with the other captains, and, if Bandello is to be believed, struck up a particular rapport with Giovanni delle Bande Nere.[90] What they spoke of probably varied, but their conversation inevitably gravitated towards warfare. It was a subject dear to both of their hearts, and each listened to the other with interest. Yet, while Niccolò was, as ever, a brilliant exponent of military theory, Giovanni soon realized that he could still teach him a thing or two about how wars were *really* fought.

One day, Bandello reported, Giovanni light-heartedly challenged Niccolò to draw up a detachment of infantrymen into one of the formations he had described in the *Arte della guerra*. Relishing the chance to put his ideas into practice, Niccolò accepted with alacrity; and, for the next two hours, he marched up and down in the scorching sun, barking out orders left, right and centre. But, try as he might, he could not get the men to form up as he wanted. As Bandello noted, they were like little birds stuck on a branch of mistletoe: the more they flailed about in the hope of escaping the mess they were in, the more hopelessly tangled they became. Eventually, Giovanni decided to put Niccolò out of his misery. With a wry smile, the *condottiere* turned to Bandello and said, 'I'm just going to pull our lads out of this mess, and then we'll go to lunch.' And, 'in the blink of an eye, with the help of his drums, he formed the men up in different ways, to the great wonderment' of everyone present. It was an eloquent, if rather shaming, lesson, but Niccolò took it in good part, and, filled with new respect for practitioners of the military art, went off to enjoy a pleasant meal with his companions.

When Niccolò was not with Giovanni and the other captains, he tried to occupy himself with correspondence. As so often in the past, it was to Francesco Vettori that he found himself pouring out his thoughts and fears. Throughout August, he wrote a series of detailed letters analysing the fortunes of the League, and proposing different ways of prosecuting the war. Though none of these have survived, Vettori's fulsome praise leaves no doubt as to their perspicacity and insight. Recognizing their value, Vettori either showed them to Cardinal Passerini and Ippolito de' Medici,[91] or sent copies to Filippo Strozzi in Rome, in the knowledge that he, in turn, would share them with Clement VII.[92] The pope was particularly impressed. According to Strozzi, he not only read them, but also re-read them and appreciated what they had to say – even if he did not always agree with Niccolò's conclusions.

But most of Niccolò's time was spent dreaming of home. He missed Marietta and the children. Most of all, he missed Barbera. Since he had been in the field, she had not written to him once. By the beginning of August, he felt so aggrieved that he wrote to Falconetti, asking for news. Dutifully, Falconetti went straight round to see her and gave her a piece of his mind.[93] Unfazed, Barbera gave him the usual, coquettish excuses. There was no man she esteemed more highly or whom she obeyed more completely than Niccolò, she claimed. If she deliberately irked him now and again – such as by not writing – it was only to see if he really loved her. And, to round her little speech off, she begged him to hurry back to Florence, protesting that she was only happy when he was there. Needless to say, this was all hot air. More likely than not, she already had a new lover in tow. But, for Niccolò, tormented by loneliness in the sweltering heat of the Lombard plain, even such empty words must have been a solace.

*

Eventually, even della Rovere had to accept that inaction could no longer be justified. Following the fall of the *castello* on 25 July, the urgency of an assault on Milan had dissipated, and, while it made good military sense to maintain the camp in its present location, the imperial forces still inside the city could be pinned down with a fraction of the troops he had stationed there. Under pressure from his captains, della Rovere therefore agreed to allow a portion of the army to break off and lay siege to Cremona while there was still time.[94] But so long did this take that, on 10 September, Guicciardini felt obliged to send Niccolò to persuade the commander, Malatesta Baglioni, either to take the city quickly, or else abandon it for an assault on Genoa instead.[95]

It was a tough and dangerous task, and it took its toll on Niccolò. Riding across Lombardy at breakneck speed, he was under greater pressure than at any point since the siege of Pisa, and it is doubtful whether he was able to take the strain. By the standards of the day, he was an old man, and after years of living quietly in the country, his frantic efforts in the field must have taxed his strength and energy further than he could bear. Enduring unbearable heat, painful saddle-sores and persistent gastric trouble, he was pushing himself to the limit – and beyond.

29

A Bang and a Whimper

(September 1526–June 1527)

Even after the retreat to Marignano, Niccolò had forced himself to remain positive. Now that his fate was bound up with that of the Medici, he needed to believe that, somehow, the League would prevail over the emperor's forces; and it was with growing insistence that he had urged the pope's counsellors to 'eradicate those savage brutes which have only the faces and voices of men.'[1] But, over recent weeks, his confidence had begun to wane. Though he still earnestly hoped for victory, he was no longer so sure that Clement VII had the decisiveness needed to conduct an effective campaign – let alone drive Charles V out of Italy.

Arriving in Cremona on 11 or 12 September, Niccolò found his worst fears confirmed. Though the League's forces vastly outnumbered the imperial garrison within, the siege was in a state of disarray. The commander, Malatesta Baglioni, appeared to have no clear strategy, and countless lives had already been lost in fruitless attempts to breach the walls.[2] On 13 September, a council of war was convened – at Francesco della Rovere's insistence – to decide whether the time had come to abandon the siege, after all. This piqued the pride of Baglioni's captains. Still smarting from their failure to take Milan, they were unwilling to be denied a second time. But, since none of them seemed to know how to press the attack, it fell to Niccolò to draw up a plan. What hopes he had for it cannot be known, but, shortly after his return to the papal camp, he received word that, on 23 September, the city had at last capitulated.[3]

Any relief Niccolò may have felt was, however, crushed by devastating news from Rome. Towards the end of the summer, the Colonna – working in collaboration with the emperor's agent, Ugo de Moncada

– had been building up their forces in the Eternal City, and by August, Sanudo reported that their troops already far outnumbered the pope's own. Unable to count on any support from France, Clement had hastily come to terms. In return for the pope's pardon, the Colonna had agreed to withdraw their men to the frontier. Believing the danger had been averted, the guileless Clement then dismissed most of his soldiers – hoping thereby to save a little money. Not for a moment did he suspect that Moncada and the Colonna might simply be lulling him into a false sense of security. On the night of 19–20 September, they smashed their way back into Rome, looted the Borgo and ransacked the Apostolic Palace. Forced to escape to the Castel Sant'Angelo, Clement lost his nerve. Before any help could arrive, he agreed to a four-month truce, and promised that, if the Colonna would pull back to Naples, he would withdraw his troops from Lombardy.

Niccolò was horrified. Writing to Bartolomeo Cavalcanti some two weeks later, he lamented that a war which was already messy enough had now become so tangled 'that not even Christ could unsnarl it.'[4] He had no doubt that it was all the pope's fault. Not only had Clement failed to raise the funds needed to conduct the campaign properly when he had had the chance, but he had then compounded his error by staying in Rome, 'where he could be taken like a baby.' Thanks to him, Niccolò ranted, the League's chances were now slight, at best. A great many mercenary captains had already left the papal army, and, with the exception of Giovanni delle Bande Nere – whose courage seemed imperturbable – those that remained were all 'ambitious and insufferable'.[5] Unless they were kept on a tight leash, Niccolò warned, they would soon start baying at each other like dogs, and the whole army would be torn apart.

Niccolò was not alone in feeling alarmed. Back in Florence, even the Medici's most loyal supporters were getting jittery.[6] Shocked that the pope had shown such 'poor judgement' and so 'little courage', they began to suspect that, if they did not reassert control over their own government soon, he might lead them to their ruin.[7] In early October, the *Otto di Pratica* therefore sent Francesco Vettori to Rome to present their case. While they would always hold Clement in the greatest affection, Vettori was to explain, they wanted to have more say over their own affairs. Not only did they want the right to appoint their own magistrates, but they also wanted to be consulted before he made any decisions that might affect them, and cautioned him not to burden them with any more demands for money. Vettori was, of course, to couch the *Otto*'s demands as delicately as he could, but there was no disguising that Florence's relationship with the Medici was beginning to fracture.

*

While Vettori wrangled vainly with the pope in Rome, Francesco Guicciardini did his best to keep what remained of the League's army in good order. But, for Niccolò, there was little left to do. Feeling thoroughly disappointed with the whole campaign, he set off for home. Along the way, he stopped in Borgo San Donnino, some twenty kilometres south of Cremona.[8] There, he managed to get into a needless squabble with the local commissioner. Perhaps offended by the commissioner's haughty manner, Niccolò insisted on addressing him as a mere *podestà*, rather than by his proper title. This sent the commissioner into a fury. Suspecting – rightly – that Niccolò was only doing this to 'mock him and make him lose prestige' in the eyes of his subordinates, he lodged a formal complaint with Guicciardini. He was in the right, of course, but, out of loyalty to his friend, Guicciardini felt obliged to give the poor commissioner a 'beautiful' chewing out.[9] Niccolò found this all very funny, but Guicciardini couldn't help feeling that he had behaved so badly that what had begun as a comedy had ended more like a tragedy.

From Borgo San Donnino, Niccolò went on to Modena, where he spent a couple of days with Filippo de' Nerli. Almost inevitably, they fell to discussing the war, and, though the tone of their conversation was light-hearted, Niccolò's humour concealed a palpable sense of disillusionment.[10] After poking fun at Nerli for worrying about his own conduct when everyone else – from the pope to the emperor – had wasted the opportunities they had been given, he and the recently arrived Guido Rangoni mocked Guicciardini for his 'blessed ill-temper'. Once he had got this off his chest, however, Niccolò went to visit a 'prophet', whose assessment was, if anything, even more damning. Claiming to have 'predicted the pope's flight and the campaign's futility,' the soothsayer warned that the 'bad times' were 'not yet over', and that a great deal more suffering still lay ahead for the pope – and for Florence.

Niccolò had never had much time for prophecies in the past.[11] Having had his fill of them while Savonarola was alive, he had poured scorn on all those who claimed to see the future in both the *Discorsi* and 'De' romiti'.[12] But, this time, even he had to admit the 'prophet' might have a point. Shortly after leaving Modena, he learned that the pope had decided to break the truce with the Colonna by sending Vitello Vitelli to attack their possessions.[13] It was, by any standards, a foolish thing to have done. Consumed by spite, the pope had failed to realize that the Colonna lands were of little strategic value, and that, by reigniting the conflict when the League's army in Lombardy was still under strength, he had placed himself and his allies at a distinct disadvantage. This was worrying enough. To make things worse, however, Niccolò learned that the pope wanted to send him to the front as a commissioner in Vitelli's army, as well.

Nothing could have appealed to Niccolò less. Though he was undoubtedly grateful to Jacopo Salviati and Francesco Guicciardini for recommending him, he had no desire to be associated with a campaign that, by common accord, was doomed to failure. But he could hardly turn the pope down, either. To get out of this potentially sticky situation, he decided to drag his heels. If he went slowly enough, he reasoned, the pressures of time would oblige the pope to choose someone else for the job, and he would still come up smelling of roses. Thankfully, his friends suspected nothing. When he eventually got back to Florence – some time before 5 November – both Salviati and Guicciardini wrote to commiserate with him on 'missing out', and promised to put in a good word for him when something better came along.[14]

As Niccolò had feared, the situation in Lombardy quickly deteriorated. On 12 November, an army of 16,000 German landsknechts commanded by Georg von Frundsberg set out from Trento. They were a fearsome prospect. Unlike other imperial troops, most of these were Lutherans, 'fired by anti-papal zeal' and bent on booty.[15] Sweeping the Venetians aside without striking so much as a blow, they advanced rapidly along the Val Lagarina, and by 20 November, they were encamped at Castiglione delle Stiviere, just south of Lake Garda. Realizing that, from there, Frundsberg could threaten Parma, or even Modena, Francesco della Rovere despatched Giovanni delle

Bande Nere to stop him crossing the Po. On 25 November, the two armies met at Governolo, a few kilometres south-east of Mantua, and, for a time, it seemed as if the battle could go either way.[16] Towards evening, however, Giovanni was hit by a cannonball, which shattered his right leg above the knee. Carried from the field in agony, he was taken hurriedly to Mantua, where his leg was amputated in an effort to save his life. But infection had already set in; within days, he was dead. It was a devastating blow. Not only had the League lost its best general, but there was now nothing to prevent the imperial forces from carrying the war into the Papal States – or even Tuscany.

The Florentines were alarmed. However much progress Niccolò had made with the walls, they had neither the men nor the money to defend themselves against an imperial onslaught.[17] They needed to know what direction Frundsberg was heading in; whether Bourbon was planning to join up with him; and – crucially – what the League would do to stop them threatening the city. To find out, the *Otto di Pratica* ordered Niccolò to ride to Modena and clarify the League's position with Guicciardini as soon as possible. He was to explain that the Florentines earnestly hoped the League would come to their aid, but that, if it did not, they would rather come to an agreement with the emperor than face destruction, and that, in such case, they would empower Guicciardini to conduct negotiations on their behalf, as he saw fit.[18]

*

Setting out on, or shortly after, 30 November, Niccolò rode through the Mugello and made for the Apennines. It was a road he had taken many times, but never had the need been more urgent, or the stakes higher. Ignoring the driving rain, the saddle sores and the stomach pains brought on by the jerking of his horse, he forced himself onwards as quickly as he could. On 2 December, he reached Modena and went straight to call on Guicciardini.[19] It quickly became apparent that the situation was worse than the Florentines had feared. Having crossed the Po five days earlier, Frundsberg was now heading south-west, towards Reggiolo and Gonzaga. He had with him between 15,000 and 16,000 men, and all the signs indicated that he was taking the road towards Milan to link up with Bourbon, who had already been offered 30,000 *fl.* to leave the city. Once they had done so, they could attack Venice, the Papal States or Tuscany, as they wished. Whether the League could stop them was, however, another matter altogether. Taken together, the League's forces comprised some 20,000 men – which, though less than the emperor had, was still a respectable number. If they were all brought together, and the pope were to keep them well supplied with money, Guicciardini opined, 'we may perhaps still be safe'. But, if the League's commanders kept their troops apart and continued to regard each other with mistrust, 'little good can be expected from them.'[20]

Should Frundsberg and Bourbon decide to march into Tuscany, the Florentines could not count on much help. Guicciardini had no more than 7,000 infantrymen, of which he could spare only a few, and he did not think the Venetians could be relied upon to provide any of their own. This being so, Florence's chances of holding out would be slim at best. Yet Guicciardini could see no point in opening negotiations on their behalf. Any attempt to come to terms with Frundsberg or to draw him away from Bourbon would 'not succeed', since, together, they formed a single unit. It would make much more sense for the Florentines to open talks directly with Charles de Lannoy or Ugo da Moncada.[21] But, if anyone was going to negotiate with the emperor's representatives, Guicciardini warned, it should really be the pope. Florence would just have to sit tight and hope for the best.

Over the next few days, Niccolò hung around, hoping that Guicciardini might change his mind – or at least give him some grounds for confidence. But the bad news continued to pour in. On 3 December, it was reported that Frundsberg's landsknechts had taken up position between Guastalla and Brescello in preparation for an attack on Piacenza or Parma.[22] That evening, Guicciardini rode in haste to meet the threat, but, before leaving, he impressed upon Niccolò that, however frightened the Florentines might be, any attempt at negotiation would be 'fruitless, damaging, and to no one's advantage.'[23]

Desolate and grief-stricken, Niccolò saw no reason to linger. Setting off from Modena the following morning – 4 December – he made his way slowly back over the Apennines.[24] It was a hard winter and, as he picked his way through the snowy passes, he felt the years weigh heavily on his shoulders. '[S]o as not to tire himself unnecessarily,' he proceeded by short, easy stages,[25] but the cold had made his bones ache, and – as the forlorn tone of his final message revealed – a weariness had entered his heart.

*

By the time Niccolò returned to Florence, the League's situation had become grave. To avoid Guicciardini's countermeasures, Frundsberg had skirted around Parma's southern edge and made for Piacenza.[26] After crossing the River Enza on 7 December, he had reached the Taro on 11 December, and, the following day, he had entered Borgo San Donnino, where his men had 'vented their Lutheran poison against holy objects and images of saints'. From there, he had gone to Firenzuola d'Arda, where he intended to await Bourbon's arrival. Neither Guicciardini nor Francesco della Rovere had been able to do anything to stop him, and, given that their captains were still refusing to unite their forces, there was little hope of them doing so now. To make matters worse, Vitello Vitelli had run into difficulties, as well. On 12 December, he informed the pope that, if the Colonna attacked him with a strong army, he would have no choice but to retreat to Rome.[27]

Even Clement VII could see how perilous his position now was. In a desperate bid to save his own skin, he let it be known that, if the emperor would grant a truce, he would gladly abandon his allies. As Francesco Vettori intimated in a letter to the papal ambassador, Nicolaus von Schönberg, the pope even went so far as to outline how Charles could use the time he would thereby gain to prepare for a renewed attack on France the following spring.[28] It was quite breathtakingly treacherous, but, as with so many of Clement's diplomatic efforts, it was also cataclysmically ill judged. Though the emperor was amenable to the pope's offer, the terms on which he would accept a truce included the surrender of Pisa and Livorno, and the payment of a crippling indemnity.[29] Clement was stunned. Anxious as he was for peace, he could never agree to such terms. Recovering his hauteur, he angrily informed Charles that they were 'tantamount to war'.[30] Yet it does not seem to have occurred to him that, in showing himself to be so willing to betray his allies, he had lost the trust of those upon whom he would have to depend.

By New Year, many leading Florentines had realized that Clement was heading for disaster, and that, if they followed him much longer, the city would be doomed. In mid-January, Niccolò Capponi asked the pope to allow Florence to govern itself, to conduct its own foreign policy and – if necessary – to negotiate a separate peace with the emperor.[31] But it was a futile effort, and everyone knew it. Realizing that Clement would never willingly relinquish his hold on Florence, the Medici's former partisans thus began to talk openly of revolution.[32] Among the most prominent were Francesco Vettori, Luigi Guicciardini and Filippo Strozzi, who had been held hostage in Naples since Clement's abortive truce with the Colonna a few months before. But theirs was to be no narrow conspiracy. Determined to save the city from ruin, they were happy to make common cause with anyone who opposed the Medici's rule. They devoted particular effort to drumming up support among young and disaffected nobles. But, as Benedetto Varchi later reported, they were also joined by Niccolò's old friends, Battista della Palla and Zanobi Buondelmonti, who had been living in exile since their botched attempt to restore the republic five years earlier.[33]

Before they took any decisive steps, however, they needed to be sure of how things stood in the field. On 31 January, Francesco Guicciardini sent word that Bourbon and Frundsberg were massing their forces near Piacenza, and that they seemed to be preparing to march on Tuscany – and then on Rome.[34] Greatly alarmed, the *Otto di Pratica* therefore decided to send Niccolò to Guicciardini's camp to report back on the enemy's progress, and to establish what – if anything – the League would do to protect the city in the event of an assault.

Still aching from his last mission, Niccolò can hardly have relished the prospect of another, but, given the gravity of the situation, he manfully hoisted himself into the saddle and set off for the front line. It was a dreadful journey. The passage of armies had thrown up innumerable obstacles along his way, and the weather was awful. Snow and rain beat down on him relentlessly, playing havoc with his health and turning the road to mud.

Not until the morning of 7 February did he reach Parma. Once he was there, however, he hastened to make up for lost time. Writing to the *Otto di Pratica* later that evening, he related that Guicciardini had been anxious to send Francesco della Rovere and the marquis of Saluzzo into Tuscany to block the imperial army's advance,[35] but there had been some disagreement over which of them was to go first. Although della Rovere had by far the most troops, he had stubbornly refused to take the lead. At his wits' end, Guicciardini had asked Niccolò to have a word with him, but, for all his eloquence, Niccolò had been unable to change the duke's mind. They had, however, agreed to meet again the following day, and Niccolò was hopeful that they would be able to find a solution that suited everyone.

As it turned out, della Rovere proved to be more pig-headed than Niccolò had expected. He was determined to keep his troops in the rear – and nothing would persuade him to do otherwise. Even so, Niccolò was optimistic that the imperial forces could still be stopped. Although no one could be sure when and where they would attack – if, indeed, they still intended to attack Tuscany at all – it was thought that, as long as the League stayed united, 'they [were] but little to be feared.'[36] Over the days that followed, Niccolò's confidence only grew. On 14 February, he reported that the enemy were so poorly led and so short of supplies that, if the League were to hold them back for just a little longer, it would be impossible for them to succeed in anything they attempted.[37] Nevertheless, he advised the Florentines to shore up their defences, just in case.

Guicciardini was not so sanguine.[38] Writing to the pope, he pointed out that, without Francesco della Rovere's support, the League's army would be unable to prevent the imperial forces from entering Tuscany.[39] It was imperative to get him back on side before it was too late. If the pope could bring himself to return the fortress of San Leo, say, the recalcitrant duke might still be induced to make the effort required of him.[40] But this was a concession that Clement would never make. Having conceived an irrational hatred of della Rovere, the pope preferred to risk everything rather than give him what he wanted. And so the League's army remained bitterly – irrevocably – divided.

*

As Romagna was blanketed in heavy snow, the two armies eyed each other warily. Still encamped outside Piacenza, the imperial army gave no sign of moving. Their resilience was surprising. Though Niccolò – like most others – had assumed that a lack of supplies would force Frundsberg and Bourbon to withdraw, they seemed utterly imperturbable. Every day, in fact, they seemed to grow stronger. By the beginning of March, their forces were reported to consist of 700 lances, 800 light horse and 18,000 infantrymen,[41] and, by mid-month, they were well on the way to solving their supply problem. With Charles de Lannoy's blessing, Frundsberg and Bourbon were negotiating with the duke of Ferrara, and it was expected that, if a deal could be reached, the duke would supply them with all the food, horses and munitions they would need.[42]

By this time, Niccolò had followed Francesco della Rovere to Bologna. There, he was warmly received by the papal governor, Cardinal Innocenzo Cybo. A worldly voluptuary, given more to poetry than to politics, Cardinal Cybo took an immediate liking to Niccolò.[43] They often dined together, and, over the next few weeks, they became 'so close' that even Niccolò was astonished.[44] He was, in truth, grateful for the company. Since arriving in the city, he had had little to do, and, as his despatches suggest, he was finding it difficult to stave off boredom. Though it seemed increasingly likely that the imperial army would march on Tuscany as soon as their supplies had been laid in, the weather kept them in camp. As Niccolò reported, the snow was lying 'a *braccio* deep' (*c.* 58 cm), and it was still falling.[45]

Sooner or later, however, the ice would clear, and when it did, the onslaught would surely begin. At last, the pope was stirred out of his complacency. Realizing the League would struggle to stem the imperial tide once it began to flow into Tuscany, he hurriedly negotiated a truce with Charles de Lannoy. For once, his timing was impeccable. Though the imperial forces had the advantage, the emperor's enthusiasm was beginning to wane. The long months of inaction had drained his coffers, and he was not sure he could sustain the costs of a protracted campaign. A brief cessation of hostilities would give him the time to put his finances in order and prepare for a renewed assault later in the year. The terms agreed were thus remarkably equitable.[46] Clement committed himself to restore any lands that he or his allies had taken from the kingdom of Naples or from the Colonna, and to pay Bourbon an indemnity of 40,000 ducats by 22 March. In return, Lannoy promised to withdraw the German landsknechts from the Romagna; to allow French and Venetian troops free passage into the Papal States; and to return any territories of the Church that had been occupied by imperial troops. As a guarantee of good faith, Lannoy also agreed to come to Rome – a gesture which so reassured the pope that he began disbanding his army.

It was, however, too late to stop the imperial forces. Having endured months of cold and discomfort, with little food and even less pay, the German landsknechts were not going to be denied the booty they had been told would be theirs when they got to Florence and Rome. When they were ordered to return to Lombardy, they steadfastly refused. Faced with growing unrest, their commanders struggled to prevent a mutiny. Bourbon felt he had no choice but to let his pavilion be ransacked, while Frundsberg – who had always suffered from a fiery temper – had a stroke trying to remonstrate with the mutineers, and had to be carried off to Ferrara to receive treatment.[47]

Niccolò did not at first realize the danger. Writing to the *Otto di Pratica* on 18 March, he seemed to be under the impression that Frundsberg's stroke would prove to be Florence's salvation.[48] Provided the Venetians could be prevailed upon to do their part, there was every chance that, if the German landsknechts tried to march into Tuscany, they could easily be drawn out into battle and defeated. The League's generals were equally optimistic. Believing that, in Frundsberg's absence, the imperial army had become little more than a disorganized rabble, Francesco della Rovere regarded victory as all but assured.

Had Frundsberg commanded any other group of soldiers, Niccolò and della Rovere would probably have had a point. But the German landsknechts were a breed apart. Although, like most armies, they fought under the banner of a single general, their command structure was unusually egalitarian. Decisions were often taken collectively, and each company – sometimes even each soldier – retained a high degree of personal autonomy. While serious, the loss of their general was therefore not as devastating a blow as it could have been – either to discipline or to strategy. Indeed, if anything, Frundsberg's stroke had actually made them more dangerous than ever. Unfettered from their erstwhile commander's fidelity to the emperor, they no longer felt obliged to respect treaties or truces, and, in the pursuit of their own enrichment, they saw no need for either negotiation or restraint.

Fearful of the havoc they might wreak, Bourbon tried valiantly to appease them by hassling the League for money. If the 40,000 ducats were paid quickly, he explained, there was still a chance of persuading them to return to Lombardy. At last, the gravity of the situation dawned on Niccolò. On 23 March, he wrote to the *Otto di Pratica*, begging them to send the cash as soon as they could. '[I]f you have ever thought of saving your country and allowing her to escape those great and momentous dangers which now loom over her,' he warned, 'then make this last effort to raise this subvention, so that this truce may be secured and these present evils avoided, in order to win us some time, or – to put it better – to postpone our ruin.'[49]

By the time Niccolò's letter arrived in Florence, however, it was no longer enough. On 29 March, Bourbon sent word that the landsknechts now wanted 150,000 ducats – and that, if it was not forthcoming, he could not be held responsible for their actions.[50] Charles de Lannoy hurried to their camp from Rome, in the hope of persuading them to settle for less, but to no avail. As Niccolò dolefully informed the *Otto di Pratica*, it now appeared to all 'that the truce [was] done for, and that there [was] nothing left except to think of war.'[51]

Within days, the landsknechts were on the move. On 31 March, they were encamped at Ponte a Reno (modern Pontecchio Marconi), less than ten kilometres south of Bologna.[52] There, they proposed to divide in two: one half threatening Bologna itself, and the other pushing on towards Imola.[53] What they would do thereafter was uncertain. Either they would regroup for a massed attack on Tuscany, or they would each cross the Apennines by a different route and strike Florence from several directions at once. Whatever they did, however, the pope urgently needed to decide what should be done. As Niccolò explained to Francesco Vettori on 5 April, Guicciardini believed two possible courses of action were open to him.[54] On the one hand, he could stand and fight – in which case, he would not only have to throw all his weight behind the struggle, but he would also have to force France and Venice to fulfil their obligations. On the other hand, however, he could stand by his agreement with the emperor and trust Charles de Lannoy to bring the mutinous landsknechts to heel. The latter was, of course, by far the most uncertain, but, because it was also the cheaper of the two, it appealed to the pope's penny-pinching ways. Heedless of the risk, Clement decided to gamble Florence's fate on his enemy's goodwill. Of all his decisions, this was certainly among the most foolish.

Oppressed by fear, Niccolò's thoughts went to his family. Taking up his pen in Imola – where he had repaired with Francesco della Rovere in the first week of April – he wrote to his young son, Guido.[55] Like any good father, he tried his hardest to seem cheerful. Rejoicing that Guido had recovered from a recent illness, he conjured up a fine future for the boy and urged him to study hard. He reminded Guido to take particular pains with Latin and music – which, as his son knew, had brought Niccolò both pleasure and honour. With a touch of humour, he offered a few words of advice about what to do with a mule that had recently gone mad, and expressed his hope that his second son, Lodovico, then in the Levant, would write soon. But, in the end, anxiety got the better of him. 'Greet Madonna Marietta for me,' he wrote, fighting back the tears, 'and tell her that I have been expecting – and still do – to leave here any day; I have never longed so much to return to Florence as I do now, but there is nothing else I can do. Simply tell her that, whatever she hears, she should be of good cheer, since I shall be there before any danger comes. Kiss Bacina, Piero, and Totto, if he is there . . . Christ watch over you all.'[56]

*

Slowly but surely, the German landsknechts drew closer. So as to force the League to spread its troops over a wide area,[57] they concealed their intentions by taking a deliberately circuitous route.[58] From Imola, they headed first towards Ravenna. Then, after taking the town of Cotignola, they turned abruptly southwards, towards Monte Poggiolo. At this point, their most natural route across the Apennines would have led them through Castrocaro and Dicomano, but instead they took the road south-eastwards, as if they were making for Città di Castello or Perugia. Following the Via di Galeata, they reached Santa Sofia on 16 April, and San Piero in Bagno the following day. Borgo Sansepolcro was only a few hours' march away. As Niccolò pointed out, from there, they could swing westwards through Arezzo, and, driving up the Valdarno, they would be able to attack Florence from the south.[59]

So successfully did the landsknechts' ruse work that the League only awoke to the imminence of the threat as they were crossing into Tuscany. Realizing how foolish he had been to place his trust in Charles de Lannoy, Clement VII hurried to patch up relations with his allies. Negotiations were opened with France and Venice (who had been on the point of leaving, only a few days before);[60] fresh subsidies were demanded of the Florentines; and Francesco della Rovere was at last offered the fortress of San Leo in return for his aid.[61] Everything would now be thrown into defending Florence. Rather than waste time chasing the 'imperial' army through the mountains, the League's forces decided to make a dash straight for the city. Taking the most direct route across the Apennines, each commander raced against the clock – hoping against hope that they would arrive before the enemy.

It quickly began to go wrong, though. As so often before, the renewed League was riven by rivalries and incompetence. Just days after its forces set out, the French and the Venetians balked at the terms Clement had proposed to their ambassadors; the various generals started squabbling over strategy; and – with food and money in short supply – the troops grew restive.

Terror spread throughout Tuscany. Acting more like a band of marauding mercenaries than an army, the German landsknechts rampaged through the countryside, raping and pillaging as they went.[62] As Guicciardini later recalled, towns were sacked, famine took hold, and the land seemed 'full of death, flight, and rapine.'[63] Observing the devastation, Niccolò plunged into a deep depression. Given how poorly the French and Venetians had behaved, 'how undisciplined [the League's] troops were . . . and how powerful and dogged the enemy' was proving, he could not help feeling that Florence was beyond saving.[64] The dangers facing it were simply too great, and, like many Florentines, he had lost any faith in the pope's ability to overcome them, either by negotiation or by force. 'I love my native city more than my own soul,' he told Vettori, but 'I tell you that, in my sixty years of experience, I do not believe there were ever more difficult problems than these, where peace is necessary and war cannot be renounced, and where we have a prince [Clement VII] on our hands, who can barely meet the needs of either peace or war.'[65] The war, he felt, had already been lost.[66]

How he must have wept when, a little later, a reply came from Guido.[67] Written with the trusting innocence that only a child can muster, it would have filled him with love for his family – and a deep sense of foreboding. At home in the Via Romana, Guido explained, they were all praying that God would soon bring him home – but, since he had promised to be with them if anything should happen, they were not as worried about the landsknechts as they had been before. Still, Guido added, with touching incomprehension, his father must be sure to tell them if there was going to be an attack on Florence, so they could bring all the produce in from the farm. Meanwhile, they were all well and he was studying hard. His music was going well. At Easter, he hoped to start singing and counterpoint. As for Latin, his teacher had read him 'almost all the first book of Ovid's *Metamorphoses*', and he wanted to recite it to Niccolò from memory as soon as he got home.

Driven by thoughts of his family, Niccolò made one last effort to steer the League – or at least Florence – away from disaster. On 18 April, he wrote to Francesco Vettori from Brisighella, just outside Faenza, with some stern advice.[68] Knowing full well how unrealistic the Florentines could be at times, he reminded Vettori that there was no point hoping the landsknechts could be manoeuvred out of Tuscany or talked into a last-minute deal. They were too cunning to be played, and too stubborn to bend. The only way of driving them out of Florentine territory was to defeat them in battle. And since delaying would only put an unbearable strain on Florence's resources, Niccolò urged Vettori to drop any negotiations with Bourbon or Lannoy straight away, to put pressure on the French and the Venetians, and to arm the city as quickly as he could.

By then, however, Niccolò's voice could no longer be heard above the clamour of war. Realizing there was nothing left for him to do in the Romagna, he set off across the Apennines for home – tired, ill and afraid.

*

On, or shortly before, 22 April, Niccolò arrived in Florence. It was an emotional return. To be with his family again after so many months of pain and worry must have been a relief beyond compare. It is easy to imagine him stepping across the threshold of the house on the Via Romana, stooped with sickness, tears falling from his eyes as Marietta and his children threw their arms around his neck, overjoyed that he had made it back alive.

His relief was, however, short lived. Tensions within Florence were rising. Although Francesco della Rovere and the marquis of Saluzzo were now within a few kilometres of the city walls, the landsknechts' approach had hardened opposition to Medici rule.[69] On 26 April, just as the neighbourhood companies were gathering to receive arms at churches across the city, it was rumoured that Cardinal Silvio Passerini had fled the city. The reality was more mundane. Seemingly unaware of how restive the people were, Cardinal Passerini and Ippolito de' Medici had actually gone to meet with the League's generals at their camp, a short distance away. But it was all too easy to believe that the rumours might be true, and it took no more than an argument over a cap to spark off a full-blown riot. Joined by crowds of citizens, the companies rushed to the Piazza della Signoria. As shouts of '*Popolo e libertà!*' echoed around the square, a band of armed youths seized control of the Palazzo and, for a moment, it seemed as if blood might be spilt. Only thanks to the timely inter-vention of Francesco della Rovere and the marquis of Saluzzo – and a few quiet words from Francesco Guicciardini – was order restored. But, though some tried to dismiss the disturbance as nothing more than a 'straw-fire', most were in no doubt that the Medici were now teetering on the brink of the abyss.[70]

Everything hung on the imperial army. Having reached Arezzo a few days before, they were widely expected to attack at any moment.[71] But the presence of the League's armies gave them second thoughts. Unwilling to risk the vicissitudes of battle, they decided to abandon their attempt on Florence and march instead towards Rome, which was tantalizingly ill defended. In haste, the League gave chase. But, once again, Francesco della Rovere allowed his nerves to get the better of him. Frightened of the consequences of defeat, he avoided making any attempt to stop the imperial forces on their march southwards, hoping instead that they might somehow falter once they reached Rome. Of all his decisions, it was by far the worst.

On 5 May, Bourbon and his men were encamped beneath Rome's walls.[72] To their delight, they found it even less well garrisoned than they had expected. The papal commander, Renzo da Ceri, had fewer than 3,000 infantrymen, and most of those were boys or old men who had been pressed into service at the last moment. The pope, however, stubbornly refused to surrender.

Early the next morning, German and Spanish troops scaled the

Leonine Walls near the Janiculum, hidden from the defenders by a heavy mist.[73] In the initial confusion, Bourbon was killed by an arquebus shot, fired (if his account is to be believed) by Benvenuto Cellini;[74] but, undeterred, the landsknechts pressed on. The Borgo was soon overrun, and, before the sun had reached its zenith, the Vatican itself was stormed. With just moments to spare, Clement managed to flee along the Passetto to the safety of the Castel Sant'Angelo with a few of his cardinals. But the struggle was already over. While the last of the Swiss Guard lay dying on the steps of St Peter's Basilica, Rome – the Eternal City, the *caput mundi*, the seat of the papacy and the repository of Clement VII's last hopes – was put to the sack.

When the news reached Florence on 12 May, the Medici regime quickly crumbled.[75] Abandoned by the pope's remaining supporters – many of whom had lost valuable investments in Rome – and with violence already spilling out onto the streets, Cardinal Silvio Passerini had no option but to relinquish his authority. On 16 May, the Signoria passed a resolution restoring the republic, and the following day, Cardinal Passerini fled the city with Ippolito and Alessandro de' Medici.

*

While these tumultuous events had been taking place, Niccolò had been rushing to Clement VII's aid at Guicciardini's side.[76] Travelling southwards through Arezzo and Montepulciano, they had been at Orvieto when news of the Sack of Rome reached them, and it was there that they parted ways. Hastily taking stock of the situation, Guicciardini sent Niccolò to Civitavecchia – where the pope had since taken refuge – to discuss matters with the commander of the French fleet. In a sign of how far his political star had fallen, however, he was to travel with Francesco Bandini, who, despite being much less experienced, insisted on signing his name directly beneath Niccolò's own in their despatches.[77]

When Niccolò returned to Florence, he found it a changed city. Though not everyone was content with the new government, his heart must have leapt for joy. He had given the best years of his life to a republican government. He had suffered for it, quite unjustly, too, and, though he had worked hard to earn the favour of the

Medici, even going so far as to repudiate his old patron, Piero Soderini, a part of him had always remained faithful to the republican dream.

In that glorious summer of freedom, all his old political dreams returned. Believing the clock had somehow been turned back to 1512, he felt sure that, having served the Republic so faithfully in the past, he would find a role in the new government. Indeed, encouraged by his old friends Zanobi Buondelmonti and Luigi Alamanni – both recently returned from exile – he even hoped he might be given his old job as second chancellor.[78] But he was too sick – or simply too confused by the speed with which things were changing – to see how impossible that would be. Despite all that he had done for the Republic, despite all that he had said and written, he had sullied himself by his association with the Medici. However much members of the new regime may have liked him at a personal level, they could neither forget the service he had rendered the Medici, nor forgive the fact that, when the new constitution had been proclaimed, he had been in Civitavecchia with the pope. On 10 June, Francesco Tarugi – the former secretary of the *Otto di Pratica* – was given the post instead.

It was a crushing blow. Over the past few months, Niccolò had given his heart and soul to keeping Florence safe, only to have the doors of the Palazzo della Signoria slammed in his face by the very Republic he had always longed to see restored. It was a pathetic way to end his career – and it must have hurt him more deeply than can be imagined. Yet he had only himself to blame. While he had been blessed with a superb mind, he had always been too hungry for glory, too painfully, catastrophically short-sighted to realize his ambitions. Whenever Florence had undergone a political transformation, he had been on the wrong side – and, though he had usually managed to correct his mistakes, he must have known it was now far too late for him to make good again.

30

The Art of Dying

(June 1527)

Confronted by the realization that he would never again return to the Palazzo della Signoria, Niccolò's already fragile health deteriorated further. He had long suffered from gastric pains, brought on by bad food and a lack of sleep, but now the agony became unbearable. Taking to his bed, he put his faith in the aloe-based pills on which he had come to rely. But his condition was too grave – or the dose too weak – for them to have any effect.[1] In desperation, he began gulping them down in ever greater quantities, until, on 20 June, he appears to have taken too many.[2]

He had neither the strength nor the will to fight on. Realizing the end was approaching fast, he tried to prepare himself as best he could. In the past, he had, admittedly, never had much time for religion. In his letters and plays, he had often ridiculed the hypocrisy of priests, while, in the *Discorsi*, he had railed against the decadence and corruption of the contemporary Church. But he had nevertheless always been a sincere believer, and, now that he saw death looming before him, he was anxious to make his peace with God.

He knew how greatly he had sinned.[3] Over the past fifty-eight years, there had been no crime he had not committed, no vice he had not indulged. He had used the 'tongue that had been meant to glorify God' to blaspheme Him; he had allowed his mouth to become 'a sewer'; he had sent men to their deaths; he had betrayed his wife; he had neglected his children; he had chased after whores and he had lusted after rent boys. At every turn, he had thought only of himself, his ambitions and desires. He had changed himself 'from a rational animal into a brute animal', from 'man to beast', from 'angel to devil' – and, for this, he knew, he deserved to be punished.

Yet he still held out some hope. Some years earlier, the Compagnia di San Girolamo – to which he had belonged since his youth – had asked him to deliver an oration on penitence.[4] In this, he had expressed his conviction that no one should despair of obtaining God's mercy. Provided a man asked for it 'with eyes full of tears, with [a] distressed heart, [and] with [a] sad voice,' he would not be denied.[5] Out of the depths of his suffering, therefore, he cried out to God. Summoning one Fra Matteo to his bedside, he confessed his sins with a sincerity that impressed his son, Pietro, and, with feverish prayers, begged for forgiveness.[6]

But it was not so easy to die 'well'. How could he be sure that God had heard him? Doubt plagued him. Like every other Florentine, he had seen the crude woodcuts in contemporary books on the *ars moriendi* ('The Art of Dying'), and he could not help suspecting that demons might be hovering beside the bed, waiting to drag him off to perdition.

As was his way, he tried to laugh it off. On 21 June, he awoke suddenly from a fitful sleep.[7] Turning to those friends who had agreed to stay with him, he described a dream he had just had. Two groups of figures had appeared to him. The first had been dressed in rags and presented a thoroughly dejected appearance. They were the blessed and were on their way to Heaven. The second group, however, were made up of richly dressed and august-looking individuals discussing history, philosophy and the affairs of state. He could not identify them all, but among them he spied Seneca, Tacitus, Plato, Plutarch and a host of other notable figures from antiquity. When he asked them where they were headed, they told him, 'We are the damned of Hell.' At this, Niccolò laughed hoarsely. If there were so many interesting people to talk to, he chuckled, perhaps he would be happier in Hell, after all.

It was typical of his dark and irreverent sense of humour. But, like so many of his jokes, this last piece of witty badinage concealed a darker and more self-critical message. Tortured though he had been by his sense of failure, it dawned on him that, in striving so ardently after glory, power and pleasure, he had not only condemned his family to 'the deepest poverty',[8] but he had also put himself beyond salvation. And, while he might have laughed at the 'good company' he was in, one can hear him inwardly shrieking with terror at the pains of Hell. Breathing his last on 21 June 1527, this most political of men had reason to rue the day he had entered politics.

Acknowledgements

No one reading Machiavelli's correspondence can fail to be struck by how much he owed to those around him. No matter how roughly Fortune treated him, or how far he was from home, he could always rely on the kindness of family, friends, and colleagues – and was never shy about expressing his gratitude. It is perhaps only fitting that, in writing his biography, I have incurred a similar debt; and it is a great pleasure finally to have the opportunity to thank the many wonderful people who have sustained me throughout.

I have been lucky to have been attached to some truly wonderful institutions while working on this book. The Centre for the Study of the Renaissance at the University of Warwick and St Catherine's College, University of Oxford – where I was fortunate enough to conduct much of my early research during the academic year 2014–15 – have been a huge support. I have benefited greatly from the resources they have made available and from the spirit of friendly collegiality at each.

At Picador, I would like to thank Georgina Morley, Laura Carr, Nicholas Blake, Penelope Price, Marissa Constantinou, Gillian Stern and Kate Green. Their patience, kindness, generosity of spirit and eagle-eyed attention to detail have been invaluable – and have made the process of bringing this book to print a true delight from start to finish.

My agent, Georgina Capel, has been wonderful. As always, she has been a pillar of encouragement and support. Without her, this book would certainly never have come into being. At Georgina Capel Associates, I would also like to thank Rachel Conway and Irene

Baldoni. They have been superbly helpful at every turn, and have put up with my endless questions with great forbearance.

I am tremendously grateful for the friendship of many extraordinary people. In particular, I would like to thank Stephen Bowd, Vicky Cornford, Luc Deitz, Luke Houghton, Paul Lay, Paul McIntosh, James O'Connor, Pit Péporté, Christina Reuterskiöld, Dilyana Valcheva, and Sr Mary Thomas. From first to last, they have cheered me with their humour, humbled me with their generosity, and inspired me with their ideas.

My family have been unfailingly brilliant. My mother, Ingrid Lee, my mother- and father-in-law, Catherine and Henri Sebban, my brother Piers, and my brother- and sister-in-law, Michaël and Julie, have sustained me at every turn with their warmth, kindness, and encouragement. They have kept me going even when times seemed hardest.

Most of all, however, I would like to thank my wife, Marie, and my daughter, Hannah. They have filled my heart with joy every single day and have made life more beautiful than I ever thought possible. There are no words to express how very much I love them.

Bibliography

Please note that this bibliography is far from exhaustive. It comprises only those works which have been cited directly in the endnotes.

Primary Sources

Alamanni, Luigi, *Flora* . . . (Florence: Lorenzo Torrentino, 1556)

———, *Versi e prose*, P. Raffaelli (ed.), 2 vols. (Florence: Le Monnier, 1859)

Alberti, Leon Battista, *Della pittura*, L. Mallè (ed.) (Florence: Sansoni, 1950)

———, *I libri della famiglia*, in *Opere volgari*, C. Grayson (ed.), 3 vols. (Bari: G. Laterza & Figli, 1960–73)

Alighieri, Dante, *La divina commedia*, M. Porena (ed.), 3 vols. (Bologna: Zanichelli, 1947)

———, *De vulgari eloquentia*, S. Botterill (ed. and trans.) (Cambridge: Cambridge University Press, 1996)

Annales Arretinorum maiores et minores: aa. 1192–1343, A. Bini and G. Grazzini (eds.), *RIS* 2nd ser. 24.1 (Città di Castello: Lapi, 1909)

Arnaldi, F., L. Gualdo Rosa and L. Monti Sabia (eds.), *Poeti Latini del Quattrocento* (Milan: R. Ricciardi, 1964)

Augustus, *Res Gestae Divi Augusti: Text, Translation, and Commentary*, A. Cooley (ed. and trans.) (Cambridge: Cambridge University Press, 2009)

Baldassarri, S. U., and A. Saiber (eds.), *Images of Quattrocento Florence: Selected Writings in Literature, History, and Art* (New Haven CT and London: Yale University Press, 2000)

Baldelli, Giovanni Battista, *Elogio di Niccolò Machiavelli* (London [Livorno?]: s.n., 1794)

Baldi, Bernardino, *Della vita e de' fatti di Guidobaldo I da Montefeltro duca d'Urbino*, C. de' Rosmini (ed.), 2 vols. (Milan: Giovanni Silvestri, 1821)

Bandello, Matteo, *Le Novelle*, G. Brognolio (ed.), 5 vols. (Bari: G. Laterza & Figli, 1910–12)

Bandini, Angelo Maria, *De Florentina Iuntarum typographia eiusque censoribus ex qua Graeci, Latini Tusci scriptores . . .*, 2 pts. in 1 vol. (Lucca: Francesco Bonsignori, 1791)

Barbaro, Francesco, *On Wifely Duties*, trans. in Kohl and Witt (eds.), *The Earthly Republic*, pp. 189–228

Beccadelli, Antonio, *The Hermaphrodite*, H. Parker (ed. and trans.) (Cambridge MA and London: Harvard University Press, 2010)

Bembo, Pietro, *History of Venice*, R. W. Ulery, Jr. (ed. and trans.), 3 vols. (Cambridge MA: Harvard University Press, 2007–9)

Binet, Étienne, *Du Salut d'Origène . . .* (Paris: Sébastien Cramoisy, 1629)

Bourrilly, V.-L., and F. Vindry (eds.), *Mémoires de Martin et Guillaume du Bellay*, 4 vols. (Paris: Renouard, 1908–19)

Bracciolini, Poggio, *Historiae Florentini populi*, L. A. Muratori (ed.), in *RIS* 20 (Milan, 1731), cols. 194–454

———, *Storie fiorentine*, Jacopo Bracciolini (trans.), E. Garin (ed.) (Arezzo: Biblioteca della Citta di Arezzo, 1984)

Brucioli, Antonio, *Dialogi*, A. Landi (ed.) (Naples: Prismi, 1982)

Bruni, Leonardo, *Laudatio Florentinae Urbis*, in Baron, *From Petrarch to Leonardo Bruni*, pp. 232–63

———, *History of the Florentine People*, J. Hankins (ed.), 3 vols. (Cambridge MA: Harvard University Press, 2001–7)

Buonaccorsi, Biagio, *Diario* (Florence: Giunti, 1568)

Buoninsegni, Domenico di Lionardo, *Storie della città di Firenze dall'anno 1410 al 1460* (Florence: Landini, 1637)

Burchard, Johannes, *Liber notarum ab anno MCCCCLXXXIII ad annum MDVI*, E. Celani (ed.), *RIS* 2nd ser. 32.1, 2 vols. (Città di Castello: Lapi, 1907–42)

Burchiello [Domenico di Giorgio], *Rime di Burchiello comentate dal Doni* (Venice: Marcolin, 1553)

Burchiello [Domenico di Giorgio] and Antonio Alamanni, *I sonetti del Burchiello et di Messer Antonio Alamanni, alla Burchiellesca . . .* (Florence: Giunti, 1552)

Busini, Giovambattista, *Lettere a Benedetto Varchi sopra l'assedio di Firenze*, G. Milanesi (ed.) (Florence: Le Monnier, 1860)

Cambi, Giovanni, *Istorie fiorentine*, ed. I. di San Luigi, 4 vols., *Delizie degli eruditi toscani*, 20–23 (Florence: Gaetano Cambiagi, 1785–6)

Canestrini, G., and A. Desjardins (eds.), *Négociations diplomatiques de la France avec la Toscane*, 6 vols. (Paris: Imprimerie Impériale / Imprimerie Nationale, 1859–86)

Cassius Dio, *Roman History*, E. Cary (trans.), 9 vols. (Cambridge MA: Harvard University Press, 1914–27)

Castiglione, Baldassare, *Lettere* . . ., P. Serassi (ed.), 2 vols. (Padua: G. Camino, 1769–71)

Cato, *Disticha Catonis recensuit et apparatu critico instruxit*, M. Boas and H. J. Botschuyver (eds.) (Amsterdam: North Holland, 1952)

Cattani da Diacceto, Francesco, *Opera omnia*, T. Zwingler (ed.) (Basel: H. Petri and P. Pernam 1563)

Cellini, Benvenuto, *Autobiography*, G. Bull (trans.), rev. ed. (London: Penguin, 1998)

Cerretani, Bartolomeo, *Dialogo della mutazione di Firenze*, R. Mordenti (ed.) (Rome: Edizioni di Storia e Letteratura, 1990)

————, *Dialogo della mutatione di Firenze*, G. Berti (ed.) (Florence: Olschki, 1993)

————, *Ricordi*, G. Berti (ed.) (Florence: Olschki, 1993)

————, *Storia fiorentina*, G. Berti (ed.) (Florence: Olschki, 1994)

Cicero, *De officiis*, W. Miller (trans.) (London, 1913)

————, *Tusculan Disputations*, J. E. King (trans.) (London, 1927)

————, *De re publica, De legibus*, C. W. Keyes (trans.) (London, 1928)

————, *Philippics*, D. R. Shackleton Bailey (trans.), J. T. Ramsey and G. Manuwald (rev.), 2 vols. (London and Cambridge MA, 2009)

Condivi, Ascanio, *Vita di Michelangelo Buonarroti*, G. Nencioni (ed.) (Florence: Studio per Edizioni Scelte, 1998)

Convenevole da Prato, *Regia carmina: dedicata a Roberto d'Angiò re di Sicilia e di Gerusalemme*, C. Grassi (ed.), 2 vols. (Cinisello Balsamo, 1982)

Crinito, Pietro, 'Ad Faustum de Sylva Oricellaria', in Comanducci, 'Gli Orti Oricellari', pp. 356–8

d'Auton, Jean, *Chroniques de Louis XII*, R. de Maulde La Clavière (ed.), 4 vols. (Paris: Renouard, 1889–95)

Dei, Benedetto, *La Cronica dall'anno 1400 all'anno 1500*, R. Barducci (ed.) (Florence: Passigli, 1985)

della Robbia, Luca, 'Narrazione del caso di Pietro Paolo Boscoli e di Agostino Capponi', *ASI* 1 (1842), pp. 273–312

Diario di Anonimo Fiorentino dall'anno 1358 al 1389, in A. Gherardi (ed.), *Cronache dei secoli XIII e XIV* (Florence: Cellini, 1876), pp. 293–481

Dumont, J., *Corps universel diplomatique du droit des gens*, 8 vols. (Amsterdam: La Haye, 1726–31)

Fachard, D. (ed.), *Consulte e pratiche della Repubblica fiorentina (1505–1512)* (Geneva: Droz, 1988)

————, (ed.), *Consulte e pratiche della Repubblica fiorentina (1498–1505)*, 2 vols. (Geneva: Droz, 1993)

Ferreti, Ferreto de', *Le Opere*, C. Cipolla (ed.), 3 vols. (Rome: Istituto Storico Italiano, 1908–20)

Ficino, Marsilio, *Opera omnia*, 2 vols. (Basel: Heinrich Petri, 1576; repr. Turin: Bottega d'Erasmo, 1959)

Giannotti, Donato, 'Trattato della Repubblica Fiorentina', 318, in Donato Giannotti, *Opere politiche e letterarie*, F.-L. Polidori (ed.), 2 vols. (Florence: Le Monnier, 1850), vol. 1, pp. 57–288

————, *Lettere italiane*, F. Diaz (ed.) (Milan: Marzorati, 1974)

Giovio, Paolo, *De vita Leonis decimi pont. max. libri quattuor His ordine temporum accesserunt Hadriani sexti pont. Max. et Pompeii Columnae cardinalis vitae . . .* (Florence: Lorenzo Torrentino, 1551)

————, *Pauli Iovii Opera*, vol. 8, R. Meregazzi (ed.) (Rome: Istituto Poligrafico dello Stato, 1972)

Giustinian, Antonio, *Dispacci di Antonio Giustinian, ambasciatore veneto in Roma dal 1502 al 1505*, P. Villari (ed.), 3 vols. (Florence: Le Monnier, 1876)

Grassi, Paride de', *Le due spedizioni militari di Giulio II*, L. Frati (ed.) (Bologna: Regia Tipografia, 1886)

Guarino, Battista, *De ordine docendi et studendi*, in Kallendorf (ed. and trans.), *Humanist Educational Treatises*, pp. 260–309

Guarino da Verona, *Epistolario*, R. Sabbadini (ed.), 3 vols. (Venice: R. Deputazione Veneta di Storia Patria, 1915–19)

Guasti, C., 'Documenti della congiura fatta contro il cardinale Giuliano de' Medici nel 1522', *Giornale storico degli archivi toscani*, 3 (1859), pp. 121–50, pp. 185–232, pp. 239–67

Guicciardini, Francesco, *Opere inedite*, 10 vols. (Florence: Barbèra, Bianchi e comp., 1857–67)

————, *Storia d'Italia*, C. Panigada (ed.), 5 vols. (Bari: G. Laterza & Figli, 1929)

————, *Dialogo e Discorsi del Reggimento di Firenze*, R. Palmarocchi (ed.) (Bari: G. Laterza & Figli, 1932)

————, *Scritti politici e ricordi*, R. Palmarocchi (ed.) (Bari: G. Laterza & Figli, 1933)

————, *Storie fiorentine*, R. Palmarocchi (ed.) (Bari: G. Laterza & Figli, 1934)

————, *Selected Writings*, C. Grayson (ed. and trans.) (Oxford: Oxford University Press, 1965)

Guicciardini, Niccolò, *Discorso del modo del procedere della famiglia de' Medici et del fine che poteva havere lo stato di quella famiglia*, in von Albertini, *Firenze dalla repubblica al principato*, pp. 365–75

Hieronimo de Bursellis, *Cronica gestorum ac factorum memorabilium civitatis Bononie*, A. Sorbelli (ed.), *RIS*, 2nd ser., 23.2 (Città di Castello: S. Lapi, 1912)

Horace, *Opera*, D. R. Shackleton Bailey (ed.) (Berlin and New York: De Gruyter, 2010)

Jacopo da Varagine, *Legenda aurea*, J. G. T. Graesse (ed.) (Leipzig: Arnoldia, 1850)

Kallendorf, C. (ed. and trans.), *Humanist Educational Treatises* (Cambridge MA: Harvard University Press, 2002)

Kohl, B. G, and R. G. Witt (eds.), *The Earthly Republic: Italian Humanists on Government and Society* (Philadelphia PA: University of Pennsylvania Press, 1978)

Kraye, J. (ed.), *Cambridge Translations of Renaissance Philosophical Texts*, 2 vols. (Cambridge: Cambridge University Press, 1997)

Le Glay, M., *Négociations diplomatiques entre la France et l'Autriche durant les trente premières années du XVIe siècle*, 2 vols. (Paris: Imprimerie Royale, 1845)

The Life of Cola di Rienzo, J. Wright (trans.) (Toronto: Pontifical Institute of Mediaeval Studies, 1975)

Livy, *Ab urbe condita*, B. O. Foster et al. (trans.), 14 vols. (Cambridge MA: Harvard University Press, 1919–59)

Lucretius, *On the Nature of Things*, W. H. D. Rouse (trans.), M. F. Smith (rev.) (Cambridge MA and London: Harvard University Press, 1975)

Machiavelli, Bernardo, *Libro di ricordi*, C. Olschki (ed.) (Florence: Le Monnier, 1954)

Machiavelli, Niccolò, *Compendium rerum decennio in Italia gestarum* (Florence: Bartolomeo de' Libri, 1506)

———, *Compendium rerum decennio in Italia gestarum* (Florence: Andrea Ghirlandi and Antonio Tubini, 1506)

———, *Lettere di Niccolò Machiavelli segretario fiorentino* . . . (Venice: Giambattista Pasquali, 1769)

———, *Opere minori di Niccolò Machiavelli*, F.-L. Polidori (ed.) (Florence: Le Monnier, 1852)

———, *Opere complete*, 1 vol. in 2 (Florence: Borghi e Compagni, 1857)

———, *Scritti inediti di Niccolò Machiavelli risguardanti la storia e la milizia (1499–1512)*, G. Canestrini (ed.) (Florence: Barbèra Bianchi e Comp, 1857)

———, *Opere*, P. Fanfani, G. Milanesi, L. Passerini (eds.), 6 vols. (Florence: Cenniniana, 1873–77)

———, *Lettere familiari*, E. Alvisi (ed.) (Florence: Sansoni, 1883)

———, *Opere*, M. Bonfantini (ed.) (Milan and Naples: R. Ricciardi, 1954)

———, *Arte della guerra e scritti politici minori*, S. Bertelli (ed.) (Milan: Feltrinelli, 1961)

———, *Lettere*, F. Gaeta (ed.) (Milan: Feltrinelli, 1961)

———, *Istorie fiorentine*, F. Gaeta (ed.) (Milan: Feltrinelli, 1962)

———, *Lust and Liberty: The Poems of Machiavelli*, J. Tusiani (trans.) (New York NY: I. Obolensky, 1963)

———, *Legazioni e commissarie*, S. Bertelli (ed.), 3 vols. (Milan: Feltrinelli, 1964)

————, *The First Decennale* (Cambridge MA: Harvard University Press, 1969)

————, *Legazioni, commissarie, scritti di governo*, vol. 1, *1498–1501*, F. Chiappelli (ed.) (Bari: Laterza, 1971)

————, *Tutte le opere*, M. Martelli (ed.) (Florence: Sansoni, 1971)

————, *Capitoli*, G. Inglese (ed.) (Rome: Bulzoni, 1981)

————, *Discorso intorno alla nostra lingua*, P. Trovato (ed.) (Padua: Antenore, 1982)

————, *Lettere a Francesco Vettori e a Francesco Guicciardini*, G. Inglese (ed.) (Milan: Rizzoli, 1989)

————, *Machiavelli: The Chief Works and Others*, A. Gilbert (trans.), 3 vols. (Durham NC and London: Duke University Press, 1989)

————, *La vita di Castruccio Castracani e altri scritti*, G. Inglese (ed.) (Milan: Rizzoli, 1991)

————, *De principatibus*, G. Inglese (ed.) (Rome: Istituto Storico Italiano per il Medioevo, 1994)

————, *Machiavelli and His Friends: Their Personal Correspondence*, J. B. Atkinson and D. Sices (eds. and trans.) (DeKalb IL: Northern Illinois University Press, 1996)

————, *Opere*, C. Vivanti (ed.), 3 vols. (Turin: Einaudi, 1997–2005)

————, *Opere politiche*, vol. 3, *L'arte della guerra. Scritti politici minori*, J.-J. Marchand, D. Fachard and G. Masi (eds.) (Rome, 2001)

————, *Art of War*, C. Lynch (trans. and ed.) (Chicago IL: University of Chicago Press, 2003)

————, *'The Prince' by Niccolò Machiavelli with Related Documents*, W. J. Connell (ed.) (Boston: Bedford/St Martin's, 2005)

————, *Opere storiche*, A. Montevecchi and C. Varotti (eds.), 2 vols. (Rome: Salerno, 2010)

Macrobius, *Commentary on the Dream of Scipio*, W. H. Stahl (trans.) (New York: Columbia University Press, 1952)

Maio, Giuniano, *De maiestate*, F. Gaeta (ed.) (Bologna: Commissione per i testi di lingua, 1956)

Martelli, Ugolino di Niccolò, *Ricordanze dal 1433 al 1483*, F. Pezzarossa (ed.) (Rome: Edizioni di Storia e Letteratura, 1989)

Masi, Bartolomeo, *Ricordanze di Bartolomeo Masi calderaio fiorentino dal 1478 al 1526*, G. Corazzini (ed.) (Florence: Sansoni, 1906)

Matarazzo, Francesco, *Cronaca della città di Perugia dal 1492 al 1503*, F. Bonaini and F. Polidori (eds.), *ASI* 16/2 (1851), pp. 1–243

Medici, Lorenzo de', *Lettere*, R. Fubini et al. (eds.), 16 vols. (to date) (Florence: Giunti Editore, 1977–2011)

Molini, G. (ed.), *Documenti di storia italiana*, 2 vols. (Florence: Tipografia all' Insegna di Dante, 1836–7)

Mussato, Albertino, *De obsidione domini Canis de Verona ante civitatem Paduanam*, L. A. Muratori (ed.), *RIS* 10 (Milan, 1727), cols. 687–714

Nardi, Jacopo, *Istorie della città di Firenze*, L. Arbib (ed.), 2 vols. (Florence: Società Editrice delle Storie del Nardi e del Varchi, 1842)

————, *Istorie della città di Firenze*, A. Gelli (ed.), 2 vols. (Florence: Le Monnier, 1858)

————, *Vita di Antonio Giacomini*, V. Bramanti (ed.) (Bergamo: Moretti & Vitali, 1990)

Nelli, G. B. C., *Discorsi di architettura del Senatore Giovan Battista Nelli* (Florence: Eredi Paperini, 1753)

Nerli, Filippo de', *Commentari de' fatti civili Occorsi dentro la Città di Firenze dall'anno MCCXV al MDXXXVII* (Augusta: David Raimondo Mertz e Gio. Jacopo Majer, 1728)

Ovid, *Fasti*, J. G. Frazier (trans.), G. P. Goold (rev.), rev. ed. (Cambridge MA: Harvard University Press, 1989)

Paoli, C., 'Convito Mediceo in Roma nel 1504', *Miscellanea fiorentina di erudizione e storia* 1 (1902), pp. 93–4

Parenti, Piero, *Storia fiorentina*, A. Matucci (ed.), 2 vols. (Florence: Olschki, 1994–2005)

Patrizi, Francesco, *De regno et regis institutione* . . . (Paris: Pierre Vidoué and Galliot du Pré, 1519)

Pazzi, Alessandro de', 'Discorso al cardinal Giulio de' Medici – anno 1522', in G. Capponi, 'Discorsi intorno alla riforma dello stato di Firenze (1522–32)', *ASI*, 1st ser., 1 (1942), pp. 411–77

Perosa, A. (ed.), *Giovanni Rucellai ed il suo Zibaldone*, 2 vols. (London: Warburg Institute, 1960–81)

Petrarca, Francesco, *Africa*, N. Festa (ed.), Edizione Nazionale delle Opere di Francesco Petrarca (Florence: Sansoni, 1926)

————, *De otio religioso*, G. Rotondi (ed.) (Vatican City: Biblioteca Apostolica Vaticana, 1958)

————, *Petrarch's Lyric Poems: The Rime Sparse and Other Lyrics*, R. M. Durling (trans. and ed.) (Cambridge MA and London: Harvard University Press, 1976)

————, *Bucolicum carmen*, M. François and P. Bachmann, with F. Roudaut (trans. and comm.) (Paris: Honoré Champion, 2001)

————, *Res seniles*, S. Rizzo and M. Berté (eds.), 3 vols. to date (Florence: Le Lettere, 2006–)

Piccolomini, *De liberorum educatione*, 10; in Kalllendorf (ed. and trans.), *Humanist Educational Treatises*, pp. 126–259

Pitti, Jacopo, 'Apologia de' Cappucci', C. Monzani (ed.), *ASI* 1st ser. 4/2 (1853), pp. 271–384

————, *Istoria fiorentina*, A. Mauriello (ed.) (Naples, 2007)

Platina, Bartolomeo, *De principe*, G. Ferraù (ed.) (Palermo: Il Vespro, 1979)

Plato, *Laws*, R. G. Bury (trans.), 2 vols. (Cambridge MA: Harvard University Press, 1984–94)

———, *Timaeus, Critias, Cleitophon, Menexenus, Epistles*, R. G. Bury (trans.) (Cambridge MA: Harvard University Press, 1929)

Plutarch, *Lives*, vol. 1, *Theseus and Romulus. Lycurgus and Numa. Solon and Publicola*, B. Perrin (trans.) (Cambridge MA: Harvard University Press, 1914)

Poliziano, Angelo, *Opera omnia*, rev. ed. (Lyon: Sébastien Gryphius, 1533)

———, *Opera omnia* (Basel: Nicolaus Episcopius, 1553)

———, *La commedia antica e l'*Andria *di Terenzio*, R. Lattanzi Roselli (ed.) (Florence: Sansoni, 1973)

———, *Coniurationis Commentarium: Commentario della congiura dei Pazzi*, L. Perini (ed.), S. Donegà (trans.) (Florence: Florence University Press, 2012)

Pontano, Giovanni Gioviano, *De fortuna* (Naples: Sigismund Mayr, 1512)

———, *De principe*, G. M. Cappelli (ed.) (Rome: Salerno, 2003)

Renaudet, A., *Le Concile Gallican de Pise-Milan: Documents Florentins, 1510–1512* (Paris: Librairie Ancienne Honoré Champion, 1922)

Ruscelli, Girolamo, *Lettere di principi . . .* (Venice: Giordano Ziletti, 1564)

Sacchetti, Franco, *Il Trecentonovelle*, E. Faccioli (ed.) (Turin: Einaudi, 1970)

Sallust, *Bellum Catilinae, Bellum Iugurthinum*, J. C. Rolfe (trans.), rev. ed. (Cambridge MA: Harvard University Press, 1931)

Salutati, Coluccio, *Epistolario*, F. Novati (ed.), 4 vols. (Rome: Istituto Storico Italiano, 1891–1911)

Sanudo, Marino, the Younger, *I diarii di Marino Sanuto: (MCCCCXCVI–MDXXXIII): dall'autografo Marciano Ital. CLVII codd. CDXIX–CDLXXVII*, R. Fulin et al. (eds.), 58 vols. (Venice: F. Visentini, 1879–1902)

Savonarola, Girolamo, *Selected Writings of Girolamo Savonarola*, A. Borelli and M. Pastore Passaro (trans. and ed.) (New Haven CT and London: Yale University Press, 2006)

Scala, Bartolomeo, *Historia florentinorum*, J. Oligero (ed.) (Rome: Nicolangelo Tinassi, 1677)

———, *Essays and Dialogues*, R. Neu Watkins (trans.) (Cambridge MA and London: Harvard University Press, 2008)

Seneca the Younger, *Moral Essays*, J. W. Basore (trans.), 3 vols. (Cambridge MA: Harvard University Press, 1928–35)

Stefani, Marchionne di Coppo, *Cronaca Fiorentina*, N. Rodolico (ed.), *RIS*, 2nd ser., 30.1 (Città di Castello: S. Lapi, 1903)

Suetonius, *Lives of the Caesars*, J. C. Rolfe (trans.), 2 vols. (Cambridge MA: Harvard University Press, 1914)

Tegrimi, Niccolò, *Vita Castrucii Antelminelli Castracani Lucensis Ducis* (Modena: Domenico Rococciolo, 1496)

————, *Vita Castrucii Antelminelli Castracani Lucensis Ducis*, in L. A. Muratori (ed.), *RIS* 11 (Milan, 1727), cols. 1308–44

Terence, *The Woman of Andros, The Self-Tormentor, The Eunuch*, J. A. Barsby (ed. and trans.) (Cambridge MA: Harvard University Press, 2001)

Tomasi, Tomaso, *La vita del duca Valentino* (Monte Chiaro: Gio. Bapt. Lucio Vero, 1655)

Vaglienti, Piero, *Storia dei suoi tempi, 1492–1514*, G. Berti, M. Luzzati and E. Tongiorgi (eds.) (Pisa: Nistri-Lischi e Pacini, 1982)

Varchi, Benedetto, *Storia fiorentina*, L. Arbib (ed.), 3 vols. (Florence: Società Editrice delle Storie Nardi e del Varchi, 1838–41)

Vasari, Giorgio, *Le vite de' piu eccelenti pittori, scultori ed architettori*, G. Milanesi (ed.), 9 vols. (Florence: Sansoni, 1878–85)

————, *Lives of the Artists*, G. Bull (trans.), 2 vols. (London: Penguin, 1987)

Velleius Paterculus and Augustus, *Compendium of Roman history. Res Gestae Divi Augusti*, F. W. Shipley (trans.) (Cambridge MA: Harvard Univeresity Press, 1924)

Vettori, Francesco, *Scritti storici e politici*, E. Niccolini (ed.) (Bari: G. Laterza & Figli, 1972)

Villani, Giovanni, *Nuova Cronica*, G. Porta (ed.), 3 vols. (Parma: Guanda, 1990–1)

Virgil, *Eclogues, Georgics, Aeneid I–VI*, H. Ruston Fairclough (trans.), G. P. Goold (rev.), rev. ed. (Cambridge MA: Harvard University Press, 1999)

————, *Aeneid VII–XII*, H. Ruston Fairclough (trans.), G. P. Goold (rev.), rev. ed. (Cambridge MA: Harvard University Press, 2000)

von Hutten, Ulrich, 'Exhortatio viri cuiusdam doctissimi ad Principes, ne in Decimae praestationem consentiant', in *Sämmtliche Werke* [=*Opera quae extant omnia*], E. J. H. Münch (ed.), 6 vols. (Berlin and Leipzig: J. G. Reimer, 1821–7), vol. 2, pp. 547–54

von Liliencron, R., *Die historischen Volkslieder der Deutschen vom 13. bis 16. Jahrhundert*, 5 vols. (Leipzig: F. C. W. Vogel, 1865–9)

Secondary Sources

Ames-Lewis, F., 'Donatello's bronze David and the Palazzo Medici courtyard', *Renaissance Studies* 3 (1989), pp. 235–51

Anglo, S., *Machiavelli: A Dissection* (London: Gollancz, 1969)

Anselmi, G. M., 'Machiavelli e l'*Istoria fiorentina* di Domenico di

Leonardo Buoninsegni', *Studi e problemi di critica testuale* 9 (1974), pp. 119–32

———, 'Il *Discursus florentinarum rerum* tra progetto politico e prospettiva storiografica', in Marchand (ed.), *Niccolò Machiavelli, politico, storico, letterato*, pp. 189–207

Arrighi, V., 'Della Valle, Antonio', *DBI*, vol. 37 (Rome, 1989), *ad voc.*

———, 'Girolami, Raffaello', *DBI*, vol. 56 (Rome, 2001), pp. 526–31

———, 'Gualterotti, Francesco', *DBI*, vol. 60 (Rome, 2003), *ad voc.*

———, 'Machiavelli, Niccolò [di Alessandro]', *DBI*, vol. 67 (Rome, 2006), pp. 79–81

———, 'Machiavelli, Totto', *DBI*, vol. 67 (Rome, 2006), pp. 105–7

———, 'Pucci, Roberto', *DBI*, vol. 85 (Rome, 2016), *ad voc.*

Atkinson, C., *Debts, Dowries, Donkeys: The Diary of Niccolò Machiavelli's Father, Messer Bernardo, in Quattrocento Florence* (Frankfurt am Main: Peter Lang, 2002)

Bainton, R. H., *Bernardino Ochino esule e riformatore del Cinquecento (1487–1563)* (Florence: Sansoni, 1940)

Barbarisi, G., and A. M. Cabrini (eds.), *Il teatro di Machiavelli* (Milan: Cisalpino, 2005)

Bardi, A., 'Filippo Strozzi (da nuovi documenti)', *ASI* 5th ser., 14 (1894), pp. 3–78

Barlow, J. J., 'The Fox and the Lion: Machiavelli Replies to Cicero', *History of Political Thought* 20 (1999), pp. 627–45

Baron, H., 'Franciscan Poverty and Civic Wealth as Factors in the Rise of Humanistic Thought', *Speculum* 13/1 (1938), pp. 1–37

———, 'Machiavelli on the eve of the *Discourses*: the date and place of his *Dialogo intorno alla nostra lingua*', *Bibliothèque d'Humanisme et Renaissance* 23 (1961), pp. 449–76

———, *From Petrarch to Leonardo Bruni* (Chicago: University of Chicago Press, 1968)

———, 'The *Principe* and the puzzle of the date of chapter 26', *Journal of Medieval and Renaissance Studies* 21 (1991), pp. 83–102

Barthas, J., 'Machiavelli e l'istituzione del conflitto', *RSI* 127 (2015), pp. 552–66

Bartoli, L. M., and G. Contorni, *Gli Orti Oricellari a Firenze: Un giardino, una città* (Florence: Edifir, 1991)

Bausi, F., 'Machiavelli e la tradizione culturale toscana', in *Cultura e scrittura di Machiavelli, Atti del Convegno di Firenze–Pisa, 27–30 ottobre 1997* (Rome: Salerno, 1998), pp. 81–115

———, *Machiavelli* (Rome: Salerno, 2005)

———, 'Machiavelli e la commedia fiorentina del primo Cinquecento', in Barbarisi and Cabrini (eds.), *Il teatro di Machiavelli*, pp. 1–20

Bazzocchi, A., *La ricerca storica e archivistica su Dionigi e Vincenzo Naldi in rapporto alla dominazione veneziana nella Valle del Lamone* (Faenza: Carta Bianca, 2010)

Bell, R. M., *How to Do It: Guides to Good Living for Renaissance Italians* (Chicago IL: University of Chicago Press, 1999)

Bellonci, M., *Lucrezia Borgia*, B. and B. Wall (trans.) (London: Phoenix Press, 2000)

Benecke, G., *Society and Politics in Germany, 1500–1750* (Abingdon: Routledge, 1974)

Benner, E., *Machiavelli's Ethics* (Princeton NJ: Princeton University Press, 2009)

Bertelli, S., 'Noterelle machiavelliane: ancora su Lucrezio e Machiavelli', *RSI* 76 (1964), pp. 774–90

———, 'Petrus Soderinus Patriae Parens', *Bibliothèque d'Humanisme et Renaissance* 31 (1969), pp. 93–114

———, 'Pier Soderini Vexillifer Perpetuus Reipublicae Florentinae: 1502–1512', in Molho and Tedeschi (eds.), *Renaissance Studies in Honor of Hans Baron*, pp. 335–59

———, 'When did Machiavelli write *Mandragola?*', *Renaissance Quarterly* 24/3 (1971), pp. 317–26

———, 'Machiavelli e la politica estera fiorentina', in Gilmore (ed.), *Studies on Machiavelli*, pp. 29–72

———, 'Constitutional Reforms in Renaissance Florence', *Journal of Medieval and Renaissance Studies* 3 (1973), pp. 139–64

———, 'Machiavelli and Soderini', *Renaissance Quarterly* 28/1 (1975), pp. 1–16

———, 'Embrioni di partiti politici alle soglie dell'età moderna', in S. Bertelli (ed.), *Per Federico Chabod (1901–1960)*, 2 vols. (Perugia: Università di Perugia, 1980–1), vol. 1, pp. 17–35

Bertelli S., and F. Gaeta, 'Noterelle machiavelliane: un codice di Lucrezio e di Terenzio', *RSI* 73 (1961), pp. 544–53

Black, R., *Benedetto Accolti and the Florentine Renaissance* (Cambridge, 1985)

———, 'Florentine Political Traditions and Machiavelli's Election to the Chancery', *Italian Studies* 41 (1985), pp. 1–16

———, 'Machiavelli, Servant of the Florentine Republic', in Bock, Skinner and Viroli (eds.), *Machiavelli and Republicanism*, pp. 71–100

———, 'New Light on Machiavelli's Education', in J.-J. Marchand (ed.), *Niccolò Machiavelli: politico, storico, letterato* (Rome: Salerno, 1996), pp. 391–8

———, *Humanism and Education in Medieval and Renaissance Italy: Tradition and Innovation in Latin Schools from the Twelfth to the Fifteenth Century* (Cambridge: Cambridge University Press, 2001)

———, 'Education and the Emergence of a Literate Society', in

Najemy (ed.), *Italy in the Age of the Renaissance* (Oxford: Oxford University Press, 2004), pp. 18–36

———, *Education and Society in Florentine Tuscany: Teachers, Pupils and Schools, c. 1250–1500* (Leiden: Brill, 2007)

———, 'A pupil of Marcello Virgilio Adriani at the Florentine Studio', in S. U. Baldassarri, F. Ricciardelli and E. Spagnesi (eds.), *Umanesimo e Università in Toscana (1300–1600): Atti del Convegno internazionale di studi (Fiesole–Firenze, 25–26 maggio 2011)* (Florence: Le Lettere, 2012), pp. 15–32

———, *Machiavelli* (Abingdon: Routledge, 2013)

———, 'Machiavelli and the grammmarians: Benedetto Riccardini and Paolo Sassi da Ronciglione', *ASI* 173/3 (2015), pp. 427–82

———, 'The School of San Lorenzo, Niccolò Machiavelli, Paolo Sassi, and Benedetto Riccardini', in A. Frazier and P. Nold (eds.), *Essays in Renaissance Thought and Letters: In Honor of John Monfasani* (Leiden: Brill, 2015), pp. 107–33

Blockmans, W., *Emperor Charles V, 1500–1558*, I. van den Hoven-Vardon (trans.) (London: Bloomsbury, 2002)

Bock, G., 'Civil discord in Machiavelli's *Istorie fiorentine*', in Bock, Skinner and Viroli (eds.), *Machiavelli and Republicanism*, pp. 181–201

Bock, G., Q. Skinner and M. Viroli (eds.), *Machiavelli and Republicanism* (Cambridge: Cambridge University Press, 1990)

Boillet, E., (ed.), *Antonio Brucioli: humanisme et évangélisme entre réforme et contre-réforme: actes du colloque de Tours, 20–21 mai 2005* (Paris: Honoré Champion, 2008)

Bolognesi, D., (ed.), *1512: La battaglia di Ravenna, l'Italia, l'Europa* (Ravenna: Angelo Longo Editore, 2014)

Bottiglioni, G., *La lirica Latina in Firenze nella seconda metà del secolo XV* (Pisa: Nistri, 1913)

Bourrilly, V.-L., *Guillaume du Bellay: Seigneur de Langey, 1491–1543* (Paris: Société nouvelle de librairie et d'édition, 1905)

Bowd, S., *Venice's Most Loyal City: Civic Identity in Renaissance Brescia* (Cambridge MA: Harvard University Press, 2010)

———, *Renaissance Mass Murder: Civilians and Soldiers during the Italian Wars* (Oxford: Oxford University Press, 2018)

Branca, V., *Poliziano e l'umanesimo della parola* (Turin: Einaudi, 1983)

Breccia Fratadocchi, M., 'Ghirlandi, Andrea', *DBI*, vol. 53 (2000), pp. 805–6

Brown, A., *Bartolomeo Scala, 1430–1497, Chancellor of Florence: The Humanist as Bureaucrat* (Princeton NJ: Princeton University Press, 1979)

———, 'Lorenzo and Public Opinion: The Problem of Opposition', in G. Gargagnini (ed.), *Lorenzo il Magnifico e il suo mondo* (Florence: L. S. Olschki, 1994), pp. 61–85

———, 'Partiti, correnti, o coalizioni: un contributo al dibattito', in A.

Fontes, J.-L. Fournel and M. Plaisance (eds.), *Savonarole: Enjeux, Débats, Questions. Actes du Colloque International (Paris, 25–26–27 Janvier 1996)* (Paris: Université de la Sorbonne Nouvelle, 1997), pp. 59–79

———, 'Ideology and Faction in Savonarolan Florence', in S. Fletcher and C. Shaw (eds.), *The World of Savonarola: Italian Elites and Perceptions of Crisis* (Aldershot: Ashgate Publishing, 2000), pp. 22–41

———, 'The Revolution of 1494 and Its Aftermath: A Reassessment', in J. Everson and D. Zancani (eds.), *Italy in Crisis – 1494* (Oxford: Legenda, 2000), pp. 13–39

———, 'Insiders and Outsiders: The Changing Boundaries of Exile', in W. J. Connell (ed.), *Society and Individual in Renaissance Florence* (Berkeley CA and Los Angeles CA: University of California Press, 2002), pp. 384–409

———, 'Philosophy and Religion in Machiavelli', in Najemy (ed.), *The Cambridge Companion to Machiavelli*, pp. 157–72

———, *The Return of Lucretius to Renaissance Florence* (Cambridge MA and London: Harvard University Press, 2010)

Brucker, G. A., *Florentine Politics and Society 1343–1378* (Princeton NJ: Princeton University Press, 1962)

Bullard, M. M., 'Marriage Politics and the Family in Florence: The Strozzi–Medici Alliance of 1508', *American Historical Review* 84 (1979), pp. 668–87

———, *Filippo Strozzi and the Medici: Favor and Finance in Sixteenth-Century Florence and Rome* (Cambridge: Cambridge University Press, 1980)

Butters, H. C., *Governors and Government in Early Sixteenth-Century Florence 1502–1519* (Oxford: Clarendon, 1985)

Cabrini, A., *Per una valutazione delle 'Istorie fiorentine' del Machiavelli: note sulle fonti del secondo libro* (Florence: La Nuova Italia, 1985)

———, *Interpretazione e stile in Machiavelli. Il terzo libro delle 'Istorie'* (Rome: Bulzoni, 1990)

———, 'Intorno al primo *Decennale*', *Rinascimento*, 2nd ser., 33 (1993), pp. 69–89

———, 'Machiavelli's *Florentine Histories*', in Najemy (ed.), *The Cambridge Companion to Machiavelli*, pp. 128–43

Cadoni, G., *Lotte politiche e riforme istituzionali a Firenze tra il 1494 ed il 1502* (Rome: Istituto Storico Italiano per il Medio Evo, 1999)

Calleri, S., *L'Arte dei Giudici e Notai di Firenze Nell'età Comunale e Nel Suo Statuto del 1344* (Milan: Giuffrè, 1966)

Campanelli, M., 'Language', in M. Wyatt (ed.), *The Cambridge Companion to the Italian Renaissance* (Cambridge: Cambridge University Press, 2014), pp. 139–63

Canfora, D., 'Culture and Power in Naples from 1450 to 1650', in
    M. Gosman, A MacDonald, and A. Vanderjagt (eds.), *Princes and
    Princely Culture, 1450–1650*, 2 vols. (Leiden: Brill, 2003–5), vol. 2, pp. 79–96
Cantimori, D., 'Bernardino Ochino uomo del Rinascimento e riformatore',
    Annali della Scuola Normale Superiore di Pisa, Classe di Lettere e Filosofia
    30/1 (1929), pp. 5–40
———, 'Rhetoric and Politics in Italian Humanism', *Journal of the
    Warburg and Courtauld Institutes* 1 (1937), pp. 83–102
———, 'Machiavelli e la religione', *Belfagor* 21 (1966), pp. 629–38
Cappelletti, L., *Storia della Città e Stato di Piombino dalle origini fino all'
    anno 1814* (Livorno: R. Giusti, 1897)
Capponi, G., 'Capitoli fatti dalla città di Firenze col re Carlo VIII, a dì
    25 novembre del 1494', *ASI* 1 (1842), pp. 362–75
Carli, E., 'Il Pio umanistico: La libreria Piccolomini', *Mensile di Franco
    Mario Ricci* 66 (1994), pp. 47–84
Carmichael, A. G., *Plague and the Poor in Renaissance Florence*
    (Cambridge: Cambridge University Press, 1986)
Casadei, A., 'Note Machiavelliane', *Annali della Scuola Normale Superiore
    di Pisa, Classe di Lettere e Filosofia*, 3rd ser., 17 (1987), pp. 447–64
Cavaluzzi, R., 'Machiavelli per *rassettare* le cose fiorentine', *Italianistica:
    Rivista di letteratura italiana* 39/1 (2010), pp. 11–21
Cecchi, A. *The Piccolomini Library in the Cathedral of Siena* (Florence:
    Scala, 1982)
Célier, L., 'Alexandre VI et la réforme de l'Eglise', *Mélanges d'Archéologie
    et d'Histoire de l'Ecole Française de Rome* 27 (1907), pp. 65–124
Ceron, A., *L'amicizia civile e gli amici del principe: lo spazio politico
    dell'amicizia nel pensiero del Quattrocento* (Macerata: EUM, 2011)
Chiappelli, F., 'Guicciardini, Machiavelli e il caso di Paolo', *Annali
    d'Italianistica* 2 (1984), pp. 53–63
Chiarelli, G., 'Il *De regno* di Francesco Patrizi', *Rivista internazionale di
    filosofia del diritto* 12 (1932), pp. 716–38
Chiesa, R., 'Machiavelli e la Musica', in *Rivista italiana di musicologia* 4
    (1969), pp. 3–31
Cipolla, C. M., *Money in Sixteenth-Century Florence* (Berkeley CA:
    University of California Press, 1989)
Ciseri, I., *L'ingresso trionfale di Leone X in Firenze nel 1515* (Florence:
    Olschki, 1990)
Clarke, P. C., *The Soderini and the Medici: Power and Patronage in
    Fifteenth-Century Florence* (Oxford: Clarendon, 1991)
———, 'Lorenzo de' Medici and Tommaso Soderini', in G. Gargagnini
    (ed.), *Lorenzo de' Medici: Studi* (Florence: Olschki, 1992), pp. 67–101
Clough, C. H., *Machiavelli Researches*, Pubblicazioni della Sezione
    Romanza dell'Istituto Universitario Orientale, Studi 3 (Naples, 1967)

Cochrane, E., *Historians and Historiography in the Italian Renaissance* (Chicago IL: University of Chicago Press, 1981)

Cohn, S. K., Jr., *Cultures of Plague: Medical Thinking at the End of the Renaissance* (Oxford: Oxford University Press, 2010)

Colish, M., 'Cicero's *De Officiis* and Machiavelli's *Prince*', *Sixteenth Century Journal* 9/4 (1978), pp. 81–93

Comanducci, R. M., 'Gli Orti Oricellari', *Interpres* 15 (1995–6), pp. 302–58

———, *Gli Orti Oricellari* (Rome: Salerno, 1997)

Connell, W. J., *La città dei crucci: fazioni e clientele in uno stato repubblicano del '400* (Simona Calvani, trans.) (Florence: Nuova Toscana, 2000)

———, 'Le molestie del Machiavelli', *Interpres* 28 (2009), pp. 266–7

Connell, W. J., and G. Constable, *Sacrilege and Redemption in Renaissance Florence: The Case of Antonio Rinaldeschi* (Toronto: Centre for Reformation and Renaissance Studies, 2005)

Cox, V., *Women's Writing in Italy, 1400–1650* (Baltimore MD: Johns Hopkins University Press, 2008)

Cox-Rearick, J., *Dynasty and Destiny in Medici Art* (Princeton NJ: Princeton University Press, 1984)

Cummings, A. M., *The Politicized Muse: Music for Medici Festivals, 1512–1537* (Princeton NJ: Princeton University Press, 1992)

D'Amico, J., 'The Virtue of Ruin in Machiavelli's "Florentine Histories"', *Renaissance and Reformation*, new ser. 8/3 (1984), pp. 202–14

Davidsohn, R., *Geschichte von Florenz*, 4 vols. (Berlin: E. S. Mittler und Sohn, 1896–1927)

———, 'L'avo di Niccolò Machiavelli: cronista fiorentino', *ASI* 93 (1935): pp. 35–47

Davies, J., *Florence and its University during the Early Renaissance* (Leiden: Brill, 1998)

Davies, M. C., 'The Senator and the Schoolmaster: Friends of Leonardo Bruni in a New Letter', *Humanistica Lovaniensia* 33 (1984), pp. 1–21

De Caro, G., 'Anguillara, Lorenzo', *DBI*, vol. 3 (Rome, 1961), pp. 309–12

———, 'Buondelmonti, Zanobi', *DBI*, vol. 15 (Rome, 1972), *ad voc*

de Grazia, S., *Machiavelli in Hell* (Princeton NJ: Princeton University Press, 1989)

de Maulde, R., 'L'entrevue de Savone en 1507', *Revue d'histoire diplomatique* 4 (1890), pp. 583–90

de Pins, J., 'Autour des guerres d'Italie: Un ambassadeur français à Venise et à Rome (1515–1525): Jean de Pins, évêque de Rieux', *Revue d'histoire diplomatique* 61 (1947), pp. 215–46, and 62 (1948), pp. 88–113

de Roover, R., *The Rise and Decline of the Medici Bank: 1397–1494* (Cambridge MA: Harvard University Press, 1963)

De Rosa, D., *Coluccio Salutati: il cancelliere e il pensatore politico* (Florence: La Nuova Italia, 1980) della Torre, A., *Storia dell' Accademia Platonica* (Florence: G. Carnesecchi e Figli, 1902)

Devonshire Jones, R. 'Some Observations on the Relations between Francesco Vettori and Niccolò Machiavelli during the Embassy to Maximilian I', *Italian Studies* 23 (1968), pp. 93–113

———, *Francesco Vettori: Florentine Citizen and Medici Servant* (London: Athlone Press, 1972)

Dionisotti, C., *Machiavellerie: Storia e fortuna di Machiavelli* (Turin: Einaudi, 1980)

Di Porto, B., 'Il problema religioso in Machiavelli', *Idea* 21 (1966), pp. 245–50

———, *Le religione in Machiavelli, Guicciardini e Pascoli* (Rome: Idea, 1968)

Doussinague, J., 'Fernando el Católico en las vistas de Savona de 1507', *Boletín de la Academia de la Historia* 108 (1936), pp. 99–146

Dunbabin, J., 'Government', in J. H. Burns (ed.), *The Cambridge History of Medieval Political Thought, c. 350–c. 1450* (Cambridge: Cambridge University Press, 1988), pp. 477–519

Ebneth, R., and P. Schmid (eds.), *Der Landshuter Erbfolgekrieg. An der Wende vom Mittelalter zur Neuzeit* (Regensburg: Kartenhaus Kollektiv, 2004)

Epstein, S. A., *Genoa and the Genoese, 958–1528* (Chapel Hill NC and London: University of North Carolina Press, 1996)

Esche, C., *Die Libreria Piccolomini in Siena – Studien zu Bau und Ausstattung* (Frankfurt: Peter Lang, 1992)

Fabronio, A., *Leonis Pontificis Maximi Vita* (Pisa: A. Landius, 1797)

Fachard, D., *Biagio Buonaccorsi* (Bologna: M. Boni, 1976)

———, 'Implicazioni politiche nell' *Arte della guerra*', in Marchand (ed.), *Niccolò Machiavelli politico, storico, letterato*, pp. 149–73

Falvo, G., 'The Art of Human Composition in Giovanni Pontano's *De principe liber*', *MLN* 129/3 (2014), pp. 21–34

Fasano Guarini, E., 'Machiavelli and the crisis of the Italian republics', in Bock et al. (eds.), *Machiavelli and Republicanism*, pp. 17–40

Faulkner, R., '*Clizia* and the Enlightenment of Private Life', in Sullivan (ed.), *The Comedy and Tragedy of Machiavelli*, pp. 30–56

Feldman, M., and B. Gordon, *The Courtesan's Arts* (Oxford: Oxford University Press, 2006)

Ferroni, G., *'Mutazione' e 'Riscontro' nel teatro di Machiavelli e altri saggi sulla commedia del Cinquecento* (Rome: Bulzoni, 1972)

Finlay, R., 'Venice, the Po expedition and the end of the League of Cambrai, 1509–1510', *Studies in Modern European History and Culture* 2 (1976), pp. 37–72

————, *Venice Besieged: Politics and Diplomacy in the Italian Wars, 1494–1534* (Aldershot: Routledge, 2008)

Fioravanti, G., 'Librerie e lettori a San Gimignano nel '400: Onofrio Coppi e Mattia Lupi', *Interpres* 18 (1999), pp. 58–73

Floriani, P., 'Trissino: la «questione della lingua», la poetica', in N. Pozza (ed.), *Atti del Convegno di Studi su Giangiorgio Trissino* (Vicenza: Accademia Olimpica, 1980), pp. 53–66

Fontana, B., 'Love of Country and Love of God: The Political Uses of Religion in Machiavelli', *Journal of the History of Ideas* 60 (1999), pp. 639–58

————, 'Sallust and the Politics of Machiavelli', *History of Political Thought* 24 (2003), pp. 86–108

Fragnito, G., 'Carvajal, Bernardino López de', *DBI*, vol. 21 (Rome, 1978), pp. 28–34

Fredona, R., 'Carnival of Law: Bartolomeo Scala's dialogue *De legibus et iudiciis*', *Viator* 39/2 (2008), pp. 193–213

Frey, L. S., and M. L. Frey, *The History of Diplomatic Immunity* (Columbus OH: Ohio State University Press, 1999)

Friedhuber, I., 'Lichtenstein, Paul von', *Neue Deutsche Biographie*, vol. 14 (Berlin, 1985), p. 464f

Frigo, D., 'Ambasciatori, ambasciate e immunità diplomatiche nelle letteratura politica italiana (secc. XVI–XVIII)', *Mélanges de l'École française de Rome* 119 (2007), pp. 31–50

Fubini, R., 'Federico da Montefeltro e la congiura dei Pazzi: politica e propaganda alla luce di nuovi documenti', in G. Chittolini, G. Cerboni Baiardi and P. Floriani (eds.), *Federico di Montefeltro: Lo stato, le arti, la cultura*, 3 vols. (Rome: Bulzoni, 1986), vol. 1, pp. 357–470

————, *Storiografia dell'umanesimo in Italia da Leonardo Bruni ad Annio da Viterbo* (Rome: Storia e Letteratura, 2003)

Garin, E., (ed.), *Il pensiero pedagogico dell'umanesimo* (Florence: Sansoni, 1958)

Gattoni, M., *Leone X e la geo-politica dello Stato pontificio (1513–1521)* (Vatican City: Archivio Segreto Vaticano, 2000)

Gavitt, P., *Gender, Honor, and Charity in Late Renaissance Florence* (Cambridge: Cambridge University Press, 2011)

Geerken, J. H., 'Heroic Virtue: An Introduction to the Origins and Nature of a Renaissance Concept' (Unpublished PhD dissertation, Yale University, 1967)

Gentile, S., 'A proposito dell'edizione del trattato *De maiestate* di Iuniano Maio', *Filologia romanza* 5/2 (1958), pp. 143–209

Gherardi, A., *Nuovi documenti intorno a Girolamo Savonarola*, 2nd ed. (Florence: Sansoni, 1887)

Gilbert, F., 'The Humanist Concept of the Prince and the Prince of Machiavelli', *Journal of Modern History* 11/4 (1939), pp. 449–83

———, 'Bernardo Rucellai and the Orti Oricellari: A Study on the Origin of Modern Political Thought', *Journal of the Warburg and Courtauld Institutes* 12 (1949), pp. 101–31

———, 'The Composition and Structure of Machiavelli's *Discorsi*', *Journal of the History of Ideas* 14 (1953), pp. 135–56

———, *Machiavelli and Guicciardini: Politics and History in Sixteenth-Century Florence* (Princeton NJ: Princeton University Press, 1965)

———, 'The Venetian Constitution in Florentine Political Thought', in N. Rubinstein (ed.), *Florentine Studies: Politics and Society in Renaissance Florence* (London: Faber, 1968), pp. 463–500

———, *History: Choice and Commitment* (Cambridge MA: Belknap Press, 1977)

Gilmore, M., (ed.), *Studies on Machiavelli* (Florence: Sansoni, 1972)

Ginzburg, C., 'Diventare Machiavelli. Per una nuova lettura dei "Ghiribizzi al Soderini"', *Quaderni Storici* 121 (2006), pp. 151–64

Giorgetti, A., 'Lorenzo de' Medici Capitano Generale della Repubblica fiorentina', *ASI* 4/11–12 (1883), pp. 194–215

Godman, P., *From Poliziano to Machiavelli: Florentine Humanism in the High Renaissance* (Princeton NJ: Princeton University Press, 1998)

Goldthwaite, R. A., 'I prezzi del grano a Firenze dal XIV al XVI secolo', *Quaderni storici* 10 (1975), pp. 5–36

———, *The Economy of Renaissance Florence* (Baltimore MD: Johns Hopkins University Press, 2009)

Gotor, M., 'Ochino, Bernardino', *DBI*, vol. 79 (Rome, 2013), pp. 90–7

Gouwens, K., *Remembering the Renaissance: Humanist Narratives of the Sack of Rome* (Leiden: Brill, 1998)

Grayson, C. 'Machiavelli and Dante', in Molho and Tedeschi (eds.), *Renaissance Studies in Honor of Hans Baron*, pp. 361–84

———, 'A proposito di una nuova edizione del *Dialogo intorno alla lingua*', *Studi e problemi di critica testuale* 16 (1978), pp. 69–80

Graziani, N., and G. Venturelli, *Caterina Sforza* (Milan: Mondadori, 2001)

Green, L., *Chronicle into History. An Essay on the Interpretation of History in Florentine Fourteenth-Century Chronicles* (Cambridge: Cambridge University Press, 1972)

Gregorovius, F., *History of the City of Rome in the Middle Ages*, A. Hamilton (trans.), 8 vols. in 13, repr. (New York: AMS Press, 1967)

Grendler, P. E., *Schooling in Renaissance Italy: Literacy and Learning, 1300–1600* (Baltimore MD and London: Johns Hopkins University Press, 1989)

———, *The Universities of the Italian Renaissance* (Baltimore MD and London: Johns Hopkins University Press, 2002)

Guidi, A., *Un segretario militante: politica, diplomazia e armi nel cancelliere Machiavelli* (Bologna: Il Mulino, 2009)

Guidi, G., 'Niccolò Machiavelli e i progetti di riforme costituzionali a Firenze nel 1522', *Il pensiero politico* 2 (1969), pp. 580–96

———, *Ciò che accade al tempo della Signoria di novembre–dicembre in Firenze l'anno 1494* (Florence: Arnaud, 1988)

Haas, L., 'Women and Childbearing in Medieval Florence', in C. Jorgensen Itnyre (ed.), *Medieval Family Roles: A Book of Essays* (New York: Garland, 1996), pp. 87–99

Hankins, J., 'The Myth of the Platonic Academy of Florence', *Renaissance Quarterly* 44/3 (1991), pp. 429–47

Hatfield, R., 'A source for Machiavelli's account of the regime of Piero de' Medici', in M. Gilmore (ed.), *Studies on Machiavelli* (Florence: Sansoni, 1972), pp. 317–33

Hauvette, H., *Luigi Alamanni. Sa vie et son oeuvre* (Paris: Hachette, 1903)

Henderson, J., *The Renaissance Hospital: Healing the Body and Healing the Soul* (New Haven CT and London: Yale University Press, 2006)

Herlihy, D., and C. Klapisch-Zuber, *Tuscans and Their Families: A Study of the Florentine Catasto of 1427* (New Haven CT: Yale University Press, 1985)

Hernando Sánchez, C. J., *El reino de Nápoles en el Imperio de Carlos V: La consolidación de la conquista* (Madrid: Sociedad Estatal para la Conmemoración de los Centenarios de Felipe II y Carlos V, 2001)

Hexter, J. H., 'Seyssel, Machiavelli, and Polybius VI: The Mystery of the Missing Translation', *Studies in the Renaissance* 3 (1956), pp. 75–96

Hirst, M., *Michelangelo*, vol. 1, *The Achievement of Fame, 1475–1534* (New Haven CT and London: Yale University Press, 2011)

Hörnqvist, M., 'Perché non si usa allegare i Romani: Machiavelli and the Florentine Militia of 1506', *Renaissance Quarterly* 55/1 (2002), pp. 148–91

———, *Machiavelli and Empire* (Cambridge: Cambridge University Press, 2004)

———, 'Machiavelli's military project and the *Art of War*', in Najemy (ed.), *The Cambridge Companion to Machiavelli*, pp. 112–27

Hughes, R. F., 'Francesco Vettori: his place in Florentine diplomacy and politics' (Unpublished PhD thesis, University of London, 1958)

Hyden, R., 'Zyprian von Serntein im Dienste Kaiser Maximilians I. in den Jahren 1490–1508' (Unpublished PhD thesis, University of Graz, 1973)

Ianziti, G., *Writing History in Renaissance Italy: Leonardo Bruni and the Uses of the Past* (Cambridge MA: Harvard University Press, 2012)

Ibler, G., 'König Maximilian I. und der Konstanzer Reichstag von 1507' (Unpublished PhD thesis, University of Graz, 1961)

Imberciadori, I., 'I due poderi di Bernardo Machiavelli, ovvero mezzadria poderale nel '400', in *Studi in onore di Armando Sapori*, 2 vols. (Milan: Istituto Editoriale Cisalpino, 1957)

Inglese, G., 'Contributo al testo critico della *Mandragola*', *Annali dell'Istituto italiano di studi storici* 6 (1979–80), pp. 129–73

———, 'Contributo al testo critico dei "Decennali" di Niccolò Machiavelli', *Annali dell'Istituto italiano per gli studi storici* 8 (1983–4), pp. 115–73

———, 'Il *Discursus florentinarum rerum* di Niccolò Machiavelli', *La Cultura* 23 (1985), pp. 203–28

———, *Per Machiavelli. L'arte dello stato, la cognizione delle storie* (Rome: Carocci, 2006)

Irace, E., 'Iacopo d'Appiano', *Enciclopedia Machiavelliana*, 3 vols. (Rome: Istituto della Enciclopedia Italiana, 2014), vol. 1, pp. 78–80

Jodogne, P., and G. Benzoni, 'Guicciardini, Francesco', *DBI*, vol. 61 (Rome, 2004), *ad voc.*

Jones, M. A., *A Catalogue of French Medals in the British Museum*, vol. 1, *1402–1610* (London: British Museum Publications, 1982)

Jones, P. J., 'The Machiavellian Militia: Innovation or Renovation?', in C.-M. de La Roncière (ed.), *La Toscane et les Toscans autour de la Renaissance: Cadres de vie, société, croyances. Mélanges offerts à C.-M. de La Roncière* (Aix-en-Provence: Publications de l'Université de Provence, 1999), pp. 11–52

Jurdjevic, M., *Guardians of Republicanism: The Valori Family in the Florentine Renaissance* (Oxford: Oxford University Press, 2008)

———, *A Great and Wretched City: Promise and Failure in Machiavelli's Florentine Political Thought* (Cambridge MA and London: Harvard University Press, 2014)

Kallendorf, C., *In Praise of Aeneas: Virgil and Epideictic Rhetoric in the Early Italian Renaissance* (Hanover NH and London: University Press of New England, 1989)

Kempshall, M. S., *The Common Good in Late Medieval Political Thought* (Oxford: Oxford University Press, 1999)

Kent, D., ' "The Lodging House of All Memories": An Accountant's Home in Renaissance Florence', *Journal of the Society of Architectural Historians* 66/4 (2007), pp. 444–63

Kirshner, J., and A. Molho, 'Niccolò Machiavelli's Marriage', *Rinascimento* 18 (1978), pp. 293–5

Klapisch-Zuber, C., 'Le chiavi fiorentine di barbablù: l'apprendimento della lettura a Firenze nel XV secolo', *Quaderni storici* 57 (1984), pp. 765–92

———, *Women, Family, and Ritual in Renaissance Italy*, L. Cochrane (trans.) (Chicago IL and London: University of Chicago Press, 1985)

Knecht, R. J., *Francis I* (Cambridge: Cambridge University Press, 1982)

Kristeller, P. O., 'Francesco da Diacceto and Florentine Platonism in the

Sixteenth Century', *Miscellanea Giuseppe Mercati* 4 (Vatican City, 1956), pp. 260–304

———, 'Cattani da Diacceto, Francesco, detto il Pagonazzo', *DBI*, vol. 22 (Rome, 1979), *ad voc.*

Kuehn, T., *Illegitimacy in Renaissance Florence* (Ann Arbor MI: University of Michigan Press, 2002)

Landon, W. J., *Lorenzo di Filippo Strozzi and Niccolò Machiavelli: Patron, Client, and the* Pistole fatta per la peste / *An Epistle Concerning the Plague* (Toronto: University of Toronto Press, 2013)

Landucci, Luca, *Diario fiorentino dal 1450 al 1516 continuato da un anonimo fino al 1542*, ed. J. del Badia (Florence, 1883)

Langdon, G., *Medici Women: Portraits of Power, Love, and Betrayal* (Toronto: University of Toronto Press, 2006)

Larosa, S., '*Sommario delle cose della città di Lucca*', *Enciclopedia Machiavelliana*, 3 vols. (Rome: Istituto della Enciclopedia Italiana, 2014), vol. 2, pp. 548–50

Lazzarini, I., *Communication and Conflict: Italian Diplomacy in the Early Renaissance, 1350–1520* (Oxford: Oxford University Press, 2015)

Lee, A., *Petrarch and St. Augustine: Classical Scholarship, Christian Theology, and the Origins of the Renaissance in Italy* (Leiden: Brill, 2012)

———, *Humanism and Empire: The Imperial Ideal in Fourteenth-Century Italy* (Oxford: Oxford University Press, 2018)

Lefort, C., *Machiavelli in the Making* (Evanston IL: Northwestern University Press, 2012)

Litta, P., et al. *Famiglie celebri italiane*, 11 vols. (Milan: P. E. Giusti, 1819–99)

Lojacono, D., 'L'opera inedita *De maiestate* di Giuniano Maio e il concetto sul principe negli scrittori della corte aragonese di Napoli', *Atti della Regia Accademia di scienze morali e politiche di Napoli* 24 (1891), pp. 329–76

Lowe, K. J. P., *Church and Politics in Renaissance Italy: The Life and Career of Cardinal Francesco Soderini, 1453–1524* (Cambridge: Cambridge University Press, 1993)

Lucarelli, G., *Gli Orti Oricellari: epilogo della politica fiorentina del quattrocento e inizio del pensiero politico moderno* (Lucca: M. Pacini Fazzi, 1979)

Luiso, F. P., 'Riforma della cancelleria fiorentina nel 1437', *ASI*, 5th ser., 21 (1898), pp. 132–41

Luzzati, M., 'Buoninsegna di Angiolino Machiavelli', *DBI*, vol. 15 (Rome, 1972), *ad voc.*

———, 'Castracani degli Antelminelli, Castruccio', *DBI*, vol. 22 (Rome, 1979), pp. 200–10

Mader, E., 'Paul von Liechtenstein, Marschall des Innsbrucker Regiments, im Dienste Kaiser Maximilians I. in den Jahren 1490 bis 1513' (Unpublished PhD thesis, University of Graz, 1973)

Malanima, P., 'Casavecchia, Filippo', *DBI*, vol. 21 (Rome, 1978), pp. 269–70

———, 'Cattani da Diacceto, Iacopo', *DBI*, vol. 22 (Rome, 1979), *ad voc.*

Mallett, M. E., *Mercenaries and Their Masters: Warfare in Renaissance Italy*, new. ed. (Barnsley: Pen & Sword, 2009)

Mallett, M. E., and C. Shaw, *The Italian Wars, 1494–1559: War, State and Society in Early Modern Europe* (London and New York: Routledge, 2012)

Mansfield, H. C., *Machiavelli's Virtue* (Chicago IL: University of Chicago Press, 1998)

———, 'The Cuckold in Machiavelli's *Mandragola*', in Sullivan (ed.), *The Comedy and Tragedy of Machiavelli*, pp. 1–29

Maracchi Biagiarelli, B., 'Niccolo Tedesco e le carte della Geografia di Francesco Berlinghieri autore-editore', in B. Maracchi Biagiarelli and D. E. Rhodes (eds.), *Studi offerti a Roberto Ridolfi, direttore de 'La Bibliofilia'* (Florence: Olschki, 1973), pp. 377–97

Marani, P. C., 'Luca Ugolini, Niccolò Machiavelli e la fama di Leonardo ritrattista nei primi anni del Cinquecento', in A. Pontremoli (ed.), *La lingua e le lingue di Machiavelli: atti del Convegno internazionale di studi, Torino, 2–4 dicembre 1999* (Florence: L. S. Olschki, 2001), 281–94

Marchand, J. J., 'I *Ghiribizzi d'ordinanza* del Machiavelli', *La Bibliofilia* 73 (1971), pp. 135–50

———, *Niccolò Machiavelli: I primi scritti politici* (Padua: Antenore, 1975)

———, (ed.), *Niccolò Machiavelli politico, storico, letterato* (Rome: Salerno, 1996)

Marietti, M., *Machiavel: Le penseur de la nécessité* (Paris: Payot, 2009)

Marks, L. F., 'La crisi finanziaria a Firenze dal 1494 al 1502', *ASI* 112 (1954), pp. 40–72

Martelli, M., 'La versione machiavelliana dell'*Andria*', *Rinascimento*, 2nd ser., 8 (1968), pp. 203–73

———, 'I *Ghiribizzi* a Giovan Battista Soderini', *Rinascimento* 9 (1969), pp. 147–80

———, *Una giarda fiorentina: il 'Dialogo della lingua' attribuito a Niccolò Machiavelli* (Rome: Salerno, 1978)

———, 'Paralipomeni alla *Giarda*: venti tesi sul *Dialogo della lingua*', *Filologia e critica* 4 (1979), pp. 212–79

———, 'Machiavelli e la storiografia umanistica', in A. Di Stefano (ed.), *La storiografia umanistica*, 2 vols. in 3 (Messina: Sicania, 1992), vol. 1, pp. 113–52

Martines, L., *The Social World of the Florentine Humanists, 1390–1460* (Princeton NJ: Princeton University Press, 1963)

———, *Lawyers and Statecraft in Renaissance Florence* (Princeton NJ: Princeton University Press, 1968)

————, *April Blood: Florence and the Plot against the Medici* (Oxford: Oxford University Press, 2003)

Martinez, R. L., 'The Pharmacy of Machiavelli: Roman Lucretia in *Mandragola*', *Renaissance Drama* 14 (1983), pp. 1–42

————, 'Benefit of Absence: Machiavellian Valediction in *Clizia*', in A. R. Ascoli and V. Kahn (eds.), *Machiavelli and the Discourse of Literature* (Ithaca NY: Cornell University Press, 1994), pp. 117–44

————, 'Comedian, tragedian: Machiavelli and traditions of Renaissance theatre', in Najemy (ed.), *The Cambridge Companion to Machiavelli*, pp. 206–22

Marzi, D., *La cancelleria della repubblica fiorentina* (Rocca San Casciano: Licinio Cappelli, 1910)

Masters, R. D., *Machiavelli, Leonardo, and the Science of Power* (Notre Dame IN: University of Notre Dame Press, 1996)

Mattingly, G., *Renaissance Diplomacy* (Boston: Houghton Mifflin Company, 1955)

May, S. J., 'The Piccolomini library in Siena Cathedral: a new reading with particular reference to two compartments of the vault decoration', *Renaissance Studies* 19/3 (2005), pp. 287–324

Mazzarosa, A., *Storia di Lucca dalla sua origine fino al 1814*, 2 vols. (Lucca: Giuseppe Giusti, 1833)

Mazzetti, A., 'Polesella 22 dicembre 1509: l'armata veneta "ruynata" in Po', *Archivio Veneto*, 5th ser. 141/210 (2010), pp. 255–84

Mazzocco, A., *Linguistic Theories in Dante and the Humanists: Studies of Language and Intellectual History in Late Medieval and Early Renaissance Italy* (Leiden: Brill, 1993)

Meld Shield, S., 'Machiavelli's Discourse on Language', in Sullivan (ed.), *The Comedy and Tragedy of Machiavelli*, pp. 78–101

Mercuri, S., 'Gli *Erudimenta grammatices* attribuiti a Benedetto Riccardini e dedicati a Niccolò e Alessandro Machiavelli (1510)', *Interpres* 32 (2014), pp. 276–89

Meschini, S., *La Francia nel ducato di Milano: La politica di Luigi XII (1499–1512)*, 2 vols. (Milan: Franco Angeli, 2006)

Molho, A., *Florentine Public Finances in the Early Renaissance, 1400–1433* (Cambridge MA: Harvard University Press, 1971)

————, *Marriage Alliance in Late Medieval Florence* (Cambridge MA: Harvard University Press, 1994)

Molho, A., and J. Tedeschi (eds.), *Renaissance Studies in Honor of Hans Baron* (Florence: Sansoni, 1971)

Momigliano, A., 'Polybius' Reappearance in Western Europe', in *Polybe*, Entretiens sur l'antiquité classique 20 (Vandoeuvres-Geneva, 1974), pp. 347–72

Moretti, S., 'Corsini, Marietta', *Enciclopedia Machiavelliana*, 3 vols. (Rome: Istituto della Enciclopedia Italiana, 2014), *ad voc.*

Morsolin, B., *Giangiorgio Trissino* (Florence: Le Monnier, 1894)

Muir, E., *Ritual in Early Modern Europe* (Cambridge: Cambridge University Press, 1997)

Murphy, N., 'Henry VIII's First Invasion of France: The Gascon Expedition of 1512', *English Historical Review*, 130/542 (2015), pp. 25–56

Mutini, C., 'Cavalcanti, Bartolomeo', *DBI*, vol. 22 (Rome, 1979), pp. 611–17

Najemy, J. M., 'Machiavelli and the Medici: The Lessons of Florentine History', *Renaissance Quarterly* 35 (1982), pp. 551–76

——, 'The controversy surrounding Machiavelli's service to the republic', in Bock, Skinner and Viroli (eds.), *Machiavelli and Republicanism*, pp. 101–17

——, *Between Friends: Discourses of Power and Desire in the Machiavelli–Vettori Letters of 1513–1515* (Princeton NJ: Princeton University Press, 1993)

——, 'Papirius and the Chickens, or Machiavelli on the Necessity of interpreting Religion', in *Journal of the History of Ideas* 60 (1999), pp. 659–81

——, ' "Occupare la tirranide": Machiavelli, the Militia, and Guicciardini's Accusation of Tyranny', in J. Barthas (ed.), *Della tirannia: Machiavelli con Bartolo* (Florence: Olschki, 2007), pp. 75–108

——, *A History of Florence, 1200–1575* (Oxford: Blackwell, 2008)

——, 'Introduction', in Najemy (ed.), *The Cambridge Companion to Machiavelli*, pp. 1–13

——, 'Society, class and state in Machiavelli's *Discourses on Livy*', in Najemy (ed.), *The Cambridge Companion to Machiavelli*, pp. 96–111

——, (ed.), *The Cambridge Companion to Machiavelli* (Cambridge: Cambridge University Press, 2010)

Nederman, C. J., 'Amazing grace: Fortune, God, and Free Will in Machiavelli's Thought', *Journal of the History of Ideas* 60 (1999), pp. 617–38

Negri, Giulio, *Istoria degli scrittori fiorentini* (Ferrara: Bernardino Pomatelli, 1722)

Nelson, E., 'The problem of princely virtue', in J. Hankins (ed.), *The Cambridge Companion to Renaissance Philosophy* (Cambridge: Cambridge University Press, 2007), pp. 319–37

Newell, W. R., 'Machiavelli and Xenophon on Princely Rule', *Journal of Politics* 50 (1988), pp. 108–30

Niccoli, O., *Prophesy and People in Renaissance Italy* (Princeton NJ: Princeton University Press, 1990)

Niccolini, B., 'Bernardino Ochino. Saggio biografico', *Biblion* 1 (1959), pp. 5–23

Niccolini, E., 'Di un frammento Machiavelliano quasi dimenticato',
    Giornale storico della lettteratura italiana 174 (1997), pp. 206–10

Olmstead, W., 'Exemplifying Deliberation: Cicero's *De Officiis* and
    Machiavelli's *Prince*', in W. Jost and W. Olmstead (eds.), *A
    Companion to Rhetoric and Rhetorical Criticism* (Malden MA:
    Blackwell, 2004), pp. 173–89

Osmond, P., 'Sallust and Machiavelli: From Civic Humanism to Political
    Prudence', *Journal of Medieval and Renaissance Studies* 23 (1993), pp.
    407–38

Padoan, G., 'Il tramonto di Machiavelli', *Lettere italiane* 33 (1981), pp.
    457–81

Parronchi, A., 'La prima rappresentazione della *Mandragola*. Il modello
    per l'apparato – l'allegoria', *La Bibliofilia* 66 (1962), pp. 37–86

Passerini, L., *Genealogia e storia della famiglia Corsini* (Florence: Cellini,
    1858)

Pecci, Giovanni Antonio, *Memorie storico-critiche della città di Siena,
    1480–1559*, 4 vols. (Siena: Pazzini, 1755–60)

Pedretti, C., 'Machiavelli and Leonardo on the fortification of
    Piombino', *Italian Quarterly* 12 (1968), pp. 3–31

———, *Leonardo: The Portrait*, H. Paterson and M. Pugliano (trans.)
    (Florence: Giunti, 1999)

Pedullà, G., *Machiavelli in Tumult: The* Discourses on Livy *and the
    Origins of Political Conflictualism*, P. Gaborik and R. Nybakken
    (trans.) (Cambridge: Cambridge University Press, 2018)

Pélissier, L.-G., 'Sopra alcuni documenti relativi all'alleanza tra
    Alessandro VI e Luigi XII, 1498–1499', *Archivio della R. Società
    romana di storia patria* 17 (1894), pp. 303–73, and 18 (1895), pp. 99–215

Pellegrini, M., 'A Turning-Point in the History of the Factional System
    of the Sacred College: The Power of the Pope and Cardinals in the
    Age of Alexander VI', in G. Signorotto and M. A. Visceglia (eds.),
    Court and Politics in Papal Rome, 1492–1700 (Cambridge: Cambridge
    University Press, 2002), pp. 8–30

Pesman Cooper, R., 'L'elezione di Pier Soderini a gonfaloniere a vita',
    ASI 125 (1967), pp. 145–85

———, 'Political survival in early sixteenth-century Florence: the case
    of Niccolò Valori', in P. Denley and C. Elam (eds.), *Florence and
    Italy. Renaissance Studies in Honour of Nicolai Rubinstein* (London:
    Committee for Medieval Studies, Westfield College, 1988), pp. 73–90

Petruccelli della Gattina, F., *Histoire diplomatique des conclaves*, 4 vols.
    (Paris: A. Lacroix, 1864–6)

Petrucci, F., 'Cibo, Innocenzo', *DBI*, vol. 25 (Rome, 1981), pp. 249–55

———, 'Colonna, Fabrizio', *DBI*, vol. 27 (Rome, 1982), pp. 288–91

———, 'Corella, Miguel', *DBI*, vol. 29 (Rome, 1983), pp. 42–6

Phillips, M., 'Machiavelli, Guicciardini, and the tradition of vernacular historiography in Florence', *American Historical Review* 84/1 (1979), pp. 86–105

———, 'Barefoot Boy Makes Good: A Study of Machiavelli's Historiography', *Speculum* 59 (1984), pp. 585–605

Pieraccioni, G., 'Note su Machiavelli storico. I. Machiavelli e Giovanni di Carlo', *ASI* 146 (1988), pp. 635–54

———, 'Note su Machiavelli storico. II. Machiavelli lettore delle *Storie fiorentine* di Guicciardini', *ASI* 147 (1989), pp. 63–98

Pieri, P., *Il rinascimento e la crisi militare* (Turin: Einaudi, 1952)

———, 'Appiano, Iacopo', *DBI*, vol. 3 (Rome, 1961), pp. 629–31

Pinto, G., *Toscana medievale: paesaggi e realtà sociali* (Florence: Le Lettere, 1993)

Pitkin, H. F., *Fortune is a Woman: Gender and Politics in the Thought of Niccolò Machiavelli* (Berkeley CA: University of California Press, 1984)

Polizzotto, L., *The Elect Nation: The Savonarolan Movement in Florence, 1494–1545* (Oxford: Clarendon, 1994)

Price, R., 'The Senses of *Virtù* in Machiavelli', *European Studies Review* 4 (1973), pp. 315–45

———, 'The Theme of *Gloria* in Machiavelli', *Renaissance Quarterly* 30 (1977), pp. 588–631

Price Zimmermann, T. C., 'Guicciardini, Giovio, and the Character of Clement VII', in K. Gouwens and S. E. Reiss (eds.), *The Pontificate of Clement VII: History, Politics, Culture* (Abingdon: Routledge, 2005), pp. 19–27

Quillen, C. E., 'Humanism and the lure of antiquity', in Najemy (ed.), *Italy in the Age of the Renaissance*, pp. 37–58

Quint, D., 'Narrative Design and Historical Irony in Machiavelli's *Istorie fiorentine*', *Rinascimento* 43 (2003), pp. 31–48

Raimondi, E., 'Machiavelli and the Rhetoric of the Warrior', *MLN* 92 (1977), pp. 1–16

———, *Politica e commedia: il centauro disarmato* (Bologna: Il Mulino, 1998)

Raimondi, F., *Constituting Freedom: Machiavelli and Florence*, M. Armistead (trans.) (Oxford: Oxford University Press, 2018)

Rajna, P., 'La data del *Dialogo intorno alla lingua* di Niccolò Machiavelli', *Rendiconti della Reale Accademia dei Lincei*, Classe di scienze morali ecc., 5th ser. 2/2 (1893), pp. 203–22

Rebhorn, W., *Foxes and Lions: Machiavelli's Confidence Men* (Ithaca NY and London: Cornell University Press, 1988)

Reinhard, H., *Lorenzo von Medici, Herzog von Urbino, 1492–1515* (Freiburg: Waibel, 1935)

Riccardi, R. 'Baldi, Pietro del Riccio (Petrus Crinitus)', *DBI*, vol. 38 (Rome, 1990), pp. 265–8

Richardson, B., 'Notes on Machiavelli's Sources and His Treatment of the Rhetorical Tradition', *Italian Studies* 26 (1971), pp. 24–48

———, 'Evoluzione stilistica e fortuna della traduzione machiavelliana dell' *Andria*', *Lettere Italiane* 25 (1973), pp. 319–38

———, 'Two notes on Machiavelli's *Asino*', *Bibliothèque d'humanisme et renaissance* 40 (1978), pp. 137–41

———, 'Per la datazione del *Tradimento del duca Valentino* del Machiavelli', *La Bibliofila* 81 (1979), pp. 75–85

———, 'La "lettera a una gentildonna" del Machiavelli', *La Bibliofilia* 84 (1982), pp. 271–6

———, *Manuscript Culture in Renaissance Italy* (Cambridge: Cambridge University Press, 2009)

Ridolfi, R., *Vita di Francesco Guicciardini* (Rome: Angelo Belardetti, 1960)

———, 'La seconda edizione della *Mandragola* e un codicillo sopra la prima', in R. Ridolfi, *Studi sulle commedie di Machiavelli* (Pisa: Nistri-Lischi, 1968), pp. 37–62

———, *Vita di Niccolò Machiavelli*, 3rd ed., 2 vols. (Florence: Sansoni, 1969)

———, 'Ultime postille Machiavelliane', *La Bibliofilia* 77 (1975), pp. 65–76

Ridolfi, R., and P. Ghigleri, 'I *Ghiribizzi* a Soderini', *La Bibliofilia* 72 (1970), pp. 52–72

Rizzo, S., *Ricerche sul latino umanistico* (Rome: Storia e Letteratura, 2002)

Rocke, M., *Forbidden Friendships: Homosexuality and Male Culture in Renaissance Florence* (Oxford: Oxford University Press, 1996)

———, 'Gender and Sexual Culture in Renaissance Italy', in J. C. Brown and R. C. Davis (eds.), *Gender and Society in Renaissance Italy* (London and New York: Longman, 1998), pp. 150–70

Roick, M., *Pontano's Virtues: Aristotelian Moral and Political Thought in the Renaissance* (London: Bloomsbury, 2017)

Rubinstein, N., 'I primi anni del Consiglio Maggiore di Firenze, 1494–1499', *ASI* 112 (1954), pp. 151–94, pp. 321–47

———, 'The beginnings of Niccolò Machiavelli's career in the Florentine chancery', *Italian Studies* 11 (1956), pp. 72–91

———, 'Firenze e il problema della politica imperiale in Italia al tempo di Massimiliano I', *ASI* 116 (1958), pp. 5–35, pp. 147–77

———, 'Politics and Constitution in Florence at the End of the Fifteenth Century', in E. F. Jacob (ed.), *Italian Renaissance Studies* (London: Faber & Faber, 1960), pp. 148–83

———, *The Government of Florence under the Medici (1434 to 1494)* (Oxford: Clarendon, 1966)

————, 'Machiavelli and the world of Florentine politics', in M. Gilmore (ed.), *Studies on Machiavelli* (Florence: Sansoni, 1972), pp. 3–28

————, 'The *De optimo cive* and the *De principe* by Bartolomeo Platina', in R. Cardini, E. Garin, L. Cesarini Martinelli and G. Pascucci (eds.), *Tradizione classica e letteratura umanistica: per Alessandro Perosa* (Rome: Bulzoni, 1985), pp. 375–89

————, *Studies in Italian History in the Middle Ages and the Renaissance*, vol. 1, *Political Thought and the Language of Politics: Art and Politics*, G. Ciappelli (ed.) (Rome: Edizioni di Storia e Letteratura, 2004)

Ruggiero, G., *Machiavelli in Love: Self, Sex and Society in the Italian Renaissance* (Baltimore MD: Johns Hopkins University Press, 2007)

Ruiz-Domènec, J. E., *El Gran Capitán: Retrato de una época* (Barcelona: Ediciones Península, 2002)

Russell Ascoli, A., and A. M. Capodivacca, 'Machiavelli and Poetry', in Najemy (ed.), *The Cambridge Companion to Machiavelli*, pp. 190–205

Sabatini, R., *The Life of Cesare Borgia* (London: Stanley Paul, 1912)

Sallaberger, J., *Kardinal Matthäus Lang von Wellenburg (1468–1540). Staatsmann und Kirchenfürst im Seitalter von Renaissance, Reformation und Bauernkriegen* (Salzburg: Anton Pustet, 1997)

Samuel Preus, J., 'Machiavelli's Functional Analysis of Religion: Context and Object', *Journal of the History of Ideas* 40 (1979), pp. 171–90

Santi, V. A., *La 'Gloria' nel pensiero di Machiavelli* (Ravenna: Longo, 1979)

Sasso, G., *Studi su Machiavelli* (Naples: Morano, 1967)

————, 'Qualche osservazione sui "Ghiribizzi al Soderino"', *Cultura* 11 (1973), pp. 129–67

————, *Machiavelli e gli antichi e altri saggi*, 3 vols. (Milan: Ricciardi, 1986)

————, 'Machiavelli, Cesare Borgia, Don Micheletto e la questione della milizia', in G. Sasso, *Machiavelli e gli antichi e altri saggi*, 4 vols. (Milan and Naples: Ricciardi, 1987–97), vol. 2, pp. 57–117

Scarpa, E., 'L'autografo del primo "Decennale" di Niccolò Machiavelli', *Studi di filologia italiana* 51 (1993), pp. 149–80

Schellhase, K. C., 'Tacitus in the Political Thought of Machiavelli', *Il pensiero politico* 4 (1971), pp. 381–91

————, *Tacitus in Renaissance Political Thought* (Chicago IL: University of Chicago Press, 1976)

Schiaparelli, A., *La casa fiorentina e i suoi arredi nei secoli XIV e XV*, M. Sframeli and L. Pagnotta (eds.), 2 vols. (Florence: Le Lettere, 1983)

Schindling, A., 'Matthäus Lang von Wellenburg', *Neue Deutsche Biographie*, vol. 16 (Berlin, 1990), pp. 394–7

Scott Baker, N., *The Fruit of Liberty: Political Culture in the Florentine Renaissance, 1480–1550* (Cambridge MA: Harvard University Press, 2013)

Searman, J., 'The Florentine *Entrata* of Leo X, 1515', *Journal of the Warburg and Courtauld Institutes* 38 (1975), pp. 136–54

Settis, S., and D. Toracca (eds.), *La Libreria Piccolomini nel Duomo di Siena* (Modena: F. Cosimo Panini, 1998)

Setton, K. M., *The Papacy and the Levant, 1204–1571*, 4 vols. (Philadelphia PA: The American Philosophical Society, 1976–84)

Shaw, C., *Julius II: The Warrior Pope* (Oxford: Blackwell, 1993)

Shaw, J. E., and E. Welch, *Making and Marketing Medicine in Renaissance Florence* (Amsterdam: Rodopi, 2011)

Silvano, G., *"Vivere civile" e "governo misto" a Firenze nel primo Cinquecento* (Bologna: Pàtron, 1985)

Simeoni, L., *Le signorie*, 2 vols. (Milan: Vallardi, 1950)

Simonetta, M., 'Machiavelli lettore di Tucidide', *Esperienze letterarie* 22/3 (1997), pp. 53–68

———, 'Federico da Montefeltro contro Firenze: retroscena inediti della congiura dei Pazzi', *ASI* 161 (2003), pp. 261–84

———, *The Montefeltro Conspiracy: A Renaissance Mystery Decoded* (New York: Doubleday, 2008)

———, 'Salviati, Giovanni', *DBI*, vol. 90 (Rome, 2017), *ad voc.*

———, 'The Lost Discourse on Governments by Machiavelli's Friend Zanobi Buondelmonti', *Culture del testo e del documento* 18/53 (2017), pp. 165–78

Skinner, Q. R. D., 'Machiavelli's *Discorsi* and the Pre-Humanist Origins of Republican Ideas', in Bock, Skinner and Viroli (eds.), *Machiavelli and Republicanism*, pp. 121–41

———, *Machiavelli*, new ed. (Oxford: Oxford University Press, 2000)

———, *Visions of Politics*, 3 vols. (Cambridge: Cambridge University Press, 2002)

Sorella, A., *Magia, lingua e commedia nel Machiavelli* (Florence: Olschki, 1990)

Spackman, B., 'Machiavelli and gender', in Najemy (ed.), *The Cambridge Companion to Machiavelli*, pp. 223–38

Spini, G., *Tra Rinascimento e Riforma. Antonio Brucioli* (Florence: La Nuova Italia, 1940)

Squires, N., 'Briton finds 500-year-old warrant for Machiavelli', *Daily Telegraph*, 15 February 2013, p. 26

Stacey, P., *Roman Monarchy and the Renaissance Prince* (Cambridge: Cambridge University Press, 2007)

Staffétti, L., *Il Cardinale Innocenzo Cybo* (Florence: Le Monnier, 1894)

Stauber, R., 'Um die Einheit des Hauses Bayern: die Wittelsbacher und König Maximilian im Landshuter Erbfolgekrieg 1504', *An der unteren Isar und Vils. Historische Heimatblätter für die Stadt und den früheren Landkreis Landau an der Isar* 29 (2005), pp. 6–31

Stein, H., 'Historical Writing and Community among the *Orti Oricellari*' (Unpublished PhD Dissertation, Johns Hopkins University, 2015)

Steiner, A., 'Petrarch's *Optimus Princeps*', *Romanic Review* 25 (1934), pp. 99–111

Stephens, J. N., *The Fall of the Florentine Republic, 1512–1530* (Oxford: Clarendon, 1983)

Stephens, J. N., and J. C. Butters, 'New Light on Machiavelli', *English Historical Review* 98 (1982), pp. 54–69

Stopani, R., *Io mi sto in villa. L'Albergaccio del Machiavelli a Sant' Andrea in Percussina* (Florence: Centro di Studi Chiantigiani, 1998)

Stoppelli, P., 'La datazione dell' *Andria*', in Barbarisi and Cabrini (eds.), *Il teatro di Machiavelli*, pp. 147–99

———, *La* Mandragola: *storia e filologia* (Rome: Bulzoni, 2005)

———, *Machiavelli e la novella* Belfagor. *Saggio di filologia attributiva* (Rome: Salerno, 2007)

Strozzi, L., *Le vite degli uomini illustri della casa Strozzi* (Florence: S. Landi, 1892)

Struever, N., *The Language of History in the Renaissance: Rhetoric and Historical Consciousness in Florentine Humanism* (Princeton NJ: Princeton University Press, 1970)

Suchowlansky, M., 'Machiavelli's *Summary of the Affairs of the City of Lucca*: Venice as *buon governo*', *Intellectual History Review* 26/4 (2016), pp. 429–45

Sullivan, V. B., 'Neither Christian Nor Pagan: Machiavelli's Treatment of Religion in the *Discourses*', *Polity* 26 (1993), pp. 259–80

———, (ed.), *The Comedy and Tragedy of Machiavelli: Essays on the Literary Works* (New Haven CT and London: Yale University Press, 2000)

Sumberg, T. A., '*Mandragola*: An Interpretation', *Journal of Politics* 23 (1961), pp. 320–40

Tabanelli, M., *Dionigi di Naldo da Brisighella, condottiero del Rinascimento* (Faenza: Fratelli Lega, 1975)

Tatum, J., *Xenophon's Imperial Fiction: On the Education of Cyrus* (Princeton NJ: Princeton University Press, 1989)

Tenenti, M., 'La religione di Machiavelli', *Studi Storici* 10 (1969), pp. 709–48

Tewes, G.-R., *Kampf um Florenz: die Medici im Exil (1494–1512)* (Cologne and Weimar: Böhlau Verlag, 2011)

Tirvoni, M., *Latino, grammatica e volgare: storia di una questione umanistica* (Padua: Antenore, 1984)

Tommasini, O., *La vita e gli scritti di Niccolò Machiavelli nella loro relazione col machiavellismo*, 3 vols. (Turin: Ermanno Loescher, 1883–1911)

Traversari, G., 'Di Mattia Lupi (1380–1468) e de' suoi "Annales

Geminianenses'", *Miscellanea storica della Valdelsa* 11 (1903), pp. 10–27, pp. 108–28

Trexler, R. C., *Public Life in Renaissance Florence* (Ithaca NY and London: Cornell University Press, 1980)

Trexler, R. C., and M. E. Lewis, 'Two Captains and Three Kings: New Light on the Medici Chapel', *Studies in Medieval and Renaissance History*, n.s. 4 (1981), pp. 93–177

Troso, M., *L'Ultima battaglia del Medioevo: La battaglia dell'Ariotta Novara 6 giugno 1513* (Mariano del Friuli: Edizioni della Laguna, 2002)

Trovato, P., *Storia della lingua: il primo Cinquecento* (Bologna: Il Mulino, 1994)

Tylus, J., 'Theatre's Social Uses: Machiavelli's *Mandragola* and the Spectacle of Infamy', *Renaissance Quarterly* 53 (2000), pp. 656–86

Vanossi, L., *Lingue e strutture del teatro italiano del Rinascimento* (Padua: Liviana, 1970)

Verde, A. F., *Lo Studio Fiorentino 1473–1503*, 3 vols. in 4 (Florence and Pistoia: Olschki, 1973–7)

———, 'Un terzo soggiorno romano del Poliziano', *Rinascimento* 22 (1982), p. 260

Verrier, F., 'Machiavelli e Fabrizio Colonna nell' *Arte della guerra*: il polemologo sdoppiato', in Marchand (ed.), *Niccolò Machiavelli politico, storico, letterato*, pp. 175–87

Villari, P., *The Life and Times of Niccolò Machiavelli*, L. Villari (trans.), 4 vols. (London: Fisher Unwin, 1878)

———, *Machiavelli e i suoi tempi*, 2nd ed., 3 vols. (Milan: Hoepli, 1895–7)

Viroli, M., *From Politics to Reason of State: The Acquisition and Transformation of the Language of Politics, 1250–1600* (Cambridge: Cambridge University Press, 1992)

———, *Niccolò's Smile: A Biography of Machiavelli*, A. Shugaar (trans.) (New York: Farrar, Straus and Giroux, 2001)

———, *Machiavelli's God*, A. Shugaar (trans.) (Princeton N.J.: Princeton University Press, 2010)

Vivanti, C., *Niccolò Machiavelli. I tempi della politica* (Rome: Donzelli, 2008)

Vivoli, C., 'Dazzi, Andrea', *DBI*, vol. 33 (Rome, 1987), pp. 184–6

Volpe, G., 'Intorno ad alcune relazioni di Pisa con Alessandro VI e Cesare Borgia', *Studi Storici* 6 (1897), pp. 495–547; and 7 (1898), pp. 61–107

von Albertini, R., *Das florentinische Staatsbewusstsein in Übergang von der Republik zum Prinzipat* (Bern: Francke Verlag, 1955)

———, *Firenze dalla repubblica al principato*, C. Cristofolini (trans.) (Turin: Einaudi, 1970)

Weinstein, D., *Savonarola and Florence: Prophesy and Patriotism in the Renaissance* (Princeton NJ: Princeton University Press, 1970)

————, 'Machiavelli and Savonarola', in M. Gilmore (ed.), *Studies on Machiavelli* (Florence: Sansoni, 1972), pp. 251–64

————, *Savonarola: The Rise and Fall of a Renaissance Prophet* (New Haven CT and London: Yale University Press, 2011)

Whaley, J., *Germany and the Holy Roman Empire*, 2 vols. (Oxford: Oxford University Press, 2012)

Whitfield, H., 'Machiavelli's Use of Livy', in T. A. Dorey (ed.), *Livy* (London: Routledge and Kegan Paul, 1971), pp. 73–96

Wiesflecker, H., *Kaiser Maximilian I: Das Reich, Österreich und Europa an der Wende zur Neuzeit*, 5 vols. (Munich: Oldenbourg, 1971–86)

Wiethoff, W. E., 'A Machiavellian Paradigm for Diplomatic Communication', *Journal of Politics* 43 (1981), pp. 1090–1104

Wilcox, D., *The Development of Florentine Humanist Historiography* (Cambridge MA: Harvard University Press, 1969)

Wilkins, E. H., *Life of Petrarch* (Chicago and London: Universtiy of Chicago Press, 1961)

Wilkins, E. H., W. A. Jackson and R. H. House, 'The Early Editions of Machiavelli's First Decennale', *Studies in the Renaissance* 11 (1964), pp. 76–104

Witt, R. G., *Coluccio Salutati and His Public Letters* (Geneva: Droz, 1976)

————, *Hercules at the Crossroads: The Life, Works, and Thought of Coluccio Salutati* (Durham NC: Duke University Press, 1983)

Wood, N., 'Some Common Aspects of the Thought of Seneca and Machiavelli', *Renaissance Quarterly* 21 (1968), pp. 11–23

————, 'The Value of Asocial Sociability: Contributions of Machiavelli, Sidney and Montesquieu', *Bucknell Review* 16 (1968), pp. 1–22

Zaccaria, R., 'Della Fonte, Bartolomeo', *DBI*, vol. 36 (Rome, 1988), pp. 808–14

————, 'Falconetti, Iacopo', *DBI*, vol. 44 (Rome, 1994), pp. 342–4

————, 'Machiavelli, Girolamo', *DBI*, vol. 67 (Rome, 2006), *ad voc.*

————, 'Note su Marietta Corsini e la sua famiglia', in L. Bertolini and D. Coppini (eds.), *Nel Cantiere degli Umanisti: per Mariangela Regoliosi*, 3 vols. (Florence: Polistampa, 2014), pp. 1353–67

Zuckert, C. H., *Machiavelli's Politics* (Chicago IL: University of Chicago Press, 2017)

Notes

Abbreviations

ASF	Archivio del Stato, Florence
ASI	*Archivio Storico Italiano*
Chief Works	Niccolò Machiavelli, *Machiavelli: The Chief Works and Others*, A. Gilbert (trans.), 3 vols. (Durham NC and London: Duke University Press, 1989)
Cons. e prat. 1498–1505	D. Fachard (ed.), *Consulte e pratiche della Repubblica fiorentina (1498–1505)*, 2 vols. (Geneva: Droz, 1993)
Cons. e prat. 1505–12	D. Fachard (ed.), *Consulte e pratiche della Repubblica fiorentina (1505–1512)* (Geneva: Droz, 1988)
DBI	*Dizionario Biografico degli Italiani*
LCSG	Niccolò Machiavelli, *Legazioni, commissarie, scritti di governo*, vol. 1, *1498–1501*, F. Chiappelli (ed.) (Bari: Laterza, 1971)
Leg. e comm.	Niccolò Machiavelli, *Legazioni e commissarie*, S. Bertelli (ed.), 3 vols. (Milan: Feltrinelli, 1964)
Lett.	Niccolò Machiavelli, *Lettere*, F. Gaeta (ed.) (Milan: Feltrinelli, 1961)
Machiavelli and His Friends	Niccolò Machiavelli, *Machiavelli and His Friends: Their Personal Correspondence*, J. B. Atkinson and D. Sices (eds. and trans.) (DeKalb IL: Northern Illinois University Press, 1996)

RIS — *Rerum Italicarum Scriptores*
RSI — *Rivista Storica Italiana*

Inauspicious Beginnings (1469–76)

1 Leonardo Bruni, *Laudatio Florentinae Urbis*, pr.; text in H. Baron, *From Petrarch to Leonardo Bruni* (Chicago: University of Chicago Press, 1968), pp. 232–63, here p. 232.

2 *Ibid.*, p. 233.

3 Benedetto Dei, *La Cronica dall'anno 1400 all'anno 1500*, R. Barducci (ed.) (Florence: Passigli, 1985), p. 77; trans. from S. U. Baldassarri and A. Saiber (eds.), *Images of Quattrocento Florence: Selected Writings in Literature, History, and Art* (New Haven CT and London: Yale University Press, 2000), pp. 84–5.

4 Bruni, *Laudatio*, 1; Baron, *From Petrarch to Leonardo Bruni*, p. 233, pp. 235–6.

5 Leon Battista Alberti, *Della pittura*, L. Mallè (ed.) (Florence: Sansoni, 1950), p. 54; trans. from Baldassarri and Saiber (eds.), *Images of Quattrocento Florence*, p. 194.

6 Benedetto Dei maintained that there were exactly 108 churches within the city proper. Dei, *Cronica*, Barducci (ed.), p. 78; trans. from Baldassarri and Saiber (eds.), *Images of Quattrocento Florence*, p. 86.

7 Bruni, *Laudatio*, 1; Baron, *From Petrarch to Leonardo Bruni*, p. 236.

8 A. Perosa (ed.), *Giovanni Rucellai ed il suo Zibaldone*, 2 vols. (London: Warburg Institute, 1960–81), vol. 1, p. 61; trans. from Baldassarri and Saiber (eds.), *Images of Quattrocento Florence*, p. 74.

9 A. Schiaparelli, *La casa fiorentina e i suoi arredi nei secoli XIV e XV*, M. Sframeli and L. Pagnotta (eds.), 2 vols. (Florence: Le Lettere, 1983), vol. 1, p. 141ff.

10 D. Kent, '"The Lodging House of All Memories": An Accountant's Home in Renaissance Florence', *Journal of the Society of Architectural Historians* 66/4 (2007), pp. 444–63.

11 C. Atkinson, *Debts, Dowries, Donkeys: The Diary of Niccolò Machiavelli's Father, Messer Bernardo, in Quattrocento Florence* (Frankfurt am Main: Peter Lang, 2002), p. 57.

12 Servants were also housed in a *casetta* in the alleyway immediately behind the *palazzo*, known as De' Ramaglianti: Bernardo Machiavelli, *Libro di ricordi*, C. Olschki (ed.) (Florence: Le Monnier, 1954), p. 168.

13 Precisely where the Machiavelli family had their origins is still a matter of some debate. On the basis that Giovanni di Angiolini de'

Machiavelli was said to have been a member of the household of
'the noble Caronidini of Giogoli', Davidsohn reasoned that it was
from this area that they must have sprung. Stopani, by contrast,
is wary of being so exact. On the basis of properties listed in
the *catasto* returns entered by various members of the family in the
fifteenth century, he has argued that it is safer to say that they
hailed from somewhere between the River Greve and the River
Pesa. R. Davidsohn, *Geschichte von Florenz*, 4 vols. (Berlin: E. S.
Mittler und Sohn, 1896–1927), vol. 2.2, p. 457; R. Stopani, *Io mi
sto in villa. L'Albergaccio del Machiavelli a Sant' Andrea in Percussina*
(Florence: Centro di Studi Chiantigiani, 1998), esp. pp. 8–9, p. 16,
p. 18.

14 Giovanni Villani, *Nuova Cronica*, 6.81.

15 Marchionne di Coppo Stefani, *Cronaca Fiorentina*, N. Rodolico
(ed.), *RIS*, 2nd ser., 30.1 (Città di Castello: S. Lapi, 1903), p. 48. The
Machiavelli are listed among the leading Guelphs of Oltrarno,
alongside the Belfradelli, Aglioni, Orciolini, Soderini and Ammirati.

16 Hieronimo de Bursellis, *Cronica gestorum ac factorum memorabilium
civitatis Bononie*, A. Sorbelli (ed.), *RIS*, 2nd ser., 23.2 (Città di
Castello: S. Lapi, 1912), p. 27.

17 Giovanni Battista Baldelli, *Elogio di Niccolò Machiavelli* (London
[Livorno?]: s.n., 1794), pp. 86–7.

18 Davidsohn, *Geschichte von Florenz*, vol. 2.2, p. 457, vol. 3, p. 53, vol.
4.1, p. 180.

19 See M. Luzzati, 'Machiavelli, Buoninsegna di Angiolino', *DBI*, vol.
15 (Rome, 1972), *ad voc.*

20 R. Davidsohn, 'L'avo di Niccolò Machiavelli: chronista fiorentino',
ASI 93 (1935), pp. 35–47, here p. 38; Luzzati, 'Machiavelli,
Buoninsegna di Angiolino'.

21 Davidsohn, 'L'avo di Niccolò Machiavelli', 38–9; Luzzati,
'Buoninsegna di Angiolino'.

22 Buoninsegna was prior in 1283, 1289, 1292, 1296, 1298, 1306, 1309, 1310,
1313, and 1314.

23 See *Diario di Anonimo Fiorentino dall'anno 1358 al 1389* in A.
Gherardi (ed.), *Cronache dei secoli XIII e XIV* (Florence: Cellini,
1876), pp. 293–481, here p. 359.

24 In 1426/7, for example, Bernardo's uncle, Guido di Buoninsegna, and
his first cousin once removed, Francesco di Lorenzo, doggedly
petitioned the Parte Guelfa to confirm them as legitimate owners of
the site once occupied by the castle of Montespertoli – which their
fathers had inherited more than thirty years earlier – even though the
expense of doing so likely exceeded the modest returns accruing from
the property. Ricordo Machiavelli, *Ricordanze*, Florence, Biblioteca

Marucelliana MS A.229.10, fols. 193–248, here 234v–235v; quoted in Atkinson, *Debts, Dowries, Donkeys*, pp. 35–6, n.37, p. 37, n.42.

25 A. Molho, *Marriage Alliance in Late Medieval Florence* (Cambridge MA: Harvard University Press, 1994), pp. 365–410, esp. p. 394.

26 P. Litta, et al. *Famiglie celebri italiane*, 11 vols. (Milan: P. E. Giusti, 1819–99), table II mentions that 'i Machiavelli vi fecero dipingere a fresco dal Ghirlandaio la deposizione di Christo della croce.' This can only refer to Ridolfo del Ghirlandaio's now lost *Deposition from the Cross with Saints*. Atkinson, *Debts, Dowries, Donkeys*, p. 35 is mistaken in suggesting that the work was commissioned from Domenico Ghirlandaio – not least because he was not born until ten years *after* the commission.

27 On the dates of Bernardo Machiavelli's birth and his father's death, see Atkinson, *Debts, Dowries, Donkeys*, pp. 41–2.

28 Atkinson, *Debts, Dowries, Donkeys*, p. 43; ASF Catasto 435, fol. 480r. It is worth noting that, in 1427, Giovanni di Buoninsegna's net capital amounted to 1,559 *fl.*: L. Martines, *The Social World of the Florentine Humanists, 1390–1460* (Princeton NJ: Princeton University Press, 1963), p. 378.

29 Ricordo Machiavelli, *Ricordanze*, Florence, Biblioteca Marucelliana MS A.229.10, fol. 233v; Bernardo Machiavelli, *Libro di ricordi*, Olschki (ed.), p. 9ff.

30 See esp. J. Davies, *Florence and its University during the Early Renaissance* (Leiden: Brill, 1998), p. 127.

31 Angelo Poliziano, *Opera omnia*, rev. ed. (Lyon: Sébastien Gryphius, 1533), p. 147; trans. from A. Brown, *Bartolomeo Scala, 1430–1497, Chancellor of Florence: The Humanist as Bureaucrat* (Princeton NJ: Princeton University Press, 1979), p. 8, n.23.

32 L. Martines, *Lawyers and Statecraft in Renaissance Florence* (Princeton NJ: Princeton University Press, 1968), p. 485; Brown, *Bartolomeo Scala*, p. 10; R. Zaccaria, 'Machiavelli, Girolamo, *DBI*, vol. 67 (Rome, 2006), *ad voc.*

33 Bartolomeo Scala, *De legibus et iudiciis*, in Bartolomeo Scala, *Essays and Dialogues*, R. Neu Watkins (trans.) (Cambridge MA and London: Harvard University Press, 2008), pp. 158–231.

34 For discussion, see Brown, *Bartolomeo Scala*, pp. 288–96; Atkinson, *Debts, Dowries, Donkeys*, pp. 149–52; and, more recently, R. Fredona, 'Carnival of Law: Bartolomeo Scala's dialogue *De legibus et iudiciis*', *Viator* 39/2 (2008), pp. 193–213.

35 Bartolomeo Scala's *De legibus et iudiciis* begins with Bernardo dropping round in such a manner. See Scala, '*De legibus et iudiciis*', 2; *Essays and Dialogues*, p. 160.

36 Atkinson, *Debts, Dowries, Donkeys*, pp. 167–8.

37 Bernardo Machiavelli, *Libro di ricordi*, Olschki (ed.), p. 14, p. 35. This 'Maestro Nicolò Tedesco' may have been either the printer Nicolò di Lorenzo della Magna, or the cartographer Nicolaus Germanus. On the identity of 'Maestro Nicolò Tedesco', see Bernardo Machiavelli, *Libro di ricordi*, Olschki (ed.), p. 236; B. Maracchi Biagiarelli, 'Niccolo Tedesco e le carte della Geografia di Francesco Berlinghieri autore-editore', in B. Maracchi Biagiarelli and D. E. Rhodes (eds.), *Studi offerti a Roberto Ridolfi, direttore de 'La Bibliofilia'* (Florence: Olschki, 1973), pp. 377–97; Atkinson, *Debts, Dowries, Donkeys*, pp. 142–3.

38 Atkinson, *Debts, Dowries, Donkeys*, pp. 168–71.

39 Petrarch was close friends with Francesco Nelli, the prior of Santi Apostoli. The two men maintained a lively correspondence over several decades. For a wider discussion of their relationship, see E. H. Wilkins, *Life of Petrarch* (Chicago and London: Universtiy of Chicago Press, 1961), pp. 94–5, pp. 101–2, pp. 109–20, p. 126, pp. 129–31, p. 133, pp. 150–8, p. 160, p. 167, p. 180, p. 177, pp. 180–3, pp. 190–1, p. 252.

40 Bernardo Machiavelli, *Libro di ricordi*, Olschki (ed.), p. 242; Atkinson, *Debts, Dowries, Donkeys*, p. 48.

41 Atkinson, *Debts, Dowries, Donkeys*, pp. 80–1.

42 Although Bartolomea's *laudi* are no longer extant, they could still be read in the Nelli family library as late as the eighteenth century: G. B. C. Nelli, *Discorsi di architettura del Senatore Giovan Battista Nelli* (Florence: Eredi Paperini, 1753), p. 8.

43 *Lett.*, p. 215 (no. 122); *Machiavelli and His Friends*, p. 222 (no. 206); Niccolò Machiavelli, *Opere*, M. Bonfantini (ed.) (Milan and Naples: R. Ricciardi, 1954), p. 1098; *Chief Works*, vol. 2, pp. 898–9, here p. 899.

44 See Atkinson, *Debts, Dowries, Donkeys*, pp. 41–2.

45 T. Kuehn, *Illegitimacy in Renaissance Florence* (Ann Arbor MI: University of Michigan Press, 2002), esp. pp. 74–9.

46 *Ibid.*, p. 80; Martines, *Lawyers and Statecraft*, p. 28; S. Calleri, *L'Arte dei Giudici e Notai di Firenze Nell'età Comunale e Nel Suo Statuto del 1344* (Milan: Giuffrè, 1966), p. 31.

47 Kuehn, *Illegitimacy*, pp. 83–4.

48 J. M. Najemy, *A History of Florence, 1200–1575* (Oxford: Blackwell, 2008), pp. 291–3.

49 *Ibid.*, pp. 293–4.

50 For what follows, see esp. N. Rubinstein, *The Government of Florence under the Medici (1434 to 1494)* (Oxford: Clarendon, 1966), pp. 89–135.

51 Domenico di Lionardo Buoninsegni, *Storie della città di Firenze dall'anno 1410 al 1460* (Florence: Landini, 1637), p. 122; Rubinstein, *Government*, p. 103, p. 109.

52 Buoninsegni, *Storie*, p. 127; Rubinstein, *Government*, p. 121.

53 Dei, *Cronica*, Barducci (ed.), p. 65.

54 R. Black, *Benedetto Accolti and the Florentine Renaissance* (Cambridge: Cambridge University Press, 1985), p. 173, p. 339; Rubinstein, *Government*, p. 294.

55 Ugolino di Niccolò Martelli, *Ricordanze dal 1433 al 1483*, ed. F. Pezzarossa (Rome: Edizioni di Storia e Letteratura, 1989), p. 292; Atkinson, *Debts, Dowries, Donkeys*, p. 40. Paolo di Giovanni was also a member of the *balìa* in 1466, 1471, and 1480: Rubinstein, *Government*, p. 294, p. 304, p. 311.

56 Buoninsegni, *Storie*, p. 122. Carlo di Piero Benizi was exiled to Avignon for twenty-five years; Antonio and Filippo di Piero Benizi – together with their sons, nephew and cousins – were exiled from Florence for twenty-five years; and Giovanni di Matteo di Piero Benizi was ordered to stay at least sixteen kilometres away from the city for ten years. All were fined, as well. See also A. Brown, 'Insiders and Outsiders: The Changing Boundaries of Exile', in W. J. Connell (ed.), *Society and Individual in Renaissance Florence* (Berkeley CA and Los Angeles CA: University of California Press, 2002), pp. 384–409, esp. pp. 367–8.

57 Atkinson, *Debts, Dowries, Donkeys*, p. 44.

58 It is not known where Bartolomea's daughter, Lionarda, was raised: Atkinson, *Debts, Dowries, Donkeys*, p. 48, n.95.

59 Bernardo Machiavelli, *Libro di ricordi*, Olschki (ed.), p. 8.

60 E.g. Martines, *Lawyers and Statecraft*, p. 32, p. 46; A. Molho, *Florentine Public Finances in the Early Renaissance, 1400–1433* (Cambridge MA: Harvard University Press, 1971), pp. 104–5, p. 167.

61 Atkinson, *Debts, Dowries, Donkeys*, pp. 92–3; Bernardo Machiavelli, *Libro di ricordi*, Olschki (ed.), p. 190. The soil around Florence was not particularly well suited to grains: see G. Pinto, *Toscana medievale: paesaggi e realtà sociali* (Florence: Le Lettere, 1993), p. 170.

62 Atkinson, *Debts, Dowries, Donkeys*, p. 92; Bernardo Machiavelli, *Libro di ricordi*, Olschki (ed.), p. 21, p. 121.

63 Atkinson, *Debts, Dowries, Donkeys*, p. 93; Bernardo Machiavelli, *Libro di ricordi*, Olschki (ed.), p. 3, p. 12, p. 13.

64 I. Imberciadori, 'I due poderi di Bernardo Machiavelli, ovvero mezzadria poderale nel' 400', in *Studi in onore di Armando Sapori*, 2 vols. (Milan: Istituto Editoriale Cisalpino, 1957), vol. 2, pp. 835–46.

65 E.g. Bernardo Machiavelli, *Libro di ricordi*, Olschki (ed.), p. 12.

66 E.g. *ibid.*, p. 3.

67 Atkinson, *Debts, Dowries, Donkeys*, pp. 128–9; Bernardo Machiavelli, *Libro di ricordi*, Olschki (ed.), p. 144ff.

68 Atkinson, *Debts, Dowries, Donkeys*, pp. 109–14; Bernardo Machiavelli, *Libro di ricordi*, Olschki (ed.), pp. 26–31, pp. 33–5.

69 Atkinson, *Debts, Dowries, Donkeys*, p. 63; Bernardo Machiavelli, *Libro di ricordi*, Olschki (ed.), p. 27, p. 34, p. 38, p. 43, p. 46.

70 When their old servant, Giusta, went blind and had to be placed in the care of the Ospedale degli Innocenti, the Machiavelli were careful to ensure that she was provided with a good supply of clothing. Atkinson, *Debts, Dowries, Donkeys*, p. 94; Bernardo Machiavelli, *Libro di ricordi*, Olschki (ed.), pp. 163–4, pp. 189–90.

71 See, for example, Atkinson, *Debts, Dowries, Donkeys*, p. 130.

72 Bernardo Machiavelli, *Libro di ricordi*, Olschki (ed.), p. 169.

73 *Ibid.*, p. 57.

74 Martines, *Lawyers and Statecraft*, p. 190.

2. The Golden Age (1476–85)

1 Ugolino Verino, *Flametta*, 2.45. ('Ad Andream Alamannum de laudibus poetarum et de felicitate sui saeculi'); text in F. Arnaldi, L. Gualdo Rosa and L. Monti Sabia (eds.), *Poeti Latini del Quattrocento* (Milan: R. Ricciardi, 1964), pp. 860–4; trans. from Baldassarri and Saiber (eds.), *Images of Quattrocento Florence*, pp. 92–5.

2 For Ficino's praise of Lorenzo, see esp. his 'De quatuor speciebus divinii furoris. Item laudes Medicis Laurentii verae', in Marsilio Ficino, *Opera omnia*, 2 vols. (Basel: Heinrich Petri, 1576; repr. Turin: Bottega d'Erasmo, 1959), p. 927.

3 Niccolò Machiavelli, *Istorie fiorentine*, 8.36; *Chief Works*, vol. 3, p. 1433.

4 Verino, *Flametta*, 2.45; trans. from Baldassarri and Saiber (eds.), *Images of Quattrocento Florence*, p. 94.

5 Angelo Poliziano, 'Monodia in Laurentium Medicem', 13–18, in Angelo Poliziano, *Opera omnia* (Basel: Nicolaus Episcopius, 1553), pp. 621–2.

6 On the character of the circle around Lorenzo, see esp. J. Hankins, 'The Myth of the Platonic Academy of Florence', *Renaissance Quarterly* 44/3 (1991), pp. 429–47.

7 C. Atkinson, *Debts, Dowries, Donkeys: The Diary of Niccolò Machiavelli's Father, Messer Bernardo, in Quattrocento Florence* (Frankfurt am Main: Peter Lang, 2002), pp. 65–8; Machiavelli, *Istorie fiorentine*, 7.13; *Chief Works*, vol. 3, p. 1353.

8 C. E. Quillen, 'Humanism and the lure of antiquity', in J. M. Najemy (ed.), *Italy in the Age of the Renaissance* (Oxford: Oxford University Press, 2004), pp. 37–58, here p. 38.

9 Leon Battista Alberti, *I libri della famiglia*, in *Opere volgari*, C. Grayson (ed.), 3 vols. (Bari: G. Laterza & Figli, 1960–73), vol. 1, pp. 1–341, here p. 68.

10   It was unusual for boys to start at such an age, but it was not unknown. In the 1480 *catasto*, 12 per cent of those boys recorded as being *alla scuola* fell within this age range, while 6 per cent of those who are known to have been learning to read and write did so before they were seven. A. F. Verde, *Lo Studio Fiorentino 1473–1503*, 3 vols. in 4 (Florence and Pistoia: Olschki, 1973–7), vol. 3, pp. 1011–1202; P. E. Grendler, *Schooling in Renaissance Italy: Literacy and Learning, 1300–1600* (Baltimore MD and London: Johns Hopkins University Press, 1989), p. 75.

11   Grendler, *Schooling*, pp. 142–6; R. Black, *Humanism and Education in Medieval and Renaissance Italy: Tradition and Innovation in Latin Schools from the Twelfth to the Fifteenth Century* (Cambridge: Cambridge University Press, 2001), pp. 36–41.

12   For discussion, see Grendler, *Schooling*, 143.

13   Grendler, *Schooling*, 149.

14   R. Black, 'Education and the Emergence of a Literate Society', in Najemy (ed.), *Italy in the Age of the Renaissance*, pp. 18–36, here p. 20.

15   Bernardo Machiavelli, *Libro di ricordi*, Olschki (ed.) (Florence: Le Monnier, 1954), p. 31. On Matteo della Rocca, see Grendler, *Schooling*, pp. 37–8; Verde, *Lo Studio Fiorentino*, vol. 2, pp. 488–9.

16   Bernardo Machiavelli, *Libro di ricordi*, Olschki (ed.), p. 45.

17   On 8 April 1478, Bernardo borrowed a copy of Pliny the Elder's *Naturalis Historia* from Battista. This was returned on 28 May. *Ibid.*, p. 70.

18   Bernardo purchased the '*donadello*' on 6 May 1476: *ibid.*, p. 31. On the '*donadello*', see R. Black, 'New Light on Machiavelli's Education', in J.-J. Marchand (ed.), *Niccolò Machiavelli: politico, storico, letterato* (Rome: Salerno, 1996), pp. 391–8, here p. 393.

19   On the *Ianua*, see esp. Grendler, *Schooling*, pp. 174–82; Black, *Humanism and Education*, pp. 44–58.

20   Grendler, *Schooling*, p. 181.

21   Q. at *ibid.*, p. 180.

22   Battista Guarino argued that pupils should be made to repeat the paradigms they learned 'over and over', to be sure that everything was firmly engrained in their memories. Battista Guarino, *De ordine docendi et studendi*, 7; text in C. Kallendorf (ed. and trans.), *Humanist Educational Treatises* (Cambridge MA: Harvard University Press, 2002), pp. 260–309, here p. 268. The same opinion had been expressed (in almost the same words) by Battista's father. See Guarino da Verona, *Epistolario*, R. Sabbadini (ed.), 3 vols. (Venice: R. Deputazione Veneta di Storia Patria, 1915–19), vol. 2, p. 498; E. Garin (ed.), *Il pensiero pedagogico dell'umanesimo* (Florence: Sansoni, 1958), p. 344.

23 Grendler, *Schooling*, p. 35.

24 Aeneas Sylvius Piccolomini, *De liberorum educatione*, 10; trans. in Kalllendorf (ed. and trans.), *Humanist Educational Treatises*, pp. 126–259, here pp. 137–9.

25 Grendler, *Schooling*, pp. 197–9.

26 Cato, *Disticha Catonis*, 1.21.

27 *Ibid.*, 4.1.

28 For what follows, see J. M. Najemy, *A History of Florence, 1200–1575* (Oxford: Blackwell, 2008), pp. 342–3; A. Brown, 'Lorenzo and Public Opinion: The Problem of Opposition', in G. Gargagnini (ed.), *Lorenzo il Magnifico e il suo mondo* (Florence: L. S. Olschki, 1994), pp. 61–85.

29 Tommaso di Lorenzo Soderini had remained loyal to Cosimo and Piero, despite the fact that his brother, Niccolò, eventually broke with them. For a splendid discussion of the Soderini brothers, see P. C. Clarke, *The Soderini and the Medici: Power and Patronage in Fifteenth-Century Florence* (Oxford: Clarendon, 1991). On Tommaso di Lorenzo Soderini in particular, see esp. L. Martines, *April Blood: Florence and the Plot against the Medici* (Oxford: Oxford University Press, 2003), pp. 83–7.

30 Clarke, *The Soderini and the Medici*, pp. 180–96; Clarke, 'Lorenzo de' Medici and Tommaso Soderini', in G. Gargagnini (ed.), *Lorenzo de' Medici: Studi* (Florence: Olschki, 1992), pp. 67–101; N. Rubinstein, *The Government of Florence under the Medici (1434 to 1494)* (Oxford: Clarendon, 1966), p. 176.

31 On the Cento, see, for example, Najemy, *History of Florence*, p. 296; Rubinstein, *Government*, pp. 113–16, pp. 120–1, p. 127, pp. 168–70.

32 Rubinstein, *Government*, pp. 177–81.

33 *Ibid.*, pp. 181–4.

34 Benedetto Dei, *La Cronica dall'anno 1400 all'anno 1500*, R. Barducci (ed.) (Florence: Passigli, 1985), p. 114.

35 For what follows, see Najemy, *History of Florence*, pp. 347–8.

36 See R. de Roover, *The Rise and Decline of the Medici Bank: 1397–1494* (Cambridge MA: Harvard University Press, 1963), pp. 358–76; Najemy, *History of Florence*, p. 352.

37 Machiavelli, *Istorie fiorentine*, 7.10; *Chief Works*, vol. 3, pp. 1349–50. Whether the Medici's foreclosures were the sole reason for the spate of bankruptcies in 1464–5 has been questioned by de Roover, *Medici Bank*, pp. 359–60.

38 Angelo Poliziano, *Coniurationis Commentarium: Commentario della congiura dei Pazzi*, L. Perini (ed.), S. Donegà (trans.) (Florence: Florence University Press, 2012), 8; English trans. (by E. B. Welles) in B. G. Kohl and R. G. Witt (eds.), *The Earthly Republic: Italian*

Humanists on Government and Society (Philadelphia PA: University of Pennsylvania Press, 1978), pp. 305–24, here p. 307; cf. Sallust, *Cat.* 23.1.

39 See Lorenzo de' Medici, *Lettere*, R. Fubini et al. (eds.), 16 vols. (to date) (Florence: Giunti Editore, 1977–2011), vol. 2, pp. 58–9.

40 Poliziano, *Coniurationis Commentarium*, Perini (ed.), 12; Kohl and Witt (eds.), *The Earthly Republic*, p. 308.

41 Machiavelli later contended that this was, in fact, the principal cause of the conspiracy. Machiavelli, *Discorsi*, 3.6; *Chief Works*, vol. 1, p. 430.

42 On Federico da Montefeltro's involvement, see esp. R. Fubini, 'Federico da Montefeltro e la congiura dei Pazzi: politica e propaganda alla luce di nuovi documenti', in G. Chittolini, G. Cerboni Baiardi and P. Floriani (eds.), *Federico di Montefeltro: Lo stato, le arti, la cultura*, 3 vols. (Rome: Bulzoni, 1986), vol. 1, pp. 357–470; M. Simonetta, 'Federico da Montefeltro contro Firenze: retroscena inediti della congiura dei Pazzi', *ASI* 161 (2003), pp. 261–84; M. Simonetta, *The Montefeltro Conspiracy: A Renaissance Mystery Decoded* (New York: Doubleday, 2008).

43 Poliziano, *Coniurationis Commentarium*, Perini (ed.), p. 18; Kohl and Witt (eds.), *The Earthly Republic*, pp. 313–14.

44 Luca Landucci, *Diario fiorentino dal 1450 al 1516 continuato da un anonimo fino al 1542*, J. del Badia (ed.) (Florence: Sansoni, 1883), p. 18; Rubinstein, *Government*, p. 196.

45 Poliziano, *Coniurationis Commentarium*, Perini (ed.), p. 22; Kohl and Witt (eds.), *The Earthly Republic*, p. 316.

46 Machiavelli, *Arte della guerra*, 1; *Chief Works*, vol. 2, pp. 574–5, p. 582.

47 Bernardo Machiavelli, *Libro di ricordi*, Olschki (ed.), p. 75f.

48 *Ibid.*, p. 99.

49 *Ibid.*, pp. 81–4, p. 86f; Atkinson, *Debts, Dowries, Donkeys*, pp. 114–17.

50 R. Black, 'A pupil of Marcello Virgilio Adriani at the Florentine Studio', in S. U. Baldassarri, F. Ricciardelli and E. Spagnesi (eds.), *Umanesimo e Università in Toscana (1300–1600): Atti del Convegno internazionale di studi (Fiesole–Firenze, 25–26 maggio 2011)* (Florence: Le Lettere, 2012), pp. 15–32, esp. pp. 20–4.

51 See V. Arrighi, 'Machiavelli, Niccolò [di Alessandro]', *DBI*, vol. 67 (Rome, 2006), pp. 79–81.

52 Niccolò di Alessandro Machiavelli was once again elected as a prior for May–June 1493 and September–October 1499, and served as one of the *Dodici Buon' Uomini* for a second time from 15 March 1501 onwards. He also served as a *gonfaloniere* (from 8 January 1486), one of the *Conservatori di Leggi* (for a term of six months, beginning 25 September 1490, and on two further occasions), *camarlingo* of the *Monte* (from 1 July 1498), and *camarlingo* of the *Gabella delle Porte*

(from 11 October 1490). In addition, he was a member of the Cento at least twice (from 1 January 1491, and 1 July 1493). Arrighi, 'Machiavelli, Niccolò [di Alessandro]'.

53 See Black, 'A pupil of Marcello Virgilio Adriani'; S. Mercuri, 'Gli *Erudimenta grammatices* attribuiti a Benedetto Riccardini e dedicati a Niccolò e Alessandro Machiavelli (1510)', *Interpres* 32 (2014), pp. 276–89.

54 See the many examples given in R. Black, *Education and Society in Florentine Tuscany: Teachers, Pupils and Schools, c. 1250–1500* (Leiden: Brill, 2007), *passim*.

55 The text of the dedication is reprinted in Black, 'A pupil of Marcello Virgilio Adriani', pp. 21–2 n.; Mercuri, 'Gli *Erudimenta grammatices*', pp. 278–9.

56 On Mantua, see, for example, A. G. Carmichael, *Plague and the Poor in Renaissance Florence* (Cambridge: Cambridge University Press, 1986), pp. 21–2, pp. 24–5.

57 Bernardo Machiavelli, *Libro di ricordi*, Olschki (ed.), p. 63; Atkinson, *Debts, Dowries, Donkeys*, p. 49.

58 J. Henderson, *The Renaissance Hospital: Healing the Body and Healing the Soul* (New Haven CT and London: Yale University Press, 2006), p. 95.

59 *Ibid.*, p. 96.

60 E.g. A. Brown, *Bartolomeo Scala, 1430–1497, Chancellor of Florence: The Humanist as Bureaucrat* (Princeton NJ: Princeton University Press, 1979), p. 87.

61 Bernardo Machiavelli, *Libro di ricordi*, Olschki (ed.), p. 93.

62 Those who died in July and August were Bernardo's cousins, Buoninsegna and Pippa, and Guido, the son of their brother, Pietro. Bernardo Machiavelli, *Libro di ricordi*, Olschki (ed.), p. 96f; Atkinson, *Debts, Dowries, Donkeys*, p. 49, p. 160.

63 See, for example, Carmichael, *Plague and the Poor*, p. 24.

64 S. K. Cohn, Jr., *Cultures of Plague: Medical Thinking at the End of the Renaissance* (Oxford: Oxford University Press, 2010), p. 33, p. 106.

65 J. E. Shaw and E. Welch, *Making and Marketing Medicine in Renaissance Florence* (Amsterdam: Rodopi, 2011), p. 248.

66 Bernardo Machiavelli, *Libro di ricordi*, Olschki (ed.), p. 99; Atkinson, *Debts, Dowries, Donkeys*, pp. 51–2, pp. 126–8.

67 Atkinson, *Debts, Dowries, Donkeys*, p. 172.

68 Grendler, *Schooling*, pp. 306–7; Black, 'Education and the Emergence of a Literate Society', pp. 22–3.

69 Alberti, *I libri della famiglia*, in *Opere volgari*, Grayson (ed.), vol. 1, p. 71.

70 Grendler, *Schooling*, pp. 308–9; Black, *Education and Society*, p. 44, pp. 237–9, pp. 322–3.

71 Grendler, *Schooling*, p. 75.

72 Bernardo Machiavelli, *Libro di ricordi*, Olschki (ed.), p. 103.

73 Black, *Education and Society*, pp. 366–7.

74 The following paragraphs are indebted to Grendler, *Schooling*, pp. 311–19.

75 *Ibid.*, p. 312.

76 *Ibid.*, pp. 313–14.

77 C. Klapisch-Zuber, 'Le chiavi fiorentine di barbablù: l'apprendimento della lettura a Firenze nel XV secolo', *Quaderni storici* 57 (1984), pp. 765–92, here pp. 766–8; Grendler, *Schooling*, pp. 76–7.

78 Bernardo Machiavelli, *Libro di ricordi*, Olschki (ed.), p. 138; Black, 'New Light on Machiavelli's Education', p. 392.

79 On Paolo Sassi da Ronciglione, see, for example, Verde, *Lo Studio Fiorentino*, vol. 2, pp. 534–6; Black, *Education and Society*, p. 361, p. 398.

80 Grendler, *Schooling in Renaissance Italy: Literacy and Learning, 1300–1600* (Baltimore MD and London: Johns Hopkins University Press, 1989), p. 204.

81 Bernardo Machiavelli, *Libro di ricordi*, Olschki (ed.), p. 123; Atkinson, *Debts, Dowries, Donkeys*, p. 171.

82 Grendler, *Schooling*, 204.

83 Piccolomini, *De Liberorum Educatione*, p. 40, p. 72, p. 89; trans. in Kallendorf (ed. and trans.), *Humanist Educational Treatises*, pp. 178–80, p. 222, p. 244.

84 Grendler, *Schooling*, p. 223.

85 This paragraph is indebted to Grendler, *Schooling*, p. 244.

86 The text is given at A. Guidi, *Un segretario militante: politica, diplomazia e armi nel cancelliere Machiavelli* (Bologna: Il Mulino, 2009), pp. 67–8; here, I follow the amended transcription given at R. Black, 'The School of San Lorenzo, Niccolò Machiavelli, Paolo Sassi, and Benedetto Riccardini', in A. Frazier and P. Nold (eds.), *Essays in Renaissance Thought and Letters: In Honor of John Monfasani* (Leiden: Brill, 2015), pp. 107–33, here p. 111, n.25. Critino dated this exercise book to the period 1486–90.

87 The following examples are indebted to Grendler, *Schooling*, p. 232.

88 On the interpretation of the *Aeneid* in the Renaissance, see esp. C. Kallendorf, *In Praise of Aeneas: Virgil and Epideictic Rhetoric in the Early Italian Renaissance* (Hanover NH and London: University Press of New England, 1989).

89 See W. J. Connell, 'Le molestie del Machiavelli', *Interpres* 28 (2009), pp. 266–7; R. Black, 'Machiavelli and the grammarians: Benedetto

Riccardini and Paolo Sassi da Ronciglione', *ASI* 173/3 (2015), pp. 427–82, esp. pp. 460–1.

90 *Lett.* p. 371 (no. 162); *Machiavelli and his Friends*, pp. 310–11 (no. 246).

91 On the career and literary pretensions of Mattia Lupi da San Gimignano, see G. Traversari, 'Di Mattia Lupi (1380–1468) e de' suoi "Annales Geminianenses"', *Miscellanea storica della Valdelsa* 11 (1903), pp. 10–27, pp. 108–28; M. C. Davies, 'The Senator and the Schoolmaster: Friends of Leonardo Bruni in a New Letter', *Humanistica Lovaniensia* 33 (1984), pp. 1–21; G. Fioravanti, 'Librerie e lettori a San Gimignano nel '400: Onofrio Coppi e Mattia Lupi', *Interpres* 18 (1999), pp. 58–73.

92 Antonio Beccadelli, *The Hermaphrodite*, 1.16; H. Parker (ed. and trans.) (Cambridge MA and London: Harvard University Press, 2010), p. 22.

93 Beccadelli, *The Hermaphrodite*, 2.16; Parker (ed. and trans.), p. 80.

94 Beccadelli, *The Hermaphrodite*, 2:24; Parker (ed. and trans.), pp. 90–1.

95 M. Rocke, *Forbidden Friendships: Homosexuality and Male Culture in Renaissance Florence* (Oxford: Oxford University Press, 1996), p. 88.

96 E.g. Beccadelli, *The Hermaphrodite*, 1.26; Parker (ed. and trans.), p. 34.

97 See, for example, Rocke, *Forbidden Friendships*, p. 94.

98 Black, 'The School of San Lorenzo', pp. 112–13.

99 Machiavelli, *Il principe*, pr.

100 Machiavelli, *Discorsi*, 3.27.

3. From a Pygmy to a Giant (1485–98)

1 Paolo Giovio, *Elogia veris clarorum virorum imaginibus apposita*, 7; text in *Pauli Iovii Opera*, vol. 8, ed. R. Meregazzi (Rome: Istituto Poligrafico dello Stato, 1972), p. 112. See R. Black, 'Machiavelli, Servant of the Florentine Republic', in G. Bock, Q. Skinner and M. Viroli (eds.), *Machiavelli and Republicanism* (Cambridge: Cambridge University Press, 1990), pp. 71–100, here p. 74; A. della Torre, *Storia dell' Accademia Platonica* (Florence: G. Carnesecchi e Figli, 1902); A. F. Verde, *Lo Studio Fiorentino 1473–1503*, 3 vols. in 4 (Florence and Pistoia: Olschki, 1973–7), vol. 3, *passim*.

2 The university year usually began on the feast of St Luke the Evangelist (18 October): P. F. Grendler, *The Universities of the Italian Renaissance* (Baltimore MD and London: Johns Hopkins University Press, 2002), p. 143.

3 L. Martines, *Lawyers and Statecraft in Renaissance Florence* (Princeton NJ: Princeton University Press, 1968), p. 80.

4 For discussion, see J. Davies, *Florence and its University during the Early Renaissance* (Leiden: Brill, 1998), pp. 125–44.

5   See esp. Grendler, *Universities*, pp. 215–16.

6   *Lett.*, p. 371 (no. 162); *Machiavelli and his Friends*, pp. 310–11 (no. 246).

7   E.g. Grendler, *Universities*, p. 500.

8   M. Rocke, *Forbidden Friendships: Homosexuality and Male Culture in Renaissance Florence* (Oxford: Oxford University Press, 1996), p. 107, p. 140.

9   Grendler, *Universities*, pp. 148–9; Davies, *Florence and its University*, p. 32.

10   Verde, *Studio Fiorentino*, vol. 4.2, pp. 632–40. For further discussion of Bartolomeo della Fonte at the Studio, see R. Zaccaria, 'Della Fonte, Bartolomeo', *DBI*, vol. 36 (Rome, 1988), pp. 808–14. On Poliziano's course on Juvenal, see also V. Branca, *Poliziano e l'umanesimo della parola* (Turin: Einaudi, 1983), p. 86, n.22; Grendler, *Universities*, p. 238.

11   Verde, *Studio Fiorentino*, vol. 4.2, pp. 685–94; Branca, *Poliziano*, p. 86, n.22; Grendler, *Universities*, p. 238.

12   Verde, *Studio Fiorentino*, vol. 4.2, pp. 771–5. For further discussion of the date of della Fonte's lectures on Juvenal, see A. F. Verde, 'Un terzo soggiorno romano del Poliziano', *Rinascimento* 22 (1982), p. 260; Verde, *Studio Fiorentino*, vol. 2, pp. 84–91.

13   Poliziano, who lectured on Terence's comedies in 1484–5, is unlikely to have been an influence, but the text was frequently on the university syllabus. S. Bertelli and F. Gaeta, 'Noterelle machiavelliane: un codice di Lucrezio e di Terenzio', *RSI* 73 (1961), pp. 544–53; B. Richardson, 'Evoluzione stilistica e fortuna della traduzione machiavelliana dell' *Andria*', *Lettere Italiane* 25 (1973), pp. 319–38, here p. 321, n.5; Verde, *Studio Fiorentino*, vol. 4.2, pp. 598–9; Grendler, *Universities*, p. 238; Branca, *Poliziano*, p. 86, n.22. For Poliziano's commentary on Terence's *Andria*, see Angelo Poliziano, *La commedia antica e l'*Andria *di Terenzio*, ed. R. Lattanzi Roselli (Florence: Sansoni, 1973).

14   For some of the more critical views of Machiavelli's early poetry, see A. Casadei, 'Note Machiavelliane', *Annali della Scuola Normale Superiore di Pisa*, classe lettere e filosofia, 3rd ser., 17 (1987), pp. 447–64, here p. 450; Niccolò Machiavelli, *Capitoli*, ed. G. Inglese (Rome: Bulzoni, 1981), p. 24; C. Dionisotti, *Machiavellerie: Storia e fortuna di Machiavelli* (Turin: Einaudi, 1980), p. 67.

15   Text in Niccolò Machiavelli, *Tutte le opere*, M. Martelli (ed.) (Florence: Sansoni, 1971), pp. 994–7.

16   Text in *ibid.*, p. 994.

17   Robert Black (*Machiavelli* [Abingdon, 2013], 27) translates ll. 1–3 as 'If I had bow and wings, Young Giulio, You would be the god

whom every man assails.' But, while this is grammatically possible, it makes no sense in the context. It is clear that *avessi* must be read as a second person singular, and that *ch'. . . assale* must pick up *giovanetto giulio.*

18 Text in Machiavelli, *Tutte le opere*, Martelli (ed.), pp. 997–8.

19 Della Torre, *Storia dell'Accademia Platonica*, p. 10ff; R. Riccardi, 'Baldi, Pietro del Riccio (Petrus Crinitus)', *DBI*, vol. 38 (Rome, 1990), pp. 265–8.

20 For what follows, see esp. N. Rubinstein, *The Government of Florence under the Medici (1434 to 1494)* (Oxford: Oxford University Press, 1966), pp. 229–35; J. Najemy, *A History of Florence, 1200–1575* (Oxford: Blackwell, 2008), pp. 375–80.

21 Francesco Guicciardini, *Storie fiorentine*, 11, R. Palmarocchi (ed.) (Bari: G. Laterza & Figli, 1934), p. 94.

22 Q. at R. Trexler, *Public Life in Renaissance Florence* (Ithaca NY and London: Cornell University Press, 1980), p. 461.

23 See esp. Guicciardini, *Storie fiorentine*, 10, Palmarocchi (ed.), pp. 84–6; Rubinstein, *Government*, pp. 230–1.

24 See, for example, Najemy, *History of Florence*, p. 375, pp. 391–2.

25 D. Weinstein, *Savonarola: The Rise and Fall of a Renaissance Prophet* (New Haven CT and London: Yale University Press, 2011), pp. 106–7; A. Brown, 'The Revolution of 1494 and Its Aftermath: A Reassessment', in J. Everson and D. Zancani (eds.), *Italy in Crisis – 1494* (Oxford: Legenda, 2000), pp. 13–39, esp. pp. 15–22.

26 Guicciardini, *Storie fiorentine*, 11; Palmarocchi (ed.), p. 94; M. E. Mallett and C. Shaw, *The Italian Wars, 1494–1559: War, State and Society in Early Modern Europe* (London and New York: Routledge, 2012), pp. 20–1.

27 Piero Parenti, *Storia fiorentina*, A. Matucci (ed.), 2 vols. (Florence: Olschki, 1994–2005), vol. 1, p. 103; Najemy, *History*, p. 377.

28 Weinstein, *Savonarola*, pp. 107–8.

29 The comparison with Lorenzo's mission to Naples is made explicit at Guicciardini, *Storie fiorentine*, 11; Palmarocchi (ed.), p. 95.

30 Parenti, *Storia*, vol. 1, p. 117; Guicciardini, *Storie fiorentine*, 11, Palmarocchi (ed.), pp. 95–6.

31 Guicciardini, *Storie fiorentine*, 11; Palmarocchi (ed.), p. 96.

32 Parenti, *Storia*, vol. 1, p. 117.

33 Luca Landucci, *Diario fiorentino dal 1450 al 1516 continuato da un anonimo fino al 1542*, J. del Badia (ed.) (Florence: Sansoni, 1883), p. 72.

34 *Ibid.*, pp. 74–5; Guicciardini, *Storie fiorentine*, 11, Palmarocchi (ed.), pp. 97–8.

35 Rubinstein, *Government*, pp. 234–5.

36 Machiavelli, *Il principe*, 12.

37 See, for example, R. A. Goldthwaite, *The Economy of Renaissance Florence* (Baltimore: Johns Hopkins University Press, 2009), p. 43, pp. 115–16, p. 119, pp. 149–51, p. 158, p. 174, p. 182, p. 186, p. 188, p. 193, p. 490, p. 514, p. 519, pp. 531–2, pp. 534–5, p. 591, pp. 595–6, p. 599.

38 Weinstein, *Savonarola*, p. 112.

39 Parenti, *Storia*, vol. 1, p. 129.

40 Landucci, *Diario*, p. 79.

41 Machiavelli, *Clizia*, 1.1; *Chief Works*, vol. 2, p. 826.

42 Landucci, *Diario*, p. 82.

43 On Savonarola's involvement, see Weinstein, *Savonarola*, pp. 116–17.

44 Landucci, *Diario*, p. 83, p. 86; for the treaty itself, see G. Capponi, 'Capitoli fatti dalla città di Firenze col re Carlo VIII, a dì 25 novembre del 1494', *ASI* 1 (1842), pp. 362–75.

45 Landucci, *Diario*, p. 87.

46 Guicciardini, *Storie fiorentine*, 12, Palmarocchi (ed.), p. 106; Parenti, *Storia*, vol. 1, p. 150. For discussion, see N. Rubinstein, 'Politics and Constitution in Florence at the End of the Fifteenth Century', in E. F. Jacob (ed.), *Italian Renaissance Studies* (London: Faber & Faber, 1960), pp. 148–83.

47 For what follows, see Weinstein, *Savonarola*, pp. 121–5.

48 *Ibid.*, p. 121.

49 For further discussion of the 'Venetian model', see F. Gilbert, 'The Venetian Constitution in Florentine Political Thought', in N. Rubinstein (ed.), *Florentine Studies: Politics and Society in Renaissance Florence* (London: Faber, 1968), pp. 463–500.

50 Parenti, *Storia*, vol. 1, pp. 156–9; Najemy, *History*, pp. 385–6; Weinstein, *Savonarola*, pp. 125–6.

51 G. Guidi, *Ciò che accade al tempo della Signoria di novembre–dicembre in Firenze l'anno 1494* (Florence: Arnaud, 1988). See also N. Rubinstein, 'I primi anni del Consiglio Maggiore di Firenze, 1494–1499', *ASI* 112 (1954), pp. 151–94, pp. 321–47.

52 See particularly L. Polizzotto, *The Elect Nation: The Savonarolan Movement in Florence, 1494–1545* (Oxford: Clarendon, 1994), esp. pp. 14–20, pp. 446–60.

53 On Francesco Valori's transition from *ottimato* to arch-Savonarolan, see esp. M. Jurdjevic, *Guardians of Republicanism: The Valori Family in the Florentine Renaissance* (Oxford: Oxford University Press, 2008), pp. 19–46.

54 See, for example, D. Weinstein, *Savonarola and Florence: Prophesy and Patriotism in the Renaissance* (Princeton NJ: Princeton University Press, 1970), pp. 185–226.

55 Giorgio Vasari, *Lives of the Artists*, G. Bull (trans.), 2 vols. (London: Penguin, 1987), vol. 1, p. 227.

56 Rocke, *Forbidden Friendships*, p. 205.

57 Girolamo Savonarola, *Selected Writings of Girolamo Savonarola*, A. Borelli and M. Pastore Passaro (trans. and ed.) (New Haven CT and London: Yale University Press, 2006), p. 256.

58 Ascanio Condivi, *Vita di Michelangelo Buonarroti*, G. Nencioni (ed.) (Florence: Studio per Edizioni Scelte, 1998), p. 62. For discussion of Michelangelo's relationship with Savonarola, see, for example, M. Hirst, *Michelangelo*, vol. 1 *The Achievement of Fame, 1475–1534* (New Haven CT and London: Yale University Press, 2011), pp. 25–6.

59 See D. Weinstein, 'Machiavelli and Savonarola', in M. Gilmore (ed.), *Studies on Machiavelli* (Florence: Sansoni, 1972), pp. 251–64.

60 Machiavelli, *Discorsi*, 1.11, 1.45; *Decennale primo*, 157–9; *Opere*, Bonfantini (ed.), p. 125, p. 186, p. 1052; *Chief Works*, vol. 1, p. 226, p. 288; vol. 3, p. 1448.

61 Machiavelli, *Il principe*, 12.

62 Machiavelli, *Discorsi*, 1.45; *Opere*, Bonfantini (ed.), p. 186; *Chief Works*, vol. 1, p. 288; Weinstein, *Savonarola*, pp. 133–4.

63 Rocke, *Forbidden Friendships*, pp. 207–21; Weinstein, *Savonarola*, pp. 155–7.

64 *Lett.*, pp. 28–9 (no. 2); *Machiavelli and his Friends*, pp. 7–8 (no. 2).

65 *Lett.*, p. 27 (no. 1); *Machiavelli and his Friends*, pp. 6–7 (no. 1).

66 Text in Casadei, 'Note Machiavelliane', pp. 450–1. For discussion, see esp. *ibid.*, pp. 451–3.

67 The original Italian (l.13: *fatti abbiàn becchi che paion d'acegge*) is, admittedly, somewhat obliquely expressed. But Gilbert seems wide of the mark in translating it as 'we have got beaks that seem like those of woodcocks' (*Chief Works*, vol. 2, p. 1012). Black's 'we have grown beaks that seem to be of woodcocks' scarcely makes any more sense (Black, *Machiavelli*, p. 24). Although it might be argued that Niccolò wanted to suggest that he and his friends were pecking like birds, woodcocks do not peck, but instead use their beaks to search for invertebrates in the ground, making a digging or probing action. That woodcock's beaks are remarkably thin, however, seems to be the point of the comparison.

68 This was the first of two occasions on which Machiavelli translated the *Andria*. For many years, it was thought that the earliest version was produced in 1517/18. Recent analysis has revealed that Machiavelli's orthography is more typical of the period 1494–8. See P. Stoppelli, 'La datazione dell'*Andria*', in G. Barbarisi and A. M. Cabrini (eds.), *Il teatro di Machiavelli* (Milan: Cisalpino, 2005), pp. 147–99; P. Stoppelli, *La Mandragola: Storia e Filologia* (Rome: Bulzoni Editore, 2005), pp. 33–6. The text of the first version is published at Stoppelli, 'La datazione', pp. 166–99.

69   For discussion, see esp. M. Martelli, 'La Versione Machiavelliana dell' *Andria*', *Rinascimento*, 2nd ser., 8 (1968), pp. 203–73.

70   E.g. Stoppelli, 'La datazione', p. 174, p. 176; cf. Terence, *Andria*, 2.1.330, 2.2.369.

71   Stoppelli, 'La datazione', p. 170; cf. Terence, *Andria*, 1.2.184.

72   Stoppelli, 'La datazione', p. 196; cf. Terence, *Andria*, 5.4.914.

73   Terence, *Andria*, 1.2.194.

74   Stoppani, 'La datazione', p. 170.

75   On Marcello di Virgilio di Andrea di Berto Adriani's life and career to 1498, see P. Godman, *From Poliziano to Machiavelli: Florentine Humanism in the High Renaissance* (Princeton NJ: Princeton University Press, 1998), pp. 144–67.

76   R. Black, 'Florentine Political Traditions and Machiavelli's Election to the Chancery', *Italian Studies* 41 (1985), pp. 1–16, here p. 12.

77   A. Brown, *Bartolomeo Scala, 1430–1497, Chancellor of Florence: The Humanist as Bureaucrat* (Princeton NJ: Princeton University Press, 1979), p. 202.

78   Verde, *Studio Fiorentino*, vol. 3.2, p. 620.

79   *Ibid.*, vol. 3.1, pp. 421–2.

80   For what follows, I am deeply indebted to Peter Godman's masterly analysis of Adriani's *prolusiones*: Godman, *From Poliziano to Machiavelli*, pp. 151–67. See also A. Brown, *The Return of Lucretius to Renaissance Florence* (Cambridge MA and London: Harvard University Press, 2010), pp. 42–67.

81   See Verde, *Studio Fiorentino*, vol 4.3, pp. 1160–3.

82   *Ibid.*, vol. 4.3, pp. 1205–8.

83   Florence, Biblioteca Riccardiana MS 811, fol. 8v; q. Lucretius 5.958–61. Trans. q. at Brown, *Return of Lucretius*, 44.

84   Florence, Biblioteca Riccardiana MS 811, fol. 20r; ref. to Plato, *Laws*, 682b–c; *Tim.* 23a; Lucretius 5.330–1; Brown, *Return of Lucretius*, p. 71; A. Brown, 'Philosophy and Religion in Machiavelli', in J. M. Najemy (ed.), *The Cambridge Companion to Machiavelli* (Cambridge: Cambridge University Press, 2010), pp. 157–72, here p. 161; Godman, *From Poliziano to Machiavelli*, p. 166; Verde, *Studio Fiorentino*, vol. 4.3, p. 1313.

85   Godman, *From Poliziano to Machiavelli*, pp. 138–9, p. 166; Florence, Biblioteca Riccardiana MS 811, fol. 23v.

86   The transcription is found in Rome, Biblioteca Vaticana MS Rossi 884. See Bertelli and Gaeta, 'Noterelle machiavelliane'; S. Bertelli, 'Noterelle machiavelliane: ancora su Lucrezio e Machiavelli', *RSI* 76 (1964), pp. 774–90. For more detailed analysis, see esp. Brown, *Return of Lucretius*, pp. 68–87, esp. pp. 74–5.

87   In what follows, I am indebted to the splendid discussion in Brown, 'Philosophy and Religion', p. 162; *Return of Lucretius*, pp. 68–72.

88 Rome, Biblioteca Vaticana MS Rossi 884, fol. 32r: '*deos non curare mortalia*'.

89 *Ibid.*, fol. 25v: '*in seminibus esse pondus, plagas et clinamen*'.

90 *Ibid.*, fol. 25r: '*motum varium esse et ex eo nos liberam habere mentem*'.

91 A. Gherardi, *Nuovi documenti intorno a Girolamo Savonarola*, 2nd ed. (Florence: Sansoni, 1887), pp. 154–6; Weinstein, *Savonarola*, pp. 219–20.

92 Parenti, *Storia*, vol. 2, pp. 83–4.

93 Landucci, *Diario*, p. 147; Parenti, *Storia*, vol. 2, pp. 98–9; Guicciardini, *Storie fiorentine*, 15, Palmarocchi (ed.), pp. 132–3.

94 Parenti, *Storia*, vol. 2, p. 100.

95 Landucci, *Diario*, pp. 147–8; see Weinstein, *Savonarola*, pp. 224–5.

96 For what follows, see Landucci, 148; Parenti, *Storia*, vol. 2, pp. 101–3.

97 E.g. Guicciardini, *Storie fiorentine*, 15, Palmarocchi (ed.), p. 135. On which see A. Brown, 'Partiti, correnti, o coalizioni: un contributo al dibattito', in A. Fontes, J.-L. Fournel and M. Plaisance (eds.), *Savonarole: Enjeux, Débats, Questions. Actes du Colloque International (Paris, 25–26–27 Janvier 1996)* (Paris: Université de la Sorbonne Nouvelle, 1997), pp. 59–79, here pp. 67–70; A. Brown, 'Ideology and Faction in Savonarolan Florence', in S. Fletcher and C. Shaw (eds.), *The World of Savonarola: Italian Elites and Perceptions of Crisis* (Aldershot: Ashgate Publishing Ltd., 2000), pp. 22–41, here pp. 28–9.

98 Landucci, *Diario*, pp. 152–3; Parenti, *Storia*, vol. 2, p. 110.

99 See Brown, *Bartolomeo Scala*, pp. 115–34.

100 Landucci, *Diario*, pp. 155–6; Parenti, *Storia*, vol. 2, pp. 119–20. For the 'peacemakers' appointed in July, see Parenti, *Storia*, vol. 2, pp. 117–18.

101 Parenti, *Storia*, vol. 2, pp. 121–2.

102 *Ibid.*, vol. 2, p. 124.

103 Weinstein, *Savonarola*, p. 243; G. Cadoni, *Lotte politiche e riforme istituzionali a firenze tra il 1494 ed il 1502* (Rome: Istituto Storico Italiano per il Medio Evo, 1999), pp. 54–5.

104 Bartolomeo Cerretani, *Storia fiorentina*, ed. G. Berti (Florence: Olschki, 1994), p. 238.

105 Machiavelli, *Discorsi*, 1.45; *Chief Works*, vol. 1, pp. 288–9.

106 On the 'envy' of Savonarola's opponents, see Machiavelli, *Discorsi*, 3.30; *Chief Works*, vol. 1, p. 497.

107 Polizzotto, *Elect Nation*, p. 48; S. Bertelli, 'Machiavelli e la politica estera fiorentina', in Gilmore (ed.), *Studies on Machiavelli*, pp. 29–72, here p. 57.

108 Machiavelli, *Decennale primo*, 160–2; *Chief Works*, vol. 3, p. 1448.

109 See D. Marzi, *La cancelleria della repubblica fiorentina* (Rocca San Casciano: Licinio Cappelli, 1910), pp. 278–86.

110 N. Rubinstein, 'The beginnings of Niccolò Machiavelli's career in the Florentine chancery', *Italian Studies* 11 (1956), pp. 72–91.

111 On the evolution of the first and second chancellorships in the fifteenth century, see, for example, R. Black, *Benedetto Accolti and the Florentine Renaissance* (Cambridge: Cambridge University Press, 2009), pp. 115–37; Marzi, *La cancelleria*, pp. 188–277, esp. pp. 211–14, pp. 236–44; F. P. Luiso, 'Riforma della cancelleria fiorentina nel 1437', *ASI*, 5th ser., 21 (1898), pp. 132–41.

112 E.g. *Machiavelli and his Friends*, p. 6; M. Viroli, *Niccolò's Smile: A Biography of Machiavelli*, A. Shugaar (trans.) (New York: Farrar, Straus and Giroux, 2001), p. 30; G. Inglese, *Per Machiavelli. L'arte dello stato, la cognizione delle storie* (Rome: Carocci, 2006), p. 11.

113 Rubinstein, 'The beginnings', p. 83; Black, *Machiavelli*, p. 35.

114 Weinstein, *Savonarola*, pp. 258–9.

115 For what follows, see *Cons. e prat. 1498–1505*, vol. 1, pp. 45–60. For discussion, see Godman, *From Poliziano to Machiavelli*, pp. 168–9; Weinstein, *Savonarola*, pp. 260–1. On divisions, see esp. Polizzotto, *Elect Nation*, p. 11ff.

116 Gherardi, *Nuovi documenti*, pp. 201–3.

117 Parenti, *Storia*, vol. 2, p. 173; Marzi, *La cancelleria*, p. 288.

4 The New Republic (June 1498–February 1499)

1 P. Villari, *Machiavelli e i suoi tempi*, 2nd ed., 3 vols. (Milan: Hoepli, 1895–7), vol. 1, p. 321; trans. from Villari, *The Life and Times of Niccolò Machiavelli*, 4 vols. (London: Fisher Unwin, 1878), vol. 2, p. 21.

2 *Lett.*, p. 77 (no. 25); *Machiavelli and His Friends*, p. 51 (no. 35).

3 V. Arrighi, 'Della Valle, Antonio', *DBI*, vol. 37 (Rome, 1989), *ad voc.* See also A. Brown, *Bartolomeo Scala, 1430–1497, Chancellor of Florence: The Humanist as Bureaucrat* (Princeton NJ: Princeton University Press, 1979), p. 124, p. 141, p. 179, p. 187, p. 192, p. 205, p. 242, p. 255, p. 256; D. Marzi, *La cancelleria della repubblica fiorentina* (Rocca San Casciano: Licinio Cappelli, 1910), p. 251, p. 255, p. 256, p. 259, p. 268. Black is strangely wide of the mark in suggesting that he was among the 'new' chancery staff: R. Black, 'Machiavelli, Servant of the Florentine Republic', in G. Bock, Q. Skinner and M. Viroli (eds.), *Machiavelli and Republicanism* (Cambridge: Cambridge University Press, 1990), pp. 71–100, here p. 84.

4 See esp. Marzi, *La cancelleria*, p. 268.

5 *Ibid.*, p. 251, pp. 254–6, p. 268, p. 284.

6 On Biagio, see esp. D. Fachard, *Biagio Buonaccorsi* (Bologna: M. Boni, 1976).

7   On Biagio's taste for dice and card games, see, for example, *Lett.*, p. 60 (no. 16); *Machiavelli and his Friends*, p. 31 (no. 18).

8   On Agostino Vespucci's career, see Marzi, *La cancelleria*, pp. 287–8, p. 292, p. 300, p. 317, p. 478.

9   *Lett.*, p. 60 (no. 16); *Machiavelli and his Friends*, p. 31 (no. 18).

10   *Ibid.* In a letter written between 20 and 29 October 1500, Agostino Vespucci related that, despite his diligence, Biagio, too, was warming 'to dice and *ronfa* playing, although Antonio della Valle keeps calling him his own tender little dove.' 'For this reason,' Vespucci continued, 'and because he never throws Venus, not out of licentiousness, he has made a complete vow with this same Antonio not to play until dawn.'

11   Piero Parenti, *Storia fiorentina*, A. Matucci (ed.), 2 vols. (Florence: Olschki, 1994–2005), vol. 2, pp. 187–8.

12   See esp. S. Bertelli, 'Embrioni di partiti politici alle soglie dell'età moderna', in S. Bertelli (ed.), *Per Federico Chabod (1901–1960)*, 2 vols. (Perugia: Università di Perugia, 1980–1), vol. 1, pp. 17–35.

13   J. M. Najemy, *A History of Florence, 1200–1575* (Oxford: Blackwell, 2008), p. 400.

14   Parenti, *Storia*, vol. 2, pp. 187–8.

15   *Ibid.*, vol. 2, p. 189; Luca Landucci, *Diario fiorentino dal 1450 al 1516 continuato da un anonimo fino al 1542*, J. del Badia (ed.) (Florence: Sansoni, 1883), p. 182.

16   See esp. L. F. Marks, 'La crisi finanziaria a Firenze dal 1494 al 1502', *ASI* 112 (1954), pp. 40–72; F. Gilbert, *Machiavelli and Guicciardini: Politics and History in Sixteenth-Century Florence* (Princeton NJ: Princeton University Press, 1965), pp. 58–9.

17   L. Martines, *Lawyers and Statecraft in Renaissance Florence* (Princeton NJ: Princeton University Press, 1968), p. 258.

18   See Gilbert, *Machiavelli and Guicciardini*, p. 59.

19   E.g. Landucci, *Diario*, p. 179.

20   On Ottaviano Riario's arrival in Florence with his troops on 28 June 1498, see *ibid.*, p. 181; Parenti, *Storia*, vol. 2, p. 187. On Jacopo d'Appiano, see esp. P. Pieri, 'Appiano, Iacopo', *DBI*, vol. 3 (Rome, 1961), pp. 629–31; E. Irace, 'Iacopo d'Appiano', *Enciclopedia Machiavelliana*, 3 vols. (Rome: Istituto della Enciclopedia Italiana, 2014), vol. 1, pp. 78–80.

21   Landucci, *Diario*, p. 182.

22   *Ibid.*, p. 183; Parenti, *Storia*, vol. 2, p. 192; Francesco Guicciardini, *Storie fiorentine*, 17, R. Palmarocchi (ed.) (Bari: G. Laterza & Figli, 1934), p. 165.

23   Landucci, *Diario*, p. 184; Guicciardini, *Storie fiorentine*, 17, Palmarocchi (ed.), p. 166.

24 Landucci, *Diario Fiorentino*, J. del Badia (ed.), p. 185; Guicciardini, *Storie fiorentine*, 17, Palmarocchi (ed.), p. 166. Cf. Machiavelli, *Discorsi*, 3.18; *Chief Works*, vol. 1, p. 473.

25 Landucci, *Diario*, p. 185; Machiavelli, *Discorsi*, 3.18; *Chief Works*, vol. 1, p. 473.

26 Landucci, *Diario*, p. 189; Guicciardini, *Storie fiorentine*, 17, Palmarocchi (ed.), pp. 167–8.

27 Landucci, *Diario*, p. 189.

28 See M. E. Mallett and C. Shaw, *The Italian Wars* (London and New York: Routledge, 2012), p. 43.

29 L.-G. Pélissier, 'Sopra alcuni documenti relativi all'alleanza tra Alessandro VI e Luigi XII, 1498–1499', *Archivio della R. Società romana di storia patria* 17 (1894), pp. 303–73, and 18 (1895), pp. 99–215, here 18 (1895), p. 133. On Cesare's marriage and the Franco-papal 'alliance', see also Guicciardini, *Storie fiorentine*, 17, Palmarocchi (ed.), pp. 160–1, pp. 168–9.

30 Landucci, *Diario*, pp. 192–3.

31 *Ibid.*, p. 193.

32 R. Black, *Benedetto Accolti and the Florentine Renaissance* (Cambridge: Cambridge University Press, 1985), pp. 118–22, pp. 164–5; 'Machiavelli, Servant of the Florentine Republic', 78; R. Black, *Machiavelli* (Abingdon: Routledge, 2013), pp. 37–8. On his responsibilities, see also Marzi, *La cancelleria*, pp. 188–277, esp. pp. 211–14, pp. 236–44; F. P. Luiso, 'Riforma della cancelleria fiorentina nel 1437', *ASI* 5th ser., 21 (1898), pp. 132–41.

33 Marzi, *La cancelleria*, p. 289; Rubinstein, 'The beginnings of Niccolò Machiavelli's career in the Florentine chancery', *Italian Studies* 11 (1956), pp. 72–91, here p. 73.

5. The First Tests (March–July 1499)

1 See M. E. Mallett and C. Shaw, *The Italian Wars, 1494–1559: War, State and Society in Early Modern Europe* (London and New York: Routledge, 2012), p. 42.

2 See esp. M. Mallett, *Mercenaries and Their Masters: Warfare in Renaissance Italy*, new. ed. (Barnsley: Pen & Sword, 2009).

3 Machiavelli, *Discorsi*, 3.18.

4 *Leg. e comm.*, p. 11.

5 On 28 December 1498, Pisan soldiers had captured Montopoli in Val d'Arno, some five kilometres east of Pontadera, and pillaged it. On 21 January 1499, they had even made a raid into the Valdinievole, further to the north-east. Luca Landucci, *Diario fiorentino dal 1450 al*

1516 continuato da un anonimo fino al 1542, J. del Badia (ed.) (Florence: Sansoni, 1883), pp. 191–2.

6 Antonio da Venafro's remarks may be found at Niccolò Machiavelli, *Opere storiche*, A. Montevecchi and C. Varotti (eds.), 2 vols. (Rome: Salerno, 2010), p. 952. For the high esteem in which Machiavelli held the Sienese chancellor, see Machiavelli, *Il principe*, 22.

7 For what follows, see *Leg. e comm.*, pp. 11–12.

8 See Landucci, *Diario*, pp. 193–4, p. 195; Giovanni Cambi, *Istorie fiorentine*, I. di San Luigi (ed.), 4 vols., *Delizie degli eruditi toscani*, 20–23 (Florence: Gaetano Cambiagi, 1785–6), vol. 2, pp. 139–40.

9 Landucci, *Diario*, p. 194.

10 *Ibid.*, p. 195.

11 *Ibid.*

12 *Lett.* p. 34 (no. 4); *Machiavelli and His Friends*, pp. 13–14 (no. 4).

13 *Lett.*, p. 35 (no. 4); *Machiavelli and His Friends*, 14 (no. 4).

14 Text in Niccolò Machiavelli, *Opere*, M. Bonfantini (ed.) (Milan and Naples: R. Ricciardi, 1954), pp. 423–7.

15 *Ibid.*, p. 423.

16 *Ibid.*

17 *Ibid.*, p. 424.

18 Landucci, *Diario*, p. 196.

19 *Ibid.*

20 *Ibid.*

21 *Lett.* p. 37 (no. 5); *Machiavelli and His Friends*, p. 15 (no. 5).

22 Landucci, *Diario*, p. 197.

23 *Lett.* p. 38 (no. 6); *Machiavelli and His Friends*, p. 16 (no. 6).

24 *Lett.* p. 37 (no. 5), p. 38 (no. 6); *Machiavelli and His Friends*, p. 15 (no. 5), p. 16 (no. 6).

25 *Lett.* p. 38 (no. 6); *Machiavelli and His Friends*, p. 16 (no. 6).

26 *Lett.* p. 37 (no. 5); *Machiavelli and His Friends*, 15 (no. 5).

27 On Antonio Guidotti da Colle's career in the chancellery, see D. Marzi, *La cancelleria della repubblica fiorentina* (Rocca San Casciano: Licinio Cappelli, 1910), p. 257, p. 267, p. 295, p. 407.

28 Q. at *Leg. e comm.*, pp. 16–17.

29 *Leg. e comm.*, Ibid., pp. 21–4.

30 *Ibid.*, 26–7.

31 *Ibid.*, *Leg. e comm.*, p. 28.

32 *Lett.*, p. 43 (no. 8); *Machiavelli and His Friends*, p. 19 (no. 8).

33 On Caterina's career, see esp. N. Graziani and G. Venturelli, *Caterina Sforza* (Milan: Mondadori, 2001).

34 *Leg. e comm.*, p. 33.

35 *Ibid.*, pp. 29–30.

36 For what follows, see *Ibid.*, pp. 30–3.
37 *Ibid.*, pp. 25–6.
38 For the following, see *Ibid.*, pp. 34–6.
39 *Ibid.*, p. 36.
40 *Ibid.*, p. 36.
41 *Ibid.*, pp. 40–2.
42 *Ibid.*, p. 41.
43 *Lett.*, pp. 39–45 (nos. 7–9); *Machiavelli and His Friends*, pp. 17–20 (nos. 7–9). At *Leg. e comm.*, p. 43, p. 46, Niccolò states that letters from Adriani, dated 19 and 20 July, had reached him on 23 July. It seems likely that the two letters Biagio wrote to him on 19 July (*Machiavelli and His Friends*, pp. 17–19 (nos. 7–8)) were dispatched by the same courier. It is, however, possible that a further letter from Biagio, written on or shortly after 20 July (*Machiavelli and His Friends*, pp. 19–20 (no. 9)), arrived at the same time.
44 *Lett.*, p. 43 (no. 8); *Machiavelli and His Friends*, p. 19 (no. 8).
45 *Lett.*, pp. 39–41 (no. 7); *Machiavelli and His Friends*, pp. 17–18 (no. 7).
46 *Lett.*, p. 41 (no. 7); *Machiavelli and His Friends*, p. 18 (no. 7).
47 Cf. Landucci, *Diario*, pp. 197–8; Francesco Guicciardini, *Storie fiorentine*, 18, R. Palmarocchi (ed.) (Bari: G. Laterza & Figli, 1934), p. 180.
48 *Leg. e comm*, pp. 37–40.
49 *Ibid.*, pp. 38–40.
50 *Ibid.*, pp. 37–8.
51 *Ibid.*, p. 37.
52 *Ibid.*, p. 46.
53 *Ibid.*, p. 43.
54 *Ibid.*, pp. 43–4.
55 *Ibid.*, pp. 44–5.
56 *Ibid.*, p. 45.
57 *Ibid.*, pp. 46–7.
58 *Ibid.*, p. 47.
59 *Lett.*, pp. 46–7 (no. 10); *Machiavelli and His Friends*, pp. 21–2 (no. 10).
60 *Leg. e comm.*, pp. 47–8.
61 *Lett.*, p. 47 (no. 10); *Machiavelli and His Friends*, p. 21 (no. 10).

6. The Fog of War (August 1499–July 1500)

1 On 31 July 1499, Landucci reported that the camp was pitched before Pisa by 11:00 p.m. Luca Landucci, *Diario fiorentino dal 1450 al 1516 continuato da un anonimo fino al 1542*, J. del Badia (ed.) (Florence, 1883), p. 198.
2 *Machiavelli and His Friends*, p. 21 (no. 10).

3   Landucci, *Diario*, p. 198.
4   *Ibid.*; Piero Parenti, *Storia fiorentina*, A. Matucci (ed.), 2 vols. (Florence: Olschki, 1994–2005), vol. 2, p. 282.
5   Parenti, *Storia*, vol. 2, p. 282.
6   Landucci, *Diario*, p. 199.
7   *Ibid.*; Parenti, *Storia*, vol. 2, p. 288, pp. 289–90.
8   See esp. Parenti, *Storia*, vol. 2, p. 281, p. 289.
9   *Ibid.*, vol. 2, pp. 291–2.
10 Niccolò alluded to this in his letter to the commissioners in the field on 1 September 1499.
11 Q. at P. Villari, *Machiavelli e i suoi tempi*, 2nd ed., 3 vols. (Milan: Hoepli, 1895–7), vol. 1, p. 340; P. Villari, *The Life and Times of Niccolò Machiavelli*, trans. L. Villari, 4 vols. (London: Fisher Unwin, 1878), vol. 2, p. 43.
12 Landucci, *Diario*, p. 200.
13 Parenti, *Storia*, vol. 2, p. 290.
14 *Ibid.*, vol. 2, p. 290, p. 293.
15 *Ibid.*, vol. 2, pp. 291–2.
16 Landucci, *Diario*, p. 200.
17 *Ibid.*, p. 201; Parenti, *Storia*, vol. 2, p. 297; Niccolò Machiavelli, *Scritti inediti di Niccolò Machiavelli risguardanti la storia e la milizia (1499–1512)*, G. Canestrini (ed.) (Florence: Barbèra Bianchi e Comp, 1857), p. 73 (letter of 4 Sept. 1499); *LCSG*, p. 221. For further discussion of the events leading up to the arrest of Paolo Vitelli, and Machiavelli's various accounts of them, see, for example, F. Chiappelli, 'Guicciardini, Machiavelli e il caso di Paolo', *Annali d'Italianistica* 2 (1984), pp. 53–63, here pp. 54–5.
18 Machiavelli, *Scritti inediti*, pp. 85–6; *LCSG*, pp. 228–9.
19 Landucci, *Diario*, p. 201.
20 Machiavelli alludes to Paolo Vitelli's 'deceit' in a letter to the commissioners on 27 October (Machiavelli, *Scritti inediti*, p. 118–19; *LCSG*, p. 259–60), and again in the *Decennale primo*, 229.
21 Machiavelli, *Scritti inediti*, pp. 95–6; *LCSG*, pp. 236–7.
22 Landucci, *Diario*, p. 202; Parenti, *Storia*, vol. 2, pp. 302–3; cf. D. Fachard, *Biagio Buonaccorsi* (Bologna: M. Boni, 1976), p. 136; Machiavelli, *Scritti inediti*, p. 98 (letter to Borgo Rinaldi, 29 September 1499); *LCSG*, p. 239.
23 Parenti, *Storia*, vol. 2, pp. 303–5.
24 *Ibid.*, vol. 2, p. 305.
25 *Ibid.*, vol. 2.
26 Landucci, *Diario*, p. 202.
27 Machiavelli, *Scritti inediti*, pp. 99–100; *LCSG*, p. 240.

28 *Lett.*, pp. 48–51 (no. 11); *Machiavelli and His Friends*, pp. 22–3 (no. 11).

29 See esp. the letters to the commissioners in the field on 5 and 7 October 1499 – *Scritti inediti*, pp. 102–6; *LCSG*, pp. 241–3.

30 *Ibid.*, p. 76; *LCSG*, pp. 223–4.

31 The treaty was signed on 12 October 1499. The text may be found in G. Molini (ed.), *Documenti di storia italiana*, 2 vols. (Florence: Tipografia all' Insegna di Dante, 1836–7), vol. 1, pp. 32–6 (doc. 14).

32 *Leg. e comm.*, pp. 55–6. Cf. the Signoria's letter to Sacierges, *Leg e comm.*, pp. 56–7.

33 For Niccolò's credentials, see *Leg. e comm.*, p. 57. On the arrival of the news, see Landucci, *Diario*, p. 206.

34 For the following, see esp. M. E. Mallett and C. Shaw, *The Italian Wars, 1494–1559: War, State and Society in Early Modern Europe* (London and New York: Routledge, 2012), p. 52.

35 Landucci, *Diario*, p. 209.

36 *Ibid.*, p. 210. In May 1500, Louis did suggest that Venice should join him in conquering Lucca and other 'faithless' allies, including the duchy of Ferrara. Mallett and Shaw, *The Italian Wars*, p. 54.

37 Landucci, *Diario*, pp. 210–11.

38 Mallett and Shaw, *The Italian Wars*, p. 56.

39 Machiavelli, *Decennale primo*, 121.

40 Machiavelli, *Discorsi*, 2.16. For his view of their fighting methods, see, for example, Machiavelli, *Arte della guerra*, 3; *Chief Works*, vol. 2, pp. 628–9, p. 639, p. 641.

41 Note esp. Landucci, *Diario*, pp. 212–13.

42 Niccolò Machiavelli, *Opere*, P. Fanfani, G. Milanesi, L. Passerini (eds.), 6 vols. (Florence: Cenniniana, 1873–77), vol. 3, pp. 52–3.

43 *Ibid.*, vol. 3, p. 54.

44 *Ibid.*, vol. 3, pp. 56–8.

45 *Ibid.*, vol. 3, pp. 58–9.

46 *Ibid.*, vol. 3, p. 55.

47 Machiavelli, *Decennale primo*, 277–8.

7. *La Chasse* (July–December 1500)

1 *Lett.*, p. 53 (no. 13); *Machiavelli and His Friends*, p. 26 (no. 13).

2 *Lett.*, p. 61 (no. 16); *Machiavelli and His Friends*, p. 32 (no. 18).

3 E.g. *Lett.*, p. 57 (no. 14); *Machiavelli and His Friends*, p. 28 (no. 14).

4 On Luca degli Albizzi's fondness for Niccolò, see, for example, *Lett.*, p. 53 (no. 13); *Machiavelli and His Friends*, p. 26 (no. 13).

5 *Leg. e comm.*, pp. 70–5.

6   *Ibid.*, p. 86.

7   *Ibid.*

8   *Ibid.*, pp. 81–3.

9   *Ibid.*, p. 82; cf. Jean d'Auton, *Chroniques de Louis XII*, R. de Maulde La Clavière (ed.), 4 vols. (Paris: Renouard, 1889–95), vol. 1, pp. 312–13.

10   *Leg. e comm.*, pp. 85–6.

11   *Ibid.*, p. 83.

12   *Ibid.*, pp. 76–81.

13   *Ibid.*, p. 78.

14   *Ibid.*, p. 81.

15   *Ibid.*

16   *Ibid.*, p. 93.

17   D'Auton, *Chroniques*, vol. 1, p. 313.

18   *Leg. e comm.*, p. 93.

19   *Ibid.*, p. 94.

20   *Ibid.*, pp. 92–3, p. 94.

21   *Ibid.*, p. 97.

22   *Ibid.*

23   *Ibid.*, p. 98.

24   *Ibid.*, pp. 98–9.

25   *Ibid.*, pp. 99–100.

26   *Ibid.*, p. 100.

27   *Ibid.*, pp. 100–1.

28   *Ibid.*, p. 102.

29   *Ibid.*, p. 101, p. 103.

30   *Ibid.*, p. 103.

31   *Ibid.*, pp. 103–6.

32   *Ibid.*, pp. 107–9.

33   *Ibid.*, pp. 110–11.

34   *Ibid.*, p. 111.

35   *Lett.*, p. 53 (no. 13); *Machiavelli and His Friends*, p. 26 (no. 13).

36   *Leg. e comm.*, p. 112. Niccolò's complaints at receiving a smaller allowance than Francesco are at *Leg. e comm.*, pp. 106–7.

37   *Machiavelli and His Friends*, p. 26 (no. 13).

38   *Lett.*, p. 55 (no. 13); *Machiavelli and His Friends*, p. 27 (no. 13).

39   D'Auton, *Chroniques*, vol. 1, p. 313; *Leg. e comm.*, p. 112, p. 116.

40   D'Auton, *Chroniques*, vol. 1, p. 313; *Leg. e comm.*, p. 117.

41   *Leg. e comm.*, pp. 117–18.

42   *Ibid.*, pp. 119–20.

43   *Ibid.*, p. 120.

44   *Ibid.*, p. 134.

45   *Ibid.*, p. 134.

46 *Ibid.*, p. 135.
47 *Ibid.*, pp. 140–4.
48 *Ibid.*, p. 141.
49 See G. Mattingly, *Renaissance Diplomacy* (Boston: Houghton Mifflin, 1955), pp. 26–33.
50 On Gualterotti, see, for example, V. Arrighi, 'Gualterotti, Francesco', *DBI*, vol. 60 (Rome, 2003), *ad voc.*
51 *Machiavelli and His Friends*, pp. 28–9 (no. 14).
52 For the following, see J. M. Najemy, *A History of Florence, 1200–1575* (Oxford: Blackwell, 2008), pp. 402–3.
53 See G. Cadoni, *Lotte politiche e riforme istituzionali a Firenze tra il 1494 ed il 1502* (Rome: Istituto Storico Italiano per il Medio Evo, 1999), pp. 114–16.
54 Francesco Guicciardini, *Storie fiorentine*, 18, R. Palmarocchi (ed.) (Bari: G. Laterza & Figli, 1934), pp. 177–8.
55 For a marvellously thorough discussion of Pistoiese factionalism and its ramifications for political divisions in Florence, see W. J. Connell, *La città dei crucci: fazioni e clientele in uno stato repubblicano del '400* (Florence: Nuova Toscana, 2000), *passim.*
56 E.g. Landucci, *Diario*, p. 214.
57 On 14 September, Niccolò and Francesco indicated that the king was to leave the following day; but on 26 September, they claimed that he had departed from Melun on the same day. The latter report seems to be the result of a faulty memory. *Leg. e comm.*, p. 146, p. 155.
58 *Leg. e comm.*, p. 155.
59 *Ibid.*
60 *Ibid.*, pp. 167–73.
61 For the election of the *Dieci*, see *ibid.*, pp. 146–9; for Niccolò's receipt of this despatch, see *ibid.*, p. 158.
62 *Lett.*, pp. 58–9 (no. 15); *Machiavelli and His Friends*, pp. 30–1 (no. 17).
63 *Ibid.*
64 *Leg. e comm.*, pp. 157–8.
65 *Lett.*, p. 62 (no. 16); *Machiavelli and His Friends*, pp. 32–3 (no. 18).
66 *Leg. e comm.*, p. 176.
67 *Ibid.*, pp. 183–4.
68 *Machiavelli and His Friends*, p. 33 (no. 19).
69 *Leg.e comm.*, pp. 179–82.
70 *Ibid.*, pp. 184–5.
71 *Ibid.*, pp. 185–6.
72 *Ibid.*, pp. 186–7.
73 *Ibid.*, pp. 201–2.
74 *Ibid.*, pp. 202–3.
75 *Ibid.*, pp. 203–4.

76 *Ibid.*, pp. 204–5.

77 *Ibid.*, p. 205.

78 *Ibid.*, pp. 205–6.

79 *Ibid.*, p. 207.

80 *Ibid.*, p. 208.

81 *Ibid.*, p. 206; *Machiavelli and His Friends*, p. 35 (no. 21). Tosinghi left Lyon on 15 November, and was at Moulins seven days later.

82 *Leg. e comm.*, p. 208.

83 *Ibid.*, pp. 208–9.

84 *Ibid.*, p. 209.

85 *Ibid.*, p. 212.

8. The Gathering Storm (January–October 1501)

1 *Lett.*, p. 56 (no. 13); *Machiavelli and His Friends*, p. 27 (no. 13).

2 *Lett.*, p. 56 (no. 13); *Machiavelli and His Friends*, p. 28 (no. 13).

3 *Lett.*, p. 60 (no. 16); *Machiavelli and His Friends*, p. 31 (no. 18).

4 E.g. Piero Parenti, *Storia fiorentina*, A. Matucci (ed.), 2 vols. (Florence: Olschki, 1994–2005), vol. 2, p. 413.

5 W. J. Connell, *La città dei crucci: fazioni e clientele in uno stato repubblicano del '400* (Florence: Nuova Toscana, 2000), p. 160.

6 Machiavelli, *Discorsi*, 3.27; *Chief Works*, vol. 1, p. 489.

7 Francesco Guicciardini, *Storie fiorentine*, 20, R. Palmarocchi (ed.) (Bari: G. Laterza & Figli, 1934), p. 207. According to Parenti, Carnesecchi was also a 'peaceful man': Parenti, *Storia*, vol. 2, p. 408.

8 Machiavelli, *Opere*, P. Fanfani, G. Milanesi, L. Passerini (eds.), 6 vols. (Florence: Cenniniana, 1873–77), vol. 3, pp. 249–50.

9 See Machiavelli, *Opere*, Fanfani et al. (eds.), vol. 3, p. 250n.

10 Luca Landucci, *Diario fiorentino dal 1450 al 1516 continuato da un anonimo fino al 1542*, J. del Badia (ed.) (Florence: Sansoni, 1883), p. 220.

11 *Ibid.*; cf. Parenti, *Storia*, vol. 2, p. 422.

12 Landucci, *Diario*, p. 221.

13 That year, Easter fell on 14 April.

14 On Soderini's coalition-building efforts, see Guicciardini, *Storie fiorentine*, 20, Palmarocchi (ed.), p. 209.

15 Parenti, *Storia*, vol. 2, pp. 423–4, p. 428; Machiavelli, *Opere*, Fanfani et al. (eds.), vol. 3, pp. 259–62. Niccolò wrote his kinsman's letters patent in his own hand (*Opere*, ed. Fanfani et al., 3:262–3).

16 Parenti, *Storia*, vol. 2, p. 424.

17 Machiavelli, *Opere*, Fanfani et al. (eds.), vol. 3, p. 268.

18 Landucci, *Diario*, p. 221.

19 See Parenti, *Storia*, vol. 2, pp. 429–30.

20 Machiavelli, *Opere*, Fanfani et al. (eds.), vol. 3, pp. 299–302.

21 Landucci, *Diario*, p. 221.

22 *Ibid.*, p. 222; Parenti, *Storia*, vol. 2, pp. 414–15, pp. 430–1.

23 Landucci, *Diario*, p. 222.

24 Machiavelli, *Opere*, Fanfani et al. (eds.), vol. 3, pp. 304–5.

25 S. Bertelli, 'Machiavelli and Soderini', *Renaissance Quarterly* 28/1 (1975), pp. 1–16, here p. 6; see also Machiavelli, *Opere*, Fanfani et al. (eds.), vol. 3, pp. 308–10.

26 Parenti, *Storia*, vol. 2, p. 438.

27 Guicciardini, *Storie fiorentine*, 21, Palmarocchi (ed.), p. 212; cf. Parenti, *Storia*, vol. 2, p. 439; Piero Vaglienti, *Storia dei suoi tempi, 1492–1514*, G. Berti, M. Luzzati and E. Tongiorgi (eds.) (Pisa: Nistri-Lischi e Pacini, 1982), p. 131; Bertelli, 'Machiavelli and Soderini', p. 7. See also S. Bertelli, 'Constitutional Reforms in Renaissance Florence', *Journal of Medieval and Renaissance Studies* 3 (1973), pp. 139–64, here pp. 161–4.

28 Landucci, *Diario*, p. 222.

29 *Ibid.*

30 Parenti, *Storia*, vol. 2, p. 440.

31 Landucci, *Diario*, p. 223.

32 Parenti, *Storia*, vol. 2, p. 440, pp. 441–2; Landucci, *Diario*, p. 223.

33 Parenti, *Storia*, vol. 2, p. 442; Landucci, *Diario*, pp. 223–4.

34 Landucci, *Diario*, p. 224.

35 *Ibid.*, pp. 225–6.

36 Machiavelli, *Opere*, Fanfani et al. (eds.), vol. 3, pp. 314–15; cf. Parenti, *Storia*, vol. 2, p. 444; Landucci, *Diario*, p. 225.

37 See, for example, Parenti, *Storia*, vol. 2, p. 447.

38 Landucci, *Diario*, p. 227.

39 Parenti, *Storia*, vol. 2, p. 449.

40 Landucci, *Diario*, p. 228.

41 *Ibid.*

42 See M. E. Mallett and C. Shaw, *The Italian Wars, 1494–1559: War, State and Society in Early Modern Europe* (London and New York: Routledge, 2012), p. 58.

43 Landucci, *Diario*, p. 229. For further details of the king's army, see Mallett and Shaw, *The Italian Wars*, p. 59.

44 Landucci, *Diario*, pp. 230–1.

45 *Ibid.*, p. 231.

46 *Ibid.*, pp. 229–30; Parenti, *Storia*, vol. 2, p. 452.

47 See Mallett and Shaw, *The Italian Wars*, p. 59.

48 See, for example, Parenti, *Storia*, vol. 2, pp. 458–9.

49 *Ibid.*, vol. 2, pp. 460–1.

50 Landucci, *Diario*, p. 232.

51 As Parenti reported, the Cancellieri had retained the services of

Count Bernardino da Marciano, while the Panciatichi had employed Count Guido dal Monte. Parenti, *Storia*, vol. 2, p. 468.

52 Machiavelli, *Opere*, Fanfani et al. (eds.), vol. 3, pp. 330–1; Parenti, *Storia*, vol. 2, p. 467.

53 Landucci, *Diario*, pp. 234–5.

54 Parenti, *Storia*, vol. 2, p. 468; Landucci, *Diario*, p. 235.

55 Landucci, *Diario*, p. 235.

56 Parenti, *Storia*, vol. 2, p. 469.

57 *Ibid.*, vol. 2, pp. 469–50. The ambassadors were Francesco Soderini, bishop of Volterra, and Luca degli Albizzi.

58 See esp. D. Herlihy and C. Klapisch-Zuber, *Tuscans and Their Families: A Study of the Florentine Catasto of 1427* (New Haven CT: Yale University Press, 1985), pp. 202–11.

59 For a discussion of the date of Niccolò's marriage to Marietta, see R. Ridolfi, *Vita di Niccolò Machiavelli*, 3rd ed., 2 vols. (Florence: Sansoni, 1969), vol. 1, pp. 74–5, vol. 2, p. 439, n.10; J. Kirshner and A. Molho, 'Niccolò Machiavelli's Marriage', *Rinascimento* 18 (1978), pp. 293–5. Cf. *Machiavelli and His Friends*, p. 42, p. 50 (nos. 25, 33). For Marietta's life and family, see S. Moretti, 'Corsini, Marietta', *Enciclopedia Machiavelliana* (Rome: Istituto della Enciclopedia Italiana, 2014), *ad voc.*; R. Zaccaria, 'Note su Marietta Corsini e la sua famiglia', in L. Bertolini and D. Coppini (eds.), *Nel Cantiere degli Umanisti: per Mariangela Regiolisi*, 3 vols. (Florence: Polistampa, 2014), pp. 1353–67. A very brief account is also to be found at L. Passerini, *Genealogia e storia della famiglia Corsini* (Florence: Cellini, 1858), p. 24, but the accompanying family tree is inaccurate.

60 On the rituals of marriage, see, for example, E. Muir, *Ritual in Early Modern Europe* (Cambridge: Cambridge University Press, 1997), pp. 31–41; C. Klapisch-Zuber, *Women, Family, and Ritual in Renaissance Italy*, L. Cochrane (trans.) (Chicago IL and London: University of Chicago Press, 1985), pp. 178–260.

61 A part of the dowry was eventually paid on 22 August 1501: Kirshner and Molho, 'Niccolò Machiavelli's Marriage'.

62 Francesco Barbaro, *On Wifely Duties*, trans. in B. G. Kohl and R. G. Witt (eds.), *The Earthly Republic: Italian Humanists on Government and Society* (Philadelphia PA: University of Pennsylvania Press, 1978), pp. 189–228, here p. 192.

63 *Ibid.*, pp. 215–20.

64 *Ibid.*, p. 208.

65 *Ibid.*, p. 202.

66 *Ibid.*, p. 196.

67 *Ibid.*, p. 194.

68 Franco Sacchetti, *Il Trecentonovelle*, E. Faccioli (ed.) (Turin: Einaudi, 1970), p. 233.

69 See esp. M. Rocke, 'Gender and Sexual Culture in Renaissance Italy', in J. C. Brown and R. C. Davis (eds.), *Gender and Society in Renaissance Italy* (London and New York: Longman, 1998), pp. 150–70.

70 Machiavelli, *Opere*, Fanfani et al. (eds.), vol. 3, pp. 358–9.

71 See Connell, *La città dei crucci*, pp. 216–17.

72 Note Landucci's enthusiasm: Landucci, *Diario*, p. 235.

73 Parenti, *Storia*, vol. 2, p. 472.

74 See, for example, W. J. Connell and G. Constable, *Sacrilege and Redemption in Renaissance Florence: The Case of Antonio Rinaldeschi* (Toronto: Centre for Reformation and Renaissance Studies, 2005), p. 55.

75 Parenti, *Storia*, vol. 2, p. 475.

76 This brief mission is attested only by the record of payments made to Niccolò for his diplomatic efforts on 30 October 1501. In this frustratingly concise document, it is recorded that he travelled to Pistoia at the Signoria's orders, ostensibly as a courier (*staffetta*). That he would also have been required to gather information at such a time of uncertainty is evident. Machiavelli, *Opere*, Fanfani et al. (eds.), vol. 3, p. 332n.

77 For what follows, see esp. Connell, *La città dei crucci*, pp. 217–22.

78 Machiavelli, *Opere*, Fanfani et al. (eds.), vol. 3, pp. 332–3.

79 For Valori's letters patent, see *ibid.*, p. 334. See also Parenti, *Storia*, vol. 2, p. 479; M. Jurdjevic, *Guardians of Republicanism: The Valori Family in the Florentine Renaissance* (Oxford: Oxford University Press, 2008), p. 55. On Niccolò's involvement, see Machiavelli, *Opere*, Fanfani et al. (eds.), vol. 3, p. 332n. et seq.

80 Machiavelli, *Opere*, Fanfani et al. (eds.), vol. 3, pp. 353–4.

81 That Niccolò returned by this date is borne out by a letter which he wrote on the prior's behalf on 28 October. This stated that he had delivered Valori's letters, together with his own report, at a meeting of the priors the previous morning (27 October), meaning that he would most likely have arrived the day before. Machiavelli, *Opere*, Fanfani et al. (eds.), vol. 3, p. 349.

9. The Whirlwind (October 1501–July 1502)

1 M. E. Mallett and C. Shaw, *The Italian Wars, 1494–1559: War, State and Society in Early Modern Europe* (London and New York: Routledge, 2012), pp. 61–2.

2 See esp. K. M. Setton, *The Papacy and the Levant, 1204–1571*, 4 vols.

(Philadelphia PA: The American Philosophical Society, 1976–84), vol. 2, pp. 526–33.

3　See, for example, R. Sabatini, *The Life of Cesare Borgia* (London: Stanley Paul, 1912), pp. 268–70, pp. 280–6; M. Bellonci, *Lucrezia Borgia*, B. and B. Wall (trans.) (London: Phoenix Press, 2000), pp. 148–70.

4　An anonymous pamphlet (published in the form of a letter to Silvio Savelli) alleged that, at one party in the Vatican, Cesare and his father caroused with fifty of Rome's finest prostitutes, while Lucrezia looked on. Sabatini, *The Life of Cesare Borgia*, pp. 271–8.

5　Piero Parenti, *Storia fiorentina*, Matucci (ed.), 2 vols. (Florence: Olschki, 1994–2005), vol. 2, p. 478.

6　On Pistoia esp., see *ibid.*, vol. 2, p. 479. For Valori's letter to Niccolò (dated 30 October 1501), see *Machiavelli and His Friends*, pp. 43–4 (no. 27).

7　Parenti, *Storia*, vol. 2, pp. 479–80.

8　For a discussion of Pisa's relations with the Borgias in late 1501 to early 1502, see G. Volpe, 'Intorno ad alcune relazioni di Pisa con Alessandro VI e Cesare Borgia', *Studi Storici* 6 (1897), pp. 495–547, here pp. 540–7; and 7 (1898), pp. 61–107, here pp. 61–9.

9　See, for example, G.-R. Tewes, *Kampf um Florenz: die Medici im Exil (1494–1512)* (Cologne and Weimar: Böhlau Verlag, 2011), p. 563.

10　Parenti, *Storia*, vol. 2, p. 481.

11　*Ibid.*, vol. 2, p. 482.

12　*Ibid.*, vol. 2, p. 481.

13　*Ibid.*, vol. 2, pp. 482–3.

14　*Ibid.*, vol. 2, p. 483.

15　Luca Landucci, *Diario fiorentino dal 1450 al 1516 continuato da un anonimo fino al 1542*, J. del Badia (ed.) (Florence, 1883), pp. 237–8; Parenti, *Storia*, vol. 2, p. 484; Biagio Buonaccorsi, *Diario* (Florence: Giunti, 1568), p. 51.

16　Landucci, *Diario*, p. 238; Parenti, *Storia*, vol. 2, p. 484; Buonaccorsi, *Diario*, p. 51.

17　Parenti, *Storia*, vol. 2, p. 488.

18　Landucci, *Diario*, p. 238.

19　Parenti, *Storia*, vol. 2, p. 488.

20　On the Signoria's fears, see esp. *ibid.*, vol. 2, pp. 488–9.

21　W. J. Connell, *La città dei crucci: fazioni e clientele in uno stato repubblicano del '400* (Florence: Nuova Toscana, 2000), p. 221f; Parenti, *Storia*, vol. 2, p. 497; Landucci, *Diario*, p. 238.

22　Machiavelli, *Opere*, P. Fanfani, G. Milanesi, L. Passerini (eds.), 6 vols. (Florence: Cenniniana, 1873–77), vol. 3, pp. 352–5.

23 The text of the '*De rebus pistoriensibus*' is published in Machiavelli, *Opere*, Fanfani et al. (eds.), vol. 3, pp. 352–5; J.-J. Marchand, *Niccolò Machiavelli: I primi scritti politici* (Padua: Antenore, 1975), pp. 409–11.

24 These are published in Machiavelli, *Opere*, Fanfani et al. (eds.), vol. 3, pp. 355–7. As Marchand rightly points out, since the only surviving manuscript of these texts is not in Niccolò's own hand, neither can be attributed to him with any certainty; but, it does not seem unreasonable to suppose that, having written the *De rebus pistoriensibus*, he would also have offered his advice about how best to proceed in separate documents. That the suggestions contained therein also appear to chime well with his later views would seem to recommend such a view. Marchand, *I primi scritti politici*, p. 45 n.9.

25 Machiavelli, *Opere*, Fanfani et al. (eds.), vol. 3, pp. 355–6.

26 *Ibid.*, vol. 3, pp. 356–7.

27 Parenti, *Storia*, vol. 2, p. 498.

28 On 20 January 1502, Vitellozzo Vitelli had already assured the Pisans that he would soon be advancing further towards Florentine territory. Volpe, 'Intorno a alcune relazioni', *Studi Storici* 6 (1897), p. 543.

29 Landucci, *Diario*, p. 239; Buonaccorsi, *Diario*, p. 54; Parenti, *Storia*, vol. 2, pp. 498–9; G. Cambi, *Istorie fiorentine*, I. di San Luigi (ed.), 4 vols., *Delizie degli eruditi toscani*, 20–23 (Florence: Gaetano Cambiagi, 1785–6), vol. 2, p. 170.

30 Buonaccorsi, *Diario*, p. 54, p. 56.

31 Landucci, *Diario*, p. 239.

32 Ridolfi seems wide of the mark in suggesting that the Florentines were able to obtain this agreement more cheaply than they had expected because Louis XII was afraid they might ally against him with Maximilian. (R. Ridolfi, *Vita di Niccolò Machiavelli*, 3rd ed., 2 vols. (Florence: Sansoni, 1969), vol. 1, p. 75.) It is, of course, true that Maximilian had been planning to venture into Italy with a view to receiving an imperial coronation in Rome, and had already despatched ambassadors to Florence (e.g. Landucci, *Diario*, p. 238; Buonaccorsi, *Diario*, p. 52; Parenti, *Storia*, vol. 2, pp. 492–5). But this appears to have had little effect on the course of negotiations with France. Not only did the priors decide to see how things went with Louis XII before giving Maximilian an answer, but they also ended up paying the king *more* than they had originally been prepared to offer. (Parenti, *Storia*, vol. 2, pp. 492–5.)

33 Buonaccorsi, *Diario*, p. 49.

34 Landucci, *Diario*, p. 239.

35 Jacopo Nardi, *Istorie della città di Firenze*, A. Gelli (ed.), 2 vols. (Florence: Le Monnier, 1858), vol. 1, p. 272.
36 *Leg. e comm.*, p. 241.
37 *Ibid.*, p. 239.
38 Landucci, *Diario*, p. 239.
39 *Ibid.*, p. 240.
40 *Ibid.*, p. 241.
41 *Ibid.*, p. 240.
42 Machiavelli, *Decennale primo*, 331–3; *Chief Works*, vol. 3, p. 1452.
43 Landucci, *Diario*, p. 241; Jacopo Pitti, *Istoria fiorentina*, 1.254–6, A. Mauriello (ed.) (Naples, 2007), p. 87.
44 Landucci, *Diario*, p. 241; Pitti, *Istoria*, 1.258; Mauriello (ed.), 88.
45 Landucci, *Diario*, p. 242.
46 *Ibid.*, p. 243.
47 *Ibid.*, p. 242.
48 *Ibid.*
49 *Ibid.*
50 *Annales Arretinorum maiores et minores: aa. 1192–1343*, A. Bini and G. Grazzini (eds.), *RIS* 2nd ser. 24.1 (Città di Castello: Lapi, 1909), p. 179. The *Dieci* was re-established on 10 June. Its members were Piero di Tommaso Soderini, Piero di Iacopo Guicciardini, Niccolò di Simone Zati, Giuliano di Francesco Salviati, Antonio di Iacopo Tebalducci, Filippo d'Andrea Carducci, Pierfrancesco di Francesco Tosinghi, Luca di Maso degli Albizzi, Giovanni di Sancti Ambruogi, and Lorenzo di Niccolò Benintendi.
51 Landucci, *Diario*, p. 243.
52 *Ibid.*
53 For Soderini's credentials, see *Leg. e comm.*, pp. 255–6.
54 *Ibid.*, p. 256.
55 *Ibid.*, pp. 256–7.
56 *Ibid.*, pp. 260–1.
57 *Ibid.*, p. 261.
58 *Ibid.*, p. 262.
59 *Ibid.*
60 *Ibid.*, pp. 262–3.
61 *Ibid.*, p. 263.
62 *Ibid.*, pp. 263–4.
63 *Ibid.*
64 *Ibid.*, p. 264.
65 *Ibid.*, pp. 259–60.
66 *Ibid.*, p. 264.
67 *Ibid.*
68 *Ibid.*, p. 265.

69 *Ibid.*

70 *Ibid.*, p. 266.

71 *Ibid.*, pp. 266–7.

72 *Ibid.*, p. 267.

73 *Ibid.*, p. 268.

74 *Ibid.*

75 *Ibid.*, p. 267, p. 271, pp. 273–4.

76 *Ibid.*, p. 279.

77 *Ibid.*, pp. 278–9.

78 Landucci, *Diario*, p. 245.

79 *Leg. e comm.*, pp. 275–7.

80 *Ibid.*, pp. 280–1.

81 *Ibid.*, p. 281.

82 *Ibid.*

83 *Ibid.*, pp. 282–3.

84 *Ibid.*, p. 283.

85 *Ibid.*, pp. 284–6.

86 On 4 July, Landucci reported that 'there were painted on the houses of the *gonfaloniere* [Filippo d'Andrea di Niccolò Carducci], of Piero Soderini, and Madonna Strozzi, pictures of gallows and all manner of other disgraceful things.' Landucci, *Diario*, p. 246; cf. Cambi, *Istorie*, vol. 2, p. 174.

87 Landucci, *Diario*, p. 246.

88 *Leg. e comm.*, p. 289.

89 *Ibid.*, pp. 292–3.

90 Landucci, *Diario*, p. 246.

91 *Leg. e comm.*, p. 297.

92 *Ibid.*; Landucci, *Diario*, pp. 246–7.

93 *Leg. e comm.*, p. 295, p. 296.

94 *Ibid.*, pp. 297–9.

95 *Ibid.*, p. 300.

96 *Ibid.*, p. 301.

97 *Ibid.*, pp. 306–7.

98 *Ibid.*, pp. 302–4.

99 *Ibid.*, pp. 304–5.

100 *Ibid.*, pp. 308–9.

101 Francesco Soderini's letter to Luca degli Albizzi may be found at *ibid.*, p. 320.

102 *Ibid.*, pp. 310–11.

103 *Ibid.*, pp. 311–12.

104 *Ibid.*, p. 316.

105 *Ibid.*, p. 303, pp. 317–18.

106 *Ibid.*, p. 317.

107 *Ibid.*, pp. 318–19.
108 Sabatini, *The Life of Cesare Borgia*, pp. 302–3.
109 Machiavelli, *Decennale primo*, 352–4; *Chief Works*, vol. 3, p. 1452.
110 *Leg. e comm.*, pp. 267–8.

10. The Eye of the Storm (August 1502–January 1503)

1 Jean d'Auton, *Chroniques de Louis XII*, R. de Maulde La Clavière (ed.), 4 vols. (Paris: Renouard, 1889–95), vol. 3, p. 28, pp. 30–1; R. Sabatini, *The Life of Cesare Borgia* (London: Stanley Paul, 1912), p. 337; M. E. Mallett and C. Shaw, *The Italian Wars, 1494–1559: War, State and Society in Early Modern Europe* (London and New York: Routledge, 2012), p. 75.

2 On 9 August 1502, Niccolò informed Antonio Giacomini that Cesare was attempting to place the blame on Vitellozzo Vitelli: Machiavelli, *Scritti inediti di Niccolò Machiavelli risguardanti la storia e la milizia (1499–1512)*, G. Canestrini (ed.) (Florence: Barbèra Bianchi, 1857), p. 23.

3 See Sabatini, *The Life of Cesare Borgia*, p. 338.

4 For what follows, see esp. F. Gilbert, *Machiavelli and Guicciardini: Politics and History in Sixteenth-Century Florence* (Princeton NJ: Princeton University Press, 1965), pp. 70–4; J. M. Najemy, *A History of Florence, 1200–1575* (Oxford: Blackwell, 2008), pp. 406–7; G. Cadoni, *Lotte politiche e riforme istituzionali a Firenze tra il 1494 ed il 1502* (Rome: Istituto Storico Italiano per il Medio Evo, 1999), pp. 155–70.

5 Q. at Gilbert, *Machiavelli and Guicciardini*, p. 71.

6 For the following, see esp. R. Pesman Cooper, 'L'elezione di Pier Soderini a gonfaloniere a vita', *ASI* 125 (1967), pp. 145–85.

7 G. Canestrini and A. Desjardins (eds.), *Négociations diplomatiques de la France avec la Toscane*, 6 vols. (Paris: Imprimerie Impériale / Imprimerie Nationale, 1859–86), vol. 1, pp. 321–4; vol. 2, pp. 15–21, pp. 31–4.

8 K. J. P. Lowe, *Church and Politics in Renaissance Italy: The Life and Career of Cardinal Francesco Soderini, 1453–1524* (Cambridge: Cambridge University Press, 1993), p. 34.

9 *Machiavelli and His Friends*, p. 47 (no. 29).

10 *Ibid.*, p. 48 (no. 31) [amended].

11 For an overview of early sixteenth-century child-rearing, see, for example, R. M. Bell, *How to Do It: Guides to Good Living for Renaissance Italians* (Chicago IL: University of Chicago Press, 1999), pp. 124–45.

12 There is no documentary evidence that the Machiavelli employed a

wet nurse for Primerana. It does, however, seem likely. It was, after all, quite common practice for well-born families in this period. That Marietta gave birth to her second child in November 1503 seems to suggest that a wet nurse had indeed been hired. Since sex while breastfeeding was frowned upon and female children were generally not weaned until they were eighteen months old, it seems more than probable that, if Marietta conceived at some point in February 1503, she was *not* nursing Primerana herself. It has been suggested that, in Florence at least, men were responsible for choosing wet nurses. See C. Klapisch-Zuber, *Women, Families, and Ritual in Renaissance Italy*, L. Cochrane (trans.) (Chicago IL: University of Chicago Press, 1985), pp. 132–64, here pp. 143–4. This view has, however, been disputed: e.g. L. Haas, 'Women and Childbearing in Medieval Florence', in C. Jorgensen Itnyre (ed.), *Medieval Family Roles: A Book of Essays* (New York: Garland, 1996), pp. 87–99, here p. 96. On the birth of the Machiavelli's second child, Bernardo, see chapter 11, 'The Wind Changes'.

13 Sabatini, *The Life of Cesare Borgia*, pp. 339–40.

14 On which, see Mallett and Shaw, *The Italian Wars*, pp. 62–3.

15 Sabatini, *The Life of Cesare Borgia*, pp. 339–40.

16 Niccolò Machiavelli, '*Descrizione del modo tenuto dal Duca Valentino nello ammazzare Vitellozzo Vitelli, Oliverotto da Fermo, il Signor Pagolo e il Duca di Gravina Orsini*', in *Opere*, M. Bonfantini (ed.) (Milan and Naples: R. Ricciardi, 1954), pp. 457–64, here p. 457; J.-J. Marchand, *Niccolò Machiavelli: I primi scritti politici* (Padua: Antenore, 1975), pp. 420–6, here p. 420; *Chief Works*, vol. 1, p. 163.

17 Those present were Viellozzo Vitelli, Paolo Orsini (together with his kinsmen Cardinal Giovanni Battista Orsini and Francesco Orsini, duke of Gravina), Oliverotto da Eufreducci, Giampaolo Baglioni, the *signore* of Perugia, and Antonio da Venafro (representing Pandolfo Petrucci). Also in attendance were Ottaviano Fregoso, representing Guidobaldo da Montefeltro, the erstwhile duke of Urbino, and Ermes Bentivoglio, standing in for his father, Giovanni, the tyrant of Bologna. See Bertelli's notes at *Leg. e comm.*, pp. 324–5; Francesco Matarazzo, *Cronaca della città di Perugia dal 1492 al 1503*, F. Bonaini and F. Polidori (eds.), *ASI* 16/2 (1851), pp. 1–243, here p. 204. Note also Machiavelli, 'Descrizione del modo', in *Opere*, Bonfantini (ed.), p. 458; Marchand, *I primi scritti politici*, p. 420; *Chief Works*, vol. 1, p. 164.

18 That the rebels wished to dispose of Cesare has been suggested by Sabatini, *The Life of Cesare Borgia*, p. 343. For criticism of this view, see, for example, Bertelli's comments at *Leg. e comm.*, p. 324.

19 Machiavelli, 'Descrizione del modo', in *Opere*, Bonfantini (ed.),

p. 458; Marchand, *I primi scritti politici*, p. 421; *Chief Works*, vol. 1, p. 164.

20 On the risings in the duchy of Urbino, see esp. Bernardino Baldi, *Della vita e de' fatti di Guidobaldo I da Montefeltro duca d'Urbino*, 7; C. de' Rosmini (ed.), 2 vols. (Milan: Giovanni Silvestri, 1821), vol. 2, pp. 7–8.

21 Machiavelli, 'Descrizione del modo', in *Opere*, Bonfantini (ed.), p. 458; Marchand, *I primi scritti politici*, p. 421; *Chief Works*, vol. 1, p. 164.

22 *Ibid.*; *Leg. e comm.*, p. 336.

23 *Leg. e comm.*, p. 335.

24 *Lett.*, p. 74 (no. 23); *Machiavelli and His Friends*, p. 50 (no. 33).

25 *Lett.*, p. 78 (no. 25); *Machiavelli and His Friends*, p. 52 (no. 35).

26 *Leg. e comm.*, pp. 335–7.

27 For the following, see *Leg. e comm.*, pp. 339–43. A partial translation may be found at *Chief Works*, vol. 1, pp. 121–3.

28 *Leg. e comm.*, pp. 344–5.

29 *Ibid.*, pp. 352–3.

30 *Ibid.*, pp. 353–4.

31 Livy 30.30.20.

32 *Leg. e comm.*, p. 345.

33 *Ibid.*, p. 350.

34 *Ibid.*, p. 351.

35 *Ibid.*

36 *Ibid.*, p. 354.

37 On 13 October, Niccolò spoke with Cesare's secretary, Agapito Gerardini, whom he had met in Urbino earlier that year. Gerardini suggested that, despite what Cesare had said, the employment of Francesco II Gonzaga might be a problem, after all. In his opinion, the Florentines had no need to employ the marquis of Mantua. If they were serious about allying with Cesare, his forces should be enough. See *ibid.*, pp. 356–8.

38 *Ibid.*, p. 356, p. 358.

39 *Lett.*, p. 81 (no. 26); *Machiavelli and His Friends*, p. 54 (no. 36).

40 *Lett.*, p. 75 (no. 23); *Machiavelli and His Friends*, p. 50 (no. 33).

41 *Lett.*, p. 78 (no. 25); *Machiavelli and His Friends*, pp. 52–3 (no. 35).

42 *Lett.*, p. 74 (no. 23); *Machiavelli and His Friends*, p. 50 (no. 33).

43 See *Lett.*, p. 84 (no. 27); *Machiavelli and His Friends*, p. 56 (no. 37).

44 For what follows, see *Lett.*, p. 74 (no. 23); *Machiavelli and His Friends*, p. 50 (no. 33).

45 *Lett.*, p. 75 (no. 23); *Machiavelli and His Friends*, p. 50 (no. 33).

46 *Lett.*, p. 82 (no. 27); *Machiavelli and His Friends*, p. 55 (no. 37).

47 *Lett.*, p. 77 (no. 25); *Machiavelli and His Friends* p. 52 (no. 35).

48 *Lett.*, p. 82 (no. 27); *Machiavelli and His Friends*, pp. 55–6 (no. 37).

49   *Lett.*, p. 86 (no. 29); *Machiavelli and His Friends*, p. 59 (no. 41).

50   *Lett.*, p. 78 (no. 25); *Machiavelli and His Friends*, p. 52 (no. 35).

51   *Lett.*, p. 78 (no. 25); *Machiavelli and His Friends.*, p. 52 (no. 35).

52   *Lett.*, p. 82 (no. 27); *Machiavelli and His Friends*, p. 55 (no. 37).

53   Cf. *Lett.*, pp. 86–7 (no. 29); *Machiavelli and His Friends*, pp. 58–9 (no. 41).

54   *Lett.*, pp. 82–3 (no. 27); *Machiavelli and His Friends*, p. 55 (no. 37).

55   *Leg. e comm.*, pp. 359–60, p. 362.

56   *Ibid.*, p. 362.

57   For what follows, see *ibid.*, pp. 365–6.

58   *Ibid.*, p. 363.

59   Cf. Luca Landucci, *Diario fiorentino dal 1450 al 1516 continuato da un anonimo fino al 1542*, J. del Badia (ed.) (Florence: Sansoni, 1883), p. 251.

60   *Leg. e comm.*, p. 368.

61   *Ibid.*

62   *Ibid.*, p. 369.

63   *Ibid.*, pp. 366–7, pp. 374–5. For the conspirators' letter, see *ibid.*, p. 538.

64   *Ibid.*, p. 374.

65   *Ibid.*, p. 375.

66   *Ibid.*

67   *Ibid.*, p. 376.

68   *Ibid.*, pp. 371–2.

69   *Ibid.*, pp. 377–82.

70   *Ibid.*, pp. 383–4.

71   *Ibid.*, p. 386.

72   *Ibid.*, pp. 392–3; *Chief Works*, vol. 1, pp. 128–9 [adapted].

73   *Ibid.*, p. 393.

74   On 28 October, Biagio told Niccolò to 'leave the judgment to others; and stick yourself in the ass'. As Atkinson and Sices note, this stinging rebuke was most likely a response to Niccolò's despatches of 15 and 23 October. Having arrived on 19 October and at some point after 25 October, respectively, these may well have seemed a little bizarre to Biagio, who was still smouldering about the errands Niccolò was asking him to run. *Lett.*, p. 90 (no. 32); *Machiavelli and His Friends*, p. 61 (no. 44), p. 449, n.1; on the receipt of Niccolò's despatches of 15 and 23 October, see *Leg. e comm.*, p. 371, pp. 388–9.

75   On 27 October 1502, Luigi della Stufa, the Florentine ambassador to France, and Ugolino Martelli, his *mandatario*, wrote to Niccolò to relay this news: *Leg. e comm.*, pp. 395–6.

76   *Ibid.*, pp. 390–1.

77   See the *Dieci*'s despatch of 25 October: *ibid.*, pp. 388–9.

78   *Ibid.*, p. 399.

79   *Ibid.*

80 *Ibid.*, p. 400.

81 *Ibid.*, p. 392.

82 Landucci, *Diario*, p. 251.

83 *Leg. e comm.*, pp. 404–5.

84 *Ibid.*, pp. 412–13.

85 For further discussion, see J. M. Najemy, 'The controversy surrounding Machiavelli's service to the republic', in G. Bock, Q. Skinner and M. Viroli (eds.), *Machiavelli and Republicanism* (Cambridge: Cambridge University Press, 1990), pp. 101–17, here pp. 106–7.

86 *Ibid.*, pp. 388–9.

87 *Ibid.*, p. 403.

88 *Lett.*, pp. 89–90 (no. 32); *Machiavelli and His Friends*, pp. 60–1 (no. 44).

89 *Leg. e comm.*, p. 412.

90 *Lett.*, pp. 93–4 (no. 35); *Machiavelli and His Friends*, p. 63 (no. 47).

91 Cf. *Lett.*, pp. 99–100 (no. 39); *Machiavelli and His Friends*, pp. 66–7 (no. 51).

92 *Leg. e comm.*, p. 413.

93 Machiavelli, 'Descrizione del modo', in *Opere*, Bonfantini (ed.), p. 459; *Chief Works*, vol. 1, p. 165.

94 *Leg. e comm.*, p. 417.

95 *Ibid.*, pp. 416–17. Niccolò's account of this audience is non-chronological.

96 *Ibid.*, p. 416. Cf. The *Dieci*'s communique of 5 November: *ibid.*, pp. 415–16. See also Canestrini and Desjardins (eds.), *Négociations diplomatiques*, vol. 2, pp. 72–5.

97 For what follows, see *Leg. e comm.*, pp. 418–23. For a partial translation of this letter, see *Chief Works*, vol. 1, pp. 130–3.

98 *Leg. e comm.*, p. 419.

99 Cesare had suggested that his three-year-old daughter, Luisa, could marry the marquis of Mantua's infant son, Federigo. The negotiations, however, came to nothing.

100 See Niccolò's explanation at *Leg. e comm.*, pp. 426–7.

101 *Ibid.*, pp. 425–6.

102 *Ibid.*, pp. 423–4.

103 *Machiavelli and His Friends*, p. 69 (no. 54).

104 *Leg. e comm.*, pp. 434–8.

105 *Ibid.*, pp. 444–5.

106 *Ibid.*, p. 445.

107 *Ibid.*

108 On 18 November 1502, Piero Soderini called upon the Council of Eighty to take notice of the services that Niccolò, Francesco della

Casa and Giovanni Ridolfi had recently rendered the Republic: *Cons. e prat. 1498–1505*, vol. 2, p. 861.

109 See the letter from Alamanno Salviati: *Machiavelli and His Friends*, p. 79 (no. 67). Although written on 23 December, we may assume that Niccolò's concern over his re-election predated this. Judging by other requests, it seems likely that he would only have asked individuals to lobby on his behalf had he already failed to convince Soderini with the same arguments.

110 *Ibid.*, p. 73 (no. 59).

111 *Leg. e comm.*, p. 452.

112 *Ibid.*, p. 464. On 22 November, Niccolò had informed the *Dieci* that an agreement had not yet been concluded: *ibid.*, p. 451. Niccolò was of the opinion that the treaty would make Cesare more disposed to listen to the Florentines' proposals. His advice was not heeded: *ibid.*, pp. 464–5.

113 *Ibid.*, pp. 467–8.

114 *Ibid.*, pp. 457–8; Sabatini, *The Life of Cesare Borgia*, p. 365.

115 *Leg. e comm.*, p. 465.

116 *Ibid.*, pp. 476–7. This question was posed by Niccolò's friend, likely Alessandro Spannocchi.

117 *Ibid.*, p. 478.

118 *Ibid.*, p. 479.

119 For the details of Niccolò's journey, see *ibid.*, p. 482.

120 Sabatini, *The Life of Cesare Borgia*, p. 367.

121 *Leg. e comm.*, p. 483.

122 Sabatini, *The Life of Cesare Borgia*, p. 367.

123 For the following, see Machiavelli, 'Descrizione del modo', in *Opere*, Bonfantini (ed.), p. 460; Marchand, *I primi scritti politici*, pp. 422–3; *Chief Works*, vol. 1, p. 166.

124 *Ibid.*

125 On Giovanni Vittorio Soderini's mission to Rome (thus far), see *Leg. e comm.*, p. 451, pp. 456–7, p. 464, pp. 481–2.

126 *Ibid.*, pp. 482–6; partial trans. in *Chief Works*, vol. 1, pp. 139–40.

127 *Leg. e comm.*, pp. 484–5; *Chief Works*, vol. 1, p. 139.

128 *Machiavelli and His Friends*, p. 79 (no. 67).

129 *Ibid.*, p. 77 (no. 65).

130 *Ibid.*, p. 79 (no. 67).

131 *Ibid.*, p. 77 (no. 64); cf. p. 79 (no. 66).

132 *Ibid.*, p. 79 (no. 66).

133 *Leg. e comm.*, pp. 494–6.

134 *Ibid.*, p. 503; trans. in *Chief Works*, vol. 1, p. 142.

135 *Leg. e comm.*, p. 500.

136 Sabatini, *The Life of Cesare Borgia*, p. 368.

137 *Leg. e comm.*, p. 502.

138 *Ibid.*, p. 503.

139 Sabatini, *The Life of Cesare Borgia*, pp. 369–70.

140 Machiavelli, 'Descrizione del modo', in *Opere*, Bonfantini (ed.), p. 460; Marchand, *I primi scritti politici*, p. 423; *Chief Works*, vol. 1, p. 166.

141 Machiavelli, 'Descrizione del modo', in *Opere*, Bonfantini (ed.), p. 461; Marchand, *I primi scritti politici*, p. 423; *Chief Works*, vol. 1, p. 166.

142 Machiavelli, 'Descrizione del modo', in *Opere*, Bonfantini (ed.), p. 461; Marchand, *I primi scritti politici*, pp. 423–4; *Chief Works*, vol. 1, p. 167 [adapted].

143 The following account is based on *Leg. e comm.*, p. 507. The version given at Machiavelli, 'Descrizione del modo', in *Opere*, Bonfantini (ed.), pp. 461–4; *Chief Works*, vol. 1, pp. 168–9 contains a good deal of embellishment. For further discussion of the differences between the two texts, see chapter 11, below.

144 *Leg. e comm.*, pp. 506–7.

145 For what follows, see *ibid.*, pp. 508–9.

146 *Ibid.*, pp. 511–12.

147 *Ibid.*, pp. 515–17.

148 For the despatch, arrival and onward progress of Jacopo Salviati, see Niccolò's despatches from 6 January 1503 on: *ibid.*, pp. 517–22, pp. 524–37.

149 Johannes Burchard, *Liber notarum ab anno MCCCCLXXXIII ad annum MDVI*, E. Celani (ed.), *RIS* 2nd ser. 32.1, 2 vols. (Città di Castello: Lapi, 1907–42), vol. 2, p. 346. Curiously, Niccolò said nothing about the execution of Paolo Orsini and the duke of Gravina.

150 *Leg. e comm.*, p. 519, p. 524, p. 528.

151 *Ibid.*, p. 528.

152 In his despatch from Castello della Pieve (13 January), Niccolò indicated that the ambassador was expected 'very soon'. Exactly when the ambassador arrived, however, is not clear. As Niccolò's letter from Castiglion Aretino (21 January) suggests, he must have arrived no later than 20 January. But beyond this, nothing can be said with any certainty. Given Niccolò's silence about the murder of Paolo Orsini and the duke of Gravina (18 January), it is *possible* that Salviati may have joined Cesare's force at Castello della Pieve at around the same time, communicating the news in a letter that has since been lost. It is, however, more likely that he caught up with them on the road over the next couple of days, when, as Burchard attests, Cesare was busy retaking the towns of Chiusi and Pienza. *Ibid.*, p. 530, p. 537; Burchard, *Liber notarum*, vol. 2, p. 347.

153 *Leg. e comm.*, p. 537.

11. The Wind Changes (January–December 1503)

1   *Lett.*, p. 112 (no. 48); *Machiavelli and His Friends*, p. 83 (no. 69).

2   Bernardo di Niccolò di Bernardo Machiavelli was born on or before 9 November 1503. As such, he was most likely to have been conceived in early February of the same year. See *ibid.*, p. 86 (no. 74), p. 88 (no. 76). For further discussion of his date of birth, see R. Ridolfi, *Vita di Niccolò Machiavelli*, 3rd ed., 2 vols. (Florence: Sansoni, 1969), vol. 1, p. 118, vol. 2, p. 451.

3   E.g. *Lett.*, p. 87, pp. 92–3 (nos. 30, 34); *Machiavelli and His Friends*, p. 59, pp. 62–3 (nos. 42, 46).

4   On Valori's influence over Piero Soderini and dedication to Niccolò, see esp. J. Najemy, 'The controversy surrounding Machiavelli's service to the republic', in G. Bock, Q. Skinner and M. Viroli (eds.), *Machiavelli and Republicanism* (Cambridge: Cambridge University Press, 1990), pp. 101–17; M. Jurdjevic, *Guardians of Republicanism: The Valori Family in the Florentine Renaissance* (Oxford: Oxford University Press, 2008), pp. 63–6.

5   *Machiavelli and His Friends*, p. 79 (no. 67); S. Bertelli, 'Machiavelli and Soderini', *Renaissance Quarterly* 28/1 (1975), pp. 1–16, here p. 11.

6   See, for example, *Cons. e prat. 1498–1505*, vol. 2, p. 872, p. 874, p. 883, pp. 888–9, p. 890.

7   *Leg. e comm.*, pp. 525–6.

8   See, for example, Antonio Giustinian, *Dispacci di Antonio Giustinian, ambasciatore veneto in Roma dal 1502 al 1505*, P. Villari (ed.), 3 vols. (Florence: Le Monnier, 1876), vol. 1, p. 364 (no. 258). Cesare had previously advised Niccolò that the *Dieci* should have no concern for the king's protection. This should, however, be regarded as nothing more than a stratagem to induce them to support his endeavour. *Leg. e comm.*, p. 530.

9   R. Sabatini, *The Life of Cesare Borgia* (London: Stanley Paul, 1912), p. 389.

10   *Leg. e comm.*, pp. 551–2 (from Bertelli's 'Nota introduttiva').

11   E.g. Johannes Burchard, *Liber notarum ab anno MCCCCLXXXIII ad annum MDVI*, E. Celani (ed.), *RIS* 2nd ser. 32.1, 2 vols. (Città di Castello: Lapi, 1907–42), vol. 2, p. 347; Luca Landucci, *Diario fiorentino dal 1450 al 1516 continuato da un anonimo fino al 1542*, J. del Badia (ed.) (Florence, 1883), p. 254; Giustinian, *Dispacci*, vol. 1, pp. 368–9 (no. 263).

12   The following is indebted to Bertelli's splendid summary at *Leg. e comm.*, p. 552.

13   Francesco Guicciardini, *Storia d'Italia*, 5.12, C. Panigada (ed.), 5 vols. (Bari: G. Laterza & Figli, 1929), vol. 2, p. 63.

14   *Ibid.*, vol. 2, p. 64; Tomaso Tomasi, *La vita del duca Valentino* (Monte Chiaro: Gio. Bapt. Lucio Vero, 1655), p. 274.

15   For the following, see M. E. Mallett and C. Shaw, *The Italian Wars, 1494–1559: War, State and Society in Early Modern Europe* (London and New York: Routledge, 2012), pp. 62–4.

16   Giustinian, *Dispacci*, vol. 1, pp. 414–15 (no. 300).

17   *Ibid.*, vol. 1, p. 415, p. 417 (nos. 301, 303).

18   *Ibid.*, vol. 1, p. 429 (no. 313).

19   *Ibid.*, vol. 1, pp. 430–1 (no. 314).

20   Giovanni Antonio Pecci, *Memorie storico-critiche della città di Siena, 1480–1559*, 4 vols. (Siena: Pazzini, 1755–60), vol. 1, p. 194.

21   *Cons. e prat. 1498–1505*, vol. 2, p. 890.

22   *Ibid.*, pp. 884–9.

23   See esp. J.-J. Marchand, *Niccolò Machiavelli: I primi scritti politici* (Padua: Antenore, 1975), pp. 57–9; N. Rubinstein, 'Machiavelli and the world of Florentine politics', in M. Gilmore (ed.), *Studies on Machiavelli* (Florence: Sansoni, 1972), pp. 3–28, here pp. 11–12. Doubts have, however, been cast on this interpretation of the text's origins, for which, see, for example, S. Anglo, *Machiavelli: A Dissection* (London: Gollancz, 1969), p. 277, n.37; R. Black, *Machiavelli* (Abingdon: Routledge, 2013), pp. 58–9.

24   E.g. *Lett.*, pp. 101–2 (no. 41); *Machiavelli and His Friends*, pp. 68–9 (no. 54).

25   Niccolò Machiavelli, 'Parole da dirle sopra la provisione del danaio'; text in *Opere*, M. Bonfantini (ed.) (Milan and Naples: R. Ricciardi, 1954), pp. 433–7; Marchand, *I primi scritti politici*, pp. 412–16. An English translation may be found in *Chief Works*, vol. 3, pp. 1439–43.

26   Machiavelli, 'Parole da dirle sopra la provisione del danaio'; in *Opere*, Bonfantini (ed.), p. 433; Marchand, *I primi scritti politici*, p. 412; trans. adapted from *Chief Works*, vol. 3, p. 1439.

27   Machiavelli, 'Parole da dirle sopra la provisione del danaio'; in *Opere*, Bonfantini (ed.), p. 434; Marchand, *I primi scritti politici*, p. 413; trans. in *Chief Works*, vol. 3, p. 1440.

28   Machiavelli, 'Parole da dirle sopra la provisione del danaio'; in *Opere*, Bonfantini (ed.), pp. 435–6; Marchand, *I primi scritti politici*, pp. 414–15; *Chief Works*, vol. 3, pp. 1441–2.

29   Machiavelli, 'Parole da dirle sopra la provisione del danaio'; in *Opere*, Bonfantini (ed.), pp. 434–5; Marchand, *I primi scritti politici*, p. 413; *Chief Works*, vol. 3, pp. 1440–1.

30   Machiavelli, 'Parole da dirle sopra la provisione del danaio'; in *Opere*, Bonfantini (ed.), p. 436; Marchand, *I primi scritti politici*, p. 415; *Chief Works*, vol. 3, p. 1442.

31   Machiavelli, 'Parole da dirle sopra la provisione del danaio'; in

Opere, Bonfantini (ed.), p. 437; Marchand, *I primi scritti politici*, p. 415; *Chief Works*, vol. 3, p. 1443.

32 Machiavelli, 'Parole da dirle sopra la provisione del danaio'; in *Opere*, Bonfantini (ed.), p. 437; Marchand, *I primi scritti politici*, p. 415; trans. adapted from *Chief Works*, vol. 3, p. 1443.

33 See n.23, above.

34 *Cons. e prat. 1498–1505*, vol. 2, pp. 912–13.

35 Giustinian, *Dispacci*, vol. 1, pp. 463–5 (no. 341).

36 See, for example, Guicciardini, *Storia d'Italia*, 5.14, Panigada (ed.), vol. 2, pp. 72–3.

37 Guicciardini, *Storia d'Italia*, 5.15, Panigada (ed.), vol. 2, pp. 74–5; Francesco Guicciardini, *Storie fiorentine*, 24, R. Palmarocchi (ed.) (Bari: G. Laterza & Figli, 1934), pp. 258–9; Giustinian, *Dispacci*, vol. 1, pp. 471–3 (nos. 345–6). Cf. *Cons. e prat. 1498–1505*, vol. 2, pp. 915–18.

38 Guicciardini, *Storie fiorentine*, 24, Palmarocchi (ed.), p. 259.

39 *Ibid.*, p. 260. On 11 April, Alexander VI also reached out to the Venetians, whose refusal to deny Spanish ships access to their ports in Southern Italy had strained relations with the France earlier in the year: Giustinian, *Dispacci*, vol. 1, pp. 476–7 (no. 348); Mallett and Shaw, *The Italian Wars*, p. 63.

40 *Cons. e prat. 1498–1505*, vol. 2, pp. 918–22.

41 *Ibid.*, vol. 2, pp. 925–8.

42 Mallett and Shaw, *The Italian Wars*, p. 64.

43 *Leg. e comm.*, pp. 557–8.

44 *Ibid.*, p. 559.

45 Giustinian, *Dispacci*, vol. 2, pp. 1–3 (no. 369); cf. Guicciardini, *Storia d'Italia*, 6.1, Panigada (ed.), vol. 2, pp. 83–4; *Storie fiorentine*, 24, Palmarocchi (ed.), p. 259.

46 On the Battle of Cerignola (28 April), see esp. Mallett and Shaw, *The Italian Wars*, pp. 64–5; Guicciardini, *Storia d'Italia*, 5.15, Panigada (ed.), vol. 2, p. 82. News of the Aragonese victory reached Rome on 4 May: Giustinian, *Dispacci*, vol. 2, p. 6 (no. 372); cf. *ibid.*, vol. 2, pp. 8–9 (no. 375). In Florence, a *pratica* was summoned to discuss the implications of the battle (and other matters) on 9 May: *Cons. e prat. 1498–1505*, vol. 2, p. 931.

47 Note, particularly, Giustinian, *Dispacci*, vol. 2, p. 7 (no. 373). In this despatch, Giustinian reported that the pope had told the ambassadors of Maximilian, Louis XII and Ferdinand the Catholic that '[t]hese Frenchmen want to send troops into the *Regno* . . .' and went on to mock the king's lack of money.

48 Guicciardini, *Storie fiorentine*, 24, Palmarocchi (ed.), p. 260.

49 Giustinian, *Dispacci*, vol. 2, pp. 3–6 (no. 370).

50 *Ibid.*, p. 34, pp. 90–92 (nos. 409 and 464). In both despatches,

Giustinian notes that Alexander had asked Maximilian to invest
Cesare with Pisa.

51   Giustinian, *Dispacci*, vol. 2, p. 9 (no. 376); Guicciardini, *Storie
fiorentine*, 24, Palmarocchi (ed.), p. 260.

52   E.g. Landucci, *Diario*, p. 255.

53   Niccolò Machiavelli, *Scritti inediti di Niccolò Machiavelli risguardanti
la storia e la milizia (1499–1512)*, G. Canestrini (ed.) (Florence:
Barbèra Bianchi e Comp, 1857), p. 151; cf. the *pratica* summoned to
discuss this same subject the following day: *Cons. e prat. 1498–1505*,
vol. 2, pp. 932–4.

54   On 14 and 16 May, Alexander VI made public his support for the
Pisans in Rome: Giustinian, *Dispacci*, vol. 2, p. 14, p. 15 (nos. 382,
384).

55   Machiavelli, *Scritti inediti*, p. 154.

56   Guicciardini, *Storia d'Italia*, 6.2, Panigada (ed.), vol. 2, pp. 89–90.

57   *Ibid.*, vol. 2, p. 90; Guicciardini, *Storie fiorentine*, 24, Palmarocchi
(ed.), pp. 260–1; Landucci, *Diario*, p. 256.

58   Landucci, *Diario*, p. 257.

59   For what follows, see Mallett and Shaw, *The Italian Wars*, p. 66.

60   Giustinian, *Dispacci*, vol. 2, p. 15 (no. 384).

61   *Ibid.*, vol. 2, p. 29 (no. 401); Guicciardini, *Storie fiorentine*, 24,
Palmarocchi (ed.), p. 261. It is worth noting that almost half of the
cardinals created at this consistory were chosen in the hope of
strengthening the planned anti-French alliance. Melchior von
Meckau, bishop of Brixen, had long been a close adviser to
Maximilian I; Niccolò Fieschi, bishop of Fréjus, was from an
influential Genoese family; and Francisco Desprats, bishop of
Astorga, had been the papal nuncio to Ferdinand the Catholic and
Isabella of Castile from 1492 onwards. The remaining five creations
were kinsmen (Francisco Lloris y de Borja, bishop of Elne, and
Juan Castellar y de Borja, archbishop of Trani), longstanding
retainers (Franciesco de Remolins was a former governor of Rome,
and Jaime de Casanova had been a papal chamberlain), or corrupt
men willing to offer massive bribes in return for a red hat (Adriano
Castellesi, bishop of Hereford).

62   Landucci, *Diario*, p. 256.

63   Francesco Soderini said Mass in Santa Maria del Fiore on 16 July.
Ibid., p. 257.

64   On the dating of this work, see Marchand, *I primi scritti politici*,
pp. 80–2. For criticisms of Marchand's analysis, see B. Richardson,
'Per la datazione del *Tradimento del duca Valentino* del Machiavelli',
La bibliofila 81 (1979), pp. 75–85; Niccolò Machiavelli, *La vita di
Castruccio Castracani e altri scritti*, G. Inglese (ed.) (Milan: Rizzoli,

1991), pp. 22–7; M. Marietti, *Machiavel: Le penseur de la nécessité* (Paris: Payot, 2009), p. 90; Black, *Machiavelli*, pp. 57–8.

65 Black, *Machiavelli*, p. 58.

66 Machiavelli, 'Descrizione del modo tenuto dal duca Valentino nell'ammazzare Vitellozzo Vitelli, Oliverotto da Fermo, il signor Pagolo e il duca di Gravina Orsini', in *Opere*, Bonfantini (ed.), p. 459; Marchard, *I primi scritti politici*, p. 421; *Chief Works*, vol. 1, pp. 164–5. Black seems to be wide of the mark in criticizing (with Marietti) 'the stylised transformation . . . of Borgia from bewildered passivity at the time of the conspiracy [of Magione] to total mastery of events at Senigallia.' It is, of course, true that Cesare was indeed 'in great fear, because suddenly and against all his expectations, since his soldiers had become hostile to him, war was upon him and he was unarmed.' But in the very next sentence, Niccolò observes that he had 'regain[ed] his courage', and decided to drag the war out with negotiations, while preparing to take his revenge. Of 'bewildered passivity' there is scarcely a trace. Black, *Machiavelli*, p. 58; Marietti, *Machiavel*, p. 90.

67 Machiavelli, 'Descrizione del modo', in *Opere*, Bonfantini (ed.), pp. 459–60; Marchand, *I primi scritti politici*, p. 422; Chief *Works*, vol. 1, p. 165.

68 Machiavelli, 'Descrizione del modo', in *Opere*, Bonfantini (ed.), p. 461; Marchand, *I primi scritti politici*, p. 423; *Chief Works*, vol. 1, p. 166.

69 *Machiavelli*, 'Descrizione del modo', in *Opere*, Bonfantini (ed.), p. 461; Marchand, *I primi scritti politici*, p. 423; *Chief Works*, vol. 1, pp. 165–6.

70 By contrast, Black argues that Niccolò's portrayal of Vitellozzo as a 'tragic hero' seems 'too favourable for a period in which his family were mortal enemies of Florence', and hence concludes that the text as a whole must have been written at 'a later date (1514–17), when the Vitelli were in the employ of the restored Medici rulers of Florence.' Black, *Machiavelli*, p. 58.

71 Machiavelli, 'Descrizione del modo', in *Opere*, Bonfantini (ed.), pp. 462–3; Marchand, *I primi scritti politici*, pp. 424–5; *Chief Works*, vol. 1, p. 168.

72 Machiavelli, 'Descrizione del modo', in *Opere*, Bonfantini (ed.), p. 464; Marchand, *I primi scritti politici*, p. 426; *Chief Works*, vol. 1, p. 169.

73 Sabatini, *The Life of Cesare Borgia*, p. 400.

74 Text in Machiavelli, *Opere*, Bonfantini (ed.), pp. 428–32; Marchand, *I primi scritti politici*, pp. 427–31.

75 On the dating of this work, see Marchand, *I primi scritti politici*, pp. 102–3.

76 Machiavelli, 'Del modo di trattare i popoli della Valdichiana ribellati', in *Opere*, Bonfantini (ed.), p. 428; Marchand, *I primi scritti politici*, p. 427; cf. Livy, 8.13.14–17.

77 At this point, Niccolò amended Livy's wording rather tellingly. Originally, Livy had stated that the walls of Velitrae were torn down (*muri deiecti*) and that its senate was ordered to dwell on the other side of the Tiber, on the understanding that, if any of its members should return, they would be fined 1,000 pounds of bronze (8.14.5–6). Niccolò, however, made the punishment far more severe. In his account, 'their city was destroyed [*fu disfatta la loro città*] and all the citizens [*tutti i cittadini*] were sent to live in Rome.' Machiavelli, 'Del modo di trattare i popoli della Valdichiana ribellati', in *Opere*, Bonfantini (ed.), p. 429; Marchand, *I primi scritti politici*, p. 428.

78 Here, Niccolò once again twisted Livy's meaning. According to Livy, new settlers were despatched to Antium, with the understanding that the Antiates would also be allowed to enlist as colonists if they wished; their warships [*naves . . . longae*] were confiscated and their people were 'forbidden the sea' [*interdictum . . . mari Antiati populo est*]. But they were nevertheless granted citizenship (8.14.8–9). By contrast, Niccolò has the Romans confiscate *all* of the Antiates' ships [*tolsero loro tutte le navi*], and omits any reference either to the Antiates' capacity to enrol as colonists or to their receipt of Roman citizenship. Machiavelli, 'Del modo di trattare i popoli della Valdichiana ribellati', in *Opere*, p. 429; Marchand, *I primi scritti politici*, p. 428.

79 Machiavelli, 'Del modo di trattare i popoli della Valdichiana ribellati', in *Opere*, p. 430; Marchand, *I primi scritti politici*, p. 429.

80 Machiavelli, 'Del modo di trattare i popoli della Valdichiana ribellati', in *Opere*, pp. 430–1; Marchand, *I primi scritti politici*, pp. 429–30.

81 This is implicit in Niccolò's statement: '*io non approvo che gli Aretini, simili ai Veliterni ed Anziani, non siano stati trattati come loro.*' Machiavelli, 'Del modo di trattare i popoli della Valdichiana ribellati', in *Opere*, p. 430; Marchand, *I primi scritti politici*, pp. 429.

82 Note Landucci, *Diario*, p. 258.

83 On the slow progress of the French army, see, for example, Mallett and Shaw, *The Italian Wars*, p. 67.

84 Landucci, *Diario*, p. 258.

85 Giustinian, *Dispacci*, vol. 2, pp. 86–8 (nos. 461–2); Sabatini, *The Life of Cesare Borgia*, p. 405.

86 See *Leg. e comm.*, p. 563.

87 In his entry for 20 August, Sanudo noted that some said Alexander VI had been poisoned. Marino Sanudo the Younger, *I diarii di*

Marino Sanuto: (MCCCCXCVI–MDXXXIII): dall'autografo Marciano Ital. CLVII codd. CDXIX–CDLXXVII, R. Fulin et al. (eds.), 58 vols. (Venice: F. Visentini, 1879–1902), vol. 5, p. 65.

88 Guicciardini, *Storia d'Italia*, 6.4, Panigada (ed.), vol. 2, pp. 96–8.

89 Burchard, *Liber notarum*, vol. 2, p. 351; Giustinian, *Dispacci*, vol. 2, p. 99 (no. 472).

90 On the death of Juan de Borja Lanzol de Romaní (1 August 1503), see, for example, Giustinian, *Dispacci*, vol. 2, p. 92 (no. 466).

91 E.g. Burchard, *Liber notarum*, vol. 2, p. 351; Giustinian, *Dispacci*, vol. 2, p. 107 (no. 479).

92 On 16 August, the Venetian ambassador reported that Cesare's case appeared to be the most serious: Giustinian, *Dispacci*, vol. 2, p. 112 (no. 482).

93 Burchard, *Liber notarum*, vol. 2, p. 351; Giustinian, *Dispacci*, vol. 2, p. 109 (no. 481).

94 Giustinian, *Discpacci*, vol. 2, pp. 113–14 (no. 483).

95 Burchard, *Liber notarum*, vol. 2, pp. 351–2; Giustinian, *Dispacci*, vol. 2, pp. 115–16 (no. 484).

96 Burchard, *Liber notarum*, vol. 2, p. 352.

97 E.g. Giustinian, *Dispacci*, vol. 2, pp. 138–40 (nos. 495–6); cf. *ibid.*, vol. 2, pp. 169–71 (no. 516); Guicciardini, *Storia d'Italia*, 6.4, Panigada (ed.), vol. 2, p. 98.

98 Giustinian, *Dispacci*, vol. 2, pp. 171–2 (no. 517); Burchard, *Liber notarum*, vol. 2, pp. 363–4; F. Petruccelli della Gattina, *Histoire diplomatique des conclaves*, 4 vols. (Paris: A. Lacroix, 1864–6), vol. 1, p. 444.

99 See, for example, Guicciardini, *Storie fiorentine*, 24, Palmarocchi (ed.), p. 263.

100 For the following, see, generally, *ibid.*, p. 264; Guicciardini, *Storia d'Italia*, 6.2, Panigada (ed.), vol. 2, p. 100.

101 Landucci, *Diario*, p. 259.

102 Giustinian, *Dispacci*, vol. 2, p. 188 (no. 534).

103 *Ibid.*, vol. 2, p. 222 (no. 571); Guicciardini, *Storia d'Italia*, 6.4, Panigada (ed.), vol. 2, p. 100.

104 *Leg. e comm.*, p. 563.

105 *Ibid.*

106 Burchard, *Liber notarum*, vol. 2, pp. 384–5. For a more detailed discussion, see Petruccelli della Gattina, *Histoire diplomatique*, vol. 1, pp. 452–4.

107 On the Piccolomini Library, see, for example, A. Cecchi, *The Piccolomini Library in the Cathedral of Siena* (Florence: Scala, 1982); C. Esche, *Die Libreria Piccolomini in Siena – Studien zu Bau und Ausstattung* (Frankfurt: Peter Lang, 1992); E. Carli, 'Il Pio

umanistico: La libraria Piccolomini', *Mensile di Franco Mario Ricci* 66 (1994), pp. 47–84; S. Settis and D. Toracca (eds.), *La Libreria Piccolomini nel Duomo di Siena* (Modena: F. Cosimo Panini, 1998); S. J. May, 'The Piccolomini library in Siena Cathedral: a new reading with particular reference to two compartments of the vault decoration', *Renaissance Studies* 19/3 (2005), pp. 287–324.

108 See L. Célier, 'Alexandre VI et la réforme de l'Eglise', *Mélanges d'Archéologie et d'Histoire de l'Ecole Française de Rome* 27 (1907), pp. 65–124; M. Pellegrini, 'A Turning-Point in the History of the Factional System of the Sacred College: The Power of the Pope and Cardinals in the Age of Alexander VI', in G. Signorotto and M. A. Visceglia (eds.), *Court and Politics in Papal Rome, 1492–1700* (Cambridge: Cambridge University Press, 2002), pp. 8–30, here pp. 15–16.

109 Burchard, *Liber notarum*, vol. 2, p. 388; Giustinian, *Dispacci*, vol. 2, p. 208 (no. 558).

110 Giustinian, *Dispacci*, vol. 2, p. 239 (no. 585).

111 On 30 September, the Venetian ambassador reported that Cesare had 1,500 infantrymen and 500 cavalrymen with him in Nepi: *ibid.*, vol. 2, p. 213 (no. 564). On the departure of the French army, see, for example, Burchard, *Liber notarum*, vol. 2, pp. 388–9; Giustinian, *Dispacci*, vol. 2, pp. 209–11 (nos. 559–60); Guicciardini, *Storia d'Italia*, 6.4, Panigada (ed.), vol. 2, pp. 99–100.

112 Giustinian, *Dispacci*, vol. 2, p. 209 (no. 559).

113 *Ibid.*, vol. 2, pp. 217–19 (nos. 566–7).

114 *Ibid.*, vol. 2, p. 223 (no. 572).

115 There were howls of protest from the cardinals. On 12 October, Giuliano della Rovere and Raffaele Riario even called on Cesare to lay down his arms. *Ibid.*, vol. 2, p. 237 (no. 583).

116 The Venetian ambassador reported that Cesare had brought only 150 men-at-arms, 500 infantrymen and 'a few light cavalry' with him. *Ibid.*, vol. 2, p. 219 (no. 567).

117 Burchard, *Liber notarum*, vol. 2, pp. 392–3; Giustinian, *Dispacci*, vol. 2, pp. 244–5, p. 249 (nos. 588, 590); Landucci, *Diario*, p. 261.

118 That Pius was having a change of heart is suggested at Giustinian, *Dispacci*, vol. 2, pp. 239–40 (no. 585). On the arrival of Bartolomeo d'Alviano and his intentions, see *ibid.*, vol. 2, p. 228, pp. 229–36, pp. 237–8 (nos. 577, 579–81, 583–4).

119 Burchard, *Liber notarum*, vol. 2, p. 392; Giustinian, *Dispacci*, vol. 2, p. 240 (no. 586).

120 Giustinian, *Dispacci*, vol. 2, p. 243 (no. 588).

121 *Ibid.*, vol. 2, p. 249 (no. 590); cf. *ibid.*, vol. 2, p. 248 (no. 589).

122 Burchard, *Liber notarum*, vol. 2, p. 393.

123 Cesare would likely have stood a better chance of breaking out in the days after Pius III's death than in the previous weeks. On 20 October, the Venetian ambassador reported that the cardinals had rejected the Orsini's request to keep the duke sequestered 'until the election of the new pontiff.' Giustinian, *Dispacci*, vol. 2, pp. 256–7 (no. 595).

124 Note, for example, *ibid.*, vol. 2, pp. 263–4, pp. 271–2 (nos. 602, 610).

125 Of the eleven cardinals, six were Cesare's relations (Luis de Milà y de Borja, Francisco Lloris y de Borja, Juan Castellar y de Borja, Francisco de Borja, Pedro Luis de Borja Lanzol de' Romaní and Juan de Vera), three had been members of Alexander VI's household, or close associates of the Borgias (Jaime de Casanova, Juan de Castro and Jaume Serra i Cau), and two were less closely associated with the family, but still shared a common Spanish heritage (Pietro Isvalies and Bernardino López de Carvajal y Sande).

126 Burchard, *Liber notarum*, vol. 2, p. 399; Giustinian, *Dispacci*, vol. 2, pp. 257–8, pp. 261–2, pp. 267–8, p. 270 (nos. 597, 601, 605, 609).

127 *Leg. e comm.*, pp. 571–3.

128 *Ibid.*, pp. 563–4.

129 *Ibid.*, pp. 589–90.

130 *Ibid.*, p. 591.

131 *Ibid.*, p. 591.

132 *Ibid.*

133 *Ibid.*, p. 593.

134 *Ibid.*

135 On Cesare's move to the Apostolic Palace, see Burchard, *Liber notarum*, vol. 2, p. 411; Giustinian, *Dispacci*, vol. 2, p. 281 (no. 618); *Leg. e comm.*, p. 599.

136 *Leg. e comm.*, p. 599.

137 On 2 November, Julius II had already told Antonio Giustinian that he would not help Cesare in the Romagna: Giustinian, *Dispacci*, vol. 2, p. 279 (no. 615).

138 *Leg. e comm.*, p. 599.

139 On 6 November, the Venetian ambassador expressed his belief that, although Cesare had a 'poor reputation', Julius would still give him Città di Castello: Giustinian, *Dispacci*, vol. 2, pp. 283–4 (no. 621).

140 *Leg. e comm.*, p. 605.

141 *Ibid.*, pp. 602–3, p. 606.

142 On Dionigi's involvement in the affairs of the Val di Lamone, see esp. M. Tabanelli, *Dionigi di Naldo da Brisighella, condottiero del Rinascimento* (Faenza: Fratelli Lega, 1975); A. Bazzocchi, *La ricerca storica e archivistica su Dionigi e Vincenzo Naldi in rapporto alla dominazione veneziana nella Valle del Lamone* (Faenza: Carta Bianca, 2010), pp. 17–40.

143 *Leg. e comm.*, p. 606.

144 *Ibid.*

145 On 8 November, the pope complained bitterly to Giustinian about the Venetians' presence in the Romagna: Giustinian, *Dispacci*, vol. 2, p. 285 (no. 623). Two days later, Giustinian reported that Cardinals Riario and Soderini had spoken to the pope about the danger of allowing them to gain any more ground: *ibid.*, vol. 2, p. 288 (no. 626).

146 *Leg. e comm.*, pp. 606–7.

147 *Ibid.*, p. 607.

148 *Ibid.*, pp. 608–9.

149 *Ibid.*, pp. 608–11.

150 *Ibid.*, pp. 612–13; Burchard, *Liber notarum*, vol. 2, p. 412; Giustinian, *Dispacci*, vol. 2, p. 286 (no. 625).

151 *Leg. e comm.*, pp. 629–30.

152 *Ibid.*, p. 631.

153 *Ibid.*, p. 632.

154 *Ibid.*, pp. 646–8.

155 *Ibid.*, p. 650.

156 *Ibid.*, pp. 650–1; p. 653.

157 *Ibid.*, pp. 645–6.

158 For the following, see *ibid.*, pp. 660–5.

159 On 19 November, Niccolò reported that Georges d'Amboise had received information from the governor of Lombardy indicating that, after seizing the Romagna, the Venetians might well attack Florence on the pretence of recovering the 180,000 *fl.* which they believed were owed them. *Ibid.*, p. 652.

160 Cf. Burchard, *Liber notarum*, vol. 2, p. 413; Giustinian, *Dispacci*, vol. 2, pp. 305–6 (no. 643).

161 *Leg. e comm.*, pp. 674–5; cf. Giustinian, *Dispacci*, vol. 2, pp. 307–9 (no. 646).

162 *Leg. e comm.*, p. 683.

163 Sabatini, *The Life of Cesare Borgia*, p. 432.

164 Julius made this point during an interview with Niccolò on 30 November: *Leg. e comm.*, p. 697.

165 According to Niccolò, there were rumours that Cesare was about to escape from Ostia as well. *Ibid.*, p. 688. Cf. Burchard, *Liber notarum*, vol. 2, p. 415.

166 Giustinian, *Dispacci*, vol. 2, p. 315 (no. 653). Niccolò does not seem to have been aware of this consistory.

167 Writing on 15 November, Biagio Buonaccorsi had specifically rejected this notion. 'We shall soon see,' he wrote, 'that the Venetians are not doing this out of hatred for the duke, but because of their unbridled greed and ambition, etc.' *Machiavelli and His Friends*, p. 88 (no. 76).

168 *Leg. e comm.*, p. 696–8.

169 Giustinian, *Dispacci*, vol. 2, pp. 310–11, p. 314, p. 317 (nos. 649, 651, 654).

170 *Leg. e comm.*, p. 679.

171 *Ibid.*, p. 702.

172 *Ibid.*, p. 705.

173 *Ibid.*

174 *Ibid.*, pp. 705–6.

175 *Ibid.*, p. 709.

176 Landucci, *Diario*, p. 263.

177 *Leg. e comm.*, pp. 718–20.

178 Ridolfi seems to be rather wide of the mark in contending that Niccolò's sojourn had been enlivened by visits to papal apartments 'crowded with ambassadors', to inns filled with fine food and to 'beautiful Roman women'. Ridolfi, *Vita di Niccolò Machiavelli*, p. 119.

179 *Leg. e comm.*, pp. 669–70. On the *carlino*, introduced in 1504, see, for example, C. M. Cipolla, *Money in Sixteenth-Century Florence* (Berkeley CA: University of California Press, 1989), p. 6.

180 *Ibid.*, pp. 679–80.

181 *Ibid.*, p. 707.

182 See Totto's reply (17 November): *Machiavelli and His Friends*, pp. 89–90 (no. 78).

183 *Lett.*, p. 115 (no. 50); *Machiavelli and His Friends*, p. 86 (no. 74).

184 *Lett.*, p. 115 (no. 50); *Machiavelli and His Friends*, p. 86, p. 87 (nos. 74, 75).

185 *Lett.*, pp. 118–19 (no. 53); *Machiavelli and His Friends*, p. 91 (no. 80).

186 *Lett.*, p. 121 (no. 55); *Machiavelli and His Friends*, p. 87, p. 93 (nos. 75, 83).

187 *Machiavelli and His Friends*, p. 87 (no. 75). On Ugolini's reference to Leonardo, see, for example, P. C. Marani, 'Luca Ugolini, Niccolò Machiavelli e la fama di Leonardo ritrattista nei primi anni del Cinquecento', in A. Pontremoli, ed., *La lingua e le lingue di Machiavelli: atti del Convegno internazionale di studi, Torino, 2–4 dicembre 1999* (Florence: L. S. Olschki, 2001), pp. 281–94; C. Pedretti, *Leonardo: The Portrait*, trans. H. Paterson and M. Pugliano (Florence: Giunti, 1999), p. 6.

188 *Machiavelli and His Friends*, p. 89 (no. 77).

189 *Lett.*, p. 121 (no. 55); *Machiavelli and His Friends*, p. 93 (no. 83).

190 *Lett.*, p. 119 (no. 53); *Machiavelli and His Friends*, p. 91 (no. 80).

191 *Lett.*, pp. 123–4 (no. 56); *Machiavelli and His Friends*, p. 95 (no. 84).

192 *Leg. e comm.*, p. 724.

193 *Ibid.*, pp. 724–5.

194 *Ibid.*, pp. 734–5.

195 *Lett.*, pp. 122–3 (no. 56); *Machiavelli and His Friends*, p. 94 (no. 84).

196 Burchard, *Liber notarum*, vol. 2, p. 423; Giustinian, *Dispacci*, vol. 2, pp. 350–1 (no. 680). Cf. Sanudo, *Diarii*, vol. 5, p. 565, p. 627.
197 Giustinian, *Dispacci*, vol. 2, pp. 367–8 (no. 693).
198 See Guicciardini, *Storia d'Italia*, 6.10, Panigada (ed.), vol. 2, pp. 136–7.

12. The Militant (January 1504–February 1506)

1 Jacopo da Varagine, *Legenda aurea*, 1.13; text ed. J. G. T. Graesse (Leipzig: Arnoldia, 1850), pp. 79–87.
2 Niccolò's attitude towards the Christian faith has been hotly debated over the years. It would be impossible to offer anything like a comprehensive bibliography of the subject, but some of the more important works include: D. Cantimori, 'Machiavelli e la religione', *Belfagor* 21 (1966), pp. 629–38; B. Di Porto, 'Il problema religioso in Machiavelli', *Idea* 21 (1966), pp. 245–50 [repr. in B. Di Porto, *Le religione in Machiavelli, Guicciardini e Pascoli* (Rome: Idea, 1968), p. 5ff.]; M. Tenenti, 'La religione di Machiavelli', *Studi Storici* 10 (1969), pp. 709–48; J. Samuel Preus, 'Machiavelli's Functional Analysis of Religion: Context and Object', *Journal of the History of Ideas* 40 (1979), pp. 171–90; S. de Grazia, *Machiavelli in Hell* (Princeton NJ: Princeton University Press, 1989); V. B. Sullivan, 'Neither Christian Nor Pagan: Machiavelli's Treatment of Religion in the *Discourses*', *Polity* 26 (1993), pp. 259–80; C. J. Nederman, 'Amazing Grace: Fortune, God, and Free Will in Machiavelli's Thought', *Journal of the History of Ideas* 60 (1999), pp. 617–38; B. Fontana, 'Love of Country and Love of God: The Political Uses of Religion in Machiavelli', *Journal of the History of Ideas* 60 (1999), pp. 639–58; J. M. Najemy, 'Papirius and the Chickens, or Machiavelli on the Necessity of interpreting Religion', in *Journal of the History of Ideas* 60 (1999), pp. 659–81; A. Brown, 'Philosophy and Religion in Machiavelli', in J. M. Najemy (ed.), *The Cambridge Companion to Machiavelli* (Cambridge: Cambridge University Press, 2010), pp. 157–72; M. Viroli, *Machiavelli's God*, A. Shugaar (trans.) (Princeton NJ: Princeton University Press, 2010).
3 *Cons. e prat. 1498–1505*, pp. 986–7; cf. Francesco Guicciardini, *Storia d'Italia*, 6.7, 10, C. Panigada (ed.), 5 vols. (Bari: G. Laterza & Figli, 1929), vol. 2, pp. 117–22, pp. 132–3; Luca Landucci, *Diario fiorentino dal 1450 al 1516 continuato da un anonimo fino al 1542*, J. del Badia (ed.) (Florence: Sansoni, 1883), p. 265 (entry for 5 January 150[4]). On the Battle of Garigliano, see M. E. Mallett and C. Shaw, *The Italian Wars, 1494–1559: War, State and Society in Early Modern Europe* (London and New York: Routledge, 2012), pp. 68–9.

4   Guicciardini, *Storia d'Italia*, 6.10, Panigada (ed.), vol. 2, p. 133.
5   *Cons. e prat. 1498–1505*, pp. 986–7.
6   See, for example, Landucci, *Diario*, p. 265.
7   Some of the Florentine elite were more pessimistic than others. At a *pratica* on 10 January, Giambattista Ridolfi queried whether Louis would be able to do *anything* to protect the city in the present circumstances. *Cons. e prat. 1498–1505*, p. 988.
8   Machiavelli, *Opere*, P. Fanfani, G. Milanesi, L. Passerini (eds.), 6 vols. (Florence: Cenniniana, 1873–77), vol. 1, pp. lxii–lxiii.
9   *Leg. e comm.*, p. 753.
10   *Ibid.*
11   The suggestion made by Atkinson and Sices that Niccolò was sent to France because the *Dieci* 'had doubts about Valori's judgement' seems rather wide of the mark, particularly given that it appears to ignore the crucial turn of events between 12 and 18 January 1504. *Machiavelli and His Friends*, p. 97.
12   *Leg. e comm.*, pp. 750–5.
13   *Ibid.*, p. 756.
14   *Ibid.*, p. 757.
15   *Ibid.*, p. 758. Fearing that Piccino would face reprisals if Niccolò's despatch was intercepted, the secretary wisely concealed his name, revealing it only a week later (*ibid.*, p. 769).
16   *Ibid.*, p. 758.
17   *Ibid.*
18   *Ibid.*, p. 759.
19   *Ibid.*
20   *Ibid.*, p. 760.
21   *Ibid.*, p. 761.
22   *Ibid.*, p. 762.
23   For what follows, see *ibid.*, pp. 763–7.
24   *Ibid.*, pp. 768–9.
25   For what follows, see *ibid.*, pp. 769–70.
26   *Ibid.*, pp. 771–2.
27   *Ibid.*, p. 771.
28   *Ibid.*, pp. 773–4.
29   *Ibid.*, pp. 777–80.
30   *Ibid.*, p. 778.
31   *Ibid.*
32   *Ibid.*, p. 780.
33   *Ibid.*, p. 782.
34   *Ibid.*, pp. 784–5; Landucci, *Diario*, p. 266.
35   *Leg. e comm.*, pp. 785–7.
36   For what follows, see *ibid.*, pp. 787–9.

37   *Ibid.*, p. 791.

38   E.g. *ibid.*, p. 794.

39   Even the cardinal kept them at arm's length. Though they sought
      audiences with him on 8, 9 and 10 February, they were turned away
      on each occasion. Only Robertet – whom they visited at Niccolò's
      suggestion – told them anything vaguely encouraging. *Ibid.*, p. 794,
      p. 795, p. 797.

40   *Ibid.*, p. 797.

41   *Ibid.*, p. 798.

42   *Ibid.*, p. 797.

43   *Ibid.*, pp. 803–4.

44   *Ibid.*, p. 802.

45   *Ibid.*, p. 813, p. 817. The text of the truce is given at J. Dumont,
      Corps universel diplomatique du droit des gens, 8 vols. (Amsterdam: La
      Haye, 1726–31), vol. 4.1, pp. 72–4.

46   *Leg. e comm.*, pp. 817–18.

47   *Ibid.*, pp. 821–2.

48   *Ibid.*, p. 827.

49   *Ibid.*, p. 834.

50   On Sunday 25 February, Niccolò informed the *Dieci* that he would
      leave Lyon 'next Friday . . . without fail' (*ibid.*, p. 834). Assuming
      that 'next Friday' refers to 1 March, and that Niccolò took a similar
      time to get back to Florence, he must have arrived on or shortly
      after 5 March.

51   Louis XII had informed Niccolò of this on 18 February: *ibid.*, p. 818.
      See also L. Cappelletti, *Storia della Città e Stato di Piombino dalle
      origini fino all' anno 1814* (Livorno: R. Giusti, 1897), p. 141ff.

52   For the following, see *Leg. e comm.*, pp. 851–2.

53   Jacopo Nardi, *Istorie della città di Firenze*, 4, A. Gelli (ed.), 2 vols.
      (Florence: Le Monnier, 1858), vol. 1, p. 282.

54   *Cons. e prat. 1498–1505*, pp. 990–3.

55   *Ibid.*, pp. 993–5.

56   *Ibid.*, pp. 997–9; H. C. Butters, *Governors and Government in Early
      Sixteenth-Century Florence 1502–1519* (Oxford: Clarendon, 1985), p. 86.

57   See Butters, *Governors and Government*, pp. 86–7.

58   On the martial associations of May Day celebrations, see R. Trexler,
      Public Life in Renaissance Florence (Ithaca NY and London: Cornell
      University Press, 1980), pp. 216–22, p. 235, pp. 510–14.

59   On Totto's ecclesiastical career, see, for example, V. Arrighi,
      'Machiavelli, Totto', *DBI*, vol. 67 (Rome, 2006), pp. 105–7.

60   *Machiavelli and His Friends*, pp. 100–1 (no. 88).

61   Several poems have been identified as those referred to in V's letter.
      One possibility – proposed by Atkinson and Sices – is the serenata

'Salve, Donna, tra le altre donne eletta'. This is, however, highly unlikely. Consisting of 264 lines, it is far too long to have been sung in any context, least of all by two friends accompanied by a rebec. Gaeta, by contrast, has suggested the *strambotti* 'Io spero e lo sperar cresce 'l tormento' and 'Nasconde quel con che nuoce ogni fera'. But these are no more plausible. As we have already noted in a previous chapter, each of these poems can reliably be dated to the period before November 1494.

62 *Machiavelli and His Friends*, p. 101 (no. 89).

63 E.g. Nardi, *Istorie*, Gelli (ed.), vol. 1, pp. 290–1.

64 E.g. Landucci, *Diario*, p. 268.

65 *Ibid.*

66 For a valuable discussion of this statue and its wider meaning, see, for example, F. Ames-Lewis, 'Donatello's bronze David and the Palazzo Medici courtyard', *Renaissance Studies* 3 (1989), pp. 235–51.

67 *Lett.*, pp. 127–8 (no. 59); *Machiavelli and His Friends*, pp. 102–3 (no. 91).

68 On the fall of Ripafratta, see, for example, Landucci, *Diario*, pp. 268–9.

69 *Cons. e prat. 1498–1505*, pp. 1005–8. On 30 May, the Signoria had convened a *pratica* to consider this question, but it was agreed that it was of such importance that a larger assembly would be needed. *Cons. e prat. 1498–1505*, pp. 1003–5; Butters, *Governors and Government*, pp. 87–8.

70 Butters, *Governors and Government*, p. 88.

71 It has sometimes been suggested that the plan to divert the Arno was devised by Niccolò and Leonardo da Vinci: e.g. C. Pedretti, 'Machiavelli and Leonardo on the fortification of Piombino', *Italian Quarterly* 12 (1968), pp. 3–31. As Fachard has demonstrated, however, this cannot be true. D. Fachard, *Biagio Buonaccorsi* (Bologna: M. Boni, 1976), pp. 126–30. See also R. D. Masters, *Machiavelli, Leonardo, and the Science of Power* (Notre Dame IN: University of Notre Dame Press, 1996), p. 19. Biagio Buonaccorsi's sketch of the planned diversion is reproduced at Fachard, *Biagio Buonaccorsi*, pp. 158–9.

72 *Cons. e prat. 1498–1505*, pp. 990–3, here p. 993.

73 *Ibid.*, pp. 1013–15; Francesco Guicciardini, *Storie fiorentine*, 25, R. Palmarocchi (ed.) (Bari: G. Laterza & Figli, 1934), p. 273; Landucci, *Diario*, p. 71.

74 This paragraph is indebted to Fachard, *Biagio Buonaccorsi*, pp. 126–30; Masters, *Machiavelli, Leonardo*, p. 19.

75 Letter q. at Fachard, *Biagio Buonaccorsi*, p. 128; trans. from Masters, *Machiavelli, Leonardo*, p. 242.

76 Biagio Buonaccorsi, *Diario* (Florence: Giunti, 1568), pp. 92–3. Cf.

Biagio's contemporaneous notes (*sunmario*), repr. at Fachard, *Biagio Buonaccorsi*, pp. 127–8, here p. 127; trans. at Masters, *Machiavelli, Leonardo*, pp. 245–6.

77 Cf. Fachard, *Biagio Buonaccorsi*, p. 128.

78 Q. at *ibid.*, p. 142, n.32.

79 Buonaccorsi, *Diario*, p. 93; Fachard, *Biagio Buonaccorsi*, p. 128.

80 Fachard, *Biagio Buonaccorsi*, p. 128; cf. Buonaccorsi, *Diario*, p. 93.

81 That Lodovico was born at the beginning of October 1504 is suggested by a letter, dated 26 October, in which Cardinal Francesco Soderini mentions that he had heard about the birth of Niccolò's son. *Lett.*, p. 135 (no. 62); *Machiavelli and His Friends*, p. 107 (no. 94).

82 *Cons. e prat. 1498–1505*, pp. 1016–19; Buonaccorsi, *Diario*, p. 94; Fachard, *Biagio Buonaccorsi*, p. 128.

83 *Cons. e prat. 1498–1505*, p. 1017. A similar criticism was made by Francesco Gualterotti and Giovanni Benitii on the following day (*Cons. e prat. 1498–1505*, p. 1018).

84 *Ibid.*.

85 Acciaiuoli's report is published in C. Paoli, 'Convito Mediceo in Roma nel 1504', *Miscellanea fiorentina di erudizione e storia* 1 (1902), pp. 93–4. It is also reprinted (with some excisions) at *Cons. e prat. 1498–1505*, pp. 1019–20, n.7. This paragraph is indebted to Butters, *Governors and Government*, pp. 76–7.

86 Butters, *Governors and Government*, p. 76.

87 *Cons. e prat. 1498–1505*, pp. 1019–20.

88 Guicciardini, *Storie fiorentine*, 25, Palmarocchi (ed.), pp. 272–3; Filippo de' Nerli, *Commentari de' fatti civili Occorsi dentro la Città di Firenze dall'anno MCCXV al MDXXXVII* (Augusta: David Raimondo Mertz e Gio. Jacopo Majer, 1728), p. 98.

89 Butters, *Governors and Government*, pp. 59–60.

90 *Ibid.*, pp. 60–5.

91 Nerli, *Commentari*, p. 99.

92 Landucci reported that, on 21 October, troops were already being moved away from Pisa, allowing the Pisans to repair their defences. Landucci, *Diario*, p. 271.

93 Three different versions of the *Decennale primo* were produced. The first was composed between 24 October and 8 November 1504. An autograph copy is today found in the Biblioteca del Seminario Arcivescovile Maggiore, in Florence. After Salviati indicated his willingness to accept the dedication, Niccolò made a few small changes to make it even more flattering. The manuscript of this second version is held by the Biblioteca Medicea Laurenziana, in Florence. Later still, in mid-1506, Agostino Vespucci arranged for

the poem to be published, allowing Niccolò another opportunity to alter the text to fit the rather different political circumstances. For discussion of the various versions of the text, see E. H. Wilkins, W. A. Jackson and R. H. House, 'The Early Editions of Machiavelli's First Decennale', *Studies in the Renaissance* 11 (1964), pp. 76–104; A. Cabrini, 'Intorno al primo *Decennale*', *Rinascimento*, 2nd ser., 33 (1993), pp. 69–89; E. Scarpa, 'L'autografo del primo "Decennale" di Niccolò Machiavelli', *Studi di filologia italiana* 51 (1993), pp. 149–80. A brief overview may also be found in R. Black, *Machiavelli* (Abingdon: Routledge, 2013), pp. 64–7. As the forthcoming discussion will demonstrate, however, I must disagree with Black's readings in several respects, particularly insofar as the poem's intended meaning for Salviati is concerned.

94   For the Italian text of the *Decennale primo* (together with the dedicatory epistles in Latin and the vernacular), see Machiavelli, *Opere*, M. Bonfantini (ed.) (Milan and Naples: R. Ricciardi, 1954), pp. 1045–65. A serviceable English translation may be found in *Chief Works*, vol. 3, pp. 1444–7.

95   Machiavelli, *Decennale primo*, 355–63; *Opere*, Bonfantini (ed.), pp. 1058–9; *Chief Works*, vol. 3, p. 1453.

96   Machiavelli, *Decennale primo*, 364–78; *Opere*, Bonfantini (ed.), p. 1059; *Chief Works*, vol. 3, p. 1453.

97   Machiavelli, *Decennale primo*, 523–34; *Opere*, Bonfantini (ed.), p. 1064; *Chief Works*, vol. 3, pp. 1456–7.

98   Machiavelli, *Decennale primo*, 547–50; *Opere*, Bonfantini (ed.), p. 1065; *Chief Works*, vol. 3, p. 1447. The closing line (*se voi el tempio riaprissi a Marte*) is most likely a reference to the Romans' practice of entering the temple of Mars to awaken the god whenever war was declared. Cf. Ovid, *Fasti*, 5.561–2; Virgil, *Aen.* 7.603–10; Suetonius, *Div. Aug.* 29. It is, however, worth noting none of these classical texts actually mentions the opening of the temple doors. This may suggest Niccolò was perhaps conflating the temple of Mars with the temple of Janus, whose doors were shut in times of peace, but *open* in times of war. Indeed, the opening of the doors of this temple was a necessary ritual for the commencement of conflict. As several ancient authorities testify, the consuls would process to the temple of Janus immediately after the declaration of war, and solemnly open its doors. See Augustus, *Res gestae*, 13; Velleius Paterculus 2.38.3; Cassius Dio 51.20, 53.27; Plutarch, *Numa* 20.1. Whatever Niccolò's sources might have been, however, scholars have often tried to suggest the opening of the temple of Mars refers to the establishment of a citizen militia. But this seems somewhat unjustified. Although Niccolò did manage to

found a militia in 1506 and discussed it with Francesco Soderini sometime earlier – as we will soon see – there is no reason to suppose this is what he had in mind when writing the *Decennale primo*. There is nothing in the text itself that supports an allusion to the militia. Nor is there any solid contextual reason to interpolate such an allusion. After all, there was no discussion of the militia in *any* of the Florentine councils or *pratiche* in October–November 1504. All that can be said with any certainty is that Niccolò believed military action against Pisa should be renewed (by whatever means), and that, in saying so, he was attempting to break the political deadlock (attested by Nerli, Guicciardini etc.) that followed from the inglorious failure of Soderini's attempt to divert the Arno.

99 Machiavelli, *Decennale primo*, 502–4; *Opere*, Bonfantini (ed.), p. 1063; *Chief Works*, p. 1456.
100 Note Niccolò's warning against opposing Soderini: 'E s'alcun da tal ordine s'arretra | per alcuna cagion, esser potrebbe | di questo mondo non buon giomètra.' Machiavelli, *Decennale primo*, 379–81; *Opere*, Bonfantini (ed.), p. 1059; *Chief Works*, vol. 3, p. 1453.
101 *Lett.*, pp. 144–6 (no. 71); *Machiavelli and His Friends*, pp. 118–19 (no. 107).
102 For what follows, see esp. Butters, *Governors and Government*, pp. 90–2.
103 *Cons. e prat. 1498–1505*, pp. 1022–3.
104 Guicciardini, *Storie fiorentine*, 26, Palmarocchi (ed.), p. 276; Guicciardini, *Storie d'Italia*, 6.1, Panigada (ed.), vol. 2, pp. 83–5.
105 *Cons. e prat. 1498–1505*, pp. 1024–5.
106 Guicciardini, *Storia d'Italia*, 6.1, Panigada (ed.), vol. 2, pp. 86–7.
107 *Leg. e comm.*, pp. 861–2.
108 *Lett.*, p. 138 (no. 65); *Machiavelli and His Friends*, p. 108, p. 110 (nos. 96, 98).
109 On Niccolò's journey to Castiglione del Lago, see *Leg. e comm.*, p. 863.
110 *Ibid.*, p. 864.
111 For what follows, see *ibid.*, pp. 865–6.
112 *Ibid.*, p. 867.
113 For what follows, see *ibid.*, pp. 867–8.
114 *Ibid.*, p. 870.
115 On the receipt of Niccolò's letter of 11 April, see *Cons. e prat. 1498–1505*, p. 1027.
116 On Fabrizio Colonna, see esp. F. Petrucci, 'Colonna, Fabrizio', *DBI*, vol. 27 (Rome, 1982), pp. 288–91.
117 *Cons. e prat. 1498–1505*, pp. 993–5; Butters, *Governors and Government*, pp. 83–4, p. 87, pp. 93–4. On his career in Aragonese service, see, for

example, Petrucci, 'Colonna, Fabrizio'; Mallett and Shaw, *The Italian Wars*, p. 59, p. 60, p. 62, p. 64, p. 65.

118 This paragraph is indebted to Butters, *Governors and Government*, p. 94.

119 The *condotta* is reproduced at *Leg. e comm.*, pp. 880–1.

120 See *ibid.*, pp. 877–8.

121 Cf. Bertelli's comments at *Leg. e comm.*, p. 885.

122 R. A. Goldthwaite, 'I prezzi del grano a Firenze dal XIV al XVI secolo', *Quaderni storici* 10 (1975), pp. 5–36, here p. 35.

123 Nardi, *Istorie*, Gelli (ed.), vol. 1, p. 312.

124 *Cons. e prat. 1498–1505*, pp. 1027–9.

125 On 23 May, for example, Francesco Pepi argued that, since the marquis's conditions could prove harmful to Florence's interests, it might not be such a good idea to retain his services. *Cons. e prat. 1505–12*, pp. 3–4.

126 *Cons. e prat. 1505–12*, p. 4. Piero del Nero's proposal was seconded by Francesco di Antonio di Taddeo and firmly supported by Soderini. See Guicciardini, *Storie fiorentine*, 26, Palmarocchi (ed.), p. 277.

127 Cf. Buonaccorsi, *Diario*, p. 106.

128 *Cons. e prat. 1505–12*, pp. 9–12.

129 On 30 May, the *Dieci* even instructed their ambassador in Rome to discuss the possibility of employing Fabrizio against the Orsini with Cardinal Giovanni Colonna. Butters, *Governors and Government*, pp. 98–9.

130 *Cons. e prat. 1505–12*, pp. 12–17.

131 On 30 May, the *Dieci* had instructed their ambassador, Francesco Pandolfini, to ask Louis XII to put pressure on the marquis, in the hope the latter might be persuaded to abandon the conditions he had requested. This was, however, unsuccessful. See Butters, *Governors and Government*, p. 98.

132 Towards the end of May, Alviano had unexpectedly suggested that Florence might employ him as its captain-general. As Butters has argued, the *Dieci* are unlikely to have taken this seriously. Even had they trusted Alviano's sincerity, they could not have concluded any agreement with the Spanish without Louis XII's express consent. But they were happy to make a pretence of considering the idea; negotiations would, after all, buy them some breathing space. See Butters, *Governors and Government*, p. 98.

133 According to Jacopo Nardi, the Florentines had refrained from attacking Pisa out of fear of Gonzalo. There is, however, little other evidence to support this contention. More likely, their failure to keep up the pressure on the city was due to political problems, financial difficulties and famine. Nardi, *Istorie*, Gelli (ed.), vol. 1, p. 313.

134 For what follows, see *Cons. e prat. 1505–12*, pp. 21–4.

135 See Bertelli's notes at *Leg. e comm.*, pp. 885–6.

136 Cf. Buonaccorsi, *Diario*, p. 107; Nardi, *Istorie*, Gelli (ed.), vol. 1, pp. 314–15.

137 The strongest opposition came from Giovanbattista Ridolfi, one of the firmest supporters of the Salviati: *Cons. e prat. 1505–12*, pp. 23–4. He reiterated his disapproval in even more forceful terms at a further *pratica* on 2 July: *Cons. e prat. 1505–12*, p. 27.

138 *Leg. e comm.*, p. 889.

139 For the remainder of this paragraph, see *ibid.*, pp. 890–1.

140 *Ibid.*, pp. 894–5.

141 *Ibid.*, pp. 895–8.

142 *Ibid.*, pp. 900–2.

143 *Ibid.*, pp. 911–12.

144 *Ibid.*, pp. 913–14. The *Dieci* did, however, accept that Gonzalo had forbidden Alviano to attack Florence. This information was duly communicated to Pandolfini in France on 27 July. ASF Dieci, Miss. 30, fols. 130v–131r; Butters, *Governors and Government*, p. 100.

145 *Leg. e comm.*, pp. 914–17.

146 *Ibid.*, pp. 917–20.

147 See, for example, Biagio Buonaccorsi's letter to Niccolò on 24 July 1505: *Lett.*, pp. 140–1 (no. 67); *Machiavelli and His Friends*, pp. 112–13 (no. 102).

148 Guicciardini, *Storie fiorentine*, 26, Palmarocchi (ed.), p. 277.

149 Butters, *Governors and Government*, pp. 100–1.

150 See Buonaccorsi, *Diario*, pp. 113–14; Guicciardini, *Storie fiorentine*, 26, Palmarocchi (ed.), p. 278.

151 Guicciardini, *Storie fiorentine*, 26, Palmarocchi (ed.), p. 278; cf. Buonaccorsi, *Diario*, p. 114.

152 As Guicciardini put it, 'the gonfaloniere's vanity [was] greatly increased by this victory, and [he] attribute[ed] it to his own genius.' Guicciardini, *Storie fiorentine*, 26, Palmarocchi (ed.), p. 278.

153 Giacomini's letter was written at the twenty-third hour of the night. See *Cons. e prat. 1505–12*, p. 45, n.2.

154 See, for example, Guicciardini, *Storie fiorentine*, 26, Palmarocchi (ed.), pp. 278–9.

155 *Cons. e prat. 1505–12*, pp. 47–51.

156 Butters, *Governors and Government*, p. 102.

157 Niccolò Machiavelli, *Scritti inediti di Niccolò Machiavelli risguardanti la storia e la milizia (1499–1512)*, G. Canestrini (ed.) (Florence: Barbèra Bianchi e Comp, 1857), p. 208.

158 See Butters, *Governors and Government*, pp. 84–5, p. 102.

159 *Ibid.*, p. 104.

160 *Cons. e prat. 1505–12*, p. 51; Buonaccorsi, *Diario*, p. 115.

161 *Machiavelli and His Friends*, p. 113 (no. 103).

162 See *Cons. e prat. 1505–12*, pp. 51–3.

163 Guicciardini, *Storie fiorentine*, 26, Palmarocchi (ed.), p. 280.

164 *Cons. e prat. 1505–12*, pp. 53–5.

165 Buonaccorsi, *Diario*, p. 115.

166 For what follows, see Buonaccorsi, *Diario*, pp. 116–17; cf. the much-abbreviated account at Guicciardini, *Storie fiorentine*, 26, Palmarocchi (ed.), p. 280.

167 This paragraph is indebted to Butters, *Governors and Government*, p. 104.

168 *Ibid.*

169 Buonaccorsi, *Diario*, p. 117; cf. Machiavelli, *Scritti inediti*, 221.

170 Guicciardini, *Storie fiorentine*, 26; Palmarocchi (ed.), p. 281. For discussion, see esp. M. Hörnqvist, 'Perché non si usa allegare i Romani: Machiavelli and the Florentine Militia of 1506', *Renaissance Quarterly* 55/1 (2002), pp. 148–91, here pp. 154–5; P. J. Jones, 'The Machiavellian Militia: Innovation or Renovation?', in C.-M. de La Roncière (ed.), *La Toscane et les Toscans autour de la Renaissance: Cadres de vie, société, croyances. Mélanges offerts à C.-M. de La Roncière* (Aix-en-Provence: Publications de l'Université de Provence, 1999), pp. 11–52; A. Guidi, *Un segretario militante: politica, diplomazia e armi nel cancelliere Machiavelli* (Bologna: Il Mulino, 2009); G. Sasso, 'Machiavelli, Cesare Borgia, Don Micheletto e la questione della milizia', in G. Sasso, *Machiavelli e gli antichi e altri saggi*, 4 vols. (Milan and Naples: Ricciardi, 1987–97), vol. 2, pp. 57–117.

171 *Machiavelli and His Friends*, pp. 101–2 (no. 90). On Cardinal Francesco Soderini's involvement in the planned revival of the militia, see K. J. P. Lowe, *Church and Politics in Renaissance Italy: The Life and Career of Cardinal Francesco Soderini, 1453–1524* (Cambridge: Cambridge University Press, 1993), pp. 60–2.

172 *Machiavelli and His Friends*, p. 107 (no. 94).

173 For what follows, see Guicciardini, *Storie fiorentine*, 26, Palmarocchi (ed.), p. 282.

174 As Hörnqvist rightly notes, 'the historians Jacopo Nardi and Jacopo Pitti both came to ascribe the idea [of reviving the militia] to Antonio Giacomini' rather than to Niccolò. Hörnqvist, 'Perché non', p. 148; Nardi, *Istorie*, Gelli (ed.), vol. 1, p. 371; cf. Jacopo Nardi, *Vita di Antonio Giacomini*, V. Bramanti (ed.) (Bergamo: Moretti & Vitali, 1990), p. 130.

175 *Leg. e comm.*, p. 926. For discussion, see Hörnqvist, 'Perché non', p. 155.

176 It was one of the coldest winters in recent years. Just two weeks later, the Arno froze over. Landucci, *Diario*, p. 272.

177 *Leg. e comm.*, pp. 926–7.

178 *Leg. e comm.*, p. 929.
179 *Ibid.*, p. 931.
180 Landucci, *Diario*, p. 273.

13. Fortune Favours the Brave (February–December 1506)

1   Niccolò's letter to Vespucci has been lost. On Vespucci, see, for
    example, Giulio Negri, *Istoria degli scrittori fiorentini* (Ferrara:
    Bernardino Pomatelli, 1722), pp. 86–7.
2   *Lett.*, pp. 129–30 (no. 60); *Machiavelli and His Friends*, pp. 103–4 (no. 92).
3   *Ibid.*, p. 118 (no. 106).
4   Niccolò received his orders on 26 February. *Leg. e comm.*, p. 932.
5   *Machiavelli and His Friends*, p. 120 (no. 109).
6   E. H. Wilkins, H. A. Jackson and R. H. House, 'The Early Editions
    of Machiavelli's First Decennale', *Studies in the Renaissance* 11 (1964),
    pp. 76–104, esp. pp. 76–88 [repr. as the introduction to Niccolò
    Machiavelli, *The First Decennale* (Cambridge MA: Harvard
    University Press, 1969)]. The *Decennale primo* was published as
    Niccolò Machiavelli, *Compendium rerum decennio in Italia gestarum*
    (Florence: Bartolomeo de' Libri, 1506).
7   *Lett.*, pp. 144–6 (no. 71); *Machiavelli and His Friends*, pp. 118–19 (no. 107).
8   For Niccolò's mission to the Casentino, see *Leg. e comm.*, pp. 933–6.
9   *Lett.*, pp. 146–9 (no. 72); *Machiavelli and His Friends*, pp. 121–3 (no.
    110); Niccolò Machiavelli, *Compendium rerum decennio in Italia
    gestarum* (Florence: Andrea Ghirlandi and Antonio Tubini, 1506).
    On Andrea Ghirlandi da Pistoia, see M. Breccia Fratadocchi,
    'Ghirlandi, Andrea', *DBI*, vol. 53 (2000), pp. 805–6.
10 Francesco Guicciardini, *Storie fiorentine*, 27, R. Palmarocchi (ed.)
    (Bari: G. Laterza & Figli, 1934), pp. 286–7; H. C. Butters, *Governors
    and Government in Early Sixteenth-Century Florence 1502–1519*
    (Oxford: Clarendon, 1985), p. 107.
11 Guicciardini, *Storie fiorentine*, 26, Palmarocchi (ed.), p. 281.
12 *Ibid.*, pp. 283–5; Butters, *Governors and Government*, pp. 108–9.
13 He seems to have been occupied primarily with arranging supplies
    for the militia in Pescia: Niccolò Machiavelli, *Scritti inediti di
    Niccolò Machiavelli risguardanti la storia e la milizia (1499–1512)*,
    G. Canestrini (ed.) (Florence: Barbèra Bianchi e Comp, 1857),
    pp. 283–95.
14 For which, see Luca Landucci, *Diario fiorentino dal 1450 al 1516
    continuato da un anonimo fino al 1542*, J. del Badia (ed.) (Florence,
    1883), p. 275.
15 Guicciardini, *Storie fiorentine*, 27, Palmarocchi (ed.), p. 287; Butters,
    Governors and Government, pp. 107–8.

16 *Lett.*, pp. 150–1 (no. 73); *Machiavelli and His Friends*, pp. 123–4 (no. 111).
17 See F. Gregorovius, *History of the City of Rome in the Middle Ages*, A. Hamilton (trans.), 8 vols. in 13, repr. (New York: AMS Press, 1967), vol. 8.1, pp. 39–40, pp. 44–7.
18 *Lett.*, pp. 151–6 (no. 74); *Machiavelli and His Friends*, pp. 124–7 (no. 112).
19 See Jean d'Auton, *Chroniques de Louis XII*, R. de Maulde La Clavière (ed.), 4 vols. (Paris: Renouard, 1889–95), vol. 4, pp. 64–6.
20 Guicciardini, *Storie fiorentine*, 27, Palmarocchi (ed.), p. 290.
21 *Cons. e prat. 1505–12*, pp. 83–94.
22 Guicciardini suggests that Gualterotti, Pepi and Salviati were problably motivated above all by a desire to harm Soderini: Guicciardini, *Storie fiorentine*, 27, Palmarocchi (ed.), p. 290. For further discussion, see Butters, *Governors and Government*, pp. 109–10.
23 *Leg. e comm.*, pp. 947–8.
24 For the following meeting with Julius, see *ibid.*, pp. 950–54.
25 *Ibid.*, pp. 954–5.
26 *Ibid.*, pp. 955–6.
27 For their route, see *ibid.*, p. 957, p. 964.
28 *Ibid.*, p. 959, pp. 960–1.
29 *Ibid.*, p. 958.
30 *Ibid.*
31 *Ibid.*, p. 963.
32 *Ibid.*, pp. 960–1.
33 As Niccolò's letters testify, Julius's route took him through Castel della Pieve and Corciano. *Ibid.*, pp. 970–3, pp. 976–9.
34 *Ibid.*, p. 965.
35 The details of the agreement are outlined at *ibid.*, pp. 970–1. This was brokered by the duke of Urbino, who commanded the pope's forces, and the papal legate, Giovanni de' Medici. See *ibid.*, p. 965, pp. 966–7.
36 *Ibid.*, p. 979, p. 980.
37 *Ibid.*, p. 980.
38 Niccolò omitted to mention that Julius did not enter Perugia alone and unaccompanied. According to Paride de' Grassi, the papal master of ceremonies, Julius was accompanied by his Swiss Guard and a sizable number of cardinals and nobles. Care also seems to have been taken to place Baglioni in the midst of this entourage. Paride de' Grassi, *Le due spedizioni militari di Giulio II*, L. Frati (ed.) (Bologna: Regia Tipografia, 1886), pp. 40–4. On this basis, Shaw has argued that it would have been 'very dangerous' for Baglioni to attempt to capture the pope. C. Shaw, *Julius II: The Warrior Pope* (Oxford: Blackwell, 1993), p. 156.
39 *Machiavelli and His Friends*, pp. 134–6 (no. 121). On the dating and

textual transmission of the letter, as well as on the identification of Giovanbattista Soderini as the likely addressee, see M. Martelli, 'I *Ghiribizzi* a Giovan Battista Soderini', *Rinascimento* 9 (1969), pp. 147–80; R. Ridolfi and P. Ghigleri, 'I *Ghiribizzi* a Soderini', *La Bibliofilia* 72 (1970), pp. 52–72; G. Sasso, 'Qualche osservazione sui "Ghiribizzi al Soderino"', *Cultura* 11 (1973), pp. 129–67; R. Ridolfi, 'Ultime postille Machiavelliane', *La Bibliofilia* 77 (1975), pp. 65–76; C. Dionisotti, *Machiavellerie. Storie e fortuna di Machiavelli* (Turin: Einaudi, 1980), pp. 74–5; C. Vivanti, *Niccolò Machiavelli. I tempi della politica* (Rome: Donzelli, 2008); B. Richardson, *Manuscript Culture in Renaissance Italy* (Cambridge: Cambridge University Press, 2009), p. 100. For a recent analysis of the intellectual background to the *Ghiribizzi* and Niccolò's possible debt to the works of Donato Acciaiuoli, see C. Ginzburg, 'Diventare Machiavelli. Per una nuova lettura dei "Ghiribizzi al Soderini"', *Quaderni Storici* 121 (2006), pp. 151–64.

40 *Machiavelli and His Friends*, p. 134 (no. 121).
41 *Ibid.*
42 *Ibid.*, p. 135 (no. 121).
43 That Niccolò intended Giovanbattista to show the letter to the *gonfaloniere* has been demonstrated in Sasso, 'Qualche osservazione'; Ridolfi, 'Ultime postille'.
44 *Machiavelli and His Friends*, p. 135 (no. 121).
45 Machiavelli, *Capitolo di Fortuna*, 25–42.
46 *Ibid.*, 107–8, 113–14.
47 *Ibid.*, 10–12.
48 For the following, see the allegorical treatment of Fortune's 'servants' at *ibid.*, 73–96.
49 *Ibid.*, 130–54.
50 *Ibid.*, 169–89.
51 *Ibid.*, 160–5.
52 *Leg. e comm.*, p. 985.
53 *Ibid.*, p. 988.
54 *Ibid.*, p. 989.
55 See, for example, Guicciardini, *Storie fiorentine*, 27, Palmarocchi (ed.), p. 292. Though Philip the Fair died on 26 September 1506, news did not reach Niccolò until 6 October: *Leg. e comm.*, p. 1013.
56 See *Leg. e comm.*, pp. 1000–1.
57 *Ibid.*, p. 981.
58 For the following, see *ibid.*, p. 984.
59 *Ibid.*, pp. 997–8.
60 The Bolognese ambassadors appear to have arrived in Cesena on the night of 30 September: *ibid.*, pp. 1004–5. For what follows, see *ibid.*, pp. 1006–8.

61 *Ibid.*, p. 1008.

62 Butters, *Governors and Government*, p. 109; cf. *Machiavelli and His Friends*, p. 136 (no. 122).

63 *Lett.*, p. 162 (no. 8); *Machiavelli and His Friends*, p. 132, p. 133 (nos. 118, 120).

64 *Leg. e comm.*, p. 1001.

65 *Ibid.*, p. 1008.

66 *Ibid.*, pp. 1019–21.

67 *Ibid.*, pp. 1024–5.

68 *Ibid.*, p. 1024.

69 *Ibid.*, p. 1025.

70 *Ibid.*, p. 1028.

71 *Ibid.*, p. 1029.

72 *Ibid.*, pp. 1030–1.

73 Cf. de' Grassi, *Le due spedizioni*, p. 68.

74 *Ibid.*, pp. 61–2; *Leg. e comm.*, pp. 1017–18; Shaw, *Julius II*, p. 159.

75 *Leg. e comm.*, p. 1029.

76 De' Grassi, *Le due spedizioni*, pp. 69–70.

77 *Ibid.*, p. 70; Shaw, *Julius II*, p. 161.

78 *Leg. e comm.*, pp. 1034–5.

79 De' Grassi, *Le due spedizioni*, pp. 79–84; Shaw, *Julius II*, p. 161.

80 De' Grassi, *Le due spedizioni*, pp. 80–1.

81 *Leg. e comm.*, pp. 1034–5.

82 For a discussion of Niccolò's return to Florence, see J.-J. Marchand, *Niccolò Machiavelli: I primi scritti politici* (Padua: Antenore, 1975), p. 132.

83 *Ibid.*, p. 128.

84 Among the most impressive was Bastiano da Castiglione, who, as Biagio Buonaccorsi noted, had successfully put together a force of 700 soldiers to be used in the event of Maximilian descending into Italy. *Lett.*, p. 157 (no. 75); *Machiavelli and His Friends*, p. 127 (no. 113).

85 On 11 October, Biagio Buonaccorsi had noted that, upon replacing Piero Guicciardini on the *Dieci*, Bernardo Nasi immediately used his influence to secure more funding for the nascent militia: *Lett.*, p. 172 (no. 83); *Machiavelli and His Friends*, p. 146 (no. 132).

86 *Lett.*, p. 163, p. 172 (nos. 79, 83); *Machiavelli and His Friends*, p. 133, p. 136, p. 146 (nos. 120, 122, 132).

87 Biagio dismissed these as 'having no value whatsoever': *Lett.*, p. 163 (no. 79); *Machiavelli and His Friends*, p. 136 (no. 122).

88 Marchand, *I primi scritti politici*, p. 128.

89 The text of *La cagione dell'ordinanza* can be found in: Niccolò Machiavelli, *Opere*, M. Bonfantini (ed.) (Milan and Naples: R. Ricciardi, 1954), pp. 465–70; *Opere*, P. Fanfani, G. Milanesi, L.

Passerini (eds.), 6 vols. (Florence: Cenniniana, 1873–77), vol. 6, pp. 330–5; Marchand, *I primi scritti politici*, pp. 432–7. For discussion of the *cagione*, see Marchand, *I primi scritti politici*, pp. 120–43.

90 Machiavelli, *Opere*, Bonfantini (ed.), p. 465; Marchand, *I primi scritti politici*, p. 432.

91 Machiavelli, *Opere*, Bonfantini (ed.), p. 465; Marchand, *I primi scritti politici*, p. 432.

92 Machiavelli, *Opere*, Bonfantini (ed.), p. 466; Marchand, *I primi scritti politici*, p. 433.

93 Machiavelli, *Opere*, Bonfantini (ed.), pp. 465–6; Marchand, *I primi scritti politici*, p. 433.

94 Machiavelli, *Opere*, Bonfantini (ed.), pp. 465–7; Marchand, *I primi scritti politici*, pp. 433–4.

95 Machiavelli, *Opere*, Bonfantini (ed.), p. 469; Marchand, *I primi scritti politici*, pp. 435–6.

96 Machiavelli, *Opere*, Bonfantini (ed.), p. 469; Marchand, *I primi scritti politici*, p. 436.

97 The text of the *Provisione della ordinanza* can be found in: Machiavelli, *Opere*, Fanfani et al. (eds.), vol. 6, pp. 339–52; Marchand, *I primi scritti politici*, pp. 450–61.

98 Machiavelli, *Opere*, Fanfani et al. (eds.), vol. 6, pp. 339–40; Marchand, *I primi scritti politici*, pp. 450–1.

99 For discussion, see, for example, Marchand, *I primi scritti politici*, pp. 144–56; R. Ridolfi, *Vita di Niccolò Machiavelli*, 3rd ed., 2 vols. (Florence: Sansoni, 1969), vol. 1, pp. 152–3; Butters, *Governors and Government*, p. 112; M. Hörnqvist, 'Perché non si usa allegare i Romani: Machiavelli and the Florentine Militia of 1506', *Renaissance Quarterly* 55/1 (2002), pp. 148–91, here p. 159.

100 Its members were: Antonio di Simone Canigiani, Francesco d'Antonio di Taddeo, Giovanni di Corrado Berardi, Chimenti di Cipriano Serrigi, Antonio di Jacopo Giacomini Tebalducci, Giovanni di Tommaso Ridolfi, Alamanno d'Averardo Salviati, Chimenti di Francesco Scarpelloni and Gulielmo d'Angiolino Angiolini. O. Tommasini, *La vita e gli scritti di Niccolò Machiavelli nella loro relazione col machiavellismo*, 3 vols. (Turin: Ermanno Loescher, 1883–1911), vol. 1, p. 367.

101 *Lett.*, p. 174 (no. 85); *Machiavelli and His Friends*, p. 150 (no. 139).

102 *Lett.*, pp. 174–5 (no. 85); *Machiavelli and His Friends*, p. 150 (no. 139).

103 As Cerretani noted, Niccolò was derided as Soderini's *mannerino* ('little man'): Ridolfi, *Vita di Niccolò Machiavelli*, vol. 1, p. 156.

104 *Lett.*, p. 168 (no. 81); 6 *Machiavelli and His Friends*, p. 141 (no. 127).

14. The Emperor (January 1507–June 1508)

1 In a letter written on 17 December 1506, Francesco Pandolfini informed Louis XII that Florence had 700 soldiers under arms and was making preparations to assemble a force of 1,200 infantrymen. G. Canestrini and A. Desjardins (eds.), *Négociations diplomatiques de la France avec la Toscane*, 6 vols. (Paris: Imprimerie Impériale / Imprimerie Nationale, 1859–86), vol. 2, p. 200.

2 Niccolò Machiavelli, *Scritti inediti di Niccolò Machiavelli risguardanti la storia e la milizia (1499–1512)*, G. Canestrini (ed.) (Florence: Barbèra Bianchi e Comp, 1857), pp. 308–9.

3 E.g. *ibid.*, pp. 305–6.

4 *Ibid.*, pp. 303–4. In this circular, Niccolò made it clear that any constable who deserted was to be put to death. The same punishment would also be imposed on those who went outside their *bandiere* to serve a private *fazione*. For further discussion, see, for example, O. Tommasini, *La vita e gli scritti di Niccolò Machiavelli nella loro relazione col machiavellismo*, 3 vols. (Turin: Ermanno Loescher, 1883–1911), vol. 1, pp. 367–8.

5 Tommasini, *Le vita e gli scritti*, vol. 1, p. 363.

6 According to Cerretani, some 3,000 men were under arms by the end of May. Bartolomeo Cerretani, *Ricordi*, G. Berti (ed.) (Florence: Olschki, 1993), p. 120; Tommasini, *La vita e gli scritti*, vol. 1, p. 362. On the deployment of the militia, see, for example, Machiavelli, *Scritti inediti*, pp. 314–16.

7 Luca Landucci, *Diario fiorentino dal 1450 al 1516 continuato da un anonimo fino al 1542*, J. del Badia (ed.) (Florence: Sansoni, 1883), pp. 280–1.

8 Cerretani, *Ricordi*, p. 120.

9 Bartolomeo Cerretani, *Storia fiorentina*, G. Berti (ed.) (Florence: Olschki, 1994), p. 347.

10 The following three paragraphs are heavily indebted to the masterful summary at H. C. Butters, *Governors and Government in Early Sixteenth-Century Florence 1502–1519* (Oxford: Clarendon, 1985), pp. 115–16.

11 Negotiations were conducted first by Jacopo Salviati and Francesco Gualterotti, and then, when they asked to be relieved, by Niccolò Valori. Francesco Guicciardini, *Storie fiorentine*, 27, R. Palmarocchi (ed.) (Bari: G. Laterza & Figli, 1934), p. 293.

12 M. E. Mallett and C. Shaw, *The Italian Wars, 1494–1559: War, State and Society in Early Modern Europe* (London and New York: Routledge, 2012), pp. 81–2; J. E. Ruiz-Domènec, *El Gran Capitán: Retrato de una época* (Barcelona: Ediciones Península, 2002),

pp. 398–9; C. J. Hernando Sánchez, *El reino de Nápoles en el Imperio de Carlos V: La consolidación de la conquista* (Madrid: Sociedad Estatal para la Conmemoración de los Centenarios de Felipe II y Carlos V, 2001), p. 125.

13 On the Genoese revolt, see S. A. Epstein, *Genoa and the Genoese, 958–1528* (Chapel Hill NC and London: University of North Carolina Press, 1996), pp. 312–13. For Louis' offer to the Florentines, see Canestrini and Desjardins (eds.), *Négociations diplomatiques*, vol. 2, pp. 222–31.

14 *Cons. e prat. 1505–12*, pp. 98–9.

15 Jean d'Auton, *Chroniques de Louis XII*, R. de Maulde La Clavière (ed.), 4 vols. (Paris: Renouard, 1889–95), vol. 4, pp. 297–8.

16 On the convention between Louis XII of France and Ferdinand of Aragon, see d'Auton, *Chroniques*, vol. 4, pp. 340–64; R. de Maulde, 'L'entrevue de Savone en 1507', *Revue d'histoire diplomatique* 4 (1890), pp. 583–90; J. Doussinague, 'Fernando el Católico en las vistas de Savona de 1507', *Boletín de la Academia de la Historia* 108 (1936), pp. 99–146.

17 For further discussion of Florence's dalliance with the emperor, see N. Rubinstein, 'Firenze e il problema della politica imperiale in Italia al tempo di Massimiliano I', *ASI* 116 (1958), pp. 5–35, pp. 147–77.

18 On the War of the Landshut Succession, see, for example, R. Ebneth and P. Schmid (eds.), *Der Landshuter Erbfolgekrieg. An der Wende vom Mittelalter zur Neuzeit* (Regensburg: Kartenhaus Kollektiv, 2004); R. Stauber, 'Um die Einheit des Hauses Bayern: die Wittelsbacher und König Maximilian im Landshuter Erbfolgekrieg 1504', *An der unteren Isar und Vils. Historische Heimatblätter für die Stadt und den früheren Landkreis Landau an der Isar* 29 (2005), pp. 6–31.

19 For discussion, see G. Ibler, 'König Maximilian I. und der Konstanzer Reichstag von 1507' (Unpublished PhD thesis, University of Graz, 1961).

20 See, for example, d'Auton, *Chroniques*, vol. 4, p. 245, pp. 335–7.

21 Guicciardini, *Storie fiorentine*, 28, Palmarocchi (ed.), pp. 298–302. For a splendid discussion of the differences between Guicciardini's account and the minutes of the *pratiche*, see Butters, *Governors and Government*, pp. 117–21.

22 Guicciardini, *Storie fiorentine*, 28, Palmarocchi (ed.), p. 297.

23 R. F. Hughes, 'Francesco Vettori: his place in Florentine diplomacy and politics' (Unpublished PhD thesis, University of London, 1958), p. 39; R. Devonshire Jones, 'Some Observations on the Relations between Francesco Vettori and Niccolò Machiavelli during the Embassy to Maximilian I', *Italian Studies* 23 (1968), pp. 93–113;

R. Devonshire Jones, *Francesco Vettori: Florentine Citizen and Medici Servant* (London: Athlone Press, 1972), pp. 10–33.

24 Salviati had been elected to the *Nove ufficiali dell'ordinanza e milizia fiorentina* in January: Tommasini, *La vita e gli scritti di Niccolò Machiavelli*, vol. 1, p. 371.

25 For a detailed discussion of the following letters, see J. Najemy, 'The controversy surrounding Machiavelli's service to the republic', in G. Bock, Q. Skinner and M. Viroli (eds.), *Machiavelli and Republicanism* (Cambridge: Cambridge University Press, 1990), pp. 101–17, here pp. 109–12.

26 *Lett.*, pp. 179–81 (no. 88); *Machiavelli and His Friends*, pp. 157–8 (no. 144). On this correspondent, see P. Malanima, 'Casavecchia, Filippo', *DBI*, vol. 21 (Rome, 1978), pp. 269–70.

27 *Lett.*, p. 182 (no. 89); *Machiavelli and His Friends*, p. 159 (no. 145).

28 Machiavelli, *Scritti inediti*, pp. 356–60.

29 *Ibid.*, pp. 360–2.

30 *Machiavelli and His Friends*, p. 159 (no. 146).

31 H. Wiesflecker, *Kaiser Maximilian I: Das Reich, Österreich und Europa an der Wende zur Neuzeit*, 5 vols. (Munich: Oldenbourg, 1971–86), vol. 3, pp. 354–79.

32 See Bertelli, 'Nota introduttiva', *Leg. e comm.*, p. 1039. For the text of '*Vom Romzug*', see R. von Liliencron, *Die historischen Volkslieder der Deutschen vom 13. bis 16. Jahrhundert*, 5 vols. (Leipzig: F. C. W. Vogel, 1865–9), vol. 3, pp. 15–17 (no. 254).

33 Bertelli, 'Nota introduttiva', *Leg. e comm.*, p. 1039. On the legate, see G. Fragnito, 'Carvajal, Bernardino López de', *DBI*, vol. 21 (Rome, 1978), pp. 28–34.

34 Landucci, *Diario*, p. 283. It is worth noting that Landucci also wildly overestimated the number of troops Maximilian had been granted by the Diet of Constance. He believed the princes had agreed to provide no fewer than 160,000 foot soldiers and 22,000 cavalry.

35 Unfortunately, Niccolò's instructions have not survived – if they ever existed in written form. His object can, however, be inferred from his despatches during the mission.

36 For the following, see *Leg. e comm.*, pp. 1041–2.

37 *Ibid.*, p. 1045.

38 *Ibid.*, p. 1046.

39 *Ibid.* (emphasis added).

40 Were this to happen, the Florentines would be able to reach an agreement with Maximilian without fear of jeopardizing their existing relationship with Louis XII. So likely was a Franco-imperial accord believed to be that, on 16 August, a *pratica*

unanimously recommended that Florence continue making payments to Louis XII. *Cons. e prat. 1505–12*, pp. 108–9; Butters, *Governors and Government*, p. 120.

41 G. Benecke, *Society and Politics in Germany, 1500–1750* (Abingdon: Routledge, 1974), p. 248; cf. J. Whaley, *Germany and the Holy Roman Empire*, 2 vols. (Oxford: Oxford University Press, 2012), vol. 1, p. 75.

42 *Cons. e prat. 1505–12*, pp. 142–8, here pp. 142–3; for discussion, see Butters, *Governors and Government*, p. 123.

43 Benecke, *Society and Politics*, p. 248; Whaley, *Germany*, vol. 1, p. 75.

44 *Cons. e prat. 1505–12*, pp. 151–2.

45 *Ibid.*, pp. 153–63.

46 *Ibid.*, pp. 159–60.

47 *Ibid.*, pp. 170–5, here p. 172.

48 For the decision to send Niccolò, see *ibid.*, p. 175. On debates about the nature of his mission, see, for example, Devonshire Jones, *Francesco Vettori*, pp. 24–5.

49 *Leg. e comm.*, p. 1069.

50 See, for example, G. Mattingly, *Renaissance Diplomacy* (Boston: Houghton Mifflin, 1955), pp. 269–82; L. S. Frey and M. L. Frey, *The History of Diplomatic Immunity* (Columbus OH: Ohio State University Press, 1999); D. Frigo, 'Ambasciatori, ambasciate e immunità diplomatiche nelle letteratura politica italiana (secc. XVI–XVIII)', *Mélanges de l'École française de Rome* 119 (2007), pp. 31–50.

51 *Leg. e comm.*, p. 1069.

52 *Ibid.*, p. 1065.

53 *Ibid.*, p. 1067.

54 *Ibid.*, p. 1066.

55 For the following, see *ibid.*, p. 1062.

56 *Ibid.*

57 *Ibid.*, p. 1069.

58 On the respective roles of Niccolò and Vettori, see Devonshire Jones, 'Some Observations'; *Francesco Vettori*, pp. 15–31.

59 For what follows, see *Leg. e comm.*, p. 1070.

60 *Ibid.*, p. 1071.

61 Butters, *Governors and Government*, p. 125; S. Bertelli, 'Petrus Soderinus Patriae Parens', *Bibliothèque d'humanisme et renaissance* 31 (1969), pp. 93–114, here pp. 113–14.

62 *Leg. e comm.*, p. 1071. On Maximilian's advisers, see, for example, R. Hyden, 'Zyprian von Serntein im Dienste Kaiser Maximilians I. in den Jahren 1490–1508' (Unpublished PhD thesis, University of Graz, 1973); E. Mader, 'Paul von Liechtenstein, Marschall des Innsbrucker Regiments, im Dienste Kaiser Maximilians I. in den Jahren 1490 bis 1513' (Unpublished PhD thesis, University of Graz, 1973); I. Friedhuber,

'Lichtenstein, Paul von', *Neue Deutsche Biographie*, vol. 14 (Berlin, 1985), p. 464f.; Pietro Bembo, *History of Venice*, 7.41, 9.54, R. W. Ulery, Jr. (ed. and trans.), 3 vols. (Cambridge MA: Harvard University Press, 2007–9), vol. 2, pp. 226–9, vol. 3, pp. 68–9.

63 For what follows, see *Leg. e comm.*, pp. 1073–4.

64 On Matthäus Lang von Wellenburg, see, for example, A. Schindling, 'Matthäus Lang von Wellenburg', *Neue Deutsche Biographie*, vol. 16 (Berlin, 1990), pp. 394–7; J. Sallaberger, *Kardinal Matthäus Lang von Wellenburg (1468–1540). Staatsmann und Kirchenfürst im Zeitalter von Renaissance, Reformation und Bauernkriegen* (Salzburg: Anton Pustet, 1997).

65 *Leg. e comm.*, p. 1074.

66 *Ibid.*, p. 1075.

67 *Ibid.*, pp. 1075–6.

68 *Ibid.*, pp. 1076–7.

69 Even Vettori seems to have realized this. In his despatch, he suggested that it might be best if the *Dieci* sent ambassadors empowered to negotiate an agreement straight away. *Ibid.*, p. 1077.

70 *Ibid.*, p. 1090.

71 *Ibid.*, p. 1094.

72 *Ibid.*, p. 1075, p. 1090. On the emperor's envoy, Giovanni Rabler (whom Vettori calls 'Rabelar'), see, for example, Tommasini, *La vita e gli scritti di Niccolò Machiavelli*, vol. 1, p. 415, n.6; Marino Sanudo the Younger, *I diarii di Marino Sanuto: (MCCCCXCVI–MDXXXIII): dall'autografo Marciano Ital. CLVII codd. CDXIX–CDLXXVII*, R. Fulin et al. (eds.), 58 vols. (Venice: F. Visentini, 1879–1902), vol. 7, p. 98, p. 103, p. 104, p. 105, p. 107, p. 108, p. 109, p. 111, p. 112, p. 126, p. 131, p. 132, p. 133, p. 192, p. 622, p. 623, p. 625, p. 626.

73 For the *Dieci*'s letter, see *Leg. e comm.*, pp. 1084–8. On Vettori's receipt of the *Dieci*'s letter, see *ibid.*, p. 1094, p. 1100; on the date of its receipt, see below, n.79.

74 For this and the following two paragraphs, see *ibid.*, pp. 1096–7; Sanudo, *Diarii*, vol. 7, p. 273, pp. 275–6, pp. 279–80, p. 282; Mallett and Shaw, *The Italian Wars*, p. 86; Wiesflecker, *Kaiser Maximilian I*, vol. 4, pp. 2–11.

75 The bulk of Vettori's despatch of 8 February (*Leg. e comm.*, pp. 1094–1101) was written in Niccolò's hand. On Niccolò's role in writing despatches, see Devonshire Jones, 'Some Observations'; *Francesco Vettori*, pp. 15–31.

76 *Leg. e comm.*, p. 1098.

77 *Ibid.*, pp. 1098–9.

78 *Ibid.*, p. 1099.

79 The despatch of 8 February claims that, on receiving the *Dieci*'s

letter of 29 January, Vettori had 'immediately' rushed off to Trento
to present their offer to Maximilian. But this seems implausible.
Although no date is given for the receipt of the *Dieci*'s letter, we are
given the impression that it arrived either shortly *before*
Maximilian's departure from Bolzano on 3 February, or on the very
same day. Had Vettori 'immediately' set off for Trento with the
intention of presenting the *Dieci*'s offer, as the despatch affirms, he
would have had ample time to reach Trento (only fifty-six
kilometres away) before Maximilian left on 5 February. But, since
Vettori is said to have been 'on the road' when he learned of
Maximilian's retreat – at least *two days later* – we must conclude
that he waited some time before leaving Bolzano, or that he was
travelling at an absurdly slow pace. Either way, he must have known
that, despite Maximilian's rejection of the *Dieci*'s initial offer, *any*
delay would have rendered their latest offer completely meaningless
(given that the *Dieci* had stipulated the first instalment was to be
handed over either in Trento, or in the first Italian city the emperor
came to that did not belong to him). As such, it seems clear that
Vettori *cannot* have set out from Bolzano on 3 (or even 4) February
with the intention of presenting the *Dieci*'s offer of 29 January. If
the letter arrived when the despatch suggests – or earlier – then his
failure to raise it with Maximilian suggests he must have discounted it
as unrealistic the moment he read it; but, if it arrived later, there would
have been no point chasing after Maximilian with an out-of-date offer.
Whichever the case, it seems much more likely that he left Bolzano at
a *later* date to find out more, and to be on hand should there be an
opportunity to reopen negotiations, but that he subsequently decided to
paint his actions in a manner that would present him as a more
devoted servant of the *Dieci*. *Ibid.*, p. 1094, p. 1100.

80 For the following, see *ibid.*, pp. 1101–2.
81 In a highly unusual move, Maximilian was proclaimed Holy Roman
     Emperor by Lang in Trento Cathedral on 8 February.
82 *Leg. e comm.*, p. 1102.
83 *Ibid.*, pp. 1103–4.
84 *Machiavelli and His Friends*, pp. 166–7 (no. 151).
85 *Leg. e comm.*, p. 1101.
86 See, for example, *ibid.*, p. 1083. A large section of this letter is written
     in cipher. Although this is omitted from Bertelli's edition, Passerini
     (Niccolò Machiavelli, *Opere*, P. Fanfani, G. Milanesi, L. Passerini
     (eds.), 6 vols. (Florence: Cenniniana, 1873–77), vol. 5, p. 271, n.2) notes
     that it contained 'burlesque or senseless things' which testified to
     'Machiavelli's eccentric character'. Passerini thus surmises that Niccolò
     had probably written it to amuse his chancellery colleagues.

87 On 14 February, Vettori noted that he would have sent Niccolò to see what was happening at court, but had not done so because 'it would anger [the court], and it would not do to disobey [Maximilian's commands], as perhaps neither he nor I would be allowed to remain in Germany'. *Leg. e comm.*, p. 1105.

88 Black has argued that Niccolò was attempting to be recalled from what he believed to be a useless mission. This, however, seems unlikely. Had Niccolò really felt the mission served no purpose, he would not have argued that it was still worth pursuing an agreement with Maximilian; nor, indeed, would he have offered to stay on. R. Black, 'Machiavelli, Servant of the Florentine Republic', in G. Bock, Q. Skinner and M. Viroli (eds.), *Machiavelli and Republicanism* (Cambridge: Cambridge University Press, 1990), pp. 71–100, here p. 88.

89 *Leg. e comm.*, p. 1108.

90 *Ibid.*, p. 1107.

91 *Ibid.*, pp. 1107–8.

92 *Ibid.*, p. 1109.

93 *Ibid.*, p. 1100.

94 *Ibid.*, p. 1111.

95 *Ibid.*, p. 1119.

96 *Ibid.*, p. 1120.

97 The following is heavily indebted to Mallett and Shaw, *The Italian Wars*, p. 86. For Bartolomeo d'Alviano's own account of the recapture of the Cadore, see Sanudo, *Diarii*, vol. 7, pp. 347–52. It is worth noting that the version Niccolò and Vettori were told is inaccurate in many important respects.

98 Sanudo, *Diarii*, vol. 7, p. 362.

99 *Ibid.*, vol. 7, p. 342ff.; cf. *Leg. e comm.*, p. 1137.

100 *Leg. e comm.*, p. 1124.

101 Cf. the letter Niccolò received from the scholar Cesare Mauro a few months later: *Lett.*, pp. 186–7 (no. 93); *Machiavelli and His Friends*, p. 167 (no. 152).

102 Although Niccolò's note has not survived, he evidently asked Cesare Mauro to procure a number of texts on his behalf. It has been suggested that these *carte* concerned political and military matters and that Niccolò needed them to check some of the points he would make in his report on German affairs. There is, however, nothing at all in Mauro's letter to support this contention. Mauro does not mention the subject of the *carte*, and says not one word about political or military affairs. E. Fasano Guarini, 'Machiavelli and the crisis of the Italian republics', in Bock et al. (eds.), *Machiavelli and Republicanism*, pp. 17–40, here p. 24, n.16;

Lett., pp. 186–7 (no. 93); *Machiavelli and His Friends*, p. 167 (no. 152).

103 *Leg. e comm.*, pp. 1122–3.

104 *Ibid.*, p. 1126.

105 *Ibid.*, p. 1127. For the *Dieci*'s letter of 4 March, see *ibid.*, pp. 1115–18.

106 See *ibid.*, pp. 1136–7, pp. 1140–1.

107 *Ibid.*, pp. 1142–3.

108 On 16 April, Niccolò – writing in Vettori's name – informed the *Dieci* that Maximilian was now inclined to make terms with the Venetians. On 22 April, Niccolò – writing in Vettori's name – noted that, a few days earlier, a Venetian secretary had arrived to discuss a truce, and that there was some disagreement over whether it was to last five years (as Venice wanted) or four months (as Maximilian preferred). *Ibid.*, p. 1138, p. 1143.

109 *Ibid.*, p. 1147.

110 *Ibid.*, pp. 1145–6.

111 *Ibid.*, p. 1145.

112 *Ibid.*, pp. 1151–2. For the text of the truce, see Sanudo, *Diarii*, vol. 7, pp. 562–67.

113 For discussion, see Mallett and Shaw, *The Italian Wars*, p. 87.

114 *Leg. e comm.*, p. 1152.

115 *Ibid.*, p. 1148.

116 *Ibid.*, pp. 1152–3; J.-J. Marchand, *Niccolò Machiavelli: I primi scritti politici* (Padua: Antenore, 1975), p. 165.

117 The text of the *Rapporto* can be found at Machiavelli, *Opere*, Fanfani et al. (eds.), vol. 6, pp. 313–22; Marchand, *I primi scritti politici*, pp. 472–81. For a splendid discussion, see Marchand, *I primi scritti politici*, pp. 157–89.

118 R. Black, *Machiavelli* (Abingdon: Routledge, 2013), p. 62.

15. Old Scores, New Enemies (June 1508–June 1509)

1 Paris, Bibliothèque Nationale de France, MS Fr. 225, fol. 1r.

2 See *Machiavelli and His Friends*, pp. 168–70 (nos. 154–5).

3 It appears that Cardinal Francesco Soderini played some role in smoothing Totto's path to ordination. See *Lett.*, pp. 187–8 (no. 94); *Machiavelli and His Friends*, p. 170 (no. 156).

4 V. Arrighi, 'Machiavelli, Totto', *DBI*, vol. 67 (Rome, 2006), pp. 105–7.

5 *Lett.*, pp. 187–8 (no. 94); *Machiavelli and His Friends*, p. 170 (no. 156).

6 The Palazzo della Signoria had caught fire on the night of *Spirito Santo*. According to Parenti, Soderini had refused to raise the alarm, fearing that, were he to ring the bells, the people would believe a coup had broken out and rise up against him. Luca Landucci,

Diario fiorentino dal 1450 al 1516 continuato da un anonimo fino al 1542, J. del Badia (ed.) (Florence: Sansoni, 1883), p. 287; H. C. Butters, *Governors and Government in Early Sixteenth-Century Florence 1502–1519* (Oxford: Clarendon, 1985), p. 129.

7   Although the reason for Don Michele's dismissal was never officially given, the possibility that he was suspected of financial misconduct appears to be suggested by Roberto Acciaiuoli's letter to Niccolò on 1 July 1508: *Machiavelli and His Friends*, p. 168 (no. 153). For further discussion, see, for example, P. Villari, *Machiavelli e i suoi tempi*, 2nd ed., 3 vols. (Milan: Hoepli, 1895–7), vol. 2, pp. 63–4; F. Petrucci, 'Corella, Miguel', *DBI*, vol. 29 (Rome, 1983), pp. 42–6. There had previously been some problems with Don Michele's heavy-handedness and poor relations with Florence's commissioners in the field. See *Machiavelli and His Friends*, pp. 159–64 (nos. 146–7).

8   On 4 December 1507, Roberto Acciaiuoli had written to ask Niccolò for advice. Since the title of *bargello* was 'hated by active men', Acciaiuoli wondered if it might not be more sensible to distinguish between a *bargello* and a disciplinarian. He also asked for clarification of the prospective replacement's rank, authority, term, stipend and contract. *Lett.*, pp. 185–6 (no. 92); *Machiavelli and His Friends*, p. 166 (no. 150). For discussion, see, for example, R. Black, *Machiavelli* (Abingdon: Routledge, 2013), p. 48.

9   Niccolò's original letter to Roberto Acciaiuoli has not survived, but that it concerned this subject is evident from Acciaiuoli's letter of 1 July: *Machiavelli and His Friends*, p. 168 (no. 153).

10 For the following, see Francesco Guicciardini, *Storie fiorentine*, 29, R. Palmarocchi (ed.) (Bari: G. Laterza & Figli, 1934), p. 307.

11 See *ibid.*, p. 308.

12 Niccolò Machiavelli, *Opere*, P. Fanfani, G. Milanesi, L. Passerini (eds.), 6 vols. (Florence: Cenniniana, 1873–77), vol. 5, p. 338.

13 *Ibid.*, vol. 5, p. 339.

14 Guicciardini, *Storie fiorentine*, 29, Palmarocchi (ed.), pp. 308–10; Biagio Buonaccorsi, *Diario* (Florence: Giunti, 1568), pp. 134–5; *Cons. e prat. 1505–12*, pp. 181–94.

15 Guicciardini, *Storie fiorentine*, 29, Palmarocchi (ed.), p. 309.

16 It had not escaped the Florentines' notice that, while the *pratiche* were debating what to do, Cardinal Georges d'Amboise had already left for Flanders and was unlikely to return for a considerable time. *Ibid.*, p. 310.

17 Note the *Dieci*'s letters to Niccolò and the commissioner in the field, Niccolò di Piero Capponi, on 26 August: Machiavelli, *Opere*, Fanfani et al. (eds.), vol. 5, pp. 340–2.

18 *Ibid.*

19 *Lett.*, pp. 188–9 (no. 95); *Machiavelli and His Friends*, pp. 170–1 (no. 157).

20 Guicciardini, *Storie fiorentine*, 29, Palmarocchi (ed.), pp. 310–11; Buonaccorsi, *Diario*, p. 135, p. 137.

21 As a letter from Giannessino da Sarzana suggests, Niccolò returned to Florence at some point before 4 September: *Machiavelli and His Friends*, p. 171 (no. 158). He was certainly back in the chancellery and attending to the sale of some wood on 18 September, as is indicated by a letter from Francesco Miniati, dated 28 September: *Machiavelli and His Friends*, p. 172 (no. 159).

22 Machiavelli, *Opere*, Fanfani et al. (eds.), vol. 5, pp. 342–3.

23 Landucci, *Diario*, pp. 288–9; Guicciardini, *Storie fiorentine*, 29, Palmarocchi (ed.), pp. 311–18; Buonaccorsi, *Diario*, p. 139; A. Mazzarosa, *Storia di Lucca dalla sua origine fino al 1814*, 2 vols. (Lucca: Giuseppe Giusti, 1833), vol. 2, p. 33. For a discussion of the negotiations and the bitter divisions among the Florentine elite, see Butters, *Governors and Government*, pp. 134–5.

24 See Machiavelli, *Opere*, Fanfani et al. (eds.), vol. 5, pp. 343–69, pp. 374–8; R. Ridolfi, *Vita di Niccolò Machiavelli*, 3rd ed., 2 vols. (Florence: Sansoni, 1969), p. 167.

25 For Capponi's complaints, see *Lett.*, p. 190, p. 191 (nos. 96, 97); *Machiavelli and His Friends*, p. 177 (nos. 162, 163); Machiavelli, *Opere*, Fanfani et al. (eds.), vol. 5, p. 354. See also J. Najemy, 'The controversy surrounding Machiavelli's service to the republic', in G. Bock, Q. Skinner and M. Viroli (eds.), *Machiavelli and Republicanism* (Cambridge: Cambridge University Press, 1990), pp. 101–17, here pp. 112–14.

26 *Lett.*, p. 190 (no. 96); *Machiavelli and His Friends*, p. 177 (no. 162) [trans. amended].

27 *Machiavelli and His Friends*, p. 179 (no. 164).

28 On the brief mission to Lucca, see Machiavelli, *Opere*, Fanfani et al. (eds.), vol. 5, pp. 369–73, p. 377. For the instructions and letter of credence given to Niccolò for his mission to Piombino, see *Leg. e comm.*, pp. 1161–3; Machiavelli, *Opere*, Fanfani et al. (eds.), vol. 5, pp. 384–6. Guicciardini, *Storie fiorentine*, 30, Palmarocchi (ed.), pp. 333–4.

29 For the following, see *Leg. e comm.*, pp. 1164–9; Machiavelli, *Opere*, Fanfani et al. (eds.), vol. 5, pp. 387–92.

30 Niccolò was certainly sending and receiving correspondence at the Palazzo della Signoria between 30 March and 14 April: Machiavelli, *Opere*, Fanfani et al. (eds.), vol. 5, pp. 392–5.

31 On the formation of the League of Cambrai, see M. E. Mallett and C. Shaw, *The Italian Wars, 1494–1559: War, State and Society in Early Modern Europe* (London and New York: Routledge, 2012), pp. 87–9;

M. Le Glay, *Négociations diplomatiques entre la France et l'Autriche durant les trente premières années du XVIe siècle*, 2 vols. (Paris: Imprimerie Royale, 1845), vol. 1, pp. 225–43. For Florentine accounts, see Guicciardini, *Storie fiorentine*, 30, Palmarocchi (ed.), pp. 334–5; Buonaccorsi, *Diario*, p. 138.

32 See, for example, *Lett.*, p. 189 (no. 96); *Machiavelli and His Friends*, p. 170, p. 179 (nos. 162, 165).

33 The accord was agreed on 13 March: see G. Canestrini and A. Desjardins (eds.), *Négociations diplomatiques de la France avec la Toscane*, 6 vols. (Paris: Imprimerie Impériale / Imprimerie Nationale, 1859–86), vol. 2, pp. 293–5. There was also a second, secret accord between Florence and France, whereby Florence would pay Louis XII 50,000 *fl.* and, if Pisa did not fall within twelve months, Louis would pay the money back. See Butters, *Governors and Government*, p. 135.

34 Mallett and Shaw, *The Italian Wars*, p. 89; Buonaccorsi, *Diario*, pp. 139–40; cf. Landucci, *Diario*, p. 291.

35 Machiavelli, *Opere*, Fanfani et al. (eds.), vol. 5, p. 398.

36 *Ibid.*, vol. 5, pp. 400–1.

37 *Ibid.*, vol. 5, pp. 401–5, pp. 408–9. The three camps were at Ripafratta, San Pietro a Grado and Mezzana: see Guicciardini, *Storie fiorentine*, 31, Palmarocchi (ed.), p. 337, p. 340.

38 Guicciardini, *Storie fiorentine*, 30; Palmarocchi (ed.), p. 333.

39 Machiavelli, *Opere*, Fanfani et al. (eds.), vol. 5, p. 410.

40 *Ibid.*, vol. 5, pp. 411–12; cf. Guicciardini, *Storie fiorentine*, 31, Palmarocchi (ed.), p. 342.

41 For the preparations that were being made for just such an eventuality, see, for example, Guicciardini, *Storie fiorentine*, 31; Palmarocchi (ed.), pp. 342–3. On the Pisans' obstinacy, see also Landucci, *Diario*, p. 292.

42 Machiavelli, *Opere*, Fanfani et al. (eds.), vol. 5, pp. 413–15.

43 *Ibid.*, vol. 5, pp. 417–19, pp. 420–2.

44 The text of the instrument of surrender is published as an appendix in O. Tommasini, *La vita e gli scritti di Niccolò Machiavelli nella loro relazione col machiavellismo*, 3 vols. (Turin: Ermanno Loescher, 1883–1911), vol. 1, pp. 685–701.

45 *Lett.* p. 194 (no. 99); *Machiavelli and His Friends*, p. 180 (no. 167).

46 Landucci, *Diario*, p. 295.

47 As will be apparent from the preceding discussion – and as Pieri has rightly noted – the fall of Pisa actually owed far more to the city's diplomats than to the militia. P. Pieri, *Il rinascimento e la crisi militare* (Turin: Einaudi, 1952), p. 442.

48 *Lett.*, p. 196 (no. 101); *Machiavelli and His Friends*, p. 182 (no. 169)

[amended]. See Najemy, 'The controversy surrounding Machiavelli's service to the republic' in G. Bock, Q. Skinner and M. Viroli (eds.), *Machiavelli and Republicanism* (Cambridge: Cambridge University Press, 1990), pp. 101–17, here p. 115.

49 On 4 October 1509, Salviati wrote a warm letter to his 'dearest Niccolò' – a clear indication of the thaw in their relations. *Machiavelli and His Friends*, pp. 186–7 (no. 173).

50 Guicciardini, *Storie fiorentine*, 29, Palmarocchi (ed.), pp. 319–20; Butters, *Governors and Government*, pp. 127–9.; J. M. Najemy, *A History of Florence, 1200–1575* (Oxford: Blackwell, 2008), p. 416; K. J. P. Lowe, *Church and Politics in Renaissance Italy: The Life and Career of Cardinal Francesco Soderini, 1453–1524* (Cambridge: Cambridge University Press, 1993), pp. 67–72.

51 For what follows, see M. M. Bullard, *Filippo Strozzi and the Medici: Favor and Finance in Sixteenth-Century Florence and Rome* (Cambridge: Cambridge University Press, 1980), pp. 45–60; M. M. Bullard, 'Marriage Politics and the Family in Florence: The Strozzi–Medici Alliance of 1508', *American Historical Review* 84 (1979), pp. 668–87; Butters, *Governors and Government*, pp. 129–34.

52 See Guicciardini, *Storie fiorentine*, 30, Palmarocchi (ed.), pp. 327–8.

53 L. Strozzi, *Le vite degli uomini illustri della casa Strozzi* (Florence: S. Landi, 1892), pp. 96–7.

54 Guicciardini, *Storie fiorentine*, 30, Palmarocchi (ed.), p. 328. For discussion of this passage, see Butters, *Governors and Government*, p. 132.

16. Walking the Tightrope (July 1509–September 1510)

1 For the following, see M. E. Mallett and C. Shaw, *The Italian Wars, 1494–1559: War, State and Society in Early Modern Europe* (London and New York: Routledge, 2012), pp. 89–93.

2 S. Meschini, *La Francia nel ducato di Milano: La politica di Luigi XII (1499–1512)*, 2 vols. (Milan: Franco Angeli, 2006), vol. 2, p. 590, p. 593.

3 C. Shaw, *Julius II: The Warrior Pope* (Oxford: Blackwell, 1993), pp. 234–5.

4 H. Wiesflecker, *Kaiser Maximilian I: Das Reich, Österreich und Europa an der Wende zur Neuzeit*, 5 vols. (Munich: Oldenbourg, 1971–86), vol. 4, pp. 44–6.

5 For what follows, see *ibid.*, pp. 46–54; Mallett and Shaw, *The Italian Wars*, pp. 93–4.

6 H. C. Butters, *Governors and Government in Early Sixteenth-Century Florence 1502–1519* (Oxford: Clarendon, 1985), p. 140; Jacopo Nardi, *Istorie della città di Firenze*, A. Gelli (ed.), 2 vols. (Florence: Le Monnier, 1858), vol. 1, pp. 359–60.

7   *Leg. e comm.*, pp. 1179–81.
8   *Lett.*, pp. 199–200 (no. 104); *Machiavelli and His Friends*, p. 187 (no. 174).
9   *Lett.*, p. 200 (no. 104); *Machiavelli and His Friends*, p. 187 (no. 174).
10   *Leg. e comm.*, p. 1183.
11   *Ibid.*, pp. 1183–4.
12   *Ibid.*, p. 1186.
13   *Ibid.*
14   *Ibid.*, p. 1188.
15   *Ibid.*, p. 1196.
16   *Ibid.*, p. 1195.
17   *Ibid.*, p. 1193.
18   *Ibid.*, pp. 1193–4.
19   *Ibid.*, p. 1194. Some translators render *lo fece appiccare* as 'had him hanged', but 'had him burned' seems closer to the original meaning. Cf. *Chief Works*, vol. 2, p. 738 n.
20   *Leg. e comm.*, p. 1199.
21   *Lett.*, p. 202 (no. 106); *Machiavelli and His Friends*, p. 189 (no. 179).
22   *Lett.*, p. 202 (no. 106); *Machiavelli and His Friends*, p. 189 (no. 179).
23   Text in Niccolò Machiavelli, *Capitoli*, G. Inglese (ed.) (Rome: Bulzoni, 1981). There is a usable (if not always strictly accurate) translation in Machiavelli, *Chief Works*, vol. 2, pp. 735–9.
24   For a brief, but splendid discussion of Niccolò's understanding of fortune in the *Capitolo dell'ambizione*, see M. Viroli, *Machiavelli's God*, A. Shugaar (trans.) (Princeton NJ: Princeton University Press, 2010), pp. 32–3.
25   *Capitolo dell'ambizione*, 1–6.
26   *Ibid.*, 13–14.
27   *Ibid.*, 28.
28   *Ibid.*, 46–8.
29   *Ibid.*, 73–81.
30   *Ibid.*, 91–3.
31   *Ibid.*, 94–9.
32   *Ibid.*, 103–8.
33   *Ibid.*, 133–8, 148–53, 157–9. Trans. adapted from Machiavelli, *Chief Works*, vol. 2, p. 738.
34   *Capitolo dell'ambizione*, 163–5.
35   *Ibid.*, 166–8. On 7 December, Niccolò reported that, in all the towns which the Venetians recaptured, they had a Saint Mark painted, but with a sword rather than a book in his hand: *Leg. e comm.*, p. 1202.
36   *Capitolo dell'ambizione*, 169–71.
37   *Ibid.*, 180.
38   *Ibid.*, 181–3.

39 *Ibid.*, 184–7.

40 *Leg. e comm.*, p. 1202.

41 *Ibid.*, pp. 1200–1.

42 *Lett.*, pp. 204–6 (no. 108); *Machiavelli and His Friends*, pp. 190–1 (no. 178). For further discussion of this letter and the amorous adventures narrated therein, see, for example, J. M. Najemy, *Between Friends: Discourses of Power and Desire in the Machiavelli–Vettori Letters of 1513–1515* (Princeton NJ: Princeton University Press, 1993), pp. 69–71; W. Rebhorn, *Foxes and Lions: Machiavelli's Confidence Men* (Ithaca NY and London: Cornell University Press, 1988), pp. 242–4.

43 *Lett.*, p. 204 (no. 108).

44 *Ibid.*

45 *Lett.*, p. 205–6 (no. 108). The translation is my own.

46 *Leg. e comm.*, p. 1206.

47 *Ibid.*, pp. 1203–4.

48 *Ibid.*, p. 1204. Niccolò had already mentioned that Pandolfini might be better informed than him in his letters of 24 November and 1 December: *ibid.*, p. 1192, p. 1200.

49 *Lett.*, p. 206 (no. 108); *Machiavelli and His Friends*, p. 191 (no. 178).

50 *Leg. e comm.*, p. 1209. On 22 November, Niccolò had noted that he was already spending 'more than the one ducat per day' he was allowed as his salary: *ibid.*, p. 1190.

51 On 8 December, Niccolò noted that he had not heard from the *Dieci* once since he had left Florence: *ibid.*, p. 1204.

52 *Ibid.*, pp. 1208–9.

53 *Ibid.*, p. 1210.

54 There was some confusion about where Maximilian was, and in what direction he was heading. On 12 December, Niccolò reported that the emperor had left Bolzano for Innsbruck some time ago, and was said to be at Augsburg, where he had convened a diet. But, on the same day, Pigello Portinari wrote to Niccolò with news that the emperor was heading in the opposite direction, and was already in Trento. *Ibid.*, pp. 1206–9; *Machiavelli and His Friends*, p. 192 (no. 180).

55 *Leg. e comm.*, p. 1207.

56 *Ibid.*, p. 1210.

57 *Ibid.*

58 See Francesco Guicciardini, *Storia d'Italia*, 8.14, C. Panigada (ed.), 5 vols. (Bari: G. Laterza & Figli, 1929), vol. 2, p. 322; Marino Sanudo the Younger, *I diarii di Marino Sanuto: (MCCCCXCVI–MDXXXIII): dall'autografo Marciano Ital. CLVII codd. CDXIX–CDLXXVII*, R. Fulin et al. (eds.), 58 vols. (Venice: F. Visentini, 1879–1902), vol. 8,

pp. 402–5; Mallett and Shaw, *The Italian Wars*, p. 95; R. Finlay, 'Venice, the Po expedition and the end of the League of Cambrai, 1509–1510', *Studies in Modern European History and Culture* 2 (1976), pp. 37–72 [repr. in R. Finlay, *Venice Besieged: Politics and Diplomacy in the Italian Wars, 1494–1534* (Aldershot: Routledge, 2008), Essay 6, pp. 46–62]; A. Mazzetti, 'Polesella 22 dicembre 1509: l'armata veneta "ruynata" in Po', *Archivio Veneto*, 5th ser. 141/210 (2010), pp. 255–84.

59 *Lett.*, p. 207 (no. 109); *Machiavelli and His Friends*, p. 192 (no. 181) [adapted].

60 V. Arrighi, 'Machiavelli, Totto', *DBI*, vol. 67 (Rome, 2006), pp. 105–7; O. Tommasini, *La vita e gli scritti di Niccolò Machiavelli nella loro relazione col machiavellismo*, 3 vols. (Turin: Ermanno Loescher, 1883–1911), vol. 1, p. 476.

61 For the following, see Mallett and Shaw, *The Italian Wars*, pp. 97–8.

62 *Leg. e comm.*, pp. 1227–9.

63 *Lett.*, pp. 209–10 (no. 110); *Machiavelli and His Friends*, p. 197 (no. 182).

64 Niccolò Machiavelli, *Opere*, P. Fanfani, G. Milanesi, L. Passerini (eds.), 6 vols. (Florence: Cenniniana, 1873–77), vol. 1, p. lxxv; vol. 6, p. 1.

65 *Ibid.*, vol. 1, pp. lxxv–lxxvi.

66 J. N. Stephens and J. C. Butters, 'New Light on Machiavelli', *English Historical Review* 98 (1982), pp. 54–69, here p. 57, p. 66.

67 Niccolò's credentials and the *Dieci*'s mandate for payment of his subsistence are both dated 20 June 1510: *Leg. e comm.*, p. 1129; Machiavelli, *Opere*, Fanfani et al. (eds.), vol. 1, p. lxxvi.

68 *Leg. e comm.*, p. 1234.

69 *Ibid.*, p. 1233, p. 1235.

70 For the following, see esp. Mallett and Shaw, *The Italian Wars*, p. 96.

71 Guicciardini, *Storia d'Italia*, 8.9, Panigada (ed.), vol. 2, pp. 295–8; Butters, *Governors and Government*, p. 141.

72 *Leg. e comm.*, p. 1241.

73 *Ibid.*, pp. 1241–2.

74 *Ibid.*, pp. 1242–3.

75 *Ibid.*, p. 1242.

76 *Ibid.*, pp. 1245–6.

77 *Ibid.*, pp. 1246–7.

78 *Ibid.*, p. 1252.

79 *Ibid.*, pp. 1240–1, pp. 1254–5.

80 *Ibid.*, pp. 1254–6.

81 *Ibid.*, p. 1269.

82 *Ibid.*, p. 1270.

83 *Ibid.*, p. 1248.

84 *Ibid.*, p. 1271.

85 *Ibid.*, p. 1281.

86 *Ibid.*, p. 1282.

87 *Ibid.*, p. 1284.

88 *Ibid.*, pp. 1282–3.

89 *Ibid.*, pp. 1293–4.

90 *Ibid.*, p. 1294.

91 *Ibid.*, p. 1295.

92 *Ibid.*, p. 1303, p. 1316; *Machiavelli and His Friends*, p. 202 (no. 188); Mallett and Shaw, *The Italian Wars*, p. 99.

93 This had first been mooted back in July: see *Leg. e comm.*, p. 1249.

94 *Ibid.*, p. 1292.

95 *Machiavelli and His Friends*, p. 198 (no. 183).

96 On 24 August, the Pistoiese banker Bartolomeo Panciatichi, then in Lyon, informed Niccolò that the most recent courier had not brought 'any letters for you, as far as I know, except for the one [enclosed]'; and even that had been sent 'under cover for [Panciatichi] without any signature'. *Machiavelli and His Friends*, pp. 202–3 (no. 189).

97 *Leg. e comm.*, p. 1298; cf. *ibid.*, pp. 1307–8, p. 1332.

98 Luca Landucci, *Diario fiorentino dal 1450 al 1516 continuato da un anonimo fino al 1542*, J. del Badia (ed.) (Florence: Sansoni, 1883), p. 302.

99 *Leg. e comm.*, p. 1308.

100 *Lett.*, pp. 213–14 (no. 112); *Machiavelli and His Friends*, pp. 201–2 (no. 187).

101 *Lett.*, p. 216 (no. 114); *Machiavelli and His Friends*, p. 204 (no. 191) [amended].

102 *Lett.*, p. 216 (no. 114); *Machiavelli and His Friends*, p. 204 (no. 191).

103 *Lett.*, p. 216 (no. 114); *Machiavelli and His Friends*, p. 205 (no. 191); q. Livy, 35.49.

104 For the following, see *Leg. e comm.*, pp. 1317–18.

105 *Ibid.*, pp. 1328–30.

106 *Ibid.*, pp. 1330–1.

107 *Ibid.*, p. 1331.

108 *Ibid.*, p. 1333.

109 *Ibid.*, p. 1341.

110 Cf. *ibid.*, p. 1347.

111 *Ibid.*, p. 1336.

112 *Ibid.*, p. 1333.

113 Exactly when Niccolò left Tours is not known.

17. Things Fall Apart (September 1510–September 1512)

1 Niccolò returned to Florence on 19 October. Niccolò Machiavelli, *Opere*, P. Fanfani, G. Milanesi, L. Passerini (eds.), 6 vols. (Florence: Cenniniana, 1873–77), vol. 1, p. lxxvii.

2 C. Shaw, *Julius II: The Warrior Pope* (Oxford: Blackwell, 1993), pp. 261–2.

3 Machiavelli, *Opere*, Fanfani et al. (eds.), vol. 1, p. lxxvii.

4 The text of the *Discorso sulla milizia a cavallo* (also known as the *Provvisione per le milizie a cavallo*) can be found in *ibid.*, vol. 6, pp. 352–8; *Opere minori di Niccolò Machiavelli*, F.-L. Polidori (ed.) (Florence: Le Monnier, 1852), pp. 161–6; *Opere politiche*, vol. 3, *L'arte della guerra. Scritti politici minori*, J.-J. Marchand, D. Fachard and G. Masi (eds.) (Rome, 2001), pp. 536–40. The following notes shall refer to the text as given in Machiavelli, *Opere*, Fanfani et al. (eds.).

5 Machiavelli, *Opere*, Fanfani et al. (eds.), vol. 6, p. 352.

6 *Ibid.*, vol. 6, pp. 353–4.

7 *Ibid.*, vol. 1, p. lxxvii.

8 *Ibid.*

9 Shaw, *Julius II*, pp. 268–9.

10 The remainder of this paragraph is deeply indebted to H. C. Butters, *Governors and Government in Early Sixteenth-Century Florence 1502–1519* (Oxford: Clarendon, 1985), p. 143.

11 S. Bertelli, 'Pier Soderini Vexillifer Perpetuus Reipublicae Florentinae: 1502–1512', in A. Molho and J. A. Tedeschi (eds.), *Renaissance Studies in Honor of Hans Baron* (Florence: Sansoni, 1971), pp. 335–59, here p. 353.

12 J. M. Najemy, *A History of Florence, 1200–1575* (Oxford: Blackwell, 2008), p. 419.

13 Luca Landucci, *Diario fiorentino dal 1450 al 1516 continuato da un anonimo fino al 1542*, J. del Badia (ed.) (Florence: Sansoni, 1883), p. 306.

14 *Ibid.*

15 *Ibid.*

16 Butters, *Governors and Government*, pp. 143–4.

17 The weather must have been terrible. On 23 January, Landucci reported that the melted snow had created so much mud that it was impossible 'to get along or go about one's business'. For a few days, makeshift gangways were the only means of crossing the street. Landucci, *Diario*, p. 306.

18 Machiavelli, *Opere*, Fanfani et al. (eds.), vol. 1, pp. lxxvii–lxxviii.

19 *Ibid.*, vol. 1, p. lxxviii.

20 *Ibid.*

21 The following three paragraphs are indebted to M. E. Mallett and C. Shaw, *The Italian Wars, 1494–1559: War, State and Society in Early Modern Europe* (London and New York: Routledge, 2012), p. 100.

22 Paride de' Grassi, *Le due spedizioni militari di Giulio II* (Bologna: Regia Tipografia, 1886), pp. 232–41.

23 *Ibid.*, pp. 262–4.

24 For what follows, see the splendid summary given in Bertelli's 'Nota introduttiva', *Leg. e comm.*, p. 1357.

25 *Ibid.*, pp. 1359–60.

26 *Ibid.*, p. 1359; Machiavelli, *Opere*, Fanfani et al. (eds.), vol. 1, p. lxxix.

27 *Ibid.*, pp. 1362–3.

28 *Ibid.*, pp. 1364–5.

29 K. M. Setton, *The Papacy and the Levant, 1204–1571*, 4 vols. (Philadelphia PA: The American Philosophical Society, 1976–84), vol. 3, p. 93. On this statue, see, for example, M. Hirst, *Michelangelo*, vol. 1, *The Achievement of Fame, 1475–1534* (New Haven CT and London: Yale University Press, 2011), pp. 79–84.

30 See de' Grassi, *Le due spedizioni*, pp. 278–9. De' Grassi reports that 'So great was the universal joy that followed that the populace exclaimed, seemingly with one voice, "blessed be the duke, blessed be that murder, blessed be the name of the Lord, from whom all good things come."'

31 *Leg. e comm.*, p. 1378. This letter is also reproduced in A. Renaudet, *Le Concile Gallican de Pise-Milan: Documents Florentins, 1510–1512* (Paris: Librairie Ancienne Honoré Champion, 1922), pp. 75–6 (no. 106).

32 De' Grassi, *Le due spedizioni*, pp. 281–4.

33 Machiavelli, *Opere*, Fanfani et al. (eds.), vol. 1, pp. lxxix–lxxx.

34 For Niccolò's letters patent, see *Leg. e comm.*, pp. 1378–9. For his instructions, see *ibid.*, pp. 1379–85.

35 *Ibid.*, p. 1389.

36 *Ibid.*, p. 1390.

37 *Ibid.*, pp. 1390–1.

38 *Ibid.*, p. 1392. A little later, Niccolò learned that Sanseverino would soon be going to Germany to try to persuade the emperor to send representatives to the council, with the promise that it would be transferred to a place of his choosing once proceedings were underway.

39 *Ibid.*, p. 1391.

40 *Ibid.*, pp. 1404–5.

41 *Ibid.*, p. 1419.

42 *Ibid.*, p. 1420.

43 *Ibid.*, pp. 1420–1.

44 *Ibid.*, p. 1422.

45 The text of the *Ritratto di cose di Francia* can be found in Machiavelli, *Opere*, M. Bonfantini (ed.) (Milan and Naples: R. Ricciardi, 1954), pp. 471–86; *Opere*, Fanfani et al. (eds.), vol. 6, pp. 297–312; *Opere minori*, Polidori (ed.), pp. 189–204; *Opere politiche*, vol. 3, *L'arte della guerra. Scritti politici minori*, Marchand et al. (eds.), pp. 536–40; J.-J. Marchand, *Niccolò Machiavelli: I primi scritti politici* (Padua: Antenore, 1975), pp. 507–24.

46 R. Black, *Machiavelli* (Abingdon: Routledge, 2013), p. 62.

47 Renaudet, *Le Concile Gallican*, pp. 246–7 (no. 240).

48 De' Grassi, *Le due spedizioni*, pp. 299–302; Renaudet, *Le Concile Gallican*, p. 332 (no. 295); G. Canestrini and A. Desjardins (eds.), *Négociations diplomatiques de la France avec la Toscane*, 6 vols. (Paris: Imprimerie Impériale / Imprimerie Nationale, 1859–86), vol. 2, p. 535. For discussion, see Mallett and Shaw, *The Italian Wars*, pp. 103–4.

49 E.g. Canestrini and Desjardins (eds.), *Négociations diplomatiques*, vol. 2, p. 539.

50 De' Grassi, *Le due spedizioni*, p. 299.

51 Machiavelli, *Opere*, Fanfani et al. (eds.), vol. 1, p. lxxx; *Leg. e comm.*, p. 1453.

52 *Leg. e comm.*, pp. 1481–3.

53 *Ibid.*, p. 1481.

54 Renaudet, *Le Concile Gallican*, p. 494, pp. 497–8 (nos. 428, 429). In the letter of Piero del Nero and Niccolò Zati, it is suggested that the spark that lit the touchpaper was an argument between a Spanish soldier and a Florentine militiaman over a woman.

55 *Ibid.*, pp. 509–12 (nos. 439–42).

56 The interdict was lifted on 1 December and came back into force on 15 December. On the lifting of the interdict, see *ibid.*, pp. 529–33, pp. 540–2, p. 543, pp. 545–6, p. 547, p. 549, pp. 551–7 (nos. 461–5, 476, 478, 481, 485, 487, 489, 492–6); Landucci, *Diario*, p. 312.

57 See Renaudet, *Le Concile Gallican*, pp. 548–9 (no. 488); Butters, *Governors and Government*, p. 157.

58 Machiavelli, *Opere*, Fanfani et al. (eds.), vol. 6, pp. 188–9.

59 See Mallett and Shaw, *The Italian Wars*, pp. 104–6; Canestrini and Desjardins (eds.), *Négociations diplomatiques*, p. 544, pp. 546–7, P. Pieri, *Il rinascimento e la crisi militare* (Turin: Einaudi, 1952), pp. 488–9; S. Bowd, *Venice's Most Loyal City: Civic Identity in Renaissance Brescia* (Cambridge MA: Harvard University Press, 2010), pp. 204–7.

60 See, for example, Mallett and Shaw, *The Italian Wars*, pp. 106–9; D. Bolognesi (ed.), *1512: La battaglia di Ravenna, l'Italia, l'Europa* (Ravenna: Angelo Longo Editore, 2014).

61 *Cons. e prat. 1505–12*, p. 289; Butters, *Governors and Government*, p. 157.

62 Butters, *Governors and Government*, p. 157.

63 N. Murphy, 'Henry VIII's First Invasion of France: The Gascon Expedition of 1512', *English Historical Review*, 130/542 (2015), pp. 25–56.

64 H. Wiesflecker, *Kaiser Maximilian I: Das Reich, Österreich und Europa an der Wende zur Neuzeit*, 5 vols. (Munich: Oldenbourg, 1971–86), vol. 4, p. 102.

65 Mallett and Shaw, *The Italian Wars*, pp. 109–10.

66 Shaw, *Julius II*, pp. 294–6.

67 *Cons. e prat. 1505–12*, p. 307.

68 E.g. Landucci, *Diario*, p. 319; Giovanni Cambi, *Istorie fiorentine*, I. di San Luigi (ed.), 4 vols., *Delizie degli eruditi toscani*, 20–23 (Florence: Gaetano Cambiagi, 1785–6), vol. 2, p. 301.

69 Landucci, *Diario*, pp. 320–1.

70 *Machiavelli and His Friends*, p. 214 (no. 203); *Lett.*, p. 223 (no. 118).

71 Francesco Vettori, *Sommario della Istoria d'Italia*, in *Scritti storici e politici*, E. Niccolini (ed.) (Bari: G. Laterza & Figli, 1972), pp. 133–246, here p. 141.

72 Bartolomeo Cerretani, *Ricordi*, G. Berti (ed.) (Florence: Olschki, 1993), p. 273; Bartolomeo Cerretani, *Dialogo della mutazione di Firenze*, R. Mordenti (ed.) (Rome: Edizioni di Storia e Letteratura, 1990), p. 43.

73 Machiavelli, *Opere*, Fanfani et al. (eds.), vol. 1, p. lxxxii. Between 23 and 29 June, Niccolò had also been raising troops in the Valdichiana.

74 Cerretani, *Ricordi*, Berti (ed.), p. 274; *Dialogo*, Mordenti (ed.), p. 44; Najemy, *History of Florence*, p. 420.

75 *Machiavelli and His Friends*, p. 214 (no. 203); *Lett.*, p. 223 (no. 118).

76 *Machiavelli and His Friends*, p. 215 (no. 203); *Lett.*, p. 224 (no. 118).

77 *Machiavelli and His Friends*, p. 215 (no. 203); *Lett.*, p. 224 (no. 118).

78 *Machiavelli and His Friends*, p. 215 (no. 203); *Lett.*, p. 225 (no. 118). That Isabella d'Este was the intended recipient of this letter has been convincingly demonstrated in B. Richardson, 'La "lettera a una gentildonna" del Machiavelli', *La Bibliofilia* 84 (1982), pp. 271–6.

79 Francesco Guicciardini, *Storia d'Italia*, 11.3, C. Panigada (ed.), 5 vols. (Bari: G. Laterza & Figli, 1929), vol. 3, p. 228.

80 Landucci, *Diario*, p. 323.

81 *Machiavelli and His Friends*, p. 215 (no. 203); *Lett.*, p. 225 (no. 118).

82 *Machiavelli and His Friends*, p. 215 (no. 203); *Lett.*, p. 225 (no. 118).

83 *Machiavelli and His Friends*, p. 213 (no. 202); *Lett.*, p. 222 (no. 117).

84 *Machiavelli and His Friends*, p. 216 (no. 203); *Lett.*, p. 226 (no. 118).

85 Cerretani, *Ricordi*, Berti (ed.), p. 279.

86 *Machiavelli and His Friends*, p. 216 (no. 203); *Lett.*, p. 226 (no. 118).

87 Vettori, *Scritti storici e politici*, p. 142; cf. Guicciardini, *Storia d'Italia*, 11.4, Panigada (ed.), vol. 3, p. 231.

88 Cerretani, *Ricordi*, Berti (ed.), p. 279; *Dialogo*, Mordenti (ed.), p. 45; Najemy, *History of Florence*, p. 420.

89 *Machiavelli and His Friends*, p. 216 (no. 203); *Lett.*, p. 226 (no. 118).

90 The following is based on Vettori, *Scritti storici e politici*, pp. 143–4.

18. 'Ministers of Violence' (September 1512–March 1513)

1 Bartolomeo Cerretani, *Dialogo della mutatione di Firenze*, G. Berti (ed.) (Florence: Olschki, 1993), p. 49.

2 For the terms of the treaty agreed by the Signoria and the *Dieci*, see Angelo Fabronio, *Leonis Pontificis Maximi Vita* (Pisa: A. Landius, 1797), pp. 266–9. For discussion, see N. Rubinstein, 'Firenze e la problema della politica imperiale in Italia al tempo di Massimiliano I', *ASI* 116 (1958), pp. 5–35, pp.147–77, here p. 173; H. C. Butters, *Governors and Government in Early Sixteenth-Century Florence 1502–1519* (Oxford: Clarendon, 1985), p. 172. Cf. Luca Landucci, *Diario fiorentino dal 1450 al 1516 continuato da un anonimo fino al 1542*, J. del Badia (ed.) (Florence; Sansoni, 1883), p. 325.

3 N. Scott Baker, *The Fruit of Liberty: Political Culture in the Florentine Renaissance, 1480–1550* (Cambridge MA: Harvard University Press, 2013), p. 63.

4 Landucci, *Diario*, p. 326. On 4 September, a Spanish soldier was murdered in the Piazza di Madonna. His body was then dragged past Santa Maria Novella, along the Via dei Fossi towards the Ponte alla Carraia, and thrown into the Arno.

5 The following two paragraphs are deeply indebted to the splendid analysis given at Butters, *Governors and Government*, pp. 166–9; J. N. Stephens, *The Fall of the Florentine Republic, 1512–1530* (Oxford: Clarendon, 1983), pp. 56–63.

6 See, for example, Bartolomeo Masi, *Ricordanze di Bartolomeo Masi calderaio fiorentino dal 1478 al 1526*, G. Corazzini (ed.) (Florence: Sansoni, 1906), pp. 101–2; Francesco Guicciardini, *Discorso del modo di ordinare il governo popolare*, in *Dialogo e Discorsi del Reggimento di Firenze*, R. Palmarocchi (ed.) (Bari: G. Laterza & Figli, 1932), pp. 218–59. For the comparison, see Butters, *Governors and Government*, pp. 175–8.

7 Landucci, *Diario*, p. 327.

8 For the following, see Bartolomeo Cerretani, *Dialogo della mutazione di Firenze*, R. Mordenti (ed.) (Rome: Edizioni di Storia e

Letteratura, 1990), pp. 52–4; cf. Bartolomeo Cerretani, *Ricordi*, G. Berti (ed.) (Florence: Olschki, 1993), p. 285.

9   Cerretani, *Dialogo*, Mordenti (ed.), p. 56.

10 Accounts of the coup can be found in *Lett.* pp. 227–8 (no. 118); *Machiavelli and His Friends*, pp. 216–17 (no. 203); Landucci, *Diario*, pp. 328–9; Francesco Guicciardini, *Storia d'Italia*, 11.4, C. Panigada (ed.), 5 vols. (Bari: G. Laterza & Figli, 1929), vol. 3, pp. 234–5; Biagio Buonaccorsi, *Diario* (Florence: Giunti, 1568), p. 184; Francesco Vettori, *Scritti storici e politici*, E. Niccolini (ed.) (Bari: G. Laterza & Figli, 1972), pp. 144–5; Cerretani, *Dialogo*, Mordenti (ed.), pp. 38–42; Masi, *Ricordanze*, pp. 103–7. See also J. M. Najemy, *A History of Florence, 1200–1575* (Oxford: Blackwell, 2008), pp. 424–5; Stephens, *The Fall of the Florentine Republic*, pp. 63–4; Butters, *Governors and Government*, pp. 183–4.

11 Masi, *Ricordanze*, p. 107.

12 Stephens, *The Fall of the Florentine Republic*, p. 64; Butters, *Governors and Government*, pp. 183–4; Najemy, *History of Florence*, p. 425; L. Polizzotto, *The Elect Nation: The Savonarolan Movement in Florence, 1494–1545* (Oxford: Clarendon, 1994), p. 246; G. Silvano, '*Vivere civile*' e "*governo misto*" a Firenze nel primo Cinquecento (Bologna: Pàtron, 1985), pp. 175–6.

13 Guicciardini, *Storia d'Italia*, 11.4, Panigada (ed.), vol. 3, p. 235; Vettori, *Scritti storici e politici*, p. 145.

14 Landucci, *Diario*, p. 329.

15 B. Richardson, 'La "lettera a una gentildonna" del Machiavelli', *La Bibliofilia* 84 (1982), pp. 271–6.

16 *Lett.*, pp. 222–8 (no. 118); *Machiavelli and His Friends*, pp. 214–17 (no. 203). For a splendid discussion of Niccolò's account of the sack of Prato in this letter, see S. Bowd, *Renaissance Mass Murder: Civilians and Soldiers during the Italian Wars* (Oxford: Oxford University Press, 2018), pp. 149–51.

17 *Lett.*, pp. 227–8 (no. 118); *Machiavelli and His Friends*, p. 217 (no. 203).

18 Niccolò Machiavelli, *Opere complete*, 1 vol. in 2 (Florence: Borghi e Compagni, 1857), pp. 1146–7. For discussion, see, for example, J.-J. Marchand, *Niccolò Machiavelli: I primi scritti politici* (Padua: Antenore, 1975), pp. 303–4; E. Niccolini, 'Di un frammento Machiavelliano quasi dimenticato', *Giornale storico della letteratura italiana* 174 (1997), pp. 206–10.

19 Giovanni Cambi, *Istorie fiorentine*, I. di San Luigi (ed.), 4 vols., *Delizie degli eruditi toscani*, 20–23 (Florence: Gaetano Cambiagi, 1785–6), vol. 2, p. 333; R. Ridolfi, *Vita di Niccolò Machiavelli*, 3rd ed., 2 vols. (Florence: Sansoni, 1969), p. 208; Butters, *Governors and Governments*, p. 203.

20 Machiavelli, *Opere complete*, p. 1146.

21 *Ibid.*, p. 1147.

22 Cerretani, *Ricordi*, Berti (ed.), p. 295; Butters, *Governors and Government*, p. 188.

23 Butters, *Governors and Government*, p. 189.

24 Cerretani, *Dialogo*, Mordenti (ed.), pp. 45–6; Landucci, *Diario*, p. 331; Najemy, *History of Florence*, p. 425; Polizzotto, *Elect Nation*, p. 241.

25 Cerretani, *Dialogo*, Mordenti (ed.), pp. 66–7; Filippo de' Nerli, *Commentari de' fatti civili Occorsi dentro la Città di Firenze dall'anno MCCXV al MDXXXVII* (Augusta: David Raimondo Mertz e Gio. Jacopo Majer, 1728), pp. 120–1.

26 Text in Niccolò Machiavelli, *Opere*, P. Fanfani, G. Milanesi, L. Passerini (eds.), 6 vols. (Florence: Cenniniana, 1873–77), vol. 5, pp. 379–81; *Tutte le opere*, M. Martelli (ed.) (Florence: Sansoni, 1971), pp. 16–17; *Opere politiche*, vol. 3, *L'arte della guerra. Scritti politici minori*, J.-J. Marchand, D. Fachard and G. Masi (eds.) (Rome, 2001), pp. 582–4; Marchand, *I primi scritti politici*, pp. 533–5. For discussion, see Marchand, *I primi scritti politici*, pp. 296–310.

27 Machiavelli, *Opere*, ed. Fanfani et al. (eds.), vol. 1, pp. lxxxiii–lxxxiv.

28 *Ibid.*, vol. 1, pp. lxxxiv–lxxxv. On 17 November, Niccolò was also banned from entering the Palazzo della Signoria. He was, however, granted permission to re-enter it so that he could answer questions about the militia on 27 November and 4 December.

29 The cardinal departed Florence on 6 November, leaving his brother, Giuliano, to watch over things in his absence. He did, however, take the precaution of asking their cousin, Giulio de' Medici, to keep an eye on Giuliano and report back to him. He returned to Florence on 19 January. Landucci, *Diario*, p. 332, p. 334; Butters, *Governors and Government*, pp. 204–5; R. Devonshire Jones, *Francesco Vettori: Florentine Citizen and Medici Servant* (London: Athlone Press, 1972), p. 69, p. 74.

30 J. N. Stephens and H. C. Butters, 'New Light on Machiavelli', *English Historical Review* 98 (1982), pp. 54–69, here p. 67.

31 Najemy, *History of Florence*, p. 426.

32 Marino Sanudo the Younger, *I diarii di Marino Sanuto: (MCCCCXCVI–MDXXXIII): dall'autografo Marciano Ital. CLVII codd. CDXIX–CDLXXVII*, R. Fulin et al. (eds.), 58 vols. (Venice: F. Visentini, 1879–1902), vol. 15, p. 554.

33 Paolo Vettori, *Ricordi di Paolo Vettori al cardinale de' Medici sopra le cose di Firenze*; trans. in J. Kraye (ed.), *Cambridge Translations of Renaissance Philosophical Texts*, 2 vols. (Cambridge: Cambridge University Press, 1997), vol. 2, p. 239.

34 Cerretani, *Dialogo*, Berti (ed.), p. 27.

35 Landucci, *Diario*, p. 334.

36 The Medici had already started rebuilding relationships with some
    of the moderates who had been marginalized the previous
    November. See, for example, Butters, *Governors and Government*,
    pp. 206–7.

37 Jacopo Nardi, *Istorie della città di Firenze*, 6, L. Arbib (ed.), 2 vols.
    (Florence: Società Editrice delle Storie del Nardi e del Varchi, 1842),
    vol. 2, pp. 25–6; cf. Vettori, *Scritti storici e politici*, p. 147.

38 Nardi, *Istorie*, 6, Arbib (ed.), vol. 2, pp. 27–8; Luca della Robbia,
    'Narrazione del caso di Pietro Paolo Boscoli e di Agostino
    Capponi', *ASI* 1 (1842), pp. 273–312, here p. 283.

39 Sanudo, *Diarii*, vol. 15, pp. 573–4; P. Villari, *Machiavelli e i suoi tempi*,
    2nd ed., 3 vols. (Milan: Hoepli, 1895–7), vol. 2, pp. 563–4.

40 A list of twelve names is appended to Giuliano de' Medici's letter
    to Piero da Bibbiena: Villari, *Machiavelli e i suoi tempi*, vol. 2, p. 564;
    Sanudo, *Diarii*, vol. 15, p. 574. A partial list is also given by Masi,
    Ricordanze, p. 118. For discussion of Valori's role, see esp. M.
    Jurdjevic, *Guardians of Republicanism: The Valori Family in the
    Florentine Renaissance* (Oxford: Oxford University Press, 2008), pp.
    96–102; R. Pesman Cooper, 'Political survival in early sixteenth-
    century Florence: the case of Niccolò Valori', in P. Denley and
    C. Elam (eds.), *Florence and Italy. Renaissance Studies in Honour of
    Nicolai Rubinstein* (London: Committee for Medieval Studies,
    Westfield College, 1988), pp. 73–90.

41 Landucci reports that fourteen of the 'conspirators' were arrested at
    midnight. Landucci, *Diario*, p. 335.

42 Ridolfi, *Vita di Niccolò Machiavelli*, vol. 1, p. 215.

43 Villari, *Machiavelli e i suoi tempi*, vol. 2, p. 566. The warrant issued
    for his arrest was recently rediscovered by Professor Stephen Milner.
    See N. Squires, 'Briton finds 500-year-old warrant for Machiavelli',
    Daily Telegraph, 15 February 2013, p. 26.

44 Stephens and Butters, 'New Light', p. 67.

45 Niccolò Machiavelli, 'Io ho, Giuliano, in gamba un paio di geti',
    ll.1–2; text in Machiavelli, *Tutte le opere*, Martelli (ed.), p. 1003.

46 *Lett.*, p. 234 (no. 122); *Machiavelli and His Friends*, p. 222 (no. 206).

47 *Lett.*, p. 232 (no. 120); *Machiavelli and His Friends*, p. 221 (no. 204).

48 See *Lett.*, p. 233 (no. 121); *Machiavelli and His Friends*, p. 221 (no. 205).

49 Machiavelli, *Tutte le opere*, Martelli (ed.), p. 1003.

50 Text in *ibid.*, pp. 1003–4. Trans. in *Chief Works*, vol. 2, p. 1014.

51 On Dazzi, see, for example, A. F. Verde, *Lo Studio Fiorentino
    1473–1503*, 3 vols. in 4 (Florence and Pistoia: Olschki, 1973–7), vol. 4,
    pp. 1464–5; P. Godman, *From Poliziano to Machiavlli: Florentine*

Humanism in the High Renaissance (Princeton NJ: Princeton University Press, 1998), p. 173, n.226, p. 193, n.67; G. Bottiglioni, *La lirica Latina in Firenze nella seconda metà del secolo XV* (Pisa: Nistri, 1913); C. Vivoli, 'Dazzi, Andrea', *DBI*, vol. 33 (Rome, 1987), pp. 184–6.

52 *Lett.*, p. 233 (no. 121); *Machiavelli and His Friends*, p. 221 (no. 205). For discussion, see Devonshire Jones, *Francesco Vettori*, p. 104.

53 Devonshire Jones, *Francesco Vettori*, p. 103.

54 *Lett.*, p. 234 (no. 122); *Machiavelli and His Friends*, p. 222 (no. 206); Devonshire Jones, *Francesco Vettori*, p. 104.

55 Nardi, *Istorie*, 6, Arbib (ed.), vol. 2, p. 27–8; Jurdjevic, *Guardians of Republicanism*, p. 98.

56 F. Petruccelli della Gattina, *Histoire diplomatique des conclaves*, 4 vols. (Paris: A. Lacroix, 1864–6), vol. 1, pp. 486–7.

57 *Ibid.*, vol. 1, pp. 490–1.

58 For discussion, see Devonshire Jones, *Francesco Vettori*, p. 90.

59 Landucci, *Diario*, pp. 335–6.

60 *Ibid.*, pp. 336–7.

19. Slumming with the Lice (March–December 1513)

1 *Lett.*, pp. 262–3 (no. 130); *Machiavelli and His Friends*, p. 239 (no. 214).

2 *Lett.*, p. 232 (no. 120); *Machiavelli and His Friends*, p. 221 (no. 204).

3 This point was made by Francesco Vettori in a letter dated 24 December 1513: *Lett.*, p. 312 (no. 142); *Machiavelli and His Friends*, p. 269 (no. 226).

4 Niccolò Machiavelli, 'Io vi mando, Giuliano, alquanti tordi'; text in Niccolò Machiavelli, *Tutte le opere*, M. Martelli (ed.) (Florence: Sansoni, 1971), p. 1004.

5 *Lett.*, p. 232 (no. 120); *Machiavelli and His Friends*, p. 221 (no. 204).

6 *Lett.*, p. 233 (no. 121); *Machiavelli and His Friends*, pp. 221–2 (no. 205) [adapted].

7 *Lett.*, p. 235 (no. 122); *Machiavelli and His Friends*, p. 222 (no. 206) [adapted].

8 *Lett.*, p. 236 (no. 123); *Machiavelli and His Friends*, p. 223 (no. 207).

9 R. Devonshire Jones, *Francesco Vettori: Florentine Citizen and Medici Servant* (London: Athlone Press, 1972), p. 101; cf. Jacopo Nardi, *Istorie della città di Firenze*, L. Arbib (ed.), 2 vols. (Florence: Società Editrice delle Storie del Nardi e del Varchi, 1842), vol. 2, p. 33.

10 Vettori had even failed to 'extract from the pope something profitable for himself and his brother'. Devonshire Jones, *Francesco Vettori*, p. 105.

11   *Lett.*, p. 239 (no. 124); *Machiavelli and His Friends*, p. 225 (no. 208) [adapted].

12   K. J. P. Lowe, *Church and Politics in Renaissance Italy: The Life and Career of Cardinal Francesco Soderini, 1453–1524* (Cambridge: Cambridge University Press, 1993), pp. 72–3, p. 74.

13   *Lett.*, p. 240 (no. 124); *Machiavelli and His Friends*, pp. 225–6 (no. 208).

14   *Lett.*, p. 244 (no. 126); *Machiavelli and His Friends*, p. 228 (no. 210).

15   *Lett.*, p. 241 (no. 125); *Machiavelli and His Friends*, p. 226 (no. 209). Although the letter is dated 9 April, Inglese and Najemy have convincingly argued that this is due to a copyist's error, and that it was actually written on 19 April: Niccolò Machiavelli, *Lettere a Francesco Vettori e a Francesco Guicciardini*, G. Inglese (ed.) (Milan: Rizzoli, 1989), p. 177; J. Najemy, *Between Friends: Discourses of Power and Desire in the Machiavelli–Vettori Letters of 1513–1515* (Princeton NJ: Princeton University Press, 1993), pp. 110–11, n.21.

16   *Lett.*, pp. 245–6 (no. 127); *Machiavelli and His Friends*, p. 229 (no. 211).

17   *Lett.*, p. 236 (no. 122); *Machiavelli and His Friends*, p. 223 (no. 206).

18   *Lett.*, p. 243 (no. 126); *Machiavelli and His Friends*, p. 227 (no. 210).

19   *Lett.*, p. 242 (no. 126); *Machiavelli and His Friends*, p. 227 (no. 210).

20   For the following, see Machiavelli, *Lett.*, pp. 242–3 (no. 126); *Machiavelli and His Friends*, p. 227 (no. 210).

21   *Lett.*, p. 243 (no. 126); *Machiavelli and His Friends*, p. 227 (no. 210).

22   *Lett.*, p. 239 (no. 124); *Machiavelli and His Friends*, p. 225 (no. 208).

23   *Lett.*, p. 243 (no. 126); q. Petrarch, *Canz.*, 102.12–14.

24   Exactly when Niccolò left Florence is not known, but it must have been at some point between 16 April (when he wrote to Vettori from the city) and 29 April (when he revealed that he was 'restricted to [his] farm'). *Lett.*, pp. 242–4, p. 516 (no. 126, *Appendice*); *Machiavelli and His Friends*, pp. 227–8, p. 236 (nos. 210, 212). Given the sorrowful tone of his letter of 16 April, it seems likely that he would have departed soon afterwards, most probably after receiving the bad news from Vettori on 19 April.

25   *Lett.*, p. 250 (no. 128).

26   See R. Stopani, *'Io mio sto in villa . . .' L'albergaccio del Machiavelli a Sant' Andrea in Percussina* (Florence: Centro di Studi Chiantigiani, 1998).

27   *Lett.*, pp. 239–40 (no. 124); *Machiavelli and His Friends*, p. 225 (no. 208).

28   For the following, see M. E. Mallett and C. Shaw, *The Italian Wars, 1494–1559: War, State and Society in Early Modern Europe* (London and New York: Routledge, 2012), pp. 116–20.

29 See Francesco Guicciardini, *Storia d'Italia*, ii.7, C. Panigada (ed.), 5 vols. (Bari: G. Laterza & Figli, 1929), vol. 3, pp. 249–54; M. Gattoni, *Leone X e la geo-politica dello Stato pontificio (1513–1521)* (Vatican City: Archivio Segreto Vaticano, 2000), pp. 318–21.

30 See Mallett and Shaw, *The Italian Wars*, p. 120; Guicciardini, *Storia d'Italia*, ii.9, Panigada (ed.), vol. 3, pp. 260–5.

31 *Lett.*, p. 249 (no. 127); *Machiavelli and His Friends*, p. 231 (no. 211).

32 *Lett.*, p. 246 (no. 127); *Machiavelli and His Friends*, p. 229 (no. 211).

33 *Lett.*, p. 249 (no. 127); *Machiavelli and His Friends*, p. 231 (no. 211).

34 *Lett.*, p. 516 (*Appendice*); *Machiavelli and His Friends*, p. 236 (no. 212). For a discussion of the phrase *uno pesce pastinaca* – translated as 'higgledy-piggledy' – see Najemy, *Between Friends*, p. 126, p. 135.

35 *Lett.*, pp. 510–16 (*Appendice*); *Machiavelli and His Friends*, pp. 231–6 (no. 212). Another version of this letter – which Gaeta appears to have believed represented the final version – is published at *Lett.*, pp. 250–8 (no. 128). Curiously, Atkinson and Sices maintain (*Machiavelli and His Friends*, p. 502 n.1) that they translated *Lett.*, pp. 250–8 (no. 128), whereas their translation is *clearly* based on *Lett.*, pp. 510–16 (*Appendice*).

36 *Lett.*, p. 510 (*Appendice*); *Machiavelli and His Friends*, p. 232 (no. 212).

37 *Lett.*, p. 512 (*Appendice*); *Machiavelli and His Friends*, p. 233 (no. 212).

38 *Lett.*, p. 513 (*Appendice*); *Machiavelli and His Friends*, p. 234 (no. 212).

39 *Lett.*, pp. 514–15 (*Appendice*); *Machiavelli and His Friends*, pp. 234–5 (no. 212).

40 *Lett.*, pp. 258–9 (no. 129); *Machiavelli and His Friends*, p. 236 (no. 213). Vettori had, in fact, been given permission to return to Florence by 4 May 1513, but Leo X repeatedly delayed his departure. As Devonshire Jones has persuasively demonstrated, the reason for this was not that Leo wanted to 'wait for the Medicean regime to become more stable' before allowing a known republican like Vettori to return to Florence, but because Vettori had become exactly 'the type of ambassador required by the Medici'. Devonshire Jones, *Francesco Vettori*, pp. 97–9.

41 For the following, see esp. Guicciardini, *Storia d'Italia*, ii.11, Panigada (ed.), vol. 3, pp. 270–3; Mallett and Shaw, *The Italian Wars*, pp. 120–1.

42 Guicciardini, *Storia d'Italia*, ii.12, Panigada (ed.), vol. 3, pp. 273–81; Mallett and Shaw, *The Italian Wars*, pp. 121–2; P. Pieri, *Il rinascimento e la crisi militaire* (Turin: Einaudi, 1952), pp. 501–2; M. Troso, *L'Ultima battaglia del Medioevo: La battaglia dell'Ariotta Novara 6 giugno 1513* (Mariano del Friuli: Edizioni della Laguna, 2002).

43 *Lett.*, p. 259 (no. 129); *Machiavelli and His Friends*, p. 237 (no. 213).

44 *Lett.*, p. 259 (no. 129); *Machiavelli and His Friends*, p. 237 (no. 213) [adapted].

45 *Lett.*, p. 261 (no. 129); *Machiavelli and His Friends*, p. 238 (no. 213).

46 *Lett.*, pp. 263–6 (no. 131); *Machiavelli and His Friends*, pp. 239–41 (no. 215).

47 *Lett.*, pp. 267–70 (no. 132); *Machiavelli and His Friends*, pp. 241–4 (no. 216).

48 *Lett.*, pp. 271–2 (no. 133); *Machiavelli and His Friends*, pp. 244–5 (no. 217).

49 See, for example, D. Herlihy and C. Klapisch-Zuber, *Tuscans and Their Families: A Study of the Florentine Catasto of 1427* (New Haven CT: Yale University Press, 1985), pp. 83–6; P. Gavitt, *Gender, Honor, and Charity in Late Renaissance Florence* (Cambridge: Cambridge University Press, 2011), pp. 31–5, p. 162, p. 184, p. 232.

50 *Lett.*, pp. 275–81 (no. 135); *Machiavelli and His Friends*, pp. 247–50 (no. 219).

51 *Lett.*, pp. 282–96 (nos. 136–8); *Machiavelli and His Friends*, pp. 251–60 (nos. 220–2).

52 Mallett and Shaw, *The Italian Wars*, p. 123.

53 *Lett.*, p. 296 (no. 138); *Machiavelli and His Friends*, p. 260 (no. 222) [adapted].

54 For what follows about Vettori's life in Rome, see *Lett.*, pp. 297–300 (no. 139); *Machiavelli and His Friends*, pp. 260–2 (no. 223).

55 For a masterly discussion of this letter, see Najemy, *Between Friends*, pp. 215–40.

56 For what follows about Niccolò's daily routine in the country, see *Lett.*, pp. 302–4 (no. 140); *Machiavelli and His Friends*, pp. 263–4 (no. 224).

57 *Lett.*, p. 305 (no. 140); *Machiavelli and His Friends*, p. 265 (no. 224).

20. Princely Aspirations (December 1513–August 1514)

1 Among the ancient historians, Niccolò's preference was for Livy, Tacitus, Xenophon, Sallust, Justin, Plutarch, Polybius and Herodian. This is evident from quotations and allusions contained in *Il principe*. As Marcia Colish has rightly noted, his classical sources 'are a subject which students of his political thought have scarcely neglected' and the bibliography is now so vast that it would be fruitless even to attempt to provide a complete conspectus. For Niccolò's knowledge and use of the authors and works mentioned, however, the following are a useful starting point. On Livy: H. Whitfield, 'Machiavelli's Use of Livy', in T. A. Dorey (ed.), *Livy* (London: Routledge and Kegan Paul, 1971), pp. 73–96. On Tacitus: K. C. Schellhase, 'Tacitus in the Political Thought of Machiavelli', *Il pensiero politico* 4 (1971), pp. 381–91; K. C. Schellhase, *Tacitus in Renaissance Political Thought* (Chicago IL: University of Chicago

Press, 1976), ch. 1. On Xenophon: M. Simonetta, 'Machiavelli lettore di Tucidide', *Esperienze letterarie* 22/3 (1997), pp. 53–68; W. R. Newell, 'Machiavelli and Xenophon on Princely Rule', *Journal of Politics* 50 (1988), pp. 108–30; J. Tatum, *Xenophon's Imperial Fiction: On the Education of Cyrus* (Princeton NJ: Princeton University Press, 1989), pp. 3–33. On Sallust: G. Sasso, *Machiavelli e gli antichi e altri saggi* (Milan: Ricciardi, 1986), vol. 1, pp. 441–60; Q. Skinner, 'Machiavelli's *Discorsi* and the Pre-Humanist Origins of Republican Ideas', in G. Bock, Q. Skinner and M. Viroli (eds.), *Machiavelli and Republicanism* (Cambridge: Cambridge University Press, 1990), pp. 121–41; P. Osmond, 'Sallust and Machiavelli: From Civic Humanism to Political Prudence', *Journal of Medieval and Renaissance Studies* 23 (1993), pp. 407–38; B. Fontana, 'Sallust and the Politics of Machiavelli', *History of Political Thought* 24 (2003), pp. 86–108. On Polybius: A. Momigliano, 'Polybius' Reappearance in Western Europe', in *Polybe*, Entretiens sur l'antiquité classique 20 (Vandoeuvres-Geneva, 1974), pp. 347–72; J. H. Hexter, 'Seyssel, Machiavelli, and Polybius VI: The Mystery of the Missing Translation', *Studies in the Renaissance* 3 (1956), pp. 75–96; F. Gilbert, *Machiavelli and Guicciardini: Politics and History in Sixteenth-Century Florence* (Princeton NJ: Princeton University Press, 1965), pp. 320–1; G. Sasso, *Studi su Machiavelli* (Naples: Morano, 1967), pp. 161–280. On Homer: J. H. Geerken, 'Heroic Virtue: An Introduction to the Origins and Nature of a Renaissance Concept' (Unpublished PhD dissertation, Yale University, 1967), chs. 4–6. On Cicero's *De Officiis*: M. Colish, 'Cicero's *De Officiis* and Machiavelli's *Prince*', *Sixteenth Century Journal* 9/4 (1978), pp. 81–93; J. J. Barlow, 'The Fox and the Lion: Machiavelli Replies to Cicero', *History of Political Thought* 20 (1999), pp. 627–45; W. Olmstead, 'Exemplifying Deliberation: Cicero's *De Officiis* and Machiavelli's *Prince*', in W. Jost and W. Olmstead (eds.), *A Companion to Rhetoric and Rhetorical Criticism* (Malden MA: Blackwell, 2004), pp. 173–89. On Seneca: N. Wood, 'Some Common Aspects of the Thought of Seneca and Machiavelli', *Renaissance Quarterly* 21 (1968), pp. 11–23; P. Stacey, *Roman Monarchy and the Renaissance Prince* (Cambridge: Cambridge University Press, 2007), pp. 205–310. Studies on Niccolò's knowledge of and relationship to Herodian seem to be rather lacking.

2 *Lett.*, p. 304 (no. 140); *Machiavelli and His Friends*, p. 264 (no. 224).
3 The following analysis of *Il principe* is based on that of Q. R. D. Skinner, *Machiavelli*, new ed. (Oxford: Oxford University Press, 2000), pp. 23–53.
4 *Lett.*, p. 304 (no. 140); *Machiavelli and His Friends*, p. 264 (no. 224) [amended].

5 *Lett.*, pp. 304–5 (no. 140).

6 Machiavelli, *Il principe*, 20; cf. 21, 23.

7 *Ibid.*, 1; Skinner, *Machiavelli*, pp. 26–7.

8 *Ibid.*, 2.

9 *Ibid.*, 2.

10 *Ibid.*, 3.

11 *Ibid.*, 1, 6–7. A little later, almost as an afterthought, he noted that a private citizen could also become a prince through crime or 'by the favour of his fellow citizens', but these were rare cases, and were accordingly given short shrift: *ibid.*, 8–9.

12 *Ibid.*, 6.

13 *Ibid.*, 7.

14 *Ibid.*

15 *Ibid.*, 15. For the following, see esp. F. Gilbert, 'The Humanist Concept of the Prince and the Prince of Machiavelli', *Journal of Modern History* 11/4 (1939), pp. 449–83.

16 Gilbert, 'The Humanist Concept of the Prince', p. 453.

17 See esp. J. Dunbabin, 'Government', in J. H. Burns (ed.), *The Cambridge History of Medieval Political Thought, c. 350–c. 1450* (Cambridge: Cambridge University Press, 1988), pp. 477–519, here p. 484.

18 Petrarch, *Sen.* 14.1; an English translation can be found in B. G. Kohl and R. G. Witt (eds.), *The Earthly Republic: Italian Humanists on Government and Society* (Philadelphia PA: University of Pennsylvania Press, 1978), pp. 35–78. For discussion, see, for example, A. Steiner, 'Petrarch's *Optimus Princeps*', *Romanic Review* 25 (1934), pp. 99–111; E. Nelson, 'The problem of princely virtue', in J. Hankins (ed.), *The Cambridge Companion to Renaissance Philosophy* (Cambridge: Cambridge University Press, 2007), pp. 319–37, here pp. 319–24.

19 Stacey, *Roman Monarchy*, p. 160; Coluccio Salutati, *Epistolario*, F. Novati (ed.), 4 vols. (Rome: Istituto Storico Italiano, 1891–1911), vol. 2, pp. 11–46. For further discussion, see D. De Rosa, *Coluccio Salutati: il cancelliere e il pensatore politico* (Florence: La Nuova Italia, 1980), p. 78, p. 131; R. G. Witt, *Hercules at the Crossroads: The Life, Works, and Thought of Coluccio Salutati* (Durham NC: Duke University Press, 1983), pp. 359–60.

20 Bartolomeo Platina, *De principe*, G. Ferraù (ed.) (Palermo: Il Vespro, 1979); for discussion, see, for example, N. Rubinstein, 'The *De optimo cive* and the *De principe* by Bartolomeo Platina', in R. Cardini, E. Garin, L. Cesarini Martinelli and G. Pascucci (eds.), *Tradizione classica e letteratura umanistica: per Alessandro Perosa* (Rome: Bulzoni, 1985), pp. 375–89; repr. in N. Rubinstein, *Studies in Italian History in*

the *Middle Ages and the Renaissance*, vol. 1, *Political Thought and the Language of Politics: Art and Politics*, G. Ciappelli (ed.) (Rome: Edizioni di Storia e Letteratura, 2004), pp. 259–72; M. Viroli, *From Politics to Reason of State: The Acquisition and Transformation of the Language of Politics, 1250–1600* (Cambridge: Cambridge University Press, 1992), p. 259.

21 Francesco Patrizi, *De regno et regis institutione* . . . (Paris: Pierre Vidoué and Galliot du Pré, 1519); for discussion, see, for example, G. Chiarelli, 'Il *De regno* di Francesco Patrizi', *Rivista internzaionale di filosofia del diritto* 12 (1932), pp. 716–38; A. Ceron, *L'amicizia civile e gli amici del principe: lo spazio politico dell'amicizia nel pensiero del Quattrocento* (Macerata: EUM, 2011), pp. 427–5; Viroli, *From Politics to Reason of State*, pp. 114–15, pp. 116–18, p. 120, pp. 121–2.

22 Giuniano Maio, *De maiestate*, F. Gaeta (ed.) (Bologna: Commissione per i testi di lingua, 1956); for discussion, see, for example, D. Lojacono, 'L'opera inedita *De maiestate* di Giuniano Maio e il concetto sul principe negli scrittori della corte aragonese di Napoli', *Atti della Regia Accademia di scienze morali e politiche di Napoli* 24 (1891), pp. 329–76; S. Gentile, 'A proposito dell'edizione del trattato *De maiestate* di Iuniano Maio', *Filologia romanza* 5/2 (1958), pp. 143–209.

23 Giovanni Pontano, *De principe*, ed. G. M. Cappelli (Rome: Salerno, 2003); for discussion, see, for example, M. Roick, *Pontano's Virtues: Aristotelian Moral and Political Thought in the Renaissance* (London: Bloomsbury, 2017), p. 3, p. 8, p. 10, p. 97, pp. 157–8, p. 166, p. 172, p. 174; G. Falvo, 'The Art of Human Composition in Giovanni Pontano's *De principe liber*', *MLN* 129/3 (2014), pp. 21–34; D. Canfora, 'Culture and Power in Naples from 1450 to 1650', in M. Gosman, A MacDonald and A. Vanderjagt (eds.), *Princes and Princely Culture, 1450–1650*, 2 vols. (Leiden: Brill, 2003–5), vol. 2, pp. 79–96, here p. 82, pp. 84–5; Viroli, *From Politics to Reason of State*, pp. 111–13.

24 Machiavelli, *Il principe*, 15.

25 *Ibid.* [emphasis added].

26 *Ibid.*, 25. Skinner, *Machiavelli*, pp. 32–3; B. Spackman, 'Machiavelli and gender', in J. M. Najemy (ed.), *The Cambridge Companion to Machiavelli* (Cambridge: Cambridge University Press, 2000), pp. 223–38, here pp. 225–6; H. F. Pitkin, *Fortune is a Woman: Gender and Politics in the Thought of Niccolò Machiavelli* (Berkeley CA: University of California Press, 1984).

27 For a discussion of Niccolò's understanding of *virtù*, see esp. R. Price, 'The Senses of *Virtù* in Machiavelli', *European Studies Review* 4 (1973), pp. 315–45; Skinner, *Machiavelli*, pp. 38–40.

28 On the role of glory in Niccolò's thought, see, for example: R. Price, 'The Theme of *Gloria* in Machiavelli', *Renaissance Quarterly* 30 (1977), pp. 588–631; V. A. Santi, *La 'Gloria' nel pensiero di Machiavelli* (Ravenna: Longo, 1979).

29 Machiavelli, *Il principe*, 19.

30 *Ibid.*, 12.

31 *Ibid.*, 13.

32 *Ibid.*, 15, 19.

33 Skinner, *Machiavelli*, p. 40. The Latin terms that Niccolò used in his chapter-headings are *liberalitas*, *pietas* and *fides*. In Italian, he rendered these as *liberalità*, *pietà* and *fede*.

34 Machiavelli, *Il principe*, 15.

35 *Ibid.*, 16.

36 *Ibid.*, 17.

37 *Ibid.*

38 Petrarch, *Sen.* 14.1.11.

39 Seneca, *De ira*, 1.20.4; q. Lucius Accius, *Atreus*. Cf. Cicero, *De off.* 3.30.82; *Phil.* 1.34.

40 Machiavelli, *Il principe*, 18.

41 *Ibid.*

42 *Ibid.*, 19.

43 *Lett.*, p. 311 (no. 142); *Machiavelli and His Friends*, p. 269 (no. 226).

44 *Lett.*, p. 319 (no. 144); *Machiavelli and His Friends*, p. 276 (no. 228). On the question of which version of the text Vettori read, see J. M. Najemy, *Between Friends: Discourses of Power and Desire in the Machiavelli–Vettori Letters of 1513–1515* (Princeton NJ: Princeton University Press, 1993), pp. 176–85.

45 H. C. Butters, *Governors and Government in Early Sixteenth-Century Florence 1502–1519* (Oxford: Clarendon, 1985), p. 243.

46 Machiavelli, *Il principe*, 20.

47 See J. N. Stephens, *The Fall of the Florentine Republic, 1512–1530* (Oxford: Clarendon, 1983), pp. 90–1.

48 Machiavelli, *Il principe*, 21–2.

49 *Ibid.*, 22.

50 *Ibid.*, 21.

51 The text of the *Decennale secondo* may be found in Niccolò Machiavelli, *Opere*, M. Bonfantini (ed.) (Milan and Naples: R. Ricciardi, 1954), pp. 1065–72.

52 On the date, see Machiavelli, *Decennale secondo*, 1–3; G. Inglese, 'Contributo al testo critico dei "Decennali" di Niccolò Machiavelli', *Annali dell'Istituto italiano per gli studi storici* 8 (1983–4), pp. 115–73, here p. 139.

53 Machiavelli, *Decennale secondo*, 43–4.

54 *Ibid.*, 181–92.

55 *Lett.*, p. 319 (no. 144); *Machiavelli and His Friends*, p. 276 (no. 228).

56 *Lett.*, p. 325 (no. 146); *Machiavelli and His Friends*, p. 279 (no. 230).

57 For the following, see *Lett.*, p. 323 (no. 145); *Machiavelli and His Friends*, pp. 278–9 (no. 229).

58 *Lett.*, p. 326 (no. 146); *Machiavelli and His Friends*, p. 280 (no. 230).

59 *Lett.*, pp. 327–30 (no. 147); *Machiavelli and His Friends*, pp. 280–2 (no. 231). For a good discussion of this letter's sexual dimension, see, for example, G. Ruggiero, *Machiavelli in Love: Self, Sex and Society in the Italian Renaissance* (Baltimore MD: Johns Hopkins University Press, 2007), pp. 98–103. Ruggiero does not, however, appear to have realized that the main character in Niccolò's tale was actually a cover for Niccolò himself. See the following note.

60 For the suggestion that 'Giuliano Brancacci' – who was then in Rome – was actually Niccolò himself, see Najemy, *Between Friends*, pp. 272–3.

61 For the following, see *Lett.*, pp. 327–30 (no. 146); *Machiavelli and His Friends*, pp. 281–2 (no. 230).

62 The text of 'De' romiti' can be found in Niccolò Machiavelli, *Opere*, C. Vivanti (ed.), 3 vols. (Turin: Einaudi, 1997–2005), vol. 3, pp. 28–9. For readable translations, see Machiavelli, *Chief Works*, vol. 2, pp. 880–1; J. Tusiani (trans.), *Lust and Liberty: The Poems of Machiavelli* (New York NY: I. Obolensky, 1963), pp. 10–12. On the date of this poem, see A. Casadei, 'Note Machiavelliane', *Annali della Scuola Normale Superiore di Pisa*, classe lettere e filosofia, ser. 3, 17 (1987), pp. 447–64, here p. 460; F. Bausi, *Machiavelli* (Rome: Salerno, 2005), p. 155. On Fra Franesco da Montepulciano's predictions, see *Lett.*, p. 308, p. 323 (nos. 141, 145); *Machiavelli and His Friends*, p. 267, p. 278 (nos. 225, 230); Stephens, *The Fall of the Florentine Republic*, pp. 77–8. For a discussion of Niccolò's relationship to these predictions, see, for example, O. Niccoli, *Prophesy and People in Renaissance Italy* (Princeton NJ: Princeton University Press, 1990), pp. 154–5.

63 Machiavelli, 'De' romiti', 23–33; adapted from Machiavelli, *Chief Works*, vol. 2, p. 881.

64 Machiavelli, 'De' romiti', 47; adapted from Machiavelli, *Chief Works*, vol. 2, p. 881.

65 The text of 'Di amanti e donne disperati' can be found in Machiavelli, *Opere*, Vivanti (ed.), vol. 3, pp. 23–4. For readable translations, see Machiavelli, *Chief Works*, vol. 2, p. 879; Tusiani (trans.), *Lust and Liberty*, pp. 5–6. On the date of this poem, see Bausi, *Machiavelli*, p. 154; O. Tommasini, *La vita e gli scritti di Niccolò Machiavelli nella*

loro relazione col machiavellismo, 3 vols. (Turin: Ermanno Loescher, 1883–1911), vol. 1, p. 115.

66 Machiavelli, 'Di amanti e donne disperati', 1–3; Machiavelli, *Chief Works*, vol. 2, p. 879.

67 Machiavelli, 'Di amanti e donne disperati', 4–8; Machiavelli, *Chief Works*, vol. 2, p. 879.

68 Machiavelli, 'Di amanti e donne disperati', 22–8; adapted from Machiavelli, *Chief Works*, vol. 2, p. 879.

69 Machiavelli, 'Di amanti e donne disperati', 36–42; adapted from Machiavelli, *Chief Works*, vol. 2, p. 879.

70 M. E. Mallett and C. Shaw, *The Italian Wars, 1494–1559: War, State and Society in Early Modern Europe* (London and New York: Routledge, 2012), pp. 125–6; see also Butters, *Governors and Government*, p. 244; L. Simeoni, *Le signorie*, 2 vols. (Milan: Vallardi, 1950), vol. 2, pp. 815–16.

71 *Lett.*, pp. 332–5 (no. 149); *Machiavelli and His Friends*, pp. 283–5 (no. 233). An early draft of this letter – containing several interesting differences – also survives, having been preserved in the *Apografo Ricci*: it is reproduced at *Lett.*, p. 335, n.1.

72 *Lett.*, pp. 336–42 (no. 151); *Machiavelli and His Friends*, pp. 286–90 (no. 235).

73 The first part of this letter, containing lurid details of Vettori's affair, was omitted by Giuliano de' Ricci.

74 See, for example, Mallett and Shaw, *The Italian Wars*, p. 126.

75 On 19 May, the *balìa* approved the revival of the militia – a proposal that had first been made by the pope, earlier in the year (see Butters, *Governors and Government*, p. 234). Since Niccolò would surely not have troubled to defend a citizen militia in *Il principe* after this day, it follows that it must have been completed *before* this. See Tommasini, *La vita e gli scritti di Niccolò Machiavelli*, vol. 2.2, p. 995.

76 *Lett.*, pp. 342–3 (no. 152); *Machiavelli and His Friends*, pp. 290–1 (no. 236).

77 *Lett.*, p. 343 (no. 152); *Machiavelli and His Friends*, p. 290 (no. 236) [adapted].

78 *Lett.*, pp. 344–6 (no. 153); *Machiavelli and His Friends*, pp. 291–2 (no. 237).

79 For the following, see *Lett.*, pp. 346–7 (no. 154); *Machiavelli and His Friends*, pp. 292–3 (no. 238). For a discussion of La Tafani's identity, see R. Ridolfi, *Vita di Niccolò Machiavelli*, 3rd ed., 2 vols. (Florence: Sansoni, 1969), vol. 1, pp. 247–9, pp. 250–1.

80 For this and what follows, see *Lett.*, pp. 346–7 (no. 154); *Machiavelli and His Friends*, p. 293 (no. 238).

21. The Garden of Delights (August 1514–March 1519)

1 It is worth noting that, on 4 December, he petitioned Vettori for help in tracking down a certain Giovanni, to whom La Tafani was betrothed, but who had since taken himself to Rome, 'oblivious to both marriage and wife'. La Tafani's brother, Niccolò, wanted Giovanni either to return to his intended bride, or to renounce her and return the portion of the dowry he had received. That this matter had now become so important suggests that, at the very least, La Tafani and her family were no longer willing to put up with the irregularity of her current lifestyle. Had her passion for Niccolò burned as brightly as once it had, it is tempting to suppose that she might perhaps have been less willing to insist on her fiancé's return/renunciation. *Lett.*, p. 350 (no. 156); *Machiavelli and His Friends*, p. 295 (no. 240).

2 *Lett.*, p. 350 (no. 156); *Machiavelli and His Friends*, p. 295 (no. 240).

3 *Lett.*, pp. 348–9 (no. 155); *Machiavelli and His Friends*, pp. 293–4 (no. 239).

4 *Lett.*, p. 348 (no. 155); *Machiavelli and His Friends*, p. 294 (no. 239).

5 *Lett.*, p. 349 (no. 155); *Machiavelli and His Friends*, p. 294 (no. 239) [adapted].

6 *Lett.*, pp. 351–61 (no. 157); *Machiavelli and His Friends*, pp. 295–302 (no. 241).

7 *Lett.*, p. 356 (no. 157); *Machiavelli and His Friends*, p. 299 (no. 241).

8 H. C. Butters, *Governors and Government in Early Sixteenth-Century Florence 1502–1519* (Oxford: Clarendon, 1985), pp. 248–9.

9 For what follows, see *Lett.*, pp. 361–3 (no. 158); *Machiavelli and His Friends*, pp. 302–3 (no. 242). Giovanni Gioviano Pontano, *De fortuna* (Naples: Sigismund Mayr, 1512). For further discussion of this letter, see J. M. Najemy, *Between Friends: Discourses of Power and Desire in the Machiavelli–Vettori Letters of 1513–1515* (Princeton NJ: Princeton University Press, 1993), pp. 308–9.

10 *Lett.*, p. 362 (no. 158) *Machiavelli and His Friends*, p. 302 (no. 242).

11 *Lett.*, pp. 363–7 (no. 159); *Machiavelli and His Friends*, pp. 303–5 (no. 243).

12 *Lett.*, p. 364 (no. 159); *Machiavelli and His Friends*, p. 303 (no. 243).

13 Cf. Machiavelli, *Il principe*, 19, 21.

14 *Lett.*, p. 364 (no. 159); *Machiavelli and His Friends*, p. 304 (no. 243).

15 *Ibid.*

16 *Lett.*, pp. 367–8 (no. 160); *Machiavelli and His Friends*, p. 306 (no. 244).

17 *Lett.*, pp. 369–70 (no. 161); *Machiavelli and His Friends*, p. 307 (no. 245).

18 For the following, see J. M. Najemy, *A History of Florence, 1200–1575*

(Oxford: Blackwell, 2008), p. 430; Butters, *Governors and Government*, pp. 249–50; R. Devonshire Jones, *Francesco Vettori: Florentine Citizen and Medici Servant* (London: Athlone Press, 1972), p. 109; Francesco Guicciardini, *Storia d'Italia*, 12.10, C. Panigada (ed.), 5 vols. (Bari: G. Laterza & Figli, 1929), vol. 3, pp. 338–42.

19 See M. E. Mallett and C. Shaw, *The Italian Wars, 1494–1559: War, State and Society in Early Modern Europe* (London and New York: Routledge, 2012), p. 127.

20 *Lett.*, p. 374 (no. 163); *Machiavelli and His Friends*. 313 (no. 247).

21 For what follows, see *Lett.*, pp. 374–5 (no. 163); *Machiavelli and His Friends*, p. 313 (no. 247).

22 Cf. chapter 10, above. Even given Niccolò's admiration for Cesare Borgia in *Il principe*, his allusion to Ramiro de Lorqua is a little surprising. Unable to believe that he could seriously have wished Paolo Vettori to emulate such a loathsome figure, some scholars have suggested his advice must have been ironic, and that the example of Ramiro was meant to warn Paolo off the whole project. As Baron, Black and Hörnqvist have pointed out, however, this simply doesn't make sense. Niccolò could only have meant his advice ironically if he had already given up all hope of securing a position with the Medici. Najemy, *Between Friends*, pp. 330–4; R. Black, *Machiavelli* (Abingdon: Routledge, 2013), p. 123; M. Hörnqvist, *Machiavelli and Empire* (Cambridge: Cambridge University Press, 2004), p. 285 n.42; H. Baron, 'The *Principe* and the puzzle of the date of chapter 26', *Journal of Medieval and Renaissance Studies* 21 (1991), pp. 83–102, here pp. 98–100.

23 *Lett.*, p. 372 (no. 163); *Machiavelli and His Friends*, pp. 311–12 (no. 247) [amended]. For further discussion of this sonnet, see Najemy, *Between Friends*, pp. 325–8.

24 C. H. Clough, *Machiavelli Researches*, Pubblicazioni della Sezione Romanza dell'Istituto Universitario Orientale, Studi 3 (Naples, 1967), p. 39; *Machiavelli and His Friends*, p. 529, n.12.

25 The following is indebted to Butters, *Governors and Government*, p. 265. For further discussion of Lorenzo's appointment, see A. Giorgetti, 'Lorenzo de' Medici Capitano Generale della Repubblica fiorentina', *ASI* ser. 4, 11–12 (1883), pp. 194–215; R. C. Trexler and M. E. Lewis, 'Two Captains and Three Kings: New Light on the Medici Chapel', *Studies in Medieval and Renaissance History*, n.s. 4 (1981), pp. 93–177.

26 Niccolò Machiavelli, *Opere politiche*, vol. 3, *L'arte della guerra. Scritti politici minori*, J.-J. Marchand, D. Fachard and G. Masi (eds.) (Rome, 2001), pp. 585–7; J.-J. Marchand, 'I *Ghiribizzi d'ordinanza* del

Machiavelli', *La Bibliofilia* 73 (1971), pp. 135–50. Though it was previously thought this text was addressed to Paolo Vettori, it has recently been shown that Niccolò intended it to be read by Lorenzo de' Medici himself – on which, see F. Bausi, *Machiavelli* (Rome: Salerno, 2005), p. 312; Black, *Machiavelli*, p. 125; Niccolò Machiavelli, *De principatibus*, G. Inglese (ed.) (Rome: Istituto Storico Italiano per il Medioevo, 1994), pp. 9–10, n.16.

27 Atkinson and Sices claim that the *Ghiribizzi d'ordinanza* failed to impress Lorenzo de' Medici. I find this a little difficult to accept. Although there is no direct evidence of Lorenzo's attitude either way, it is logical to infer from Niccolò's rededication of *Il principe* the following year that he must have reacted positively. Had the *Ghiribizzi* been given a frosty reception, Niccolò would surely not have considered trying his luck again. *Machiavelli and His Friends*, p. 309.

28 Guicciardini, *Storia d'Italia*, 12.12, Panigada (ed.), vol. 3, pp. 351–2; Mallett and Shaw, *The Italian Wars*, p. 128.

29 For the following, see esp. Najemy, *History of Florence*, p. 431; Butters, *Governors and Government*, pp. 268–71; Devonshire Jones, *Francesco Vettori*, p. 113; Giorgetti, 'Lorenzo de' Medici', pp. 212–13.

30 Francesco Vettori, *Scritti storici e politici*, E. Niccolini (ed.) (Bari: G. Laterza & Figli, 1972), p. 169; Devonshire Jones, *Francesco Vettori*, p. 113.

31 H. Reinhard, *Lorenzo von Medici, Herzog von Urbino, 1492–1515* (Freiburg: Waibel, 1935), p. 52.

32 For the following, see Mallett and Shaw, *The Italian Wars*, pp. 128–30.

33 On this medal, see M. A. Jones, *A Catalogue of French Medals in the British Museum*, vol. 1, *1402–1610* (London: British Museum Publications, 1982), p. 218, p. 222.

34 See, for example, J. N. Stephens, *The Fall of the Florentine Republic, 1512–1530* (Oxford: Clarendon, 1983), p. 102.

35 For the following, see Najemy, *History of Florence*, p. 432; Butters, *Governors and Government*, p. 273; I. Ciseri, *L'ingresso trionfale di Leone X in Firenze nel 1515* (Florence: Olschki, 1990); J. Cox-Rearick, *Dynasty and Destiny in Medici Art* (Princeton NJ: Princeton University Press, 1984), pp. 34–6; A. M. Cummings, *The Politicized Muse: Music for Medici Festivals, 1512–1537* (Princeton NJ: Princeton University Press, 1992), pp. 67–82; J. Searman, 'The Florentine *Entrata* of Leo X, 1515', *Journal of the Warburg and Courtauld Institutes* 38 (1975), pp. 136–54.

36 Vettori, *Vita di Lorenzo de' Medici, duca di Urbino* in *Scritti storici e politici*, pp. 259–72, here p. 266.

37 *Lett.*, p. 377 (no. 165); *Machiavelli and His Friends*, p. 314 (no. 249).

38 Machiavelli, *Il principe*, pr.

39 *Lett.*, p. 378 (no. 166); *Machiavelli and His Friends*, p. 315 (no. 250).

40 Riccardi's story about the dogs was first published in Niccolò Machiavelli, *Lettere familiari*, E. Alvisi (ed.) (Florence: Sansoni, 1883), p. xiv. For discussion, see *'The Prince' by Niccolò Machiavelli with Related Documents*, W. J. Connell (ed.) (Boston: Bedford/St Martin's, 2005), p. 142; C. H. Zuckert, *Machiavelli's Politics* (Chicago IL: University of Chicago Press, 2017), p. 42 n.

41 Francesco Guicciardini, *Del modo di assicurare lo stato ai Medici*, in Guicciardini, *Dialogo e Discorsi del Reggimento di Firenze*, R. Palmarocchi (ed.) (Bari: G. Laterza & Figli, 1932), pp. 267–81.

42 Paolo Giovio, *De vita Leonis decimi pont. max. libri quattuor. His ordine temporum accesserunt Hadriani sexti pont. Max. et Pompeii Columnae cardinalis vitae* . . . (Florence: Lorenzo Torrentino, 1551), p. 95.

43 Ulrich von Hutten, 'Exhortatio viri cuiusdam doctissimi ad Principes, ne in Decimae praestationem consentiant', in *Sämmtliche Werke* [=*Opera quae extant omnia*], E. J. H. Münch (ed.), 6 vols. (Berlin and Leipzig: J. G. Reimer, 1821–7), vol. 2, pp. 547–54, here vol. 2, p. 553.

44 See Butters, *Governors and Government*, p. 278.

45 *Lett.*, pp. 379–80 (no. 168); *Machiavelli and His Friends*, p. 316 (no. 252).

46 K. M. Setton, *The Papacy and the Levant, 1204–1571*, 4 vols. (Philadelphia PA: The American Philosophical Society, 1976–84), vol. 2, p. 171.

47 *Lett.*, pp. 378–9 (no. 167); *Machiavelli and His Friends*, p. 315 (no. 251).

48 By far the best study of the Orti Oricellari as a garden and a gathering place is R. M. Comanducci, 'Gli Orti Oricellari', *Interpres* 15 (1995–6), pp. 302–58.

49 F. Gilbert, 'Bernardo Rucellai and the Orti Oricellari: A Study on the Origin of Modern Political Thought', *Journal of the Warburg and Courtauld Institutes* 12 (1949), pp. 101–31, here p. 114. This article is reprinted in F. Gilbert, *History: Choice and Commitment* (Cambridge MA: Belknap Press, 1977), pp. 215–46.

50 Pietro Crinito, 'Ad Faustum de Sylva Oricellaria', 63–6; text in Comanducci, 'Gli Orti Oricellari', pp. 356–8.

51 For the following, see esp. Gilbert, 'Bernardo Rucellai and the Orti Oricellari'.

52 On the composition and character of the second Orti Oricellari group, see Gilbert, 'Bernardo Rucellai and the Orti Oricellari'; F. Gilbert, 'The Composition and Structure of Machiavelli's *Discorsi*', *Journal of the History of Ideas* 14 (1953), pp. 135–56 [repr. in Gilbert,

History: Choice and Commitment, pp. 115–33]; D. Cantimori, 'Rhetoric and Politics in Italian Humanism', *Journal of the Warburg and Courtauld Institutes* 1 (1937), pp. 83–102; R. von Albertini, *Das florentinische Staatsbewusstsein in Übergang von der Republik zum Prinzipat* (Bern: Francke Verlag, 1955), pp. 67–85; G. Lucarelli, *Gli Orti Oricellari: epilogo della politica fiorentina del quattrocento e inizio del pensiero politico moderno* (Lucca: M. Pacini Fazzi, 1979); L. M. Bartoli and G. Contorni, *Gli Orti Oricellari a Firenze: Un giardino, una città* (Florence: Edifir, 1991); R. M. Comanducci, *Gli Orti Oricellari* (Rome: Salerno, 1997); H. Stein, 'Historical Writing and Community among the *Orti Oricellari*' (Unpublished PhD Dissertation, Johns Hopkins University, 2015).

53 On these figures, see generally, Gilbert, 'Bernardo Rucellai and the Orti Oricellari'. On Francesco Cattani da Diacceto, see, for example, P. O. Kristeller, 'Cattani da Diacceto, Francesco, detto il Pagonazzo', *DBI*, vol. 22 (Rome, 1979), *ad voc.*; 'Francesco da Diacceto and Florentine Platonism in the Sixteenth Century', *Miscallanea Giuseppe Mercati* 4 (Vatican City, 1956), pp. 260–304; Gilbert, 'Bernardo Rucellai and the Orti Oricellari'. On Zanobi Buondelmonti, see G. De Caro, 'Buondelmonti, Zanobi', *DBI*, vol. 15 (Rome, 1972), *ad voc.* On Luigi Alamanni: H. Hauvette, *Luigi Alamanni. Sa vie et son oeuvre* (Paris: Hachette, 1903). On Jacopo da Diacceto: P. Malanima, 'Cattani da Diacceto, Iacopo', *DBI*, vol. 22 (Rome, 1979), *ad voc.* On Antonio Brucioli: G. Spini, *Tra Rinascimento e Riforma. Antonio Brucioli* (Florence: La Nuova Italia, 1940); É. Boillet (ed.), *Antonio Brucioli: humanisme et évangélisme entre réforme et contre-réforme: actes du colloque de Tours, 20–21 mai 2005* (Paris: Honoré Champion, 2008); Cantimori, 'Rhetoric and Politics'.

54 *Lett.*, p. 199 (no. 103); *Machiavelli and His Friends*, p. 186 (no. 172).

55 Kristeller, 'Cattani da Diacceto, Francesco, detto il Pagonazzo'.

56 Text in Niccolò Machiavelli, *Tutte le opere*, M. Martelli (ed.) (Florence: Sansoni, 1971), pp. 954–76; trans. in *Chief Works*, vol. 2, pp. 750–72.

57 Machiavelli, *L'asino*, 7.28–33; *Chief Works*, vol. 2, p. 767.

58 Machiavelli, *L'asino*, 7.115–8.151; *Chief Works*, vol. 2, pp. 769–72.

59 Niccolò left his poem incomplete – most likely because of concerns about how it might be received. Writing to Francesco Vettori on 3 March 1518, Giuliano Brancacci intimated that Niccolò feared he would end up paying the price for his poem, without gaining anything in return. R. Ridolfi, *Vita di Niccolò Machiavelli*, 3rd ed., 2 vols. (Florence: Sansoni, 1969), vol. 2, p. 502, n.7; Bausi, *Machiavelli*, p. 148.

60   For a splendid discussion of the literary reminiscences in *L'asino*,
     see, for example, A. Russell Ascoli and A. M. Capodivacca,
     'Machiavelli and Poetry', in J. M. Najemy (ed.), *The Cambridge
     Companion to Machiavelli* (Cambridge: Cambridge University Press,
     2010), pp. 190–205, here pp. 198–200, pp. 202–3, p. 204.
61   Niccolò's gentle mockery of Ariosto was born of a genuine
     admiration, tempered by mild umbrage. On 17 December 1517, he
     wrote to Ludovico Alamanni, who was then in Rome, praising
     Ariosto's poetry, yet criticizing his taste in poets. 'Lately,' he wrote,
     'I have been reading Ariosto's *Orlando furioso*; the entire poem is
     really fine and many passages are marvellous. If he is there with
     you, give him my regards and tell him that my only complaint is
     that in his mention of so many poets, he has left me out like some
     prick and that he had done to me in his *Orlando* what I shall not
     do to him in my *Ass*.' *Lett.*, p. 383 (no. 170); *Machiavelli and His
     Friends*, p. 318 (no. 254).
62   Machiavelli, *L'asino*, 1.28–90.
63   It has proved difficult – if not impossible – to establish to whom
     the animals were intended to refer. See Giovambattista Busini,
     Lettere a Benedetto Varchi sopra l'assedio di Firenze, G. Milanesi (ed.)
     (Florence: Le Monnier, 1860), p. 243; B. Richardson, 'Two notes on
     Machiavelli's *Asino*', *Bibliothèque d'humanisme et renaissance* 40 (1978),
     pp. 137–41; Bausi, *Machiavelli*, pp. 151–2.
64   Cf. Machiavelli, *L'asino*, 8.82–7.
65   The Latin text of the *Panegyricus in amorem* can be found in
     Francesco Cattani da Diacceto, *Opera omnia*, T. Zwingler (ed.)
     (Basel: H. Petri and P. Pernam, 1563), pp. 130–8. A splendid English
     translation by Luc Deitz can be found in J. Kraye (ed.), *Cambridge
     Translations of Renaissance Philosophical Texts*, 2 vols. (Cambridge:
     Cambridge University Press, 1997), vol. 1, pp. 156–65.
66   Luigi Alamanni, *Flora* . . . (Florence: Lorenzo Torrentino, 1556); also
     published in Luigi Alamanni, *Versi e prose*, P. Raffaelli (ed.), 2 vols.
     (Florence: Le Monnier, 1859), vol. 2, pp. 321–403.
67   Although the surviving manuscript has been dated to 1525–7, it has
     been observed that this may have been a copy of a rather earlier text,
     written perhaps during Niccolò's time in the Orti Oricellari. Black,
     Machiavelli, p. 194, pp. 345–6, n.104; Bausi, *Machiavelli*, p. 272; P.
     Stoppelli, *Machiavelli e la novella* Belfagor. *Saggio di filologia
     attributiva* (Rome: Salerno, 2007), pp. 80–1; P. Stoppelli, *La
     Mandragola: storia e filologia* (Rome: Bulzoni, 2005), pp. 40–1; P.
     Stoppelli, 'La datazione dell' Andria', in G. Barbarisi and A. M.
     Cabrini (eds.), *Il teatro di Machiavelli* (Milan: Cisalpino, 2005),
     pp. 147–99; M. Martelli, 'La versione machiavelliana dell'Andria',

Rinascimento, s. 2, 8 (1968), pp. 203–73; Richardson, 'Two Notes', pp. 323–4, p. 329.

68 For discussion, see Black, *Machiavelli*, p. 186.

69 See R. L. Martinez, 'Comedian, tragedian: Machiavelli and traditions of Renaissance theatre', in Najemy (ed.), *The Cambridge Companion to Machiavelli*, pp. 206–22, here p. 207.

70 On *Le maschere*, see, for example, *ibid.*, p. 207; F. Bausi, 'Machiavelli e la commedia fiorentina del primo Cinquecento', in Barbarisi and Cabrini (eds.), *Il teatro di Machiavelli*, pp. 1–20; E. Raimondi, *Politica e commedia: il centauro disarmato* (Bologna: Il Mulino, 1998), pp. 82–4, p. 111; P. Godman, *From Poliziano to Machiavelli: Florentine Humanism in the High Renaissance* (Princeton NJ: Princeton University Press, 1998), p. 241.

71 Text in Machiavelli, *Tutte le opere*, Martelli (ed.), pp. 868–90; trans. in *Chief Works*, vol. 2, pp. 776–821.

72 Machiavelli, *Mandragola*, 1.1; *Chief Works*, vol. 2, p. 780.

73 For discussion, see H. C. Mansfield, 'The Cuckold in Machiavelli's *Mandragola*', in V. B. Sullivan (ed.), *The Comedy and Tragedy of Machiavelli: Essays on the Literary Works* (New Haven CT and London: Yale University Press, 2000), pp. 1–29.

74 Martinez, 'Comedian, tragedian', p. 215; T. A. Sumberg, '*Mandragola*: An Interpretation', *Journal of Politics* 23 (1961), pp. 320–40; A. Parronchi, 'La prima rappresentazione della *Mandragola*. Il modello per l'apparato – l'allegoria', *La Bibliofilia* 66 (1962), pp. 37–86; G. Inglese, 'Contributo al testo critico della *Mandragola*', *Annali dell'Istituto italiano di studi storici* 6 (1979–80), pp. 129–73; A. Sorella, *Magia, lingua e commedia nel Machiavelli* (Florence: Olschki, 1990), pp. 9–99.

75 See esp. R. L. Martinez, 'The Pharmacy of Machiavelli: Roman Lucretia in *Mandragola*', *Renaissance Drama* 14 (1983), pp. 1–42, esp. pp. 7–9; J. Tylus, 'Theatre's Social Uses: Machiavelli's *Mandragola* and the Spectacle of Infamy', *Renaissance Quarterly* 53 (2000), pp. 656–86.

76 It is worth noting that Nicia's name may be derived either from the Latin verb *nictare* ('to wink'), or, more likely, from the Greek noun νίκη ('victory'). The latter etymology would seem to support an identification of the character with the Medici, as they could well be said to have 'won' the city.

77 *Lett.*, pp. 385–6 (no. 172); *Machiavelli and His Friends*, pp. 319–20 (no. 256).

78 *Lett.*, pp. 383–4 (no. 170); *Machiavelli and His Friends*, p. 318 (no. 254).

79 *Leg. e comm.*, pp. 1505–8. For a detailed treatment of this mission, see Bertelli's 'Nota introduttiva' at *Leg. e comm.*, p. 1503.

22. The Radical Conservative

1   Antonio Brucioli, *Dialogi*, A. Landi (ed.) (Naples: Prismi, 1982).

2   Machiavelli, *Discorsi*, 1, pr.; *Chief Works*, vol. 1, p. 190.

3   Machiavelli, *Discorsi*, 1, pr.; *Chief Works*, vol. 1, p. 191.

4   *Ibid.*

5   For a splendid overview of debates about the dating of the *Discorsi*, see R. Black, *Machiavelli* (Abingdon: Routledge, 2013), pp. 130–8.

6   This was thoroughly in keeping with how Livy wanted his history to be read. As he wrote at the very beginning of *Ab urbe condita*: 'What chiefly makes the study of history wholesome and profitable is this, that you behold the lessons of every kind of experience set forth as on a conspicuous monument; from these you may choose for yourself and for your own state what to imitate, from these mark for avoidance what is shameful in the conception and shameful in the result.' Livy 1. pr. 10; B. O. Foster et al. (trans.), 14 vols. (Cambridge MA: Harvard University Press, 1919–59), vol. 1, p. 7.

7   Machiavelli, *Discorsi*, dedication; *Chief Works*, vol. 1, pp. 188–9.

8   Skinner, *Machiavelli*, p. 57; Machiavelli, *Discorsi*, 1.1; *Chief Works*, vol. 1, p. 192. The following discussion largely follows Skinner, *Machiavelli*, pp. 56–87.

9   Machiavelli, *Discorsi*, 2.2; *Chief Works*, vol. 1, p. 329; Skinner, *Machiavelli*, p. 58.

10 Cf. Machiavelli, *Discorsi*, 3.41; *Chief Works*, vol. 1, p. 519.

11 Q. at R. G. Witt, *Coluccio Salutati and His Public Letters* (Geneva: Droz, 1976), p. 54.

12 Skinner, *Machiavelli*, p. 58.

13 On the two *fundamenta iustitiae* (equity and the common good), see Cicero, *De off.* 1.10.31. On equity, in particular, see Cicero, *De off.* 1.9.28; 1.34.124; 2.23.83.

14 Machiavelli, *Discorsi*, 2.2; *Chief Works*, vol. 1, p. 329.

15 On 'force and *virtù*' as the foundation of a city's liberty and greatness, see, for example, Machiavelli, *Discorsi*, 3.27; *Chief Works*, vol. 1, p. 492.

16 Q.v. Machiavelli, *Discorsi*, 2.1; *Chief Works*, vol. 1, p. 326.

17 Albertino Mussato, *De obsidione domini Canis de Verona ante civitatem Paduanam*, L. A. Muratori (ed.), *RIS* 10 (Milan, 1727), cols. 687–714, here col. 689A–D. For discussion, see A. Lee, *Humanism and Empire: The Imperial Ideal in Fourteenth-Century Italy* (Oxford: Oxford University Press, 2018), pp. 36–7, pp. 44–5.

18 Ferreto de' Ferreti, *De Scaligerorum origine*, 2.19–31; in Ferreto de' Ferreti, *Le Opere*, C. Cipolla (ed.), 3 vols. (Rome: Istituto Storico Italiano, 1908–20), vol. 3, pp. 1–100, here vol. 3, p. 28; Lee, *Humanism and Empire*, p. 48.

19 Petrarch, *Ecl.* 5; Lee, *Humanism and Empire*, p. 109.
20 Cicero, *De off.* 1.5.15; 1.43.153; *Tusc.* 1.39.94; 5.5.14; I *Cor.* 13. This understanding of the political virtues is found, for example, in Convenevole da Prato's *Regia carmina*, 55.63–6; 56.6–8, 56.10–13. For discussion, see Q. R. D. Skinner, *Visions of Politics*, 3 vols. (Cambridge: Cambridge University Press, 2002), vol. 2, pp. 61–3; Lee, *Humanism and Empire*, pp. 114–15.
21 Cicero, *Rep.* 6.13.13; 6.16.16; Macrobius, *Somn. Scip.* 1.8.4, 11. A good illustration of this can be found in Petrarch, *Africa*, 1.482–6, 490–3. For discussion, see Lee, *Humanism and Empire*, pp. 115–16.
22 Skinner, *Machiavelli*, p. 61.
23 Machiavelli, *Discorsi*, 3.41; *Chief Works*, vol. 1, p. 519.
24 Machiavelli, *Discorsi*, 1.3; *Chief Works*, vol. 1, p. 201.
25 Machiavelli, *Discorsi*, 1.1; cf. Skinner, *Machiavelli*, pp. 59–60.
26 Machiavelli, *Discorsi*, 1.49; *Chief Works*, vol. 1, p. 295.
27 Machiavelli, *Discorsi*, 1.2; *Chief Works*, vol. 1, pp. 196–7. The English versions of Niccolò's names for the six different types of constitution are taken from J. Najemy, 'Society, class and state in Machiavelli's *Discourses on Livy*', in J. M. Najemy (ed.), *The Cambridge Companion to Machiavelli* (Cambridge: Cambridge University Press, 2010), pp. 96–111, here p. 98.
28 For the following, see Machiavelli, *Discorsi*, 1.2; *Chief Works*, vol. 1, pp. 197–8.
29 Cf. Machiavelli, *Discorsi*, 1.10; *Chief Works*, vol. 1, p. 220.
30 Machiavelli, *Il principe*, 9.
31 On the notion of 'institutionalized' conflict in the *Discorsi*, see, for example, N. Wood, 'The Value of Asocial Sociability: Contributions of Machiavelli, Sidney and Montesquieu', *Bucknell Review* 16 (1968), pp. 1–22; C. Lefort, *Machiavelli in the Making* (Evanston IL: Northwestern University Press, 2012), p. 173; J. Barthas, 'Machiavelli e l'istituzione del conflitto', *RSI* 127 (2015), pp. 552–66; G. Pedullà, *Machiavelli in Tumult: The Discourses on Livy and the Origins of Political Conflictualism*, P. Gaborik and R. Nybakken (trans.) (Cambridge: Cambridge University Press, 2018), pp. 182–3.
32 Machiavelli, *Discorsi*, 1.4; *Chief Works*, vol. 1, p. 202.
33 Machiavelli, *Discorsi*, 1.6; *Chief Works*, vol. 1, pp. 207–8.
34 Machiavelli, *Discorsi*, 1.6; *Chief Works*, vol. 1, p. 208.
35 Machiavelli, *Discorsi*, 1.6; *Chief Works*, vol. 1, p. 210.
36 Machiavelli, *Discorsi*, 1.5; *Chief Works*, vol. 1, pp. 204–5.
37 On which see, for example, Pedullà, *Machiavelli in Tumult*, p. 142.
38 Machiavelli, *Discorsi*, 1.7; *Chief Works*, vol. 1, p. 211.
39 Machiavelli, *Discorsi*, 1.7; *Chief Works*, vol. 1, p. 212.
40 Machiavelli, *Discorsi*, 1.33; *Chief Works*, vol. 1, p. 265 [adapted].

41 Machiavelli, *Discorsi*, 1.33; *Chief Works*, vol. 1, p. 266 [adapted].

42 Machiavelli, *Discorsi*, 1.46; *Chief Works*, vol. 1, pp. 290–1; cf. Livy 3.56.

43 Machiavelli, *Discorsi*, 1.52; *Chief Works*, vol. 1, pp. 300–2.

44 Machiavelli, *Discorsi*, 1.57; *Chief Works*, vol. 1, pp. 312–13.

45 Machiavelli, *Discorsi*, 1.53–4; *Chief Works*, vol. 1, pp. 302–6.

46 This paragraph is based on the splendid analysis at Skinner, *Machiavelli*, pp. 76–7.

47 Najemy, 'Society, class and state', p. 100.

48 Machiavelli, *Discorsi*, 1.46; *Chief Works*, vol. 1, p. 291.

49 Machiavelli, *Discorsi*, 1.33; *Chief Works*, vol. 1, p. 266.

50 Machiavelli, *Discorsi*, 1.34; *Chief Works*, vol. 1, p. 269.

51 Cf. Machiavelli, *Discorsi*, 1.35; *Chief Works*, vol. 1, p. 270; Skinner, *Machiavelli*, p. 79.

52 Machiavelli, *Discorsi*, 1.34; *Chief Works*, vol. 1, pp. 267–9.

53 Machiavelli, *Discorsi*, 3.31; *Chief Works*, vol. 1, p. 498.

54 Machiavelli, *Discorsi*, 3.16; *Chief Works*, vol. 1, p. 469. Cf. Machiavelli, *Discorsi*, 1.37; 3.25; *Chief Works*, vol. 1, p. 272, p. 486.

55 Machiavelli, *Discorsi*, 1.55; *Chief Works*, vol. 1, p. 308 [adapted].

56 Machiavelli, *Discorsi*, 1.3; *Chief Works*, vol. 1, p. 201; Skinner, *Machiavelli*, pp. 72–3. For recent discussions of this point in a wider context, see, for example, E. Benner, *Machiavelli's Ethics* (Princeton NJ: Princeton University Press, 2009), p. 191; H. C. Mansfield, *Machiavelli's Virtue* (Chicago IL: University of Chicago Press, 1998), p. 297.

57 This and the following two paragraphs are based on Skinner, *Machiavelli*, p. 70.

58 M. Viroli, *Machiavelli's God*, A. Shugaar (trans.) (Princeton NJ: Princeton University Press, 2010), p. 177.

59 Machiavelli, *Discorsi*, 1.11; *Chief Works*, vol. 1, p. 225.

60 Machiavelli, *Discorsi*, 1.12; *Chief Works*, vol. 1, p. 226.

61 Machiavelli, *Discorsi*, 1.11; *Chief Works*, vol. 1, p. 225 [adapted].

62 Machiavelli, *Discorsi*, 1.11; *Chief Works*, vol. 1, p. 224.

63 Machiavelli, *Discorsi*, 2.4; *Chief Works*, vol. 1, p. 339.

64 Machiavelli, *Discorsi*, 1.15; *Chief Works*, vol. 1, pp. 233–4.

65 Machiavelli, *Discorsi*, 1.12; *Chief Works*, vol. 1, p. 228.

66 Machiavelli, *Discorsi*, 1.12; *Chief Works*, vol. 1, p. 228.

67 Machiavelli, *Discorsi*, 1.12; *Chief Works*, vol. 1, p. 229.

68 See M. S. Kempshall, *The Common Good in Late Medieval Political Thought* (Oxford: Oxford University Press, 1999).

69 Ferreto de' Ferreti, *Historia rerum in Italia gestarum ab anno MCCL usque ad annum MCCCXVIII*, 3; in Ferreto de' Ferreti, *Le Opere*, Cipolla (ed.), vols. 1–2, here vol. 1, pp. 281; *The Life of Cola di Rienzo*, J. Wright (trans.) (Toronto: Pontifical Institute of Mediaeval

Studies, 1975), pp. 34–5; Petrarch, *Africa*, 1.482–6; Lee, *Humanism and Empire*, p. 54, p. 68, p. 112, p. 116.

70 Viroli, *Machiavelli's God*, p. 185.

71 Machiavelli, *Discorsi*, 1.12; *Chief Works*, vol. 1, p. 227.

72 Machiavelli, *Discorsi*, 2.2; *Chief Works*, vol. 1, p. 331.

73 Machiavelli, *Discorsi*, 2.2; *Chief Works*, vol. 1, pp. 330–1.

74 Machiavelli, *Discorsi*, 1.12; *Chief Works*, vol. 1, pp. 228–9.

75 For a brief overview, see Machiavelli, *Discorsi*, 3.1; *Chief Works*, vol. 1, pp. 421–2.

76 Skinner, *Machiavelli*, pp. 66–8. This and the following four paragraphs are based on Skinner's masterly overview, and it is with pleasure that I acknowledge myself to have been guided by his argument.

77 *Ibid.*, p. 66.

78 Machiavelli, *Discorsi*, 3.1; *Chief Works*, vol. 1, p. 421.

79 Machiavelli, *Discorsi*, 3.22; *Chief Works*, vol. 1, p. 481.

80 Machiavelli, *Discorsi*, 3.1; *Chief Works*, vol. 1, p. 421.

81 Machiavelli, *Discorsi*, 3.21; *Chief Works*, vol. 1, p. 479.

82 Machiavelli, *Discorsi*, 3.22; *Chief Works*, vol. 1, pp. 479–81.

83 Machiavelli, *Discorsi*, 3.22; *Chief Works*, vol. 1, p. 479, p. 481.

84 Machiavelli, *Discorsi*, 3.21; *Chief Works*, vol. 1, p. 477.

85 Machiavelli, *Discorsi*, 3.22; *Chief Works*, vol. 1, p. 482.

86 Machiavelli, *Discorsi*, 3.22; *Chief Works*, vol. 1, pp. 483–4.

87 Machiavelli, *Discorsi*, 3.12; *Chief Works*, vol. 1, p. 462.

88 Machiavelli, *Discorsi*, 3.30; *Chief Works*, vol. 1, p. 495.

89 Machiavelli, *Discorsi*, 3.47; *Chief Works*, vol. 1, p. 526.

90 Machiavelli, *Discorsi*, 3.38; *Chief Works*, vol. 1, p. 515.

91 Niccolò did note that Piero Soderini had 'acted in all his affairs with kindness and patience', but, while this had served him perfectly well in times of prosperity, it became a weakness in times of strife. Soderini, he claimed, did not know when to 'break off his patience and humility'. Machiavelli, *Discorsi*, 3.9; *Chief Works*, vol. 1, p. 453.

92 Machiavelli, *Discorsi*, 3.30; *Chief Works*, vol. 1, p. 497.

93 A good example of the Florentines' credulity was provided by their decision to accept the emperor's (empty) offer of help against the Visconti in return for a subvention of 100,000 ducats. That he turned back after advancing only as far as Verona served to illustrate just how gullible they had been. Machiavelli, *Discorsi*, 3.43; *Chief Works*, vol. 1, pp. 521–2.

94 According to Niccolò, the two Catos had been able to accomplish nothing good because they had lived too long after Rome's last *virtuoso* figures, and because the one was also too distant from the other. Machiavelli, *Discorsi*, 3.1; *Chief Works*, vol. 1, pp. 421–2.

95 '[T]o praise disunity,' wrote Guicciardini, 'is like praising a sick man's disease because of the virtues of the remedy applied to it.' Francesco Guicciardini, 'Considerazioni sui Discorsi del Machiavelli', IV; text in *Scritti politici e ricordi*, R. Palmarocchi (ed.) (Bari: G. Laterza & Figli, 1933), pp. 1–65, here pp. 10–11; trans. from 'Considerations on the "Discourses" of Machiavelli', in Francesco Guicciardini, *Selected Writings*, C. Grayson (ed. and trans.) (Oxford: Oxford University Press, 1965), p. 68.

23. Deaths and Resurrection (March 1519–April 1520)

1 See, for example, Francesco Petrarca, *De otio religioso*, 2.2, text G. Rotondi (ed.) (Vatican City: Biblioteca Apostolica Vaticana, 1958), p. 62, ll.16–29; p. 63, ll.10–11. For discussion, see esp. A. Lee, *Petrarch and St. Augustine: Classical Scholarship, Christian Theology, and the Origins of the Renaissance in Italy* (Leiden: Brill, 2012), p. 135.

2 For the following, see J. N. Stephens, *The Fall of the Florentine Republic, 1512–1530* (Oxford: Clarendon Press, 1983), p. 108.

3 Niccolò Guicciardini, *Discorso del modo di procedere della famiglia de' Medici in Firenze et del fine che poteva havere lo stato di quella famiglia*, in R. von Albertini, *Firenze dalla repubblica al principato*, C. Cristofolini (trans.) (Turin: Einaudi, 1970), pp. 365–75.

4 On Cardinal Giulio's indecisiveness, see T. C. Price Zimmermann, 'Guicciardini, Giovio, and the Character of Clement VII', in K. Gouwens and S. E. Reiss (eds.), *The Pontificate of Clement VII: History, Politics, Culture* (Abingdon: Routledge, 2005), pp. 19–27.

5 L. Polizzotto, *The Elect Nation: The Savonarolan Movement in Florence, 1494–1545* (Oxford: Clarendon, 1994), p. 248.

6 Stephens, *The Fall of the Florentine Republic*, p. 109.

7 On the powers and revivial of the Seventy and the Hundred, see H. C. Butters, *Governors and Government in Early Sixteenth-Century Florence 1502–1509* (Oxford: Clarendon, 1985), pp. 17–19, pp. 226–9; Stephens, *The Fall of the Florentine Republic*, pp. 67–9.

8 J. M. Najemy, *A History of Florence, 1200–1575* (Oxford: Blackwell, 2008), p. 433.

9 Jacopo Nardi, *Istorie della città di Firenze*, 7, L. Arbib (ed.), 2 vols. (Florence: Società Editrice delle Storie del Nardi e del Varchi, 1842), vol. 2, p. 73.

10 This paragraph is indebted to R. Ridolfi, *Vita di Niccolò Machiavelli*, 3rd ed., 2 vols. (Florence: Sansoni, 1969), vol. 1, pp. 276–7.

11 For the following, see M. E. Mallett and C. Shaw, *The Italian Wars, 1494–1559: War, State and Society in Early Modern Europe* (London and New York: Routledge, 2012), p. 136.

12 *Ibid.*

13 For the following, see R. Devonshire Jones, *Francesco Vettori: Florentine Citizen and Medici Servant* (London: Athlone Press, 1972), pp. 148–9.

14 Filippo de' Nerli, *Commentari de' fatti civili Occorsi dentro la Città di Firenze dall' anno MCCXV al MDXXXVII* (Augusta: David Raimondo Mertz e Gio. Jacopo Majer, 1728), p. 134. This contradicts Cambi's claim that the cardinal left Florence for Rome: Giovanni Cambi, *Istorie fiorentine*, I. di San Luigi (ed.), 4 vols., *Delizie degli eruditi toscani*, 20–23 (Florence: Gaetano Cambiagi, 1785–6), vol. 3, p. 152. Cf. Stephens, *The Fall of the Florentine Republic*, p. 112.

15 Devonshire Jones, *Francesco Vettori*, pp. 148–9.

16 Cf. Nerli, *Commentari*, p. 138.

17 Niccolò Machiavelli, *Arte della guerra*, 1; *Chief Works*, vol. 2, p. 569.

18 M. Hörnqvist, 'Machiavelli's military project and the *Art of War*', in J. M. Najemy (ed.), *The Cambridge Companion to Machiavelli* (Cambridge: Cambridge University Press, 2010), pp. 112–27, here p. 121.

19 On Fabrizio Colonna as a mouthpiece for Niccolò's own views, see esp. F. Verrier, 'Machiavelli e Fabrizio Colonna nell' *Arte della guerra*: il polemologo sdoppiato', in J.-J. Marchand (ed.), *Niccolò Machiavelli politico, storico, letterato* (Rome: Salerno, 1996), pp. 175–87.

20 Machiavelli, *Arte della guerra*, pref.; *Chief Works*, vol. 2, p. 567; cf. *Discorsi*, 2.16.

21 Machiavelli, *Arte della guerra*, 7; *Chief Works*, vol. 2, p. 718.

22 For discussion, see esp. D. Fachard, 'Implicazioni politiche nell' *Arte della guerra*', in Marchand (ed.), *Niccolò Machiavelli politico, storico, letterato*, pp. 149–73.

23 R. Black, *Machiavelli* (Abingdon: Routledge, 2013), p. 216. The remainder of this paragraph is based on Black's excellent analysis.

24 Machiavelli, *Arte della guerra*, 1; *Chief Works*, vol. 2, pp. 590–2.

25 *Chief Works*, vol. 2, p. 585.

26 *Ibid.*, pp. 585–6. For discussion, see esp. Black, *Machiavelli*, p. 216; J. M. Najemy, '"Occupare la tirranide": Machiavelli, the Militia, and Guicciardini's Accusation of Tyranny', in J. Barthas (ed.), *Della tirannia: Machiavelli con Bartolo* (Florence: Olschki, 2007), pp. 75–108.

27 Hörnqvist, 'Machiavelli's military project', pp. 122–3; Black, *Machiavelli*, p. 218.

28 E.g. Machiavelli, *Arte della guerra*, pref., 4, 6; *Chief Works*, vol. 2, p. 566, p. 661, pp. 701–2.

29 Machiavelli, *Arte della guerra*, 4, 6; *Chief Works*, vol. 2, pp. 661–2, p. 691.

30 Black, *Machiavelli*, p. 221.

31 Machiavelli, *Il principe*, 20.
32 Machiavelli, *Arte della guerra*, 3; *Chief Works*, vol. 2, pp. 636–40.
33 Machiavelli, *Arte della guerra*, 2; *Chief Works*, vol. 2, pp. 607–8.
34 Niccolò Machiavelli, *Art of War*, C. Lynch (trans. and ed.) (Chicago IL: University of Chicago Press, 2003), p. 188; cf. Black, *Machiavelli*, p. 221.
35 For the following, see Hörnqvist, 'Machiavelli's military project', pp. 124–5.
36 Machiavelli, *Arte della guerra*, 1; *Chief Works*, vol. 2, pp. 572–3.
37 Machiavelli, *Arte della guerra*, 7; *Chief Works*, vol. 2, p. 725.
38 *Lett.*, p. 389 (no. 174); *Machiavelli and His Friends*, p. 325 (no. 260).
39 Filippo Strozzi's letter of 17 March 1520 is reproduced at O. Tommasini, *La vita e gli scritti di Niccolò Machiavelli nella loro relazione col machiavellismo*, 3 vols. (Turin: Ermanno Loescher, 1883–1911), vol. 3, pp. 1081–3, here p. 1082.
40 *Lett.*, p. 387 (no. 173); *Machiavelli and His Friends*, p. 324 (no. 259).
41 *Lett.*, p. 389 (no. 174); *Machiavelli and His Friends*, p. 325 (no. 260) [amended].

24. A Second Apprenticeship (April–December 1520)

1 The following is based on the excellent summary given in Bertelli, 'Nota introduttiva', *Leg. e comm.*, pp. 1511–12.
2 *Ibid.*, p. 1533.
3 *Ibid.*, pp. 1527–8.
4 *Ibid.*, pp. 1529–30.
5 *Ibid.*, p. 1529; cf. Bertelli, 'Nota introduttiva', *Leg. e comm.*, p. 1512.
6 *Ibid.*, p. 1529.
7 *Lett.*, pp. 391–3 (no. 176); *Machiavelli and His Friends*, pp. 326–8 (no. 262).
8 *Lett.*, p. 392 (no. 176); *Machiavelli and His Friends*, p. 327 (no. 262).
9 Text in Niccolò Machiavelli, *Opere storiche*, A. Montevecchi and C. Varotti (eds.), 2 vols. (Rome: Salerno, 2010), pp. 7–66; *La vita di Castruccio Castracani e altri scritti*, G. Inglese (ed.) (Milan: Rizzoli, 1991), pp. 107–36; *Opere*, M. Bonfantini (ed.) (Milan and Naples: R. Ricciardi, 1954), pp. 552–9. English trans. in *Chief Works*, vol. 2, pp. 553–9.
10 On Castruccio Castracani, see, for example, M. Luzzati, 'Castracani degli Antelminelli, Castruccio', *DBI*, vol. 22 (Rome, 1979), pp. 200–10.
11 F. Bausi, 'Machiavelli e la tradizione culturale toscana', in *Cultura e scrittura di Machiavelli, Atti del Convegno di Firenze–Pisa, 27–30 ottobre 1997* (Rome: Salerno, 1998), pp. 81–115, here pp. 101–8;

F. Bausi, *Machiavelli* (Rome: Salerno, 2005), pp. 246–53; R. Black, *Machiavelli* (Abingdon: Routledge, 2013), pp. 223–8; R. Bruscagli, *Machiavelli* (Bologna: Il Mulino, 2008), pp. 112–14; Machiavelli, *La vita di Castruccio*, Inglese (ed.), p. 30.

12 Machiavelli, *Chief Works*, vol. 2, pp. 534–5.

13 Niccolò Tegrimi, *Vita Castrucii Antelminelli Castracani Lucensis Ducis* (Modena: Domenico Rococciolo, 1496); text also publ. in L. A. Muratori (ed.), *RIS* 11 (Milan, 1727), cols. 1308–44.

14 Machiavelli, *Chief Works*, vol. 2, pp. 535–6.

15 *Ibid.*, vol. 2, pp. 555–9.

16 *Ibid.*, vol. 2, pp. 533–4.

17 *Ibid.*, vol. 2, p. 535.

18 *Ibid.*, vol. 2, p. 536.

19 *Ibid.*, vol. 2, p. 536 [amended].

20 *Ibid.*, vol. 2, p. 537.

21 *Ibid.*, vol. 2, p. 555.

22 *Ibid.*

23 For the following, see *ibid.*, vol. 2, pp. 546–8.

24 For the following, see *ibid.*, vol. 2, pp. 537–8.

25 *Ibid.*, vol. 2, pp. 540–1.

26 For the following, see *ibid.*, vol. 2, p. 543.

27 *Ibid.*, vol. 2, p. 552.

28 *Ibid.*, vol. 2, pp. 553–4.

29 *Ibid.*, vol. 2, p. 554.

30 *Ibid.*, vol. 2, pp. 554–5.

31 *Lett.*, pp. 394–5 (no. 177); *Machiavelli and His Friends*, p. 328 (no. 263).

32 *Lett.*, p. 394 (no. 177); *Machiavelli and His Friends*, p. 328 (no. 263).

33 *Lett.*, p. 395 (no. 177); *Machiavelli and His Friends*, pp. 328–9 (no. 263).

34 *Lett.*, p. 395 (no. 177); *Machiavelli and His Friends*, p. 328 (no. 263).

35 *Lett.*, p. 397 (no. 179); *Machiavelli and His Friends*, p. 329 (no. 264).

36 See the letters from Giovambattista Bracci (7 and 14 September 1520): *Leg. e comm.*, pp. 1533–5, pp. 1537–8.

37 *Ibid.*, pp. 1359–60. The deliberations of the Lucchese Consiglio generale may be found at *ibid.*, pp. 1543–4.

38 Text in Niccolò Machiavelli, *Opere politiche*, vol. 3, *L'arte della guerra. Scritti politici minori*, J.-J. Marchand, D. Fachard and G. Masi (eds.) (Rome, 2001), pp. 613–20.

39 S. Larosa, '*Sommario delle cose della città di Lucca*', *Enciclopedia Machiavelliana*, 3 vols. (Rome: Istituto della Enciclopedia Italiana, 2014), vol. 2, pp. 548–50, here p. 548.

40 Machiavelli, *Opere politiche*, vol. 3, *L'arte della guerra. Scritti politici minori*, Marchand et al. (eds.), p. 616.

41 For a recent discussion of Niccolò's comparison between Lucca and Venice, see M. Suchowlansky, 'Machiavelli's *Summary of the Affairs of the City of Lucca*: Venice as *buon governo*', *Intellectual History Review* 26/4 (2016), pp. 429–45.

42 The contract can be found at Niccolò Machiavelli, *Opere*, P. Fanfani, G. Milanesi, L. Passerini (eds.), 6 vols. (Florence: Cenniniana, 1873–77), vol. 1, p. lxxxix.

43 For discussion, see D. Wilcox, *The Development of Florentine Humanist Historiography* (Cambridge MA: Harvard University Press, 1969); E. Cochrane, *Historians and Historiography in the Italian Renaissance* (Chicago IL: University of Chicago Press, 1981); R. Fubini, *Storiografia dell'umanesimo in Italia da Leonardo Bruni ad Annio da Viterbo* (Rome: Storia e Letteratura, 2003).

44 Leonardo Bruni, *History of the Florentine People*, J. Hankins (ed.), 3 vols. (Cambridge MA: Harvard University Press, 2001–7); Poggio Bracciolini, *Historiae Florentini populi*, L. A. Muratori (ed.), in *RIS* 20 (Milan, 1731), cols. 194–454 (for a facsimile of the Italian translation by his son, Jacopo Bracciolini, see Poggio Bracciolini, *Storie fiorentine*, E. Garin (ed.) (Arezzo: Biblioteca della Citta di Arezzo, 1984)); Bartolomeo Scala, *Historia florentinorum*, J. Oligero (ed.) (Rome: Nicolangelo Tinassi, 1677). For discussion of these works, see, in addition to the works listed in the previous note, A. Brown, *Bartolomeo Scala, 1430–1497, Chancellor of Florence: The Humanist as Bureaucrat* (Princeton NJ: Princeton University Press, 1979), pp. 297–306; N. Struever, 'Rhetoric, Ethics, and History: Poggio Bracciolini', in N. Struever, *The Language of History in the Renaissance: Rhetoric and Historical Consciousness in Florentine Humanism* (Princeton NJ: Princeton University Press, 1970), pp. 144–99; G. Ianziti, *Writing History in Renaissance Italy: Leonardo Bruni and the Uses of the Past* (Cambridge MA: Harvard University Press, 2012), pp. 91–146, pp. 204–33.

45 *Lett.*, p. 397 (no. 178); *Machiavelli and His Friends*, p. 330 (no. 265).

46 Text in Machiavelli, *Opere politiche*, vol. 3, *L'arte della guerra. Scritti politici minori*, Marchand et al. (eds.), pp. 624–41; Niccolò Machiavelli, *Tutte le opere*, Martelli (ed.) (Florence: Sansoni, 1971), pp. 24–31. A useable English translation may be found in Machiavelli, *Chief Works*, vol. 1, pp. 101–15. On the dating of the *Discorso delle cose fiorentine dopo la morte di Lorenzo*, see Black, *Machiavelli*, p. 232. For discussion of this text, see, for example, R. Cavaluzzi, 'Machiavelli per *rassettare* le cose fiorentine', *Italianistica: Rivista di letteratura italiana* 39/1 (2010), pp. 11–21; G. M. Anselmi, 'Il *Discursus florentinarum rerum* tra progetto politico e prospettiva storiografica', in J.-J. Marchand (ed.), *Niccolò Machiavelli, politico,*

storico, letterato (Rome: Salerno, 1996), pp. 189–207; G. Inglese, 'Il *Discursus florentinarum rerum* di Niccolò Machiavelli', *La Cultura* 23 (1985),

pp. 203–28; J. M. Najemy, 'Machiavelli and the Medici: The Lessons of Florentine History', *Renaissance Quarterly* 35 (1982), pp. 551–76; J. M. Najemy, *A History of Florence, 1200–1575* (Oxford: Blackwell, 2008), pp. 437–40; and (with caution) Black, *Machiavelli*, pp. 231–8.

47 Machiavelli, *Chief Works*, vol. 1, pp. 102–3.

48 In *Il principe*, Niccolò had acknowledged that 'there is nothing more difficult to manage, more doubtful of success, and more dangerous to carry through than initiating changes in a state's constitution.' Machiavelli, *Il principe*, 5.

49 Machiavelli, *Chief Works*, vol. 1, p. 101.

50 *Ibid.*, vol. 1, p. 107.

51 *Ibid.*, vol. 1, p. 108.

52 For the following, see *ibid.*, vol. 1, pp. 108–9.

53 *Ibid.*, vol. 1, p. 110.

54 *Ibid.*

55 *Ibid.*, vol. 1, pp. 109–10.

56 *Ibid.*, vol. 1, p. 113.

57 For the following, see *ibid.*, vol. 1, pp. 111–12.

58 *Ibid.*, vol. 1, p. 114.

59 *Ibid.*, vol. 1, p. 115.

60 *Ibid.*, vol. 1, p. 114.

25. The Republic of Clogs (January–December 1521)

1 *Lett.*, pp. 398–9 (no. 180); *Machiavelli and His Friends*, p. 333 (no. 266). For Vernacci's reply, see *Lett.*, pp. 400–1 (no. 182); *Machiavelli and His Friends*, pp. 334–5 (no. 268).

2 Soderini's first letter has not survived. For the second, see *Lett.*, p. 399 (no. 181); *Machiavelli and His Friends*, p. 334 (no. 267).

3 This suggestion is made in R. Ridolfi, *Vita di Niccolò Machiavelli*, 3rd ed., 2 vols. (Florence: Sansoni, 1969), vol. 1, p. 289.

4 *Lett.*, p. 399 (no. 181); *Machiavelli and His Friends*, p. 334 (no. 267).

5 This paragraph and the next are based on the masterly overview given at M. E. Mallet and C. Shaw, *The Italian Wars, 1494–1559: War, State and Society in Early Modern Europe* (London and New York: Routledge, 2012), pp. 139–40.

6 See Francesco Guicciardini, *Storia d'Italia*, 14.1, C. Panigada (ed.), 5 vols. (Bari: G. Laterza & Figli, 1929), vol. 4, p. 81; W. Blockmans, *Emperor Charles V, 1500–1558*, I. van den Hoven-Vardon (trans.) (London: Bloomsbury, 2002), pp. 51–2.

7   On this treaty, see esp. M. Gattoni, *Leone X e la geo-politica dello Stato pontificio (1513–1521)* (Vatican City: Archivo Segreto Vaticano, 2000), pp. 306–12.

8   That Niccolò had kept abreast of developments can be inferred from the 'barstool gossip' he exchanged with Sigismondo Santi on 18 May 1521: *Lett.*, pp. 409–10 (no. 187); *Machiavelli and His Friends*, p. 340 (no. 273).

9   The following is indebted to the splendid summary given by Bertelli, 'Nota introduttiva', *Leg. e comm.*, pp. 1547–8.

10   See, for example, H. Baron, 'Franciscan Poverty and Civic Wealth as Factors in the Rise of Humanistic Thought,' *Speculum* 13/1 (1938), pp. 1–37.

11   On Bernardino Ochino, later condemned for heresy, see, for example, D. Cantimori, 'Bernardino Ochino uomo del Rinascimento e riformatore', *Annali della Scuola Normale Superiore di Pisa, Classe di Lettere e Filosofia* 30/1 (1929), pp. 5–40; R. H. Bainton, *Bernardino Ochino esule e riformatore del Cinquecento (1487–1563)* (Florence: Sansoni, 1940); B. Niccolini, 'Bernardino Ochino. Saggio biografico', *Biblion* 1 (1959), pp. 5–23; M. Gotor, 'Ochino, Bernardino', *DBI*, vol. 79 (Rome, 2013), pp. 90–7.

12   *Leg. e comm.*, pp. 1551–3.

13   *Ibid.*, p. 1552.

14   *Ibid.*

15   *Ibid.*, pp. 1553–4.

16   *Ibid.*, pp. 1555–6.

17   *Lett.*, p. 407 (no. 186); *Machiavelli and His Friends*, p. 339 (no. 272).

18   On the likelihood of Niccolò's visit to Modena, see, for example, J. Najemy, 'Introduction', in J. M. Najemy (ed.), *The Cambridge Companion to Machiavelli* (Cambridge: Cambridge University Press, 2010), pp. 1–13, here pp. 1–2.

19   See *Leg. e comm.*, p. 1553.

20   On Carpi's dishonesty, see *Lett.* 402 (no. 183); *Machiavelli and His Friends*, p. 335 (no. 269).

21   *Lett.*, p. 407 (no. 186); *Machiavelli and His Friends*, p. 339 (no. 272).

22   *Lett.*, p. 404 (no. 184); *Machiavelli and His Friends*, p. 336 (no. 270).

23   *Lett.*, p. 405 (no. 184); *Machiavelli and His Friends*, p. 337 (no. 270).

24   Guicciardini, *Storia d'Italia*, 16.8, Panigada (ed.), vol. 4, pp. 312–13.

25   *Lett.*, p. 408 (no. 186); *Machiavelli and His Friends*, p. 339 (no. 272).

26   Cf. *Leg. e comm.*, p. 1559.

27   For the circumstances of the letter's arrival, see *Lett.*, p. 402 (no. 184); *Machiavelli and His Friends*, p. 336 (no. 270). For the letter itself, see *Lett.*, pp. 401–2 (no. 183); *Machiavelli and His Friends*, p. 335 (no. 269).

28 *Lett.*, p. 402 (no. 183); *Machiavelli and His Friends*, 335 (no. 269).

29 *Lett.*, pp. 402–5 (no. 184); *Machiavelli and His Friends*, pp. 336–7 (no. 270).

30 *Lett.*, p. 403 (no. 184); *Machiavelli and His Friends*, p. 336 (no. 270); ref. to Boccaccio, *Decameron*, 4.2.

31 *Lett.*, p. 404 (no. 184); *Machiavelli and His Friends*, p. 337 (no. 270).

32 *Lett.*, p. 404 (no. 184); *Machiavelli and His Friends*, p. 337 (no. 270).

33 *Lett.*, p. 406 (no. 185); *Machiavelli and His Friends*, p. 338 (no. 271).

34 *Lett.*, p. 409 (no. 187); *Machiavelli and His Friends*, p. 340 (no. 273).

35 *Lett.*, p. 409 (no. 187); *Machiavelli and His Friends*, p. 340 (no. 273).

36 *Lett.*, pp. 409–10 (no. 187); *Machiavelli and His Friends*, p. 340 (no. 273).

37 *Lett.*, p. 410 (no. 187); *Machiavelli and His Friends*, p. 340 (no. 273).

38 *Lett.*, pp. 410–11 (no. 187); *Machiavelli and His Friends*, p. 341 (no. 273).

39 *Lett.*, p. 407 (no. 186); *Machiavelli and His Friends*, p. 339 (no. 272).

40 Cf. *Lett.*, pp. 412–13 (no. 188); *Machiavelli and His Friends*, p. 342 (no. 274).

41 *Lett.*, p. 408 (no. 186); *Machiavelli and His Friends*, p. 339 (no. 272).

42 *Lett.*, pp. 411–13 (no. 188); *Machiavelli and His Friends*, pp. 341–2 (no. 274).

43 *Lett.*, p. 411 (no. 188); *Machiavelli and His Friends*, p. 341 (no. 274).

44 *Lett.*, p. 411 (no. 188); *Machiavelli and His Friends*, p. 341 (no. 274).

45 *Lett.*, pp. 411–12 (no. 188); *Machiavelli and His Friends*, p. 341 (no. 274).

46 *Lett.*, p. 412 (no. 188); *Machiavelli and His Friends*, p. 341 (no. 274).

47 *Lett.*, p. 412 (no. 188); *Machiavelli and His Friends*, p. 341 (no. 274).

48 For the following, see *Leg. e comm.*, pp. 1556–9.

49 This can be inferred from Fra Ilarione's suggestion that he leave Carpi straight away so as to reach Florence 'by Wednesday evening' – that is, by the evening of 22 May. *Leg. e comm.*, p. 1559.

50 The following three paragraphs are deeply indebted to Mallett and Shaw, *The Italian Wars*, pp. 140–1.

51 On Prospero Colonna's overall command, see, for example, Guicciardini, *Storia d'Italia*, 14.4, Panigada (ed.), vol. 4, p. 95.

52 Guicciardini, *Storia d'Italia*, 14.3, Panigada (ed.), vol. 4, pp. 91–3. On Guicciardini's appointment, see, for example, P. Jodogne and G. Benzoni, 'Guicciardini, Francesco', *DBI*, vol. 61 (Rome, 2004), *ad voc.*

53 See Guicciardini, *Storia d'Italia*, 14.4, Panigada (ed.), vol. 4, pp. 96–8.

54 Angelo Maria Bandini, *De Florentina Iuntarum typographia eiusque censoribus ex qua Graeci, Latini Tusci scriptores . . .*, 2 pts. in 1 vol. (Lucca: Francesco Bonsignori, 1791), part 2, p. 171.

55 On Salviati, see M. Simonetta, 'Salviati, Giovanni', *DBI*, vol. 90 (Rome, 2017), *ad voc.*

56 *Lett.*, p. 414 (no. 189); *Machiavelli and His Friends*, pp. 342–3 (no. 275).

57 In this regard, it is perhaps worth noting that Cardinal Giulio de' Medici had left Florence for Lombardy, where he was to act as legate to the papal armies, leaving the city in the hands of Silvio Passerini, cardinal of Cortona. Filippo de' Nerli, *Commentari de' fatti civili Occorsi dentro la Città di Firenze dall'anno MCCXV al MDXXXVII* (Augusta: David Raimondo Mertz e Gio. Jacopo Majer, 1728), p. 134; R. Devonshire Jones, *Francesco Vettori: Florentine Citizen and Medici Servant* (London: Athlone Press, 1972), p. 151.

58 For the following, see Mallett and Shaw, *The Italian Wars*, p. 141.

26. Love, Labour, Loss (December 1521–March 1525)

1   Exactly when Niccolò returned to Sant'Andrea in Percussina is unclear. All that can be said with any certainty is that he arrived at some time before 26 December, as a letter to Francesco Vettori testifies: *Machiavelli and His Friends*, p. 343 (no. 276).

2   Paride de' Grassi reported that he had died from an 'excess of catarrh'; q. at K. M. Setton, *The Papacy and the Levant, 1204–1571*, 4 vols. (Philadelphia PA: The American Philosophical Society, 1976–84), vol. 3, p. 196.

3   Francesco Vettori, *Sommario della Istoria d'Italia*, in *Scritti storici e politici*, E. Niccolini (ed.) (Bari: G. Laterza & Figli, 1972), p. 196.

4   Francesco Guicciardini, *Storia d'Italia*, 14.10, Panigada (ed.), 5 vols. (Bari: G. Laterza & Figli, 1929), vol. 4, p. 131.

5   For the following, see M. E. Mallett and C. Shaw, *The Italian Wars, 1494–1559: War, State and Society in Early Modern Europe* (London and New York: Routledge, 2012), p. 142; Guicciardini, *Storia d'Italia*, 14.10, Panigada (ed.), vol. 4, p. 132.

6   J. N. Stephens, *The Fall of the Florentine Republic, 1512–1530* (Oxford: Clarendon, 1983), p. 118.

7   K. J. P. Lowe, *Church and Politics in Renaissance Italy: The Life and Career of Cardinal Francesco Soderini, 1453–1524* (Cambridge: Cambridge University Press, 1993), p. 121.

8   Guicciardini, *Storia d'Italia*, 14.11, Panigada (ed.), vol. 4, pp. 140–1.

9   Marino Sanudo the Younger, *I diarii di Marino Sanuto: (MCCCCXCVI–MDXXXIII): dall'autografo Marciano Ital. CLVII codd. CDXIX–CDLXXVII*, R. Fulin et al. (eds.), 58 vols. (Venice: F. Visentini, 1879–1902), vol. 32, p. 195.

10 *Ibid.*, vol. 32, pp. 404–5, p. 408.

11 Guicciardini, *Storia d'Italia*, 15.3, Panigada (ed.), vol. 4, p. 187; R. J. Knecht, *Francis I* (Cambridge: Cambridge University Press, 1982), p. 114.

12 For the following, see Mallett and Shaw, *The Italian Wars*, p. 145.

13 Stephens, *The Fall of the Florentine Republic*, p. 118; Guicciardini,

Storia d'Italia, 14.15, Panigada (ed.), vol. 4, p. 165; Vettori, *Scritti storici e politici*, p. 200; Lowe, *Church and Politics*, p. 127. Cf. M. M. Bullard, *Filippo Strozzi and the Medici: Favor and Finance in Sixteenth-Century Florence and Rome* (Cambridge: Cambridge University Press, 1980), p. 99. On Renzo da Ceri, see G. De Caro, 'Anguillara, Lorenzo', *DBI*, vol. 3 (Rome, 1961), pp. 309–12.

14 Lowe, *Church and Politics*, p. 127.

15 Stephens, *The Fall of the Florentine Republic*, p. 118; Baldassare Castiglione, *Lettere . . .*, P. Serassi (ed.), 2 vols. (Padua: G. Camino, 1769–71), vol. 1, pp. 63–69 (nos. viii–xviii).

16 Vettori, *Scritti storici e politici*, p. 200.

17 Stephens, *The Fall of the Florentine Republic*, p. 118; J. de Pins, 'Autour des guerres d'Italie: Un ambassadeur français à Venise et à Rome (1515–1525): Jean de Pins, évêque de Rieux', *Revue d'histoire diplomatique* 61 (1947), pp. 215–46, and 62 (1948), pp. 88–113; here 62 (1948), pp. 107–9.

18 Stephens, *The Fall of the Florentine Republic*, p. 118.

19 Bartolomeo Cerretani, *Ricordi*, G. Berti (ed.) (Florence: Olschki, 1993), p. 393, pp. 398–9.

20 Filippo de' Nerli, *Commentari de' fatti civili Occorsi dentro la Città di Firenze dall'anno MCCXV al MDXXXVII* (Augusta: David Raimondo Mertz e Gio. Jacopo Majer, 1728), p. 136; L. Polizotto, *The Elect Nation: The Savonarolan Movement in Florence, 1494–1545* (Oxford: Clarendon, 1994), p. 326.

21 Cf. Machiavelli, *Il principe*, 5.

22 Nerli, *Commentari*, p. 137; O. Tommasini, *La vita e gli scritti di Niccolò Machiavelli nella loro relazione col machiavellismo*, 3 vols. (Turin: Ermanno Loescher, 1883–1911), vol. 2, p. 449; Stephens, *The Fall of the Florentine Republic*, p. 113.

23 Nerli, *Commentari*, p. 137; R. Black, *Machiavelli* (Abingdon: Routledge, 2013), p. 239; Stephens, *The Fall of the Florentine Republic*, p. 114; M. Simonetta, 'The Lost Discourse on Governments by Machiavelli's Friend Zanobi Buondelmonti', *Culture del testo e del documento* 18/53 (2017), pp. 165–78.

24 Alessandro de' Pazzi, 'Discorso al cardinal Giulio de' Medici – anno 1522', in G. Capponi, 'Discorsi intorno alla riforma dello stato di Firenze (1522–32)', *ASI*, 1st ser., 1 (1942), pp. 411–77, here pp. 420–32.

25 Text in Machiavelli, *Opere politiche*, vol. 3, *L'arte della guerra. Scritti politici minori*, J.-J. Marchand, D. Fachard and G. Masi (eds.) (Rome, 2001), pp. 643–4. For the following, see Black, *Machiavelli*, p. 329; G. Guidi, 'Niccolò Machiavelli e i progetti di riforme costituzionali a Firenze nel 1522', *Il pensiero politico* 2 (1969), pp. 580–96.

26 Black, *Machiavelli*, p. 239.

27 For discussion of the dating of the 'Draft', and of Cardinal de' Medici's role in commissioning Niccolò, see Guidi, 'Niccolò Machiavelli e i progetti'; Stephens, *The Fall of the Florentine Republic*, pp. 114–15; Black, *Machiavelli*, p. 240.

28 Text in Machiavelli, *Opere politiche*, vol. 3, *L'arte della guerra. Scritti politici minori*, Marchand et al. (eds.), pp. 646–54; *Opere*, C. Vivanti (ed.) (Turin: Einaudi, 1997–2005), vol. 1, pp. 746–52. Also repr. in W. J. Landon, *Lorenzo di Filippo Strozzi and Niccolò Machiavelli: Patron, Client, and the* Pistole fatta per la peste/*An Epistle Concerning the Plague* (Toronto: University of Toronto Press, 2013), pp. 241–9. The following analysis is based on Black, *Machiavelli*, pp. 240–1; F. Raimondi, *Constituting Freedom: Machiavelli and Florence*, M. Armistead (trans.) (Oxford: Oxford University Press, 2018), pp. 124–9.

29 Jacopo Pitti, 'Apologia de' Cappucci', C. Monzani (ed.), *ASI* 1st ser. 4/2 (1853), pp. 271–384, here p. 326.

30 For the following, see Mallett and Shaw, *The Italian Wars*, pp. 143–4; Knecht, *Francis I*, pp. 114–15; Giucciardini, *Storia d'Italia*, 14.14, Panigada (ed.), vol. 4, pp. 158–60; Sanudo, *Diarii*, vol. 33, pp. 197–8, p. 200, p. 211, pp. 213–14, pp. 288–94; Vettori, *Scritti storici e politici*, p. 200; V.-L. Bourrilly and F. Vindry (eds.), *Mémoires de Martin et Guillaume du Bellay*, 4 vols. (Paris: Renouard, 1908–19), vol. 1, pp. 224–30.

31 Castiglione, *Lettere*, vol. 1, p. 26 (no. xxi).

32 C. Guasti, 'Documenti della congiura fatto contro il cardinale Giuliano de' Medici nel 1522', *Giornale storico degli archivi toscani*, 3 (1859), pp. 121–150, pp. 185–232, pp. 239–67; here p. 122.

33 Vettori, *Scritti storici e politici*, p. 201.

34 Lowe, *Church and Politics*, p. 129.

35 Stephens, *The Fall of the Florentine Republic*, p. 122.

36 Machiavelli, *Opere*, M. Bonfantini (ed.) (Milan and Naples: R. Ricciardi, 1954), p. 1075; trans. *Chief Works*, vol. 3, p. 1463 [adapted].

37 Totto had until then been in the service of Cardinal Salviati. See V. Arrighi, 'Machiavelli, Totto', *DBI*, vol. 67 (Rome, 2006), pp. 105–7.

38 *Lett.*, pp. 414–15 (no. 190); *Machiavelli and His Friends*, pp. 345–6 (no. 277). On Pucci, see V. Arrighi, 'Pucci, Roberto', *DBI*, vol. 85 (Rome, 2016), *ad voc.*

39 *Machiavelli and His Friends*, pp. 346–7 (no. 278).

40 *Ibid.*, pp. 347–8 (no. 280).

41 *Lett.*, p. 415 (no. 191); *Machiavelli and His Friends*, p. 347 (no. 279).

42 For discussion, see V. Arrighi, 'Girolami, Raffaello', *DBI*, vol. 56 (Rome, 2001), pp. 526–31.

43 Text in Machiavelli, *Opere*, Vivanti (ed.), vol. 1, pp. 729–32; Niccolò Machiavelli, *Arte della guerra e scritti politici minori*, S. Bertelli (ed.) (Milan: Feltrinelli, 1961), pp. 285–6; English trans. in *Chief Works*, vol. 1, pp. 116–19.

44 For discussion, see, for example, W. E. Wiethoff, 'A Machiavellian Paradigm for Diplomatic Communication', *Journal of Politics* 43 (1981), pp. 1090–1104; I. Lazzarini, *Communication and Conflict: Italian Diplomacy in the Early Renaissance, 1350–1520* (Oxford: Oxford University Press, 2015), p. 117, p. 165, pp. 194–5.

45 Machiavelli, *Chief Works*, vol. 1, p. 119.

46 *Ibid.*, vol. 1, p. 118.

47 *Ibid.*

48 The text of this will may be found in Niccolò Machiavelli, *Lettere di Niccolò Machiavelli segretario fiorentino . . .* (Venice: Giambattista Pasquali, 1769), pp. 432–6.

49 Niccolò Machiavelli, *Lettere a Francesco Vettori e a Francesco Guicciardini*, G. Inglese (ed.) (Milan: Rizzoli, 1989), pp. 304–6; *Machiavelli and His Friends*, p. 349 (no. 281).

50 Machiavelli, *Lettere*, Inglese (ed.), pp. 303–4; *Machiavelli and His Friends*, p. 348 (no. 281).

51 Guicciardini, *Storia d'Italia*, 14.14, Panigada (ed.), vol. 4, p. 164.

52 Guicciardini, *Storia d'Italia*, 15.1, Panigada (ed.), vol. 4, p. 169.

53 For the following, see Mallett and Shaw, *The Italian Wars*, p. 146.

54 For a list of the cardinal electors present at the beginning of the conclave, and details of the money they had brought with them, see Sanudo, *Diarii*, vol. 35, pp. 61–2. Additional French cardinals arrived a few days later.

55 Guicciardini, *Storia d'Italia*, 15.5, Panigada (ed.), vol. 4, pp. 200–1.

56 Guicciardini, *Storia d'Italia*, 15.4, Panigada (ed.), vol. 4, pp. 195–7.

57 For the following, see Stephens, *The Fall of the Florentine Republic*, pp. 164–5; R. Devonshire Jones, *Francesco Vettori: Florentine Citizen and Medici Servant* (London: Athlone Press, 1972), p. 162.

58 Vettori, *Scritti storici e politici*, pp. 207–8.

59 For the following, see Mallett and Shaw, *The Italian Wars*, pp. 146–8.

60 Guicciardini, *Storia d'Italia*, 15.6, Panigada (ed.), vol. 4, p. 212.

61 Guicciardini, *Storia d'Italia*, 15.8, Panigada (ed.), vol. 4, pp. 220–4.

62 Stephens, *The Fall of the Florentine Republic*, pp. 165–6; Devonshire Jones, *Francesco Vettori*, pp. 163–5; Vettori, *Scritti storici e politici*, pp. 208–9.

63 On Falconetti, see R. Zaccaria, 'Falconetti, Iacopo', *DBI*, vol. 44 (Rome, 1994), pp. 342–4.

64 In Domenico Puligo's portrait of Barbera Salutati (private collection), she is shown seated at a table, holding an open book of

music and a volume of Petrarch's verse, on which can be read the first stanza of *Canz.* 213:

> Graces that generous Heaven allots to few,
> virtues rare beyond the custom of men,
> beneath blond hair the wisdom of grey age,
> and in a humble lady high divine beauty.

Trans. from *Petrarch's Lyric Poems: The* Rime Sparse *and Other Lyrics*, R. M. Durling (trans. and ed.) (Cambridge MA and London: Harvard University Press, 1976), p. 366. On Puligo's portrait, see, for example, G. Langdon, *Medici Women: Portraits of Power, Love, and Betrayal* (Toronto: University of Toronto Press, 2006), p. 26, p. 164; M. Feldman and B. Gordon, *The Courtesan's Arts* (Oxford: Oxford University Press, 2006), pp. 146–7.

65 Giorgio Vasari, *Le vite de' piu eccelenti pittori, scultori ed architettori*, G. Milanesi (ed.), 9 vols. (Florence: Sansoni, 1878–85), vol. 4, p. 465.

66 See, for example, V. Cox, *Women's Writing in Italy, 1400–1650* (Baltimore MD: Johns Hopkins University Press, 2008), pp. 83–4.

67 This description is based on Puligo's portrait.

68 Q.v. *Lett.*, p. 427, p. 449 (nos. 202, 210); *Machiavelli and His Friends*, p. 360, p. 377 (nos. 294, 303).

69 *Lett.*, p. 428 (no. 202); *Machiavelli and His Friends*, p. 361 (no. 294).

70 This letter was published in Tommasini, *La vita e gli scritti di Niccolò Machiavelli*, vol. 3, p. 1148.

71 Machiavelli, 'S'a la mia immensa voglia'; text in Machiavelli, *Opere*, Bonfantini (ed.), p. 1080; Machiavelli, *Tutte le opere*, Martelli (ed.) (Florence: Sansoni, 1971), pp. 1004–5; J. Tusiani (trans.), *Lust and Liberty: The Poems of Machiavelli* (New York NY: I. Obolensky, 1963), pp. 41–2. For discussion, see M. Viroli, *Machiavelli's God*, A. Shugaar (trans.) (Princeton NJ: Princeton University Press, 2010), pp. 73–4; M. Viroli, *Niccolò's Smile: A Biography of Machiavelli*, A. Shugaar (trans.) (New York: Farrar, Straus and Giroux, 2001), p. 227.

72 Machiavelli, 'Amor, I' sento l'alma'; text in Machiavelli, *Opere*, Bonfantini (ed.), p. 1079.

73 *Lett.*, p. 417 (no. 194); *Machiavelli and His Friends*, p. 351 (no. 285).

74 For useful introductions to *la questione della lingua*, see, for example, M. Campanelli, 'Language', in M. Wyatt (ed.), *The Cambridge Companion to the Italian Renaissance* (Cambridge: Cambridge University Press, 2014), pp. 139–63; A. Mazzocco, *Linguistic Theories in Dante and the Humanists: Studies of Language and Intellectual History in Late Medieval and Early Renaissance Italy* (Leiden: Brill, 1993); S. Rizzo, *Ricerche sul latino umanistico* (Rome: Storia e Letteratura, 2002), esp. pp. 15–27; M. Tirvoni, *Latino, grammatica e volgare: storia di una questione umanistica* (Padua: Antenore, 1984).

75 Dante Alighieri, *De vulgari eloquentia*, S. Botterill (ed. and trans.) (Cambridge: Cambridge University Press, 1996).

76 *Lett.*, p. 392 (no. 176); *Machiavelli and His Friends*, p. 327 (no. 262).

77 On Trissino, see esp. B. Morsolin, *Giangiorgio Trissino* (Florence: Le Monnier, 1894). On the *Epistola*, see, for example, P. Trovato, *Storia della lingua: il primo Cinquecento* (Bologna: Il Mulino, 1994), p. 109; P. Floriani, 'Trissino: la «questione della lingua», la poetica', in N. Pozza (ed.), *Atti del Convegno di Studi su Giangiorgio Trissino* (Vicenza: Accademia Olimpica, 1980), pp. 53–66.

78 Niccolò Machiavelli, *Discorso intorno alla nostra lingua*, P. Trovato (ed.) (Padua: Antenore, 1982). For discussion of the contents and date of this treatise, see, for example: P. Rajna, 'La data del *Dialogo intorno alla lingua* di Niccolò Machiavelli', *Rendiconti della Reale Accademia dei Lincei*, Classe di scienze morali ecc., 5th ser. 2/2 (1893), pp. 203–22; H. Baron, 'Machiavelli on the eve of the *Discourses*: the date and place of his *Dialogo intorno alla nostra lingua*', *Bibliothèque d'Humanisme et Renaissance* 23 (1961), pp. 449–76; C. Grayson, 'Machiavelli and Dante', in A. Molho and J. Tedeschi (eds.), *Renaissance Studies in Honor of Hans Baron* (Florence: Sansoni, 1971), pp. 361–84; C. Grayson, 'A proposito di una nuova edizione del *Dialogo intorno alla lingua*', *Studi e problemi di critica testuale* 16 (1978), pp. 69–80; M. Martelli, *Una giarda fiorentina: il 'Dialogo della lingua' attribuito a Niccolò Machiavelli* (Rome: Salerno, 1978); M. Martelli, 'Paralipomeni alla *Giarda*: venti tesi sul *Dialogo della lingua*', *Filologia e critica* 4 (1979), pp. 212–79; S. Meld Shield, 'Machiavelli's Discourse on Language', in V. B. Sullivan (ed.), *The Comedy and Tragedy of Machiavelli: Essays on the Literary Works* (New Haven CT and London: Yale University Press, 2000), pp. 78–101; F. Bausi, *Machiavelli* (Rome: Salerno Editrice, 2005), pp. 69–80; Black, *Machiavelli*, pp. 200–1.

79 See esp. Machiavelli, *Istorie fiorentine*, 1.5; *Chief Works*, vol. 3, pp. 1039–41.

80 Meld Shield, 'Machiavelli's Discourse on Language', p. 97.

81 Machiavelli, *Discorso intorno alla nostra lingua*, 10–11, Trovato (ed.), pp. 9–10.

82 Machiavelli, *Discorso intorno alla nostra lingua*, 13–14, Trovato (ed.), pp. 12–13.

83 Machiavelli, *Discorso intorno alla nostra lingua*, 17, Trovato (ed.), p. 15.

84 Machiavelli, *Discorso intorno alla nostra lingua*, 28, Trovato (ed.), p. 28.

85 Meld Shield, 'Machiavelli's Discourse on Language', p. 85.

86 Matteo Bandello, *Le Novelle*, 40, G. Brognolio (ed.), 5 vols. (Bari: G. Laterza & Figli, 1910–12), vol. 2, pp. 83–4.

87 Text in Machiavelli, *Tutte le opere*, Martelli (ed.), pp. 919–23; *Opere*, Bonfantini (ed.), pp. 1035–44. Translation in *Chief Works*, vol. 2, pp. 869–77.

88 For discussion of this point, see Black, *Machiavelli*, p. 195; Bausi, *Machiavelli*, p. 298.

89 Machiavelli, *Opere*, Bonfantini (ed.), p. 1035; *Chief Works*, vol. 2, p. 869.

90 Machiavelli, *Opere*, Bonfantini (ed.), p. 1037; *Chief Works*, vol. 2, p. 871.

91 Machiavelli, *Opere*, Bonfantini (ed.), p. 1038; *Chief Works*, vol. 2, p. 871.

92 Machiavelli, *Opere*, Bonfantini (ed.), pp. 1040–1; *Chief Works*, vol. 2, pp. 873–4.

93 Machiavelli, *Opere*, Bonfantini (ed.), p. 1044; *Chief Works*, vol. 2, p. 877 [adapted].

94 Vasari, *Le vite de' piu eccelenti pittori*, Milanesi (ed.), vol. 6, p. 437.

95 Translation in *Chief Works*, vol. 2, pp. 822–64. The bibliography on the *Clizia* is considerable, but particular mentions should be made of the following works: L. Vanossi, *Lingue e strutture del teatro italiano del Rinascimento* (Padua: Liviana, 1970), pp. 57–108; E. Raimondi, *Politica e commedia: il centauro disarmato* (Bologna: Il Mulino, 1972), pp. 84–7; G. Ferroni, *'Mutazione' e 'Riscontro' nel teatro di Machiavelli e altri saggi sulla commedia del Cinquecento* (Rome: Bulzoni, 1972), pp. 19–137, esp. pp. 120–37; G. Padoan, 'Il tramonto di Machiavelli', *Lettere italiane* 33 (1981), pp. 457–81; R. L. Martinez, 'Benefit of Absence: Machiavellian Valediction in *Clizia*', in A. R. Ascoli and V. Kahn (eds.), *Machiavelli and the Discourse of Literature* (Ithaca NY: Cornell University Press, 1994), pp. 117–44; R. L. Martinez, 'Comedian, tragedian: Machiavelli and the traditions of Renaissance theatre', in J. M. Najemy (ed.), *The Cambridge Companion to Machiavelli* (Cambridge: Cambridge University Press, 2010), pp. 206–22, here pp. 216–19; R. Faulkner, '*Clizia* and the Enlightenment of Private Life', in Sullivan (ed.), *The Comedy and Tragedy of Machiavelli*, pp. 30–56.

96 The following is based on Black, *Machiavelli*, pp. 203–4.

97 For discussion of the date of the *Clizia*'s first performance, see Tommasini, *La vita e gli scritti di Niccolò Machiavelli*, vol. 2, p. 414.

98 *Lett.*, p. 418 (no. 195); *Machiavelli and His Friends*, p. 354 (no. 286); Vasari, *Le vite de' piu eccelenti pittori*, Milanesi (ed.), vol. 6, p. 438; Donato Giannotti, 'Trattato della Repubblica Fiorentina', 318, in Donato Giannotti, *Opere politiche e letterarie*, F.-L. Polidori (ed.), 2 vols. (Florence: Le Monnier, 1850), vol. 1, pp. 57–288, here p. 228.

99 Vasari, *Le vite de' piu eccelenti pittori*, Milanesi (ed.), vol. 6, p. 438.

NOTES

100 For discussion of Niccolò's relationship with Philippe Verdelot, see
R. Chiesa, 'Machiavelli e la Musica', in *Rivista italiana di
musicologia* 4 (1969), pp. 3–31, esp. p. 12, p. 15.
101 *Lett.*, p. 418 (no. 195); *Machiavelli and His Friends*, p. 354 (no. 286)
[adapted].

27. 'This Ruined World'

1 Niccolò Machiavelli, *Istorie fiorentine*, F. Gaeta (ed.) (Milan:
Feltrinelli, 1962); trans. in *Chief Works*, vol. 3, pp. 1025–1435.
2 On the rhetoric and style of the *Istorie fiorentine*, see esp. A. M.
Cabrini, *Interpretazione e stile in Machiavelli. Il terzo libro delle
'Istorie'* (Rome: Bulzoni, 1990); D. Quint, 'Narrative Design and
Historical Irony in Machiavelli's *Istorie fiorentine*', *Rinascimento* 43
(2003), pp. 31–48; E. Raimondi, 'Machiavelli and the Rhetoric of the
Warrior', *MLN* 92 (1977), pp. 1–16; B. Richardson, 'Notes on
Machiavelli's Sources and His Treatment of the Rhetorical
Tradition', *Italian Studies* 26 (1971), pp. 24–48.
3 Machiavelli, *Istorie fiorentine*, 'Al Santissimo e Beatissimo Padre
Signore Nostro Clemente Settimo'; *Chief Works*, vol. 3, p. 1030.
4 *Lett.*, p. 417 (no. 194); *Machiavelli and His Friends*, p. 351 (no. 285).
5 Besides Leonardo Bruni and Poggio Bracciolini, the authors whose
works Niccolò consulted included: Giovanni Villani, Giovanni
Cavalcanti, Giovanni di Carlo, Angelo Poliziano, Flavio Biondo,
Neri di Gino Capponi, Giovanni Simonetta, Bernardino Corio,
Niccolò Valori, and his friend Francesco Guicciardini. On Niccolò's
sources for the *Istorie fiorentine*, see esp. G. M. Anselmi, 'Machiavelli
e l'*Istoria fiorentina* di Domenico di Leonardo Buoninsegni', *Studi e
problemi di critica testuale* 9 (1974), pp. 119–32; R. Hatfield, 'A source
for Machiavelli's account of the regime of Piero de' Medici', in
M. Gilmore (ed.), *Studies on Machiavelli* (Florence: Sansoni, 1972),
pp. 317–33; A. M. Cabrini, *Per una valutazione delle 'Istorie fiorentine'
del Machiavelli: note sulle fonti del secondo libro* (Florence: La Nuova
Italia, 1985); G. Pieraccioni, 'Note su Machiavelli storico. I.
Machiavelli e Giovanni di Carlo', *ASI* 146 (1988), pp. 635–54; 'Note
su Machiavelli storico. II. Machiavelli lettore delle *Storie fiorentine*
di Guicciardini', *ASI* 147 (1989), pp. 63–98.
6 On Niccolò's relationship with Renaissance historiography see, for
example, C. Dionisotti, 'Machiavelli storico', in C. Dionisotti,
Machiavellerie. Storie e Fortuna di Machiavelli (Turin: Einaudi, 1980),
pp. 365–409; M. Martelli, 'Machiavelli e la storiografia umanistica',
in A. Di Stefano (ed.), *La storiografia umanistica*, 2 vols. in 3
(Messina: Sicania, 1992), vol. 1, pp. 113–52; M. Phillips, 'Barefoot Boy

Makes Good: A Study of Machiavelli's Historiography', *Speculum* 59 (1984), pp. 585–605.

7   Leonardo Bruni, *History of the Florentine People*, pr. 1, J. Hankins (ed. and trans.), 3 vols. (Cambridge MA: Harvard University Press, 2001–7), vol. 1, p. 3.

8   For discussion, see esp. G. Ianziti, *Writing History in Renaissance Italy: Leonardo Bruni and the Uses of the Past* (Cambridge MA: Harvard University Press, 2012), pp. 186–233.

9   Machiavelli, *Istorie fiorentine*, pr.; *Chief Works*, vol. 3, p. 1031. As several scholars have rightly pointed out, however, Bruni and Bracciolini were, in this regard, quite untypical. Giovanni Villani, Marchionne di Coppo Stefani, Giovanni Cavalcanti, Piero Parenti, Bartolomeo Cerretani, Francesco Guicciardini and a host of other Florentine historians had made a point of examining and condemning the divisions by which the city had been rent for centuries past. See G. Bock, 'Civil discord in Machiavelli's *Istorie fiorentine*', in G. Bock, Q. Skinner and M. Viroli (eds.), *Machiavelli and Republicanism* (Cambridge: Cambridge University Press, 1990), pp. 181–201, here p. 183; G. A. Brucker, *Florentine Politics and Society 1343–1378* (Princeton NJ: Princeton University Press, 1962), pp. 131–2; D. Wilcox, *The Development of Florentine Humanist Historiography* (Cambridge MA: Harvard University Press, 1969), pp. 73–81; N. C. Struever, *The Language of History in the Renaissance: Rhetoric and Historical Consciousness in Florentine Humanism* (Princeton NJ: Princeton University Press, 1970), pp. 115–43; L. Green, *Chronicle into History. An Essay on the Interpretation of History in Florentine Fourteenth-Century Chronicles* (Cambridge: Cambridge University Press, 1972), esp. pp. 39–43, pp. 95–102, pp. 106–7; M. Phillips, 'Machiavelli, Guicciardini, and the tradition of vernacular historiography in Florence', *American Historical Review* 84/1 (1979), pp. 86–105, esp. p. 102.

10   Machiavelli, *Istorie fiorentine*, pr.; *Chief Works*, vol. 3, p. 1031.

11   Here and in the following three paragraphs, I broadly follow Q. R. D. Skinner, *Machiavelli*, new ed. (Oxford: Oxford University Press, 2000), pp. 95–6. See also Bock, 'Civil Discord in Machiavelli's *Istorie fiorentine*'.

12   Machiavelli, *Istorie fiorentine*, 7.1; *Chief Works*, vol. 3, p. 1336.

13   Machiavelli, *Istorie fiorentine*, 3.1; *Chief Works*, vol. 3, p. 1140.

14   Machiavelli, *Istorie fiorentine*, 7.1; *Chief Works*, vol. 3, p. 1336.

15   Machiavelli, *Istorie fiorentine*, 4.1; *Chief Works*, vol. 3, p. 1187.

16   Machiavelli, *Istorie fiorentine*, 2.3–4; *Chief Works*, vol. 3, pp. 1083–5.

17   Machiavelli, *Istorie fiorentine*, 2.34–6; *Chief Works*, vol. 3, pp. 1121–30.

18   Machiavelli, *Istorie fiorentine*, 2.39; *Chief Works*, vol. 3, pp. 1133–5. On the depiction of Walter of Brienne's fall in the *Istorie fiorentine*, see,

for example, M. Jurdjevic, *A Great and Wretched City: Promise and Failure in Machiavelli's Florentine Political Thought* (Cambridge MA and London: Harvard University Press, 2014), p. 191, pp. 202–3.

19 Machiavelli, *Istorie fiorentine*, 3.12–18; *Chief Works*, vol. 3, pp. 1158–69.

20 Machiavelli, *Istorie fiorentine*, 3.20–1, 3.24, 4.2; *Chief Works*, vol. 3, pp. 1171–4, p. 1178, p. 1188.

21 This represents a break with the *Discorsi*. It may be remembered that, in the earlier work, Niccolò had argued that greatness could not be achieved without liberty. Here, however, the two concepts are uncoupled. See A. M. Cabrini, 'Machiavelli's *Florentine Histories*', in J. M. Najemy (ed.), *The Cambridge Companion to Machiavelli* (Cambridge: Cambridge University Press, 2010), pp. 128–43, here pp. 131–2.

22 Machiavelli, *Istorie fiorentine*, 2.15; *Chief Works*, vol. 3, p. 1097.

23 Machiavelli, *Istorie fiorentine*, pr.; *Chief Works*, vol. 3, p. 1032.

24 Skinner, *Machiavelli*, p. 94. The remainder of this paragraph is indebted to Skinner's analysis.

25 Machiavelli, *Istorie fiorentine*, 4.6; *Chief Works*, vol. 3, pp. 1192–3.

26 Machiavelli, *Istorie fiorentine*, 5.33; *Chief Works*, vol. 3, p. 1280.

27 Donato Giannotti, letter to Marcantonio Micheli, 30 June 1533; Donato Giannotti, *Lettere italiane*, F. Diaz (ed.) (Milan: Marzorati, 1974), p. 35.

28 Machiavelli, *Istorie fiorentine*, 4.16; *Chief Works*, vol. 3, p. 1204.

29 Machiavelli, *Istorie fiorentine*, 7.5; *Chief Works*, vol. 3, p. 1342.

30 Machiavelli, *Istorie fiorentine*, 8.36; *Chief Works*, vol. 3, p. 1434.

31 E.g. Machiavelli, *Istorie fiorentine*, 4.26, 5.4; *Chief Works*, vol. 3, pp. 1217–18, pp. 1236–8. For discussion, see, for example, Cabrini, 'Machiavelli's *Florentine Histories*', pp. 138–9.

32 Machiavelli, *Istorie fiorentine*, 8.1; *Chief Works*, vol. 3, p. 1383.

33 Machiavelli, *Istorie fiorentine*, 8.8; *Chief Works*, vol. 3, p. 1393. Skinner, *Machiavelli*, p. 97; Jurdjevic, *A Great and Wretched City*, p. 92; J. M. Najemy, 'Machiavelli and the Medici: The Lessons of Florentine History', in *Renaissance Quarterly* 35 (1982), pp. 551–76.

34 Machiavelli, *Istorie fiorentine*, 5.1; *Chief Works*, vol. 3, p. 1232. For a discussion of this passage, see, for example, J. D'Amico, 'The Virtue of Ruin in Machiavelli's "Florentine Histories"', *Renaissance and Reformation*, new ser. 8/3 (1984), pp. 202–14.

35 Machiavelli, *Istorie fiorentine*, 5.1; *Chief Works*, vol. 3, p. 1233 [amended].

36 See esp. Najemy, 'Machiavelli and the Medici'.

28. An Old Man in a Hurry (March 1525–September 1526)

1   R. Devonshire Jones, *Francesco Vettori: Florentine Citizen and Medici Servant* (London: Athlone Press, 1972), p. 171.

2   *Lett.*, p. 419 (no. 196); *Machiavelli and His Friends*, pp. 354–5 (no. 287).

3   Francesco Guicciardini, *Storia d'Italia*, 15.9, C. Panigada (ed.), 5 vols. (Bari: G. Laterza & Figli, 1929), vol. 4, pp. 228–30.

4   Guicciardini, *Storia d'Italia*, 15.10, Panigada (ed.), vol. 4, pp. 232–7.

5   See M. E. Mallett and C. Shaw, *The Italian Wars, 1494–1559: War, State and Society in Early Modern Europe* (London and New York: Routledge, 2012), p. 149.

6   Guicciardini, *Storia d'Italia*, 15.12, Panigada (ed.), vol. 4, pp. 240–1.

7   G. Canestrini and A. Desjardins (eds.), *Négociations diplomatiques de la France avec la Toscane*, 6 vols. (Paris: Imprimerie Impériale / Imprimerie Nationale, 1859–86), vol. 2, pp. 812–14; Guicciaridni, *Storia d'Italia*, 15.11, Panigada (ed.), vol. 4, p. 238.

8   On the Battle of Pavia, see esp. Mallett and Shaw, *The Italian Wars*, pp. 150–2.

9   Guicciardini, *Storia d'Italia*, 16.2, Panigada (ed.), vol. 4, pp. 275–6.

10 Guicciaridni, *Storia d'Italia*, 16.7, Panigada (ed.), vol. 4, pp. 301–2; Francesco Vettori, *Scritti storici e politici*, E. Niccolini (ed.) (Bari: G. Laterza & Figli, 1972), p. 216.

11 Q. at R. Ridolfi, *Vita di Niccolò Machiavelli* 3rd ed., 2 vols. (Florence: Sansoni, 1969), vol. 1, p. 330.

12 Q. at *ibid.*, vol. 1, p. 331.

13 For a discussion of the date of Niccolò's arrival in Rome, see *ibid.*, vol. 2, p. 533, n.25.

14 Q.v. O. Tommasini, *La vita e gli scritti di Niccolò Machiavelli nella loro relazione col machiavellismo*, 3 vols. (Turin: Ermanno Loescher, 1883–1911), vol. 2, p. 769, n.5.

15 *Leg. e comm.*, p. 1567.

16 *Ibid.*, pp. 1570–2. The previous day, Guicciardini had prepared a draft of this letter, which still survives, and which contains several noteworthy differences of style and emphasis. His criticisms, however, remain the same. *Ibid.*, pp. 1568–9.

17 *Lett.*, p. 420 (no. 197); *Machiavelli and His Friends*, p. 356 (no. 289).

18 *Lett.*, p. 422 (no. 199); *Machiavelli and His Friends*, p. 357 (no. 291).

19 Guicciardini, letter to Cesare Colombo, 26 July 1525, in Francesco Guicciardini, *Opere inedite*, 10 vols. (Florence: Barbèra, Bianchi e comp., 1857–67), vol. 8, p. 287 (no. 139).

20 *Lett.*, p. 421 (no. 198); *Machiavelli and His Friends*, pp. 356–7 (no. 290).

21 *Machiavelli and His Friends*, pp. 355–6 (no. 288).

22 *Lett.*, p. 422 (no. 199); *Machiavelli and His Friends*, p. 357 (no. 291).

23 *Lett.*, pp. 423–6 (no. 200); *Machiavelli and His Friends*, pp. 358–9 (no. 292).

24 *Lett.*, p. 426 (no. 201); *Machiavelli and His Friends*, pp. 359–60 (no. 293).

25 For this and what follows, see *Lett.*, pp. 427–30 (no. 202); *Machiavelli and His Friends*, pp. 360–2 (no. 294).

26 Guicciardini wrote to thank Niccolò for the copy of the *Mandragola* in a (now lost) letter of 12 August. Niccolò refers to this at the beginning of his letter of 17 August: *Lett.*, p. 432 (no 205); *Machiavelli and His Friends*, p. 363 (no. 296).

27 *Lett.*, pp. 432–4 (no. 204); *Machiavelli and His Friends*, pp. 363–5 (no. 296).

28 For this and what follows, see *Lett.*, pp. 436–7 (no. 205); *Machiavelli and His Friends*, p. 366 (no. 297).

29 The date is given in a letter by Ludovico Canossa: Ridolfi, *Vita di Niccolò Machiavelli*, vol. 2, p. 537, n.54.

30 *Lett.*, p. 435 (no. 205); *Machiavelli and His Friends*, p. 365 (no. 297).

31 *Lett.*, p. 432 (no. 204); *Machiavelli and His Friends*, p. 363 (no. 296). In thanking Guicciardini for his suggestion, Niccolò did not specify where the play was to be performed, but that Faenza was intended is evident. Not only was Guicciardini in Faenza when Niccolò replied to his (now lost) letter, but, on 26 December 1525, he later wrote from the town explaining that he was planning to put it on 'a few days before Carnival' and asking Niccolò to come and stay 'here' until Lent: *Lett.*, p. 447 (no. 209); *Machiavelli and His Friends*, p. 372 (no. 302). Cf. *Lett.*, p. 449 (no. 210); *Machiavelli and His Friends*, p. 377 (no. 303).

32 *Lett.*, p. 440 (no. 206); *Machiavelli and His Friends*, p. 368 (no. 299).

33 *Lett.*, p. 447 (no. 209); *Machiavelli and His Friends*, p. 372 (no. 302).

34 Machiavelli, *Mandragola*, pr.; Niccolò Machiavelli, *Opere*, M. Bonfantini (ed.) (Milan and Naples: R. Ricciardi, 1954), p. 983, trans. from *Chief Works*, vol. 2, p. 776.

35 Charles V sent Lopes Urtado to request the necessary dispensation from the pope in late July 1525: Guicciardini, *Storia d'Italia*, 16.7, Panigada (ed.), vol. 4, p. 305.

36 Guicciardini, *Storia d'Italia*, 16.9, Panigada (ed.), vol. 4, p. 318.

37 *Lett.*, pp. 438–40 (no. 206); *Machiavelli and His Friends*, pp. 367–8 (no. 299).

38 Machiavelli, *Mandragola*, 3.6; *Chief Works*, vol. 2, p. 799.

39 *Lett.*, p. 439 (no. 206); *Machiavelli and His Friends*, p. 368 (no. 299).

40 Q. at *ibid.* The text given by Niccolò differs slightly from that given in both the 1552 Giunti edition and the 1553 Marcolin edition: *I sonetti del Burchiello et di Messer Antonio Alamanni, alla Burchiellesca*

... (Florence: Giunti, 1552), fol. 14v.; *Rime di Burchiello comentate dal Doni* (Venice: Marcolin, 1553), p. 139. The principal differences are as follows:

Machiavelli		1552 Giunti / 1553 Marcolin
l.2	Si mandò imbasciator	V'andò Imbasciadore
l.2	paiol	Paiuol
l.3	molle	molli
l.3	palletta	paletta
l.4	Che se ne trovò	Perch'ella tornò
l.5	Ma l'erpice	E l'Erpice

41 *Lett.*, p. 440 (no. 206); *Machiavelli and His Friends*, p. 368 (no. 299).

42 The following is indebted to Mallett and Shaw, *The Italian Wars*, p. 154.

43 For this and what follows, see Guicciardini, *Storia d'Italia*, 16.10, Panigada (ed.), vol. 4, pp. 318–21.

44 *Lett.* 444 (no. 207); *Machiavelli and His Friends*, p. 371 (no. 300); cf. Dante, *Purg.* 20.86–7: 'veggio in Alagna entrar lo fioraliso | e nel vicario suo Cristo esser catto.' (*I see Agnani yield to the fleur-de-lys, | and in his vicar, Christ held captive*). Diplomatically, Niccolò gave only the first four words. He assumed that Guicciardini would know the rest. It is worth noting that Niccolò appears to have quoted Dante's lines from memory, giving *'d'Alagna tornar'* for *'in Alagna entrar'*. Since the alteration makes little historical sense, it seems plausible that his intended meaning was that of Dante's original.

45 Guicciardini, *Storia d'Italia*, 16.11, Panigada (ed.), vol. 4, pp. 323–4.

46 Mallett and Shaw, *The Italian Wars*, p. 155; Guicciardini, *Storia d'Italia*, 16.11, Panigada (ed.), vol. 4, pp. 324–5.

47 *Lett.*, p. 446 (no. 208); *Machiavelli and His Friends*, p. 372 (no. 301).

48 *Lett.*, p. 446 (no. 208); *Machiavelli and His Friends*, p. 372 (no. 301).

49 *Lett.*, p. 447–8 (no. 209); *Machiavelli and His Friends*, p. 373 (no. 302).

50 See Guicciardini, *Storia d'Italia*, 16.11, Panigada (ed.), vol. 4, pp. 326–7.

51 *Lett.*, pp. 447–8 (no. 209); *Machiavelli and His Friends*, p. 373 (no. 302).

52 *Lett.*, p. 450 (no. 210); *Machiavelli and His Friends*, p. 378 (no. 303).

53 *Ibid.*; Mallett and Shaw, *The Italian Wars*, p. 155; Guicciardini, *Storia d'Italia*, 16.15, Panigada (ed.), vol. 4, pp. 348–50.

54 *Lett.*, p. 451 (no. 210); *Machiavelli and His Friends*, p. 378 (no. 303).

55 Marino Sanudo the Younger, *I diarii di Marino Sanuto: (MCCCCXCVI–MDXXXIII): dall'autografo Marciano Ital. CLVII codd. CDXIX–CDLXXVII*, R. Fulin et al. (eds.), 58 vols. (Venice: F. Visentini, 1879–1902), vol. 32, p. 458. See S. Bertelli, 'When did Machiavelli write *Mandragola*?', *Renaissance Quarterly* 24/3 (1971), pp. 317–26, here p. 317.

56 R. Ridolfi, 'La seconda edizione della *Mandragola* e un codicillo

sopra la prima', in R. Ridolfi, *Studi sulle commedie di Machiavelli* (Pisa: Nistri-Lischi, 1968), pp. 37–62.

57 For this and what follows, see *Lett.*, pp. 452–3 (no. 211); *Machiavelli and His Friends*, p. 379 (no. 304) [adapted].

58 *Lett.*, pp. 454–8 (no. 212); *Machiavelli and His Friends*, pp. 380–3 (no. 305).

59 *Lett.*, p. 456 (no. 212); *Machiavelli and His Friends*, p. 381 (no. 305).

60 *Ibid.*

61 *Lett.*, p. 457 (no. 212); *Machiavelli and His Friends*, p. 382 (no. 305).

62 *Lett.*, p. 458 (no. 212); *Machiavelli and His Friends*, pp. 382––3 (no. 305).

63 *Lett.*, pp. 459–61 (no. 213); *Machiavelli and His Friends*, pp. 383–5 (no. 306).

64 *Lett.*, p. 460 (no. 213); *Machiavelli and His Friends*, p. 384 (no. 306).

65 *Lett.*, pp. 460–1 (no. 213); *Machiavelli and His Friends*, p. 384 (no. 306).

66 On Francis' release, see Guicciardini, *Storia d'Italia*, 16.17, Panigada (ed.), vol. 4, pp. 355–6. On the reaction in Italy, see Guicciardini, *Storia d'Italia*, 17.1, Panigada (ed.), vol. 5, pp. 1–2.

67 Niccolò Machiavelli, 'Argo'; trans. *Chief Works*, vol. 3, p. 1463 [adapted]. Niccolò had previously referred to the myth of Argus in *L'Asino*, 1.97–9; *Chief Works*, vol. 2, p. 752: 'But the present age so grudging and evil, without a man's having the eyes of Argus, makes him always see bad more quickly than good.'

68 Vettori, *Scritti storici e politici*, pp. 222–3; Guicciardini, *Storia d'Italia*, 17.2, Panigada (ed.), vol. 5, pp. 8–11.

69 *Lett.*, pp. 462–3 (no. 214); *Machiavelli and His Friends*, pp. 385–6 (no. 307).

70 Text in Niccolò Machiavelli, *Opere politiche*, vol. 3, *L'arte della guerra. Scritti politici minori*, J.-J. Marchand, D. Fachard and G. Masi (eds.) (Rome, 2001), pp. 662–70; *Opere*, P. Fanfani, G. Milanesi, L. Passerini (eds.), 6 vols. (Florence: Cenniniana, 1873–77), vol. 6, pp. 364–70.

71 This is also discussed at length at *Lett.*, pp. 462–3 (no. 214); *Machiavelli and His Friends*, p. 385 (no. 307).

72 In a letter dated 27 April, Francesco Guicciardini told his brother, Luigi, that Niccolò had just left Rome. This letter is reproduced in Tommasini, *La vita e gli scritti di Niccolò Machiavelli*, vol. 2, p. 1157.

73 See *Lett.*, p. 465 (no. 215); *Machiavelli and His Friends*, p. 387 (no. 308); Ridolfi, *Vita di Niccolò Machiavelli*, vol. 1, p. 354.

74 The text of the *Provvisione per la istituzione dell'ufficio de' cinque provveditori delle mure della città di Firenze* (Provision for the institution of the office of the five procurators of the walls of the

city of Florence) can be found in Machiavelli, *Opere politiche*, vol. 3, *L'arte della guerra. Scritti politici minori*, Marchand et al. (eds.), pp. 671–5; *Opere*, Fanfani et al. (eds.), vol. 6, pp. 360–2.

75 *Lett.*, pp. 464–5 (no. 215); *Machiavelli and His Friends*, pp. 386–7 (no. 308). On the ambassador's attempts to reach an accord, see Guicciardini, *Storia d'Italia*, 17.4, Panigada (ed.), vol. 5, pp. 21–2, pp. 24–5.

76 *Lett.*, p. 464 (no. 215); *Machiavelli and His Friends*, p. 386 (no. 308).

77 See Mallett and Shaw, *The Italian Wars*, p. 155.

78 Guicciardini, *Storia d'Italia*, 17.3, Panigada (ed.), vol. 5, p. 20.

79 Guicciardini, *Storia d'Italia*, 17.5, Panigada (ed.), vol. 5, p. 28.

80 Guicciardini, *Storia d'Italia*, 17.6, Panigada (ed.), vol. 5, p. 38.

81 *Lett.*, pp. 467–8, 470 (nos. 217, 219); *Machiavelli and His Friends*, p. 388, p. 390 (nos. 310, 312).

82 Ridolfi, *Vita di Niccolò Machiavelli*, vol. 1, p. 356.

83 R. Ridolfi, *Vita di Francesco Guicciardini* (Rome: Angelo Belardetti, 1960), p. 245.

84 E.g. *Lett.*, p. 471, p. 490 (nos. 219bis, 226); *Machiavelli and His Friends*, pp. 390–1, p. 404 (nos. 313, 323). Niccolò's 'we' could refer either to the army in whose train he was following, or simply to the League's forces.

85 *Lett.*, pp. 471–3 (no. 219bis); *Machiavelli and His Friends*, pp. 390–2 (no. 313). For discussion, see Ridolfi, *Vita di Niccolò Machiavelli*, vol. 1, p. 357.

86 See C. Mutini, 'Cavalcanti, Bartolomeo', *DBI*, vol. 22 (Rome, 1979), pp. 611–17.

87 *Lett.*, pp. 471–3 (no. 219bis); *Machiavelli and His Friends*, pp. 390–2 (no. 313).

88 Guicciardini, *Storia d'Italia*, 17.9, Panigada (ed.), vol. 5, p. 53.

89 Guicciardini, *Storia d'Italia*, 17.9, Panigada (ed.), vol. 5, p. 54.

90 For the following, see Matteo Bandello, *Le Novelle*, 40, G. Brognolio (ed.), 5 vols. (Bari: G. Laterza & Figli, 1910–12), vol. 2, pp. 83–4.

91 *Lett.*, pp. 478–9 (no. 222); *Machiavelli and His Friends*, p. 396 (no. 317).

92 *Lett.*, p. 485 (no. 224); *Machiavelli and His Friends*, p. 400 (no. 319).

93 *Lett.*, pp. 473–4 (no. 220); *Machiavelli and His Friends*, p. 393 (no. 315).

94 On the siege of Cremona, see Guicciardini, *Storia d'Italia*, 17.10, 11, Panigada (ed.), vol. 5, pp. 59–60, pp. 65–8.

95 *Leg. e comm.*, pp. 1591–2.

29. A Bang and a Whimper (September 1526–June 1527)

1 *Lett.*, p. 465 (no. 215); *Machiavelli and His Friends*, p. 387 (no. 308).

2 See Francesco Guicciardini, *Storia d'Italia*, 17.11, C. Panigada (ed.), 5 vols. (Bari: G. Laterza & Figli, 1929), vol. 5, pp. 65–6.

3 *Ibid.*, vol. 5, pp. 70–1.

4 *Lett.*, p. 491 (no. 226); *Machiavelli and His Friends*, p. 405 (no. 322).

5 *Lett.*, p. 492 (no. 226); *Machiavelli and His Friends*, p. 405 (no. 322).

6 For the following, see R. Devonshire Jones, *Francesco Vettori: Florentine Citizen and Medici Servant* (London: Athlone Press, 1972), p. 179.

7 Francesco Vettori, *Scritti storici e politici*, E. Niccolini (ed.) (Bari: G. Laterza & Figli, 1972), p. 232.

8 For the following, see *Lett.*, pp. 494–5 (no. 227); *Machiavelli and His Friends*, pp. 406–7 (no. 323).

9 *Machiavelli and His Friends*, p. 407 (no. 324).

10 For the following, see *Lett.*, pp. 495–6 (no. 228); *Machiavelli and His Friends*, p. 408 (no. 325).

11 The only occasion on which Niccolò seems to have been tempted to believe such prophecies was in December 1513, when a Franciscan preacher, Fra Francesco da Montepulciano, had predicted the defeat of the king of France: *Lett.*, pp. 308–9 (no. 141); *Machiavelli and His Friends*, p. 267 (no. 225).

12 Cf. Machiavelli, *Discorsi*, 1.14; 'De romiti'.

13 Guicciardini, *Storia d'Italia*, 17.15, Panigada (ed.), vol. 5, pp. 87–8.

14 *Lett.*, p. 497, p. 498 (nos. 229, 230); *Machiavelli and His Friends*, pp. 409–10 (nos. 326–7).

15 M. E. Mallett and C. Shaw, *The Italian Wars, 1494–1559: War, State and Society in Early Modern Europe* (London and New York: Routledge, 2012), p. 158.

16 Guicciardini, *Storia d'Italia*, 17.16, Panigada (ed.), vol. 5, pp. 92–3.

17 See *Leg. e comm.*, p. 1599.

18 *Leg. e comm.*, pp. 1599–1600.

19 *Leg. e comm.*, p. 1601.

20 *Leg. e comm.*, p. 1602.

21 *Leg. e comm.*, pp. 1602–3.

22 *Leg. e comm.*, p. 1604.

23 *Leg. e comm.*, p. 1605.

24 *Ibid.*

25 *Ibid.*

26 For the following, see Guicciardini, *Storia d'Italia*, 17.16, Panigada (ed.), vol. 5, p. 94.

27 Marino Sanudo the Younger, *I diarii di Marino Sanuto:*

(MCCCCXCVI–MDXXXIII): dall'autografo Marciano Ital. CLVII codd. CDXIX–CDLXXVII, R. Fulin et al. (eds.), 58 vols. (Venice: F. Visentini, 1879–1902), vol. 43, pp. 448–9.

28 The text of this letter can be found in Girolamo Ruscelli, *Lettere di principi . . .* (Venice: Giordano Ziletti, 1564), fols. 98r–99v. For discussion, see Devonshire Jones, *Francesco Vettori*, p. 182.

29 Ruscelli, *Lettere di principi . . .*, fols. 100r–101r; Devonshire Jones, *Francesco Vettori*, p. 183.

30 Devonshire Jones, *Francesco Vettori*, p. 183.

31 See Ruscelli, *Lettere di principi . . .*, fol. 206v; Devonshire Jones, *Francesco Vettori*, p. 189.

32 A. Bardi, 'Filippo Strozzi (da nuovi documenti)', *ASI* 5th ser., 14 (1894), pp. 3–78, here p. 51.

33 Benedetto Varchi, *Storia fiorentina*, L. Arbib (ed.), 3 vols. (Florence: Società Editrice delle Storie Nardi e del Varchi, 1838–41), vol. 1, p. 111.

34 *Leg. e comm.*, p. 1617.

35 *Ibid.*, pp. 1618–19.

36 *Ibid.*, p. 1622.

37 *Ibid.*, p. 1624.

38 This paragraph is indebted to M. Viroli, *Niccolò's Smile: A Biography of Machiavelli*, A. Shugaar (trans.) (New York: Farrar, Straus and Giroux, 2001), pp. 249–50.

39 Francesco Guicciardini, *Opere inedite*, 10 vols. (Florence: Barbèra, Bianchi e comp., 1857–67), vol. 5, p. 226 (no. 97).

40 *Ibid.*, vol. 5, p. 228 (no. 98).

41 Mallett and Shaw, *The Italian Wars*, pp. 158–9.

42 *Leg. e comm.*, p. 1632.

43 On Cardinal Cybo, see, for example, L. Staffétti, *Il Cardinale Innocenzo Cybo* (Florence: Le Monnier, 1894); F. Petrucci, 'Cibo, Innocenzo', *DBI*, vol. 25 (Rome, 1981), pp. 249–55.

44 *Lett.*, p. 499 (no. 231); *Machiavelli and His Friends*, p. 413 (no. 328).

45 *Leg. e comm.*, p. 1634.

46 Guicciardini, *Storia d'Italia*, 18.5, Panigada (ed.), vol. 5, p. 122.

47 Mallett and Shaw, *The Italian Wars*, p. 159.

48 For this and what follows, see *Leg. e comm.*, pp. 1635–6.

49 *Ibid.*, p. 1637.

50 Mallett and Shaw, *The Italian Wars*, p. 159.

51 *Leg. e comm.*, p. 1642.

52 *Ibid.*, p. 1644.

53 *Ibid.*, p. 1640.

54 *Lett.*, pp. 501–2 (no. 232); *Machiavelli and His Friends*, pp. 414–15 (no. 329).

55   *Lett.*, pp. 499–500 (no. 231); *Machiavelli and His Friends*, pp. 413–14 (no. 328).

56   *Lett.*, p. 500 (no. 231); *Machiavelli and His Friends*, pp. 413–14 (no. 328).

57   Cf. *Leg. e comm.*, p. 1649.

58   For the following, see Guicciardini, *Storia d'Italia*, 18.6, Panigada (ed.), vol. 5, pp. 127–8.

59   See *Leg. e comm.*, pp. 1651–2.

60   Mallett and Shaw, *The Italian Wars*, p. 159; V.-L. Bourrilly, *Guillaume du Bellay: Seigneur de Langey, 1491–1543* (Paris: Société nouvelle de librairie et d'Édition, 1905), pp. 42–3.

61   Guicciardini, *Storia d'Italia*, 18.6, Panigada (ed.), vol. 5, p. 129.

62   *Leg. e comm.*, p. 1653.

63   Guicciardini, *Storia d'Italia*, 18.1, Panigada (ed.), vol. 5, p. 101.

64   *Lett.*, p. 503 (no. 233); *Machiavelli and His Friends*, p. 415 (no. 330).

65   *Lett.*, p. 505 (no. 234); *Machiavelli and His Friends*, p. 416 (no. 331) [adapted].

66   *Lett.*, p. 503 (no. 233); *Machiavelli and His Friends*, p. 415 (no. 330).

67   For the following, see *Lett.*, pp. 505–6 (no. 235); *Machiavelli and His Friends*, pp. 416–17 (no. 332).

68   *Lett.*, pp. 507–8 (no. 236); *Machiavelli and His Friends*, pp. 417–18 (no. 333).

69   The following is indebted to Devonshire Jones, *Francesco Vettori*, p. 190. See also J. N. Stephens, *The Fall of the Florentine Republic, 1512–1530* (Oxford: Clarendon, 1983), pp. 198–9; Guicciardini, *Storia d'Italia*, 18.7, Panigada (ed.), vol. 5, pp. 131–2; Vettori, *Scritti storici e politici*, pp. 240–1.

70   The suggestion that the *tumulto di venerdì* was nothing more than a 'straw-fire' appears in a letter written by Pagolo Beniventi to Bernardo Segni on 2 May 1527. See Stephens, *The Fall of the Florentine Republic*, p. 199.

71   Guicciardini, *Storia d'Italia*, 18.7, Panigada (ed.), vol. 5, p. 131.

72   Guicciardini, *Storia d'Italia*, 18.8, Panigada (ed.), vol. 5, pp. 135–8.

73   For what follows, see esp. Mallett and Shaw, *The Italian Wars*, p. 160; Guicciardini, *Storia d'Italia*, 18.8, Panigada (ed.), vol. 5, pp. 138–42; Vettori, *Scritti storici e politici*, pp. 243–4. For a splendid discussion of how this most devastating of events was portrayed in the literature of the time, see K. Gouwens, *Remembering the Renaissance: Humanist Narratives of the Sack of Rome* (Leiden: Brill, 1998).

74   Benvenuto Cellini, *Autobiography*, G. Bull (trans.), rev. ed. (London: Penguin, 1998), p. 60.

75   Vettori, *Scritti storici e politici*, p. 245.

76 The following is indebted to R. Ridolfi, *Vita di Niccolò Machiavelli*, 3rd ed., 2 vols. (Florence: Sansoni, 1969), vol. 1, p. 386.

77 Machiavelli, *Opere*, P. Fanfani, G. Milanesi, L. Passerini (eds.), 6 vols. (Florence: Cenniniana, 1873–77), vol. 6, pp. 265–6.

78 Giovambattista Busini, *Lettere a Benedetto Varchi sopra l'assedio di Firenze*, G. Milanesi (ed.) (Florence: Le Monnier, 1860), p. 85.

30. The Art of Dying (June 1527)

1 If Niccolò was suffering from a gastric ulcer or appendicitis, as has sometimes been suggested, it is possible that a large dose of aloe vera might actually have *worsened* his condition. On the identification of his illness, see R. Ridolfi, *Vita di Niccolò Machiavelli*, 3rd ed., 2 vols. (Florence: Sansoni, 1969), vol. 2, p. 556, n.23.

2 See Piero Machiavelli's letter to Francesco Nelli on 22 June 1527: *Lett.*, p. 509 (no. 238); *Machiavelli and His Friends*, p. 425 (letter F).

3 For the following, see Niccolò Machiavelli, 'Exortatione alla penitenza', in *Opere*, C. Vivanti (ed.), 3 vols. (Turin: Einaudi, 1997–2005), vol. 3, pp. 247–50, here p. 248; trans. in *Chief Works*, vol. 1, pp. 171–4, here p. 172.

4 On the 'Exortatione alla penitenza', see esp. M. Viroli, *Machiavelli's God*, A. Shugaar (trans.) (Princeton NJ: Princeton University Press, 2010), pp. 62–3, pp. 67–8, pp. 143–4.

5 Machiavelli, 'Exortatione alla penitenza', in *Opere*, Vivanti (ed.), vol. 3, p. 247; trans. in *Chief Works*, vol. 1, p. 171.

6 *Lett.*, p. 509 (no. 238); *Machiavelli and His Friends*, p. 425 (letter F).

7 Our knowledge of Niccolò's dream derives from Étienne Binet, *Du Salut d'Origène* . . . (Paris: Sébastien Cramoisy, 1629), pp. 359–61. Unfortunately, Binet made no mention of the sources on which he drew. For a discussion of this account and its authenticity, see Ridolfi, *Vita di Niccolò Machiavelli*, vol. 1, pp. 390–1; vol. 2, pp. 556–7, n.24. Binet's text is also reproduced in P. Villari, *Machiavelli e i suoi tempi* 2nd ed., 3 vols. (Milan: Hoepli, 1895–7), vol. 3, p. 370, n.1.

8 *Lett.*, p. 509 (no. 238); *Machiavelli and His Friends*, p. 425 (letter F).

Index